DATE DUE			

Mass Communication Review Yearbook

Editorial Board

Mass Communication Review Yearbook

Volume 6

1987

Michael Gurevitch
Mark R. Levy

Editors

Steve M. Barkin
Edward L. Fink
Contributing Editors

Published in cooperation with the
Center for Research in Public Communication,
University of Maryland

SAGE PUBLICATIONS
The Publishers of Professional Social Science
Newbury Park   Beverly Hills   London   New Delhi

For information address:

SAGE Publications, Inc.
2111 West Hillcrest Drive
Newbury Park, California 91320

SAGE Publications Inc.
275 South Beverly Drive
Beverly Hills
California 90212

SAGE Publications Ltd.
28 Banner Street
London EC1Y 8QE
England

SAGE PUBLICATIONS India Pvt. Ltd.
M-32 Market
Greater Kailash I
New Delhi 110 048 India

Printed in the United States of America

ISBN 0-8039-3112-3
ISSN 0196-8017

FIRST PRINTING

302.23
M38
144155
may 1988

Contents

About the Editors

MICHAEL GUREVITCH is a Professor in the College of Journalism and Director of the Center for Research in Public Communication at the University of Maryland. His current research interests include the relationship between media organizations and political institutions and media portrayal of public issues. He is coauthor (with Elihu Katz) of *The Secularization of Leisure* and (with Jay Blumler) of *The Challenge of Election Broadcasting,* as well as articles on political communication and uses and gratifications. He is also coeditor of *Mass Communication and Society* and *Culture, Society, and the Media,* and Volume 5 of the *Mass Communication Review Yearbook.* He earned his Ph.D. from the Massachusetts Institute of Technology. Prior to joining the University of Maryland, he worked at the Open University and the University of Leeds, England, and the Hebrew University of Jerusalem.

MARK R. LEVY is a Professor in the College of Journalism and a Research Associate of the Center for Research in Public Communication at the University of Maryland. His principal research interests are audience decoding and comprehension of news; uses and gratifications theory; and the impact of new technologies, particularly home video cassette recorders, on audience behavior. His publications include *The Audience Experience with Television News* and (with John Robinson) *The Main Source: Learning from Television News.* He is coeditor of Volume 5 of the *Mass Communication Review Yearbook,* and was guest editor of "The VCR Age" (*American Behavioral Scientist,* May/June 1987). Before earning his Ph.D. from Columbia University, he was a reporter with *The Record* in Hackensack, New Jersey; a writer, editor, and associate producer with NBC News in New York; and an associate national affairs editor with *Newsweek.*

INTRODUCTION

Michael Gurevitch and Mark R. Levy

Volume 6 in the *Mass Communication Review Yearbook* series continues the two-fold mission of *MCRY*: first, to anthologize those recent studies in mass communication that exemplify the more interesting and significant work in the field, and to open up new themes and issues or direct attention to fresh avenues of research; second, to provide a forum for original contributions that explore and reflect upon basic theoretical issues.

In Volume 5 we sought to order the materials along a rough "micro" to "macro" continuum. Articles in this volume are arranged topically. While we still believe that the "micro-macro" dimension is useful for organizing both old and newly produced knowledge in this field, the articles collected here settled more comfortably into categorization by topic and subject matter. Two examples are the articles assembled in Sections 2 and 3: In Section 2 we offer articles that in different ways illustrate past and present practices in mass communication research in different countries. In Section 3 we assembled articles dealing with the relationship between communication technologies and cultural change. Both sections defy the "micro-macro" organizing principle.

As is clearly inevitable in editing a volume of previously published articles, we were again "held hostage" by the materials available. Moreover, our selection is clearly constrained by the materials with which we were familiar, and those brought to our attention by members of the *MCRY* editorial board. Thus we are unavoidably vulnerable to charges of omission and, perhaps, parochialism. Still, from the more than 250 items nominated, we were able to select many pieces that might be "new" to *MCRY* readers and that were published in journals and books few of us routinely see.

We wish to thank the members of our editorial board and contributing editors Steve Barkin and Ed Fink for their prodigious efforts and insights. Thanks are also due to Jay Blumler, who contributed to the selection process. Our graduate assistants, Peggy DeBona, Min-Sun Kim, and Ray MacDougall, helped to assemble the materials and performed other administrative chores. We are also grateful to Dean Reese Cleghorn of the College of Journalism, University of Maryland, for his continuing interest and support. Finally, we wish to thank those friends and colleagues whose original contributions to Volume 6 have provided us with some of our greatest pleasure and challenge as editors of *MCRY*.

PART I

EXPLORING NEW DIRECTIONS

INTRODUCTION

Michael Gurevitch

One of the major purposes of the *Mass Communication Review Yearbook,* as we saw it when we assumed the editorship of the series, is to "alert mass communication scholars to the shifting contours of the field." We have tried to accomplish that goal not only through the selection of the articles included in *MCRY,* but also by using the yearbook as a vantage point from which to reflect on present dilemmas and future developments of the field.

Our first opportunity to operationalize this exploratory and reflective spirit came in Volume 5 of *MCRY.* There we presented our own "agenda for mass communication research," in which we outlined what we considered to be the significant issues in the field. We also invited five prominent scholars to contribute "personal statements" describing their views of current and future issues and directions.

Part I of the present volume continues the exploration of new directions for mass communication research. The first part of this section presents a discussion of the issues raised in the Research Agenda offered in the Introduction to Volume 5, and a debate about the merits and demerits of research agendas in general. The second part consists of three original contributions concerning major theoretical issues in the field.

To facilitate discussion of the Research Agenda, we convened at the University of Maryland a meeting of a dozen researchers and scholars concerned with the directions of future research. We asked the participants to consider three sets of questions:

(1) Does the field of mass communication research "need" an agenda? Would the field benefit from having a coherent and agreed statement identifying the significant issues and areas to be explored in the future? Conversely, might the formulation of an "agreed" agenda be potentially detrimental to the development of the field?

(2) Does the "Maryland Agenda" identify the most significant questions? Which areas or issues were ignored or neglected? Which questions included in the agenda

statement do not merit the title "significant" and should be deleted from such statement?
(3) How does that agenda relate to the main paradigms in the field? More generally, do research agendas merely serve to reflect, and thus reinforce, current thinking, or do they help to bring about progress?

Under the title "A Debate over the Research Agenda" we offer the conference participants' thoughts on these questions. Not surprisingly, these contributions vary, both in focus and in scope. Some participants addressed the questions above more or less directly; others chose to depart from our questions and to "do their own thing." Some thought it useful to formulate an agenda, others did not. And while some participants endorsed the general contents of our agenda, others advocated attention to different issues. Taken together, these contributions offer a diversity of ideas that should be taken on board in future discussions of the development and direction of the field.

The second half of this section offers three original essays, each devoted to reconsideration of a major theoretical issue. In the first essay, Eric Rothenbuhler argues for the reintroduction of functionalist—or, more properly, neofunctionalist—thinking to mass communication theory. At a time when many scholars have noted "a virtual explosion . . . in the acceptance and availability of critical analysis in mass communication" (Real, 1986), Rothenbuhler's plea for the return to the much-maligned theoretical base of functionalism might seem surprising. Yet Rothenbuhler argues that the current "Parsonian revival" in sociology has led to a resurgence of interest in functionalist theory; that in sociology and in communication research functionalism was never really rejected; and that neofunctionalist theory holds the promise of an important "potential payoff" in exploring various issues in mass communication. He proceeds to illustrate that promise by outlining the possible contribution of neofunctionalism to a reformulation of the "uses and gratifications" approach.

Larry Grossberg's essay comes from the opposite theoretical pole. A certified member of the "critical school," Grossberg nevertheless argues against continuing to structure mass communication research "in terms of the institutionalized oppositional and often antagonistic relations" between "critical" and "empirical" research, and against seeing a necessary disjunction between the two. Research methods, he contends, whether qualitative, interpretive, or quantitative/statistical, "are not intrinsically politically good or bad, humane or mechanical, progressive or regressive." And building on the work of Pierre Bourdieu, he suggests the possibility of bringing quantitative methods into work conducted from the critical perspective.

The final essay, by W. Phillips Davison, offers a different challenge. Known for many years for his work on public opinion and media effects, Davison attempts to "climb out" of what he describes as the "intellectual trap" into which he and many others have fallen in the past, namely, "the notion that communication content and channels have effects." Indeed, Davison argues, "our time, and other people's money, could have been more wisely spent if we had realized at the outset that communications have no effects; they merely make effects possible." Davison's alternative is to view the role of communications in the production of effects not directly, but via the establishment of linkages between "two or more disparate elements." Davison realizes that some might regard the distinction between "no direct effects" and "making effects possible" as mere quibble, but claims that "in any event, examination of a quibble can sometimes lead to new insights, or to interpretations of old ones."

In sum, the voices and arguments heard in this section are diverse, even discordant. Often they start from different, apparently incompatible theoretical perspectives, and sometimes they seem to be talking past each other. We make no apologies for this "lack of internal coherence." In fact, we view this diversity as a sign of the energy of the field. Here we disagree with the argument made by Fink (in the introduction to Part V in this volume) and wish to endorse a point made by James Carey in his contribution to the "A Debate over the Research Agenda." In that essay, Carey expresses a preference for the rule of the "republican tradition" in scholarship. Republics, he reminds us, "are noisy places, filled with the cacophony of competing and discordant voices." It is our hope that a genuine and productive conversation will grow out of the cacophony of voices represented here.

THE PERSONAL AND THE PUBLIC
Observations on Agendas in
Mass Communication Research

Jay G. Blumler and Michael Gurevitch

The psychoanalyst Erik Erikson, famed for his innovative psychohistorical studies of Luther and Gandhi (Erikson 1962, 1969), once remarked that revolutionaries are individuals who resolve their personal conflicts in the largest possible public arena. Luther's assault on the authority of the Pope was rooted, according to Erikson, in his struggle against the authority of his father. The formation of research agendas is interpretable in like terms (albeit more modestly and less dramatically): They too emerge from commingled personal and public concerns.

Thus our choices of questions as sufficiently significant to merit a major intellectual investment, however personal, are not at all private. They are shaped by professional socialization, modified by awareness of colleagues' writings and shifting academic trends, and are bounded by the contours of the field as generally perceived at a given moment. At career turning points (e.g., as graduate students, entrants to the field from other disciplines, or when moving to a new position) we may purposively scan the range of available study options (including agenda statements by leading scholars) to help settle on an inquiry path. Personal research agendas, then, are very much a product of public agendas. At the same time they may be eventually offered back to colleagues as a sort of public property.

This blend of personal commitment and public concern emerges when we list the main sources of researchers' decisions to investigate particular topics. These include:

sheer curiosity and interest
a sense of a question unduly neglected
a sense of what is focusing activity and controversy among prominent scholars
awareness of theoretical problems requiring attention
values relevant to the organization of communication in society
paradigm allegiances

Thus, on the more personal side, one finds the role of curiosity and interest often anchored in an individual's history and background. Personal value commitments further shape decisions about which questions are significant, while linking scholarship to the public good. Allegiances to one or another major paradigm can also steer people toward certain research priorities. On the public side of the equation, the search for direction may be guided by a sense of the "new" and where the cutting edge of the discipline is located; a sense of what has hitherto been neglected (invoking values again); an awareness of unresolved problems in important theoretical approaches; and last (but not least), the need to gain experience and attempt to secure publication and recognition by following intellectual fashions.

WHY BOTHER?

Mass communication research has been, since its early days, a notoriously eclectic enterprise, drawing on and borrowing from a wide range of social science and humanistic disciplines. This has been due in part to the inherent complexity of mass communication processes, raising questions open to study at several levels and from various points of departure, and in part to the manner in which the field has developed, recruiting into its ranks researchers trained and socialized in different disciplines, who were attracted to the field in accordance with shifting definitions of, and preoccupations with, different "significant issues" at different times. As a result of that eclectic history, the media are today examined as organizations (deploying a sociological perspective); as industries and businesses (economics); for their relations to government, public opinion, and various social groups (political science); as suppliers of patterned texts and discourses (cultural and rhetorical studies); and as builders of audiences seeking certain gratifications and open to certain effects (social psychology). It follows that no single research agenda can aspire to comprehensiveness or claim superiority over all others. Indeed, since intellectual creativity and innovation are offsprings of conflict, diversity, and debate, a widespread and unquestioning consensus over research priorities would be a sign of stultification rather than vigor. Yet much scholarly blood has been shed in vain attempts to establish and demolish such imperialist claims. Should we not therefore follow Cole Porter and "call the whole thing off"?

The answer turns on the advantages of formally formulated research agendas, a number of which occur to us:

First, such agendas could promote programmatic order, placing prospective lines of inquiry in coherent relations to each other and facilitating cumulative theoretical and empirical advance.

Second, they provide explicit rationales for research priorities, clarifying the grounds of choices, and so highlighting their strengths and limitations.

Third, they could offer considered guidance on which other scholars (perhaps especially younger ones) may draw when canvassing the research directions that it might be worthwhile for them to follow.

PARADIGM JOSTLING

In recent years, the communication research agendas of American scholars have been formed in a climate of intensified paradigm jostling. Certain European critics have taxed them for adhering to a "dominant paradigm," which paradoxically is alleged to rest on shaky and outmoded foundations—as if they were blindly saddled to a huge academic dinosaur. Labelled as crudely behaviorist and naively positivist, they are said to have presumed without warrant a consensual social order (Hall, 1982) and to have been overly preoccupied with individual-level audience phenomena. In quantitative content analyses, they are accused of having fragmented meanings that should never have been sundered. In effects research, they allegedly looked for evidence of media impact in the least likely and most trivial places. They also ignored, it is charged, more meaningful issues about the ideological role of the media, the location of media organizations in the nexus of power relations in society, the nature of the production process, and the values of media professionals.

For some researchers, a consequence of exposure to this phase of paradigm jostling was a sharpened imperative of making choices. In a field structured by a single paradigm, there is perhaps less felt need for self-conscious choice making. Consensus on approaches, issues, and methodologies is less likely to generate debate; live and let live prevails (as Blumler, 1978, noticed when examining American journalism research from a "transatlantic perspective" some years ago). But in a field where controversy is waged over alternative approaches, choices are more insistently forced on scholars. The tension between the personal and the public becomes not only more publicly visible but also a more urgent source of personal concerns. Research agendas may then become solutions to personal dilemmas highlighted by public debates.

Faced by that mixture of the valid and the unfair that typifies keen polemic, American academics have reacted to the European gauntlet in a variety of ways—sometimes reminiscent of the range of audience responses discussed in the literature on media effects. A few bought the new approach more or less wholesale (conversion?). Some stoutly reasserted the claims of "scientific" research models (reinforcement?). Some admired, even applauded, the new doctrines from afar, without modifying the essential thrust of their own strategies (minimal effects?).

OUR OWN RESPONSE:
CRITICAL PLURALISM

Euro-American in intellectual background, affiliations, and experience, our personal response to the dilemma presented by jostling paradigms has taken the form of "negotiation," involving a recognition of the validity of certain critical theory stances without accepting all their elements. The core of our position is that the study of mass communication "could be enriched by adoption of a systems outlook" (Gurevitch and Blumler, 1977). Thus our perspective is holistic, not in the sense of recommending "attempts . . . to arrive at total analysis and total explanation" (McLeod and Blumler, 1987), but in the belief that the mass communication process should

> be viewed as an integrated whole in which the various actors and institutions are linked and interdependent: investigation of any part or aspect of this process ought to be located in its social, cultural and political context [Gurevitch and Levy, 1986].

That is why we recommend greater attention to what we have termed "level-spanning" phenomena, reconciling boundedness of communication inquiry with sensitivity to system influences. Thus, for example, we have sought to integrate our interest in audiences' uses and gratifications into a systems perspective by translating the psychological notion of audience motivations into the sociological one of audience roles (Blumler, 1985). As another example, in a recent policy paper on factors responsible for the failure of the news media to serve democratic values, we have attributed this in part to "the fact that in large, complex, industrialized societies, political messages emanate from more or less rigidly structured and enduring political communication systems" (Gurevitch and Blumler, 1985).

Nevertheless, certain key features distinguish our concept of a communication system from those explicit or implicit in much system-oriented writing. We would argue that:

(1) Monocausal approaches are inappropriate. The mass communication process is a site on which multiple and contending forces impinge. While these forces may be differentially powerful and their impact on communication processes unevenly significant, none is completely reducible to any other force or totally derivable from it.

(2) Communication systems differ—that is, they do not conform to some universally applicable pattern that scholars should strive to discover and explicate. Instead, the presumption should be that "different system parameters, i.e., different manners in which systems are structured, will differentially encourage or constrain communication roles and behaviors belonging to, organized by or exposed to them" (McLeod and Blumler, 1987). A significant conceptual challenge is therefore the task of postulating and applying potentially formative dimensions of cross-system variation, exploring how they differentially affect the activities and attitudes of producers, processors and receivers of communication.

(3) Analysis of media systems should consider the role of incongruities, cross-level disparities, and internal contradictions within them. This may offer clues over how and in which directions media systems change over time. We suspect that a view of communication systems as "muddling through" in response to internal and external pressures will generally be more applicable than either (a) those which perceive them as largely dominated by integrative and

stabilizing forces (Alexander, 1981), or (b) those which assume that they must eventually collapse under the weight of their own contradictions.

(4) Methodologically, scholars should be open to both qualitative and quantitative sources of evidence. To insist that the form of evidence gathering should be considered strictly for its appropriateness to the question under investigation is to state a truism that regrettably is often ignored.

(5) A holistic approach implies that all parts of a communication system are equally worthy of investigation. In the past, more partial approaches have predominated, including Marxist emphases on ownership, control, and content unmatched by audience research, and American work on audience phenomena rarely related to political and institutional factors. The consequences of such partiality have included not only skewed perceptions of the communication process, but also a tendency to fall unwittingly prey to misleading assumptions— the audience as victim in the former case and the audience as unconstrained agency in the latter.

(6) Media organization per se may matter. Exploration of its dependence on political, economic, and cultural systems should not blind us to variable factors within media structures, roles, and cultures that may play back onto such systems, not only as props but also as change agents.

Taken together, these features provide some of the elements of a philosophy of "critical pluralism." Such a position gives research priority to those system characteristics that may significantly shape and constrain media performance, including its implications for other institutions and individuals. Its proponents, regarding communication processes as value-impregnated, are ready to criticize media performance in the light of normative criteria, which are themselves open to deliberation and debate. However, such a standpoint declines to treat communication systems, either as seamless webs or as set on some predetermined and irrevocable course. And among the diverse forces that may shape media systems, it would allow room for beliefs and expectations about the functions that communication should serve, to be found among media-dependent elites, mass media professionals, and audiences.

A WORD FOR THE SKEPTICS

There is no consensus in the research community about the advantages of formulating enquiry agendas. In the essays that follow the reader will encounter some persuasive arguments against engaging in such exercises. These have alerted us, however, to two additional reasons for setting up explicit rationales for research agendas.

First, we should entertain no illusions about the fact that research priorities are constantly being set, both implicitly and explicitly. Published articles often conclude with "suggestions for further research." Even if the editors of the main journals in the field see themselves as no more than "gatekeepers," the decisions they take clearly shape the broad contours of the field and favor certain agendas rather than others. A similar role is played by the major publishers who specialize in communication books. Last, and certainly not least, a powerful influence is exercised by those who hold the purse strings—foundations, government agencies, and the like—who make decisions about the allocations of funds for research. Although some of those listed above are bona fide members of the research community, others are "outsiders" whose decisions might be based on criteria external to the field. To avoid being instruments of the priorities of others, should we not try, so far as possible, to keep the agenda setting power firmly in our own hands? This is not to recommend a single-minded obliviousness to issues of public concern voiced by outsiders, but rather their incorporation into a set of priorities based firmly on our own judgments.

Second, apart from their other functions, enquiry agendas might also be read as "autobiographical statements." They reveal the research preoccupations of scholars as well as the philosophical underpinnings of their interests. Had all of us been required to make such statements periodically, say every 5 or 10 years, we would have created a record, documenting not only the intellectual growth and change of individual scholars, but also, cumulatively, the historical development of the field. And in a field characterized by much flux, debate, "ferment" or, indeed, battle, such a record, by itself, could be worth whatever price it might exact.

REFERENCES

Blumler, Jay G. (1978) "The purposes of mass communication research: a transatlantic perspective." Journalism Quarterly 55, 2: 219-230.
Blumler, Jay G. (1985) "The social character of audience gratifications," in Karl-Erik Rosengren et al. (eds.) Media Gratifications Research: Current Perspectives. Newbury Park, CA: Sage.
Erikson, Erik (1962) Young Man Luther. New York: Norton.
Erikson, Eric (1969) Gandhi's Truth: The Origins of Militant Nonviolence. New York: Norton.
Gurevitch, Michael and Jay G. Blumler (1977) "Linkages between the mass media and politics: a model for the analysis of political communication systems," in James Curran et al. (eds.) Mass Communication and Society. London: Edward Arnold.
Gurevitch, Michael and Jay G. Blumler (1985) "Political communication systems and democratic values." Presented to the Working Group on "News, Mass Media and Democratic Values," Washington, DC.
Gurevitch, Michael and Mark R. Levy (1985) "Introduction," in Michael Gurevitch and Mark R. Levy (eds.) Mass Communication Review Yearbook, Vol. 5. Newbury Park, CA: Sage.
McLeod, Jack and Jay G. Blumler (1987) "The macrosocial level of communication science," in Charles Berger and Steven H. Chaffee (eds.) Handbook of Communication Science. Newbury Park, CA: Sage.

AGENDAS FOR
MASS COMMUNICATION RESEARCH

Robert K. Avery

ON THE QUESTION OF AGENDAS

Our task is to respond—at several levels of abstraction—to the research agenda described in the introduction to Volume 5 of the *Mass Communication Review Yearbook.* My own response is grounded in the assumption that, whether we like it or not, we cannot avoid setting research agendas. Just as some scholars have argued that "we cannot not communicate," I would contend that our intellectual efforts and the published works resulting from those efforts constitute a continuous, evolving research agenda for our discipline. We cannot escape the conclusion that the writings of Blumler, Carey, Gerbner, Hall, McGee, and Newcomb—to name but a representative sampling of our contemporary communication scholars—are having a direct impact on judgments regarding what is "significant," and what is worth doing. The obvious agenda-setting function of these and other authors is readily apparent as we move from one professional conference to another and take stock of the ideas, research questions, and methodological approaches that fill the convention programs. At the Iowa Television Criticism Conference I came face-to-face with the disciples of John Cawelti, John Fiske, and Horace Newcomb. At the annual meeting of the Association for Education in Journalism and Mass Communication I witnessed the enormous influence of James Carey on a generation of journalism historians. The 1986 Culture and Communication Conference in Philadelphia would have been a mere skeleton without the work of Raymond Williams, Stuart Hall, and Lawrence Grossberg. At the International Communication Conference we saw the living legacy of George Gerbner, and at the Speech Communication Association conference the rhetoricians flocked to hear the latest presentation of Michael McGee. The work of each of us makes a public statement about our individual judgments regarding the significance of our personal research contributions. And just as we, as individual scholars, contribute to the agenda-setting process for our discipline, the institutions that we represent are not unaware of the importance of establishing research agendas that contribute to their own future success and the collective mix of scholarly discourse. The research agenda that we've been asked to examine serves as perhaps the most vivid evidence that the ongoing process of academic discourse functions to set the research agendas that guide our discipline.

If we recognize the inevitable outcome of agenda-setting as a product of virtually all scholarly enterprise, we move to asking whether it is healthy for some agent to intentionally *set* the agenda or some agent to force a periodic *evaluation* of the agenda(s) most responsible for scholarly productivity at any given point in time. My own position is that a critical appraisal of the state of the art can be a constructive enterprise that contributes to the maturation of our collective efforts. The fear, of course, is that the very process of evaluation can become self-defeating, negative, and counterproductive to the serendipitous explorations of true creativity and scholarly imagination. There is, after all, some danger that, by making a declaration as to the relative importance of a line of inquiry, we may undermine the free flow of native inquisitiveness that produces the quantum leaps. While this danger does exist, I believe that it is offset by the potential sparks of intellectual life it can kindle in the mind of the solid, though average, academic. The gifted minds will continue to pursue their own fertile courses regardless of the claims or condemnation of others. But for many, it does require an external endorsement from a recognized agent to enable one to believe in the integrity and potential significance of his or her own efforts, or even to focus in on a question deserving of serious study.

Although I would not go as far as Percy Tannenbaum in characterizing most of current communication research as "dreary and uninteresting," I would suggest that there is much too little work that deserves to be labeled "significant." My experience as editor of *CSMC* leads me to conclude that a sizable portion of our academic community would welcome, and profit from, the formulation and publicizing of a research agenda. The manuscript rejection rate of the new journal speaks to the volume of uninspired or ill-conceived projects that failed to benefit either author or discipline. The valuable time and energy that is invested in the rehashing of old issues, the restatement of old findings, and the rediscovery of old "givens" is disheartening. It is no longer a mystery why the same handful of authors keep reappearing in our journals. They represent that segment of the community that continues to conduct research and prepare writings that offer original ideas and shape the research agenda. Unfortunately, without a more prescriptive set of guidelines, these writings often fail to cultivate new extensions in the minds of many readers. Hence, much of the research generated by these original works is not only "dreary and uninteresting"—to use Tannenbaum's words—but wasted effort as well.

Before moving to an assessment of the "Maryland Agenda," let me restate my position. I believe that the setting of research agendas is inherent in the process of academic scholarship. Some agendas will retard the collective efforts of a discipline while others will accelerate the significant work of the community. Given the present state of communication research, the advantages to be derived from the advancement of multiple research agendas clearly outweigh their potential dangers.

ON THE "MARYLAND AGENDA"

Whether made explicit or not, every research agenda has an underlying assumption or position. It is to the credit of Gurevitch and Levy that the general research philosophy and orientation that guided the preparation of their agenda is set forth at the outset. Few would argue, I think, with the basic premise that the communication process should be viewed as an integrated whole and hence investigations of this process should be adequately contextualized. Similarly, the position that we are living in a world "in which global communication assumes ever-growing significance" is widely accepted and argues for an agenda that encourages comparative, cross-cultural research efforts. However, the stated goal of the research agenda—"enhancing the contribution of mass communication research to the promotion of democratic institutions and practices"—is the statement that appears to embody the thrust of the underlying philosophy that sets the agenda. It is, in fact, the authors' interpretation of this goal statement that establishes the political significance of the research priorities. The four major headings appear to be situated in a descending order of significance. This appearance results from not only the perceived ranking of topics, but from the authors' treatment, which affords decreasing detail and creative exploration of the "levels" of scholarly attack. One cannot avoid the fundamental assumption that is inherent in the authors' orientation: That is, to set an agenda that promotes democratic institutions and practices is by definition to focus on media as active agents within the matrix of political/social power.

This is an important and justified position, and one that yields an exciting agenda for research. It is a position to which I have become increasingly sensitized during the past three years. But even though I agree with the basic tenets that underlie the authors' call for research, I cannot help wondering how the agenda might differ if the guiding objective were stated in other terms. For example, what if the goal were to contribute to the collective mental health of our society? Or our social well-being? Or the basic issue of quality of human life? Would such a reorientation reverse the order of headings, thus making communication technology and media representations of social issues higher ranking topics than those outlined within the discussion of media and power relations? Would such a shift increase the emphasis on micro approaches, and would the unit of analysis move away t. m media organizations in the direction of individual consumers? None of these questions should be taken as a negative reaction to the agenda set forth, but rather to suggest the multilayered nature of the research agenda itself.

Looking at the specific questions proposed by the agenda, there is much here that deserves to be considered as significant avenues for scholarly inquiry. Let me point to just a few of the research topics that have been called to my attention recently—in other words, topics that have received external validation or endorsement by others.

First, the authors' call for more work that is empirically grounded was echoed at the 1986 Culture and Communication Conference by Larry Grossberg. If I understand his position accurately, he has reached the point in his own thinking where the feud between logical positivists and critical theorists is no longer generating constructive outcomes. Arguments to advance the critique that he advocates must begin to take advantage of empirical evidence. Current critical scholarship can benefit from the tools of the empiricist in order to move beyond the stage of theoretical debate to the arena of practical application.

The topics of "media-social elite integration" and "source-professional communicator relations" are especially significant and deserve the top billing received in the agenda. Anyone closely related with the workings of political and news elites intuitively recognizes the importance of this line of research. The issue of "journalists' orientations toward social institutions" was a matter of special concern in the October 1986 issue of *The QUILL,* the publication of The Society of Professional Journalists. Called into question was journalists' coverage of religious institutions and the implications of current practices. In an age when religion and politics are inseparable, the responsibility of journalistic coverage of "sacred" institutions must be seen as an important area for research. In my own conservative state, there are daily occurrences of what media critics identify as preferential journalistic treatment. The idea of constructing a media view of the core consensual values of society could yield valuable insights that go well beyond our present level of understanding.

If manuscript submissions to *CSMC* during the past three years can be used as an index of individual research agendas, the topic of "media representation of social issues" is a priority item that is widely shared. There is little question that increasing numbers of text-bound scholars are attempting to explicate the ideological struggle for social and institutional meaning embedded in media texts, especially television. Interestingly, much of the work submitted to *CSMC* locates the struggle in the entertainment programming, as opposed to the news programs, which have served as the primary focus for much of the British work in this area. If there is a weakness in the authors' agenda here, it is that the research directions appear sketchy and seem to follow rather than lead the more promising textual analyses. Comparative investigations, such as the international popular music project, are already generating the kinds of cross-cultural findings called for by the authors.

As a communication researcher whose roots are intertwined with those of the cognitive psychologist, I can only applaud the authors' identification of human information processing as an agenda priority. Unfortunately, this subject area is receiving even less attention within our discipline than it garnered in the authors' priority scale. The current criticism of logical positivism as a respectable paradigm would appear to have contributed to a reduction in the quantitative investigation of the encoding/decoding process by a new generation of mass communication researchers. Work within the growing field of information science is making some progress in this area, but the integrated perspective advocated by the authors is largely absent from existing literature.

Communication is well situated within the academy to make the kind of necessary connections that will enable integrated research projects that fulfill the authors' expectations—examining program construction and audience interpretation within a single analytical framework. Perhaps of equal importance are studies to determine the way our cognitive processes are being altered by patterns of media consumption. There is some physiological evidence that suggests that our mental capabilities are undergoing subtle changes as we engage in thought processes dictated by an increasingly visual culture. In my opinion, the field of visual communication holds some of the most exciting potential for those interested in the encoding and decoding of mediated messages. Work in this area is highly fragmentary and most of the serious scholarship is being done outside communication. As critical and empirical approaches achieve a greater balance within our communication programs, I would predict important advances in our understanding of the human visual experience from a communication perspective.

The authors' agenda is brought full circle with their identification of "communication technology and policy" as important research topics for a democratic society. The authors are quite right in characterizing the existing literature as a collection of "disparate efforts." Anyone who has taught graduate level courses on these subjects has been challenged with the task of conceptual integration and sense-making. Perhaps more than any of the topics contained within the authors' research agenda, the questions outlined under this heading have suffered from a failure to locate the work within its social, cultural, and political context. It may be that those engaged in these efforts feel that the called-for contextualization is so self-evident that it does not need further grounding, but I suspect that the problem really stems from the kind of task- or issue-related questions that generate this body of research.

My overall reaction to the "Maryland Agenda" is quite favorable. It does reflect the research interests and preferences of its authors, but the range of significant questions affords any serious scholar with ample food for thought. Other than generating discussion and stimulating individual research programs that build upon the ideas shared by the authors, one might speculate as to the impact of such an agenda. But then, this very response serves as evidence that the public statement of research agendas can encourage reflection and promote dialogue. While the formulation of agendas may be regarded as a fairly idealistic exercise, the process does permit us to identify and shift the boundaries of our work.

WILL THE CENTER HOLD?

James W. Carey

Once upon a time, or so the story goes, there was an age when mass communication research possessed a more or less "paradigmatic" unity, in which certain methods were pretty much agreed upon and shared, in which an agenda of research was available so that studies connected with one another—*The People's Choice* gave rise inevitably to *Personal Influence*—and findings accumulated in a more or less orderly way. It was research that had a story to tell, a story at once social and political, as well as scientific, and mass communications researchers were the proprietors of the telling.

That my caricature is overdrawn is irrelevant. Mass communication research may never have been particularly well laid out or orderly, particularly consensual or "paradigmatic." It nonetheless had a clear center of gravity and a preferred style of community life. By contrast, things have of late fallen apart, the center no longer holds. The individuals who engage in mass communication research no longer have much, if anything, in common. They share neither a "paradigm," nor an agenda, nor a method, nor a philosophy of science. They have been thrown into one another's company by the vagaries of fate: an increasingly international community whose lives have fallen together by accident. They are united neither by method or purpose nor, if the truth be known, subject matter. For some this is a deeply disquieting state and they yearn to put humpty-dumpty together again, yearn for a discipline with a "paradigm" and an agenda, though a discipline as they define it and a paradigm and agenda they are currently peddling.

If those are the choices—a recovery of paradigmatic unity or the anarchy of a fractured field—I much prefer the disarray that is the current state of affairs, for it maximizes the degrees of freedom available in scholarship. It suits, so much the better, the republican tradition. Republics, we have often been reminded, are noisy places, filled with the cacophony of competing and discordant voices. What republicans fear in politics, they fear in scholarship: a monopoly of knowledge that under a different label parades as a shared "paradigm" and agenda.

But I do not think that those are the only options open to us. We can secure the benefits of the current disarray if we adopt an evolutionary or ecological model of scholarship: If we recognize, in short, that a proliferation of perspectives, concepts, and methods maximizes the chances that many ideas will find a favorable ecological niche in which to flourish and grow. However, and this is the critical point, there is no way of predicting in advance which concepts, perspectives, or methods will work, which will move us toward a web of beliefs of cognitive power and moral efficacy. All thought is an experiment without guarantees and all we can do is create conditions favorable to such experimentation. Paradigmatic scholarship, by contrast, seeks guarantees and determinations in advance. It seeks, implicitly, to close down the conversation, to eliminate options, because it assumes a given form of theory, method, or morals—a form known in advance—contains the one right position. The paradigmatic spirit in scholarship enters conversation as an afterthought, as an attempt to merely correct and complete a position *by* discourse rather than as an attempt to discover a position *in* discourse. It has little need for conversation because it has already experienced an epiphany.

Thought is, to use a Dewey metaphor, like the unforced flowers of spring; left to itself, thought proliferates in dazzling variety. A clash of doctrines, then, is not a disaster but a triumph and an opportunity. However, the conditions supporting ecological variety do not come about automatically. Critical theory should have taught us, though we could have learned it elsewhere, that dominion is the more natural condition of discourse, as of other human relations.

How are we to resist the temptation to dominion? How are we to secure a center that will tolerantly hold? We have before us a grand opportunity, and we may not get another one, for securing the conditions supporting diversity, a grand opportunity to constitute a genuine conversation about this field. We are at a moment when, if we learn to listen and genuinely argue with one another, we can build an agenda around a willingness to tolerate and embrace competing articulations, a willingness to try anything, a willingness to express explicit discontent and debate fundamentals. We are, in short, at a moment when we can move, following Thomas Kuhn (1970: 9), whose language I am pirating, from normal to extraordinary discourse. All we need to do this is a commitment to the minimum level of agreement necessary to a civic and civil life. United neither by method nor purpose nor subject, we can be wedded only in community, in civility, in the hope that if we just keep the conversation going, can just keep talking, there may be a chance we will agree about something. But it must be a conversation grounded in certain republican habits, habits that are not, at the moment, in long supply in the academy. If it is to be a conversation, it must be one in Gadamer's (1975: 347) sense: "It is characteristic of every true conversation that each opens himself to the other person, truly accepts his point of view as worthy of consideration and gets inside the other to the extent that he understands not a particular individual but what he says." To use language with which I am more comfortable, it must be a fiduciary conversation—one grounded in trust—about the content of a living tradition, an extended, socially embedded argument about the Good which constitutes that tradition (MacIntyre, 1981).

Let me illustrate. Those of us working this field in the United States have inherited a particular tradition. Call it what you will—behaviorism, functionalism, the "effects" tradition, the dominant paradigm, the positive sciences—all of us define ourselves in relation to it. This tradition and the reactions to it define not only an intellectual community, but a moral and psychological one as well: It confers individual identity as well as social purpose. I have argued, as best I can, against this tradition, as a deeply flawed one, bound up with an unhelpful philosophy of science and politics. Yet, as I have also argued (Carey, 1985), there is a sound and substantial reason why people cling to this tradition, and no one has effectively argued against it. The tradition of anti-ideological liberalism at its core has provided one defense against many, though not all, of the depredations of this century. As I put it earlier (Carey, 1985: 32-33), the attack on the positive sciences "seems to buy into a moral and political vocabulary that is, if not antidemocratic, at least insufficiently sensitive to the ways in which valued political practices intertwine with certain intellectual habits. . . . Positive science, anchored as it was in a notion of truth independent of politics, arrived at by open communication and in the doctrine of natural rights, was one means of withstanding the totalitarian temptation." In short, there is sound though misplaced political reason behind the dominant paradigm, but until its defenders actually and explicitly defend it or until someone actually and explicitly dismantles it, there is little possibility of constituting a conversation within the only tradition available to us.

I have grossly simplified this matter, of course, but to a particular end. William James has a meditation somewhere in which he considers a set of arguments and wonders whether they are positions in a conversation or staging sites in a battle. "Somehow," he concludes, "it feels like a battle." That's what the debate about mass communication research feels like—a battle, and a peculiar battle at that: one in which people are being forced to take sides, often to join camps, with which they do not agree, in which many feel like outsiders, in which there is a lot of repression of true feelings and irrational reaction formations, in which there are attempts at cooptation, and, even worse, polite disregard and bad faith. As a result, ever more dangerous options get opened up whereby arguments are settled ascriptively—by class, nationality, gender, or race—or, because we never learn by our own work, the application of power. The potential diversity of the argument about mass communication research is reduced to a dialogue—better a duologue in Abraham Kaplan's (1969) sense—between what I'll call a party of representation and a party of power. The party of representation seeks a cognitively privileged site to secure the *Truth* "out there" via *method*. The party of power seeks a morally privileged site to secure the *Good* "out there" via *critique*. Both parties seek a guarantee, a metaphysical comfort: a means of transcending their political communities, a means of escaping the burdens of citizenship, a way of becoming an outsider, whether scientist or critic, that grants one a privileged voice and a privileged view. More than that, these parties do everything but listen—really listen—to one another and hardly ever read one another, at least in the hermaneutic sense of attempting to capture, fully and sympathetically, what is being said.

I think these are bad choices, but I have nothing—indeed, I want to have nothing—to put in their place. I, of course, have notions of things we might try, of concepts that look promising, of studies that might open fresh possibilities, but I have no candidates for Truth and Goodness—no theory, method, or concepts, not the Text, not Technology, not Postmodernism, to replace all the failed candidates that have come before. All I can suggest is that we get rid of the notion that intellectual work is something other than conducting a conversation, that there are standards of evidence other than conversational ones, that there is some way we can guarantee in advance that we are going to end up on the side of the good, the true, and the beautiful. I do know that if we are going to get out of this situation, we are going to have to ventilate this conversation both with new ideas and new procedures. For example, can anyone any longer bear the deadly repetitive harangue between two equally sentimental notions, one that looks at freedom as an individual expression and one that looks at freedom, to give it Marcuse's twist, as merely repressive tolerance or disguised domination? Does anyone seriously think that the frequently uncivil and generally anticommunal habits that dominate our conventions and our universities are getting us anywhere? If *we*, the relatively privileged, leisured members of the theory class, cannot constitute a genuine conversation of our culture, there is little likelihood that it will be achieved in the wider society. But, in the absence of that conversation, which party to the duologue do we choose? That we will have to choose I have no doubt, but I do not find the current alternatives particularly appetizing.

REFERENCES

Carey, James W. (1985). "Overcoming resistance to cultural studies," pp. 27-40 in Mass Communication Review Yearbook, vol. 5. Newbury Park, CA: Sage.

Gadamer, Hans-George (1975). Truth and Method. New York: Crossroad.

Kaplan, Abraham (1969). "The life of dialogue," pp. 87-108 in J. D. Roslansky (ed.) Communication. Amsterdam: North Holland Publishing.

Kuhn, Thomas J. (1970). The Structure of Scientific Revolutions (2nd, enlarged ed.). Chicago: University of Chicago Press.

MacIntyre, Alasdair (1981). After Virtue. South Bend, IN: University of Notre Dame Press.

A RESEARCH AGENDA
FOR THE INFORMATION AGE
A Personal and Institutional Response

Oscar H. Gandy, Jr.

While I understand the canons of academic freedom and the inherent value of scholarly autonomy, it would be disingenuous for me to suggest that I had no interest in influencing the research agenda within mass communications. Clearly the publication of my research and critical analyses represent an effort to influence others to join with me in addressing one pressing problem or another. Indeed, I have had the audacity from time to time to suggest what I thought critical scholarship "ought to be about." I have attempted on numerous occasions in the past, and will try increasingly in the future, to influence the formation of research agendas by private and public agencies that fund social research. I believe it is not only my right but my responsibility to try to influence the research agenda.

Scholars are never truly free to pursue any subject which interests them. Some investigations are forbidden by law, others by custom, some by policies of "institutional review boards," and still others by lack of access to necessary "puddles of data," or the analytical machinery to wade through them.

It might be, of course, that the work we do as social scientists is really inconsequential in the great scheme of things. Thus, if what we produced neither caused harm, nor contributed to the general welfare, then it might not really matter what we studied, as long as we were "productive." That is, social scientists might be like artists, supported by our universities, foundations, or other patrons to pursue whatever subjects interested us, as long as we met some minimal criteria for scholarship. In reality, however, research activity places claims upon limited social resources and someone (and hopefully, the community of scholars is included in that set of policymakers) must decide about their allocation.

Although I don't intend to extend the already well-worn debate about critical versus administrative research, as it has been thrashed over quite well in the *Journal of Communication* (1983), some trends are still worth noting. There has been a general tendency for research within the discipline to justify its claim on resources in terms of some ultimate social benefit. Lowery and De Fleur (1983) describe 11 important "milestones" in mass communications research, only one of which can be said to have been guided by a general theoretical orientation, rather than some affirmative social purpose. Thus it would appear that the research establishment already places some operational, if nonbinding, limits on the range of research questions we pursue as a discipline.

With this in mind, I would suggest that it is not enough for us to understand *how,* or by what process the media might influence individuals, groups, and relationships; it is also necessary to determine the extent to which such influence is *actually* produced, on whose behalf, for what purposes, and with what results in terms of the quality of life experienced by individuals within a given society.

INFORMATION AND SOCIAL POWER

In large part, my research and writing has been concerned with the relationship between information and social power. As a critical political economist by orientation, this work has sought to describe the means through which information has been used by the elite or ruling segments to influence the allocation of the society's resources. To a lesser extent, no doubt reflecting the pessimistic tendencies of those in the critical camp, this work has also explored the use of information by the underclass to redress the balance of power. Over time, this work has moved back and forth from micro to macro levels of analysis, but it has always been linked to the fundamental question of power.

Research under this broad umbrella of research can take a number of productive directions. As suggested by Gurevitch and Levy in the last volume of *MCRY,* it is important to identify and clarify the role of the mass media in the "nexus of power relations." My orientation has traditionally favored a more deterministic analytical model, one which sees social outcomes as the result of considered, and purposeful action, rather then the unpredictable result of the accidental or coincidental confluence of forces. Thus I see the efforts by Graham Murdock (1982) to specify the ways in which control is exercised over the mass media as important for us to continue and extend. Ownership, management, sponsorship, professional leadership, and mutually beneficial exchange relationships are all means by which the content of media channels may be influenced. Each should be the subject of extended theoretial and empirical work.

While it is important for us to consider how factors beyond the control of individual actors serve to constrain or limit their abilities to produce influence at will, it is perhaps more important for us to understand how they respond in order to overcome those constraints. We might note, for example, that the nature of competition in media markets is not under the control of policy actors seeking to use the media to influence the public's perception of one issue or another. Indeed, increasing competition in media markets has resulted in increasingly fractionated and homogeneous audiences, making it more difficult to capture a mass audience with a single well-placed information subsidy (Gandy, 1982). In response to this reality, the twin marketing research technologies of segmentation and targeting have been pursued with a great sense of urgency. Mass communication theorists must help us to understand how changes in the nature of the audience production process facilitate or constrain efforts at the management of demand and the formation of public policy.

I have argued, for example, that contrary to traditional views of diversity, one may see the growth of alternative media channels as potentially more supportive of elite social control—sort of "patching the cracks in a leaky hegemony." Stuart Hall suggests that the consensus of the majority is the regulator which makes the alignment between power and consent possible: "If the consensus of the majority can be so shaped so that it squares with the will of the powerful, then particular (class) interests can be represented as identical with the consensus will of the people. This, however, requires the shaping, the educating, the tutoring of consent." And, as current educational experience would suggest, all students cannot progress equally well in the same classroom with the same instructional material.

Our experience with ability grouping and individualized instruction demonstrates that learning improves when instructors are able to provide examples which resonate with the life experiences of their students, and when the level of difficulty matches the level of their students' preparation. Learning from television is no different. For some, the material is irrelevant, outside the realm of their experience; for others, the media portrayals are "true to life" and reinforce, albeit selectively, key components of the emerging consensus. Multiple channels could conceivably increase the achievement of the necessary hegemonic consensus through a kind of individualized instruction. Content analysis of media channels designed for more specialized audiences may help us to determine if there are ideological differences which make a difference.

I believe more researchers should explore the extent to which audience segmentation and targeting results in greater efficiency in the production of influence in specific behavioral and policy areas. Examination of the marketing efforts behind the historic privitization of British Telecom reveals the degree of sophistication which has been achieved in the segmentation and targeting of mass media appeals (Newman, 1986). To quote one observer, "The techniques of planning and executing an unprecedented campaign were involved. It deployed the whole modern armory of marketing strategies and tactics. Large-scale and continuous market research, sophisticated audience analysis, and versatile use of advertising media were coupled with the largest direct-mail campaign the world has yet seen" (Newman, 1986).

The principal architect behind this overwhelmingly successful marketing effort has been identified as a specialist in political consulting who created the overall marketing design on the basis of a modified version of his "political decision and forecasting model."[1] Research surveys were used to construct a decision model for different potential buyers, then subsequent tracking studies assessed the changes in attitudes brought about by the targeted communications. The direct mail effort is reported to have achieved a 61% conversion rate. This change in the technology for providing information subsidies should be studied, especially with regard to the use of what we refer to as the new, demassified media.

Many of the new computer-based systems represent not only new ways of distributing information, but the twin attributes of addressability and verifiability increase their potential for use as aids to increased hegemonic control. Addressability makes it possible for programmers to selectively include or exclude individuals or households from the audience for any particular program or message. The initial use of this capacity in the entertainment realm is to deny programming to those who have not paid a premium for access. The same technology can be used to bar access to audiences for whom the content is deemed inappropriate for one reason or another. Perhaps parents will want to limit their children's access to adult channels. But we should note that content is also selectively delivered to households with different demographic profiles in order to evaluate the productivity of marketing appeals when delivered in different editorial contexts.[2] Verifiability makes it possible to determine, almost on a continuous basis, whether a household has been exposed to a particular message. Recognizing the limitations of passive measurement devices, competitors in the ratings business are rushing to introduce "people meters" which facilitate the construction of detailed demographic portraits of the audiences for particular program segments.

With regard to the broader social implications of this response to competition and diversity in the media marketplace, it is important to note that targeting is also used to *avoid* market segments estimated to have a low potential as consumers, being politically inactive, or likely to vote against the preferred candidate or referendum position. Research and theoretical work should address the impact on political participation which may result from systematic exclusion of segments of the population on the basis of some behavioral profile.

Finally, a concern with mass communications and social power relations would lead us to examine the ways in which communications technology, especially the computer, is being brought into play in an attempt to respond to greater global competitiveness and economic uncertainty. The new information age has been described by some as the age of surveillance and control.[3] Scientific management techniques in the workplace are being facilitated by automated surveillance of worker productivity. Psychological batteries and analyses of bodily fluids and brain waves warn employers of potentially nonproductive or disloyal employees. Telecommunications systems support the growth of distributed processing of the information, which allows management to shift production to more productive (less costly, more profitable) units on a continuing basis, weakening the power of labor to resist.

At the same time that information technology (IT) is used to further rationalize the production process, and increase management's control over its work force, computer-based models developed through surveillance of consumer behavior help to reduce uncertainty in the management of demand. While watching these trends within the corporate sector, we should not lose sight of similar patterns in the behavior of government agencies. Computerized searches of public and private records are performed routinely as a part of a process of "front-end verification." A variety of behavioral profiles aid the federal, state, and local governments in their efforts to eliminate "waste, fraud, and abuse" in the provision of government services.

A social power orientation would lead us to chronicle the uses to which such information is being put, including the description of its use within the realm of electoral and issue politics. The ability of bureaucratic organizations to gather information about individuals and "person types" contributes to a growing sense of powerlessness among the citizenry. An analysis of these trends should contribute to our understanding of the continuing decline in political participation and the growing sense of alienation being expressed by the public.

Because of our concern with Black and other populations that have traditionally been outside the mainstream, research organized through the Center for Communications Research at Howard University will reflect a particular interest in identifying those forces which contribute to a deepening of the inequality we already experience. Questions of media ownership, management, sponsorship, and control are high on our agenda. We have already noted the differences in the portrayal of Black and White political figures, and we plan to explore whether minority participation at management levels makes a difference in those portrayals.

We have also noted the striking disparity in health outcomes between Blacks and others in the United States, which we attribute in part to the quality of information about health provided through the mass media. The way people respond to perceived health threats depends in part on the kinds of images of both the threats and the treatment or prevention alternatives they are able to construct for themselves. The health of Black people is rarely the focus of content in mainstream media, and we suspect that minority media are also seriously constrained. We are especially interested in the relationship between dependence upon alcohol and tobacco revenue and the health-related editorial content of Black periodicals.

We agree with Gaye Tuchman (1973) that we learn more about media systems by observing how they respond in unusual situations, when circumstances cause them to depart from the routine. These are very unusual times. We believe as well that we best understand the hegemonic process when we observe how the media system operates to incorporate groups and individuals at the periphery into mainstream social consensus. Studying media and the ethnically diverse populations that make up the growing information underclass represents a vitally challenging opportunity for us to advance our understanding. We invite you to join us.

NOTES

1. Bob Worcester of Market and Opinion and Research International (MORI).
2. See Gandy and Simmons (1986) and Gandy (1987, in press). These papers discuss the dual technology of segmentation and targeting which are facilitated by changes in distribution systems that permit narrowcasting.
3. See Marx (1985) and Webster and Robins (1986).

REFERENCES

Ferment in the Field (Summer, 1983). J. of Communications 33, 3.
Gandy, Oscar H., Jr. (1982) Beyond Agenda Setting: Information Subsidies and Public Policy. Norwood, NJ: Ablex.
Gandy, Oscar H. Jr. (1987, in press) "The political economy of communications competence," in V. Mosco and J. Wasko (eds.) The Political Economy of Information. Madison: Univ. of Wisconsin Press.
Gandy, Oscar H. Jr. and Charles E. Simmons (1986) "Technology, privacy and the democratic process." Critical Studies in Mass Communications 3: 155-168.
Hall, Stuart (1982) "The rediscovery of ideology: return of the repressed in media studies," in M. Gurevitch, T. Bennett, J. Curran, and J. Woollacott (eds.) Culture, Society and the Media. New York: Methuen.
Lowery, Shearon and Melvin DeFleur (1983) Milestones in Mass Communication Research. New York: Longman.
Marx, Gary (1985) "I'll be watching you." Dissent (Winter): 26-34.
U.S. Congress, Office of Technology Assessment (June, 1986). Federal Government Information Technology: Electronic Records Systems and Individual Privacy. OTA-CIT-296. Washington, DC: Government Printing Office.
Murdock, Graham (1982) "Large corporations and the control of the communications industries," in M. Gurevitch, T. Bennett, J. Curran, and J. Woollacott (eds.) Culture, Society and the Media. New York: Methuen.
Newman, Karin (1986) The Selling of British Telecom. New York: St. Martin's.
Tuchman, Gaye (1973) "Making news by doing work: routinizing the unexpected." Amer. J. of Sociology 79: 110-131.
Webster, Frank and Kevin Robins (1986) Information Technology (a Luddite analysis). Norwood, NJ: Ablex.

THE MEDIUM AND THE EXPERIENCE
Further Gropings Toward
the Conceptualization of Effects

Elihu Katz

Before long, television-as-we-know-it will be gone, drowned in competition and confusion. I fear that we shall not be able to state, even then, wherein lie its powerful effects, although these may become clearer with historical distance. The agenda still calls for answers to the most elementary questions. I shall address two of them here, both designed to redirect attention to more sociological analysis. One question has to do with whether television is better conceived as technology or as text, and, if the latter, whether it consists in programs to which viewers pay attention or in a never-ending "flow" or "supertext," which viewers enter and exit as if in a trance. The second question presumes that at least certain programs are decoded as such—media events, for example, or best sellers such as "Dallas"—and asks what we might learn about effect from studies of the experience of viewing them. For purpose of this discussion, I propose (1) to reopen the hypothesis that the technologies of communication, independent of their content, have powerful consequences, albeit in combination with the nature of their deployment by social forces; and (2) to invoke the concepts of role and involvement in order to investigate the nature of the experience of viewing programs. I urge attention to these two agenda items—the medium and the experience.

THE MEDIUM

It is ironic that the empirical study of media effects has so much difficulty in identifying individual-level changes (McGuire, 1986; Katz, 1980), even while students of media technology insist that each new medium has brought revolutionary change at the societal level. For example, historians connect the technical attributes of print—rapid reproduction and exactitude ("fixity" in Eisenstein, 1978; "hot" in McLuhan, 1964)—with the Protestant Reformation and with the rise of science. By the same token, the newspaper is credited with describing boundaries for European nationalism; the telegraph is associated with the integration of economic markets in the United States (Carey, 1983); portable "media of space" (such as papyrus) are said to have been prerequisite to the bureaucratic empires of Egypt and Rome (Innis, 1951); the Book as "collective memory"—and substitute homeland—may be said to have contributed to the survival of the geographically dispersed Jewish people.

I suggest that technological theories, often discredited for their crude determinism, deserve our reconsideration in the search for powerful effects. Compared with the more common theories of media effects, technological theories are characterized by their emphasis (1) on how we think, rather than what we think, that is, on the ways in which our mental processing of different media give rise to different styles of thought; (2) on information and its diffusion, rather than on influence; (3) on boundary-setting for social systems such as empires, nations, churches—sometimes in concert, sometimes in conflict, with agencies of established power.

I think it is important to encourage study of the "careers" of media technologies and the struggles they engender in the effort to harness them, now for one cause or one class, now for another. The "revolutions," I suspect, result from these struggles rather than from simple cooptation by established power. If we can find regularities in these "careers," we shall have gotten somewhere. Such an approach also puts the new media technology into perspective. It calls for classifying the new media more strictly, some as point-to-point, others as broadcast technologies; some as media that "segment" societies and others as media that "integrate" them; some that inform, others that influence. It raises the question of whether media have "immanent" tendencies to perform one function or another, or to "resist" being confined to boundaries that are narrower than their reach. I don't want to anthropomorphize, but I do want to dramatize the issues.

I believe that we are now entering a phase where television will go the segmented way of radio, with nothing in sight to replace its integrative role. Lang (1979) disagrees in a thoughtful anticipation of media proliferation in the United States. The explosive multiplication of new channels and new media seems to be leading to highly specialized elite networks of communication on the one hand, and to international pop networks on the other, that is, to social structures that are both less than, and more than, the nation state. Indeed, the new media seem to be presiding over the dismemberment of the nation-state and its culture. European national public broadcasting systems—which perfected the art and sometimes the politics of television—are disintegrating before our eyes.

THE EXPERIENCE

At the other pole stands the "message." But there is a great, still unresolved debate about the nature of the message. There are those who see television simply as a nonstop tease, inviting a regressive posture, promising satisfaction but providing only frustration and addiction. This is the argument of cultural elitists (Postman, 1986; Mander, 1978), cinema theorists (Houston, 1984), and even certain empiricists (Csikszentmihalyi and Kubey, 1981). The opposing position sees "programs" that the viewer actively decodes, whether hegemonically, oppositionally, or in negotiation with the text. Clearly, we need closer observation of the viewing experience using a variety of methods, but especially anthropological ones, if only to distinguish the conditions under which we view television as zombies or as humans. In this connection, it is interesting to note the surprising convergence on the empirical study of "reading" by gratificationists who are rediscovering the text, and by critical and literary theorists who are discovering "real" readers.

The empirical study of types of involvement seems to be a high priority. If slow and alpha waves characterize one kind of viewing and certain kinds of programs (Krugman, 1971), we know that the live broadcasting of historic ceremonies (e.g., Greenberg and Parker, 1965) or of popular television serials evokes another kind of involvement. For this more active involvement, it is surprising how little we have adopted and applied relevant concepts from the psychology of drama such as "identification" or the symbolic interactionism of Horton and Wohl (1956).

The key to patterns of involvement, I believe, is to be found in the concept of role. Viewers who saw the Kennedy funeral as mourners, the Watergate trial as jurors, or the Royal Wedding as Her Majesty's subjects (Dayan and Katz, 1985) were enlisted by television to perform—and thus to be affected—in their ceremonial roles. By the same token, entering into a dialogue with "Dallas" as the representative of another culture (Liebes and Katz, 1986) or assuming a ludic stance toward the program as "play" (Stephenson, 1967) involves different kinds of experience, and, concomitantly, different kinds of effects, as Carey and Kreiling (1974) once proposed. Ostensibly, it would appear that referential readings may be more involving than ludic or metalinguistic ones, but we believe that the roles of critic or fantasy-game player may be as involving as referential or parasocial roles. Both the text and our social situations bear upon the reading roles we assume.

Studies of involvement suggest studies of noninvolvement or, to take a further step, of active disinvolvement or "denial." Lazarsfeld and Merton (1948) noted the narcotizing dysfunction of mass communications that gives us the illusion of participation. Knowledge gap studies show how we selectively avoid information that might, if we took note, improve our lot. Critical studies argue that we are victims of false-consciousness for failing to decode hegemonic messages oppositionally, or for cowering in the unpopularity to which the media have (falsely) assigned us or our views. The study of what commands whose attention, how it is decoded, and whether or how it is translated into action are central issues in the study of political communication. Not acting, not knowing, not believing, not doubting, not caring, not wanting to know, not wanting others to know may sometimes be functional, but at other times it may be costly indeed, as the Holocaust proved too well (Lipstadt, 1985).

REFERENCES

Carey, J. (1983) "Technology and ideology: the case of the telegraph," in J. Salzman (ed.) Prospects: The Annual of American Cultural Studies (vol. 8). Cambridge University Press.

Carey, J. and A. Kreiling (1974) "Popular culture and uses and gratifications: notes toward an accommodation," in J. Blumler and E. Katz (eds.) The Uses of Mass Communication. Newbury Park, CA: Sage.

Csikszentmihalyi, M. and R. Kubey (1981) "Television and the rest of life: a systematic comparison." Public Opinion Quarterly 45: 317-328.

Dayan, D. and E. Katz (1985) "Electronic ceremonies: television performs a royal wedding," in M. Blonsky (ed.) On Signs. Baltimore: Johns Hopkins.

Eisenstein, E. (1978) The Printing Press as an Agent of Change. New York: Cambridge University Press.

Greenberg, B. and E. Parker (1965) "Social research on the Kennedy Assassination," in B. Greenberg and E. Parker (eds.) The Kennedy Assassination and the American Public: Social Communication in Crisis. Stanford, CA: Stanford University Press.

Horton, D. and R. Wohl (1956) "Mass communication and para-social interaction." Psychiatry 19: 215-229.

Houston, B. (1984) "Viewing television: the metapsychology of endless consumption." Quarterly Journal of Film Studies 9: 183-95.

Innis, H. (1951) The Bias of Communication. Toronto: University of Toronto Press.

Katz, E. (1980) "On conceptualizing media effects." Studies in Communication 1: 119-142.

Krugman, H. (1971) "Brain wave measures of media involvement." Journal of Advertising Research 11, 1: 3-9.

Lang, K. (1979) "Media abundance: the American case." Communications (International Journal of Communication Research) 5 :171-201.

Lazarsfeld, P. and R. Merton (1948) "Mass communication, popular taste and organized social action," in L. Bryson (ed.) The Communication of Ideas. New York: Harpers.

Liebes, T. and E. Katz (1986) "Patterns of involvement in television fiction: a comparative analysis." European Journal of Communication 1 (2): 151-171.

Lipstadt, D. (1985) Beyond Belief. New York: Free Press.

Mander, J. (1978) Four Arguments for the Elimination of Television. New York: Morrow Quill.

McGuire, W. (1986) "The myth of massive media impact: savagings and salvagings." Public Communication and Behavior 1: 173-257.

McLuhan, M. (1964) Understanding Media. New York: McGraw-Hill.

Postman, N. (1986) Amusing Ourselves to Death: Public Discourse in the Age of Show Business. New York: Viking.

Stephenson, W. (1967) The Play Theory of Mass Communication. Chicago: University of Chicago Press.

THE PERSONAL AND THE PUBLIC
A Very Personal Public Response

Gladys Engel Lang

The research agenda for any discipline is a collective product and, necessarily, always in flux. It emerges as researchers go about their work, talking about projects they propose to undertake or propose as worthful undertakings for others. The many efforts by individuals, organizations, and ad hoc groups of scholars to set their own agenda, as well as the debates that ensue over the comparative merits of competing research agenda, are a vital part of the process by which a collective agenda emerges, "vital" not in the sense that, without them, no agenda would emerge, but in the sense that the emergent agenda would be different.

This distinction between formal agenda and collective agenda seems basic in answering the question, "Why bother?" Why should we devote so much time and energy to devising agenda? Some academics, it would seem, spend as much, or perhaps more, time debating the merits of alternative agendas—searching for "new paradigms" or "new directions"—than in getting on with their research. [Present company excepted, of course!] I firmly believe that the most meritorious agendas are never set but evolve collectively. It's not just that personal research agendas are the products of public agendas modified by awareness of what others are doing, personal curiosity, professional socialization, and so forth—"of the commingling of personal and public concerns"—but that the collective agenda is constantly being modified and evolving in response to all these private and public efforts to set the agenda. The debate over alternative agenda may be more determining of where research moves than the efforts to put into effect the proposed agenda themselves.

No one individual or group of individuals ultimately dictates the collective agenda. Nor do most of them have this purpose in mind when drawing up formal agenda for research. Agenda can be devised to serve different ends, so the first and basic question is: "Agenda for what?" What function is it intended to serve, and does it serve that function? The intended benefits of any agenda have to be weighed against its costs—and either of these can be anticipated or unanticipated. With no intent of setting up any systematic typology of agenda, based on function, let me illustrate:

Agendas can be used to set boundaries to a field, to give it an identity. Though admittedly not their primary function, the availability of such an agenda provides us with ready answers when skeptics insist on asking, "What is this field called 'communications'? Is there a discipline and how do you define it?" Questions like this are not unique to communications; each emergent discipline has had to endure such skepticism. Therefore, until communications becomes, like political science, "communication science," or, like psychology, sociology, and anthropology, "communicology," research agendas may serve us to justify and explain ourselves to other academics and to the professional community.

Some agendas, whether or not they were intended to do so, signal to others what is trendy, where the cutting edge is. Or, they may stake out a claim for a particular theory or approach. At its best, this serves to concentrate attention and efforts, to direct attention to problems central to the field, and, in this way, sometimes to create order out of chaos. At its worse, this kind of agenda-manufacture, in asserting the case for a given theoretical or methodological approach, has the, perhaps unintended, consequence of staking out a "turf"—of attracting money and brainpower so that everybody "runs" in the same direction—without examining whether this is the direction in which we should be moving, or whether this is where we want to go. Over the years some agendas have been more successful than others in staking out a claim; sometimes this has amounted to nothing more than successfully coining a catchword to describe the thrust of research on which disparate individuals have been working for some time.

Perhaps most frequent is the use of an agenda to codify the field—to take stock of "where we are, where we need to go, and what gaps there are to fill." Put to the best of uses, this programmatic "state-of-the-art" exercise can clarify and inspire; used badly, it can stifle creativity by reinforcing any tendency toward closure—that is, by making research fit into given slots, or by an insistence on overclassifying. In the effort to fit everything everyone is doing—or can think of doing—into some slot, there is also the danger of simply ending up with a smorgasbord of areas into which the field may be divided. But then, in all agenda-manufacture, there are certain potential dangers in restricting imagination and dictating direction.

Agendas, for analytic purposes, may be divided between those that are discipline-oriented and those that are policy-oriented. Of course, they can be both and usually are. Still, there are agendas that are drawn up for the express purpose of promoting research that will advance knowledge in the field, help to clarify concepts, and help to build that theory that mass communications is so often said not to have. Policy-oriented research, on the other hand, starts with goals that you believe in, or, at least, intend to achieve, and is oriented to providing guidance toward achievement of those goals. In calling for studies that look at the role of mass communications in the survival of democratic institutions, the Maryland agenda—as set out in Volume 5—is basically policy-oriented. But in proposing to focus on such matters as the intersection between political elites and communication elites, theirs is an agenda that is also discipline-oriented.

My own inclination, in drawing up an agenda, is to be less concerned with advancing the discipline than in ensuring that the discipline advances the cause of humankind. I have a kind of naive faith that if we ask the right questions the advancement of the discipline will somehow take care of itself. But, if we don't focus our questions so as to find some answers to urgent social problems, then what will it matter if we contribute to the discipline? I share the basic concern of the Maryland Center for focusing on the role of mass communications in the survival of democratic institutions and putting top priority on the intersection between political and communication elites. But, beyond that, I'd propose focusing on the role of mass communications in the survival of the world. Maybe the world will outlive those of us who attended this conference, but is it going to be there—and in what shape—for our children and grandchildren?

The difference between a discipline-oriented agenda and a problem-oriented agenda is basically a difference in orientation—the end product may not be much different. For instance, my own predilection—were I drawing up your agenda— would be to start by formulating an agenda for studying the preservation of democratic institutions and then, within this context, deciding what it is that we ought to study about the role of political and communication elites. Put another way, I would not be so much interested in studying a subject such as the social interlock between political and communication elites as understanding how public images of and participation in the political process are shaped by this overlap. Likewise, I'm less interested in demonstrating with scientific certainty that televised violence promotes unhealthy aggression in children than under-standing how television can be utilized to contribute to the guidance and supportive environment that is missing in the lives of disadvantaged children.

My sense is that what made the field of mass communications attractive to many communication scholars was that its research agenda evolved out of a concern with problem solving, and I would also argue that the most important theoretical advances in the field have been the result of trying to get answers to pressing social problems. The collective agenda has been the product of individuals' curiosity and desire to find answers to questions that not only intrigued them but had policy implications. The infant field was nurtured in a concern about the power of the media for good and evil—about the misuses of propaganda in promoting war hysteria, in fostering facism, and in domestic demagoguery. There was the interest in "ballyhoo" and whether you could indeed fool some of the people all of the time. I think a good cause can be made that, as a field, mass communications made most of its giant steps forward whenever researchers were focusing their empirical attention on tough and pressing "real-life" problems—like urban violence (in all its forms), censorship, political and community controversies, the threat of disaster, social movements for civil, gender, and social equities, along with voter apathy and other behavior problems involving the body politic and threatening to undermine the democratic process.

Has the consequence of exposure to the climate of "intensified paradigm jostling" forced researchers to make choices? Perhaps, insofar as their main concern has been for formulating an agenda that is predominantly discipline-oriented. But, from the perspective of the problem-oriented researcher—whether "crudely behaviorist" or "holistic" in orientation—I find it difficult to imagine that the controversy waged over alternative approaches—mainly having to do with methodology—has made much of a difference in the formulation of personal agendas. Yet, insofar as the formulation of a formal agenda is part of a battle for power and influence reflecting divisions in the political world, then the controversy will have had, in the not-so-long run, a very real effect on what emerges as the collective agenda for mass communication research. In this respect, "critical pluralism" (or "negotiation") would seem a logical personal response to an academic war, but I doubt that it will lead to a truce.

THE PROCESS OF AGENDA DEVELOPMENT

Kurt Lang

Research agendas are projections into an uncertain future. All too often the impetus comes from potential sponsors who want certain things studied or are simply looking for reassurance that a particular line of inquiry will pay off. Nevertheless, developing an agenda encourages stock-taking, a look at our complex field from a broad perspective to assess what we think we already know and to see what further questions this raises. One cannot do this without some codification of a complex field. There are different approaches. Some agendas seek to be all-encompassing; others set up priorities together with justifications for them.

I nevertheless have some doubts that the creative process can be programmed in this precise way. Historians of science have distinguished between the discovery of solutions to problems defined in advance and other accidental discoveries of a phenomenon the investigator could not at first understand because it contradicted the assumption on which the research was conducted and therefore forced a reformulation. One never knows in advance where idle curiosity will lead. In this profound sense, at least, research agendas will remain personal. It strikes me therefore that the *process* of developing an agenda, to the extent that it helps channel curiosity, is probably more useful than any set of questions on which participants in such discussions are likely to agree.

Although I have always pretty much gone my own way wherever my curiosity has led me, this has not been without some general orientation (or theory), which I do indeed share with others. I refer specifically to what the introduction by Gurevitch and Levy to Volume 5 of the *MCRY* identifies as an interest in the relationship between media and society, which subsumes comparisons of social reality with the media representation of that reality. The latter and other macrolevel issues have been a specific interest of mine.

My approach diverges from what has been the dominant orientation in American communication research with its emphasis on the individual and the determinants of his or her response. Although the member of the audience remains an indivisible unit of observation, it need not and should not be the only unit of analysis. The *social* effects we need to focus on involve the analysis of some collectivity. They also need to be perceived as process. In this connection, I propose a reformulation of the media versus reality problem to account for the fact that what we call reality is itself a social construction that arises in communication. The media, as major communication agencies, do not merely reflect or distort events; rather, they participate as actors in these events and help weave a tissue of meaning of which they, along with other actors, take account.

I am aware, of course, that it is often useful to examine whether a particular message in a distinct code and with a specific structure (or syntax) is accurately reproduced by journalists—Was the name right? Who and how many were present at some event? Is the quotation, already an encoded script, correct or not? To seize on these and other specifics can easily divert attention from the more complex interactions between reporters and their sources and between political actors attempting to use the media. The process of reality construction is and will always remain essentially a political process.

This is a good place to recall the dictum of W. I. Thomas that when people define a situation as real it is real in its consequences. Similarly, the definition of an issue as it emerges through the media has consequences because of the way actors respond to it. Gladys Engel Lang and I have repeatedly called attention to this under the rubric of "refraction." By our choice of that term we wanted to acknowledge that the image disseminated by the media, just as the view of any participant in an event, is shaped by what is accessible through the channels on which each one depends for information. *Collective* definitions are the result of pooling information that results in an image that most people consider valid.

This notion of collective definition has a certain similarity with what more recently has been lumped together under the label of agenda-setting research. But the exponents of this approach, in reviving the old idea that the media structure issues, gradually extended the concept of an agenda to apply to anything of which people were aware, to topics of their concern, to the subjects they talked about, and so forth. The question of how a public agenda relates to the various institutional agendas, which Cobb and Elder had raised in their original articles, was redefined in terms of how people perceived and learned about specific subjects and how they became aware of their importance.

Important as the above type of data are as a foundation on which to build an understanding of the political process, the categorization of issues that go into the agenda has by and large been too superficial to be of much use. It fails to deal adequately with the content of the images that affect the actions of individuals, groups, and organized entities in relation to one another. The list of relevant images includes self-images; it includes, in fact, anything that impels people, especially significant actors, to act in order to control and/or manipulate their own image and to counteract and refute competing images. On the political level, one has to deal with the various media strategies the competitors employ to achieve an objective. The social effect to be looked for is how the availability of the media for such strategies affects the outcome of particular controversies and whether the implementation of a policy is facilitated or made more difficult.

Other social effects become manifest only over long periods. Among these I mention the possibility that the present media structure, as well as its omnipresence, may contribute to or undermine national unity, the diffusion of projective distrust, and the credibility and legitimacy of major institutions; that it may raise or lower the level of conflict within a society; that it may create new social, cultural, and intellectual cleavages or bridge existing ones; and that it may influence the ethos governing community life in a number of ways difficult to specify.

Having outlined how I view mass communications and mass communicators as ongoing participants, not only in the creation of issues but also in the production of culture, let me briefly make some specific observations and suggestions.

(1) Too many issues and controversies have been studied only in the context of electoral contests, events that are predictable and where the cleavages usually follow established conventional lines. Other long-standing conflicts have not had nearly as much attention from mass communication research. We should redirect our effort.

(2) Another important question that has not received enough attention from social scientists is how particular technological innovations affected political strategies, especially when one can target and "personalize" promotional messages much more than ever before.

(3) Closely related to the above is how these innovations affect the distribution of power among skill groups. For example, campaign managers seem to be replacing newspaper publishers as chief political advisers.

(4) These and other changes also have implications for how the game of politics is played, for the production of culture, for the distribution of knowledge within a society. Harold A. Innis was one who dealt with these problems in a broad historical sweep, but there has not been enough of a follow-up.

(5) What is the flow or distribution of "information" from the center to the periphery? This problem affects not only nations and how they see their

relationship to each other (as expressed by the demands for a New World Information Order), but also regions and the different levels of the same society. An event communicated as news will be "local" for some, but quite distant or even foreign to others. Perceptions of and reactions to the event and of the reporting of the event are apt to differ accordingly.

(6) One question of particular interest to me relates to the effect of publicity in various contexts—international diplomacy, collective bargaining, and even athletic contests. The public is brought in and sees more than ever before. In the area of sports, to cite one example, umpires are "corrected" by replays. Media representatives take pride in what they can show, but are reluctant to be forced into the role of adjudicators.

(7) Studies of all these and other questions should be comparative, but not only in the mistaken sense of using identical indicators from six or eight nations but, rather, by going back to the Weberian "thought experiment," which draws on intensive case studies of phenomena or events that are, at least in some sense, similar. The comparison need not be national but can use several communities, time zones, and historical eras, especially when these are associated with the difference in modes of communication (e.g., literate-nonliterate, visual-auditory, analog-binary) or access to information (e.g., media rich versus media poor).

(8) Although policy-orientation can make a study more relevant, it has been my experience that research on almost any problem, conducted from a broad intellectual perspective, will yield findings that are policy relevant. One is not required to remain in a strictly managerial framework. Problems should be redefined to encompass the whole range of possible side effects, including such costs and benefits as may not have occurred to the manager or client.

(9) Finally, while many of the most interesting research questions will be self-generated, researchers should also be responsive to external requests as long as they develop their research in ways that does not compromise their intellectual and scholarly commitments.

THE END OF COMMUNICATION
AND THE BEGINNING OF IDEOLOGY

Thelma McCormack

The foundations of modern media research in the United States are a strong emphasis on the empirical method, an interactive model of communication, and a concept of media institutions as independent of the state and accountable in a free society. In one way or another, each of these propositions has been challenged, yet they survive, alone or in combination, if only because the critique of them proved even more frangible. It is, then, a deeply flawed yet resilient tradition that keeps rising, like the phoenix out of its own ashes, but each time flying lower with more wobble and less grace.

There are many things we do that are right, and should continue to do and do better. I recently returned from Chile, where I was invited to talk about content analysis because they were using an article I had done on content analysis. I have never been very enthusiastic about counting and measuring or the conventional methods of doing content analysis. Yet in Chile, a country struggling with its own tragic Orwellian nightmare, where history goes down the memory hole and is replaced by the paranoid scenarios of General Pinochet, I began to understand that content analysis could be a form of political praxis. The small cadre of people in Santiago who have been analyzing media content—the regime's media (newspapers and broadcasting) and the opposition media—has provided the only record we have of what has been taking place in recent Chilean history, and the best documentation we could possibly find of the complicity of the prestige media in the Pinochet government. These studies have kept alive a past of a socialist and democratic Chile, and they have protected the present day opposition to Pinochet from falling prey to mental depression and a sense of political despair.

And there are other examples of monitoring research that lack some of the style, some of the haute couture of newer forms of research, but are important in building a data base over time that will allow us to distinguish between long-term trends and short-term variations. But on the down side, on the negative side, is the return of communication models that most of us thought were dead and buried. In our discipline, it seems, we are never able to retire old hypotheses.

The new pornography research is a case in point. Carried out mainly by experimental psychologists and based on behavioral theory, it has revived the old hypodermic needle model that we long ago discarded. The recent studies that are not based on either communication theory or cultural theory are widely accepted now as evidence of how the media influence our behavior. Communication scholars have been remarkably, indeed, conspicuously silent in the public debates about pornography research and public policy. Is it because we have some doubts in our minds about our own models of media effects? Or is it some "failure of nerve" in a conservative political environment?

Our record, then, is mixed. We have made a great deal of progress in both our research and theory in a short time. Indeed, the time frame is itself a problem. The largest part of our research has been carried out since World War II. Only a small fraction belongs to the Depression years, and although some of the most important research was done during the war, it tends to be overlooked. What stands, then, as the corpus of work, what a contemporary student regards as "media research," may, in retrospect, be atypical, the special product of a distinctive period whose ethos and culture, political economy and division of labor, social cleavages and political consensus are all unusual when viewed from the longer-range perspective of history. If we were to do a sociology of knowledge on ourselves, on our intellectual history, on the template of our tradition, what parochialisms emerge and characterize the work as belonging to a certain period in our history? And what kinds of exogenous constraints are being imposed on us now that we are unaware of? Can they be anticipated and dealt with by a more reflexive research?

I'm going to suggest that it can or that we ought to try. Meanwhile, our day-to-day research is only indirectly affected by the politics of the postwar period because we are not a mirror of reality. Rather we are a mirror of the mirror; that is, our agendas are set by the media. Our research has been a response to last night's television, last month's press, last year's movies. We are more directly influenced by the media—their organization and production, content and style—than by the social order. The media, regrouping themselves after the war and realigning themselves after the introduction of television, became the effective voice of the new lifestyles of the middle class, as well as of its political withdrawal from the larger and more complex world outside of the United States. So did our research that focuses on entertainment and on the integrative functions of the media, that is, on pleasure, peace, and harmony. And, then, as the media themselves became more and more removed from social reality, scholars began to refer to news and public affairs as "myth" in order to draw attention to the dramaturgical structure of what was supposed to be a relatively scientific and unmythological treatment of a subject. In short, our media research took its cues from the media themselves. If there was a distortion, it became a double distortion that we, in turn, passed on to the next generation of young scholars.

They say generals are always fighting the last war. What I have been suggesting is that the media are too. And I mean this both symbolically and literally. Television coverage of Vietnam were the newsreels of World War II. G.I. Joe in Italy became G.I. Joe in Saigon. Street fights in Beirut look like the old movies of Allied troops taking towns left in ruins by fleeing Germans. Girls and women greeting troops on tanks look like the footage of Americans arriving in Paris. It is not, then, just generals who fight the last war; it is journalists as well, and they, in turn, shape our agendas.

Instead of being the conscience of the media, we have been their faithful Eckermanns, recording the wisdom of others without questioning it.[1] When the media were apolitical, so were we. Nothing demonstrates this more clearly and more poignantly than Deborah Lipstadt's study of how the American press treated, or, more accurately, failed to treat the Holocaust. The under reporting, she says, was a form of self-censorship that she attributes to a psychological block, an inability on the part of reporters and editors to grasp the true dimensions of the deportations, the camps, and the final solution. It was, she said, simply beyond their belief.

But it was not beyond ours, not beyond the belief of a community of scholars that included a significant number who were refugees. Had we in the research community defined ourselves independently and as the conscience of the media, had we opted to be political precisely because the media were in this period apolitical, there would at least have been a debate on record. As it was, we were captives of a model that studied the media and focused on what was there, that is, what the media defined as important; we had neither theory nor precedent to make the media accountable for their disbelief, for their caution, although we had enough people who knew from firsthand experience the consequences of this self-censorship, this denial.

As long as the conventions remain intact, as long as we react to the media's behavior and media content, we risk making the same mistake again. I am concerned that we have a great deal of abstruse discussion of "news"-as-"myth," but no theory of disinformation when our government openly acknowledges that it practices disinformation. Our students are apt to know more about cockfights in Indonesia or the prison notebooks of Gramsci than they do about history. How will we be judged 30 years from now? How do we do research on disinformation? What kind of a theory, what kind of a model do we need? And if we move toward a model of media research as the conscience of the media, what kinds of restraints are needed?

Media research has *not* been the conscience of the media. It has been the bad conscience. And I would like to illustrate this in the way our studies have treated women, for, as I have suggested elsewhere, there is as much "machismo" in media research as there is in media content.

First, the women's movement owes nothing to the media or to media research. Both ignored the changes taking place in the labor force with more women returning to work or remaining in their jobs; both ignored, too, the changes taking place in family structure with more families headed by single parents. And both treated as whining the complaints of women about their cultural and social isolation in the suburbs, as neurotic their complaints about the sexist abuses in the health care system. These are some of the demographic and sociopsychologial factors that account for the recent development—more accurately, the recent revival—of a more or less dormant women's movement. The larger framework is, of course, the aspirations on a worldwide scale for structural equality and political liberation. (It is no accident that the rhetoric of the women's movement is similar to the rhetoric of Third World countries in their anticolonial struggles for independence.) But whether we are talking about the larger frameworks and an ideological program or the smaller, immediate grievances, the media showed very little interest unless a group of women was disrupting a "Miss America" contest.

As for the present, media research continues to treat gender as an attribute, an ascriptive characteristic that does not have the dynamic or potential volatility as the most preferred and privileged variable, namely, income. Gender is treated more like "age": maybe you use it, maybe you don't, but there is no theory that makes it imperative, and that gives it a priority over other variables. This tendency in our studies to minimize gender, to make it an optional table, is a measure of indifference rather than a conviction that gender differences are disappearing. The fact is, as I learned in reviewing voting studies, there is no consistency: in one study the data are broken down by "sex"; in another on the same subject, they are not.

It is not sufficient, however, to use gender. The challenge is to use it as an active variable, and as a potential focus of an insurgent social movement. The second bias, then, is an equilibrium model of society that would view the current women's movement as a bleep on a radar screen, a signal of a need for minor adjustment. Hence it is not a failure on the part of the media if news about the movement is not given a prominent place. But, alternately, a conflict model of society would lead to a different kind of analysis of how the media depict the movement. The hypothesis would be that in a social structure based on gender inequality, the media marginalize the movement by treating it as a deviant phenomenon attracting deviant women, and that the media attempt to defuse the militancy by devaluing the movement. Thus, if we continue in media research to use an equilibrium model of society, our research on gender will be inadequate, a classification rather than a relationship based on differential authority, power, and privilege. To take a very simple example, "male" and "female" are not the same as "husband" and "wife." The former is a classification; the latter, a relationship.

I have suggested here that conflict theory may be more appropriate for understanding gender and gender differences in media research than equilibrium or systems theory. But conflict theory may not be sufficient for understanding the nature of women's behavior and their responses to the mass media. We have to account for the fact, borne out by our demographic studies, that women are the most faithful members of audiences, and, with few exceptions, they are overrepresented proportionately. Thus women have a power, but do not use it. And, they seem most devoted, most loyal in their audience behavior to programs that provide a number of obvious gratifications but are, nevertheless, androcentric in their value system, and patriarchal in the gender relationships. Why have women been content to be depicted as objects, as innately inferior, as less able than men to think, plan, or take adult responsibility? And why have women who are employed outside of the home found the same pleasures as their counterparts at home in movies, magazine fiction, and TV programs that see women only as homemakers?

Our theories do not, I suggest, account for this behavior. And the male researchers who do so typically fall back on some version of motivational theory that sees women as immature, looking for escape, seeking role models, or some other explanation that assumes a very low level of reality testing. Indeed, there is a double standard that male researchers use. When women write to their favorite TV star, it is seen as childish fan behavior; when men write to their favorite TV anchor man, it is "feedback." When young girls scream at "rock" concerts, it is hysteria; when adult men scream at an umpire whose decision they did not like, it is seen as a cognitive response—slightly excessive, but still a person playing a game, a more intelligent, higher-order response than a female's.

A double standard is involved, too, in the presumption of male investigators that they are qualified to understand the gratifications women experience in soap operas or movies made for women, but women investigators are not qualified to understand the gratifications of men watching sports. I have some personal experience here, having done a study of boxing films. I am continually asked to explain this strange interest, although no man, to my knowledge, has ever been asked to explain his competence to review the ballet. In a patriarchal society, male expertise is a generalized ability, while female expertise is specialized and domestic.

Putting aside, however, the politics of media research and the double standard, there is a question of whether we have a theory to account for the behavior of women, whether communication theory can compete with the newly developing feminist theory. The most serious objection to communication theory and communication research is that they depict women as passive and indirectly contribute to that passivity. We see this in various kinds of audience research where the creative roles are less apparent, and in the management-oriented studies that invite the participation of women but for purposes of improved management. We see it, also, in the way findings are interpreted either through traditional sex roles or through sex-role theory rather than stratification.

The passivity of women is both real and symbolic, but in reality women are less passive than they are in the minds of men; the symbolic or perceived passivity is greater than reality. In the case of the fine arts, women are as active as men, but outside of the market sectors in the semiprofessional and nonmonetized parts of art worlds. But those who study the study of distribution of people in the arts and who focus only on the prestige or monetized areas are apt to conclude from the absence of women that they are passive. What these historians, men or women, are expressing is a social prejudice and a system of discrimination.

But given that most of our research is directed to the commercial or popular media, not the amateur or semiprofessional milieu, women appear passive in the sense that they seldom express any criticism or use their clout. Nevertheless, from a management perspective the behavior of female audiences may not be a good fit for managerial objectives; it may even be too erratic although still highly passive. Thus we have audience research shaped by the interests of management or by the more creative cultural workers: writers, producers, actors, musicians, and others. In this research, women's opinions are solicited, they are invited to participate in panels, and someone listens to them as they ventilate their grievances. Yet this is as far as it goes, for the results of the studies are never returned to the audiences, and the opportunities for a genuine two-way dialogue do not exist. Thus what appears to be cultural democracy is not; what alarms elitist critics about audience control is unfounded. The overall result of these studies may be more audience satisfaction, but not a more active audience; the women who participate as subjects still have no voice in planning or in making major decisions within the systems.

The analysis of the findings of the studies is often very sophisticated statistically, but any differences in gender are attributed to different patterns of socialization and sex roles. Thus the preferences of women for drama, religious programs, and consumer information, and the preferences of men for sports, adventure, and nature programs, are explained in terms of their sex roles. But sex roles are no longer complementary; they overlap and are canceled by other roles—occupational and professional—that men and women also play. What is problematic is whether the differences are the result of our fondness for sex role theory and whether, if the differences are real, they can be accounted for in different ways.

The key to these gender patterns may be inequality rather than sex roles. Increasingly, feminists have been dissatisfied with sex-role theory because it leaves intact the larger social structure with its power differentials. For our purposes, it led people in advertising research to believe that if only sex-role images could be changed, if more women were seen in the executive offices and more men in the kitchen, that if the negative stereotypes of women could be removed and replaced by prosocial images, that equality would be achieved. Structural inequality and the concomitant patterns of sex roles or definitions of femininity and masculinity can account for differences; that is, women's sex roles may change, but their dependency does not.

What I have tried to suggest here is that the major bias in media research, and the one that future media research must address, is the emphasis on the passivity of women. This passivity is, as I indicated earlier, both fact and fiction. When I said earlier that media research had a bad conscience, I was suggesting that we may have contributed to the fiction in the way we have carried out our research, the way we have interpreted our results, and the methods we have used. But these are not simply methodological biases that could be eliminated with more care and sensitivity, tighter controls, and stricter rules. They are in the nature of the discourse itself so that contemporary feminists, starting from a different set of assumptions about gender and about texts, are moving toward a different theory. To put the matter bluntly, I see a time coming when we may have to choose between communication theory and feminist theory.

The latter has a special interest in the way women construct their own texts and the way they deconstruct the texts of men. Communication theory has never been interested in the gendering of texts. It has been interested in how novels became films, but not how feminist novels became sexist films; nor has it been interested in avant-garde feminist films. Yet communication theory has a great deal to say on how we deconstruct texts. But have we been too facile in our assumption that women have selectedly reinterpreted the messages in the media? These are questions that are now in contention, and where a real break may occur.

The contemporary fascination with texts in both the humanities and the social sciences sensitizes us to the structure of our own texts and the way the media construct and package reality. If, as I suggested earlier, we seem to be dealing with today's history through yesterday's cameras, can we envisage a different type of format that would come closer to our experience? And, if there are other formats, how can we study them?

These are some of the questions that come to mind in viewing the eight-hour documentary film on the Holocaust, *Shoah*, made by French filmmaker Claude Lanzmann. *Shoah* consists mainly of interviews with concentration camp survivors, people who lived in the villages near the camps, and some of the functionaries responsible for the camps. As a film it is so underproduced and unstructured it makes any kind of sequential, linear documentary seem false. In addition, it is uninteresting cinematically; there are no great angles or shots, no interesting special effects. No one would consider it an art film, yet it is as important in communication history as Picasso was for modern art.

Shoah, like the Watergate hearings or the more recent Iran-Contra hearings, is addictive. Normal spans of attention are extended, and the impact is seldom emotional; the redundancy alone is numbing. And yet it engages us far more than the more consciously dramatized narrative. But to do research on this form is to do research on research, for this format is a form of inquiry.

Thus it is the end of research as we have known it. Our research and the media may become fused into a new form of communication and a new form of research. We will not be studying programs; we will be the programs, or the programs will be studying us. Taking this one step further, how would we do our research if we saw it as a documentary, if tomorrow we saw ourselves not as observers, outside of a process, but as interviewers and interviewees? At the very least, it calls for a radically new communications paradigm.

NOTE

1. J. P. Eckermann was a young man who greatly admired Goethe. They met when Goethe was in his 70s and Eckermann in his early 30s. Shortly after Eckermann devoted his life to editing Goethe's works and the famous conversations.

BARRIERS TO CARRYING OUT
A RESEARCH AGENDA

Jack M. McLeod

Insofar as it is restricted to the suggestion of new topics and approaches, the setting of a research agenda presents no problem for me. If, on the other hand, such an agenda stipulates topics that should *not* be studied and methods that should *not* be used, then the smell of the académie can become off-putting. The latter is common enough in the pretentious "paradigm" arguments on all sides; happily, Blumler and Gurevitch restrict themselves to a critical pluralism that welcomes a wide variety of viewpoints and strategies.

Even a research agenda without restrictions raises a number of questions, however. For example, what, if anything, can be achieved collectively from a "consensual" agenda that would not be obtained individually from a "semi-free marketplace of ideas?" Increasing the possibilities for accumulating knowledge is one answer to this question, but there are some real structural barriers to collective efforts that should be discussed.

Before discussing these barriers more fully, some mention should be made of the difficulties with the Gurevitch and Levy goal of "enhancing the contributions of mass communication research to the promotion of democratic ideals and practices." Which democratic practices and goals are to be given priority? How are we to adjust our research priorities when, for example, the ideals of freedom and equality are in conflict?

With respect to research goals, it also seems important to distinguish between *being conscious* of the policy implications of communication research and the *doing* of policy research as defined by others. In the latter case, the media organization (e.g., credibility) and the government agency (e.g., violence) define the problem as they see it. Critical scholars point out the obvious status quo biases of such "administrative" research; more subtle are the potential restrictions externally defined problems place on theoretical development. With the problem come sponsor-defined effect criterion variables that are overly broad and usually multidimensional. Complex behaviors such as "aggressiveness" and "school achievement," not surprisingly, have many determinants. As a result, whatever effect television use or other media variables might have is likely to be buried amidst a host of other influences. Alchemistic prediction rather than theoretical accumulation is apt to be the result.

Although I am very sympathetic to both the spirit and the detail of the key features outlined in the Blumler and Gurevitch agenda statement, I wonder if they haven't put the research agenda "cart" before the research organization and training "horse." That is, we are less deficient in having appropriate topics of research than we are in having suitable facilities and strategies for the accumulation and communication of knowledge and for the training of future scholars who would make things better. Some of the topics and problems presented here also puzzled the "founding fathers" of the field and today we "tribal elders" seem not much closer to a solution. The carrying out of any agenda seems to belong to the next generation of communication scholars. We would do well to ponder the barriers that are likely to frustrate the scholars who follow us.

Today's graduate students are presented with some very confusing intellectual signals by their elders. They are urged to study theory, but they have difficulty finding good examples of it. Close inspection shows not lack of assertions; rather, the problem stems from a failure to clearly state definitions and assumptions behind the assertions. It is odd that a field called communication is most deficient in its attention to the problems of language. In my judgment, all our intellectual and ideological perspectives share this problem.

Students are urged to adopt systematic methods in the pursuit of research questions, but there seems to be little interelder agreement as to which approaches are systematic and which are not. The adviser's pet method is the safest out. Ironically, the basic journalistic skills of *observation,* which could be a common meeting ground for varying perspectives, seems to be given relatively little attention in our research methods training. My own bias is that both hard and soft data can make important contributions to any research problem worth studying—the problem is combining such data when few researchers are good at using more than one method.

The received wisdom has it that one of the attractive features of the communication field is that it is eclectic in incorporating a number of perspectives; yet what the entering student sees is a set of warring camps, each intolerant of all "paradigms" but its own. All varieties of the "enemy" are put into one stereotypic boat, which is then set intellectually adrift and sunk with a clever turn of phrase.

Another enticing feature of the communication field offered down to our students is its multilevel multidisciplinary nature. Yet few guidelines are given on how to build theory at one level (e.g., macrosocial, cognitive, physiological) based on or consistent with data obtained at a different level. Before the upcoming Chaffee and Berger volume, this problem was not even discussed. The student also gets mixed signals about the relative autonomy of communication theory in terms of how much is to be borrowed and how much is or can be uniquely developed. This ambivalence is also reflected in students' doctoral work, which at worst poses a choice between becoming a borrowing psychologist, and so forth, or a self-conscious communicologist.

Our students come to see that, although mass communications includes the study of many parts of as "model"—sources, media organizations, content, audiences, and so forth—research on these various parts tends to stand in splendid isolation, each separate from the other. However much we may urge the "horizontalizing" of research to make connections between the parts, our students perceptively see the practical difficulties of doing so with limited resources. The best students also become aware of the American focus of the existing literature. They see the desirability of doing comparative research across nations, organizations, communities, and also time to test and clarify theoretical generalizations. But financial and other constraints make this comparative strategy seem, at best, an item on their "someday" list.

Today's graduate students are faced with problems more pressing than a distant research agenda, however attractive. Faced with the increasingly high cost of education and lessened levels of financial support, they are apt to begin their academic careers tens of thousands of dollars in debt. Job openings in journalism education seem narrowly defined in specifying skills teaching while teaching theory and research methods appear as special interests to be tolerated. The tenure hustle is anticipated and quick-and-dirty research looks more feasible than pursuing the more long-term features of agendas such as we have considered. Cross-national research may be feasible in Europe, where boundaries are close, but what prospects are there for travel, much less for data gathering, for the growing numbers of Asian and African scholars? Opportunities for Americans to do overseas research have also lessened considerably in the past two decades.

Lest I appear to be overly cranky and pessimistic, let me say that there are positive aspects to a communication research career that should not be overlooked. There are more job openings in communication at major universities than in almost any other field. Publishing opportunities are certainly far greater than they were 20 years ago, and the new journals provide forums for a wide range of approaches to research. Thanks to people like Blumler and Gurevitch, there are now appropriate models of comparative research available. They have provided logical argument for multicausality, systemic comparison, and eclecticism, which should give encouragement to future scholars, whatever constraints are present. It is my belief, however, that pursuit of a common agenda requires collective and structural solutions to conditions that cannot be overcome solely by individual effort.

COMMUNICATION AND CULTURE

Horace Newcomb

My concerns with the "Maryland Agenda" have to do with the fact that, while many of my interests are touched on there, none of "my" language is used. I don't mean to suggest personal, individual ownership of this language; I'm not talking about references to my own published work. I'm talking about a set of terms used in the body of work I read—text, narrative, or, more basically, fiction. Other terms—portrayal, representations—*are* used, but in ways not common to the work I follow, the ongoing scholarly and research traditions in which I feel included. I will comment briefly on some of the details of this fact, pointing to some implications, then go on to equally brief suggestions about how the use of that "other" language might refocus some of the expressed concerns of the Maryland writers.

To begin, I find some problems in the paragraph devoted to "cultural studies." It is now clear, of course, that this "field" is itself multiple, fraught with internal distinctions bordering on the usual scholarly disagreements, and quite fuzzy about common goals. Perhaps the single, lumped term used by the Maryland authors accounts for their puzzlement that, while Carey "sees entrenched resistance to cultural studies among American researchers," they feel that "the doors for cultural studies in the United States have been thrown wide open." This is all the more curious when they close their paragraph by saying that "attention still must be paid to finding a place in and establishing the relevance of cultural studies for schools of journalism and mass communication." Should we be concerned that the doors have been thrown open to a field of study whose relevance is unclear, and for which there seems to be no place? Are the doors open in other departments in American universities? Do those other departments have a clearer notion of the relevance of cultural studies?

I don't mean to be picky here. In fact, I probably come closer to the Maryland view than to Carey's. My sense is that much work that could be loosely collected under the heading of cultural studies is being done, much of it in departments named or associated with journalism and mass communication, and much of it having a strong influence on other, more traditional forms of analysis. Still, the anomalous sentence in the Maryland paper—find a place, establish the relevance—helps explain other factors within that work which bear on my own concerns for future developments.

Central here is the nearly exclusive attention to news as the subject for analysis in mass communication studies. This is doubtless an expression of the authors' affiliation and prior research, but I also think it an expression of a lingering hesitance—often *in* departments of journalism and mass communication—to deal with mass mediated fiction. The hesitance is related to a deeply ingrained reluctance to deal with material not central (or not admitted to be central) to the researchers' lives. "Popular culture," "TV," "hit movies, records, books," are still suspect. And it should be clear that I write from a comfortable professional affiliation in a department not of journalism, or even mass communication, but of Radio-Television-Film. My own shaping forces are fully as involved as those of the Maryland writers.

It is not surprising, then, that the term "stories" appears only in the context of discussing news professionals and their relation to social elites, and is flagged with the sign of the strange, the quotation marks. Nor is it surprising that "media portrayals" also refers to news portrayals of issues. Nor again, that the field of "decoding" strategies is cited as undeveloped, when it comes to news "(as well as of other media contents)"—the double flag of quotes *and* parentheses.

Again, none of this is meant to carp. I agree totally with the Maryland paper that "the public (or mass) communication process ought to be viewed as an integrated whole in which the various actors and institutions are linked and interdependent; investigation of any part of this process ought to be located in its social, cultural, and political context." The problem is, however, that, in order to do this, one must have an articulated theory of culture. This is still missing from the Maryland paper and from its calls for further research. I suggest the lack goes far in accounting for the absence of certain terms, foci, and methods, and helps explain the all-but-contradictory early comment on the place of cultural studies.

Let me suggest, then, that my own first order of research would be to focus on just such a question/problem, on the relationships among various under-standings of "communication" and "culture." Work is proceeding apace on this topic in various versions of cultural studies in this country and abroad, in anthropology and sociology, in literary and cinematic studies. From my personal perspective, various approaches to the study of television—approaches that are aside from or challenges to older social-psychological approaches—have caused much of this discussion. Television—as technology, as content, and as socioeconomic system—poses problems for almost every discipline, much as written communication did before it.

And central to an understanding of the cultural roles of mass-mediated communication are terms often associated with those other disciplines. What happens when we change "Sender-Message-Receiver" to "Author-Text-Reader," of to "Authorship-Signification-Meaning Making?" Here, I again agree with the Maryland authors. I believe that the social construction of reality is a possible area in which our various approaches will come together. We will have to see, however, that that construction process takes fiction as one of its central components, that the producers of fictions, no less than the audiences for them, struggle over that construction process, and that our systems of distribution—the political economy of the process—must also be studied within a cultural framework. Economics, policy, distribution, reception can all be translated from their traditional languages into the language of cultural and textual analysis. This should not happen in every study, nor should the translation remain final. It is another way to understand. But if we are to engage these issues, we must *all* begin to be familiar with, begin to use, the terms. It is only in the interest of "equal time" that I've concentrated on problems with the Maryland paper. While I shy away from directives of any sort, content to pursue, with Tannenbaum, the things that most interest me, I remain grateful for those statements that require me to clarify my own. It is, after all, communication that we study.

AGENDAS IN
MASS COMMUNICATION RESEARCH
A View from Britain

Colin Seymour-Ure

British scholars might greet the idea of pondering a research agenda for mass communications with a shrug of tolerant skepticism. After all, it is difficult actually to be *against* the idea; and if you like doing that sort of thing, then that is the sort of thing you will like doing. Engagement in the activity might produce a more constructive reaction. The value of drawing up an agenda as an intellectual "mapping" exercise would become clear, much as drafting a budget helps one to appraise one's potential, even though it does not itself make you richer or poorer. Like a budget, too, a research agenda may make plain the difference between a scholar's view of what is desirable and what is practical.

But skepticism might endure, even so. Admittedly, any generalization about British media researchers is unreliable, because of their diversity. Yet this diversity is the chief ground on which the skepticism would rest. British researchers are typically located, intellectually and institutionally, in disciplines and departments whose vantage points encourage them to view most important questions about communications as questions essentially about something else—whether it be political leadership, social class, economic power, technology, health education, leisure, international relations, or an infinite range of possibilities. Agendas, by comparison at least with the United States, will surely be fairly personal and individual (not to say idiosyncratic). More than a hint of a prescriptive intention would seem hubristic, if not ridiculous.

This individuality derives from the particular forces shaping mass communications research in Britain. These scarcely need elaborating. British institutions of higher education, still comparatively few in number (only 44 universities, for instance) are geared primarily to undergraduate teaching. The tendency to link teaching and research is strong. Graduate schools are small. Schools of Communication and of Journalism, no longer entirely nonexistent, remain pitifully few—as do research institutes like those at Leeds and Leicester. (Units at Manchester, City University, Central London Poly, and Goldsmiths College, among others, have begun to swell the ranks, as have non-university-based organizations such as the Broadcasting Research Unit in London.) Research fundors such as the Economic and Social Research Council, the major fundor, still seem unsure where to fit mass communications into their grant-making arrangements. Research too often gets a bad press from media professionals, who dub it nasty, brutish, and long—jargon-ridden and "too sociological." British ethnocentrism and linguistic incompetence cut off too many scholars from continental European work. The accessible literature from overseas was for years largely North American. Of course, these features change. But the research community remains—if less so than 10 years ago—small, dispersed, based in traditional disciplines, lacking a large audience for detailed, specialist work and which serves as a pool of talent.

The overall "research agenda" produced from these conditions resembles more the raggedy garb of a derelict than a Harlequin's brightly patterned cloth. Within their own particular disciplines or groups of disciplines, one might nonetheless expect to find in scholars' own agendas a number of general characteristics. First is the continuing disinclination to view Communications as a discipline rather than as a field or process. But with changing technology has come a new interest in defining the boundaries of the field. How to define a mass medium is a preoccupation of British scholars as of scholars elsewhere, and the surge of new media has given an impetus to studies of how people use media and for what purposes. The theoretical frameworks to which such concerns are related remain, however, those of traditional disciplines in the arts and social sciences.

In the 1950s and 1960s personal agendas were strongly influenced by American scholarship. This provided, in the behavioral sciences, models of empirical work to which there were few counterparts in Britain. Studies of the impact of press and television reflected the formulation of questions about violence or voting behavior, for instance, in ways that seemed as appropriate to British as to American life. Thus the first comprehensive national study of voting behavior in Britain (which was not, in fact, strong on the media side) was published by an Anglo-American team of whom the American half provided the bulk of the methodological expertise (Butler and Stokes, 1969). But at a time when higher education was expanding very rapidly and young scholars were increasingly keen to do research about communications, few indeed were able to find finance for studies of that kind. This alone may have been a major reason (alongside others implicit in the conditions outlined earlier) for a cavalier approach to methodology bordering on indifference. To put it another way, British scholars have shown a willingness to ask "large questions" in mass communications without too much concern about their ability to answer them with a precision satisfying rigorous canons of social scientific "proof." The complimentry way of judging this tendency would be to say that British scholars are not hidebound; that they have avoided triteness and banality (in this form at least); that they do not lose sight of the wood for the trees; and that they have been uninhibited by problems of methodology from tackling questions about the broad social effects of media, during a time when TV has come to so permeate social life that more rigorous methodologies cannot easily be applied. In contrast, an uncomplimentary evaluation could stress the overassertiveness, tendentiousness, sloppy arguments, exaggerated claims, and inadequate evidence in too much British work.

Finally, personal research agendas in Britain are constrained more severely than in the United States, it seems, by academic condition. This is a matter of degree, and no doubt American researchers are subject to some different constraints (e.g., of the needs of the marketplace or of graduate students) from which the British may be free. Within the picture drawn above, two examples may be highlighted. The first is the dominance of Sociology. The 10 years 1965 to 1975 were goldrush years for Sociology in Britain, compared with anything earlier or since. This was partly because the subject was poorly established beforehand and was bound to develop disproportionately fast in a period of rapid general expansion. It was fueled further by student demand, and its theories and methods seemed to offer more comprehensive and successful means of studying mass communications than what was available earlier. By the late 1970s the boom was over. It was succeeded by a boom in "policy studies." In Mrs. Thatcher's Britain, policy studies offered an instrumental legitimacy unnecessary—indeed disdained—in the boom years. Besides, the developments in technology were forcing governments and corporate decision makers to make policy choices with apparently far-reaching and (possibly) exciting consequences. "Research" itself was not yet a contaminated idea. Thus funding, media developments, and the needs of researchers came into a mutually satisfactory new alignment. Free of such constraints, however, would media policy studies have become quite so much the flavor of the month?

To many media researchers—working away, say, at television's role in mother-infant interaction—those comments might seem about a different world. The importance of the individuality of research agendas as the dominant British theme must at this point be reemphasized. Moreover, all these remarks are drawn with a very broad brush and could be challenged at every line. That is inevitable with such a topic as this—and immaterial. Any comparison of research agendas, especially in different countries, quickly shows how much they meet different needs in each. In Britain they may help, so to speak, the private professional needs of any scholar who plays the game of drawing them up. Beyond that, they surely serve as a means of delineating what scholars feel they ought to be able to do and of gauging the forces that constrain them. The very absence of a communications discipline means that research agendas in the field can help to constitute a necessary, constant reminder to the established discipline, in which mass communications have so long been marginalized, that the subject must be taken seriously—and never more so than now.

REFERENCE

Butler, E. E. and Donald Stokes (1969) Political Change in Britain. New York: Macmillan.

THOUGHTS ON AN AGENDA
FOR MASS COMMUNICATION RESEARCH

David Weaver

As one who often struggles with the conflicting demands of academic freedom on the one hand and the need for a cumulative body of research on the other, it is with mixed feelings that I commit to paper my thoughts on an agenda for mass communication research. Like Percy Tannenbaum (1985), I am reluctant to impose on others my personal views on what is needed in mass communication research, but at the same time, as I've written elsewhere, I believe the field needs more structure, more replication, and more focus on important social and scholarly issues.

Thus it is with some relief that I find myself responding to an agenda for the field advanced by my colleagues at Maryland's Center for Research in Public Communication. It is always easier to respond than to create.

IS AN AGENDA NEEDED?

The first question we were asked to address was whether the field of mass communication research requires, or needs, an agenda—a coherent set of suggestions about the significant questions and areas to be explored in the future. Given what I have previously written about trends and problems in the field, I can hardly disagree with the need for such an agenda (Weaver and Gray, 1980; Weaver, 1985). I think that even the attempt to come to some kind of agreement on the most important questions and areas can help lead to more systematic and cumulative programs of research in several areas, especially those concerned with the effects of society upon mass communication.

In addition, a research agenda could help shift the focus of discussion from methods to substance. Although methods cannot be ignored, no study's findings are likely to be regarded as significant unless interesting and important questions are asked at the beginning, regardless of level of sophistication in methods or the statistical significance of the findings. We need to keep asking, in Peter Clarke's (1973) words, "whether the results of a proposed inquiry—any of its results—would make a difference if known" (p. 5).

A research agenda, or even the discussion of one, could also help mass communication researchers steer a course between the "two great errors of communication research"—defining communication so broadly that it loses any special meaning, and being so obsessed with precise measurement that our studies proclaim more and more about less and less (Nord, 1985). An agenda that includes questions that are neither too specific nor too general could do much to help researchers stay on track and could increase the chances of such research having an impact on mass communication practice and policy.

In short, I think a research agenda has the potential for helping mass communication research to become less piecemeal, ad hoc, and atheoretical. An agenda could also introduce more continuity to a field racing to keep up with changes in the structure and technology of mass communication, and perhaps generate some centripetal force to counter the centrifugal tendencies of the field without unduly restricting the academic freedom of individual researchers.

WHAT ARE THE
MOST SIGNIFICANT QUESTIONS?

Gurevitch and Levy's (1985) introduction to Volume 5 of the *MCRY* highlights many of what I consider to be the most significant issues and areas for research in mass communication. These include questions of:

(1) the integration of media and social elites
(2) relations between sources and mass communicators
(3) journalists' orientations toward various social institutions
(4) orientations toward mass media by groups, institutions, and public
(5) media treatment of specific public issues
(6) the impact of news as a constructor of interpretive frameworks for audiences
(7) the impact of new technologies on democratic processes

While I would not delete any of these areas from a proposed agenda for mass communication research, I would be inclined to put less emphasis on areas 1, 4, and 7 than they perhaps might. And I would suggest the following areas of research be added to the agenda:

(1) the role of journalism/mass communication education and media organizational constraints in shaping journalists' orientations and perceived role self-concepts
(2) the impact of journalists' perceived roles, orientations, and organizational environments upon media coverage
(3) the impact of news on government elites and policymakers, as well as on more general audiences
(4) the impact of new technologies on media organizations and media treatment of public issues

I realize that these are somewhat more specific suggestions than the ones proposed by Gurevitch and Levy, and that at least two of them (numbers 3 and 4) could be included under their numbers 6 and 7. Nevertheless, I think these proposed additions call attention to the need to study the influences on, and the relations between, mass communication sources, messages, and receivers. In doing so, they hopefully reinforce the Maryland group's basic assumption "that the public (or mass) communication process ought to be viewed as an integrated whole in which the various actors and institutions are linked and interdependent" (Gurevitch and Levy, 1985).

These suggestions also reflect my own interests in journalistic organizations, journalists, and agenda setting (see, for example, Weaver and Wilhoit, 1986; Weaver et al., 1981). In fact, I'm convinced that the agenda-setting framework offers one of the most promising ways of connecting mass communication sources, messages, and receivers under one theoretical framework, and of balancing the prodigious body of research on media effects on society with more research on the effects of society upon the media.

When we begin to look more systematically at the influences on journalists' orientations and the influences of these orientations on the media agenda, as several of us here are presently doing in our joint project on the formation of campaign agendas in the United States and Britain (Gurevitch et al., 1986; Weaver et al., 1986), then we begin to achieve a more complete picture of the mass (or public) communication process. This is especially true if the research on agenda-building (the influences on the media agenda) can be linked with the research on agenda-setting (the influences of the media agenda on various audiences).

I think there are some promising trends in the field of mass communication research, as revealed in previous volumes of the *MCRY*, that support this argument for more research on societal influences on the media. These trends include greater concern about the development, control, support, and institutional context of mass communication, especially from European scholars interested in broader social theories and a more critical approach to communication research; a shift in attention among media effects researchers from attitudes and opinions to cognitions that has been accompanied by more compelling evidence that mass media are important institutions, leading to more interest in what influences shape media messages; a realization that multiple methods often provide more complete and valid insights into mass communication processes than reliance upon a single method; and a greater concern with the implications of mass communication research for policymaking in media organizations as well as in government, especially by scholars in Europe and in Canada.

All of these trends point toward a view of the mass communication process that is more balanced and complete than that provided by the media effects paradigm alone, but a view that does not neglect or reject media effects research as having something important to say.

PARADIGM REFLECTIONS OR REFRACTIONS?

The third question we were asked to address was whether any research agenda is merely a reflection of the dominant paradigms in which we work, or whether a research agenda can accelerate changes in such paradigms. My own view is that research agendas, especially those of individuals, reflect our paradigms to a considerable extent, but not perfectly. Because research agendas are both descriptive and normative (reflections of what we actually do as well as what we think we *should* do), they are not simply passive reflections of dominant paradigms, but are rather refractions of these paradigms. They both reflect and distort the dominant paradigms in ways that can lead to change.

One example of this ability of a research agenda to lead, as well as to follow, is the Maryland group's own agenda. It does not simply reflect the once dominant paradigm of effects research in U.S. mass communication research, nor does it completely reject the study of effects. Rather, it places more emphasis on the study of the creation and nature of media messages than on their effects on audiences. This kind of reordering of priorities can result in the acceleration of changes in the major paradigms of the field, even if the overall agenda is anchored in these paradigms. This seems especially true if the research agenda is the product of scholars who subscribe to different paradigms of mass communication research.

I don't fully agree with my colleague Cleve Wilhoit (1981) that the eclecticism of the mass communication field is centripetal, but I am hopeful that efforts to construct a research agenda stand a good chance of helping mass communication researchers remain focused on significant problems and of welding the diverse ideas of the field into a more integrated whole within their social, cultural, and political contexts.

One of the most significant problems is the question of the power of mass media—the power to shape political agendas, to determine which versions of reality are acceptable on a widespread basis, and to shape the values of a society. Whether one is most concerned with the influences of society upon the media, or vice versa, many of the topics on the Maryland research agenda and on my own are subsumed under a general concern with the amount and the nature of the power of mass communication—cultural as well as economic and political power—as compared with (or linked to) the power of parents, preachers, teachers, experts, politicians, public relations practitioners, labor leaders, public interest groups, celebrities, political action committees, and so forth.[1]

Once this concern with power is made more explicit and more carefully defined, the study of the mass (or public) communication process stands a good chance of becoming less fragmented and more integrated within various social, cultural, and political contexts.

NOTE

1. Many of the ideas in this paragraph come from Jay Blumler (remarks at Maryland seminar) and from Lears's 1985 article, which was brought to my attention by my colleague at Indiana, David Nord.

REFERENCES

Clarke, Peter (1973) "How much of communication research is worth knowing about?" Theory and Methodology Newsletter (Association for Education in Journalism) (December): 5.

Gurevitch, Michael, Jay G. Blumler, and David Weaver (1986) "The formation of campaign agendas in the U.S. and Britain: a conceptual introduction." Presented at the annual conference of the International Communication Association, Chicago, May.

Gurevitch, Michael and Mark R. Levy (1985) "Introduction," pp. 15-21 in M. Gurevitch and M. R. Levy (eds.) Mass Communication Review Yearbook (vol. 5). Newbury Park, CA: Sage.

Lears, T. Jackson (1985) "The concept of cultural hegemony: problems and possibilities." American Historical Review 90 (June): 567-593.

Nord, David Paul (1985) "Career narrative," p. 1. Indiana University, School of Journalism.

Tannenbaum, Percy H. (1985) "To each his/her own: a personal research agenda for micro issues in communication," pp. 41-47 in M. Gurevitch and M. R. Levy (eds.) Mass Communication Review Yearbook (vol. 5). Newbury Park, CA: Sage.

Weaver, David (1985) "Mass communication research: problems and promises." Prepared for a conference, "Communications Research: What, Why, and How?" at the S.I. Newhouse School of Public Communications, Syracuse University, Syracuse, New York, December 6-8, 1985.

Weaver, David H., Doris A. Graber, Maxwell McCombs, and Chaim H. Eyal (1981) Media Agenda-Setting in a Presidential Election. New York: Praeger/Greenwood.

Weaver, David H. and Richard G. Gray (1980) "Journalism and mass communication research in the United States: past, present and future," pp. 124-151 in G. C. Wilhoit and H. de Bock (eds.) Mass Communication Review Yearbook (vol. 1). Newbury Park, CA: Sage.

Weaver, David H. and G. Cleveland Wilhoit (1986) The American Journalist: A Portrait of U.S. News People and Their Work. Bloomington: Indiana University Press.

Weaver, David, G. Cleveland Wilhoit, and Holli Semetko (1986) "The Role of the press in the formation of campaign agendas in Britain and the United States." Presented at the annual conference of ICA, Chicago, May.

Wilhoit, G. Cleveland (1981) "Introduction," pp. 13-33 in G. C. Wilhoit and H. de Bock (eds.) Mass Communication Review Yearbook (vol. 2). Newbury Park, CA: Sage.

PARADIGM LOST
A Personal Postscript to
the Maryland Conference
on Media Research Agendas

Jay G. Blumler

The "dominant paradigm," once an "impressive but nevertheless rather rambling, exposed, and vulnerable giant" (Blumler, 1978) is now merely a straw man. That paradigm—determinedly positivist, individualistic, value-neutral, interested in audiences but indifferent to media organizations and social systems, and available for administrative research exploitation—no longer shapes the work, thinking, and research of many senior American scholars. Its loss of intellectual authority was signalled by five features of the discussion of media research agendas at the Maryland conference.

First, there were no defenders of the social-psychological tradition of concentrating the research unit of analysis on the individual-level audience member, despite the fact that several conference participants had been reared in that approach. Instead, what Nordenstreng (1976) a decade ago termed the "characteristically holistic approach of European communication science" has evidently crossed the Atlantic Ocean and sunk sturdy roots in American soil.

Second, there is no longer a "curious hesitation to address in any sustained way those larger themes and controversies from which the real world of mass communications cannot be isolated" (Blumler, 1978). At bottom, this is because American scholars now recognize—and also reflect in their work and writings— the fact that mass media organizations and mass communication processes lie at the heart of social and political power in several senses:

(1) Through the cumulating evidence that, with respect to a number of "dependent variables," mass communications do exert an influence on the awareness and ideas of at least significant subsets of the mass audience—particularly on what they may think about and possibly also on how to think.

(2) Through the assertion of a structural power, compelling all sorts of institutional and personal adaptations by those seeking office, policy influence and backing for their causes and interests, in order to gain access to a public opinion, which is itself largely represented through mass media outlets (Lang and Lang, 1983).

(3) As a source of representational power, by virtue of how images of key groups (e.g., women, blacks, other ethnics, businessmen, trade unionists, etc.) are repeatedly delineated and projected in fictional and news forms, confirming certain identities and roles, marginalizing others, flouting others, ignoring and excluding yet others.

(4) Through the tendency for mass communication itself to have become an object of power struggle in society, bringing in its wake not only highly organized news management strategies but also such "pathologies" as disinformation campaigns and concerted attempts at censorship, control, and intimidation.

More aware of media power processes in all these senses, scholars can no longer stay aloof from debates over how such power is or ought to be exercised.

Third, a convergence of several influences has also ensured that American scholars' value orientations are less detached and compartmentalized off from, are more closely a part and parcel of, what they now say and do as academics. These include:

- The very centrality of a power perspective on mass media organization.
- The impact on established media systems, ostensibly wedded to certain social values and functions, of disruptive new communication technologies.
- The pressure on the mass media—and also on media researchers—of diverse social movements, challenging them to say where they stand.
- Complex cross-currents, unleashed by research into the manufacture of news, involving values in the mesh of what professional journalists claim to do, what they do not do and what in the circumstances they might be expected to do.
- Third World/First World confrontations over appropriate communication system values.

Fourth, their more central normative commitments have forced scholars to face several other problems unfamiliar to upholders of the once-dominant paradigm. One is to find adequate ways of articulating appropriate values for communication organizations, as they respond to pressures of technological change and new social expectations. Another is to situate themselves stably on a scale of optimism versus pessimism over the prospects of realizing suitable values through mass media organization.

Yet another involves a heightened awareness of a whole host of constraints on the capability of scholars to implement their research programs and associated policy aspirations.

It was in this last, fifth context, therefore, that the conference participants, far removed from an administrative mentality, found the most compelling case for communication research agenda making: to defend their integrity in a world in which many powerful forces continually press them to serve the agendas of other interests.

REFERENCES

Blumler, Jay G. (1978) "Purposes of mass communication research: a transatlantic perspective." Journalism Quarterly 55, 2: 219-230.
Lang, Gladys and Kurt Lang (1983) The Battle for Public Opinion. New York: Columbia University Press.
Nordenstreng, Kaarle (1976) "Recent developments in European communication theory," in Heinz-Dietrich Fischer and John C. Merril (eds.) International and Intercultural Communication. New York: Hastings House.

1

NEOFUNCTIONALISM FOR
MASS COMMUNICATION THEORY

Eric W. Rothenbuhler

Functionalism, or at least functionalist tendencies, have been common throughout the history of mass communication research; Kline's (1972) 15-year-old observation remains as true of the ensuing work as it was for the then extant. Any new developments in functionalist theorizing, then, should be of interest to the field.

Currently within American and German sociological circles there is a resurgence of interest in functionalist theory. This revolves principally around a revival of attention to the work of Talcott Parsons (see Sciulli and Gerstein, 1985) and reformulations and new applications of Parsonian concepts. Some of this revival has been principally exegetical; other examples are adaptations and syntheses that put the works of Parsons into dialogue with subsequent work and later concerns. Still other work is not so explicitly Parsonian, but is concerned with the same problematics that have preoccupied analysts in the Parsonian tradition. This whole package of tendencies is what is traveling under the name *neofunctionalism*.

Many in sociology have met neofunctionalism and the Parsons revival with scorn. Having once won a fight to rid their field of functionalist and, more specifically, Parsonian theorizing, they are not anxious to join battle again (e.g., Page, 1985; Sica, 1983). Many in communication are likely to feel the same. We also have rejected functionalism. What's further, Parsons was never important to our field in the first place; why should we turn to him now, in revival?

One reason is that, in both sociology and communication, functionalism was never really rejected. Functional logic and functionalist concepts remain in

AUTHOR'S NOTE: Work on this article was partially supported by an Old Gold Summer Fellowship from the University of Iowa. An earlier version was presented to the Ph.D. seminar of the Department of Communication Studies, University of Iowa. This article makes clear my intellectual debt to Jeff Alexander, whose teaching and generosity are in no way yet repaid. I also benefited considerably from the comments of John Peters, Sam Becker, Michael Gurevitch, and Mark Levy.

abundance throughout our literatures. Rather than being rejected, functionalism became the object of a critical discourse that prevented its being taken for granted, denied it its once persuasive prestige, and worked that it should no longer be thoughtlessly applied. Gone are the days when a Kingsley Davis (1959) could claim that functionalism was isomorphic with good science. But functionalism itself is not really gone, only its confidence. Functionalism is nowadays used only apologetically, some practitioners refusing to use the name and denying that there is anything functional about their work, rather than rationally facing their critics.

Neofuntionalism, in contrast, is a product of the rational reconsiderations engendered by the critics of the older functionalisms. Neofunctionalism is built on the strengths of the functionalist tradition, and is systematically rejecting or revising the weaknesses. Neofunctionalism has the power that derives from explicit, disciplined attention to theoretical logic and from striving for maximum generality and deductive strength.

Even if neofunctionalism is more rational and more powerful than implicit and remaindered versions of older functionalisms, the question still remains: Why should we in communication be concerned with a Parsons revival? Parsons was never important to us at the height of his sway over American (and German and English) sociology; in the meantime, he's been subjected to years of disparagement in his own field. Merton has been much more important to us, and his middle-range conceptions are more appropriate to our own concern with communications. Any resurgent functionalism in our field is more likely to be Mertonian.

We should pay attention to the Parsons revival because it was Parsons, and not Merton, that was chosen for revival in the reexaminations of functionalism engendered by its critics. The feeling among neofunctionalists is that they should distance their work from Merton because he does not hold up under serious exegesis; Parsons does (Sciulli, 1986).

THE PARSONS REVIVAL

The Parsons revival has taken various forms: first, the publication of an increasing number of exegeses of the works of Talcott Parsons in English or English translation (e.g., Alexander, 1978, 1983; Bershady, 1973; Bourricaud, 1977; Münch, 1981, 1982a). A second form is the increasing appearance of Parsonian concepts and logics in places where they would not have been expected 10 years ago (most notably in Habermas, 1981a, 1981b; also in the French literature, Bourricaud, 1977). Accompanying these publications was recognition among American theorists of the continuing growth of Parsons's popularity in Germany, in stark contrast to the situation in the United States (e.g., Habermas, 1981a, 1981b; Luhmann, 1979, 1981; Münch, 1982b; and Schluchter, 1979, 1981; see also, Alexander, 1984a).

It is not as paradoxical as it at first seems that the critics of Parsons and functionalism have indirectly brought about a revival of interest in both. The critics motivated a more disciplined attention to the whole of Parsons efforts than had previously been present anywhere but among his own students. This disciplined rereading came about in a period characterized by a widespread recognition of the power of hermeneutics and the ever-presence of the problem of interpretation. These rereadings placed Parsons in theoretical, empirical, and political contexts he may never have considered and put him in dialogue with authors he may never have read. Parsons's work thus becomes a shifting mosaic, the value of the elements dependent upon the reader's problematic. This is more, though, than a willy-nilly picking and choosing of interesting concepts; the neofunctionalists see their rereadings as disciplined efforts in theory revision (Alexander's, 1983, volume on Parsons is self-conscious regarding the reader-centered hermeneutics of theory revision; his (1982) rationale for such practices is in Volume 1 of that work; and his attention to the reconstructive readings of Parsons by others can be found in Alexander, 1981a, 1984a, 1985).

The result of these efforts to check critics of Parsons against Parsons's own texts is the realization, as Alexander puts it, that, while the major charges made against Parsons were with some validity, his critics have mistaken these parts of Parsons work for the whole of his efforts. These parts can be abandoned or fixed while the problematics motivating the whole and the remaining useful parts are salvaged. Or as Sciulli (1986) puts it, neofunctionalism is about rehabilitating selected Parsonian concepts, but not necessarily Parsons's uses for them.

But still, why should we work so hard on an author if later authors have made clear the necessity of revision? For a great variety of reasons, and each reader must have his or her own, but three that figure near the top of any list will be his sustained attention to overcoming the dilemma of the material/ideal duality within the realm of social theory, the importance of his distinguishing the analytic from the concrete and the ways that distinction is worked out in his theory, and the unparalleled example of generality and scope in his theory. Jürgen Habermas has this to say about Parsons's work and its current relevance:

> Talcott Parsons ... even while still living had attained the status of a classic. ...
> No one of his contemporaries developed a theory of society of comparable complexity. ... With regard to its level of abstraction, its complexity, theoretical scope, systematicity, and grounding in the literature of relevant branches of research his published work simply has no competitor at this time. Furthermore, no one else among the productive theorists of society has conducted a continuing debate with the classics of our discipline with equal intensity and persistence in order to build on received tradition. ... Any theoretical work in sociology today that failed to take account of Talcott Parsons could not be taken seriously [Habermas, 1981a: 173-174].

Taking account of Parsons and becoming an epigone are two different things. The authors working within the neofunctionalist movement recognize the reasons Parsons was criticized. In certain aspects of his work and at certain points in his 50 years of writing, he was guilty of too little attention to social conflict, of inadequately theorizing social change, of being too abstract, of certain idealistic tendencies, and of undervaluing the Marxist tradition. Neofunctionalist authors have responded to the critiques of Parsonianism by themselves addressing problems of social conflict (e.g., Colomy, 1985; Lechner, 1985; also the earlier work of Coser, 1956, and Smelser, 1962), by reformulations of Parsonian theories of social change (e.g., Gould, 1985; Rossi, 1985; and the earlier work by Smelser, 1959), by creative synthesis of aspects of Parsons's work with aspects of other traditions, including that established by Marx (e.g., Sciulli, 1985; Luhmann, 1979, 1981; Habermas, 1981b; Gould, 1981), and by increased attention to empirical problems and more concrete modes of analysis, including attention to historical social forms, and their interests and conflicts (this tendency is present in nearly every essay of the 1985 neofunctionalism book). A major theme of Alexander's (esp. 1983) work is a rereading of Parsons that emphasizes those moments of analytically overcoming the old subject/object::ideal/material dualities as opposed to the clearly contradictory idealistic tendencies. Others are engaged in a serious exegesis of Parsons's philosophical underpinnings and the implications for social theory (e.g., Münch 1981, 1982a, and others cited above; see Sciulli and Gerstein, 1985; Alexander, 1983, 1984a, 1985 for reviews).

It would be inappropriate to attempt a listing of neofunctionalist responses to specific criticisms made of Parsons's work. Such a defensive approach to scholarly work is foreign to neofunctionalists' thinking. As Alexander puts it, "Sociologists of varied interests and in diverse countries have begun to respond to the antifunctionalist critique not by reasserting Parsonian orthodoxy, the reflective response of earlier loyalists, but by developing original permutations, and often far-reaching revisions, of earlier functionalist work" (1986: 5).

No one wants to have another debate, after which the points can be chalked up and the winners announced. Good theory-building is harder work than that. Neofunctionalism is an exercise in intellectual honesty: Can it be for no reason that functionalisms of one or another form have dominated a century of Western social science? No, probably not. Can those reasons be explained away by the sort of sociology of knowledge and ideology critique attempted by Gouldner (1970)? No, not really. But are all of the charges made against functionalist theory without grounding? No again. And has everything done in the name of functionalism been good and appropriate theory? No, definitely not.

Functionalism must, then, be reconsidered. But it must be a rational reconsideration without prior commitment to defending this theoretical system or attacking that one. It is impossible to say where such a reconsideration may lead; it would be impossible to judge its value by simply counting the number of criticisms neutralized.

A REVIEW OF NEOFUNCTIONALISM

The public announcement of the neofunctionalist movement came with a special miniconference on the topic at the 1984 meetings of the American Sociological Assocation, the papers for which are collected in a volume titled *Neofunctionalism* (the papers were presented under the auspices of the Theory

Section, chaired that year by Jeffrey Alexander, who also coined the term *neofunctionalism* and edited the book). The miniconference was intended to call wider attention to existing trends in sociology; in coining a new name, debate over these trends was also focused and intensified.

As with any school of thought, the neofunctionalists have made moves to codify their position and to read history back from that position. In the editorial introduction to the neofunctionalism book, Alexander provides a rationale for the term and a listing of six analytic elements that distinguish the functionalist tradition from others in sociological thought. This is no simple description; this is an interpretation that selects and values some elements of theoretical work over others. In offering this particular interpretation of functionalism, Alexander is both offering a selective reading of the history of functionalism and advocating a set of evaluative standards for neofunctionalism.

(1) Alexander's first point:

> Although not providing a model in an explanatory sense, functionalism does provide a general picture of the interrelation of social parts, a model in a more descriptive sense. Functionalism models society as an intelligible system. It views society as composed of elements whose interaction forms a pattern that can be clearly differentiated from some surrounding environment
> [Alexander, 1985: 9].

This first proposition is essentially a commitment to functional logic on the level of societies—societies are taken to be systems composed of interacting subsystems, themselves composed of interacting subsystems, and so on. At each level one can analyze the actions of parts in terms of their significance for the larger systems in which they are implicated.

(2) "Functionalism concentrates on action as much as on structure" (Alexander, 1985: 9). The point here is twofold: first, to give equal treatment to the constraining shape of a society and to the actions of its members. Then, within the analysis of social actions, to give equal treatment to adaptations to structural constraints and to enactments of nonstructural elements such as belief and value systems. Following Parsons's (1937/1968) *Structure of Social Action,* the former are conceived as the conditions of action, the later the ends of action and normative regulation of its conduct, and the two are linked by means and effort. The functionalist analysis, then, focuses on the normative integration of conditions, means, and ends in situations of social action (see Parsons and Shils, 1951). The "ends" of action are the differences between "desired states of affairs" and what the situation would be at a designated time without the actor's acting. This is the "voluntaristic" element of action for Parsons; the hypothesized existence of integrated systems of ends is the basis of his nondeterministic theory of social order (see esp. Parson, 1935, 1937/1968).

(3) "Functionalism is concerned with integration as a possibility and with deviance and processes of social control as facts. Equilibrium is taken as a reference point for functionalist systems analysis, though not for participants in actual social systems as such" (Alexander, 1985: 9). The meanings of these terms,

their usefulness, and their assumed relations are highly controversial. In that these terms were brought into sociological theory for purposes of explaining social order, this aspect of the functionalist tradition could be rephrased less controversially, as a concern with how social systems tend to reproduce themselves within sets of conditions, and adapt between sets of conditions. This focuses on the issue of social order, and leaves the terms by which order will be explained unspecified.

Alexander's statement of integration as a possibility and deviance and social control as facts is a decided reformulation of earlier functionalist positions. In Parsons it is often possible—especially in his 1951 book, *The Social System*—to read between the lines that integration is a fact, deviance only a possibility, and social control a natural response to it. By reversing that theme, Alexander implies the possibility of a society happier than the existing one. This leaves open the possibility of important relations between a functionalist theory and a reformist or revolutionary program of social change—something of which older versions of American sociological functionalism were never accused (e.g., Gouldner, 1970).

(4) "Functionalism posits the distinctions between personality, culture, and society as vital to social structure, and the tensions produced by their interpenetration as a continuous source of change and control" (Alexander, 1985: 10). This derives explicitly from the work of Parsons and his colleagues in the early 1950s. In *Toward a General Theory of Action* and *The Social System,* three interdependent but distinct analytic systems were said to be present in all social action: the social system, the cultural system, and the personality system.

Patterns of social interaction, patterns of culture, and patterns of personality are considered indicative of these three analytic systems. Each is present to some degree in all concrete instances of social action; no general analytic priorities can be made amongst them. Culture is not, then, in general a reflection (even in the last instance) of some base of social interaction, though the relation may work out that way in some concrete instances. The same holds true for all of the other combinations of the three. Within each system there are strains toward consistency, both synchronically and diachronically, as well as strains toward adaptation to new conditions. Between each the same types of strains exist. Each provides both conditional constraints and enablements for the others. The interaction of any two is an important component of the constitution of the third, but none can be analytically reduced to either of the others or any form of their combination.

(5) "Functionalism implies a recognition of differentiation as a major mode of social change—whether cultural, social, or psychological—and of the individual and institutional strains that this historical process creates" (Alexander, 1985: 10). Differentiation is the replacement of one multiple function unit with multiple single function units; it implies an increase in efficiency at the cost of an increase in complexity.

Why differentiation? Amongst all modes of social change, why should differentiation be singled out?

The straightforward rationale for attention to differentiation is derived directly from principles of systems theory (see e.g., Parsons and Smelser, 1956: 246). Because systematicity requires expenditures of energy to maintain order in an environment characterized (relative to the system) by scarcity and tension, systems cannot grow indefinitely. As they grow, components become spread further apart and the maintenance of order becomes more difficult. At some point on a growth curve, then, systems must reorganize. At this point they either segment, creating smaller duplicates of the larger system, or they differentiate. Segmentation reduces the load on the system, differentiation increases its efficiency. Segmentation is a relatively uninteresting type of social change and it is seldom observed on the level of whole societies anyway. Differentiation would appear to be one of the major dimensions of transitions to modernity—the core obsession of classical sociology. (This idea that growth produces segmentation or differentiation is common and often taken as axiomatic, e.g., Hawley, 1986; Spencer, 1868, and Durkheim, 1893/1964, are just two classic examples.)

The distinction and interpenetration of cultural systems and social systems (position 4) and the focus on the role of nonsituational ends in guiding situated action (position 2) requires attention to what is called specification. Specification is the process by which general phenomena become adapted at more particular levels. In the Parsonian tradition it is usually construed as a problem of value specification (e.g., Parsons, 1961) or cultural specification (Alexander, 1984b)— the process by which general values, ultimate ends, primary beliefs, and so on, become a component of orientations to action in specific situations. The language from Smelser's (1962) book on collective action is typical: Values are specified as norms that are specified as motivations that are specified in situational facilities.

Differentiation describes a major dimension of variation in the specification process. Several questions illustrate: Will conflicting values in a society—for example, liberty and equality—be fused within a civil religion and specified in a single institutional structure (say, government), or will the values be differentiated and specified in distinct and competing institutional structures (such as business and judiciary)? Will one functional subsystem—for example, mass communication—be differentiated from other such subsystems—for example, state, religion, labor, business—to become specified in its own institutional structure (as is the dominant pattern in the United States), or be a functional activity carried on by other institutional structures (as was once dominant in Europe; see Alexander, 1981b)? Will the values of the polity be specified in offices or incumbents? If the latter, then values are embodied in the person of the leader and opposition to the current regime is tantamount to opposition to the sacred, legitimating values of the governing structure. If values are specified in office, then contemporary leaders are differentiated from the legitimating values of leadership; incumbents can be held up to the values specified in the office as to standards of judgment. Here opposition is legitimate within the system (see Bellah, 1970; Bellah and Hammond, 1980). The role of journalism, to take only one clear example, is going to be sharply differently defined and regulated in systems with differing patterns of value differentiation and specification.

(6) "Functionalism implies the commitment to the independence of conceptualization and theorizing from other levels of sociological analysis" (Alexander, 1985: 10). The point here is that the empirical cannot and should not be the final arbiter of theoretical value; theoretical work *qua* theoretical work is a legitimate, in fact necessary, activity.

The progress of science does not depend on empirical procedures alone. We do not choose between competing theories only on the basis of empirical test, but also on the basis of logic, aesthetics, and tradition. This aspect of the neofunctionalist movement is a positive recognition of these elements of scientific practice: Rather than apologize for the nonempirical criteria used in our work, we should work to make them elements that are objectively agreed upon, to make them recognized rules of the community. Alexander's four-volume *Theoretical Logic in Sociology* is an extended argument for the utility of one set of these standards.

NEOFUNCTIONALISM APPLIED
TO MASS COMMUNICATION THEORY

Functional analysis has been used throughout the mass communication field, and so neofunctionalism has a correspondingly wide area of potential applicability. But nowhere in our field has functionalism been discussed more than in reference to media uses and gratifications. It is to that area, then, that the discussion now turns.

Earlier, what we now call *uses and gratifications studies* were known simply as *functional studies* (Bauer, 1964; Klapper, 1960). The revival of uses and gratifications studies following Katz, Gurevitch, and Haas (1973) was hailed by some as a return to functional analysis (Wright, 1974), condemned by others for the same reasons (Carey and Kreiling, 1974; Elliott, 1974). Even some of its practitioners asked if it couldn't "be detached from its former functionalist moorings" (Blumler and Katz, 1974: 16). That functionalism was a bad thing and that a research approach clearly based on it, like uses and gratifications is, could be improved by distancing itself came to be the accepted common sense. Recently some have asserted that, due to hard work in the intervening years, uses and gratifications is somehow no longer functionalist (Palmgreen et al., 1985: 16)—this while their explanatory logic remains essentially unchanged from earlier work.

It could be, however, that the weaknesses of uses and gratifications theory could be more readily rectified by disciplined attention to its functionalism than by denying it—that is, after all, its conceptual system and some rational attention would probably be a good thing.

What follows is an outline for a neofunctionalist reformation of uses and gratifications theory and some research ideas based on that reformation. This is not intended to be a full reconstruction of uses and gratifications—such an effort would require considerably more page space. Rather, this is an illustration of part of what would be possible by reapproaching uses and gratifications in a neofunctionalist spirit. Following these necessarily schematic proposals, the criticisms conventionally made of uses and gratifications theory are examined. This demonstrates that a neofunctionalist uses and gratifications would, when fully reconstructed, be superior to currently available alternatives.

The first neofunctionalist reformulation of the uses and gratifications paradigm is to make it Parsonian rather than Mertonian. In this case it is best done by following the general theory of action in the version outlined by Parsons and Shils (1951) in the essay "Values, Motives, and Systems of Action," and the "General Statement" with their colleagues in that same volume.

The advantages to be gained include: (1) The assumptions about the active nature of the audience member become integrated within a logically consistent theoretical structure rather than being ad hoc features of particular investigations. (2) The conceptualization of the audience member is in the terms of a *general* theory of action, so follows the conceptualization of social actors in their other capacities as well. (3) The pattern variable scheme within the general theory of action captures five analytically distinguishable aspects of orientations of actors in situations that can organize extant knowledge about audience members' patterns of orientation to media and guide future uses and gratifications research. (4) The general theory of action is associated with a theory of socialization that can help us begin to theorize the genesis of audience motivations, roles, and gratifications. (5) The general theory of action conceives personality systems, social systems, and cultural systems as three analytically distinct but concretely interpenetrating components of action situations (with actors conceived either as individuals or collectivities), so that our theorizing of the media audience member can be tied into theories of institutional structure and larger social processes.

The conceptualization begins with actors in situations. Actors are those phenomena (in our case, they will be concrete people or collectivities) capable of action, defined as "behavior . . . oriented [implying subjective meaning, see below] to the attainment of ends in situations, by means of the normatively regulated expenditure of energy" (Parsons and Shils, 1951: 53).

Situations contain objects of three types: social, physical, and cultural. Social objects are actors; both ego and alter may be objects of orientation for an actor. Social objects are capable of response and interaction; nonsocial objects do not respond or interact. Physical objects are empirical things with physical position in the situation (Parsons and Shils say "located in time and space," p. 58). Cultural objects are ideas, beliefs, symbols, or value patterns to the extent that they are oriented to as objects and not internalized. The most fundamental distinction between cultural patterns and physical ones is that the former can be internalized and so may be both aspects of actor and of situation (a key to theorizing social integration), while the latter can only be situational objects.

Objects in situations—whether social, physical, or cultural—can be means, ends, conditions, or expressively significant symbols for actors; cultural objects may also be norms. (Remembering de Saussure's, 1915/1966, signifier/signified distinction helps differentiate cultural aspects from physical aspects of the same objects—something Parsons intends anyway, since he defines *objects* analytically rather than concretely.)

Action is said to be oriented "when it is guided by the meaning that the actor attaches to it in its relationship to his [or her] goals or interests" (Parsons et al., 1951: 4). There are five dilemmas of any orientation to action. These are captured in a set of five dichotomies known as the *pattern variable scheme*.

(1) Will the orientation be *affective* or *affective neutrality*? This is akin to seeking immediate gratification without regard to further consequences, or submitting to some form of discipline, allowing one's actions to be guided by evaluative standards of some sort.

(2) *Self-orientation* or *collectivity-orientation*? Will one's actions be oriented or evaluated in terms of one's own goals or interests, or in terms of those of a collectivity of which one is a member?

(3) *Universalism* or *particularism*? Will one's orientation to an object be guided by standards applying to all such situations and objects, or by some particular aspect of this situation, this object, or its relationship to ego or ego's collectivity?

(4) Will objects be judged by standards of *ascription* or *achievement*? Will one evaluate objects and orient to them in terms of the categories of which they are members, in terms of what they are, or in terms of their performance, what they are doing or have done?

(5) *Specificity* or *diffuseness*? The question here is the scope of the significance of an object of orientation for the actor. What is the range of "demands" that it may make on an actor, or an actor on it; are they very specific or completely diffuse?

The cross-classification of these five dilemmas yields 32 logically possible modes of orientation. But some of these are less likely to be real than others. (Parsons and Shils are ambiguous on this issue.) Collectivity orientations are probably affectively neutral for the individual actor, even if the collective standards applied are affective. Universalism must almost surely be affectively neutral. But these distinctions are analytic; they are meant to illuminate aspects of orientation and should not be confused with types of orientation. Concrete action situations will show mixtures and layerings of the modes of orientation.

Discussion of actors, means, ends, and situations has an individualistic appearance. If that holds of the concepts as well as the terminology, then this Parsonian reconstruction of uses and gratifications will have failed to overcome a major weakness of the approach. But the individualistic appearance is only an appearance; the technical use of words in this conceptual system must be carefully distinguished from the connotations of their everyday usage.

In the first place, the conception *actor* may refer to individuals or collectivities, or indeed any phenomenon or any aspect of any phenomenon capable of pursuing action as defined above. Thus the actor pursuing ends via means in situations may be an individual (usually, more properly designated as a role-segment of an individual), a group, an organization, a movement, a society, or many phenomena between. This is a fairly straightforward problem of the empirical specification of the analytic system for a particular investigation.

The more profound supraindividualist aspects are those built into the analytic system itself. These have to do with the relations among the personality system, the social system, and the cultural system. Any concrete actor or action is to be understood as a manifestation of a personality system, a social system, a cultural system, an action situation, and their interaction, simultaneously. Our subjects in uses and gratifications studies, then, are walking and talking bits of their social circumstances and should be studied as such. This means we need ways to operationalize the conditions of the systems that constitute the actors we study. This is what the pattern variable scheme was designed for.

In terms of the pattern variables, there is a certain symmetricality between the personality system and the social system. They each make demands, of a sort, on the other. The social system has role-expectations for the personality, while the personality system poses need-dispositions for the society. The place of the cultural system in this phase of the conceptualization is as the major environment on the metaphysical or transcendent end of a continuum—the other end being the material arrangements of the situation, its physical contingencies. Action situations (including actors, objects, ends, means, contingencies, and orientations) are constructed of the interpenetration of material and ideal environments, and personality and social systems. (Some of these points are more clearly formulated in Parsons's later work; see Parsons and Smelser, 1956; Parsons, 1961; Parsons, 1966; and Parsons and Platt, 1973, for the four function paradigm, the generalized media of exchange, and the hierarchy of control.) Consequently, no reference to actor or action within this conceptual scheme can properly be taken as individualist. It is always a reference to interpenetrating systems of four distinct analytic levels.

To summarize: The action frame of reference delimits actors in situations oriented to social, physical, or cultural objects as means, ends, conditions, or symbols in terms of the five pattern variables. These actors are socialized; both they and their situation of action are located within a social structure. Action is the normative expenditure of energy toward the attainment of ends by an oriented actor in such situations.

Mass communication researchers may want to limit their attention to actors in their capacity as audience members, or, somewhat more broadly, actors with goals in situations such that attention to mass communication is a viable choice object.

The standard terms of analysis in uses and gratifications research can be reconceived into those of the general theory of action. Audience "needs" become a negative form of statement of the ends of action. "Uses" become the means of action. Needs, uses, gratifications, audience activity all become ways of talking about factors in audience-role orientations to communicative objects in socially structured situations, but reference will also be made to other concepts in the general theory of action. In this way uses and gratifications can be considerably broadened beyond the analysis of needs leading to need gratifying behavior.

Three examples of the usefulness of this reformulation follow:

(1) Existing typologies of audience needs could be reorganized along the pattern variable line. One recent effort at summary and reorganization by Dobos, Dimmick, and Calabrese (1986) proposed that nearly all of the variance in existing need inventories could be captured by the cognitive/affective dichotomy. This is equivalent to the affective/affective-neutrality pattern variable. We might hypothesize that, within each category of affectivity/ affective-neutrality, other clusterings of orientations to media will occur following the other pattern variables. Self versus collectivity might be exemplified in items such as what I need or want to know from the media versus what I need to know in my role as mother or teacher or voter.

(2) Blumler's (1985) and Blumler et al.'s (1985) calls for attention to media audience roles (normative structurings of orientation and action, as opposed to idiosyncratic seeking of need satisfaction) and the media texts' offering of roles can begin immediately with the pattern variable scheme. For examples: The ideal citizen voter might be oriented to news and public affairs media along the lines of an affectively neutral, universalistic, collectivity orientation, evaluating politicians in diffuse, achievement terms. The straight-ticket voter sees politicians in ascriptive terms; the special interest voter might be particularistically or self oriented. Negative campaigns and horse-race journalism appeal to affectivity rather than affective neutrality.

But these roles should be expected not only as patterns of activity, they should also have counterparts embedded in symbol systems, texts, and communicative interaction. This is a point anticipated in Parsons's own work on propaganda and on personality and social structure (Parsons, 1954, 1964), though here we do not want to follow him closely. Advantages will accrue from synthesizing the action frame of reference and the pattern variable scheme with more recent, more subtle attention to the relationship of reader and text (e.g., Dayan, 1976; Silverman, 1983; Tompkins, 1980).

Work in this area is well prepared by the classic studies of Herzog (1944), Arnheim (1944), Lowenthal (1944), Warner and Henry (1948), and others of the early Columbia group, and by the more recent work of Liebes and Katz (Liebes, 1986; Liebes and Katz, 1986), Morley (1980), and Radway (1984). But we have yet to see the full analysis needed. We must bring together, on the one hand, the roles offered to audiences in texts produced by concrete actors (with goals in situations, etc.) operating in functional roles within concrete organizations (with goals in situations, etc.) operating in functional subsystems and concrete social exigencies with, on the other hand, roles constructed in the reading of texts by concrete actors (with goals in situations, etc.) characterized by a location in a social structure that is both functionally and concretely defined.

(3) Though it has not been discussed here, this general action frame of

reference has served as the basis for a theory of social systems (Parsons, 1951) and, in a revised form, a theory of the institutional structure and process within societies (Parsons and Smelser, 1956; Parsons and Platt, 1973). Because these extensions are logically consistent, conceptualizations of audience members in these terms can be integrated with conceptualizations of the media as both functioning subsystems and concrete organizational entities, in a manner that is not ad hoc.

A neofunctionalist uses and gratifications could be, then, theoretically integrated with a theory of society, a general theory of action, and with theories of the socialization of individuals into social roles. Mass communication activity is one amongst the forms of activity conceived by the theory; this allows conceptualization of the choice of mass communication activity in a way impossible with theories that take mass communication as their sole object.

How does this reformulation answer to criticisms conventionally made of uses and gratifications? Those of Carey and Kreiling (1974), Elliott (1974), and Swanson (1977, 1979) can be taken as representative and condensed into a list of five charges:

(1) Uses and gratifications is a mentalistic theory and a psychological reduction of social phenomena.
(2) Uses and gratifications is individualistic, with social structure introduced only ad hoc as a set of demographic variables, if at all.
(3) Depending on the author, uses and gratifications is atheoretical, theoretically eclectic and potentially inconsistent, characterized by vague and inconsistent use of terms, or an inventory rather than a theory.
(4) Uses and gratifications offers no explanation for the origin of needs or the patterning of needs, and often slips into deterministic accounts of these issues inconsistent with the voluntaristic commitment to an active audience conception.
(5) Uses and gratifications is functionalist in a way that is bad because (a) it is utilitarianism in another guise, (b) it is a circular argument, or (c) it supports the status quo by explaining that it is functional.

A neo-Parsonian version of uses and gratifications would be superior on every one of these accounts to any other currently available uses and gratifications conception. Each charge is addressed in order.

(1) In that it makes reference to mental states as *part* of an explanation of action, this version of uses and gratifications has mentalistic components. But these features do not make it psychologically reductive, for the personality system is only one component of the system of action, and is itself interpenetrated by the cultural and social systems.

(2) A Parsonian version of uses and gratifications is clearly not individualistic. This point has already been discussed. The very starting point for a conception of the actor is the place of that actor in the social structure.

(3) Conceived as one application of Parsons's general theory of action, uses and gratifications becomes a logically consistent system of precisely defined terms and relations, integrated within a larger theoretical structure.

(4) The issues surrounding voluntaristic versus deterministic explanations for the origin and patterning of needs are difficult.

Uses and gratifications begins with the voluntaristic assumption that audience members are willful, what we call active. But as Swanson (1977, 1979) asks (although not as directly as I am asking), how can we explain patterns in what people will and in the resulting actions without violating that voluntaristic assumption? Parsons's theory is uniquely able to help us here, for this is just another form of the fundamental dilemma that he devoted his career to: how to explain social order within a voluntaristic theory of action.

In briefest outline, social action can become nondeterministically integrated when the terms of its coordination are located within personality systems. For Parsons, this requires a theory of socialization in which aspects of cultural and social systems are internalized in personality. Once internalized, these are no longer components of situations or system environments, but components of actors. As such, they become patterns of will rather than patterns of condition or constraint, and thus voluntaristic rather than deterministic.

This seems a neat trick of logic, but on more examination one must ask, how is explaining social order via the social construction of the subject any less deterministic than via some other means, say the social control of the subject?

This explanation of social order is voluntaristic because internalization and enactment are ultimately semiotic (here I am going beyond Parsons). It is only as symbols that internal patterns and external patterns can be articulated one with another. This articulation of signifier with signified is willful in that it need not be that way—the individual may deny the correctness of it. That individuals often do not is what enables Parsons's theory of social order. That they may is the voluntaristic component of the theory. In certain historical circumstances it is clear that large numbers of people have denied the correctness of certain cultural specifications. A Parsonian theory of social order can, in fact, predict the conditions, though not necessarily the directions, of certain forms of changing order based on this voluntarism.

In uses and gratifications we would explain patterns of media use by reference to norms associated with role-segments of personality systems. Both the learning of the norms and their enactment are matters of interpretation, a problem of the articulation of signifier and signified. "Reading" becomes a double problem for uses and gratifications: The reading of, say, the televisual text so that light and sound become meaning, and the reading of the self so that motivation becomes action, in this case television viewing.

The Parsonian reformulation of uses and gratifications not only handles the voluntarism/determinism problem in the explanation of what are called needs. But the way in which it does so is evocative of rich possibilities for synthesis with semiotics and structuralist theories of the subject.

(5) To the extent that being functionalist is a sin, a Parsonian reformulation is no remedy. But the spirit of neofunctionalism is that such ascriptive criticisms are irrational. The more rational criticisms are those addressed to traits related to the

specific form functionalism has usually taken in uses and gratifications research.

(a) Many accuse uses and gratifications of being a form of utilitarianism, and in the hands of many analysts there would appear to be little reason not to. If media use is explained as a rational choice among alternative modes of want satisfaction, the choice being based on a calculation of efficiency in achieving self-interest, then the explanation is a form of utilitarianism. This is clearly an incomplete explanation of human motivation and action, as well as being unable to account for order among rational actors without reference to deterministic factors outside the logical structure of the theory. Neither of these charges would be true of a neofunctionalist uses and gratifications. First, because the explanations of media use would make at least as much reference to emotions, norms, beliefs, institutional structures, social constraints, and so forth, as to the efficiency of need gratification. Second, because a critique of, and movement beyond, these very problems in utilitarian theory was the starting point of Parsons's career and his theoretical structure (Parsons, 1937/1968).

(b) Uses and gratifications is sometimes accused of engaging a circular argument characteristic of some functionalisms: The recurrent pattern of media use is explained by reference to its functionality, the primary evidence of which is the recurrence of use.

In the Parsonian theory of action, concrete action situations, personality systems, social systems, and cultural systems act as environments for each other. Explanations of actions taken refer to elements of these environments—amongst which for us will be not only needs, but norms, organizations, economics, regulation, and so on. The presence of these elements can then be explained by use of revised versions of the Parsonian theories of socialization, system change, specification, differentiation, and evolution. Because these systems operate independently of the systems that bring about the action explained, the circular argument is avoided.

(c) Uses and gratifications is sometimes accused of being a form of functionalism that supports the status quo because, in demonstrating that current media structures and processes are functional, no rationale for change is offered. The observation that no rationale for change has been offered is correct, but the interpretation that that supports the status quo is not.

Two mistakes are being made here. First, an explanation is being mistaken for a justification. A rationale for change is not logically required by an explanation of why things are the way they are. Fascist, liberal democratic, and socialist societies all require integration, for example; explaining how that integration works and positively evaluating the terms around which it occurs are two different activities. If analysts are to be criticized for not offering rationales for change, it cannot be on the grounds of the logic of their explanations.

The second mistake is that the level of adaptedness implied by a functional explanation is being overestimated. A functional explanation never correctly implies that the action being explained is the only or the best way to bring about the criterion consequences; it need not even be better than others. A functional explanation correctly implies only that the action being explained is one amongst many possible actions that are "good enough," given the prevailing selective forces in the environments of action, importantly affected by distributions of power (Rothenbuhler, 1986).

Despite the fact that it often has been done, a functional explanation of audience activity should never be taken as evidence that current media fare is good enough for the audience (and thus that there is no reason for change), only that it is good enough to bring about forms of audience attention that are, in turn, good enough for media institutions (and there may be a great variety of reasons for change). A neofunctionalist reformulation of uses and gratifications would be less likely to make that error.

CONCLUSION

The purpose of this article has been to introduce neofunctionalist ideas to the mass communication field. No more than an introduction has been offered. A great deal of hard work lies between here and any potential payoff in neofunctionalist theory.

REFERENCES

Alexander, J. C. (1978) "Formal and substantive voluntarism in the work of Talcott Parsons: a theoretical and ideological reinterpretation." American Sociological Review 43: 177-198.

Alexander, J. C. (1981a) "The French correction: revisionism and followership in the interpretation of Parsons." Contemporary Sociology 10: 500-505.

Alexander, J. C. (1981b) "The mass news media in systemic, historical, and comparative perspectives," in E. Katz and T. Szecsko (eds.) Mass Media and Social Change. Newbury Park, CA: Sage.

Alexander, J. C. (1982) Theoretical Logic in Sociology, Volume 1: Positivism, Presuppositions, and Current Controversies. Berkeley: University of California Press.

Alexander, J. C. (1983) Theoretical Logic In Sociology, Volume 4: The Modern Reconstruction of Classical Thought: Talcott Parsons. Berkeley: University of California Press.

Alexander, J. C. (1984a) "The Parsons revival in German sociology," in R. Collins (ed.) Sociological Theory 1984. San Francisco: Jossey-Bass.

Alexander, J. C. (1984b) "Three models of culture and society relations: toward an analysis of Watergate," in R. Collins (ed.) Social Theory 1984. San Francisco: Jossey-Bass.

Alexander, J. C. (1985) "Introduction," in J. C. Alexander (ed.) Neofunctionalism. Newbury Park, CA: Sage.

Alexander, J. C. (1986) "Why neofunctionalism?" Footnotes. Washington, DC: American Sociological Association, January.

Arnheim, R. (1944) "The world of the daytime serial," in P. F. Lazarsfeld and F. N. Stanton (eds.) Radio Research 1942-1943. New York: Duell, Sloan & Pearce.

Bauer, R. A. (1964) "The obstinate audience: the influence process from the point of view of social communication," in W. Schramm and D. F. Roberts (eds.) (1974) The Process and Effects of Mass Communication. Urbana: University of Illinois Press.

Bellah, R. N. (1970) Beyond Belief: Essays on Religion in a Post-Traditional World. New York: Harper & Row.

Bellah, R. N. and P. E. Hammond (1980) Varieties of Civil Religion. New York: Harper & Row.

Bershady, H. J. (1973) Ideology and Social Knowledge. New York: John Wiley.

Blumler, J. G. (1985) "The social character of media gratification," in K. W. Rosengren, L. A. Wenner, and P. Palmgreen (eds.) Media Gratifications Research: Current Perspectives. Newbury Park, CA: Sage.

Blumler, J. G., M. Gurevitch, and E. Katz (1985) "Reaching out: a future for gratification research," in K. E. Rosengren, L. A. Wenner, and P. Palmgreen (eds.) Media Gratifications Research: Current Perspectives. Newbury Park, CA: Sage.

Blumler, J. G. and E. Katz [eds.] (1974) "Forward" in J. G. Blumler and E. Katz (eds.) The Uses of Mass Communications: Current Perspectives on Gratifications Research. Newbury Park, CA: Sage.

Bourricaud, F. (1977) The Sociology of Talcott Parsons (A. Goldhammer, trans.). Chicago: University of Chicago Press (Translation, 1981).

Carey, J. W. and A. L. Kreiling (1974) "Popular culture and uses and gratifications: notes toward an accommodation," in J. G. Blumler and E. Katz (eds.) The Uses of Mass Communications: Current Perspectives on Gratifications Research. Newbury Park, CA: Sage.

Colomy, P. (1985) "Uneven structural differentiation: toward a comparative approach," in J. C. Alexander (ed.) Neofunctionalism. Newbury Park, CA: Sage.

Coser, L. (1956) The Function of Social Conflict. New York: Free Press.

Davis, K. (1959) "The myth of functional analysis as a special method in sociology and anthropology." American Sociological Review 24: 757.

Dayan, D. (1976) "The tutor code of classical cinema," in B. Nichols (ed.) Movies and Methods. Berkeley: University of California Press.

de Saussure, F. (1915) Course in General Linguistics. New York: McGraw-Hill (Paperback edition, 1966).

Dobos, J., J. Dimmick, and A. Calabrese (1986) "On theory-building: factor analysis and gratification constructs." Presented to the International Communication Association, May, Chicago.

Durkheim, E. (1893) The Division of Labor in Society. New York: Free Press (Paperback translation, 1964).

Elliott, P. (1974) "Uses and gratifications research: a critique and a sociological alternative," in J. G. Blumler and E. Katz (eds.) The Uses of Mass Communications: Current Perspectives on Gratifications Research. Newbury Park, CA: Sage.

Gould, M. (1981) "Parsons versus Marx: an earnest warning. . . . " Sociological Inquiry 51: 197-218.

Gould, M. (1985) "Prolegomena to any future theory of societal crisis" in J. C. Alexander (ed.) Neofunctionalism. Newbury Park, CA: Sage.

Gouldner, A. W. (1970) The Coming Crisis of Western Sociology. New York: Basic Books.

Habermas, J. (1981a) "Talcott Parsons: problems of theory construction." Sociological Inquiry 51: 173-196.

Habermas, J. (1981b) The Theory of Communicative Action (T. McCarthy, trans.). Boston: Beacon Press (Translation, 1984).

Hawley, A. H. (1986) Human Ecology: A Theoretical Essay. Chicago: University of Chicago Press.

Herzog, H. (1944) "What do we really know about daytime serial listeners?" in P. F. Lazarsfeld and F. N. Stanton (eds.) Radio Research 1942-1943. New York: Duell, Sloan & Pearce.

Katz, E., M. Gurevitch, and H. Hass (1973) "On the use of mass media for important things." American Sociological Review 38: 164-181.

Klapper, J. T. (1960) The Effects of Mass Communication. New York: Free Press.

Kline, F. G. (1972) "Theory in mass communication research," in F. G. Kline and P. J. Tichenor (eds.) Current Perspectives in Mass Communication Research. Newbury Park, CA: Sage.

Lechner, F. J. (1985) "Modernity and its discontents," in J. C. Alexander (ed.) Neofunctionalism. Newbury Park, CA: Sage.

Liebes, T. (1986) "On the convergence of theories of mass communication and literature regarding the role of the 'reader.'" Presented to the Conference on Culture and Communication, October, Philadelphia.

Liebes, T. and E. Katz. (1986) "Patterns of involvement in television 'fiction,' a comparative analysis." European J. of Communication 1.

Lowenthal, L. (1944) "Biographies in popular magazines," in P. F. Lazarsfeld and F. N. Stanton (eds.) Radio Research 1942-1943. New York: Duell, Sloan & Pearce.

Luhmann, N. (1979) Trust and Power (H. Davis, J. Raffan, and K. Rooney, trans.). London: John Wiley (Editions published 1973, 1975).

Luhmann, N. (1981) The Differentiation of Society. New York: Columbia University Press.

Morley, D. (1980) The "Nationwide" Audience: Structure and Decoding. London: British Film Institute.

Münch, R. (1981) "Talcott Parsons and the theory of action, I: the structure of the Kantian core." American Journal of Sociology 86: 709-739.

Münch, R. (1982a) "Talcott Parsons and the theory of action, II: the continuity of the development." American Journal of Sociology 87: 771-826.

Münch, R. (1982b) Theorie des Handelns—Zur Rekonstruktion der Beiträge, von Talcott Parsons, Emile Durkheim, und Max Weber. Frankfurt: Suhrkamp.

Page, C. H. (1985) "On neofunctionalism." Footnotes (October): 10.

Palmgreen, P., L. A. Wenner, and K. E. Rosengren (1985) "Uses and gratifications research: the past ten years," in K. E. Rosengren, L. A. Wenner, and P. Palmgreen (eds.) Media Gratifications Research: Current Perspectives. Newbury Park, CA: Sage.

Parsons, T. (1935) "The place of ultimate values in sociological theory," in L. H. Mayhew (ed.) (1982) Talcott Parsons on Institutions and Social Evolution. Chicago: University of Chicago Press.

Parsons, T. (1937) The Structure of Social Action. New York: Free Press (Paperback edition, 1968).

Parsons, T. (1951) The Social System. New York: Free Press (Paperback edition, 1964).

Parsons, T. (1954) Essays in Sociological Theory (rev. ed.). New York: Free Press.

Parsons, T. (1961) "An outline of the social system," in T. Parsons, E. Shils, K. D. Naegele, and J. R. Pitts (eds.) Theories of Society. New York: Free Press.

Parsons, T. (1964) Social Structure and Personality. New York: Free Press.

Parsons, T. (1966) Societies: Evolutionary and Comparative Perspectives. Englewood Cliffs, NJ: Prentice-Hall.

Parsons, T. and G. M. Platt (1973) The American University. Cambridge, MA: Harvard University Press.

Parsons, T. and E. A. Shils [eds.] (1951) Toward a General Theory of Action. Cambridge: Harvard University Press.

Parsons, T. and E. A. Shils (1951) "Values, motives, and systems of action," in T. Parsons and E. A. Shils (eds.) Toward a General Theory of Action. Cambridge: Harvard University Press.

Parsons, T., E. A. Shils, G. W. Allport, C. Kluckhohn, H. A. Murray, Jr., R. R. Sears, R. C. Sheldon, S. A. Stouffer, and E. C. Tolman (1951) "Some fundamental categories of the theory of action: a general statement," in T. Parsons and E. A. Shils (eds.) Toward a General Theory of Action. Cambridge: Harvard University Press.

Parsons, T. and N. J. Smelser (1956) Economy and Society: A Study in the Integration of Economic and Social Theory. London: Routledge & Kegan Paul (Reprint, 1984).

Radway, J. A. (1984) Reading the Romance: Women, Patriarchy, and Popular Literature. Chapel Hill: University of North Carolina Press.

Rossi, I. (1985) "Predicting technological innovation through a dialectic reinterpretation of the four-function paradigm," in J. C. Alexander (ed.) Neofunctionalism. Newbury Park, CA: Sage.

Rothenbuhler, E. W. (1986) "Relativizing the evolutionary model for a neofunctionalist theory." Presented to the Conference on Culture and Communication, October, Philadelphia.

Schluchter, W. (1979) Verhalten Handeln und System. Frankfurt: Am Main.

Schluchter, W. (1981) The Rise of Western Rationalism: Max Weber's Developmental History. Berkeley: University of California Press.

Sciulli, D. (1985) "The practical groundwork of critical theory: bringing Parsons to Habermas (and vice versa)," in J. C. Alexander (ed.) Neofunctionalism. Newbury Park, CA: Sage.

Sciulli, D. (1986) "Comments on neofunctionalism." Theory Section Roundtable, American Sociological Association Annual Convention, August, New York.

Sciulli, D. and D. Gerstein (1985) "Social theory and Talcott Parsons in the 1980s." Annual Review of Sociology 11: 269-287.

Shils, E. (1975) Center and Periphery: Essays in Macrosociology. Chicago: University of Chicago Press.

Sica, A. (1983) "Parsons, Jr." American Journal of Sociology 89: 200-219.

Silverman, K. (1983) The Subject of Semiotics. New York: Oxford University Press.

Smelser, N. J. (1959) Social Change in the Industrial Revolution. Chicago: University of Chicago Press.

Smelser, N. J. (1962) Theory of Collective Behavior. New York: Free Press.

Spencer, H. (1868) The Principles of Sociology. New York: Appleton.

Swanson, D. L. (1977) "The uses and misuses of uses and gratifications." Human Communication Research 3: 214-221.

Swanson, D. L. (1979) "Political communication research and the uses and gratifications model: a critique." Communication Research 6: 37-53.

Tompkins, J. P. [ed.] (1980) Reader-Response Criticism: From Formalism to Post-Structuralism. Baltimore: Johns Hopkins University Press.

Warner, W. and W. Henry (1948) "The radio daytime serial: a symbolic analysis." Genetic Psychology Monographs 37: 3-71.

Wright, C. R. (1974) "Functional analysis and mass communication revisited," in J. G. Blumler and E. Katz (eds.) The Uses of Mass Communications: Current Perspectives on Gratifications Research. Newbury Park, CA: Sage.

2

CRITICAL THEORY AND THE POLITICS OF EMPIRICAL RESEARCH

Lawrence Grossberg

ABSTRACT: This chapter offers a framework for understanding critical work as an open-ended theoretical practice, using the concepts of difference, struggle, and empowerment. It argues that the politics of research practices are not inherent in the practices themselves but are the result of struggles to articulate their significance. Using the work of Pierre Bourdieu, it suggests the possibility for a rearticulation of quantitative methods into a critical perspective.

Like other social and humanistic disciplines, the study of communication is mapped by a number of taken-for-granted oppositions: Two axes in particular define the dominant conception of the field, a conception most recently resanctified in *Ferment in the Field* (1983). This way of structuring knowledge first differentiates between "critical" (or utopian) and "empirical" (or administrative) research, and between qualitative and quantitative research. But it quickly assumes a necessary correspondence between the two axes, thus effectively collapsing them: For example, empirical research is quantitative, critical research is qualitative. Debates, as well as educations, occur within the terrain that is thus constructed, and the field is continuously reproduced in terms of the institutionalized oppositional and often antagonistic relations between two homogeneous camps, perspectives, and traditions. I want, in this essay, to challenge this framework and to argue against seeing a necessary disjunction between these two traditions. This taken-for-granted organization is based partly in the very connotations of *critical* within our discipline,[1] which always appears to register a radical distinction from, and a marginal status in relation to, a

AUTHOR'S NOTE: I would like to acknowledge the assistance, suggestions, and encouragement provided by Jennifer Daryl Slack, Martin F. Allor, Ellen Wartella, Charles Whitney, and Janice Radway. I would also like to acknowledge my debt to Stuart Hall: My understanding of critical theory is to a large extent drawn from his work. I would also like to thank the graduate students at the Annenberg School of Communication at Los Angeles, whose invitation to lecture provided the original stimulus for this article, and whose interest provided the motivation to continue.

supposedly dominant empirical or scientific tradition.[2] But if neither of these traditions is as homogeneous as its opponents assume, then this way of structuring the field glosses over significant distinctions within each camp as well as alliances that cut across the opposition. If it is too early to declare war, then it may be fruitful to deconstruct—or at least rattle—the distinction a bit, especially at the level of research practices.

I will offer an alternative framework for critical research, drawn from cultural studies and built upon three concepts: difference, struggle, and empowerment. Then, bringing these concepts to bear upon research methods, I will argue that the politics of research methods are not intrinsic to them and that, in fact, critical researchers can and should take advantage of the full range of sophisticated methodological tools available, rearticulating the practices of the so-called empirical tradition into their own theoretical and political projects.

Research methods—whether qualitative, interpretive, or quantitative (in the narrow sense, e.g., forms of statistical analysis)—and the knowledge they offer us are not intrinsically politically good or bad, humane or mechanical, progressive or regressive. On what basis do we assume that they simply reflect a taken for granted political opposition? Even though there are historical links between politics and practices, political positions are not necessarily inscribed into the research practices that define our intellectual resources. For the missing term in such arguments is the larger interpretive context out of which they emerge, into which they are inserted, and within which their theoretical and political consequences are articulated. But this is not to suggest, at the other extreme, that research practices are, in themselves, innocent and benign, for they never appear "in themselves." Nor can one embrace all the work that has been or is being done in either tradition, as if all descriptions and accounts were entirely open to be reread and reappropriated. They are always already articulated into larger political/theoretical frameworks, and I am not suggesting that one can free them from all such frameworks and discover a pure neutrality. Metaphorically, research practices are like chemical radicals; while they may momentarily appear to be free-floating during some disruptive experimental intervention, their identity and power depends upon their re-entrance into particular relationships. Thus I am suggesting that we can struggle to rearticulate such practices, that is, to construct them within a different set of relations, to locate them in different contexts, recognizing the constraints that always limit the possibilities for winning such struggles. I am proposing that we appropriate such practices for different political and theoretical projects, acknowledging that this will involve transforming them.

I will make my claim even stronger: We need to bring some of the sophisticated research techniques available to us today into critical research. At the very least, the nature of the mass media and the sheer size of its audiences (not to mention the differences within them) seems to demand new forms of critical research. As younger generations of scholars seek out the sorts of linkages that would enable them to bring together the disparate discourses constituting our field, it becomes obvious that the differences between us and the multiplicity of research practices we use, although they appear to constrain us, may, in fact, become a significant resource if turned to our advantage.

DEFINING CRITICAL WORK

Three criteria are commonly proposed for defining critical research: (1) It recognizes the close, even necessary, relationship between knowledge and politics and thus demands that researchers declare their political allegiances, (2) it understands the complex causal relations between communicative practices and the social totality, and (3) it locates communicative practices and elements within the already structured social formation and thus sees communication itself as the expression of already existing relations of power.

However, there are significant problems with each of these attempts to characterize the essential conditions of critical research. The first quite correctly rejects the innocence and neutrality of knowledge and the possibility that researchers and the knowledge they produce can escape having their own impact upon the context they purport to describe and explain. Descriptions and explanations are, after all, an important part of how we come to organize our everyday lives and social policies. Neutrality is not an objective stance but a privilege available to those with power, and a value defined within the cultural habits of particular social groups. However, this too often sounds like a claim that knowledge constitutes or is responsible for the evils with which it is implicated. But the relation of knowledge and social power is more complex and contradictory: It is not easy to simply judge, a priori, the political implications of particular research programs. Moreover, the demand that one declare one's political allegiance is, in many senses, a rather simplistic illusion. There are not two sides—good and bad, powerful and powerless. Critical researchers must, in fact, begin with the recognition of their own paradoxical situation—existing in the heart of the beast, so to speak, in one of the most powerful and complex ideological institutions. Declaring oneself to be on the side of the oppressed too often serves as a way of avoiding the more difficult task of locating the points at which one already identifies and is identified with those who hold power in our society. One of the most surprising and disturbing tendencies of critical (as well as mainstream) researchers is their elitism, which often expresses the power they claim to oppose. That elitism dictates that it is the critical researcher's task to identify the existing structures of power—structures of which ordinary people are always unaware—and to become the vanguard of a truly (so they confidently assume) liberatory, even revolutionary, politics. I remain rather uncomfortable with this set of attitudes, which often defines the tone of critical research, just as I am suspicious of anyone who is secure enough in his or her utopian vision to be willing to impose it on others.

The second criterion, which defines critical research by notions of causality, also seems fundamentally misplaced, for it mistakes epistemological issues for the demands of knowledge in particular historical contexts. This displacement is often disguised by the vocabulary of determination—whether Williams's (1980) notion of the exertion of pressures and constraints or Althusser's (1970) multiplicity of structural determinations, the conceptual equation of determination and causality seems to always lead one back into examining historical processes as if they were simply a matter of explaining the origin of practices, or the configuration of structures. The third criterion allows critical researchers to merely insert the practices with which they are concerned into the already existing social structures and relations of power. Consequently, the social formation is too often conceptualized as if its parameters were predictable in advance, as if power were a reified structure that we stand outside of by virtue of our moral righteousness and a scientific epistemology of causality. This produces a politics defined by the success or failure of the processes of the reproduction of the social order.

It is not that these criteria do not describe some of what is actually done by critical researchers; rather, it is their claim to be able to draw the boundaries of critical research—creating a dialectic of inclusion and exclusion—by defining its project and commitments beyond its existing practices that is problematic. The question is whether there is a way of understanding these limited descriptive concepts as useful tools on the road to a more adequate sense of critical theory and practice. Because the site of critical theory is, at least in part, the relationship between its own discourses and the historical context it attempts to comprehend and intervene into, critical theory is always in process. If neither history nor politics ever comes to an end, then theory (as well as research) is never completed and our accounts can never be closed or totalized. On this model, the goal of theory is to offer not a polished representation of the truth, but simply a little help in our efforts to better understand our world. If we refuse to see critical work as a finished theory, or even as a set of conceptual and methodological commitments seeking closure, is there a way of describing this as yet unrealized project? Are there broader, more open-ended ways of characterizing the thrust of critical research, of its views of power and the social formation, of the nature of its account-giving practices, and of its own place within the questions it raises?

I want to start then by suggesting that the cornerstone of critical work is its committed opposition to any reductionism, its recognition that concrete reality is always more complex and contradictory than our intellectual schemes can represent. The task is more than learning to acknowledge this as a footnote to our analyses, and even more than learning to live with this complexity. The unfulfilled promise of critical work is to find ways of incorporating this fundamental insight into its most basic theoretical and analytic tools, to recognize that the truth is always concrete. As Hall (1985a) puts it, we must "bend against the wind" and actively seek out that which, for whatever reasons, is being kept off the agenda (including our own), whatever is being silenced in the production, not only of social reality, but of social knowledge as well.

Of course, we must also recognize that there is some truth in each of the three criteria discussed above: Critical theory is concerned with power and the social formation; it is based upon a set of assumptions about the relations between reality and human practices; and it is committed to reflecting upon the relationship of knowledge and power so that it can actively use its own interpretations to intervene into contemporary social relations of power. But these three notions need to be reread in a more generous and less dogmatic way. I will offer three concepts, not simply as isomorphic substitutes but, rather, as three inflections of the commitment to concrete complexity and contradiction into the different arenas of critical concern; they are "difference," "struggle" and "empowerment." They are not intended to describe the actual commitments of critical researchers but to provide the broadest possible context within which such work might be located.

Difference

The concept of difference brings the commitment to complexity to bear upon the analysis of specific events at every level: It says, most fundamentally, that the outcomes of particular historical events and processes are never guaranteed in advance, that history is contingent and not necessary. In epistemological terms, it is characterizable as antitranscendentalism, antiessentialism, overdetermination, or even deconstructionism. In analytic terms, it is what Hall (1985b), Laclau and Mouffe (1985), and others call "articulation theory," or what Foucault (1981) presents as a theory of effectivity.[3] While Marx (1975) described human nature as the ensemble of social relationships—thereby denying it any essential or universal status by making it the product of a particular social and historical formation—it is structuralism that, for critical theory, has provided new ways of understanding and describing such specific, context-dependent (or, in Gramscian terms, conjunctural) identities. Let me elaborate this, for the claim is both normative and descriptive.

Structuralism (and its various "posts") argues that no element is definable in and of itself; it exists—its identity takes shape—only in its complex relations to, its differences from, its others (and, of course, there can be no single definition of the other, i.e., contradiction is itself a complex and historical relationship). Structuralism calls into question any easy identification between a text (as a set of signifiers) and its meaning, politics, or reference to a reality outside itself. It refuses to see the meanings and effects of a text guaranteed by either the text itself or its origin. It points to the text's existence within, and determining relations to, a complex field of differences. There is always a space between mobile signifiers and their meanings and references, producers and consumers.

If the meaning and politics of a text (in fact, its very identity) cannot be guaranteed by, or even read off of, the surface of the text itself, then one has to analyze the network of relations (or lines of effects) within which it comes to have the identity, and hence, the effects, it does. Moreover, such relations cannot be reduced to a single plane; for example, they include not only the structure of the text itself but also its intertextual relations within and across media and genre. They include not only the text's relation to its producers but also to its consumers, both of which may be equally active and complex. They include not only the meanings the text eventually offers, but its relationships to broader contexts of reality and its claims to represent aspects of them; and they include not only the text's contributions to the determinations of its effects, but the audience's ability to appropriate those determining effects.

But critical theory cannot rest with the deconstruction of any structure into its constituent differences, for the fact remains that structures are real and have their own effects in the world, although they are themselves produced. Critical work is located in the dialectic between deconstruction and reconstruction. If it rejects the essentialism of theories that assume "necessary correspondences," it also rejects the theoreticism of theories that assume "necessary noncorrespondence." Essentialism assumes that anything can be explained by appealing to its intrinsic and invariant features; theoreticism assumes that empirical questions can be resolved by conceptual work. Alternatively, the radical contextuality of critical theory defines a position in which, while there are "no necessary correspondences," there are always historically real correspondences (Hall, 1985b). It does not propose that preconstituted elements (with their own already defined unified identities, whether as texts, meanings, political or subject positions) are inserted into already waiting contexts. Rather, it asserts that both elements and contexts articulate each other. Contexts (or structures) have no identity apart from their articulated relations to the elements that constitute them; both elements and structures are the ongoing productions of articulating practices. Of course, any practice carries with it the different contexts and struggles that have produced it, but it remains always open to be redefined, rearticulated into new contexts, which produce it as a slightly different practice, with different meanings and effects.

Structuralism has rearticulated the critical terrain and old maps will no longer suffice: Rather than a hierarchical model of the critic standing above the producer, who stands above the text, which stands above the consumer, the critical researcher now confronts a complex array of signifying practices, intertextual connotations, historical contexts, social relations, and modes of production, distribution, and consumption. I am not suggesting that we all become structuralists, as if it were a finished and correct position (and, obviously, my description deviates significantly from the classic positions of de Saussure, Jakobsen, and Levi-Strauss). But I am suggesting that, at least within critical theory, we already are (or ought to be) "post" structuralists (taking that literally, rather than paradigmatically). I am suggesting that structuralism has reshaped the terrain on which we must begin to rethink questions of the relationships between knowledge, communicative practices, and power. If structuralism too easily limits the context and ignores history (thus essentializing the structure rather than the elements), if it too easily dismisses questions of subjectivity, if it too easily reduces reality and power to questions of signification, if it too easily accedes to the necessity of existing structures of power, these are the sites at which critical theory needs to develop. These questions, both theoretical and empirical, are, in fact, being raised quite explicitly, not only in Marxism (in its efforts to rethink theories of ideology, power, and material determination), but also in psychoanalysis (with its theories of desire and subject-formation), poststructuralism (with its radical sense of underdetermination and contextualization), and feminism (which is challenging many fundamental notions of power and value, of the relations between nature and culture in the always contextualized production of gendered subject-identities, and of the very nature of interpretive and political intervention). Hence I am suggesting that one must argue against it, fight to win its insights into a more open-ended practice of theorizing.

The concept of difference functions here, not as an abstract epistemological commitment but as a more adequate, nonreductionist form of conjunctural or contextual analysis. When critical theory argues that communication (as practices, institutions, and relationships) must be located within the social formation, that it is linked to different elements and levels of social life, it is arguing that the privileged self-identity and assumed self-sufficiency of communication (as if it could be understood in isolation, in its own terms) must be deconstructed in order to reveal how it is constituted, defined, and constructed—how its effects are determined—by its complex contextual relations. However, without the notion of difference, the commitment to contextualism often becomes quite ambiguously intertwined with reductionist notions of causality, and one forgets that all such relations are themselves complex and contradictory. Whether one defines all relations of power by appealing to a single social plane (the economic or the ideological/epistemic), or whether one ignores the contradictions within the different planes themselves, conjunctural analysis gives way to causal reductionism. The analytic demand of the commitment to difference is to avoid such reductionist tendencies (which are always present), whether the reduction of reality to communication or to economics, the reduction of power to manipulation, or the reduction of people to "cultural dopes." Such tendencies tell us where to lay the blame and reassure us, not only that the truth has already been found, but further, that we have fulfilled our intellectual and political responsibilities as critics.

Struggle

Critical research is concerned with the the complex and often contradictory effects of particular social practices—effects that are manifested in the production of capital, money (for the two are not equivalent), meanings, subject identities, desires, and affects. Continuing the economic metaphor, however, it is also concerned with their unequal distribution, for it is this that is the concrete expression of power. Power shapes relationships, structures differences, draws boundaries, delimits complexity, reduces contradictions to claims of unity, coherence, and homogeneity, and organizes the multiplicity of concrete practices and effects into predefined identities, unities, hierarchical categories, and apparently necessary relationships. Critical research attempts to analyze how particular practices (or texts) have been and are being inserted into, and thus articulated within, more complex contexts. If the notion of difference makes the meaning of a text or practice and its power to affect our lives an open question, the product of contingent historical events and contexts, we cannot begin an explanation of particular communicative practices by assuming that its meanings (politics or other effects) are essential—inherent and necessary—to it. Such an "essentialism" (whether of texts or social practices or human nature) would allow us to read their significance off their surfaces or out of their origins. But such moments of identity (for example, as if a text had a single meaning or a predefined political position) cannot be the starting point of our investigations; they are precisely that which we must construct by working through the analysis concretely.

The commitment to notions of struggle defines the middle term in the investigation, for such effects (or articulations) must be seen as the product of real historical struggles and contradictions, of people making history, but in conditions not of their own making (Marx). To treat reality conjuncturally (i.e., in its specific configurations and contextual identities) then involves seeing it as the active struggle to produce the contexts within which any practice is determined, that is, within which its effects are actualized. Articulation, the construction of contexts by inflecting practices into particular relations, is an active struggle, carried out by real historical individuals and groups, within the determining limits and contradictions of their lives and their historical contexts. Three points need to be emphasized here.

First, critical research seeks to identify not only the possibilities of struggles to rearticulate particular practices into different contexts, to link them to different effects, but also the limits and constraints on such struggles at particular sites within the social formation. The recognition of the historical limits on struggle prevents critical research from falling back into a negative essentialism that would define the identity of any practice as an empty space that can never be entirely filled, as if the field were entirely open, as if our possibilities for struggle were unlimited, as if structures of power did not have their own real historical effects, even if they are neither essential nor necessary. There are real historical tendencies and historically powerful articulations that cannot be ignored; not every site in the social field is a site for struggle (or if it is, there may be good reasons for assuming that one is unlikely to win anything).

Second, critical research must have a notion of historical actors as real people. Marx (1973) understood that wherever there is domination, there is subordination, and that with subordination comes resistance. Not because—as Foucault (1980) would sometimes have it—resistance is necessarily present, but because reality is always complex and contradictory, and because people are themselves complex and contradictory subjects, always struggling to "make history but in conditions not of their own making." If the origin of a particular text does not guarantee its politics, it is also the case that living a particular (objective) social position does not guarantees one's experiences (i.e., how one lives the objective conditions), interests, or values. Critical research must resist both a "humanistic pull" that would essentialize human nature and a "discursive pull" that would reduce subjectivity to an abstract and empty epistemological subject-position within discourse.[4] While humanism makes undetermined human subjects into the active agents of history, discursive theories make discourse itself into the active force of history. Both pulls fall back into assuming necessary correspondences; for both, positions (whether in social or discursive formations) directly determine experience. The notion of struggle demands that the agent of struggle—people—be understood as concrete, historically overdetermined subjects, positioned in contradictory ways by the range of discourses and social practices within which they live out their lives. This "sociological pull" sees the subject as a "structure in dominance," a historically constructed hierarchical structure of identities, never free from social determination but never reducible to the necessary determinations of any single material level.

Third, critical theory sees history as a contingent and changing field, and it sees its own descriptions as interventions that necessarily, although in perhaps unpredictable ways, will reshape it. Its politics is always strategic rather than utopian (which is not to deny the importance and effectiveness of utopian motivations). Our theories become dysfunctional when they allow us to become complacent, when we think we can take for granted the significance or politics of any practice. It is only with a commitment to struggle that critical research can describe the ways in which concrete practices enter into concrete social life, as sites of potential and sometimes real struggles by real people. People struggle with what they are given, and sometimes against what they are given, although they don't always win. Thus the notion of struggle defines a different political practice for the critical researcher. Too often, because "the masses" do not speak when we want them to and, when they do, they too often do not say what our theories had predicted or what we want them to, we assume they are necessarily silent, passive, colonized victims, cultural dopes. But we should not confuse our analyses of particular practices (and the evaluations these often carry) with their actual insertion into everyday life, as if we were always capable of seeing what the masses never can, as if we could assume their absolute ability, if not willingness, to be manipulated. For, at the most practical level, it is simply ineffective to try to organize political opposition in the modern world by telling people that they are oppressed but don't know it, that we understand their real interests better than they do. Further, if people are actively appropriating what they are given in unpredictable ways, constantly attempting to bend what they have had no control over to their own advantage, to win a bit of purchase on their situation, then it seems inappropriate as well for us, as critical researchers, to define what constitutes real or appropriate opposition for everyone.[5] Rather we should locate such questions within the ongoing struggles of concrete people in concrete situations; we should be content to identify such struggles, to help articulate them, to nurture them and, perhaps, to bring them into visible relations with other struggles, constantly trying to draw connections that might organize concrete struggles into larger forms of opposition.

This positions the critical researcher as another historical actor, and rejects the privileged status of the analyst over that of the everyday consumer (as well as the implicit "vanguardism" of much of critical research). The critic is another consumer, admittedly standing in a different position, within a different network of codes and practices, struggling to articulate (in both senses, to speak and to produce) the meaning and effects of particular practices. This does not mean that critical theory cannot make normatively based political arguments. Rather than dismantling itself, critical theory needs to locate its own position within a unique institutional context (one of the projects of Pierre Bourdieu, of whom I will say more below), and hence, as always, be implicated within the social and historical relations of power. At the very least, this means that critical theory must consider the place of its own categories within the contemporary relations of power.[6]

Empowerment

The notion of struggle makes clear that power cannot be conceptualized as either simple domination or manipulation. Power is not an abstract concept, nor a reified set of presupposed structures, nor a universal process replicated over and over again, nor a subjective experience entirely dependent upon our interpretations. Yet power is real and operates at every level of our lives. At its most concrete, we might define power as the enablement of particular practices, that is, as the conditions of possibility that enable a particular practice or statement to exist in a specific social context, and that enable people to live their lives in different ways. And, of course, every such practice itself enables other practices to exist.

Empowerment points to the fact that people live in a complex and changing network of social relationships, that they are implicated in contradictory ways in hierarchical relations of power. Whether a particular group is empowered or disempowered, whether a particular practice empowers or disempowers its subjects, is never a simple matter; it depends upon where one positions those subjects—as well as oneself as a researcher—within the social field. That is to say, whether someone has power over someone else depends upon where you and they stand, and it is worth repeating that the two are not always the same, despite our assumptions that we can or do occupy the same positions as those we study.[7]

Moreover, concrete relationships of power are themselves always multiple and contradictory. Wherever people and practices are organized around particular social contradictions or differences, there is a differential distribution of power. Hence, the politics of any communicative practice cannot be limited to its relation to the state or to the economic sector. Relations of gendered, sexual, racial, class, national, and age differences are all part of the organization of power in the contemporary world. And the relations between these different structures of power are themselves complex; we cannot assume that by overthrowing capitalism, we have guaranteed a society that is not racist or sexist. Similarly, if we were able to overthrow the particular historical form of patriarchy in our society, this would not guarantee the elimination of racial or economic oppression (in their various forms, for we must not forget that each is itself a complex phenomenon). Consequently, the critical researcher is compelled, if not to simultaneously explore all of these structures, at least to recognize their relative autonomy, their complex relations to one another and to their specific historical context. While they may be organized hierarchically in particular contexts, critical theory is obliged to refuse to make any one structure of power fundamental, as if we could know in advance that this was the real locus of power and oppression. At the very least, it is incumbent upon us to open spaces for and to support the efforts of those who seek to understand and oppose the dominant structures of power in their complex and contradictory forms.

Furthermore, we cannot take for granted the meanings by which we already organize relations of power in any particular context; we cannot assume that the meaning or difference signalled by such notions as gender, race, or class are available to us apart from the particular context. They are themselves the result of struggles to articulate their meanings and effects. For example, skinheads (a British youth subculture) apparently redefined racial difference so that West Indians were on the side of the whites while Pakistanis were on the side of the blacks. Similarly, many liberal men have not overcome or even denied sexism but have merely redrawn the line between acceptable female behavior (i.e., when a woman is allowed to "act" like a man) and required female behavior. And it is quite obvious that the meaning of the different classes (where they are to be found, how the lines are to be drawn around them, and the nature of their relationships) is not easily assimilable into the rather romantic and nostalgic notions that still permeate so much of contemporary critical work.[8]

Finally, the notion of empowerment suggests the complexity of the political effects of any social event or practice: that it may have multiple and contradictory effects even within a single register and that one cannot know in advance and apart from concrete analysis what the effects of that practice are in the relations of power. People can win something and lose something simultaneously. For example, buying commodities also gives one access to new forms of social production (e.g., "remaking" records so as to eliminate politically obnoxious songs) and social knowledge, to new languages of social and political calculation; participating in apparently sexist cultural forms—such as popular music, dance, and fashion—may also empower women to discover new relations with their own bodies and identities that were simply unavailable to them before; the exportation of American cultural products certainly contributes to the continued redistribution of international wealth, and it may have real consequences on the production or destruction of traditional cultural forms, but it may also empower its audiences by giving them a common language (in those countries where the state uses tribal languages as a form of disempowerment) or new visions of social and political possibilities. One can gain power in the economic domain, while losing power over one's emotional life. One can be empowered through cultural consumption, even while still disempowered productively. Sexual empowerment may have complex relations to economic, interpersonal, and affective relations of power. Thus, not only can't we be sure whether any practice is empowering or disempowering, but the question makes no sense apart from concrete contexts and concrete political struggles.

THE POLITICS OF EMPIRICAL RESEARCH

There is an admitted relativism to this position but it is not antiempirical; it is a relativism of "no guarantees" that sees knowledge implicated in struggles for empowerment. It sees truth precisely as a measure of our ability to "cut into"[9] the surfaces of historical and social reality in order to win some purchase on the relations of power and resistance within the world as it is historically being made around us. It does not attempt to offer global accounts or metanarratives of social life, for it recognizes that theory, like any practice, cannot be abstracted out of its contexts; nor can its empirical questions ever be entirely free of political relations. For if one is always "theorizing the concrete," it is also the case that the concrete is always the result of the detour through theory. If theory is a struggle over how we represent and engage the world, it is also a political practice attempting to make its own articulation dominant (i.e., taken up as the representation of the truth) and thus to affect the very ways in which we live that reality. Such conjunctural theories are not caught in the constant (modernist) dilemma between truth and falsity, or success and failure, but rather, operate in the ongoing articulation of political and cultural struggles.

It is in this context that I wish to turn to the question of empirical research practices and empiricism, for I think it important to distinguish the two.[10] Critical theory, in its attacks on what it assumes to be the dominant paradigm, often ignores the power and value of the latter's research and methods because it confuses them with the framework out of which they may have emerged (which still guarantees nothing) and into which they are regularly inserted. Critical researchers often act as if numbers (except for their own economic analyses) necessarily misrepresent the world. They forget that it is not the numbers or correlations that offer a representation, but the context within which they are articulated, the words and meanings with which empiricists construct and interpret them. Not only do I want to take exception to such a confusion (and the assumption of the necessary political inflections of statistics) but also, I want to suggest that the attempt to study communication in the contemporary world—in which messages are effective in part because of their proliferation and repetition, and in which the mass audience is no longer conceivable as either a simple aggregate of sociological fractions or a common psychological structure—may, in fact, demand the appropriation of such research practices. Otherwise, we are likely to produce ever more schizophrenic researchers, despairing of ever reconciling their sophisticated capabilities with their political and even theoretical commitments[11]

However, we need to carefully separate the ideology of empiricism from the statistical production of data. In the earlier part of this century, when interpretive social theorists were attempting to justify their research and negotiate a peace treaty with the so-called scientists, they often were willing to take the role of data-gatherers. Schutz (1971), for example, offered a historic compromise in which phenomenological social science would provide the raw material for scientific explanations. I want to reverse the roles of the negotiated treaty, to argue that it is statistics that, in the contemporary world, produces the data that critical theorists should be interpreting. But again, this is not to argue that statistical methods exist as neutral terms outside of any context; it is, rather, to argue that we must rethink the statistical practices and designs that we use by rearticulating them into a new, critical theoretical context, always recognizing the constraints operating, limiting our chances of winning. That is to say, we need a critical theory of research (and of the terms of measurement) built upon the concepts of difference, struggle, and empowerment.

My argument is, then, with empiricism as an interpretive practice that can be partly separated from the construction of correlations. By empiricism I mean the set of assumptions that privilege the given (the phenomenon, experience)—whether found or constructed—as the transparent window on truth. Empiricism takes the raw material of experience as the surface of an essential reality innocently waiting below the surface to be read off the "facts." Empiricism is connected, on the one hand, with utility theory (and its paradoxical commitment to rationality, accomplished only by relegating the irrational to a space outside of knowledge) and, on the other hand, to liberalism (with its faith that the free flow of information would inevitably result in the maximization of truth as social utility). Mattelart's (forthcoming) statement that "the observation of empirical facts is too important to be left to the empiricists" needs to be taken literally: It is not a rejection of empirical methods but of a theoretical and political ideology that assumes that correlations can themselves represent or offer an account of a reality behind the surface level of experience, as if they were intrinsically self-explanatory. Critical theory takes the correlation as the object of interpretation—as that which is in need of an account.

The work of Pierre Bourdieu (1984) offers a powerful example of the attempt to combine critical theory and statistical analysis, to define an antiessentialist articulation of statistical research, to reconceptualize statistical research practices (in particular, survey research) in ways consistent with the framework of critical theory. I want here to simply summarize his critique of how empiricism articulates empirical methods. Bourdieu sees empiricism as an intuitionism that universalizes particular social experiences across the contradictory field of social practices. It assumes not only a transparent meaning, but a simple (i.e., noncontradictory) one as well. That is, a critical analysis of sociological correlations would have to carry on an "interminable analysis of the social value of each of the properties or practices considered" (p. 20), in order to understand "what is designated in the particular case by each term" (p. 18). Variables—whether dependent or independent, whether sociological properties or cultural practices—do not "impose the self-evidence of a universal, unanimously approved meaning" (p. 100). The empiricist's assumption of the constancy of the variable is an illusion resulting from its nominal identity and the researchers' failure to locate themselves within the field of social positions. That is, the taken-for-granted meaning of a variable is merely the reproduction of the researcher's own social perspective. For Bourdieu, if we are to successfully establish a science, we need a reflective analysis that will simultaneously focus on the complex social conditions that overdetermine or make possible particular practices, and on the historically determined limits of available truths (e.g., the systematic blindspots and structured absences of any theory). Only in that way can we both gain some truth and recognize our own role, always located with a political field, in the construction of that truth.

Bourdieu argues that both dependent and independent variables are themselves complex entities rather than simple monistic measures. Moreover, the specific configuration of any variable depends upon the social field within which it is deployed in specific research. And, because different fields of social life have their own logics, their own forces at work, and their own struggles already ongoing, it is not a matter of merely contextualizing the data or of limiting their validity to a particular context, but of recognizing that the correlation already articulates a particular context. Consequently, Bourdieu argues, the critical researcher cannot take for granted what is determining in the independent variable or what is determined in the dependent variable. Because each variable is always a particular arrangement of different features, one must seek out those "pertinent properties" that are actively involved in the particular relationship and that are inseparable from the relationships within which they act; one must identify the actual conditions that are determining and being determined, what Bourdieu calls the concrete "conditions of possibility" that enable particular effects to result. (For example, Bourdieu attacks those who treat educational level as a property attached to agents, as if they operated as independent forces.)

That is, Bourdieu argues that we must "deconstruct" the illusory unity of our variables in order to understand them as social and historical productions (both in everyday life and in scientific practice) that are the sites of complex and active articulations: "What are grasped through indicators such as educational level or social origin—or, more precisely, in the structure of the relations between them, are different modes of production of the cultivated habitus, which engender differences not only in the competencies acquired but also in the manner of applying them" (p. 66). That is, we can only understand the concrete effects being measured in something like educational level if we realize that it is already determined by complex relations to dominant social and cultural sensibilities. Similarly, Bourdieu argues that the researcher must take into account—without privileging lived experience (for it is an ideological production)—"how the perception and appreciation of what is designated by the dependent variable vary" (p. 100). Only in this way can we "move beyond the abstract relation between consumers with interchangeable tastes and products with uniformly perceived and appreciated properties to the relation between tastes, which vary in a necessary way according to their social and economic conditions of production, and the products on which they confer their different social identities" (pp. 100-101). This enables Bourdieu to understand how it is that social struggles may often continue to reproduce the established, dominant social order, since what is struggled over may not be different conditions but, rather, differences between the active effects of the same conditions. Thus one may be struggling, not to change the structures of education but, rather, simply the ways in which they are available to different populations, or the ways in which they are taken to express important social differences. The "nature" of the conditions may change while the structure of the social relations of power remains.

An Empirical Map of
the Social Conjuncture

Having drawn upon Bourdieu's critique of empiricism's appropriation of statistics, it may be useful to further explicate his position. Having argued that it is not simply a matter of limiting data to a context but of contextualizing the data themselves, Bourdieu's "theory of practices" offers one of the few explicit examples of statistically based critical analysis. Rejecting essentialist models of cultural consumption (taste, needs) and production (creativity, intentionality), which assume that effects are determined by the inherent properties of the subject or agent of the practice, Bourdieu attempts to describe the material conditions that, on the one hand, make possible the relative autonomy of cultural practices (including intellectual work), and on the other hand, implicate such practices within social structures as organizations of "symbolic power." He attempts to provide a statistically based map of the different social and cultural fields, and of the general sociocultural space of a particular historical conjuncture.

More accurately, he superimposes maps of three different levels of the social formation, each with its own practices, effects, and conditions, and its own logic of transformation and possibility: The first describes the historically determined distribution of economic and cultural capital (the two forms of capital can be exchanged for one another, but the forms and rates of exchange are themselves contextually determined). The second maps out the historically determined distribution of cultural and social practices (the space of lifestyles and distinctions). That is, it describes where in the social population particular practices are likely to be found (e.g., museumgoing is decidedly middle-class, as are certain forms of fashion, of foods, and of media consumption). Once again, while practices can be appropriated and taken up elsewhere on the map, the likely trajectories, and the possibilities, of such movements depend upon where one is positioned on the map, both as social subject and as researcher. The third map describes the historically determined distribution of the "habitus." Bourdieu postulates the existence of an objectively determined, internalized set of dispositions that both fits the individual into a particular set of economic and life-style sites and enables that individual to improvise creatively within those sites. It is, basically, the psychological mechanism by which individuals are positioned within (socialized into) their specific place upon the social field, mediating between the structures of capital distribution and those of the distribution of social practices. By mapping these three levels, as it were, onto one another, Bourdieu attempts to describe the complex relations and determinations between economic relations, sociocultural practices, and subjective positions, and the ways in which each can serve as the condition of possibility for the others. That is, Bourdieu attempts to find, using statistics, the correlations between the distribution of economic positions,[12] cultural practices, and socially shared dispositions toward different forms of practice. But his interpretation does not offer a static description of an internally stable structure, as if these relations were forged once and for all times in every social formation. For Bourdieu additionally charts the lines of movement and change that are possible within particular social spaces, both internally (within each map) and externally (in the relations amongst the three), always recognizing that such possibilities depend upon where one starts from within the social space. Having constructed a dynamic system of statistical correlations, Bourdieu's interpretations of the significance of any correlation (which in practice would define the sociological identity of particular subject positions) depends upon the fact that every variable at each social position is overdetermined by its relations with the other variables also constituting the specific social site. Consequently, we can see that what people are likely to struggle over in their attempts to redefine and contest specific social distinctions (and relations of power) are precisely the ways in which the meanings and conditions of particular forms of capital, or of cultural and social practices, are being constructed.

It is an ambitious and, I would argue, significant project. It is, in fact, often quite compelling, but it becomes less so as Bourdieu moves from societies and practices that are permeated by class structures to questions revolving around mass media and mass audiences. There are two reasons for this failure: First, the ways in which Bourdieu superimposes the three maps on one another often represent, not concrete articulations, but presupposed homologies or correspondences. In the end, the entire topography is defined by assumptions of utility (people act to maximize their economic and cultural capital) and class determination. Second, Bourdieu assumes an encoding/decoding model that separates cultural production and consumption, although both are active struggles to appropriate cultural objects and practices according to the possibilities, trajectories, and utilities of a particular site. That is to say, the audience always appropriates particular texts into the resources (as capital and practices) already defined by its sociocultural position. Obviously, I want to agree with the notion that the effects of a text are the product of potential or actual struggles embodied within the text-audience interaction and with the recognition that the audience is defined historically rather than psychologically. And I want as well to embrace Bourdieu's recognition that such effects are not limited to questions of meaning, but include matters of attention, attitude, affect, and so forth.

But I want to draw back from the view that these struggles are defined by particular social positions identifiable independently of the struggles themselves. Leaving aside the problems with notions of encoded or preferred meanings (Morley, 1981), the model is easily reduced to a transmission model of subjects existing outside of the particular context of the textual encounter, as if the audience already and always existed. The subject is no longer the container of self-determined intentions but, rather, a walking bank account of socially determined capital (codes, competencies, etc.). But if there is no guaranteed relation between any social practice and a particular set of cultural resources (i.e., an ideological position), Bourdieu himself essentializes the analysis because he fails to take into account the multiple and contradictory subjectivities of the masses (and hence of their cultural capital) and instead assumes a necessary and stable nature of the subjects in the mass. The theory cannot account for how particular resources become activated contextually (for different groups are located, with the texts, in different contexts), or for resources that are distributed in other than class terms (e.g., the mass media distribute cultural capital in complex ways), or for the contradictory ways in which texts are constructed and appropriated (e.g., Benjamin's, 1986, distinction between distracted and absorbed viewing: "The critical and receptive attitudes of the public coincide. The decisive reason for this is that the individual reactions are predetermined by the mass audience they are about to constitute" [p. 236], or notions of flow in television texts).

We need ways of describing the contextual determination of the subject without forgetting that it is not an empty space but a historically articulated subject that must be won into particular positions. That is, the subject is always a particular conjunctural articulation of cultural and social practices. Thus I would propose that the empirical task of critical research is to construct a map of the practices or effects that produce a specific local conjuncture, without privileging any of the theoretical categories that are themselves effective within the context. Rather than inserting an already existing audience into a conjuncture, we need to see the complex, contradictory, but always active struggles within which audiences, texts, and effects are constructed. Rather than beginning with a sociology of culture and tracing that out upon the conjuncture, we need a topography of the conjuncture that may connect to or disrupt our sociological schemas. The critical task is to identify the ways in which particular audiences (fragments or holograms of the masses) are empowered or disempowered by their conjunctural articulation.[13] Such a theoretical model is necessary if we are to avoid the easy path of simply trying to use the empiricist's data and, instead, follow the more arduous but rewarding path of attempting to win statistical and empirical techniques into a more self-consciously political position. Reconciliation is, after all, not the same as struggle and rearticulation is not the same as attributing innocence.

CONCLUSION

I have attempted to present a model of critical work that, although different from many commonly offered, does not exclude those who would articulate their positions differently. I have proposed a framework that is antireductionist, activist and antielitist. The notions of difference, struggle, and empowerment would seem to demand that the critical researcher must always be a bit humble:

on the one hand, content to provide a piece of the larger puzzle, a limited (and always determined) perspective on contemporary historical relations and, on the other hand, always reluctant to privilege their own position too much (that is, always fighting against the elitism that seems at times an almost irresistible product of the social position of the intellectual in capitalism). I want to emphasize the image of critical theory and research (and, I would add, teaching and politics as well) as an open-ended struggle, historically defined and socially realized, an ongoing social project in which the differences amongst us need to be made into a strength rather than a divisive weakness.

But, at the same time, we cannot forget that knowledge is implicated in questions of power and is not an idealized dialogic search for "truth," and that there are real political oppositions amongst scholars that cannot be deferred forever. Recognizing that political struggles are fought out in part within the discourses of knowledge does not mean, however, that we can confidently predict this ahead of time, or that we can read it off of particular intellectual and research practices. It is best to give each other the respect I would hope we give to those whose lives we describe. (After all, the masses are neither a manipulated object nor a collection of individually alienated subjects. Researchers need to remember that we are the masses as well, no matter how hard we work to deny that self-representation.) However, to end on a cynical note, we should also learn to recognize the weaknesses of our allies (this does not make them any less an ally) and the strengths of our enemies. And we should not reject the possibilities of appropriating those strengths for our own ends, bending them to our political and intellectual projects. There is no reason to assume that the real political oppositions that exist between people are directly and simply reproduced upon everything they do, or upon every practice they appropriate. The real danger is that, without such a commitment in our own work, we will always remain blind to such commitments in everyday life, and we will, once again, fall into what Benjamin (1978: 191) described as an "organization of pessimism." Against that, the critical scholar must always oppose Gramsci's (1971) dictum, "pessimism of the intellect, optimism of the will."

NOTES

1. The term *critical* is itself problematic. First, it is ambiguous, oscillating between a political and a methodological (interpretive, textual) register. Second, it resonates with a kind of arrogance that assumes that the speaker has a privileged handle, not only on self-reflection, but also on political values. Thus an account of critical research can deteriorate into the claim that no one else's efforts are really critical; definitions then become manifestos, full of normative statements disguised as descriptive interpretations. This is, of course, a trap that I too am unable to totally avoid. After all, one's own position is always shaped in part by one's research project, by its object of study and its intellectual history. While *critical* may be an unfortunate choice of terms—after all, is there any scholar whose work is not "critical" in some sense?—I have no other term to offer in its place. "Marxist" and "utopian," both obvious alternatives, have their own problems, although I am

sympathetic to their clear connotations of political dissent in the current political context.

2. Of course, we should at least note as well the arrogance implicit in those positions that describe themselves as "scientific" or "empirical." Also, while my argument is, in its current form, addressed to critical researchers, a similar argument needs to be made to empirical researchers in the field who continue to try to forcefully separate their politics from their research.

3. My own impulse is to locate it first at the level of historical specificity: That is, it is a theory of the contemporary social formation, of hegemony and postmodernity. See Grossberg (1984). For a more complete discussion of "articulation," see Hall (1986), Hall with Slack and Grossberg (forthcoming), and Grossberg (1986). For a discussion of essentialism, see Grossberg (forthcoming).

4. The distinction between these two traditions in cultural studies has been widely discussed. The typical form of the difference opposes humanism to structuralism: See, for example, Hall (1980). Allor (1977) extends and refines this distinction—since there is an antihumanistic, antistructuralist position (Stuart Hall's current work is the best example)—to point to the "sociological" pull that continues to oppose the discursive priorities of the structuralist tradition.

5. Examples can be found in many of the typical Left responses to new technologies and cultural forms. For example, arguments that the very use of computers, or the very act of enjoying popular music, entails the incorporation of the audience into structures of capitalist domination ignore the powerful role that these forms have in people's everyday lives, as well as the fact that they are, in many cases, what Hall has called the "languages of calculation" of the future. The goal should not be to avoid capitalist technologies and forms but, rather, to find ways of appropriating them for activities that the capitalists never imagined.

6. For example, what effects does the concept of communication have upon our theories and experiences? What struggles does it engage with, and how has it already been implicated in struggles to articulate reality in particular ways? In fact, a critical theory of communication faces a rather unique dilemma, since its very discourses reproduce some of the very relations of power that it seeks to identify and oppose. In particular, three strategies commonly articulate the political implications of communication theory: Communication is given a transcendental status as the fundamental process of human existence; a widely diverse set of practices is subordinated to an imposed identity; and a particular reduction of the multiple and contradictory subject positionings of cultural practices is accomplished—the communicative subject is located as the source of our freedom and agency. Questions of power are reduced to those of communicative equality, freedom of participation, the distribution of competencies, and the free flow of information (as if these were either real historical events or guaranteed utopian relationships). Thus, within the contemporary historical and intellectual context, we cannot ignore the political effects of our own discourses that purport to explain and describe a finite set of human practices.

7. For that reason, critical researchers would do well to listen more attentively to those for whom the two positions commonly coincide—I am thinking here of women, third world, and minority scholars.

8. Even more controversially, I remain unconvinced that the forms of economic power in so-called late capitalism are organized primarily around the capital/labor contradiction, which is to say, in class terms. Instead, I would argue, the weight of the structure of capitalism's power has moved into the second aspect that Marx (1973) described: the contradictions between the forces and relations, not only of production, but of distribution and consumption as well. I am proposing that an understanding of contemporary forms of economic domination requires us to rethink the meaning of what Marx called commodity fetishism in the context of a world in which everything (including class identity) has become a commodity, in which, in fact, the distinction between use and exchange value has been eroded.

9. I am using Benjamin's (1986) metaphor of the surgeon as opposed to the empiricist cum magician who is content to merely "lay" his or her hands upon reality.

10. I do not mean to equate empirical research with quantitative methods. On the contrary, such an analysis must be undertaken for the full range of rich research practices—literary critical, ethnographic, and so forth. Moreover, each must be recognized as having its own power, rigor, and "scientificity." Thus I would argue for those who use literary critical techniques, it is a grave error to

continue to appeal to intuitivist notions rather than incorporating some of the important gains of structuralist, semiotic, and feminist criticism. Finally, I do not mean to suggest that all quantitative research is based in empiricism; the best of such work is struggling, precisely, to move away from such an interpretive framework.

11. This is a visible dilemma for many feminists, who must confront the argument made by at least some feminists that certain forms of experimental and/or statistical research are inherently patriarchal. Obviously, my own position is that practices are not inherently anything. Of course, the same thing is true of qualitative methods: Their politics is similarly not inherent to them but is rather the site of articulation and struggle.

12. It is important to acknowledge that class fractions are, for Bourdieu, overdetermined by the three planes of social logic and not reducible to simple economic conditions. Furthermore, they are characterized by contradictory relations between the distribution of economic and cultural capital, thus creating dominant and dominated fractions within both the dominant and the dominated classes.

13. I recognize that this is quite an abstract description of an empirical project. This itself raises a significant issue: the burdensome use of technical language (jargon) in much of critical theory after structuralism. Here, I wish to make two points: First, politically, there is, I believe, a necessary displacement between theory and popular struggle; second, what defines an "obscurantist" or mystifying use of language is itself culturally determined, that is, it is the site of ideological struggle. Returning to the question of empirical work itself, there is some work that has already begun to concretize something like Bourdieu's model: See Bennett and Woollacott's (1987) notion of "regimes of reading," Hall and Jacques's (1983) studies of Thatcherism, or my own efforts to describe the apparatuses of pop music (Grossberg, 1984). In addition, the work of the International Communication and Youth Consortium promises to be a significant effort to bring together critical theory and quantitative research around issues of cultural politics.

REFERENCES

Allor, Martin F. (1977) Cinema, Culture and the Social Formation: Ideology and Critical Practice. Dissertation. Urbana, IL.

Althusser, Louis (1970) For Marx (B. Brewster, trans.). New York: Vintage.

Benjamin, Walter (1986) Illuminations (H. Arendt, ed.). New York: Harcourt, Brace & World.

Benjamin, Walter (1978) Reflections (P. Demetz, ed.). New York: Harcourt Brace Javonovich.

Bennett, Tony and Janet Woollacott (1987) Bond and Beyond: The Political Career of a Popular Hero. New York: Methuen.

Bourdieu, Pierre (1984) Distinction: A Social Critique of the Judgement of Taste (R. Nice, trans.). Cambridge, MA: Harvard University Press.

Ferment in the Field (Summer 1983) Journal of Communications 33, 3.

Foucault, Michael (1980) Power/Knowledge: Selected Interviews and Other Writings (C. Gordon, ed.). New York: Pantheon.

Foucault, Michael (1981) "Questions of method." I&C 8: 3-14.

Gramsci, Antonio (1971) Selections from the Prison Notebooks (Q. Hoare and G. N. Smith, trans.). New York: International Publishers.

Grossberg, Lawrence (1984) "'I'd rather feel bad than not feel anything at all': Rock and roll, pleasure and power." Enclitic 8 (Spring/Fall): 94-110.

Grossberg, Lawrence (1986) "History, politics and postmodernism: Stuart Hall and cultural studies." Journal of Communication Inquiry 10: 61-77.

Grossberg, Lawrence (forthcoming) "Postmodernist elitisms and postmodern struggles." Graduate Faculty Philosophy Journal.

Hall, Stuart (1980) "Cultural studies: two paradigms." Media, Culture, Society 2: 57-72.

Hall, Stuart (1985a) "Authoritarian populism: a reply." New Left Review 151: 115-124.

Hall, Stuart (1985b) "Signification, representation, ideology: Althusser and the post-structuralist debates." Critical Studies in Mass Communication 2: 91-114.

Hall, Stuart (1986) "On postmodernism and articulation: an interview." Journal of Communication Inquiry 10: 45-60.

Hall, Stuart and Martin Jacques [eds.] (1983) The Politics of Thatcherism. London: Lawrence & Wishart.

Hall, Stuart with Jennifer Daryl Slack and Lawrence Grossberg (forthcoming) Cultural Studies: A Theoretical History (The Illinois Lectures). London: Macmillan.

Laclau, Ernesto and Chantal Mouffe (1985) Hegemony and Socialist Strategy: Towards a Radical Democratic Politics. London: Verso.

Marx, Karl (1973) Grundrisse (M. Nicolaus, trans.) New York: Vintage.

Marx, Karl (1975) "Theses on Feuerbach," in Early Writings. New York: Vintage.

Mattelart, Armand (forthcoming) "Communications in socialist France: the difficulty of matching technology with democracy," in C. Nelson and L. Grossberg (eds.) Marxism and the Interpretation of Culture. Urbana: University of Illinois Press.

Morley, David (1981) "'The Nationwide Audience'—A critical postscript." Screen Education 39: 3-14.

Schutz, Alfred (1971) "Concept and theory formation in the social sciences," in M. Natanson (ed.) Collected Papers (vol. 1). The Hague: Martinus Nijhoff.

Williams, Raymond (1980) Problems in Materialism and Culture. London: Verso.

3

A LINKAGE THEORY
OF COMMUNICATION EFFECTS

W. Phillips Davison

When one is incautious enough to fall into an intellectual trap, the resulting embarrassment can sometimes be minimized by pretending that everyone else fell into the same trap. Then one can at least comfort oneself by imagined company while trying to climb out.

The trap in this case is the notion that communication content and channels have effects. All of us engaged in communication research have assumed this at one time or another (or so I shall argue) and have therefore devoted great effort to discovering these effects and the conditions under which they occur. The results have been chaotic when not contradictory, hedged with enough provisos, reservations, and escape clauses to shame a Philadelphia lawyer. We have found that the effects of communications can be massive or minimal, are controlled or not controlled by the audience, and serve to reinforce or to undermine the existing social order.

Our time, and other people's money, could have been more wisely spent if we had realized at the outset that communications have no effects; they merely make effects possible. They are like the cables that connect appliances with power sources. The communication process as a whole can have massive consequences, but within this process the content and channel serve merely a connective function. With this realization, our attention would have been directed more to the elements that are linked, and to the way they interact in order to produce certain outcomes. We could still have examined the qualities and quantities of the linkages provided by content and channels, but would not have committed the error of concluding that one can turn on a light bulb by attaching a bit of wire to it.[1]

Actually, many researchers sensed that something was wrong. Discussions of communication effects are almost always accompanied by disclaimers. Joseph Klapper, the first scholar to inventory systematically the findings of "disciplined social research," as he labeled it, regarding mass media effects, proposes that "mass communication *ordinarily* does not serve as a necessary and sufficient cause of audience effects, but rather functions among and through a nexus of mediating factors and influences" (Klapper, 1960: 8).

He also observed that "almost every aspect of the life of the audience member and the culture in which the communication occurs seems susceptible of relation to the process of communication effect" (Klapper, 1960: 4). These reservations, taken together, invite the hypothesis that the various aspects of life and culture cause the observed effects when they are appropriately linked by communication, although Klapper didn't go this far.

The present writer included a less explicit disclaimer in a discussion of communication effects published 22 years after Klapper's groundbreaking work: "Although we speak about the 'effects of communication' as a convenience, the term may be misleading. For communication is like air or water; it is found everywhere that human society exists. We are not likely to ask, 'What are the effects of water?'" (Davison et al., 1982: 120). As Father Noah may have had occasion to remark, as he gazed beyond the rail of the Ark, it is not the effects of water but the effects that water makes possible with which we should be concerned. The same is true of communication.

In spite of reservations such as these, most students of communication, including the two cited above, then proceed to catalog and analyze communication effects, unimpressed by their own qualms. Indeed, Klapper specified that there are certain residual situations in which mass communication seems to produce direct effects—to serve certain psycho-physical functions directly and of itself. Yet even this affirmation carries with it seeds of doubt, since the idea that the media might serve "psycho-physical functions" suggests that they are perhaps forming linkages in the manner of nerves or sensory organs, and are not themselves motors.

Another indication that communications are actually without effect is the extraordinarily wide range of effects attributed to them. These effects can, in many cases, be observed and documented; there is no question about the existence of at least some of them. What is open to question is that the observed phenomena are caused by communications. Would it not be more reasonable to conclude that the wide range of effects can be accounted for by a wide range of causes? Communication channels merely serve the function of linking together the causative factors with the persons or groups that are affected. They make effects possible.[2] Again, there is a suggestion that Klapper entertained this notion, although he did not follow up on it. He observes: "The relative efficacy of the mass media varies so widely from one topical area to another as to defy generalization" (1960: 130).

Numerous other scholars have expressed reservations about the assumed direct connection between communication and effect. The "systems" approach to communication research, for example, postulates that outcomes are the product of interactions among a number of variables, thereby questioning the direct causative role of communications. Functionalists frequently explain what appear to be communication effects by reference to preexisting requirements of the audience. Yet all of us (or so I shall persist in maintaining) continue to speak about communication effects and to assume their existence in the design of our research.

Why is this? What accounts for the persistence of the notion that communications have effects, in and of themselves, even though so many scholars have given evidence that they do not believe it? A variety of explanations might be advanced.

First, and perhaps most important, is the historical explanation. People—and even serious scholars are after all also people—have always believed that communications have effects. Is there a society that does not harbor a strong tradition of verbal magic? I doubt it. Words are known to have power. Even Goethe's Faust, an obviously overeducated man, since he had the equivalent of doctorates in philosophy, law, medicine, and theology, used a magic combination of phrases to conjure up the devil. And in our own society, highly skilled copywriters search diligently for verbal formulas that will compel shoppers to reach for Crispy Crunchies or Bubbly Bleach, or that will induce voters to pull down the lever under the name of Joe Blow. To suggest that communication content and channels are without direct effects is to defy deeply held beliefs.

Besides, the concept that communications have effects that can be tested and measured works fairly well. Research based on this hypothesis has paid off. The avenue of inquiry started by Lazarsfeld and his colleagues in the 1940s (Lazarsfeld et al., 1944), and updated by Mendelsohn and O'Keefe (1976), Patterson (1980), and others, continues to provide useful guidance to both commercial and political salespeople. The Newspaper Advertising Bureau has demonstrated that even "one little ad" can have an appreciable impact on buying behavior (Bureau of Advertising, 1969). Publicity campaigns frequently succeed in raising the information level among the population at large about subjects ranging from insecticides to football stars.

At this point, one might object that if the concept works then it must be correct. But this reasoning is not conclusive. Many theories that have served mankind well have later been found to be erroneous. Ptolemaic astronomy, which turned the universe on its head, provided people with useful guidance for many centuries. It was wrong, but it worked fairly well. Then it turned out that the Copernican system worked even better. Nevertheless, people are understandably reluctant to abandon ideas that have proved their serviceability.

A third factor favoring belief in the direct effects of communications is that the methodologies most widely used in communication research are well adapted to exploring the effects of specific messages—especially their effects on individuals. Experimentalists can control channels and communication content and can select and manipulate audiences in such a way that hypotheses can be tested. Content analysis allows concise description and quantification of information in the channel. Survey research makes it possible to relate message exposure to individual characteristics and actions. Increasingly powerful statistical techniques enable the researcher to separate out the effects of a communication from the effects of other influences. Acceptance of the proposition that communications do not cause effects would not necessitate the abandonment of currently popular research techniques, but at least some of these techniques would have to be rethought and adapted to new designs.[3] For example, procedures used to determine how much of a given variance can be explained by exposure to a communication, as opposed to other variables, would become meaningless if one postulated that the communication itself had no effect. One would be left with a figure that had no readily identifiable referent.

SOME RESEARCH IMPLICATIONS
OF THIS OUTRAGEOUS HYPOTHESIS

If we accept, at least for purposes of argument, the hypothesis that communications have no independent effect, but achieve effects only by establishing relationships between two or more disparate elements, then we probably would conduct our research with somewhat different questions in mind. First, we would want to establish as definitely as possible what was being linked with what. This may not always be obvious. Then, we would be interested in the dynamics of the relationships that had been established: why the linked elements behaved as they did, and whether changing the nature of the linkage would change this behavior. Third, we would probably want to examine a wide range of behaviors with a view to determining what communication linkages made them possible. Fourth, we might reverse the above procedure, and start by examining major communication linkages in order to identify the implications these might have for individual and group behavior. We would continue to be concerned, as we are now, with the quality and quantity of the linkages: how faithfully are ideas and images transmitted by the communication channels that are involved? Let us look briefly at each of these questions.

First, what is being linked with what? Let us imagine a tired commuter viewing the evening television news. Is a link established between ideas already in the mind of the viewer and any of the ideas, personalities, scenes, or events featured in the newscast? And if the viewer reacts to any of these ideas or images, should the reaction be attributed to their existence in the outside world or to the information (perhaps erroneous) that the viewer has received about them?[4] Or is it that the viewer is not paying attention to the newscast's content, but has fallen in love with the photogenic anchorman or anchorwoman, and that the major link is between the anchorperson (regardless of what he or she says) and the unknown admirer? Perhaps the link is with this particular channel, which the viewer regards as the most prestigious and which can be counted upon to cover the subjects that the boys in the bar will be talking about later in the evening. Aha! The linkage is not only with the channel and certain news stories but indirectly, with the boys in the bar as well.[5]

And so it goes. The relationships established, if any, are usually determined not by the manifest content of a communication but by the audience. Indeed, this approach tends to downgrade the importance of manifest content, thus limiting the usefulness of content analysis. One cannot necessarily ascertain what linkages are established by examining the messages carried by the communication channel. Furthermore, some linkages may be in the nature of a loop connecting a person's consciousness with images and memories stored in the memory or subconscious. An advertisement may remind a person that he or she enjoys a given product, even though the specific message in the ad may not be attended to. Or, a communication may remind people of their group memberships and of the behavior expected of them as group members.

Having identified the principal linkages that have been established, the researcher will probably then want to examine the dynamics implicit in the resulting relationships. Let us assume that the newscast referred to above identifies a political candidate as belonging to the same ethnic or religious group as the viewer, and that the viewer is paying sufficient attention to become aware of this. What behaviors does this connection make more likely? Is there a strong tradition of cohesion within this group? Do group members customarily help each other? Or does the group's self-image emphasize individualism and impartiality? A vote may hang in the balance.

Or, to revert to the commercial world, an advertisement reminding the viewer that a particular product has been enjoyed in the past may carry with it the admonition to buy the product again. If the ad carries the reminder that other people are also likely to enjoy the product, it may establish a linkage with friends and activate gift-giving impulses associated with friendship. Advertising and political researchers have often explored the associations that a message about a particular product or candidate arouses. The approach suggested here would extend this exploration to include empirical research on the varied action implications of these associations, and not only in connection with messages that are intended to be persuasive. What behaviors, if any, are suggested by news reports about a major earthquake in a distant country?

A further research approach suggested is that it may prove rewarding to take almost any behavior and inquire into the role played by communication in making it possible. We know that a large proportion of human behavior involves linkages produced by social communication in some form, and many of these linkages are formed by public communication. Categories of effects that have received little attention from researchers thus far, since they do not appear to be related directly to communication, would thus be brought under scrutiny. For example, what linkages are associated with the incidence of broken hips among the aged? It may be that this expensive and debilitating medical problem is most often avoided by old people whose friends are predominantly in their own age group. By precept and example, group members warn each other about hazards that might lead to falls. Or, the reverse may prove to be the case: that younger friends say and do things that promote fitness and the preservation of agility.

Either way, if a relationship is discovered, it would suggest that the promotion of desirable linkages by appropriate communications could lead to a reduction in human and financial costs associated with broken hips.

Similarly, it would be useful to know if there is a relationship between certain communication linkages and ability in mathematics, languages, or other branches of learning. Once the importance of particular linkages had been established—for example, between role models and grade school students—then the question would arise whether the same connections could be brought about through the use of the mass media or other available channels.

One could turn this research approach on its head, and start not by examining the role of communication in explaining various behaviors, but by looking instead at various kinds of communication linkages and asking what kinds of behavior they made possible, directly and indirectly. What are the effects of the linkages established by community newspapers or by personal acquaintance networks? A research approach along these lines has the virtue of focusing attention on collectivities as well as individuals.

For example, we are aware that communication channels play a role in the formation of social groups, business enterprises, and public opinion, as well as in the establishment of laws, norms, and other social conventions. Nevertheless, relatively little systematic research has been devoted to studying exactly how these processes occur. Charles Cooley, Robert Park, and other classical sociologists thought about such questions, but later researchers have tended to avoid them, possibly because the questions do not lend themselves easily to treatment by quantitative techniques. As a result, we are relatively ignorant about the ways that communication, through its capabilities to link individuals together, makes cooperation and collective action possible. Yet communication-induced linkages that allow the formation of public opinion, enable people to join together in associations, and lead to formation of laws and norms may be the most significant contribution of communication channels to society.

As an illustration of the importance of communication channels to social life, it can be argued that survival of any community as a good place to live in is heavily dependent on linkages among community leaders and between these leaders and their existing and potential followers. These linkages make possible the functioning of existing neighborhood organizations, and the formation of new ones. They help build public opinion on issues affecting the community and community morale in general. They enable public concerns to be expressed to government and can greatly facilitate civil administration. It is primarily the influence of organized groups, laws, public opinion, and strong personalities (sometimes including government officials) that induces people to cooperate in the public welfare, but this influence is transmitted largely through existing formal and informal communication channels. A community with a strong local newspaper, among other channels, is more likely to survive threats to its integrity than a community without one.[6]

Would it be possible to inventory all the major linkages that communication channels bring about in a given area, or among a particular population group? This has never been attempted. There may be some linkages, previously given little attention, that help explain significant social phenomena. It would be fascinating to explore the behavioral implications of reading detective stories or spy novels, especially because these works seem to be favored as aids to relaxation by so many influential members of our society.

Researchers who accept this model of the communication process, like those who favor other models, are likely to be interested in the quality of communication—the faithfulness with which an idea or image is transmitted from source to receiver. There is a long tradition of research on channel "noise" and on other factors that reduce or distort message content, such as the selectiveness of the receiver. In that approach it is agreed that there are three messages in every communication transaction: the message intended by the source, the message in the channel, and the message as received. The quality of communication can be measured by the degree of correspondence of the three messages, although distortions may have nothing to do with the message's encoding or decoding.

If one accepts the "linkage" approach, it becomes clear that the quality of transmission may be poor but the linkage may still be strong. At least, this is worth exploring. There are abundant cases of people who speak different languages and don't understand each other very well, but who nevertheless experience a mutual attraction—or revulsion.[7] And a diplomatic note that is misunderstood (for example, is interpreted as a sign of weakness when it is intended to express forbearance) may lead to more vigorous interaction than a communication that transmits the sender's meaning accurately.

This approach suggests also that the receiver may learn to compensate for distortions of the intended message (or of external reality) that are introduced in the channel. Researchers have frequently pointed out that information in the news media may be shaped by journalistic conventions, bias on the part of media personnel, or pressures from government or advertisers, so that the message in the channel differs substantially from the message at the source. The capabilities of audiences to correct, or exaggerate, these distortions are less often taken into account. Physiologists inform us that the eye actually perceives the world upside down, but that we learn at an early age to correct for this misperception. The linkage to the environment provided by the eye is thus fairly good, even though the transmitted image is faulty. Can the same be said of the mass media? It is a reasonable hypothesis that those who have learned to interpret media messages (including advertising and entertainment) receive a fairly adequate picture of reality. One can argue further that people become expert at interpreting communications about subjects that are important to them, whether received through the mass media or through other channels, and that as a result they become even more accurately informed about these subjects.

In countries where the press is controlled, skills of "reading between the lines" and "writing between the lines" sometimes become highly developed. It is thus possible for a dissident journalist to compose a text that will satisfy the censor but will still enable sophisticated readers to decipher the intended message.

The observation that examination of the message in the channel does not necessarily tell us very much about the quality of a communication link does nothing to minimize the importance of clear writing and exposition. It does remind us, however, that communication skills by themselves are not always sufficient to transmit ideas from a source to an audience.

REINTERPRETING OBSERVED EFFECTS
OF COMMUNICATION

If one accepts the hypothesis that communications, as linking mechanisms, do not exert influence but merely establish relationships that sometimes have attitudinal or behavioral consequences, then one is faced with the task of reinterpreting data on communication effects that have been compiled by generations of communication researchers. Does the linkage theory explain these observations better than the established view that words and images have power of their own? Even more critical for validation of the approach is whether it can help to eliminate the contradictions and qualifications that have bespattered existing research results.

A serious reexamination of these voluminous data would be an enormous task, probably requiring years. But in the meantime one can speculate. Let us, for example, consider the finding that the mass media serve as agenda setters, telling us what to think about, even though they are less successful in telling us what to think. According to our hypothesis, this effect must result not from the content of the mass media as such but from the influence of something with which this content has connected us. With what have we been linked? One possibility is that we see the mass media as reflecting public opinion. The subjects discussed there are the subjects that everyone is talking about, or will be talking about. It is therefore the power of public opinion that induces us to adopt a particular agenda—not the power of the media.

This interpretation would not be difficult to test. If it is true, then those individuals who do *not* believe that the media reflect public opinion about what is important will be less likely to adopt the agenda set forth by the media than those who do. It may be that some mass media are regarded as reliable indicators of public interest while others are not. If so, only the former should be efficacious as agenda setters.

Another possible interpretation is that the primary linkage established is between audience members and the mass media institution itself. The medium becomes an authority, and the fact that a subject is discussed makes that subject important. The important consideration is not what is said, but the fact that expert journalists consider it worth saying. This interpretation makes it necessary to distinguish sharply between media as institutions and media as purveyors of information. To test it, one could attempt to determine whether media institutions with low prestige are as influential in setting agendas as those with higher prestige.

Reinterpretation of findings with regard to the persuasive effects of communications could be more straightforward. When the received message carries inducements to action or attitude change that are sufficient to overcome the existing resistance to such action or attitude change, then persuasion results. Otherwise, there will be no persuasive effects. The inducements are not in the message itself, however. They are merely reported, or the audience believes they are reported. Thus advertisements announcing a sale are able to bring potential customers to the point of purchase when previous messages promoting the same product could not. Or, the second ad may overcome resistance by doing a better job of describing the advantages of the product. In either case, the resistance remains the same, but the perceived inducement increases.

One can also find cases where the inducement remains constant and resistance decreases, as when the necessity of finding a birthday gift for Aunt Millie makes a high price more tolerable.

Similarly, activation and reinforcement can be explained by postulating that a communication provides a link between stored memories and a person's current conscious state. The communication thus releases impulses that are already present. If no such impulses exist, there will be no activation or reinforcement.

Is it a quibble to distinguish between the manifest content of a communication and the ideas, events, or persons to which this content refers? Philosophers since Plato's parable of the cave have argued about this distinction, but their disputations do not necessarily make it a quibble. In any event, examination of a quibble can sometimes lead to new insights, or to new interpretations of old ones. So, even if we all continue to refer to the effects of communication, and to search diligently for them, as I am sure we will do, perhaps the linkage hypothesis will provide a little more light for the search.

NOTES

1. The wary reader may suspect at this point that we may be belaboring a quibble—that "linkage" is simply being used as another word for "effect." Whether or not this is indeed the case it is the prerogative of the reader to decide. The author will continue to maintain that no quibble is involved, and that researchers are likely to focus their attention on different questions if they view communication channels and content as linking mechanisms that have no independent effects.

2. The notion that communication channels are neutral and do not in themselves cause effects seems to fly in the face of the widely accepted dictum that new communication technologies can bring about massive social changes, and that it is the existence of a channel that is significant. But perhaps the contradiction is more apparent than real. New technologies for conveying messages are significant factors in social change in that they make new linkages possible. Indeed, H. A. Innes (1950), one of the first to consider the global impact of communication technology, pointed out explicitly, for example, that light and transportable writing materials changed the structure of empires by making it possible for officials at the capital to exercise greater control over what happened in the provinces.

3. Lazarsfeld (1957), in *Public Opinion and the Classical Tradition,* pointed out that survey research techniques could be useful in exploring theoretical approaches quite different from the ones with which they customarily are associated.

4. This raises a troublesome question about the linkage approach. If a reaction follows a false report, is not the communication content itself the causative factor? It must be, one could reason, because there is no other possible cause—there is no referent for the report in the environment. But one could also argue that it is not the false report that causes the reaction, but rather belief in the false report. In other words, the linkage is between an imagined reality and ideas already in the mind of the subject. If the report is not believed, then there is no linkage with the external environment, real or imagined, although there may be linkages with the media institution itself. For example, the viewer may regard the report as one more indication that you can't believe everything in a newscast.

5. Observations along these lines have frequently been made by scholars following the "uses and gratifications" approach to the study of the communication process. The approach holds that the effect of a communication is determined not by its manifest content but by the uses that members of the audience make of the communication (Blumler and Katz, 1974).

6. This argument is made in a qualitative pilot study of a number of New York City neighborhoods that was recently completed by the writer. It is tentatively scheduled for publication as an Occasional Paper of the Gannett Center for Media Studies, Columbia University. Its working title is "Communication Channels and the Quality of Life in an Urban Neighborhood."

7. When studying in Stockholm, the writer had a Danish landlady who attempted to explain the degree of difference in the spoken language in various parts of Scandinavia. Her deceased husband had been from the north of Sweden, she said, and during the first six months of their marriage, she could scarcely understand him.

REFERENCES

Blumler, Jay G. and Elihu Katz [eds.] (1974) The Uses of Mass Communications: Current Perspectives on Gratifications Research. Newbury Park, CA: Sage.

Bureau of Advertising, A.N.P.A. (1969) "What Can One Newspaper Ad Do? An Experimental Field Study of Newspaper Advertising Communication and Sales Results." New York: Author.

Davison, W. Phillips, James Boylan, and Frederick T.C. Yu (1982) Mass Media: Systems and Effects (2nd ed.). New York: Holt, Rinehart & Winston.

Innes, Harold A. (1950) Empire and Communication. London: Oxford Univ. Press.

Klapper, Joseph T. (1960) The Effects of Mass Communication. New York: Free Press.

Lazarsfeld, Paul F. (1957) "Public opinion and the classical tradition," pp. 39-53 in Public Opinion Quarterly 21, 1.

Lazarsfeld, Paul F., Bernard Berelson, and Hazel Gaudet (1944) The People's Choice. New York: Duell, Sloan & Pearce.

Mendelsohn, Harold, and Garrett J. O'Keefe (1976) The People Choose a President. New York: Praeger.

Patterson, Thomas E. (1980) The Mass Media Election. New York: Praeger.

PART II

DOING MASS COMMUNICATION RESEARCH
Practices and Traditions

INTRODUCTION

Michael Gurevitch

One feature of the growth of mass communication research in the last two decades is the increasing internationalization of the field. The appearance of new journals with proclaimed cross-national editorial policies (e.g., *Media, Culture and Society, Critical Studies in Mass Communication* and *The European Journal of Communication*), the internationalization of the professional associations (e.g., ICA and IAMCR), and the opportunities thus afforded for cross-national contacts and dialogue in professional meetings, have eroded the isolationist impact of national boundaries, which in the past had also demarcated schools of thought and directions of research. Admittedly, the United States and Europe are still the "super powers" in the field, whether judged by the number of researchers, the volume of published research, or the intellectual influence exerted. But the flow of influence, both between American and European researchers, and between them and scholars in other countries, is increasingly reciprocal. In this section we sought to document and illustrate this trend with examples of the development of mass communication research in three non-American settings: Australia, Italy, and Latin America. In addition, the section includes two essays examining the historical development of research in the United States in two specific areas: children and the media, and telecommunication policy.

Two major (and related) characteristics of the development of mass communication research in these three settings (but especially in Italy and in Latin America) emerge from the articles by Putnis, Mancini, and Roncagliolo. First, they document the significant impact of politics on the development of mass communication research in their countries. Second, they highlight the influence of Marxist/critical work on the direction of research. Putnis frames the history of mass communication research in Australia primarily in terms of the cross-currents of British ("a story of colonial dependence") and American influences, and the debate/competition between "American empiricist functionalism" and European linguistic/structuralist/semiotic approaches. In Putnis's words, "Far from being isolated, Australia is, if anything, too closely locked into the international scene; each overseas controversy is played out, in miniature, on Australian soil." Not wishing to remain merely another site for international controversies, Australian researchers are now also searching for the "distinctively Australian" element in their work.

The forces that have shaped media research in Italy are more explicitly political. Mancini traces them both to the influence of Catholicism and to the country's system of mass communication, primarily to the structure and the ideology of the Italian Broadcasting Company (RAI) and the research commissioned by it. Political changes in Italy that, in turn, have led to changes and reforms in RAI also had consequences for the direction of media research. But the political nature of Italian mass communication research is due not only to the impact of these forces, but also to the influences of Marxist scholarship. Thus Italian researchers are currently "giving maximum space to the macroconstruction of the economy of media and of its use in the production of social consensus."

Although the political circumstances in Latin America are different from those in Italy, the general tendencies in the work on what Roncagliolo prefers to label "popular culture" appear to be largely similar. Latin American researchers were influenced by the intellectual resistance to Western cultural imperialism and by a "concern for democratically regulating the culture industry through National Policies on Communication and Culture that secure participation of consumers in the production and circulation of messages." Two competing trends have evolved from this: Resistance to "cultural transnationalization" led to preoccupation with "big international themes," while concern with the democratization of the media resulted in "enchantment with small media," and disregard for national communication structures and policies. Both, however, are reflections of Roncagliolo's concluding description of the position of communication and popular culture research in his continent: "Here in Latin America, research is and will continue to be what it has always been: a form of social commitment."

The essays by Wartella and Reeves, and Rowland return to mass communication research in the United States and examine aspects of its history. Wartella and Reeves carefully document the argument that the "received history" of American mass communication research "does not describe scholarship about children and the media . . . [which has] developed independently of the broader media effects tradition." They claim that "the origin of research about children lies in concern expressed by the public about each medium as it was introduced. Public debate helped shape research agendas . . . rather than research shaping public concerns or policy." They suggest that, while expressions of concern about the impact of twentieth-century media highlight the "novel attributes of each new medium, the bases of objections and promises have been similar."

Rowland offers a critical examination of the origins of American telecommunication policy research. He identifies a number of sources of influence here: the "deep-set pattern of American attitudes toward intellectual activity and about the accommodations among public and private interests"; "the common positivism of mid-twentieth-century communication research and of the more general fields of American policy studies"; the "blue-sky" approach of American work to issues of technological change, which perceives new communication technologies as essentially "technologies of abundance"; and the uncritical reliance on conservative work in law and economics. In more recent work he discerns the beginnings of critical research in this area, but recognizes that the road to "more autonomous critical policy studies" is still long and fraught with difficulties.

Mass communication research is still sometimes described as a "young science" with a relatively brief history. But, on the evidence of the articles assembled here, this history is not sufficiently rich to merit historical and developmental examination. It is, perhaps, not surprising that that examination, as illustrated in these articles, is animated by a critical spirit. Self-reflection is always critical. It is also, perhaps, a sign of growing maturity.

4

COMMUNICATION STUDIES IN AUSTRALIA
Paradigms and Contexts

Peter Putnis

Can one speak of communication studies in Australia as a discipline in its own right or even as a single field of study? Certainly in recent years there have been steps towards the construction and institutionalization of such a field. Communication studies courses, combining, in varying degrees, studies in language, the media, social psychology and information management, have been established at degree level in at least a dozen tertiary institutions; an Australian Communication Association was established in 1979 and now conducts annual conferences; the *Australian Journal of Communication* (formerly the less broadly-based *Australian Scan: Journal of Human Communication*) had its first issue in 1982. However, these are recent and tentative steps and cannot be taken as evidence of the emergence of any single dominant Australian paradigm of communication studies.

Communication teaching and research in Australia are characterized by great diversity of organizational settings, individual and institutional purposes, disciplinary starting points and ideological positions. This is hardly surprising. Given the ubiquitousness and centrality of communication, teaching and research inevitably reflect or engage large social, ideological and epistemological debates. Such issues as utilitarian versus liberal approaches to education, the relative weight given to determinism and human volition in explanations of behaviour, and the critique and defence of empiricism find their analogues in communication teaching and research.

From Peter Putnis, "Communication Studies in Australia: Paradigms and Contexts," *Media Culture and Society,* Vol. 8, pp. 143-157. Copyright © 1986 by Sage Publications, Ltd.

Furthermore, particular characteristics of the Australian situation contribute to a diversity of approach. There is the two-tier system of tertiary education — universities emphasizing 'academic' degrees and pure research, and colleges of advanced education emphasizing vocational degrees and applied research. There is the fact that most communication scholars come into the field from related, better established disciplines and, most importantly, there are the substantial and diverse overseas influences on curriculum development and research.

This paper examines the interplay of these approaches and forces as they are reflected in the emergence of communication studies in Australia as an arena for competing paradigms. The particular focus is on an assessment of the influence of recent British work in Australia.

British and American influence: an overview

The history of Australian education is essentially a story of colonial dependence. British educational institutions and ideologies were re-created on Australian soil with minimal adaptation. Educational leaders were imported from Britain; Australian students who aspired to such leadership sought to complete their education at Oxford or Cambridge.

The dependence on British models included all levels of education and extended to details of the curriculum. For example, in Queensland primary schools English schoolbooks were exclusively used well into the twentieth century. At tertiary level the teaching of Australian literature and history is a relatively recent development. 'Real culture', culture worth studying, resided in Britain and Europe.

The 1960s and 1970s were a period of Australian cultural self-assertion and this was reflected in curriculum developments in tertiary institutions. Australian Studies emerged as a distinct field of study in some new universities and colleges. However, as late as 1973 Geoffrey Serle still located the universities as 'almost the last strangleholds of the "cultural cringers" ':

> The important battle still has to be joined: acceptance of the simple point that it is the duty of Australian universities to emphasise Australian studies, as almost every other country does with its own. (Quoted by Alomes, 1981:68)

A recognition of the traditional Australian dependence on British curriculum models and of the reluctance to develop courses focusing on Australian society and culture seems a logical starting point for a consideration of communication studies in Australia. To what extent has this emerging and growing field fallen into the traditional pattern? Is it merely coincidence that the current expansion of communications courses in Australia follows hard on the heels of British expansion in the field? What kinds of discourses and institutions mediate British influence?

The received view is that British influence on the pattern of research and teaching is less evident in communication studies than in the older, more traditional humanities and social sciences. This, however, is less because of the development of any indigenous approach, than because of the growing influence of American culture and ideology on Australian institutions since the second world war.

Australia is in the cross-current of Anglo-American influence. Lewis (1982) has outlined the main trends in the development of Anglo-American models of communications education and related these to current Australian practices. Features of the American emphasis include:

(i) a pragmatic, 'professional communicator', skills approach where the development of mass communications study originates from practically-oriented schools of journalism and the study of interpersonal communication grows out of a strong interest in rhetoric and persuasion;

(ii) stress on detailed empirical research rather than broad cultural analysis;

(iii) arguably, a tendency to take the message as a 'given' in the communication process, rather than taking the construction of meaning as the focus;

(iv) strong links between communications studies and business education.

Features of the British/European emphasis include:

(i) communication viewed in the context of larger societal and cultural considerations, sociological perspectives more influential than psychological ones;

(ii) stress on critical analysis in a broadly Marxist tradition;

(iii) focus not so much on communication as the transmission of messages as upon the production and consumption of meaning in society;

(iv) a separation between practical communication training in areas such as journalism, and theoretical/critical studies in degree-level courses.

Such an opposition between North American and British/European approaches is over-schematic and misleading if taken too literally. The 1983 special issue of the *Journal of Communication*, 'Ferment in the Field', amply demonstrated the diversity of American approaches. As Steven H. Chaffee put it:

> There is not so much agreement today on the unique promise of behavioural research. Scholars who specialize in historical, legal, critical, and other methods of inquiry are challenging the behavioural approach, and some of us who used to think of ourselves as mainly concerned with individual behaviour are now attempting to study structural factors and historical contexts of communication systems more carefully. (Rogers and Chaffee, 1983:22)

At the same time, in Britain, recent curriculum and professional developments point towards the growing influence of pragmatic, vocational approaches to communication studies. These include:

(i) the development of some degree-level, directly vocational courses. For example at Trinity and All Saints College, Leeds, students are able to combine an academic study, 'Communication and Cultural Studies' with a professional strand entitled 'Public Media'. This strand is seen as a preparation for careers in advertising, public relations, marketing and information services and includes twelve weeks of professional attachment.

(ii) a growing emphasis on practical work in media production in a number of other degrees including those at Wales and Coventry Polytechnics.

(iii) the growing polytechnic involvement in journalism education at institutions like the London College of Printing and Preston Polytechnic.

Furthermore, an analysis of two 1984 British conferences in the field (Putnis, 1984) suggests a partial breakdown of the characteristically British nexus between communication studies and cultural studies. However, despite its limitations, the 'cross-currents', American versus British/European paradigms, idea has become the dominant way of situating teaching and research in Australia (for the most recent example, see King and Muecke, 1984).

Lewis (1982) has argued that Australian communication programmes take their point of departure from one of the two dominant overseas paradigms, and it is possible to locate Australian courses and communications scholars accordingly. For example, both at the Queensland Institute of Technology and Kuring-gai College of

Advanced Education, communications courses have developed in the context of business and administrative education. The former stresses advertising, public relations and journalism while the latter, inter-personal and organizational communication in business. At the South Australian College of Advanced Education and the New South Wales Institute of Technology the emphasis has been on critical and/or linguistic approaches. With respect to research, Lewis points out that while American empiricist functionalism has been the most common research model, there is a strong minority approach drawing on linguistic, structural, historical or semiotic British and European models. Lewis places work by Edgar (1977, 1979, 1980), Galloway (1980/81) Murray (1979) Pingree and Hawkins (1981), Crocker et al. (1979) Irwin (1980/81) and Hansford and Aveyard (1980/81) in the former category and work by Kress (1980/81), Tulloch (1977), Bonney (1980) and Sless (1980/81) in the latter. Later it will be argued that, since Lewis's review, there has been a marked shift away from empiricist approaches towards cultural studies perspectives.

Discussion about the direction of communication studies in Australia has continued within the cross-currents framework, with its attendant opposing of empirical and critical perspectives. Penman (1982) highlighted the failure of empiricist approaches to develop a comprehensive theory of communication with generalizable, predictive laws and, following Shotter (Shotter, 1975, Gauld and Shotter, 1977), turns to the idea of communication studies as a 'moral science' emphasizing human involvement and human responsibility and taking its epistemological stance from the hermeneutical perspective as articulated by Giddens (1977). The approach emphasizes the view that the social world, unlike the natural world, has to be compre-hended as the skilled accomplishment of active human beings, and that generating descriptions of social conduct requires the inter-pretative task of penetrating the frames of meanings which humans drawn upon in constituting and reconstituting their social world.

The 1981 National Conference of the Australian Communication Association (ACA) took as its theme 'Differing Perspectives on Human Communication'. As Irwin and More (1983: vii) have pointed out, the differing perspectives in question were directly related to recent European and American debates. The framework of debate was in fact remarkably similar to that later presented by the 'Ferment in the Field' issue of the *Journal of Communication*. A key paper was Bonney's (1983) 'Two Approaches to Communication' which contrasted approaches 'which draw primarily upon psychology and take face-to-face communication between individuals as the basic model, and those which bring to bear some form of sociological approach.' Bonney argued that only the latter 'can deal adequately with unquestioned assumptions underlying the other approach'. This debate was taken a step further at the 1983 Conference of the ACA where, in a keynote paper, Gunther Kress (1983 b) argued that if *meaning* — how it is constituted, how produced, how controlled and consumed — is recognized as the central issue in communication studies, the traditional separation of mass communication and inter-personal communication is exposed as unfounded and fundamentally misconceived: 'The participants in communication can no longer be seen as either individual on the one hand or as institutional on the other. Individuals speak through the discourses available to them.'

The use of the notion of competing paradigms as a way of making sense of communication studies is predominant not only in discussions of the field as a whole but also in the way research in particular branches such as interpersonal communication or media studies is represented.

Irwin (1983) has argued that the major movement in interpersonal communication in the past quarter-century has been a paradigm shift from a monologic to a dialogic view: 'All contemporary approaches in the field . . . embrace a two-way interactional view which is meaning centred rather than a linear one-way view of communication where the emphasis is upon message transmission.' Yet within the dialogic framework there is a methodological pluralism. While interpersonal communication research has been dominated by the empirical school (characterized by quantitative empiricism, positivism and behaviourism), inroads are being made by the critical school (characterized by qualitative methods of inquiry, structuralism, philosophical analysis and interest in the broader contexts of communication). Similarly, Mayer (1983) introduces a survey of recent literature on media studies with the observation that 'the fundamental split between positivist and alternative methodological approaches continues'.

Paradigmatic trends

As the foregoing indicates, debate about the direction of communi-cation studies in Australia closely reflects the international debate.

Far from being isolated, Australia is, if anything, too closely locked
into the international scene; each overseas controversy is played out,
in miniature, on Australian soil.

But what of trends within and between the paradigms? Lewis
(1982), it will be recalled, argued that the most common research
model in Australia was American empiricist functionalism while
linguistic/structural/semiotic approaches formed a strong minority
approach. Since Lewis's review there has been a marked shift towards
the latter approach. This can be demonstrated by briefly reviewing
recent developments in three areas: discussion and implementation of
curriculum models, approaches to media studies, and directions
taken by the Australian Communication Association.

Curriculum issues

Debate about the objectives and content of communication courses
in Australia is situated within the larger debate between utilitarian/
vocational and liberal/critical approaches to tertiary education. This
is partly a matter of institutional location. Whereas the two
universities which predominate in the field, Griffith University in
Brisbane and Murdoch University in Perth, feel free to offer theory-
centred courses (set firmly within European structuralism/semiotics),
colleges of advanced education, where the most spectacular recent
growth has been, must couch courses in terms of vocational
reference. For example, even the promoters of such a clearly
generalist degree as the BA in Communication Studies at the South
Australian College of Advanced Education take as their primary
justification for the course structure the (real or imagined) needs of
the employment market (South Australian College of Advanced
Education, 1982). Secondly, there is considerable diversity in the
avowed objectives of communication studies courses: there are
marked distinctions between those degrees which offer a generalist
arts/social science type education, those which focus on business
education and those which offer a professional qualification in a
communication-related work area, e.g. journalism, media production.
Within each category there are specific areas of debate. For example,
in 1982, the journal *Media Information Australia* conducted a forum
on journalism education in which a central question was the
appropriate balance between critique and practice. Similarly, within
media education the status of studio work remains problematic. Is its

primary purpose to supplement theoretical work (i.e. use the studio as a laboratory to further critical understanding of codes and practices) or is the aim to teach students how to produce a commercially acceptable product? While the former approach might emphasize the conventionality of current production routines and televisual codes and would try to explore the medium 'afresh', the latter might have as its prime purpose the inculcation of established routines and practices. This debate, in turn, raises the general question of the extent to which courses should be concerned with communication skills. There is understandable concern that 'skills' will be viewed narrowly and reductively by educational managers who promote utilitarian communication studies courses. The term may set up unhealthy oppositions, e.g. academic work versus skills, and even skills versus understanding.

These, then, are the general debates. Evidence for a trend towards the ascendancy of linguistic/semiotic/critical approaches comes from reports of recent curriculum development. Hodge (1982) of Murdoch University argues for a merging of communication and cultural studies: 'Communication and culture are so intrinsically related that culture *is* communication, and the scope of communication studies should reflect this condition.' He goes on to argue that semiotics can provide an overarching theory for communication studies and that courses in semiotic method should be the core course in all such programmes. That his suggestion has borne some fruit is indicated by Fiske's (1983) review of course development in Western Australia significantly entitled 'Communication: Curriculum and Consensus in the West'. The consensus to which he refers is the belief that the focus of study should be to explore how texts interrelate with larger social structures moving from a semiotic consideration of human sign systems and codes, their manifestation in texts (both 'written' and 'lived') and thence to 'the culture and social structure within which all communication occurs and which all communication helps to shape'. Similarly, Muecke (1983) of the South Australian College of Advanced Education notes the 'ascendancy of the concepts of "sign" and "discourse" ' (the latter term in Foucault's usage) in communication studies courses in Australia, while Kress (1983) of the New South Wales Institute of Technology sees the social production and consumption of meaning as the central concern of communication studies. He highlights the inadequacy of traditional disciplinary accounts and argues for a new discipline closely related to semiotics.

Media studies

Hall (1980) has described the development of media studies at the Centre for Contemporary Cultural Studies at Birmingham as a movement away from 'mass-communications research' as defined by American empirical social science practice, i.e. a movement away from 'research of a largely empirical kind, based on audience-survey method, quantitative content analysis and a preoccupation with questions of the debasement of cultural standards through trivialization, pinpointed in the issue of the media and violence'. The Centre's redefinition of work on the media in the broader framework of cultural studies has involved:

(i) a break with models of direct influence and instead a framework drawing on the ideological role of media;

(ii) a challenge to the notion of media texts as transparent bearers of meaning via closer attention to their linguistic and ideological structuration;

(iii) the replacement of passive and undifferentiated conceptions of audience with more active conceptions taking into account the 'reading' process and the variation of audience decodings;

(iv) concern with the role of the media in circulating and securing dominant ideological definitions and representations.

Recent developments in media studies teaching and research in Australia closely parallel the movements described by Hall. This is largely a matter of direct influence by work either from the Centre for Contemporary Cultural Studies itself or by other British work influenced by its construction of media studies. It should be noted here that a number of factors have facilitated the expansion of British influence:

(i) Textbooks: while ten years ago books in the field were few and far between there has been a boom in British publishing in this area in recent years. A growing number of Australian courses are based on British textbooks and readers in communication and cultural studies, the most popular being Fiske and Hartley (1978), Curran et al. (1977), Gurevitch et al. (1982), Fiske (1982), Corner and Hawthorn (1980), Hall et al (1980), Bennett et al. (1981a, 1981b).

(ii) Curriculum models: here one should particularly note the influence of the Open University course *Mass Communication and Society* and the way it constructed media studies in terms of alternative and competing theoretical accounts of how the media work. As the authors (Gurevitch et al., 1982) note, the course focused on the division and opposition between liberal-pluralist and Marxist views of the media and tended to favour Marxist explanations. The more recent Open University course *Popular Culture* and its associated readers (Bennett et al., 1981a, 1981b) have also been influential.

(iii) Flow of staff: there is a steady flow of staff in the area from the UK to Australia, with these staff often taking key planning positions. Many Australian staff take sabbaticals in Britain.

Nixon's (1972) review of the few Australian communication research studies then undertaken indicates the early dominance of behaviouristic experimental and survey and questionnaire studies. For example, Emery and Martin (1957) constructed experiments to assess the psychological effects of western films; Thomson (1959) studied the emotional effects of viewing television crime drama on secondary school children; while Campbell and Keogh (1962) used survey techniques to assess children's attitudes to television in Sydney. Dissatisfaction with these approaches and with the growing popularity of uses and gratifications research (for Australian examples, see Noble, 1975, and Kippax and Murray, 1979), was expressed in Edgar's (1975) assessment of directions in mass communication research. Experimental methods mistakenly assumed that cause/effect relationships took place in a social vacuum, while uses and gratifications research tended to ignore social structures which create needs in the first place. Edgar recommends instead the reality constructionist perspective of Berger and Luckmann (1967) and uses this in her own study of children and screen violence (Edgar, 1977).

The rejection of experimental and survey methods and their empiricist assumption also provides the starting point for Bonney and Wilson's (1983) study, *Australia's Commercial Media*. This book, already a widely-used text in Australian tertiary courses, avowedly derives its orientation from British work on media and culture, especially that done at the Centre for Contemporary Cultural Studies and at the Centre for Mass Communication Research at Leicester. It echoes the points made by Hall about the textual construction of reality and its ideological dimensions and also argues for the location of texts in the appropriate discourses which structure particular conceptions of reality. As Muecke (1983) has pointed out, the term 'discourse' has become one of the major categories articulating newer European theories of language and the media including the application to media studies of 'Marxist and psychoanalytical theories of literary discourse'. Evidence of activity in this area in Australia is in the work of Kress (1983a) and others in *Media Information Australia* (No. 28) which had a special section devoted to the subject, and in the fact that Nos. 5 and 6 of the *Australian Journal of Communication* (1984) were devoted to media in relation to discourse analysis.

The Australian Communication Association

The Australian Communication Association was formed in 1979 at a Conference held in Armidale, New South Wales, on 'Developing Oral Communication Competencies in Children'. Its first president sought to define its proper constituency as follows:

> My view is that the focus of A.C.A. is on interpersonal communication. Under this term I would include person-to-person communication, group discussion, public speaking and writing and the applications of theory and skills in these areas to such activities as teaching, counselling, business, politics, social work, administration and personal relationships . . . It is not centrally concerned with mass media, communication arts or communication technology. (Crocker, 1979)

However, this attempt at demarcation proved relatively short-lived. While the founding president continued to promote the association as representing 'communication professionals' whose major emphasis was on applied communication (Crocker, 1981:2), others sought to broaden the association. Against the background of the 'cross-currents' debate outlined earlier, the association has broadened its membership and has officially recognized the impact of cultural studies on the field through its sponsorship of the *Australian Journal of Cultural Studies*, established in 1983.

Distinctively Australian?

Australia is sometimes perceived as being partially removed from European and American cultural and intellectual developments by virtue of its geographical isolation. A major social history of Australia is called *The Tyranny of Distance* (Blainey, 1966). But, of course, as far as cultural and intellectual influences are concerned, the world has shrunk.

Communication studies in Australia has been presented in this paper as an arena for competing Anglo-European and American paradigms. The three aspects of communication studies development reviewed — curriculum models and issues, approaches to media studies, and directions within the Australian Association — point towards the growing influence of Anglo-European perspectives at the expense of earlier American-inspired approaches. One might comment in passing that perhaps there is a tendency to overcompensate for geographical isolation and to be only too ready to adopt the latest American or European development. Where does this leave distinctively Australian approaches?

There have been regular calls for some distinctively Australian approach, coupled with the view that Australian teachers and researchers too readily adopt overseas models. Irwin and More (1983:vii) bemoan the tendency 'for Australian scholars to copy slavishly one or other overseas approach without full consideration of the alternatives, or without any attempt to develop from the alternatives a uniquely Australian approach'. Further, they warn against Australian scholars becoming too preoccupied with the struggle between contending epistemologies and methodologies lest Australia become 'yet another faction ridden hotbed where different groups adhere to specific positions and methods' (vii–viii).

Some evidence for these assertions might be gleaned from the recent development of cultural studies in Australia.

At the first major Australian Conference on Interpersonal and Mass Communications held at the New South Wales Institute of Technology in Sydney in 1976, Terry Mohan (1977) introduced participants to cultural studies as it was being developed in conjunction with communication studies, in Britain, but emphasized the need to adapt the approach for Australia. He suggested as possible points of reference for an Australian cultural studies:

Cultural isolation and the absence of substantial influential artistic and intellectual élite groups; relative egalitarianism; pervasive philistinism; old and neo-nationalism; hedonism; social mobility; relative affluence (through luck); relative absence of cultural snobbery; masculinity as a pervasive ethic. (Mohan, 1977: 372).

While many would argue with this list, most (one suspects) would agree with Mohan's basic point that 'Cultural Studies arose very specifically out of the British social experience and that any Australian version would have to take into account real differences in the two societies'. However, when the *Australian Journal of Cultural Studies* was inaugurated in 1983 the editors expressed no such reservations. The impulse was to key in to exciting Anglo-European developments as quickly as possible. The journal is less one of

Australian cultural studies than the Australian arm of what is seen as an international, though Eurocentric, enterprise. The first article of the first issue asserts confidently: 'Readers of the *Australian Journal of Cultural Studies* shouldn't need convincing that there *is* a single enterprise that can be labelled "cultural studies" which has a fundamental coherence and importance, whether Australia is the object or only the unwary host of such a study' (Hodge and Kress, 1983:1). The editorial policy indicates that articles with a linguistic, semiotic, or structuralist theoretical base will be preferred. This is, of course, defensible. However, the cost is that cultural studies in Australia and the approaches to communication studies that it has fostered are as yet insufficiently linked to mainstream Australian social history, and with research and course development in the growing fields of Australian studies (see the *Journal of Australian Studies* published since 1977) and Asian studies (though for perspectives on Australia, Asia and the media, see Broinowski, 1982).

However, it is not the purpose of this paper to bemoan overseas influences, nor the growing impact of Anglo-European approaches. Much of the intellectual excitement of communication studies in Australia derives from the challenges of the new theories and approaches. Given the very recent development of the field in Australia, much energy has quite rightly been spent catching up and keeping up with these developments. Furthermore, there has been more research and publishing on communication forms and processes in Australia in the last ten years, albeit often adopting overseas models, than in all previous decades.

Nevertheless, it does seem appropriate to end with a note of caution and once again to mention the tradition of Australian dependence on British curriculum models noted at the beginning of this paper. Arguably, an earlier phase of British influence stifled proper consideration of Australian literature, history and society in Australia's tertiary institutions within the context of traditional disciplines. It is hoped that this new phase of influence will inform and illuminate studies of Australia's communication patterns and institutions and not weigh too heavily upon them.

Bibliography

Alomes, S. (1981) 'Exploring the Satellite Society', *Journal of Australian Studies*, 10:64–8

Bennett et al. (eds) (1981a) *Culture Ideology and Social Process: A Reader.* London: Batsford Academic.

Bennett et al. (eds) (1981b) *Popular Television and Film.* London: Open University Press.

Berger, P. and T. Luckmann (1967) *The Social Construction of Reality.* New York: Doubleday.

Blainey, G. (1966) *The Tyranny of Distance.* Melbourne: Sun Books.

Bonney, G. (1980) 'W. Packer and Televised Cricket', NSW IT Occasional Media Paper, No. 2.

Bonney, W.L. (1983) 'Two Approaches to Communication' pp. 1–5 in Ted J. Smith, III (ed.), *Communication in Australia.* Warrnambool: Warrnambool Institute Press.

Bonney, B. and H. Wilson (1983) *Australia's Commercial Media.* Melbourne: Macmillan.

Broinowski. A. (ed.) (1982) *Australia, Asia and the Media.* Centre for the Study of Australian-Asian Relations, Griffith University.

Campbell, W.J. and R. Keogh (1962) *Television and the Australian Adolescent, a Sydney Survey.* Sydney: Angus and Robertson.

Corner, J. and J. Hawthorn (eds) (1980) *Communication Studies: An Introductory Reader.* London: Edward Arnold.

Crocker, W. et. al. (1979) 'Communication Apprehension', *Australian Journal of Education,* 23 (3): 262–70

Crocker, B. (1979) 'A Note From the President', *Australian Communication Association Newsletter,* (1), 1–2.

Crocker, B. (1981) 'The Communication Professional and the Professional Association', *Australian Communication Association Newsletter,* 2 (1): 1–3.

Curran, J. et al. (eds) (1977) *Mass Communication and Society.* London: Edward Arnold.

Edgar, P. (1975) 'Directions in Mass Communication Research', *Australian and New Zealand Journal of Sociology,* 11 (2): 21–7.

Edgar, P. (1977) *Children and Screen Violence.* Brisbane: Old University Press.

Edgar, P. (1979) *The Politics of the Press.* Melbourne: Sun Books.

Edgar, P. (1980) *The News in Focus.* Melbourne: Macmillan.

Emery, F.E. and D. Martin (1957) *Psychological Effects of the Western Film, a Study in Television Viewing.* University of Melbourne, Dept of Audio-Visual Aids.

Fiske, J. and J. Hartley (1978) *Reading Television.* London: Methuen.

Fiske, J. (1982) *Introduction to Communication Studies.* London: Methuen.

Fiske, J. (1983) 'Communication, Curriculum and Consensus in the West', *Australian Communication Review,* 4 (2): 12–17.

Galloway (1980/81) 'Communication Networks. State of the Art', *Australian Scan,* 9 & 10: 17–22.

Gauld, A. and J. Shotter (1977) *Human Action and its Psychological Investigation.* London: Routledge & Kegan Paul.

Giddens, A. (1977) *New Rules of Sociological Method.* London: Hutchinson.

Gurevitch, M. et al. (eds) (1980) *Culture, Society and the Media.* London: Methuen.

Hall, S. et al. (eds) (1980) *Culture, Media, Language.* London: Hutchinson.

Hall, S. (1980) 'Introduction to Media Studies at the Centre' pp. 117–21 in S. Hall et al. (eds), *Culture, Media, Language.* London: Hutchinson.

Hansford, B.C. and B.C. Aveyard (1980/81) 'Communication Apprehension, Self-Acceptance and Behavioural Attitudes of Trainee Teachers', *Australian Scan,* 9&10: 42–8.

Hodge, R. (1982) 'Culture as Communication: Towards a Theoretical Basis for Communication Studies', *Australian Journal of Communication*, 1&2: 76–83.

Hodge, R. and G. Kress (1983) 'Functional Semiotics', *Australian Journal of Cultural Studies*, 1 (1): 1–17.

Irwin, H. (1980/81), 'Communication Competence: A Framework for Interpersonal Communication Research in Dyads, Groups and Organizations', *Australian Scan*, 9&10: 35–41.

Irwin, H. (1983), 'Interpersonal Communications: Contemporary Issues and Directions in Theory and Research', *Australian Journal of Communication*, 3: 1–11.

Irwin, H. and E. More (1983) 'Differing Perspectives and the Development of Communication Studies in Australia' pp. vii–viii in Ted J. Smith III (ed.) *Communication in Australia*. Warrnambool: Warrnambool Institute Press.

King, N. and S. Muecke (1984) 'Caught Between Two Paradigms: Communication Studies in Australia', *Australian Journal of Communication*, 5&6: 1–2.

Kippax, S. and J. Murray (1979) *Small Screen, Big Business*. Sydney: Angus and Robertson.

Kress, G. (1980/81) 'Ideological Unity of Discourse: The Concept of Textual Congruence', *Australian Scan*, 9&10: 71–8.

Kress, G. (1983a), 'Media Analysis and the Study of Discourse', *Media Information Australia*, 28: 3–11.

Kress, G. (1983b), 'Directions in Communication Studies', *Australian Journal of Communication*, 4: 1–6.

Lewis, G. (1982) 'The Anglo-American Influence on Australian Communication Education', *Australian Journal of Communication*, 1&2: 14–20.

Mayer, H. (1983) 'Mass Media Studies: Survey Comments', *Australian Journal of Communication*, 3: 27–30.

Mohan, T. (1977), 'Mass Media and Cultural Studies' pp. 350–80 in *Conference of Interpersonal and Mass Communication: Proceedings*. Sydney: Clarendon Press.

Muecke, S. (1983) 'Teaching About Language in Communication Studies Courses: Some Developmental Perspectives', *Australian Journal of Communication*, 3: 17–25.

Murray, J.P. (1979) 'Television', pp. 94–121 in A. Burns (ed.), *Children and Families in Australia*. Sydney: Allen and Unwin.

Nixon, M. (1972) 'Mass Media' pp. 178–99 in F.J. Hunt (ed.), *Socialisation in Australia*. Sydney: Angus and Robertson.

Noble, G. (1975) *Children in Front of the Small Screen*. London: Constable.

Penman, R. (1982) 'Problems in Human Communication Studies: Another Argument', *Australian Journal of Communication*, 1&2: 52–7.

Pingree, S. and R. Hawkins (1981) 'U.S. Programs on Australian TV', *Journal of Communication*, 31 (1): 97–106.

Putnis, P. (1984) 'Communication and Cultural Studies in Britain: Two Conferences, Two Paradigms', *Australian Communication Review*, 5 (3), 15–26.

Rogers, E.M. and S.H. Chaffee (1983) 'Communication as an Academic Discipline', *Journal of Communication*, 33 (3): 18–30.

Sless, D. (1980/81) 'Semiotics: Survey', *Australian Scan*, 9&10, 1–4.

Shotter, J. (1975), *Images of Man in Psychological Research*. London: Methuen.

South Australian College of Advanced Education (1982) *Handbook*.

Thomson, R.J. (1959) *Television Crime-Drama: Its Impact on Children and Adolescents*. Melbourne: Cheshire.

Tulloch, J. (1977) *Conflict and Control in the Cinema*. Melbourne, Macmillan.

5

BETWEEN NORMATIVE RESEARCH AND THEORY OF FORMS AND CONTENT
Italian Studies on Mass Communication

*Paolo Mancini**

This article discusses the combination of influences on the focus and direction of Italian media research after its beginnings over thirty years ago, through the 1970s and up to and including current research efforts. During the 1950s and 1960s, Catholic culture was a strong influence and this combined with normative goals in the research commissioned by RAI. An important political and ideological debate on the future of the Italian broadcasting system influenced the direction and subjects of research in the 1970s. Present day research seems more influenced by the start of competition between public service broadcasting and commercial networks in Italy.

Introduction

Mass media scholarship in Italy can be divided into three main phases which correspond roughly to the last three decades. The boundaries of these phases are not rigid, however; they are rather more indicative of prevalent trends within time periods whose limits often expand and overlap. The 1960s was the first phase, when studies in mass communication initially began in Italy. The second phase began in the early 1970s and was a period of critical reflection on the limits of the discipline; this period witnessed an abundance of literature in a political key. Of primary concern here, however, is the third and present phase which began in the early 1980s. Italian studies in this current period seem profoundly influenced by the changes which have taken place over the years in the country's system of mass communication.

Although there are references to studies of a broad range of forms of mass communication, namely cinema, journalism and advertising, Italian studies of television are the predominant subject of this article.

*The author is based at the Instituto di Studi Sociali, Via Pascoli, 06100 Perugia, Italy.

From Paolo Mancini, "Between Normative Research and Theory of Forms and Content: Italian Studies on Mass Communication," *European Journal of Communication*, Vol. 1, pp. 97-115.

The Shadow of Didacticism

Much of Italian sociology — and of particular interest here is semiology — was born and developed around university and other research centres with strong ties to Catholic culture. Catholicism in Italy has a unique way of interpreting interest in research, associating it with civil and religious involvement, a sense of community, and an increased potential for human growth. Research is seen as a service, the process of which can be accelerated and directed within well-defined social parameters. An important part of mass communication research in Italy developed, or had strong bonds with, scholars holding this concept of their work.

Indeed, the first empirical research in the field was carried out at the Agostino Gemelli Institute, founded in 1960 for the experimental study of social problems on the initiative of the Provincial Administration of Milan and the National Centre of Social Prevention and Defence, in close contact with the Catholic University of Milan. Within this Institute scholars came together and were educated. They were not all Catholic, most came from academic settings, and they both directed and shaped the subsequent course of Italian mass communication research until the present time. They included Francesco Alberoni, Gianfranco Bettetini, Maria Angela Croce, Cesare Musatti, Assunto Quadrio and Franco Rositi amongst others. The Institute's Journal, *IKON*, published the findings of the first investigations and it progressively became an important instrument through which this newborn field of study in Italy made contact with the experience of research conducted in other countries.

One of the principal characteristics of the early empirical research carried out by the Institute was a social-psychological approach. Eminent scholars — such as Cesare Musatti, Assunto Quadrio, Marcello Cesa Bianchi — were students of psychology and members of the Institute's Board of Directors as well as *IKON*'s editorial staff. This group of scholars was also responsible for applying psychological methodologies to studies of learning processes and the socializing effects of television messages. Because of this emphasis, studies were published with particular attention to violence in programmes. Much of this literature concerned children and teaching problems connected with the use of the mass media. Amenable to the same social-psychological approach, and of equal importance at this time, was the analysis of French films. In these years, much of the research published in *IKON* was characterized by this social-psychological emphasis, much of which was empirical, covering the vast field of the cognitive effects of mass communication and its role in the process of socialization. This early Italian audience-effects research and the analysis of transmitted messages, albeit conducted in laboratory settings, came to shape the policy later adopted by the Italian Broadcasting Company (RAI) for its internal research.

The Catholic vision was at the base of the positive functional interpretation of the role of the mass media, which would later become functionalist in Parsonian terms. This interpretation conceived of the mass media as facilitating the process of civil maturation and the development of both social and individual potentialities. This is generally defined as the so-called current of 'social communication'. In those years, even non-Catholic intellectuals were attracted to such a positive view of the role of the media, for it was set against a Marxist pessimism which, under the influence of the Frankfurt School, tended to 'demonize' the mass media and which lacked an empirical base to its research work. The influence of the Catholic vision on research resulted in great importance being placed on the educational functions of the media. Studies focused on the effects of television and other media on the process of socialization and offered broad policy prescriptions urging the media toward educational objectives or, at least, programming that would not be harmful to the concept of human identity and social cohesion that was so widespread among supporters of social involvement in those years. The social-psychological perspective fits very well with the needs for knowledge so-defined, thus making both possible and methodologically operational the study of the modalities of reading and interpreting television and film messages and their possible effects.

But these problems of methodology and approach were not the only developments in Italian media research in the 1960s. Another trend began with RAI television's internally commissioned polls. Since the mid-1960s, RAI has been the major supporter of mass communication research in Italy. The birth of television and the consolidation of its position as the primary medium, rather than radio as had happened in other Western countries, made the research activity a major component of the social and cultural role played by state television. RAI's objectives in commissioning research conformed to the popularizing and educational character which typified radio and television broadcasts of those years. Indeed during that period, RAI conformed to its public service obligations by releasing programmes which had an educational purpose.[1] Of course much of this was made possible by RAI's monopoly status which sheltered it from commercial competition. The educational emphasis appeared in a range of television programmes as well as in other cultural functions (meetings, seminars) organized by RAI around the country. RAI focused its greatest attention on 'erudite' broadcasts, programmes based on famous works of literature, and was in close collaboration with socially involved cinema, without losing sight of light entertainment. Above all, this cultural emphasis resulted in careful programme control which, on the one hand, sometimes functioned as a form of censorship while, on the other, limited the amount of advertising and the importation of foreign programmes. RAI's cultural emphasis was also reflected in the many national events it organized and promoted, such as conferences, exhibitions and meetings, the most famous of which is the annual *Prix Italia* in which all European television organizations participate. The importance of RAI's contribution to the support and development of mass communication research cannot be underestimated.

During this period, as was also true in later years, RAI directed the choice of its studies and defined the general field in which all its research was conducted. At that time RAI's largest research office was *Il Servizio Opinioni* (Audience Research Department) which carried out part of the commissioned studies using small sample audience surveys. A major project was launched at this time to investigate processes of comprehension of different types of programmes. The project had two aims: first, to characterize the gratifications which the public derived from the programmes; and secondly, to improve these programmes' information dissemination function by analysing the relationship between the transmitted messages and common cultural standards.

The study of violence on television began during this period and continues today, in an effort to discover and limit the effects that might increase criminal potential and aggression. In line with RAI's aim of raising the general public's level of cultural sophistication, the following subjects have been studied: Italian musical preferences, the public's level of comprehension of films based on classic novels, and also, for example, comprehension of economic terminology. Although methodology varies from study to study, in general a content analysis is accompanied by a study of audience reception of the message in terms of gratifications and comprehension.

Thus, a continuity was established between the activities of the Gemelli Institute and the research commissioned by RAI. Many of the same scholars (e.g. Alberoni and Rositi) were involved in both organizations, thus guaranteeing a similarity of methodology and approach. In addition, the aims that inspired research in both organizations were based on a common orientation which can be defined as *normative*. As a result, several social objectives existed, either implicitly, due to the cultural and ideological background of the researcher or, more explicitly, because of the particular research questions chosen, to which research tried to find answers by developing instruments for the characterization, definition and empirical verification of norms and rules that could be applied to television programming. The civil and social involvement of the researcher in the endeavour to promote the cultural growth of both the individual and community adapted perfectly to educational objectives, which, in the case of RAI, helped it to carry out its institutional goals.

Finally, during the 1960s numerous texts on mass communication were translated into Italian. As a result, Italian research benefited from reference to the latest research conducted in other Western countries. Of particular significance here was the 1969 anthology by Marino Livolsi (1969).

Towards Political Involvement
Media studies in the 1970s were characterized by two main tendencies. The first was a great improvement in methodology which coincided with the enormous amount of research commissioned by RAI. This was closely connected, especially in the early 1970s, to research conducted in the late 1960s so that results became more detailed and precise. Secondly, the 1970s witnessed a progressive growth in political discussions about mass communication and television in particular. Both politicians and intellectuals of a more or less Marxist leaning took part in these discussions and produced numerous newspaper and specialist magazine articles as well as books on the subject.

Between 1973 and 1976, RAI published a series of studies, *Televisione e ragazzi* (Television and children), exploring the influence of different types of programmes on different age groups of young people. These studies focused mainly on children's television programmes. Their level of comprehension of both film and spoken language was analysed and, more generally, television's role in the socialization process and the various functions of the different media were investigated. During this period, Sabino Acquaviva (1975) completed his research series on the role played by the mass media, particularly television, in the process of cultural development. This research began in 1971 with the publication of *La Montagna del Sole* (The Sun Mountain), one of the most important studies on cultural change.

RAI also developed another important field of research: content analysis. In the early 1970s Italian mass communication research became influenced by research efforts undertaken in the USA, the findings of which were translated into Italian. Gianni Statera's 1972 work was of particular importance in describing the progress of such research in Anglo-Saxon countries.

Content analysis became an important analytical tool of Italian scholars, producing both theoretical research and, following subsequent discussion, empirical application. In effect, many of the methodological problems connected with content analysis had already been dealt with in preceding years. After the 1970s and the publication of several significant works, however, critical analysis came to evaluate the potential and reveal the limits of this methodology. Theoretical studies of particular importance were those by De Lillo (1971) and Rositi (1970), the latter a study commissioned by RAI. The empirical research that particularly stands out is that conducted by Alberoni (1973), in which the methodologies of content analysis are first critically discussed and then applied to a highly significant body of research on television programmes, periodicals and films. From this, the importance of the contents or forms of mass communication were revealed. Further research during these years conducted by Rositi (1970) — on television news of four European countries — was presented at the convention, *L'attualita in TV* (News on TV), as part of the *Prix Italia*, held in Florence in September 1975.

Another important discussion developed over the application of semiotical analysis in mass communication research. But in this case new ground was not being broken since research appeared in the Journal, *IKON*, as early as the 1960s, which was similar to French film analysis by Metz (1974) and Cohen-seat (1946). Later, the attempt to apply semiotical methodology shifted from studies of cinema to studies of television, triggering a heated debate that is still going on today. Semiotical analysis found its first application in the notion of genre and in the definition of its meaningful structures. In accordance with studies from other European countries, there was a tendency to define the structural characteristics of the notion of genre so that they could also be used to contribute to the organization of the schedule of everyday transmissions (Bettetini et al., 1977). Among the particularly important semiotical approaches are the theoretical and empirical works by Umberto Eco (1964).

A political approach to the study of mass communication espoused predominantly by Marxist intellectuals, was a second main development in Italian media studies in the 1970s. The work of Althusser (1970) was an obvious influence and this combined with the greater political awareness brought about in Italy and other Western European countries by the events of May 1968. According to this political perspective, the mass media were the strongest means for promulgating the dominant capitalist ideology.

Another more circumstantial occasion for the political interpretation of the media emerged from the debate over control of RAI. Until that time, RAI had been controlled by the government and hence the Christian Democrats, the majority party since 1945. Much of the research of these years focused on policy options for reforming the public communication system and on the resulting modifications and future possibilities. RAI TV was reformed in 1975. The large number of publications and conferences resulting from this debate, however, was not matched by a corresponding increase in the number of empirical studies. Not much attention was paid to empirical research which might demonstrate ideological positions, since the emphasis was on the changes that were taking place in the media due to the political struggle for its control and, in particular, for the control of the news. Consequently, theoretical and political debates and sociological macro-constructions were chosen, tendencies that perfectly compounded with a philosophic and humanistic tradition that had begun with the studies of Benedetto Croce and their Marxist interpretation by Antonio Gramsci.

Gramsci's concept of hegemony was used to demystify and fight against the use of the media as a tool for perpetuating the dominant capitalist ideology. Althusser's theory of the 'ideological state apparatus' (ISA) was taken up by Cesareo (1974) and specifically adapted to the study of the organization of media production. The division of labour within the ISA reflected the roles determined by the capitalist mode of production and hence limited the power of television as an instrument of liberation. In this period, neither the concept of hegemony nor that of the ISA received sufficient empirical verification; they continued to be theoretical notions by which different political positions could be measured.

Several important editorial events occured during this decade. In 1976 Paolo Murialdi, journalism historian and a journalist himself, founded the magazine *Problemi dell 'informazione* (Problems of Information) which soon became the medium for the exchange of research on journalism, as well as research into advertising, and television programmes. From 1976 to 1977, this magazine became the important organ for a debate between scholars over the question of the existence of a Marxist theory of the media. This magazine was also a forum for the comparison of the problems in Italian media studies with developing European Marxist theoretical positions (see Enzensberger, 1970). The belief that the sociology of mass communication was in a period of crisis, the parameters of which were essentially political and ideological, was gaining ground. *IKON* was the origin of another important editorial event when Giovanni Cesareo became its director and changed the entire editorial staff in September, 1978. (The new *IKON* was to be short-lived, however, since the journal stopped publication in the spring of 1981.) Cesareo's (1978: 8) words in the editorial that inaugurated the new *IKON* series reflected the increasingly political element in the macro-sociological dimension of media research: '. . . with that we reject, in fact, a neutral position; it is our intention that . . . this new series of *IKON* must serve to point out the possible new processes of communication, the production of consciousness and of knowledge, and identify their antagonists, old and new.'

One important consequence of the intellectual ardour of these years was the creation of a theoretical body of writing that would subsequently be drawn upon to provide a framework for a large amount of empirical research. Finally, we should not forget an often neglected area of mass communication: the legal aspect of media systems that was especially prominent after the reform of RAI TV.

The Present
The present state of mass communication research in Italy cannot be understood without reference to two events which took place in 1975 and 1976 respectively and which defined certain research trends that had previously existed to a lesser degree. Previous lines of research were continued but, at the same time, with an overlapping of different approaches that still characterizes present day Italian research.

The first significant event was in 1975 with the reform of RAI TV. Until then, RAI had been the most important commissioner of research. It is not an easy task to summarize the Reform Act of April, 1975 and this discussion is therefore limited to the major consequences this Act had on the evolution of research. Of primary importance was the passing of control of Italian National Television from the government to Parliament. As a consequence, all the political parties represented in Parliament came to have a far greater influence on the workings of RAI in proportion to their electoral strength. This process (described as *lottizzazione*) created a need for mechanisms to control the production of messages and to check whether they were in accordance with the directives released by the *Commissione Parlamentare di Vigilanza* (The Parliamentary Board for RAI), the organ that connects RAI with Parliament. Another office, *Verifica Programmi Trasmessi* (Broadcast Programme Verification), was established which is now an essential reference service for anyone analysing television broadcasts.[2] These were added to other previously existing research offices including: *La Documentazione e Studi* (Documentation and Studies), in charge of collecting national and international material possibly of use to the company; *Sperimentazione e Ricerca* (Experimentation and Research), which studies new forms of television expression as well as conducting analysis of the different structures and types of communication and messages in the mass media, with particular emphasis on television serials; *Il Servizio Opinioni* (Audience Research Dept.), formerly in charge of analysing programme content but presently limited to conducting audience opinion surveys; and the Marketing Department was created for market research into improving the Company's image. The latter two departments have become increasingly restricted to company business and administration, losing their theoretical and scientific reputation as the results of their studies are not publicized. *La Documentazione e Studi* and *Verifica Programmi Trasmessi* have sought to unite the Company's aims with the promotion of scientific research on mass communication.

The liberalization of the airwaves was the second major reform to influence the focus of Italian media research. Two decisions by the Constitutional Court in 1976 allowing the existence of private television companies put an end to the RAI monopoly. Successive decisions limited the range of possibilities of inter-station connection making it impossible to broadcast a single live news programme simultaneously throughout the country. As a consequence of these two decisions, a great number of local television stations sprang up across the country. A process of concentration has resulted in the present arrangement of three main ccmmercial networks — Canale 5, Rete 4, Italia 1 — which have, in turn, become part of a single corporation.[3] By the start of the present decade, the process of consolidation of this mixed system in which public television operates alongside private, was already well advanced. Indeed, RAI found itself in such a competitive situation that it was in danger of losing its audience and, hence, advertising revenue. At present, there are no laws regulating the competition between RAI and the other networks; apart from that which forbids inter-company link-ups for live broadcasting of news. The RAI reform of 1975 has not been adapted to the circumstances of this new competitive situation. Nevertheless, both the reform law and the competition that exists among networks direct the aims and methods of Italian media research today.

At present RAI places primary importance on research designed to verify the performance of broadcast output. Indeed, the commissioned studies have been exclusively directed to the verification of broadcast messages to determine if they are in line with the policy of the *Commissione Parlamentare di Vigilanza*, and the *Consiglio di Administrazione* (Governing Board of RAI). All of the most important intellectuals in Italy contribute to this research. *La RAI sotto Analisi* (RAI Under Analysis), edited by Giorgio Grossi, which includes all the studies commissioned by *Verifica Programmi Trasmessi* up to and incuding 1980, has recently been published by ERI (a publishing house owned by RAI).

A number of distinct areas of interest can be found in these studies. Most of the studies focus on journalistic information and go beyond an analysis of RAI's presentation of various themes on television to draw comparisons with that of the press. News is the primary object of investigation, and the relationship between the media and political systems, analysed through message content, is a predominant theme. Another major subject of study is terrorism, a phenomenon which came to the forefront in Italy during the late 1970s and early 1980s (Morcellini et al., 1981). The mass media paid so much attention to terrorism that, according to many, its very existence became connected with publicity in the news. Other aspects of social change, such as the presentation of women and the family on television are also studied (Buonanno, 1983). Comparative research has also not been neglected: during the 1979 European elections the content of the Italian mass media was analysed in a research project involving a number of European countries (Bechelloni, 1980).

More recently, the competitive situation has made it necessary for *Verifica Programmi Trasmessi* to broaden the area of interest of a number of its research projects to include the output of private networks.[4] Again, the analysis of the relationship between political and mass media systems is based on the comparison between public and private television, and on the changes that the latter have brought about in traditional communication policy and programming structures (Grossi et al., 1984).

Television serials, on both private and public stations, form another subject of study. This subject in fact is the largest field of RAI commissioned research today, after information. Indeed, with the advent of private television, the educational character that distinguishes RAI programming and limits both the importation of foreign programmes and the number of light entertainment shows, disappears. While the commercial networks draw from the vast array of North American productions, without regard to organic programming, RAI is progressively changing its programming structures to keep up with the competition. The recent discussions, research, and meetings on the theme of serials is the result of this sudden overwhelming flood of American television films after years of culturally and educationally focused programming. The attention paid by Italian intellectuals to serials is not mere curiosity for a new subject, but is stimulated by the desire to compete with American predominance in television productions. This was the topic of discussion of the most important meetings on television in 1983 and 1984, to which there was a strong political flavour. Although the title of the 1983 *Prix Italia* was 'Nothing but the News', the main theme of the conference was the possibility of autonomous European production. Even more explicit was the theme of the conference *Teleconfronto*, held in Chianciano in 1984: 'Films and TV Films: Europe Strikes Again?'

The subject of television serials did not remain the exclusive property of academicians for long; it was soon taken up by people working directly in communications, as well as politicians, and directors thus extending discussion and debate on the subject to a wide variety of spheres. This time, however, the research went beyond the ideological and theoretical level of interpretation. For example, Francesco Casetti, semiologist and organizer of the recent conferences (noted above) on the relationship between cinema films and TV films at the International Centre for Semiotics and Linguistics in Urbino, conducted a study commissioned by *Verifica Programmi Trasmessi* on the cognitive frameworks and techniques of communication in American serials (Casetti, 1984). Abruzzese (1984) directed another study which was part of a much larger project promoted by RAI's *Sperimentazione e Ricerca* in an effort to find Italy's answer to American serials.

Italian research of the last few years has focused on the message and this determines the methodology to a great extent. Previous areas of research, such as the studies conducted by *Il Servizio Opinioni* which investigated public gratification from and comprehension of television programmes, and those of the Gemelli Institute which considered audience reactions in experimental settings, have now been abandoned.

Today the message is essentially studied using content analysis techniques. The critical revision carried out in past years along with the more sophisticated theories that accompanied political discussion on media, have made the critical use of an increasingly more refined methodology of content analysis both possible and necessary. The latter is often accompanied by investigations carried out according to essentially semiotic techniques, not only into the connotative dimension of the broadcast message but also into communication structures and strategies. In this respect analyses of content are able to define the objective 'indicators' whose characterization is not left to the discretion of other analysts. The category of 'subject' (or the actors — those who speak, or about whom the news speaks) can be isolated, cross-classified against other variables, allowing the measurement of the varied appearances of social actors and the modality of their referent actions. In this way the roles of the different subjects making up the political and social reality are defined. News content analysis is often accompanied by an investigation into the different speakers' roles, based on the principles of symbolic interactionism and linguistic pragmatics (Mancini, 1985). Similarly, the narrative structures of television and journalistic information have been investigated using methodologies mostly based on Van Dijk's linguistic studies. One of these studies was the significant research carried out by Rositi (1982) on behalf of VPT.

It is mainly in entertainment and TV film analysis, however, that various semiotic theories have served as the principal approach to interpretation. Casetti's (1984) analysis of American TV films in Italy greatly relies on Greimas's semiotics, while Wolf (1982) attempts to investigate *programmi a contenitore* (all-afternoon variety shows) using many ideas borrowed from Goffman's works.

An interesting characteristic of several of the many studies commissioned by RAI is the mention of some possible policy prescriptions based on an interpretation of the results of research. Italian mass communication research is presently characterized by the combination of social involvement, due to the politicization over the years of the Italian intellectuals, with research objectives confirming the normative dimension which had previously come to light. This is evident in recent studies into whether the transmitted messages correspond to the norms which, however tentatively, seek to define strategies and methods of communication to be used to give incentive to Italian film production. Or conversely, the norms designed to limit the tendency to give preference to emphasis on light entertainment which the coming of commercial competition has encouraged in the Italian television system.

The recent trend to return to more concrete empirical research is confirmed by other symptomatic events. Although *IKON* ceased publication in 1981, there is available a bi-annual review entitled *IKON Ricerche sulla Comunicazioni* (IKON Research on Communication), directed by the *Consiglio Scientifico dell 'Istituto Gemelli* (Scientific Committee of the Gemelli Institute), which is not an autonomous committee as in the case of *IKON Nuova Serie* (IKON New Series) Another journal, *Sociologia della Comunicazione* (Sociology of Communication), launched recently, and stemming from an idea of the late Giorgio Braga, pays particular attention to the themes of symbolic interactionism and the sociology of knowledge.

Outside RAI's sphere, other areas of research have sprung up which, regrettably, are often unable to find sufficient means of publication and circulation. These are usually concerned with problems in written journalism. Indeed, the regulation that introduced the study of newspapers in Italian schools requires theoretical and methodological research into the structure, language, and pedagogic uses of newspapers. More empirical knowledge is needed concerning the much debated theme of schools of journalism. As is well known, no Faculty of Communication exists in Italy (the only exception is the Department of

Communicative Arts (DAMS), founded in Bologna in 1970), nor any School of Journalism that sufficiently enjoys the necessary juridicial and functional recognition. Bechelloni (1982) and others have made important contributions in comparing the Italian situation to that of the rest of Europe in this area of journalism studies.

Conclusion: Some Interpretative Directions

In concluding, it is possible to advance several interpretations of current mass communication research in Italy. One emerges clearly at the outset: although Italy, in comparison with other European countries as well as the USA, was late in embarking upon media research, Italian scholars have made ample use of the methodologies, hypotheses and findings that have come out of research in these countries. Many classic texts as well as the most innovative works in sociology, mass communication, semiotics and linguistics are translated into Italian soon after publication. In spite of its late start, therefore, Italian research has caught up with that of other countries. The reverse, however, is rarely the case. Few Italian studies are translated and therefore are not widely circulated in other countries. This is particularly unfortunate since many Italian empirical analyses have a comparative dimension, bringing to light the unique aspects of the Italian media system as well as its similarity to those in other countries.

Within the Italian intellectual community, there is also a problem of circulation of research and of relation with other branches of sociology. One problem is that the focus of many studies stems from the immediate needs of the commissioning agent and they are therefore often not of high theoretical or methodological calibre. As a consequence, not only do such studies not obtain the necessary circulation but the findings do not arouse adequate debate and critical review.

The facility and willingness with which Italian researchers borrow theories and empirical methodologies is one reason why it is impossible to find a single dominant approach to the study of mass communication in this country. A second distinctive characteristic of Italian research is, therefore, its use of a number of different methodologies. This is true for social-psychological approaches, but perhaps the most obvious case is the use of sociological and semiotic tools for the analysis of the same body of material. Sociological content analysis brings to light characteristics and typologies at the semantic level of the text while the semiotical tools work on the communication and structural strategies present. At the same time, there is ongoing discussion as well as a number of theoretical studies on the attempts to integrate different methodologies of analysis. The limits of traditional methodologies and content analysis are evident when one tries to study, within the message, modes of involving the television audience, the construction of images deployed by the programme makers and the processes of audience recognition and identification.

A third previously mentioned characteristic which has been typical of Italian research on mass communications since its beginning is the normative dimension. Both empirical research and the rich theoretical debate often tend to focus on, and create rules and behavioural standards, to confirm, strengthen and contrast trends and theories of change when they are not directly involved in heated political debate. Few studies can avoid one of the characteristics of Italian research, its social relevance and application, and this is not only found in research on mass communication. This tendency has been reinforced by RAI which (up to 1980) defined research aims as being connected with its teaching functions and, later, as depending on its new organization and relation to the political system, and the logic of competition which has a permanent character. The prevalence of the normative dimension is connected with the macro-sociological character of much Italian research and debate, mainly during the middle years of the 1970s, although it still directs some studies today.

In this sense, Italian research confirms, and even pushes to their limits, some of the typical characteristics of European research as described by Blumler (1978). Normativism is connected with a trend towards macro-sociological approaches that are applied to the mechanisms of legitimation and delegitimation of the political system through the media. Marxism, the Frankfurt School, functionalism and, lastly, the influence of Luhmann's (1971) hypothesis on the processes of thematization are macro-theoretical reference points of a highly politically involved mode of research. This research has, at different times, deployed empirical data in support of its hypotheses. All the problems arising within the system of mass communication have been studied with great attention to possible lines of operational intervention. The concept of journalistic objectivity, the relation between the media and the political system, the mechanisms that facilitate social consensus and the possible dimensions of a theory of cultural hegemony have been privileged 'sites' for intellectual investigation using theoretical structures of macro-sociological paradigms. At the same time it is possible to point out the normative dimension even in a not inconsiderable body of empirical research which has been guided, as we have already demonstrated, by cognitive objectives inherent in pedagogic theory or critical perspectives.

Another distinctive characteristic of Italian media scholarship is to be found in the specific objects studied. Following the early RAI effects studies, attention has been focused in recent years exclusively on the broadcast message whose content has been analysed, together with its narrative structures. Here again, preoccupation has been normative, intended to characterize those communications which are most conducive to an appropriate civil and social maturity. There is also a need, however, to study, through the content, the modalities through which the system of politics and media systems are correlated and therefore the weight and influence of the different political tendencies in television programming. The cross-cutting analysis of the content of different media, usually the press and television, permits the investigation of the role which each medium plays in this process of constructing consensus. The contemporary investigation of forms and message structures brings to light the modality of spectator involvement and, therefore, the assumed persuasive value and also makes it possible to establish correlations between cinema and television and between different forms of entertainment.

A prevalent focus on the message is certainly still at the base of the current development, deepening a utilization of techniques of research relating to content analysis, to semiotics, to symbolic interactionism and to pragmatics. Although there is a great deal of attention to the message, its content and structure, it is not always possible to find lines of interpretation which have much in common with the macro-sociological tendency that also characterizes Italian debate and research.

There is a wealth of studies and although they are often diverse and fragmented, they are all characterized by a normative and critical emphasis and an applicability to immediate social policy objectives. The basic criteria for research is a social purpose; this stems from the researcher's expectations, manner of involvement and his or her relation with social reality, confirming the close correlation and interdependence between the focus of Italian research and the environment that surrounds it.

Italian studies of mass communication are a faithful reflection of this interdependence. Methodologies imported from abroad and those produced at home were first utilized from a perspective which exalted the media's positive educational function, with the social aim of stimulating cultural enrichment among the general public and limiting possible negative (violent or anti-social) effects. Later, with the increase of political influence, debate and the ideological use of scientific theorization were encouraged, by giving maximum space to the macro-construction of the economy of media and of its use in the production of social consensus. This was in complete harmony with the humanistic tradition of the Italian academy.

More recently, there has been a revival of interest in applied research arising from a need to respond to contingent objectives of knowledge. New research projects on the problems of analysing content have begun and more are foreseen in the field of audience reception and effects as private television restructures the political and cultural market, freeing it from the chains of ideological faith and community localism that for a long time made audience research seem unnecessary.

In this way the relative decline of the political aspect of research has made room, on the one hand, for an essential and circumscribed normativism and on the other to more profound methodological approaches that do not lead down the road of macro-theorizing even if they still focus on mechanisms of legitimation and delegitimation, on the construction of social consensus, and on investigations of cognitive processes connected with media functions. All this seems to be one of the directions which foreshadows more attention to theories of symbolic exchange and of the symbolic construction of reality, but, even more, towards the theory of systems.

Notes

1. RAI is owned by IRI and the Italian State is its major stock-holder. In the 1960s and 1970s it had a monopoly on television broadcasting and was under government control. This situation remained unchanged until 1975 when RAI was reformed. The next year two decisions by the Constitution Court 'freed the air', permitting private television broadcasting.

2. *Verifica Programmi Trasmessi* (Broadcast Programme Verification) is the RAI office responsible for research designed to check the performance of broadcast output.

3. The term network used for these three private Italian television companies is somewhat inappropriate. The programmes are broadcast simultaneously with

cassettes by each of the local stations that make up the company. The stations connected to Italia 1 and Canale 5 (the most diffused network) are all owned by the same company.

4. The research promoted by *Verifica Programmi Trasmessi* are published by RAI in a series called 'Dati per la verifica dei programmi trasmessi'.

References

Abruzzese, Alberto (ed.) (1984) *Ai Confini della Serialità*. Napoli: Società Editrice Napoletane.

Acquaviva, S., I. De Sandre, G. Guizzardi and G. Sarpellon (1975) *Cambiamento Sociale e Sistema di Comunicazione in un'Area in via di Sviluppo*. Roma: RAI Appunto del Servizio Opinioni.

Alberoni, Francesco (1973) *Risultati di un'Indagine Sperimentale sui Contenuti dei Principali Mezzi di Communicazione negli Anni 1969-1970*. Roma: RAI Quaderni del Servizio Opinioni.

Althusser, Louis (1970) 'Idéologie et Appareils Idéologiques d'Etat' *La Pensée*, 151: 3-38.

Bechelloni, Giovanni (ed.) (1980) *TV ed Elezioni Europee 1979. Ricerca Comparata nei Nove Paesi della CEE. Il caso Italiano*. Roma: RAI Verifica Programmi Trasmessi.

Bechelloni, Giovanni (ed.) (1982) *Il Mestiere di Giornalista*. Napoli: Liguori.

Bechelloni, Giovanni (1984) 'Le Tre Televisioni. Limiti e Porteri della TV', *Problemi dell'Informazione*, 2: 151-68.

Bettetini, G., F. Casetti, P. Fabbri, S. Fuà, A. Lombezzi and M. Wolf (1977) *Contributi Bibliografici ad un Progetto di Ricerca sui Generi Televisivi*. Roma; RAI Appunto del Servizio Opinioni.

Blumler, Jay G. (1978) 'Purposes of Mass Communications Research: A Transatlantic Perspective', *Journalism Quarterly*, 2: 219-30.

Braga, G., C. Cipolli, E. Mascilli Migliorini and E. Monti Civelli (1982) *Accostarsi al Quotidiano*. Torin: ERI.

Buonanno, M. (1983) *Cultura di Massa ed Identità Femminile*. Torino: ERI.

Casetti, Francesco (ed.) (1984) *Un'altra volta ancora*. Torino: ERI.

Cesareo, Giovanni (1974) *La Televisione Sprecata*. Milano: Feltrinelli.

Cesareo, Giovanni (1978) 'La Nuova Serie di IKON' *IKON*, 1 (2): 7-16.

Cohen-Séat, Gilbert (1946) *Essai sur les principes d'une philosophe du cinema*. Paris.

De Lillo, Antonio (1971) *L'Analisi del Contenuto*. Bologna: Il Mulino.

Eco, Umberto (1964) *Apocalittici ed Integrati*. Milano: Bompiani.

Eisermann, G. and S. Acquaviva (1971) *La Montagna del Sole*. Milano: Comunità.

Enzensberger, Hans M. (1970) 'Constituents of a Theory of the Media', *New Left Review*, 64.

Greimas, Algirdas J. (1970) *Du sens*. Paris: Le Seuil.

Grossi, G., P. Mancini and G. Mazzoleni (1984) *Guigno 1983: Campagna Elettorale*. Roma: RAI Verifica Programmi Trasmessi.

Grossi, Giorgio (ed.) (1984) *La RAI sotto Analisi*. Torino: ERI.

Livolsi, Marino (ed.) (1969) *Comunicazioni e Cultura di Massa*. Milano: Hoepli.

Luhmann, Niklas (1971) *Politische Planung*. Opladen: Westdeuscher Verlag GMBH.

Mancini, Paolo (1985) *Videopolitica, Telegiornali in Italia e in USA*. Torino: ERI.

Mascilli Migliorini, Enrico (1983) 'Gli Studi sulle Comunicazioni di Massa in Italia dal dopoguerra ad oggi (1945–1982)', *Sociologia della Comunicazione*, 4: 113–37.

Metz, Christian (1974) *Film Language: A Semiotics of the Cinema*. New York: OUP.

Morcellini, M., F. Avallone and D. Ronci (1981) *Terrorismo e TV: Italia, Gran Bretagna, Germania Occidentale*. Roma: RAI Verifica Programmi Trasmessi.

Rositi, Franco (1970) *L'Analisi del Contenuto come Interpretazione*. Roma: RAI Quaderni del Servizio Opinioni.

Rositi, Franco (1978) *Informazione e Complessità Sociale*. Bari: De Donato.

Rositi, Franco (1982) *I Modi dell'Argomentazione e l'Opinione Pubblica*. Torino: ERI.

Statera, Gianni (1972) *Società e Comunicazioni di Massa*. Palermo: Palumbo.

Wolf, Mauro (ed.) (1982) *Tra Informazione ed Evasione: i Programmi Televisivi di Intrattenimento*. Roma: RAI Verifica Programmi Trasmessi.

6

POPULAR CULTURE

Rafael Roncagliolo

"Culture" and "popular" are both debatable terms, but an enormous amount of scholarly work in Latin America falls under this topic. In fact, there is even a journal produced by the University of Minnesota-Morris in the United States called *Studies in Latin American Popular Culture*. A newsletter, *Materiales para la Comunicacion Popular* (Materials for Popular Communication), published quarterly by the Centro de Estudios sobre Cultura Transnacional (Center of Transnational Cultural Studies) in Lima, connects more than a thousand groups in this region of the Western Hemisphere devoted to popular communication.

Three basic features characterize Latin American production of culture. First, the political and academic spheres walk hand in hand. This research can only be understood from a perspective of the type applied by Alvin Gouldner (1970) and Perry Anderson (1976) to Western sociology and Marxism—due to the social organization of intellectual practice and because of historical background and context—have increasingly taken refuge in universities. In contrast—yet for similar reasons—Latin American production yields an opposite result. Research

takes root in political life; its topics, inquiries and analyses respond to non-academic needs. It is no mere coincidence that Latin American researchers exchange, through time, academic roles with political ones. Three examples illustrate this phenomenon: Paulo Freire headed the Brazilian literacy campaign under Goulart's administration and was then jailed and expatriated; Augusto Salazar Bondy after fruitful intellectual work on cultural identity assumed public responsibilities with the Peruvian government in carrying out educational reform; and Nestor Garcia Canclini, Argentinian intellectual, developed most of his scholarship while exiled in Mexico.

The second feature concerns institutional frameworks. In Latin America, universities are not the sole habitat of intellectual production. Political changes in recent decades have affected the university and the labor market in such a manner that they spawned a wave of research centers. These centers are non-profit associations, generally of a private nature and nearly always independent, which tend to obtain foreign financing and carry out quite original lines of intellectual work.

These centers are not federations of isolated researchers, each covering its own topic. Rather, they are think tanks, exchange groups in continual dialogue. This is the

Mr. Roncagliolo directs the Centro de Estudios sobre Cultura Transnacional in Lima, Peru.

From Rafael Roncagliolo, "Popular Culture," *Critical Studies in Mass Communication*, Vol. 3, pp. 230-235. Copyright © 1986 by Speech Communication Association. Reprinted by permission.

third feature to be mentioned—the highly gregarious, dialogic and collective nature of Latin American research. Very few individual researchers work on their own. For this same reason, scientific seminars and meetings within the region are not summaries of many individual papers. On the contrary, the meetings tend to be small with few papers submitted, but with extensive discusison.

This gregarious nature results in a trade union attitude. Latin American researchers perceive themselves as workers sharing collective interests. Thus a Latin American Association of Researchers in Communication has emerged, as well as two commissions of the Latin American Council of Social Sciences (CLASCO)[1] concerned with the topic of communication and culture.

Historical Overview

A list of the historical factors which have influenced research on culture and communications since its appearance two decades ago, among other things must include the following:

1. A form of conscience has been strengthened which opposes national popular culture (in the sense defined by Gramsci) to cultural imperialism. There has been resistance to cultural transnationalization since the 1960s, when transnational culture corporations (e.g., news, advertising, cinema, television, music companies) started their big expansion.

2. Related to this resistance has been the increase of Latin American participation within the Third World block, especially in the Movement of Non-Aligned Countries. During the 1960s, Latin America was included with the Afro-Asiatic nations in demanding economic sovereignty along with political sovereignty. In 1973 the summit conference of non-aligned countries in Algiers introduced the concept of information colonialism and with it the idea of cultural sovereignty.

3. There is a concern for democratically regulating the culture industry through National Policies on Communication and Culture which secure participation of con-

sumers in the production and circulation of messages. Concepts like participatory research, conscientization, alternative communication and many others are developed as a consequence. These concepts point to a type of reflection intending to walk alongside everyday experience.

4. A whole series of national political processes instituted by governments to gain support for popular cultural expressions have been attempted (Goulart in Brazil, Velasco Alvarado in Peru, Torrijos in Panama, Campora in Argentina, Allende in Chile, etc.). These governments to different degrees, however, have been followed by highly repressive regimes in which work on the cultural base and microinstruments of communication are strongly resisted. But the trauma has stimulated reflection on important theoretical issues and on political strategies for organizing popular movements. This critical self-reflection has led to the recognition that science and action have paid insuffi cient attention to the problem of culture. A total reformulation which brings culture into adequate perspective has taken place throughout Latin America. Interest in Gramsci and in Jose Carlos Mariategui—a Peruvian Marxist who died in 1930 and who successfully linked politics and trade unionism with press and culture—are two examples.

Contemporary Currents

Gramsci and Mariategui are just antecedents which help us trace the present interest in popular culture. But if we had to define the starting point of the contemporary current we must go to Paulo Freire.

Freire's thought took shape during the fifties and early sixties when he developed his method of adult education in the Brazilian northeast, the country's poorest region. Freire (1963) published in the Universidade de Recife's magazine his "Conscientizacao e Alfabetizacao: Uma nova visao do processo." It became the prolific starting point of the stream of popular culture developing in Latin America during the last two decades.

Following an especially sharp commentator on Freire, Venicio Artur de Lima (1981), we should stress that the power of Freire's work results from (a) its renewal and enlargement of the cultural approach to communications; (b) its establishing a balance between communication and education at the philosophical as well as the social level, since both are ways of legitimation and/or socialization par excellence; and (c) its moving away from patterns of cultural dependence. Actually, Freire (1959) had received his doctorate in the History and Philosophy of Education with a thesis on "Education and the Brazilian Reality." Freire, a radical Catholic activist, created a literacy method whereby reading and writing abilities could be developed within forty hours. Even more important, through literacy people could gain an awareness of their social condition. Hence, it was not surprising that after the military coup of 1964, the army invaded the Service of Cultural Expansion of the University of Recife, and Freire spent 70 days in prison. After his imprisonment he found refuge in the Bolivian Embassy and, after the military coup in that country, he took asylum in Chile. This is a normal route which illustrates once again the identification between intellectual and politician so common in Latin America.

This approach to popular culture from the standpoint of education and communication occurs simultaneously with the appearance of what we might call the Latin American critical tradition in communication. In the same year as Freire's first work, Venezuelan Antonio Pasquali (1963) published in Caracas "Communicacion y Cultura de Masas." This is also a founding work of research and reflection, a tradition expanded by such outstanding representatives as Luis Ramiro Beltran, Juan Diaz Bordenave, Eleavar Diaz Rangel, Juan Gargurevich, Luis Anibal Gomez, Jose Marques de Melo, Armand Mattelart and Hector Schmucler. It is noteworthy to see how the concern for two-sided communication and culture appears in Pasquali as well as in Freire. Another similarity is that Pasquali also goes into politics, as main propellant of the RATELVE project (Venezuelan Radio Television) which was a

big unsuccessful effort to rationalize radio and television in that country. Pasquali fights against the effects of mass culture, whereas Freire is concerned with unveiling popular culture—the culture of the oppressed, those overwhelmed and suffocated by the mass media. And citing one more connection, Freire and Pasquali both avoid an analysis of communications as a universe closed in itself. From both origins there is a multidisciplinary approach. Educators, philosophers and historians subsequently have converged on the topic.

Freire, Pasquali and several others have laid the foundations for popular culture analysis as an answer to a range of questions about cultural imperialism, underdevelopment, and alienation. In this manner, culture is no longer the hodgepodge of economics and other social sciences; it becomes an object of analysis in its own right. Thus, many Latin American social scientists in the seventies turned to cultural problems in general and popular culture in particular.

Probably it is in Brazil where reflection and practical experiences of all types flourish: in the favelas, in the nanica (small) press, in cord literature, in the theater, and so forth. Octavio Ianni's book (1979) is a classic of the general type analysis, for instance, which treats culture in its economic, political, and military context. On the other side, it is worth mentioning Frei Clarencio Neotti's edition of the book Comunicacao e Consciencia Critica (1979) which gathers accounts of concrete experiences. This book presents work carried out in small groups, in church based communities, in cooperatives and also in what is known as the critical reading of messages. In this type of task, receivers are helped in unveiling meta-meanings and informational and ideological biases of the messages transmitted by the media. It is a rudimentary semantic-structural analysis made in groups with extraordinary practical results.

Of course, studies of popular culture are constantly changing. One useful technique has been recovering oral history as a way of maintaining the collective memory of communities. For instance, there are group interviews on the history of the marginal populations (*barriadas* [quarters]), when the invasion took place, and how neighborhood organizations occurred. Once more, research is linked to pedagogy, to communication (small, simple newspapers are edited, loudspeakers are used, and sometimes radio programs), and to organization. Many research centers in Chile, Peru, and Costa Rica are at the same time promotion centers, where this relationship between research and action develops.

On the other hand, communication researchers as their careers became more professional in the 1970s tended to privilege such national and international topics as national communication policies; international news, advertising, and television; and new technologies of information. By the end of the decade terms like alternative, horizontal, and participatory communication entered the vocabulary. But communication was still considered a closed space. This restriction was only overcome when communication terminology was replaced by cultural terminology, and communication topics were considered as an element of the culture industry and the arena of ideological confrontations.

Probably the most relevant author for the contemporary encounter between communication and culture is Nestor Garcia Canclini. His book (1982) provides a global structure for situating the problems of popular culture and its relationship—of contradiction, complementarity, juxtaposition, and so forth—with mass and transnational culture. Canclini supplies specific empirical research where this documentary evidence is tested.

In the same year, by way of illustration, publications appeared in Latin America based on a symposium held in the Catholic University of Sao Paulo (including such authors as Valle, Weffort, Bosi Wanderly, Cinira M., Beisiegel, Garcia, Monteiro, Alves, Queiroz, Ianni, and Chau). In addition, Aldolfo Colombres (1982) edited a book of articles by Rodolfo Stavenhagen, Mario Margulis, Guillermo Bonfil Batalla, Jas Reuter, Eduardo Galeano, Adolfo Colombres and Amilcal Cabral. The Consejo

Latinoamericano de Ciencias Sociales (CLASCO) and Centro de Estudios y Promocion del Desarrollo (DESCO) in Lima published pieces by Fox, Schmucler, Terrero, Munizaga, Gonzaga Motta, Peirano, Capriles, Fernandez, and Martinez. Anibal Quijano's book (1982) was edited also in Lima. Most of the names may be unknown to the non-Latin American reader, but among them we find some of the most outstanding social scientists of the region. This listing of authors proves that the topic has definitely arrived in the region to stay.

New Tendencies

From here on, what will happen with the study of communication and popular culture? In our opinion it is now facing new fundamental problems that enrich the problematic and put it farther away from the previous perspective in which there existed an autonomous alternative communication, micromedia, and popular circuits of communication that demanded top priority from researchers and politicians. Maybe 1985 was the year in which the jump became more obvious, as illustrated by two seminars during this time.

The first one took place in the suburbs of Santiago, Chile. Its topic was "Cultural Policies in the Transition to Democracy in South America: The Cases of Argentina, Brazil, Chile, Peru and Uruguay." The meeting was the outcome of a joint initiative of Sociedade Brasileira de Estudos Interdisciplinares da Comunicacao (INTERCOM) of Brazil, Centro de Indagación y Expresión Cultural y Artistics (CENECA) of Chile. Also participating in the meeting was the Centro Latinoamericano de Economia Humana (CLAEH) of Uruguay, and the Grupo de Estudios y Desarrollo (GREDES) and the Centro de Estudios sobre Cultura Transnacional (IPAL), both in Peru. This seminar served to regain the importance of culture to rebuild and strengthen democracy. Discussions developed around an unpublished text of Jose Joaquin Brunner (1985b) which outlines the matrix lines, or to put it in other words, the map of areas to be considered when talking about a democratic cultural policy. As is clearly appreciated, the topic itself (democratic cultural policies in transition) arises from the political context of present day South America, with the fall of military regimes in Argentina, Bolivia, Uruguay and Brazil. The relationship between culture and democracy is a relevant line of research for the near future.

The second seminar was organized by the Instituto para America Latina (IPAL) and was held in Bogota in June 1985. The work there centered around an unpublished text of Nestor Garcia Canclini, "Transnational Culture Versus Popular Cultures: Theoretical-Methodological Foundations for Research" (1985). At this Bogota meeting, the second line of future concern took shape: how to systematically research the existing complex contradictions between transnational culture, mass culture and popular culture? How is research on mass media redefined within the cultural sphere?

It is necessary to stress that in Bogota, the main document criticizing Nestor Garcia Canclini's text was Brunner's (1985a) which gives an idea of the ongoing dialogue social researchers maintain in Latin America. In the Bogota seminar, Jesus Martin Barbero submitted a paper (1985) also; he is presently researching the production and consumption of soap operas in Latin America. Barbero, Garcia Canclini, and Brunner represent probably the main lines of research on popular culture at the moment.

We are stressing these new tendencies because they mean a revival of the main concerns of their founders two decades ago. We have returned—with more experience and after many defeats—to the starting point. In the interim, a divorce occurred between concern for big international themes and enchantment with small media. National communication structures, communication policies (which always exist implicitly or explicitly), and, above all, the culture were disregarded. During that interim, consideration was given to media democratization and to the usage of the media for democracy, while overlooking ownership, financing, statism, and so forth. In all this, there were victories of sophistry over research, of accusation over explanation, and of naivete over science. It is very important to formulate this precisely because here in Latin America research is and will continue to be what it has always been: a form of social commitment.

NOTE

[1]The following is an alphabetical list of Spanish and Portugese acronyms and their referents which are used in this essay:

CENECA   Centro de Indagacion y Expresion Cultural y Artistica (Center of Cultural and Artistic Research and Expression).

CLAEH   Centro Latinamericano de Economia Humana (Latin American Center of Human Economy).

CLASCO   Consejo Latinamericano de Ciencias Sociales (Latin American Council of Social Sciences).

DESCO   Centro de Estudios y Promocion del Desarrollo (Center of Study and Promotion of Development).

GREDES   Grupo de Estudios y Desarrollo (Study and Development Group).

INTERCOM   Sociedade Brasiliera de Estudos Interdisciplinares da Comunicacao (Brazilian Society of Interdisciplinary Study of Communication).

IPAL   Instituto para America Latina (Institute for Latin America).

RATELVE   Radio Televisión Venezuela (Radio Television Venezuela).

REFERENCES

Anderson, P. (1976). *Considerations on western Marxism*. London: Newleft Book LTD.

Barbero, J. M. (1985, June). *La comunicación desde la cultura: Crisis de lo nacional y emergenicade lo popular* [Cultural communication: National crisis and popular emergency]. Paper presented at the Latin American Seminar on Transnational Culture, Popular Cultures and Cultural Policies, Bogota, Colombia.

Brunner, J. J. (1985a, June). *La comunicación desde la cultura: Crisis de lo nacional y emergenica de lo popular* [Cultural communication: National crisis and popular emergency]. Paper presented at the Latin American Seminar on Transnational Cultures, Popular Cultures and Cultural Policies, Bogota, Colombia.

Brunner, J. J. (1985b). *Políticas culturales para la democracia* [Cultural politics for democracy]. Paper presented to the International Seminar on Cultural Policies in Transition to Democracy in South America, Santiago, Chile.

Colombres, A. (Ed.). (1982). *La cultura popular* [Popular culture]. Mexico City, Mexico: Premia.

Freire, P. (1959). *Educacao e atualidade Brasileira* [Education and the Brazilian reality]. Unpublished doctoral dissertation. University of Recife, Brazil.

Freire, P. (1963, April-May-June). Conscientizacao e alfabetizacao: Umo nova visao do processo [Understanding literacy: A new vision of process]. *Revista de Cultura da Universidade do Recife, 4*, 5-23.

Garcia Canclini, N. (1982). *Las culturas populares en el capitalismo* [Popular culture and capitalism]. Mexico City, Mexico: Siglo XXI.

Garcia Canclini, N. (1985, June). *Cultura transnacional y culturas populares: Bases teórico-methodologicas para la investigacion* [Transnational culture versus popular cultures. Theoretical-methodological foundations for research]. Paper presented at the Latin American Seminar on Transnational Culture, Popular Cultures and Cultural Policies, Bogota, Colombia.

Gouldner, A. (1970). *The coming crisis of western sociology*. New York: Basic Books.

Ianni, O. (1979). *Imperialisimo e cultura* [Imperialism and culture]. Rio de Janeiro, Brazil: Vozes.

Lima, V. A. de. (1981). *Comunicacao e cultura: As idéias de Paulo Freire* [Communication and culture: The ideas of Paulo Freire]. Rio de Janeiro, Brazil: Paz e Terra.

Neotti, C. (Ed.). (1979). *Comunicacao e consciencia critica* [Communication and critical consciousness]. Sao Paulo, Brazil: Edicoes Loyola.

Pasquali, A. (1963). *Comunicacion y cultura de masas* [Communication and mass culture]. Caracas, Venezuela: Monte Avila.

Quijano, A. (1982). *Dominación y cultura* [Domination and culture]. Lima, Peru: Mosca Azul.

7

HISTORICAL TRENDS IN RESEARCH ON CHILDREN AND THE MEDIA 1900-1960

Ellen Wartella and Byron Reeves

*Similar questions have been asked about "effects"
as each new medium appeared on the scene, and
precursors of current concerns with developmental
and social factors were found in the period of
the most research on media and children—the 1930s.*

For the past several years, scholars of mass communication have reflected on the history of American media research and found it lacking. Gerbner, for instance (26), has noted that the "received history" of mass communication research "should not be taken literally." Rowland (64) has argued for a revision of early American media research history and a recovery of the cultural studies traditions that predate the era of Paul Lazarsfeld and the Columbia school. And Chaffee and Hochheimer (8) were critical of the dogma that followed from the political communication studies of the 1940s.

This article is an attempt to address questions about the history of mass communication research in the United States by examining a particular research domain, that of media effects on children. Our study is part of a larger ongoing analysis of the history of public controversy about media effects on children and youth.

A major thesis of our project is that the traditional history of media effects research is biased toward considerations of public opinion, propaganda, public affairs, and voting. As embodied in basic textbooks, this history can be outlined as follows. Earliest concerns about the mass media at the turn of the century and through the 1920s and early 1930s took the form of the direct effect or "hypodermic needle" model of media impact. The latter term, coined by political scientist Harold

Ellen Wartella is Research Associate Professor, Institute of Communications Research, University of Illinois at Urbana-Champaign. Byron Reeves is Professor, Mass Communication Research Center, School of Journalism and Mass Communication, University of Wisconsin-Madison. Support for Wartella's participation was provided by an Arnold O. Beckman research award from the University of Illinois.

From the *Journal of Communication*, 1985; 35(2): 118-33. © 1985 *Journal of Communication*. Reprinted by permission.

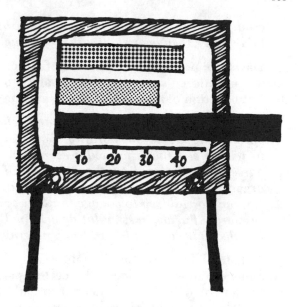

Lasswell during his analysis of World War I propaganda techniques, reflects an assumption that messages have a direct and undifferentiated impact on individuals. In the 1940s, Lasswell's ideas were challenged by studies that questioned the ability of media to influence directly important political decisions. What little influence was found was thought to operate through opinion leaders who in turn influenced others. This idea about indirect effects was crystallized in the "two-step flow" theory and was applied to other areas of media content, most notably fashion, product choices, and movie attendance (38). The research characterized a trend toward practical and applied communication research that looked at immediate short-term effects of messages for the benefit of communication administrators in advertising, public relations, and government information campaigns (39).

There are many contexts in which this history has been recounted (6), although most discussions preface current research in all media effects areas (e.g., 39). Moreover, even scholars who are critical of the mainstream of media effects research, such as Gitlin (27) and Rowland (63), recite essentially the same history, although for the purposes of uncovering the roots of administrative emphasis. Consequently, it is important to examine the accuracy of this received view.

With the development of each modern means of storytelling—books, newspapers, movies, radio, comics, and television—social debates regarding their effects have recurred. A prominent theme in all these debates has been a concern with media's impact on youth, a concern which in fact predates the modern era. Plato's *Republic* (58) warned about storytellers:

Children cannot distinguish between what is allegory and what isn't, and opinions formed at that age are usually difficult to eradicate or change; it is therefore of the utmost importance that the first stories they hear shall aim at producing the right moral effect.

Davis (16) noted the prominence of issues surrounding the impact of media on children's morality in an analysis of popular arguments about the introduction of film, radio, and television into American society:

A major attack on movies, radio and television involved the influence of the media on morality. Both sides (opponents and proponents) agreed that the media exerted a moral influence. The disagreements centered on the direction of that influence. Attackers argued that the media undermined conventional systems of morality, caused children to engage in illicit sexual adventure and were a primary influence in stimulating criminal lessons and might be used to substitute for real life in learning ethical principles (p. 142).

Although much of the literature has been lost to contemporary students of television effects, the earlier part of the twentieth century was a time of active and substantial research on children and youth. In this article we review this early research and examine how well it fits the received history of mass communication research.

We have three major points. First, the traditional history of American mass communication research, whatever its faults and biases, does not describe scholarship about children and media. The study of media effects on youth has developed independently of the broader media effects tradition. Second, the origin of research about children lies in concern expressed by the public about each medium as it was introduced. Public debate helped shape research agendas—at least with respect to topics—rather than research shaping public concerns or policy. Third, arguments about twentieth-century media have recurred throughout the century. Although the expression of concern highlights novel attributes of each medium, the bases of objections and promises have been similar.

> *Although the period from 1900 to 1940 has been labeled the "direct effects era," one in which media were thought to have a direct and undifferentiated impact on all audience members, this is not the case for research on children and media.*

Some histories suggest that the "direct effects" model derives from learning theory and simple stimulus-response models in behavioristic psychology (39, 40). Yet the best-known research from this era contradicts a direct effects conclusion. The 1933 Payne Fund studies—twelve volumes of research conducted by the most prominent psychologists, sociologists, and educators of the time—represent a detailed look at the effects of film on such diverse topics as sleep patterns, knowledge about foreign cultures, attitudes about violence, and delinquent behavior. These studies have not often been cited in the last 25 years, despite the fact that they represent a research enterprise comparable to the 1972 Surgeon General's Committee on Television and Violence. But at the time the Payne studies generated significant press attention, academic review, and critical comment, and were the basis of recommendations for government action on what the authors believed were significant social problems.

A major conclusion of the report was that the same film would affect children differently depending on each child's age, sex, predispositions, perceptions, social environment, past experiences, and parental influence. In this sense, the report was similar to the most current summaries of research about children and television. Further, the effects were said to be conditional on whether the criterion concerns were behaviors, attitudes, emotions, or knowledge about people and events. For example, Blumer's study of *Movies, Delinquency and Crime* (5) concluded that the effects of film on criminal behavior may be diametrically opposed, depending on the diversity of themes presented and the social milieu, attitudes, and interests of the observer.

Although Blumer's contingencies were largely sociological, the conclusions of several other researchers involved affective and psychological differences. Dysinger and Ruckmick (19) studied emotional reactions and concluded, based on a physiologic measure, that children varied widely in emotional stimulation. They suggested that age differences in response were caused by varied abilities to comprehend information on the screen. For example, young children tended not to understand the romantic scenes to which adolescents responded enthusiastically.

Cognitive variables received similar attention elsewhere in the Payne Fund volumes. In a study about learning from film, Holoday and Stoddard (33) focused on information retention as a function of grade in school. Not only did they look at individual differences in relation to long- and short-term effects, but they examined retention in relation to specific message content, thereby foreshadowing research to come a half-century later. The authors concluded that action was remembered best when it was about sports, action, and crime, when the information had an emotional component, and when the action occurred in a familiar background such as home or school. Such attention to age differences can be found in research on film attendance conducted prior to the Payne Fund studies, such as a 1917 survey of children's leisure activities (49) and Mitchell's (50) 1929 survey of Chicago children's attendance and reactions to films.

Nor is it true that the logic of this research depended on stimulus-response models. There are several different meanings for the phrase "stimulus-response," each with different theoretical assumptions, but none applies to the research about children. One definition links stimulus-response with a strict behavioristic notion of reinforcement and a scientific philosophy that ignores what cannot be objectively observed—namely, mental concepts. As Katz and Lazarsfeld (38) commented about the scheme with which media research began, this idea was "that of the omnipotent media, on the one hand, sending forth the message, and the atomized masses, on the other hand, waiting to receive it—and nothing in-between" (p. 20). Even though this conception was not explicitly pro-behaviorist, it still implied that intervening mental processes were irrelevant. Such a conclusion is clearly not applicable to the Payne Fund studies or to writing earlier in the century. In fact, the Blumer studies of movies and criminal behavior were the only research in the Payne series to measure behavior; the remainder of the research dealt with mental concepts assumed to intervene between exposure and effect. The psychologists and educators on the Payne committee studied ideas and factual learning (34), social attitudes (56), emotions (19), sleep patterns (60), and moral development (12).

A cognitive orientation was not new even in 1933, however. An important book by Hugo Munsterberg (52), published in 1916, had also focused on mental processes. The author was one of the first laboratory psychologists and a student of Wilhelm Wundt, the acknowledged father of experimental psychology and an avowed introspectionist. Munsterberg devoted the first half of his book to comments on mental attention, memory, imagination, and emotions.

Nor is it true that the Payne Fund studies were anomalous in the 1930s. Other research of that era similarly was concerned with how children use and are affected by the media. Eisenberg (20), for instance, conducted the first major study of radio's effects on child audiences, surveying over 3,000 New York children and their parents. In addition to examining the frequency of radio listening and children's preferences for radio programs, he assessed the impact of radio on children's factual learning about the world, attitudes, imitation of radio characters' language and behavior, and requests for advertised products.

In short, the pre-1940 period included study of cognitive concepts, attention to developmental differences in children's use of media, and a focus on children's knowledge of the world, their attitudes and values, and their own moral conduct. Although the commentators felt that media effects could be powerful, they also recognized that other factors, such as the child's developmental level or social class, could modify the media's impact. It is difficult to find evidence of the "hypodermic needle" model of media effects in pre-1940 studies of children and media.

> *Nor, as is commonly assumed, did theorizing*
> *about media effects on children in the period*
> *1940–1960 follow an "indirect effects" model.*

For example, Herzog's 1941 review of research on children's radio listening habits has a developmental emphasis in demonstrating age differences in children's attraction to and preference for radio programming (31). She also notes evidence of children's direct learning of information and standards of conduct from radio. Later radio studies in the 1940s examined a wide range of "effects," such as the influence of radio drama in producing differential emotional reactions in children (17, 18), psychological differences in children's abilities to distinguish between reality and fantasy (35), and the influence of radio on children's school performance (31). The commercial nature of radio was noticed as well. Surveys of mothers documented the appeal of radio ads to children (31) and the effects of premium advertising on children's responses to advertising and product requests (29).

The few studies on children and media related to the Columbia Bureau of Applied Social Research did not use an indirect effects model of media impact on youth. For example, studies by Meine (47) and Wolf and Fisk (72) are noteworthy both for what they include—psychological explanations of media effects—and what they do not—the model of "indirect media effects" most identified with the Columbia school that predicts different effects based on sociological ideas about "opinion leadership" or "multiple steps in information dissemination." Meine (47) found a direct relationship between children's consumption of newspaper and radio news and their knowledge of current affairs, even after controlling for age, sex, and intelligence. Similarly, Wolf and Fisk (72) conducted an extensive study of children and comics that previewed many concepts that would be discussed as new ideas in later television research. Children were thought to progress through three qualitatively different stages of sophistication in their ability to read and understand comics. Parental mediation of media experiences was advocated by almost all mothers, yet few actually prohibited their children from reading the comics.

Attention to questions about use and preference for television programs predominated in the literature of the 1950s, when the "indirect effects" model is said to have become "reified" (28, 63) and when the earliest studies of television influence on children were being conducted. Not only were notions of indirect effects not articulated, however; they were not even implied by the authors. A far more common theme in the 1950s, illustrated by Shayon's 1952 book (67), is a concern with gauging the impact of television, widely thought to have enormous influence on children and labeled by Shayon the new "Pied Piper."

If studies about media and children do not follow the received history of media effects research, then how can the research history be described? It is our contention that emphasis on research topics was influenced by public debate about changing media technologies. That is, as public concerns about film gave way to concern about radio and then television, academic research made corresponding shifts.

Has the quantity of research on a medium changed as popular attention shifted?

Evidence about the relationship between media research and media popularity comes from two sources: (a) a bibliography, compiled by us, of academic studies published between 1900 and 1960 about the effects of media on youth, and (b) statistics about the growth of film, radio, and television as popular entertainment. In the bibliography of published studies we included articles and books that meet three criteria. The reference must have addressed the issue of media effects on children and youth, been written for an academic or professional audience, and been published in the United States. Technical reports and research papers were excluded. The bibliography was compiled from printed and on-line bibliographies and published references on media effects (e.g., 3, 53). The final bibliography contains 242 entries from the period between 1900 and 1960—a time frame corresponding to the introduction of film, radio, and television into American life.

Each study was classified by the type of medium addressed: film, radio, television, print (newspapers, comics, magazines, and reading in general), or cross-media issues (any combination of media effects, such as comparison of radio and print or TV and movies). Five studies of print media and 21 cross-media studies were found. The remaining 216 studies were about electronic media.

Figure 1 shows the number of citations to studies about children between 1900 and 1960. There are three identifiable epochs of research,

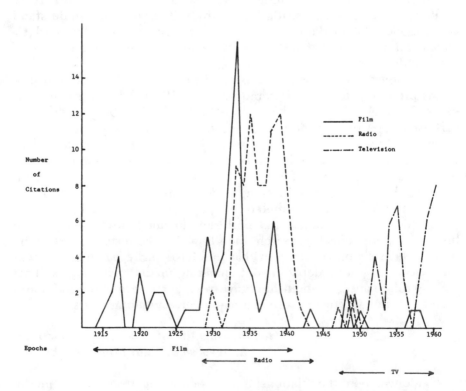

Figure 1: Number of citations about children and film, radio, and television, 1900–1960

one associated with each electronic medium. The film epoch begins in 1904, ends in 1939, and reaches a peak in 1932 during the Payne Fund investigations (9). The radio epoch begins in 1930 and ends just before World War II. There is some overlap in the beginning of the period with the decline of film research. The television epoch, the period most separated from other research, begins in 1949 and builds through 1960, with a one-year lapse in 1957.

Our major emphasis is on variance in research activity *within* each epoch; however, features of the entire distribution are both apparent and counterintuitive. First, the *cumulative* number of studies did not increase monotonically prior to 1960. Most research activity occurred during the 1930s. In fact, two-thirds of the research on children prior to 1960 was completed by 1939. Second, it is clear that the 1940s, a time of active research on politics and persuasion, lacked such activity in the area of children and media.

The three epochs obviously correspond to the introduction and dissemination of the three technologies. The clearest relationship is for television, a medium that came on the market at an identifiable time (about 1948) and diffused rapidly. By 1954, a mere seven years after its introduction, 55 percent of American households had a television set (68). The number of television receivers in use by year is correlated at .82 (n = 13, p < .05) with the number of studies on television and children published each year. The same relationship for the diffusion of radio receivers and radio research is also positive, but smaller (r = .55, n = 15, p < .05). The smallest correlation is between studies of film effects on children and annual film audience data (r = .20, n = 23, n.s.).

Figure 2 shows two time series for each medium—one for the number of research citations and one for the rate of diffusion (number of TV sets, number of radio receivers, and average weekly film audience). Cross-correlations between these two series indicate that the relationship between research activity and media popularity is not simultaneous. For the film epoch, the highest correlation between film audience data and film research is .25, with a positive three-year lag. The lag for television is also three years, when the correlation reaches its highest level of .80. On the other hand, the highest lagged correlation between radio receivers in use and research on radio and children (.63) is reached with a negative six-year lag, suggesting that research on children and radio anticipated the rise in radio's growth.

Unlike the television epoch, the film and radio epochs show a decline in research activity, although audience use of the medium continues. In the case of radio, the number of receivers in use actually grows during the late 1940s and 1950s. All of these lagged correlations, however, are positive and they do not show substantial increases over the correlations matched in time. Although the rise in research interest corresponds to the growth of audiences for film, radio, and television, abatement of the research has no counterpart in diminishing audiences for these media. Rather, the quantity of research shifted as a result of the *growth* of each new medium.

Have researchers addressed the same kinds of questions about the effects of film, radio, and television?

Our review found a progression from early attention to studies of media use to increasing emphasis on issues of physical and emotional harm, and changes in children's knowledge, attitudes, and behaviors. In addition, studies about violence, sex, and advertising recur.

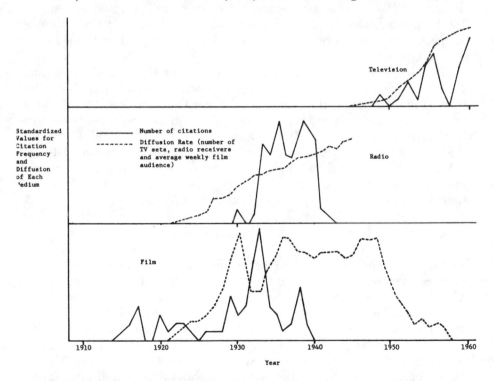

Figure 2: Number of citations about media and youth by diffusion rate for film, radio, and television, 1910–1960

Note: This scale represents the association between citations and diffusion rates. The absolute values cannot be compared because each function represents a different metric, as follows: The number of citations per year ranges from 0 to 16 in 1933 for film, from 0 to 12 in 1935 and 1939 for radio, and from 0 to 8 for television in 1960. The diffusion rate scales for each medium are taken from Sterling and Haight (68). Film audience attendance data begin in 1922, when the average weekly attendance is 40,000 people; it peaks in 1930 and 1946 through 1948, with average weekly attendance at 90,000 people (68, p. 352). Households with radio receivers range from 60,000 in 1922 to a high of 35.9 million in 1947 (68, p. 367). There were 8,000 television sets in use in American homes in 1946; in 1960, 45.7 million homes had TV sets (68, p. 372).

Media use studies are not published exclusively in the earliest part of an epoch, but they are most likely in the years right after a medium's introduction. In the case of film, only a few of the pre-1930 studies in the bibliography (e.g., 25) deal with effects of movies. Most studies are either discussions of the need for children to see wholesome family-oriented programs (e.g., 22, 36, 49, 54, 62, 73) or, beginning in the late 1920s, reports about audience attendance and the type of movies that appeal to children (e.g., 11, 37, 50, 70, 74). Mitchell's (50) examination of children's attendance at Chicago theaters is the best-known early study of children's film use.

Similarly, the earliest studies of radio effects are examinations of children's listening habits and preferences (e.g., 10, 15, 28, 32). Here, too, many of the early studies are catalogues of available radio programs and/or extended discussions (without evidence) of their likely impact on listeners (e.g., 2, 40, 43, 71). A landmark study of children's radio listening and preferences by Eisenberg (20), for which over 3,000 children were surveyed, received the same attention in the subsequent radio literature as the early study of film audiences by Mitchell (50) received in the film literature.

The television literature, too, began with studies of children's use of the medium and preference for different types of programming. The earliest study of television effects in our bibliography (42) is about teenage viewing preferences and is similar to most of the television studies in the early 1950s (e.g., 44, 45, 61, 66). Although what is frequently referenced as the landmark study of the impact of television on children, Schramm, Lyle, and Parker's *Television in the Lives of Our Children* (65), did not appear until 1960, considerable research on TV's impact on knowledge, attitudes, and behavior preceded this study (e.g., 1, 23, 30, 46, 51, 57).

In reviewing these pre-1960 studies, two observations are particularly pertinent. First, there is a surprisingly large scientific literature on children and media, and we continue to discover more, particularly that which precedes the television era. Second, and more important, we are impressed by the overwhelming similarity in the research studies from epoch to epoch, with a new technology substituted as the object of concern. How can we account for these similarities?

One obvious explanation for similarities in research is that earlier studies may have set the agenda for later research.

There is limited evidence that later scientists either attempted to replicate research from an earlier epoch or were at least enough aware of past efforts to cite them in their own work. For instance, radio and film studies may have influenced each other. DeBoer's work on children's emotional responses to radio (17, 18) made frequent reference to the

Dysinger and Ruckmick (19) research on film. Herzog (31), in her review of radio research on children, also cited a number of earlier film studies. The extent to which television research was influenced by the earlier studies of film and radio is far less clear, however. The first studies on television made infrequent reference to earlier media studies on children and youth, and then chiefly to the Payne Fund studies (see, e.g., 65, 66).

There is also evidence from cross-media studies that direct comparison between radio and movie effects on children was a popular topic only in the 1940s (24, 34, 41, 48, 59, 69, 75). Moreover, we found only four people who conducted research that spanned at least two decades and that addressed different media. Rather, the bibliography suggests that *different* scholars conducted the research about each medium and that these people came from diverse disciplines: psychology, sociology, education, communications, and social work.

It may be, however, that earlier research, particularly the Payne Fund studies, set future agendas even though they were not cited. In particular, the strategies for studying media as a social problem that surrounded the Payne Fund may have had an influence on the later efforts of both organized commissions and individual researchers. In order to understand such an influence, we need to locate the Payne Fund studies within their social and cultural milieu and ask why the academics who conducted these studies defined media's influences as they did. As Rowland (63) has pointed out, the Payne Fund researchers chose to study film impact in terms of film content, film use, film's short-term effects, and approaches to teaching children how to use film more selectively. Charters's overview of the studies (9) acknowledges that they ignored questions about the structure of the film industry and the larger institutional arrangements that gave rise to the film culture of the United States in the 1920s. This is not to imply, however, that the Payne Fund researchers were uninterested in changing the film industry. As Charters concludes:

> *Certainly the problem of the movies and children is so important and critical that parents, producers, and the public must willingly and intelligently cooperate to reach some happy solution. The producers occupy the key position. The public at present must take, within the limits of the censorship of the states, whatever pictures are made. . . . The simple obligation rests upon the producers who love children to find a way of making the motion picture a beautiful, fascinating, and kindly servant of childhood* (9, p. 63).

Throughout the 1930s, Charters championed the development of films directed to and intended for the juvenile market (see 14) and addressing the particular needs of youth.

What influenced the Payne Fund approach to studying film effects as a social problem? One possibility is the University of Chicago's program on communication. As Pecora (55) has noted, seven of the twelve Payne Fund volumes were written by University of Chicago faculty or former students (4, 5, 9, 12, 13, 14, 55). In addition, authors of two other earlier influential studies, Mitchell (50) and DeBoer (17, 18), received Ph.D.s from the same university. Chicago's commitment to scientific research about visible social problems may have encouraged attention to questions of media's impact on youth.

Precisely how and why the studies were conceptualized as they were, however, is not readily explained. Although the University of Chicago approach to communications studies is frequently identified with symbolic interactionism (63), as represented by Blumer's (4) approach to studying film's influence through the use of life histories, the Chicago school had broader definitions of appropriate research methods and definitions of effects. For instance, Peterson and Thurstone's experimental studies of children's attitudes toward ethnic groups (56) employed some of the earliest interval measures of attitude change. The highly quantitative content analysis of film themes and portrayals by Dale (14), and the survey research of Mitchell (50) and Dale (13), also represent methods identified with the University of Chicago.

In locating effects studies at an individual rather than cultural level and in connecting film portrayals to short-term changes, the Payne Fund studies utilized a definition of "effect" that runs throughout U.S. media research. Some critics have mistakenly suggested that such a definition came from Lazarsfeld's administrative research on radio in the 1940s (see 27, esp. p. 79). That such a definition of media effects both predates Lazarsfeld and appears in a literature widely separate from the "received history" of media effects research suggests that we need to look elsewhere to account for its presence. It is far more likely that such definitions of "effects" were responsive to deeper roots in American social science.

> *Another likely influence of the whole body of research on media and youth is the social reform movement early in the century.*

Rowland (63) locates the roots of media violence research in the progressive era of social reform before World War I. Indeed, throughout the literature on children and media, there is a recurring self-professed interest in addressing what scientists perceive to be public concerns. In the early studies within each epoch, scholars introduced their research with self-conscious acknowledgments of widespread public concern about the influence of media on children (see, e.g., 9, 20, 40, 42, 66). For instance, Eisenberg (20) comments:

> *The popularity of this new pastime [radio] among children has increased rapidly. This new invader of the privacy of the home has*

brought many a disturbing influence in its wake. Parents have become aware of a puzzling change in the behavior of their children. They are bewildered by a host of new problems, and find themselves unprepared, frightened, resentful, helpless (pp. 17–18).

It may be that such public concerns were only one part of a group of middle-class progressive reforms. However, an argument can be made that researchers more specifically directed their inquiries to questions posed by an anxious public composed of worried parents. Theorizing about "effects" at the individual level—how children acquire discrete knowledge and perform discrete behaviors—can be seen as responsive to the questions of parents and teachers about media's impact on "their children."

The roots of this paradigm for media research are not as clear as critics of U.S. media effects research would imply. There are a few glaring exceptions of studies that directly try to examine children's media use for market exploitation (e.g., 7, 29), but it is difficult to see how the research is necessarily tied to the administrative interests of media industries.

In sum, we observe a history much different from the received history of U.S. media effects research, one that is characterized by trends in research epochs that focus on different media and recurring topics. The roots of these trends are not easily characterized and probably reside in an understanding of the nature of public controversy about the adoption of new media technology into American life.

We are not the first to note recurrences in the literature. This is more apparent now that we are at the threshold of yet another set of new communication technologies such as cable and computers. Over thirty years ago Mary Seagoe observed:

Television is the newest addition to the illustrious family of our mass entertainment enthusiasms. We have had dime novels, movies, radio, comics—and now television. Each time we seem to go through the same stages. We remember the alarm raised soon after the advent of the talking picture, which in time gave rise to the Payne Fund studies, which in turn showed that the same movies might either help or hinder growth, reinforce social standards, or teach the techniques of crime, depending upon the person who saw them and the attitudes he took to the seeing. For a while films seemed designed more for children than adults: then when we had examined the matter and learned how to use movies, the alarm died away. The same thing happened with the widespread use of radio, leading to the studies of Eisenberg and others. The same thing went on in relation to the comics. Now we are starting that cycle with television. Whenever there is a new social invention, there is a feeling of strangeness and a distrust of the new until it becomes familiar (66, p. 143).

As we stand at the threshold of research about new technologies, a look back at public controversy and concern about older media is useful both to point out where we have been and to determine how we might proceed in the future. The recurring nature of public concern for and scientific study of media influence on youth thus speaks to our field's responsiveness to the wider social and cultural context of American media.

REFERENCES

1. Banning, E. L. "Social Influences on Children and Youth." *Review of Educational Research* 25, 1955, pp. 36–47.
2. Beuick, M. D. "The Limited Social Effect of Radio Broadcasting." *American Journal of Sociology* 32, January 1927, pp. 615–622.
3. Blum, E. *Basic Books in the Mass Media.* Urbana: University of Illinois Press, 1972.
4. Blumer, H. *Movies and Conduct.* New York: Macmillan, 1933.
5. Blumer, H. and P. M. Hauser. *Movies, Delinquency and Crime.* New York: Macmillan, 1933.
6. Brown, R. "Approaches to Historical Development of Mass Media Studies." In J. Tunstall (Ed.) *Media Sociology: A Reader.* Urbana: University of Illinois Press, 1970, pp. 41–57.
7. Brumbaugh, F. N. "What Effect Does TV Advertising Have on Children?" *Educational Digest* 19, 1954, pp. 32–33.
8. Chaffee, S. and J. L. Hochheimer. "Mass Communication and American Politics: A New Look at the Early Studies." Paper presented to the conference of the International Communication Association, Dallas, Texas, May 1983.
9. Charters, W. W. *Motion Pictures and Youth.* New York: Macmillan, 1933.
10. Child Study Association. "Radio for Children: Parents Listen In." *Child Studies* 10, April 1933, pp. 44–48.
11. Cressey, G. "The Motion Picture as Informal Education." *Journal of Educational Sociology* 7, April 1934, pp. 504–515.
12. Cressey, P. G. and F. M. Thrasher. *Boys, Movies and City Streets.* New York: Macmillan, 1934.
13. Dale, E. *Children's Attendance at Motion Pictures.* New York: Macmillan, 1935.
14. Dale, E. *Content of Motion Pictures.* New York: Macmillan, 1935.
15. Darrow, B. H. "The Child and the Radio." *Parental Education* 4, April 1934, pp. 84–95.
16. Davis, R. "Response to Innovation: A Study of Popular Arguments About New Mass Media." Unpublished Ph.D. dissertation, University of Iowa, 1965.
17. DeBoer, J. J. "Determination of Children's Interests in Radio Drama." *Journal of Applied Psychology* 21, 1937, pp. 456–463.
18. DeBoer, J. J. "Radio and Children's Emotions." *School and Society* 50, 1939, pp. 290–295.
19. Dysinger, W. S. and C. A. Ruckmick. *The Emotional Responses of Children to the Motion Picture Situation.* New York: Macmillan, 1933.
20. Eisenberg, A. L. *Children and Radio Programs.* New York: Columbia University Press, 1936.

21. Ervy, H. "TV Murder Causes Bad Dreams." *Film World* 8, 1952, p. 247.
22. Ferguson, I. M. "Movies for Children." *Minnesotan*, August 1917, pp. 30–31.
23. Feshbach, S. "The Catharsis Hypothesis and Some Consequences of Interaction with Aggressive and Neutral Play Objects." *Journal of Personality* 24, 1956, pp. 449–462.
24. Frank, J. *Comics, Radio and Movies and Children.* New York: Public Affairs Office, 1949.
25. Geiger, J. R. "Effects of Motion Pictures on the Mind and Morals of the Young." *International Journal of Ethics* 34, October 1923, pp. 69–83.
26. Gerbner, G. "The Importance of Being Critical—In One's Own Fashion." *Journal of Communication* 33(3), Summer 1983, pp. 355–362.
27. Gitlin, T. "Media Sociology: Dominant Paradigm." *Theory and Society* 6, 1978, pp. 205–253.
28. Gruenberg, S. M. "Radio and the Child." *Annals of the American Academy of Political and Social Science*, June 1935, pp. 123–130.
29. Grumbine, E. E. *Reaching Juvenile Markets.* New York: McGraw-Hill, 1938.
30. Haines, W. H. "Juvenile Delinquency and Television." *Journal of Social Theory* 1, 1955, pp. 192–198.
31. Herzog, H. *Children and Their Leisure Time Listening to the Radio.* New York: Radio Council on Children's Programs, 1941.
32. Hewes, R. K. "A Study of 1,000 High School Listeners." *Education on the Air: Fourth Yearbook.* Columbus: Ohio State University, 1933, pp. 326–329.
33. Holaday, P. W. and G. D. Stoddard. *Getting Ideas from the Movies.* New York: Macmillan, 1933.
34. Jersild, A. T. "Radio and Motion Pictures." *Thirty-Eighth Yearbook for the Study of Education.* Bloomington, Ill.: Public School Publishing Co., 1939.
35. Jersild, A. T. *Child Psychology.* New York: Prentice-Hall, 1940.
36. Johnson, J. S. "Children and Their Movies." *Social Service Review* 6, September 1917, pp. 11–12.
37. Jones, H. E. "Attendance at Movie Pictures as Related to Intelligence and Scholarship." *Parent-Teacher*, March 1928.
38. Katz, E. and P. Lazarsfeld. *Personal Influence.* New York: Free Press, 1955.
39. Klapper, J. *The Effects of Mass Communication.* Glencoe, Ill.: Free Press, 1960.
40. Langworthy, B. F. "More About Children's Programs." *Education by Radio* 3, 1936, p. 26.
41. Lazarsfeld, P. F. "Motion Pictures, Radio Programs, and Youth." In F. Henne, A. Brooks, and E. R. Ersted (Eds.) *Youth, Communication and Libraries.* Chicago: American Library Association, 1949.
42. Lewis, P. "TV and Teenagers." *Educational Screen* 28, 1949, pp. 159–161.
43. Longstaff, H. P. "Effectiveness of Children's Radio Programs." *Journal of Applied Psychology* 20, June 1936, pp. 264–279.
44. Lyness, P. "The Place of the Mass Media in the Lives of Boys and Girls." *Journalism Quarterly* 29, 1952, pp. 43–54.
45. Maccoby, E. E. "Why Do Children Watch Television?" *Public Opinion Quarterly* 18, 1954, pp. 239–244.
46. Meerlo, J. A. "Television Addiction and Reactive Empathy." *Journal of Nervous and Mental Diseases*, 1954, pp. 290–291.
47. Meine, F. J. "Radio and the Press Among Young People." In P. Lazarsfeld and F. Stanton (Eds.) *Radio Research.* New York: Duell, Sloan and Pearce, 1941.
48. Merry, F. K. and R. V. Merry. "Children's Interest in the Radio and Movies." *From Infancy to Adolescence.* New York: Harper Brothers, 1940, pp. 236–256.
49. Michael, R. "Better Films." *Child Welfare Magazine* 12, November 1917, pp. 41–42.
50. Mitchell, A. M. *Children and Movies.* Chicago: University of Chicago Press, 1929.
51. Munn, M. "The Effect on Parental Buying Habits of Children Exposed to Children's Television Programs." *Journal of Broadcasting* 2, 1958, pp. 253–258.

52. Munsterberg, H. *The Photoplay*. New York: Appleman, 1916.
53. Murray, J. P. *Television and Youth: 25 Years of Research and Controversy*. Boys Town, Neb.: Boys Town Center, 1980.
54. Nutting, D. B. "Motion Pictures for Children." *The Woman Citizen* 5, November 1920, pp. 659–660.
55. Pecora, N. "Children, Mass Media and the University of Chicago." Paper presented to the Conference on Culture and Communication, Temple University, Philadelphia, 1983.
56. Peterson, R. C. and L. K. Thurstone. *Motion Pictures and the Social Attitudes of Children*. New York: Macmillan, 1933.
57. Pittman, D. "Mass Media and Juvenile Delinquency." In R. J. Roucek (Ed.) *Juvenile Delinquency*. New York: Philosophical Library, 1958, pp. 230–247.
58. *Plato's Republic*. Cambridge: Cambridge University Press, 1966.
59. Preston, M. "Children's Reactions to Movie Horrors and Radio Crime." *Journal of Pediatrics* 19, 1941, pp. 147–168.
60. Renshaw, S., V. L. Miller, and D. P. Marquis. *Children's Sleep*. New York: Macmillan, 1933.
61. Riley, J. W., F. V. Cantwell, and K. F. Muttiger. "Some Observations on the Social Effects of Television." *Public Opinion Quarterly* 13, 1949, pp. 223–234.
62. Rogers, A. and C. Rowland. "Can the Movies Teach?" *Transactions*, 1922, pp. 125–135.
63. Rowland, W. *Politics of TV Violence*. Beverly Hills, Cal.: Sage, 1982.
64. Rowland, W. "Recreating the Past: Problems in Rewriting the Early History of American Communication Research." Paper presented to the conference of the International Association for Mass Communication Research, Prague, September 1984.
65. Schramm, W., J. Lyle, and E. B. Parker. *Television in the Lives of Our Children*. Stanford, Cal.: Stanford University Press, 1960.
66. Seagoe, M. V. "Children's Television Habits and Preferences." *Quarterly of Film, Radio and Television* 6, 1952, pp. 143–152.
67. Shayon, R. L. *Television and Our Children*. New York: Longman, 1952.
68. Sterling, C. H. and T. R. Haight. *The Mass Media: Aspen Institute Guide to Communication Industry Trends*. New York: Praeger, 1978.
69. Sterner, A. P. *Radio, Motion Pictures and Reading Interests: A Study of High School Pupils*. New York: Bureau of Publications, Columbia University, 1947.
70. Sullenger, T. E. "Modern Youth and the Movies." *School and Society*, October 1930, pp. 459–461.
71. Thomas, C. "A Comparison of Interests of Delinquent and Non-Delinquent Boys." *Journal of Juvenile Research* 16, 1932, pp. 310–318.
72. Wolf, K. M. and M. Fisk. "The Children Talk About Comics." In P. Lazarsfeld and F. Stanton (Eds.) *Communications Research 1948–1949*. New York: Harper, 1949.
73. Woodard, A. P. "Motion Pictures for Children." *Social Service Review* 6, September 1917, pp. 10–11.
74. Woodbury, R. F. "Children and Movies." *Survey* 62, May 1929, pp. 253–254.
75. Witty, P., S. Garfield, and W. Brink. "Interests of High School Students in Motion Pictures and the Radio." *Journal of Educational Psychology* 32, 1941, pp. 176–184.

8

AMERICAN TELECOMMUNICATIONS POLICY RESEARCH
Its Contradictory Origins and Influences

Willard D. Rowland

In recent years there has emerged as an offshoot of several disciplines, including communications, a loose, general field of telecommunications policy research. Precisely because the work in this area is so variously rooted — in law, economics, political science, sociology and so forth — it is a field whose contours are quite difficult to map and interpret. Indeed, one might argue that there is as yet no central, coherent set of questions and approaches that could confidently be considered to constitute a clearly identifiable field of telecommunications policy research (Rowland, 1984). Furthermore, it is an area full of many troublesome, fundamental ambiguities and contradictions. It embodies all the recent struggles in North America and Europe about the meanings and roles of science, research, technology and policy-making, and as such it reflects all the socio-cultural and political economic conflicts of values, interests and needs in a rapidly changing, post-industrial, international capitalist information order.

Yet for all its vagaries and contradictions, telecommunications policy research is an area of inquiry which for better or worse has gained some currency in both the academy and applied communications policy-making activities. Increasingly, in the English-speaking, industrialized West, as well as in several other nations, one finds new programmes in university curricula that include courses with 'telecommunications policy' or something similar in their titles. A number of scholars from North America and, to a certain extent, Western Europe have been regular participants in a gathering that,

From Willard D. Rowland, "American Telecommunications Policy Research: Its Contradictory Origins and Influences," *Media, Culture and Society*, Vol. 8, pp. 159-182. Copyright © 1986 by Sage Publications, Ltd.

for over a decade, has become a spring ritual in the Washington DC area, namely the 'Annual Telecommunications Policy Research Conference'. Increasingly one finds that communication research graduates have arrived alongside attorneys, economists and engineers to hold jobs in government agencies where their responsibilities are to monitor and generate research of various kinds that bears on and even defines the principal telecommunications policy issues.

Given this situation and assuming the need for regular critical reflexivity about the origins and trends of thought across the range of communication and cultural studies, it would seem appropriate to try to say something about those general contours of the research in telecommunications policy. Accordingly, this paper tries to outline a few of the key issues that must be faced as work proceeds in the area. The essay is not so much concerned with defining the field of telecommunications policy research as with trying to take account of those intellectual and structural influences that have tended to shape it and to give it whatever identity it seems variously to invoke.

The origins of communication research

Perhaps the first general point to which attention should be called is the deeper history of communication research and its involvement in public policy deliberations. As I have been at pains to show elsewhere (Rowland, 1983), the growth of a certain style and content of social research in the United States has been directly related to a deep-set pattern of American attitudes toward intellectual activity and about accommodations among public and private interests. From the earliest days of the republic and even well before, during the colonial period, there was a strong tradition of intermixture among moral philosophy, political theory and applied scientific research. The American experience was a child of the Enlightenment and in its particular material forms of expression it was seen as a series of practical experiments to be carried out across the range of human activity and into the future. The constitutional provisions for separation of powers, the emerging American economic structure, the country's developing transportation and communication systems, its various forms of religious organization, and its patterns of education and study were all seen as wide open to testing, tinkering and presumably progressive improvement.

Whether in fact they were all so open and in any way truly

revolutionary is now largely doubtful. But such a conclusion, albeit accurate, may also be beside the point for our argument here, for what has always been crucial in the American experience is that such matters were *felt* to be open and accessible to change. The ideology of liberal progress has always been central to the American imagination, and it has been nowhere as apparent as in the expectations for science and the role of an applied academy. From the era of Franklin and Jefferson to the programmes of the Great Society there is an unbroken string of concrete examples of widespread, authoritative faith in the power and positive influence of the natural, engineering and social sciences and in the need for co-operation between government, private enterprise and academic interests in pursuing the necessary material, social and political experiments. The way in which we came to develop and evaluate social research was clarified and reinforced in various aspects of the Morrill Land Grand Act of 1862, the anti-trust and interstate commerce legislation of the 1880s and 1890s, the language and ethnography research for the Bureau of Indian Affairs, and the mobilization, planning and intelligence testing needs of the first world war.

These well-rehearsed predispositions and social arrangements were crucial in shaping the terms under which the dominant forms of communication and policy research would initially emerge. By the time of the post-first world war rise of radio, the re-expansion of popular film and the full flowering of a commercial press, the patterns of co-operation among state, business and academy were well-developed and particularly close. During the 1920s these patterns were fostered by a growing belief in the several efficacies of scientifically-based professional management, a set of notions embodied in calls by Herbert Hoover and other 'ballyhoo' years leaders for socially responsible 'progressive individualism' among private and public leaders, the practical expression of those ideas in a series of pre- and mid-Depression study commissions whose members were predominantly prominent business and government figures, and proposals by Walter Lippmann and others for various sorts of 'intelligence bureaus' in the government, the academy and business, to help guide public policy in various economic and social affairs (Lyons, 1969: 34–5; Schlesinger, 1957; Steel, 1980: 180–5).

Far from dampening the enthusiasm for the interactions among the public, private and intellectual realms, the Depression, New Deal and second world war experiences only heightened the felt need for such co-operation, so that by the late 1940s the American academy had become closely entwined with the government and vast ranges of private enterprise. Contradicting the ancient mythologies of 'academic freedom', the modern university had become highly entrepreneurial and thoroughly integrated into the contemporary state. It is in this light that one wants to consider the purposes, structures and legacies of such new institutions as Paul Lazarsfeld's Bureau of Applied Social Research at Columbia (1930s) and the several journalism and communication research institutes appearing (1940s and 1950s) at other, often land-grant universities around the country. The marketing and administrative research needs of the various private and public clients served by such bureaux and institutes fit well in the tradition of an applied practical role for the academy, and that much of their work should turn on communications is merely a reflection of the substantial and growing commercial and political interest in the powers and potentials of the modern mass media.

The intellectually debilitating results of this administrative bias in the early days of communication research are becoming increasingly understood (Rowland, 1983; Robinson, 1984). American communication studies became captured early by the most positivistic debates over media effects (direct, indirect, uses and gratification). It let itself be drawn into the politically-loaded mass culture debate, and in the process it forgot or ignored much of its own more interpretative social science and humanistic heritage. In all this work for the clients of Lazarsfeld's Bureau and like institutions, the emerging model of communication was essentially an amalgam of organic and mechanical images, of behaviouristic/stimulus-response and transportation/transmission processes. In these views culture was simply a product of an industrial, commodity manufacturing process, and depending upon one's socio-political outlook these images were acceptable, frightening or, most typically, vaguely disquieting. Again, the acceptance of such models was due in a large part to their emergence in a period particularly interested in the applicability of social science. The economic and international crises during the first half of the century were serious, immediate experiences in the lives of all Americans, and they seemed to threaten much of the material well-being and the spirit of individual freedoms that had been promised for 'the American century'. It would simply be too difficult for the more metaphysical aspects of social science discourse to find prominence in the academy at large, let alone in its application in a field whose emergence was so closely associated with the spread of new waves of applied technology. As a consequence, much of the older, more interesting theoretical explorations of society, culture, language and ideas tended to be ignored in communication research.

This is not to say that the academic debates were ignorant of the richer social science and philosophic traditions. Far from it. Indeed, many of the founders of the American social sciences had studied in the late-nineteenth century continental academies. They were close, knowledgeable students of Weber, Durkheim, Tonnies, and Simmel, among others, and in their various Harvard, Chicago and Columbia manifestations they took note of how their work was rooted in the European efforts to create a formal science of society and in a common interest in explaining the changes associated with industrialism and urbanization. But there was tremendous selectivity in tracing that lineage, as, for instance, in oversimplifying much of the more ambiguous theoretical and methodological characteristics of the European scholars — traditions of inquiry that were not in fact as subject to positivistic empiricism as the American academy (e.g. Parsons, 1964) would try to have it. Furthermore, American social scientists largely ignored other aspects of the European heritage – most notably Marx – and therefore had weak notions about class, power, ideology and economic factors in social analysis. In fact, as with some of their liberal late-nineteenth-century European mentors, there was a tendency to adopt perspectives and techniques of social inquiry that would seek explanations in terms precisely opposed to matters of historical dialectics, economic structures and related social contradictions. Whether or not these programmes of social investigations were consciously anti-radical, they had that effect, and there thus developed in the American social sciences a substantial epistemological naïvety that, in conjunction with their pragmatic tendencies, would prove to restrict the range of inquiry and theoretical sophistication in communication research as it emerged.

To the extent, then, that communication research was beginning to have a bearing on public policy considerations about the media, it was doing so within the confines of a series of all-important intellectual, social and political compromises. In addressing the nature and role of newspapers and modern industrial communication in the early-twentieth-century urban environment, Robert Park, John Dewey and others in the Chicago Schools of sociology and pragmatic philosophy were working within the ethics of a liberal reform progressivism. Genuinely concerned with the well-being of the urban poor (largely eastern and southern European immigrants), their programmes for change and improvement were still rooted in libertarian ideas of individual fulfilment and private enterprise, coloured now though by nativist perceptions of appropriate social and political order. Hardly unaware of the new socio-economic conditions of industrial capitalism, they none the less had difficulty breaking through the progressivist imagery of a hope for return to some mythical conditions of a small-town Jeffersonian or *Gemeinschaft* community. In these reformed urban neighbourhoods the new patterns of communication would aid the advance of education and science and therefore integrally contribute to the emergence of an informed, responsible citizenry in which class, economics and status differentials would be eroded (Quandt, 1970). The social science reformers had little basis for any substantial, wide-ranging critical inquiry into the inherited cultural traditions, economic structures or political processes of American society, and they therefore tended to take the existing communications media on their own terms.

Similarly, the somewhat later work of the Payne Fund studies on film is notable for its historical and cultural innocence. Here was one of the first organized media research efforts that seemed to have certain communications policy implications. In that light the project was highly revealing and, albeit unintentionally, prophetic. The Payne reports were conducted and written in the depths of the nation's most serious and potentially revolutionary economic depression, yet they seemed oblivious to those events. All the fuss and bother about film's impact on youngsters was articulated in relation to an idealized imagery of bourgeois youth and adolescence. One searches that research in vain for any consciousness of the deep-set social and political struggles of the period. It is as if the concern for film effects on children is a diversionary interest of the funders and researchers. One is tempted to argue that, to avoid confronting the more serious issues of the day, attention was focused on a question that in the context of the period was largely trivial. Then, of course, the results were inconclusive and incapable of sustaining any reassessment of film industry purpose and structure. The policy significance of that research — its essential irrelevance — is manifest in the fate of the film industry regulation legislation proposed at the time. Without necessarily endorsing any of those mid-1930s proposals for film statutes and regulation, it is sufficient to note that the Payne Fund research programme and most government studies of the period did not permit addressing questions of film industry ownership, funding, control and public oversight.

Common models in communication and policy science

A second general point about the influence on telecommunications policy research has to do with the common positivism and shared perspectives of mid-twentieth-century communication research and the initial phases of the more general fields of American policy studies. Again, as I have argued elsewhere (Rowland, 1984), in all the recent enthusiasm for communication policy research and with only one problematic exception (Harms, 1980), almost no one has observed the extent to which the first generation of American communication research science emerged simultaneously with and out of the same administrative research programme that engendered the first attempts to create a formal science of policy studies (Lerner and Lasswell, 1951; Lasswell, 1971; Lazarsfeld, 1975). All of these men were principal actors in both movements, and for a full generation key elements of each continued to bear the stamp of their behavioural, normal science origins. Although policy research has become more self-conscious as a field, as in the formation of professional policy studies and policy analysis organizations (PSO and APPAM) and the creation of several journals and book series, its orientation remains closely associated with the liberal positivism and industrial/informatic state capitalism of its initial formulations (see the Lasswell, Lerner and Lazarsfeld citations, plus Nagel, 1975, 1977, and almost any issue of the *Policy Studies Journal* or *Policy Studies Review*).

As reflected in Fig. 1, the official logotype of the PSO is revealing in this regard. Employing one-way arrows that depict flow from 'causes' through 'policy' to 'effects', complete with feedback loops, the logo closely resembles the old behaviouristic models of experimental psychology that Schramm (1954) and others had married to information theory models during the post-war political science enthusiasm for systems analysis and cybernetics. Embodying a decidedly mechanistic view of communication, the parallel imagery suggests a continuing parallel theory of society, culture and politics.

The more recent research published in some policy journals, such as *Policy Analysis, Policy Sciences, Public Policy* and *Journal of Applied Policy Analysis and Management*, has become somewhat more eclectic and critically reflective. But the contradictory Lasswellian influence remains strong in such forums. In promoting the field of policy sciences, Lasswell was far from narrow and unimaginative, for instance calling for links 'with law and jurisprudence, political theory

FIGURE 1
Similar behaviouristic policy studies and communication models
(i) Official logotype of the Policy Studies Organization

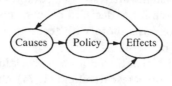

Source: Letterhead, journal covers and other materials of the Policy Studies
Organization.

(ii) Early communication process models

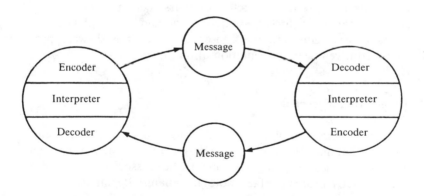

Source: Schramm (1954): 4, 8.

and philosophy' and for approaches steeped in 'contextuality'. Yet his examples of the important developments in the field emphasize such innovations as 'operations research, linear and dynamic programming . . . systems analysis . . . computer simulation and gaming', and the search for a 'decision process model', all of which ultimately reflects concerns more with technique than philosophy (Lasswell, 1971: xiii–ix, 14–33).

By the early 1970s Ithiel de Sola Pool was proclaiming the existence of a communication policy research field (1974). But his description of it was based on a celebration of technological change and the academic entrepreneurship that in the 1960s and 1970s was rushing uncritically to secure the federal and business grants for its study and that Nisbet (1971), Horowitz (1977) and others have correctly seen as so troublesome. Pool was careful to cite the 'bigger role in policy research' of 'values and social philosophy', but there is much in his paper that, as with Lasswell, suggests a narrow appreciation of the terms and implications of that change. In this regard one wants to pay particular attention to his discussion of the policy research grants actually funded by NSF and to his notions about 'free flow' in the international satellite debate. The most significant legacy in all this formative activity therefore may be the theoretical naivety of communication policy research. To the extent that both the broader fields of communication research and policy science eschewed epistemologically serious theoretical discourse, communication policy studies began to develop without reliable guidance as to all the facets of its own origins and the consequences of the skewed, pro-administrative research orientation of that history.

The embrace of technology

A third significant problem in the historical backdrop to contemporary communication policy research is revealed in the way in which most communication policy literature has been associated with, if not dominated by, problems of technological change. Beginning with the principal public and private studies of common carrier, information, broadcasting and cable communications (US President's Task Force, 1968; Sloan Commission, 1971) and continuing through the subsequent critiques of FCC policy (Le Duc, 1973; US Cabinet Committee, 1974) most of the discussions of public policy for the mass media during the past fifteen years have been driven by questions about the role and promises of the 'new technologies'. Particularly during the more recent phases of policy debate, beginning perhaps with the proposals for major communication legislation and regulatory change (US House of Representatives, 1976, 1977), the primary assumptions in the literature have been the inevitability of technological change — broadband cable, satellites, miniaturization, fibre optics, computerization and so on — the economic and social advantages that presumably can occur with it, and therefore the need to adjust public policy accordingly. The principal conclusion of much of that literature, particularly most of the official congressional and administrative agency reports, has been that this 'technology of abundance' would so alter the conditions of communication access, production, and distribution — the 'marketplace of ideas' — that the central argument for electronic communication regulation (spectrum scarcity) would fall, and with it much of the rationale for traditional regulatory procedures (see, for example, Fowler and Brenner, 1982). In short, the new technologies would justify substantial deregulation and further privatization.

The power and appeal of these assumptions and conclusions have been so great that as applied, and to a great extent initiated, in the practical political sphere they have had substantial influence. In conjunction with resurging neo-conservative and neo-libertarian views in economic and social issues at large, they have defined much of the recent centre of the communication policy agenda. For the most part the normal journal, review and book literature has tended to follow and support that line of argument. There have been exceptions in a small and growing body of dissenting literature (see below), but for a considerable period little critical distance was achieved in communication policy research, and a major reason for this condition has been the general weakness in the field's ability to know how to deal, intellectually, with matters of technology.

Reflecting a long tradition of American literary enthusiasm for the presumed liberating consequences of general technological advance, those contemplating the policy implications of the current changes in electronic communication have by and large demonstrated little familiarity with the paradoxes and failures in the heritage. There has always been a tension between hope and anxiety over the prospects for electronic technology (Czitrom, 1982), and it would be incorrect to claim that there has been no legacy of critical concern. But the terms of that critique have regularly tended to be liberally pragmatic, perceiving whatever problems there might be as subject to some combination of administrative tinkering and appeals to the social conscience of technology manufacturers and media owners and managers. Whether it was nineteenth-century reform campaigns against obscenity in cheap literature and the mass press (Comstock, 1883), city council concerns about motion pictures during the early 1900s, or eventually educator and psychologist complaints about violence and pornography on television, there has always also been a certain hopefulness about the potential for turning the successive media to more progressive ends, an ambivalence that was frequently expressed by the same reform critics or their professional research colleagues.

Simultaneously, constitutional considerations have always tended to constrain any concerted efforts of what might be considered censorship, particularly in the print and film media. Government authority was more readily invoked in electronic media implementation. The 'natural monopoly' characteristics of telegraphy and telephony, and the limited spectrum realities of broadcasting permitted the introduction of some administrative oversight. Yet, industry laments notwithstanding, such restrictions as were imposed tended to have more to do with technical standards than content matters, and they were usually *post hoc* — established after the principal purposes and structures of the industry had already been settled — and with results tending to favour the economic stability of existing parties rather than any substantial reform. Efforts to make the critical argument scientifically have proven equally futile. The entire positivistic social science enterprise was compromised from the start, it shared many of the liberal reform ambivalences and its 'evidence' simply could neither overcome the general public contentment with the media nor therefore sufficiently convince the political process of its case (Rowland, 1983).

The strength of the positive hopes for electronic technology, the uncertainties about how to take a priori steps to guide it without violating deep-seated and closely associated first amendment and private enterprise values, and the inherent weakness of the scientific case have regularly checked the critical thrust. It is not so much that no one has observed that the respective electronic 'revolutions' over a century and a half have never delivered on the full panoply of promised social and intellectual liberation, it is more that the grip of that liberating mythos (Carey and Quirk, 1970) has been so great and the other concomitant beliefs and commitments so deeply embedded that it has been difficult to confront the anomalies in the actual applied uses of each generation of electronic communication. Further, since the general intellectual realm has for so long been such a considerable part of the problem, by failing to perceive and address those inconsistencies, communication research at large and communication policy research specifically have not been well tutored in those lessons about technology and their implications for communication policy questions.

These difficulties become apparent in the various technology and policy publications of, for instance, the Rand Corporation, the Harvard Program on Information Resources Policy and the Aspen Institute Program on Communication and Society. Carried along on the strength of industrial and government grants, the research conducted by or on behalf of these groups has done much to lay out the detailed terms of the changing communication technologies and to articulate many of the issues associated with the passage into the 'post-industrial' or 'information society'. But while often empirically sophisticated, as for example in analysis of short-term economic and work-place social dislocations attendant upon telecommunications changes, and while even relatively alert to such global problems as technology transfer, transborder data flow and cultural dependency, the discussions of those matters are largely technocratic, administrative and only narrowly historical. Beyond the ritualistic bows to Daniel Bell (1973) or generalized third-world concerns, there is little analysis that is deeply social, political or cultural, and most of the discussions of domestic and international policy problems are presented from perspectives that, whether conscious or not, are ultimately protective of the fundamental structures and global status of the American corporate welfare state (particularly good examples of the strengths and weaknesses outlined here can be seen in Baer, 1978; Baer et al., 1974; Homet, 1979; and Robinson, 1978).

During its initially optimistic years the Aspen programme repeatedly asserted its interest in asking the 'important questions', facing the 'critical choices', establishing the 'vital linkages' between research and public policy action, invoking 'humanistic values', and doing so all from a position of neutrality in which specific policy recommendations were not made (see, for instance, Cater, 1975). Yet this posture ignores the terms of funding behind such programmes and the social and political relations among their boards, staffs, consultants and regular conferees, with all their implicit limitations on what real intellectual and democratically significant change they could foster. While the arrangements vary among these programmes, their ties to the academy are almost entirely contractual, providing for the lease of its space, name (prestige) or personnel, but involving little or no direct involvement in its formal teaching and intellectual life.

Obviously there are significant differences among the structures, funding and purposes of these and other institutions. There is perhaps a continuum among them, running from the strictly private, commercial firms (Arthur D. Little, Kalba-Bowen, Rand), to the non-profit and non-attached enterprises (Aspen, Brookings) to the loosely attached (Harvard) and more formally integrated programmes, institutes or departments (MIT, Illinois, Stanford, Annenbergs, and many others), among all of whom the exact amount of teaching, thesis advising and general academic involvement varies considerably. Drawing from all of these are the staff and consulting opportunities presented by various industries and government agencies. Altogether, then, there is a substantial interpenetration among private, public, foundation and academic interests — a set of interrelationships that has considerable influence on the agenda of communication policy research. In many ways these programmes represent the apotheosis of the Lippmann and Lazarsfeld intelligence bureaux, but as such they continue to carry with them the scholarly contradictions and implicit political commitments of the original models.

The influence of law and economics

A fourth characteristic of communication policy research (and one that deserves extended treatment and debate) has been its uncritical reliance on at least two other fields of research — law and economics — without much awareness of the biases and difficulties implicit there. Along with engineers (whose own socio-economic perspectives are no less problematic) attorneys long dominated the process of broadcasting and common-carrier policy studies. Placed in the formal, adversary settings of regulatory proceedings, the research they conducted or commissioned tended to be guided by the prior interests of contending private parties and the rules of pre-structured administrative practice. Further, as broadcasting, journalism, and mass communication programmes all became more professional in orientation, simultaneously with the rise of an ever-more positivistically empirical approach to research in the general field, and as communication on legal matters expanded and became more complex, there was a tendency to treat the first amendment, press law and electronic media regulatory issues from the perspective of professional legal training. Research and instruction in these matters became the study of precedents and guidelines, all with an eye to helping aspiring journalists, media managers and communication attorneys learn as much as possible about the litigation trends in issues they were likely to confront once working in the industries. Operating in this context, regulatory and policy instruction tended to assume that the public interest in broadcasting policy was adequately served by the provision of the regulatory and federal court forums in which the proceedings took place and by the results of competition of viewpoint among those parties.

It took nearly forty years of broadcast regulation before, as in the WLBT/UCC cases of the mid- and late-1960s, it became more widely apparent that there was a series of fundamental contradictions in those neo-libertarian notions about the workings of the administrative process. It turned out that there had been severe restrictions on who could participate in regulatory proceedings, narrow definitions of the public interest, and little awareness of how the law and the legal process themselves sustained those limitations. An apparent major shift seemed to be taking place with the rise of 'public' or 'citizens interest' law and its apparent success in expanding notions of parties-at-interest, liberalizing opportunities for comparative licence renewal proceedings and settlement agreements, and revitalizing inquiries into children's television, affirmative action, network controls and economic concentration. Yet just as these activities began to gather momentum and appeared to be making some impact — and perhaps precisely because this was happening — the counter-currents of private, industrial self-interest and deregulation began to assert themselves, to the point now that the reform successes of a decade or more ago have largely been swept away (Rowland, 1982).

To a considerable degree broadcasting, journalism and communication research long ignored the constraining influences and tacit commitments of normal legal research perspectives. To attend Broadcast Education Association or AEJ regulatory workshops or convention sessions was to enter a realm where applied legal models dominated and where broadcast and journalism instructors, anxious about their lack of formal legal knowledge, would attempt to out-lawyer the lawyers. Part of the more immature, and always somewhat academically-suspect, aspects of professional education programmes in radio, television and journalism, many instructors in the broadcast rules and policy portions of the curriculum could often be seen to be envying the status and authority of the older legal professional training system, and they would try to adopt its methods and earn its respect. Often quite good technically, in the sense of providing exhaustive, detailed legal literature reviews and the empirical facts of the cases, the actual historical and theoretical consciousness of such research and teaching, as might be expressed in any contextual sensitivity to long-term political, social and economic trends, tended to be nearly non-existent.

Usually ignoring questions about the world-views of the law, communications legal and policy studies tended never to confront their own liberal, ideological perspectives and how those perspectives embody significantly limited capacities for comprehending not only American administrative law and process, but also essential realities of American politics, communication and power. By and large, American communication legal and policy studies have taken the standard issues — privacy, free press/fair trial, defamation and libel, obscenity, copyright, licensing, political broadcasting, fairness doctrine and administrative procedures — as given and subject to straightforward debate in traditional legal form. It is not so much that the issues are not seen as complex and often ambiguous. The typical law and communication journal articles and the materials filed in formal regulatory proceedings do attend to such problems. But what they usually do not do is frame those issues against the broader intellectual traditions, social conditions and economic forces out of which they rise in the first place. One may debate the outcome of a particular case by reviewing its 'facts', precedents and internal logic, but one does not question the issue as a whole, asking how its very existence might reflect a series of central patterns in American culture and history and therefore be fundamentally problematic. Much communication policy research therefore tends to deal with narrow problems within that 'closed system' in which many of the most crucial issues are out of bounds.

Similar questions bear on the economic research literature invoked in communications policy-making. Blessed with considerably more 'hard' data than that available to other social scientists, communication economists have been able to fold that information into general economic notions about such matters as market theory, efficiency, elasticity and public vs private goods. These efforts to model dimensions of media performance from economic perspectives have gained considerable sway in recent policy debates. They have been crucial to the deregulation debate, providing much of the empirical evidence of the failures of previous regulatory schemes which have proven to be so protectionist as to undermine aspects of the very public interest they were to serve. Indeed, in this respect, in the critique of the 'captured agency' nature of much public regulation, the economists have had strong critical, citizen-interest-group support. Together these views have helped establish a political climate in which substantial rethinking of the statutory and regulatory structure for communication policy could be undertaken, with the particular expectation of so changing the conditions for dealing with the new technologies as to permit a presumably less monopolistic, more openly competitive process for market entry and public service.

But as it developed, that critique relied too heavily on economic as opposed to social considerations, with the consequence that conditions of real access, real diversity, real freedom of choice have proved to be far more difficult to secure than normal economic theory can acknowledge. For, despite the many progressive aspects of its orientation, the neo-classic economic logic here ultimately supports the private ownership origins of all American communication media with their seemingly indissoluble free expression–free enterprise associations. The reformist fascination with deregulatory economics thus contains the usual progressive trap. Shaped within the context of a liberal industrial capitalism, normal and even opposed schools in American economics are no freer of structural and ideological limits than the law or other social sciences, and to the extent they rely on existing dominant models for the economy at large they have a relatively narrow sense of real social and political alternatives for communication policy.

Towards an improved communication policy research discourse

In a close parallel with the theoretical blinders of positivistic communication research at large, broadcast and journalism educators tended to fail to recognize that in much of their own humanistic and interpretative social science heritage there were approaches to regulatory and policy questions that might serve as significant correctives to the unspoken assumptions and commitments of normal legal and economic research. It was not as if critical insights into conventional views of communication policy-making never existed (see, for example, Smythe, 1957; Edelman, 1964; Skornia, 1965; Network Project, 1970–75; Melody, 1973; Friendly, 1976;

Schmidt, 1976; and Bunce, 1976), but it has been only recently that some of the corrections have begun to be made more systematically. There is now a body of critical policy research that is asserting itself more self-consciously, dealing with the underlying historical contradictions in broadcast law and regulation, with the anomalies in the 'diversity' and the 'marketplace' notions, and with the social and economic power struggles over new technologies, citizen interests, violence and legislative and regulatory change (see, variously, Glasser, 1984; Haight, 1979; Le Duc, 1982; Mosco, 1979, 1982; Rowland, 1982, 1983; Schiller, 1982; and Smythe, 1982).

This collection of work is hardly monolithic and much of it is internally contentious on many fundamental questions. If pressed firmly enough, various of these critiques would reveal important disputes over assumptions about such essential issues as material reality, ideology and culture itself. For example, it would appear that Le Duc and Mosco would have rather serious differences about the nature of the state. The former's views are more implicit and thus difficult to gauge, but aspects of them would seem to be subject to the latter's critique of pluralism from instrumentalist and structuralist perspectives (Domhoff, 1978, and Poulantzas, 1973).

On the whole, though, the new phase of American communication policy research is ever more consciously linked to the theoretical and epistemological debates in the contemporary social sciences and humanities at large. To varying degrees it rises within, responds to and even reflects back upon the paradigmatic shifts associated with recent developments in British and American cultural studies, Frankfurt School sociology, critical political economics, structuralist and post-structuralist semiotics, the sociology of knowledge and the philosophy of science, and various phenomenological and hermeneutic reformulations of interpretive theory. Some work has already begun to clarify the newer forms of linkage between communication and policy studies. For instance, Halloran's analysis (1981) of the differences between policy research and policy-oriented research emerges from the administrative-critical distinction discussed above, and it points to the ground towards which a more autonomous critical policy studies must move. It makes somewhat more explicit in policy-studies terms aspects of the efforts by Hall (e.g., 1982) and several others to reformulate media research problems in the light of the complex current discourses about power, ideology, the state, social structure, symbolic reality and cultural meaning that are otherwise becoming increasingly central to

European and American communication and media studies.

The availability of critical strains of policy research and recognition of their potential is only a start, however. There is much yet that needs to be done before these approaches to communication policy matters can become more central to the public debate, particularly in the United States. For one thing, they must extend the kind of connections they have already made between critical policy studies and the ferment in the social sciences and humanities to parallel developments in other disciplines, particularly in law and economics.

It turns out, for instance, that there is an entire body of research and debate in a growing field known as 'critical legal studies' (*George Washington Law Review*, 1984; Kairys, 1982; *Stanford Law Review*, 1984; *Yale Law Journal*, 1981). This work has tended to be organized round an annual conference on the topic, and it counts between a hundred and two hundred contributing scholars from various, mostly élite, law schools in the United States (Cahan, 1984; Trillin, 1984). More importantly, it is asking precisely the sorts of questions about the law and legal scholarship that are proposed here about communication policy studies. It tends to deal with

> ... the idea of law as a legitimator of false ideologies or oppressive social orders or as a defense mechanism against the recognition of tensions in those orders; attacks on the alleged superiority of law and economics as a framework for legal analysis and on the alleged coherence of law and of liberal ideology; critiques of the notion that particular legal practices derive inevitably from doctrine, principles, or functional social needs or, more generally, that history follows an inevitable, predetermined path; and calls for personal participation and acceptance of responsibility. (*Stanford Law Review*, 1984: i)

Initially dismissed in conventional legal forums as 'trashing' and as unworthy of the label scholarship, critical legal research is proving to be far more impressive in both theory and method than its detractors would have it. As Robert Gordon, Mark Tushnet, Alan Freeman and others have suggested, critical legal studies make explicit appeals precisely to the varieties of critical social science discourse invoked above (*Yale Law Journal*, 1981: 1017–56, 1205–23, 1229–37). It is epistemologically sophisticated, recognizing the relationships between knowledge and power and introducing matters of class, structure, legitimation and normativism into the formalism and doctrinal analysis of traditional legal scholarship. As such, much of its literature demonstrates a convincing grasp of the themes — and controversies — among social and cultural theory, intellectual history, and the philosophy of science, making its own productive use of Hegel, Marx, Weber, Durkheim, Gramsci, Foucault, Habermas, Kuhn, Thompson and Geertz, to name just a few of those recognized as central to critical cultural studies in communication. Indeed, there even is evidence that some critical legal studies work has been shaped in direct reference to certain British strains of cultural studies (e.g., Hunt, 1985). Critical legal research is also empirically rigorous, often constituting close examination of legal texts — statutes, rules and cases — but doing so from perspectives of critical textual exegesis and history that recognize matters of material and ideological context, that refuse to take the law in isolation and as sufficiently self-explanatory.

As has already been suggested, neo-classical economics have been closely associated with the principal trends in the conservative political resurgencies of the deregulatory era, and nowhere so cosily as in the work on telecommunications policy. There simply is no critical dimension to the marketplace rhetoric of the Fowler FCC.[1] However, it would be a mistake to assume that the Chicago monetarists and the supply-siders have had total control of American economic theory. As in the law there have emerged critical factions of various post-Keynesian, neo-Marxist and institutionalist perspectives (Kuttner, 1985). The leakiness of neo-classical hegemony is all too apparent in the work of Samuel Bowles, David Gordon and their colleagues in the Union for Radical Political Economy. Their work on various contemporary economic problems (Bowles et al., 1983) as well as a regular specific focus on labour (Braverman, 1974) has constituted a major challenge to traditional liberal and neo-conservative views. Most such research has even found a regular outlet in the *Review of Radical Political Economy* and in such other academic forums as the *Journal of Economic Literature*, the *History of Political Economy*, the *Journal of Economic History*, and even such bastions of liberal thought as the *Brookings Papers on Economic Activity*.

Given the obvious Marxian heritage in economics, a critical focus has been there all along, particularly in Europe. However, at least in North America, the critical economics literature has only relatively recently become coherently self-conscious. As with the parallel work in the law, formal critical economic perspectives have begun to emerge in part as a response to the critiques of their dominant forms of professional education and the related efforts to reinterpret carefully the rise and development of economic thought. As is proving to be the case in other social and cultural sciences, the history of economics leads to confrontation with the workings of ideological and institutional structures and the consequent patterns of association between power and intellectual endeavour (North, 1981).

The existence of these sorts of critiques in such traditional, heretofore seemingly intractable professional fields suggests that it will be incumbent upon American communication policy students to take cognizance of them and to insist that they be applied to those forums where normal legal and economic perspectives prevail. This suggestion should lead to the introduction of certain new faces in various of those communication conferences in which policy questions might have some salience. At the very least it would seem appropriate that in subsequent telecommunications policy research conferences the likes of a David Kairys, Duncan Kennedy, Alan Hunt, Samuel Bowles or Robert Kuttner should appear.

Meanwhile, the critical and cultural studies policy research already rising out of communication should continue to be pursued and entered more directly into the public policy debates. In the light of all the related work in the social sciences, law and economics, there is no longer any excuse for permitting policy debate to proceed without close, hard review of some of its very terms and assumptions. There is a huge research project lying ahead of us that will require exhaustive reanalysis of the legislative and regulatory history of the Communications Act, the notions and functions of administrative law inherited by and worked out through the FCC, the practical applied meaning of the public interest standard, and all the other principal regulatory doctrines and practices. Implicit here is a thoroughgoing critique of our notions and myths about freedom, the marketplace, regulation, the state and public–private distinctions.

The published research cited above is surely a start in that process, but it is as yet unclear how much influence, if any, it is having in the practical world of federal and state telecommunications policy-making. The old administrative research siren continues to sing her seductive song and the dilemmas of appropriate academic response persist. Congressmen, executive agency officials and regulators all live in a rapidly moving, highly charged atmosphere of immediate economic pressures and political needs. In that environment there is an almost irresistible temptation to continue to see communication research solely and simply as a tool in the short-term struggle over specific problems, rather than as a potentially principal framework for re-examining basic questions about power, cultural values and social well-being. Living in an equally contradictory practical environment of disciplinary in-fighting, curricular struggles and promotion, tenure and salary problems, communication policy scholars are no less susceptible to the temptations of trafficking in the more immediately practical, applied aspects of their work. The mutual attraction here for the pursuit of the less critical, less metaphysical and less epistemologically conscious form of communication policy studies is undeniable. It is also deeply threatening to prospects for improvements in the intellectual substance of communication research and progressive social change in American telecommunications.

Note

1. As an example, efforts by the author to find a spectrum of economic views among economists working on American telecommunications policy questions for a plenary session of the 1984 convention of the Association for Education in Journalism and Mass Communication (AEJMC) met with mixed success. There appear to be no Americans with anything approaching radical economic perspectives working in any federal agency dealing with telecommunications, and their primary, private, think-tank and university consultant colleagues are also all largely neo-classicists. The one exception was an independent consultant, a Welshman trained at the London School of Economics. But his views were most notable for how remarkably unique and isolated they seemed to be in contemporary Washington communications economic research circles.

References

Baer, Walter S. (1978) *Telecommunications Technology in the 1980s*. Santa Monica: Rand Corporation, P-6725.

Baer, Walter S., Henry Geller, Joseph A. Grundfest and Karen B. Possner (1974) *Concentration of Mass Media Ownership: Assessing the State of Current Knowledge*. Santa Monica: Rand Corporation, R-1584-NSF.

Bell, Daniel (1973) *The Coming of Post-Industrial Society*. New York: Basic Books.

Bowles, Samuel, David M. Gordon and Thomas E. Weisskopf (1983) *Beyond the Waste Land: A Democratic Alternative to Economic Decline*. Garden City, NY: Doubleday.

Braverman, Harry (1974) *Labor and Monopoly Capital: The Degradation of Work in the Twentieth Century*. New York: Monthly Review Press.

Bunce, Richard (1976) *Television in the Corporate Interest*. New York: Praeger.

Cahan, Catherine C. (1984) 'Rebels Without a Pause', *Student Lawyer*, October.

Carey, James W. and John J. Quirk (1970) 'The Mythos of the Electronic Revolution',

Parts I and II, *The American Scholar*, 39 (2): 219–41; (3): 395–424.

Cater, Douglass (1975) 'Communications Policy Research: The Need for New Dimensions', in Rivers and Slater (1975).

Comstock, Anthony (1883), *Traps for the Young*. New York: Funk & Wagnalls. (See Robert Bremmer [ed.] [1967] *Traps for the Young* by Anthony Comstock. Cambridge, Mass.: Harvard University Press.)

Czitrom, Daniel J. (1982) *Media and the American Mind: From Morse to McLuhan*. Chapel Hill: University of North Carolina Press.

Domhoff, William G. (1978) *The Powers That Be*. New York: Vintage.

Edelman, Murray (1964) *The Symbolic Uses of Politics*. Urbana: University of Illinois Press.

Fowler, Mark S. and Daniel L. Brenner (1982) 'A Marketplace Approach to Broadcast Regulation', *Texas Law Review*, 60: 207.

Friendly, Fred W. (1976) *The Good Guys, the Bad Guys, and the First Amendment: Free Speech vs. Fairness in Broadcasting*. New York: Random House.

George Washington Law Review (1984) 'Perspectives on Critical Legal Studies, 52 (2): 239–88.

Glasser, Theodore L. (1984) 'Competition and Diversity among Radio Formats: Legal and Structural Issues', *Journal of Broadcasting*, 28 (2): 127–42.

Gurevitch, Michael, Tony Bennet, James Curran and Janet Wollacott, (eds) (1982) *Culture, Society and the Media*. New York: Methuen.

Haight, Timothy R. (ed.) (1979) *Telecommunications Policy and the Citizen: Public Interest Perspectives on the Communications Act Rewrite*. New York: Praeger.

Hall, Stuart (1982) 'The Rediscovery of "Ideology". Return of the Repressed in Media Studies', in Gurevitch et al. (eds.) *Culture, Society and the Media*, New York: Methuen.

Halloran, James D. (1981) 'The Context of Mass Communication Research' in McAnany et al. (eds) *Communication and Social Structure*. New York: Praeger.

Harms, L.S. (1980) 'Appropriate Methods for Communication Policy Science: Some Preliminary Considerations', *Human Communication Research*, 7(1): 3–13.

Homet, Roland S. Jr (1979) *Politics, Cultures and Communication: European vs. American Approaches to Communication Policymaking*. New York: Aspen Institute for Humanistic Studies.

Horowitz, Irving Louis (1977) *Ideology and Utopia in the United States: 1956–1976*. New York: Oxford University Press.

Hunt, Alan (1985) 'The Ideology of Law: Advances and Problems in Recent Applications of the Concept of Ideology to the Analysis of Law', *Law and Society Review*, 19 (1): 11–37.

Kairys, David (ed.) (1982) *The Politics of Law: A Progressive Critique*. New York: Pantheon.

Kuttner, Robert (1985) 'The Poverty of Economics' *The Atlantic*, 255 (2): 74–84.

Lasswell, Harold D. (1970) 'The Emerging Conception of the Policy Sciences', *Policy Sciences*, 1 (1): 3–14.

Lasswell, Harold D. (1971) *A Pre-View of Policy Sciences*. New York: American Elsevier.

Lazarsfeld, Paul F. (1975) 'The Policy Science Movement', *Policy Sciences*, 6 (3): 211–22.

Le Duc, Don R. (1973) *Cable Television and the FCC*. Philadelphia: Temple University Press.

Le Duc, Don R. (1982) 'Deregulation and the Dream of Diversity, *Journal of Communication*, 32 (4): 164–78.

Lerner, Daniel and Harold D. Lasswell (eds) (1951) *The Policy Sciences: Recent Developments in Scope and Method*. Stanford: Stanford University Press.

Lyons, Gene M. (1969) *The Uneasy Partnership*. New York: Russell Sage Foundation.

McAnany, Emile G., Jorge Schnitman and Noreene Janus (eds) (1981) *Communication and Social Structure: Critical Studies in Mass Media Research*. New York: Praeger.

Melody, William (1973) *Children's TV: The Economics of Exploitation*. New Haven: Yale University Press.

Mosco, Vincent (1979) *Broadcasting in the United States: Innovative Challenge and Organizational Control*. Norwood, NJ.: Ablex.

Mosco, Vincent (1982) *Pushbutton Fantasies: Critical Perspectives on Videotex and Information Technology*. Norwood, NJ: Ablex.

Nagel, Stuart S. (ed.) (1975) *Policy Studies and the Social Sciences*. Lexington, Mass.: Lexington Books.

Nagel, Stuart S. (1977) *Policy Studies Annual Review Vol. 1*. Beverly Hills: Sage.

Network Project (1970–75). (A series of over a dozen monographs and reports published by the Network Project, Earl Hall, Columbia University Law School, New York.)

Nisbet, Robert A. (1971) *The Degradation of the Academic Dogma: The University in America. 1945–1970*. New York: Basic Books.

North, Douglass C. (1981) *Structure and Change in Economic History*. New York: W.W. Norton.

Parsons, Talcott (1964) *Essays in Sociological Theory* (rev. ed.). New York: Free Press.

Pool, Ithiel de Sola (1974) 'The Rise of Communications Policy Research', *Journal of Communication*. 24 (2): 31–42.

Poulantzas, Nicos (1973) *Political Power and Social Classes*. London: New Left Books.

Quandt, Jean B. (1970) *From the Small Town to the Great Community: The Social Thought of Progressive Intellectuals*. New Brunswick, NJ: Rutgers University Press.

Robinson, Gertrude Joch (1984) 'The Study of "Schools of Thought" in Communication Studies: A Paradigmatic Approach'. Paper presented at the International Association for Mass Communication Research, Prague, 30 August.

Robinson, Glen O. (ed.) (1978) *Communications for Tomorrow: Policy Perspectives for the 1980s*. New York: Praeger.

Rowland, Willard D. Jr (1982) 'The Illusion of Fulfilment: The Broadcast Reform Movement', *Journalism Monographs* No. 79.

Rowland, Willard D. Jr (1983), *The Politics of TV Violence*. Beverly Hills: Sage.

Rowland, Willard D. Jr (1984) 'Deconstructing American Communications Policy Literature', *Critical Studies in Mass Communication*, 1 (4): 423–35.

Schiller, Dan (1982) *Telematics and Government*. Norwood, NJ: Ablex.

Schlesinger, Arthur M. Jr (1957) *The Age of Roosevelt: The Crisis of the Old Order, 1919–1933*. Boston: Houghton Mifflin.

Schmidt, Benno C. Jr (1976) *Freedom of the Press vs. Public Access*. New York: Praeger.

Schramm, Wilbur (ed.) (1954) *The Process and Effects of Mass Communication*. Urbana: University of Illinois Press.

Skornia, Harry J. (1965) *Television and Society: An Inquest and an Agenda for Improvement*. New York: McGraw-Hill.

Sloan Commission (1971) *On the Cable: The Television of Abundance*. New York: McGraw-Hill.

Smythe, Dallas W. (1957) *The Structure and Policy of Electronic Communication.* Urbana: University of Illinois Press.

Smythe, Dallas, W. (1982), 'Radio: Deregulation and the Relation of the Private and Public Sectors', *Journal of Communication*, 32 (1): 192–200.

Stanford Law Review (1984) 'Critical Legal Studies Symposium' 36 (1-2) : 1–674.

Steel, Ronald (1980) *Walter Lippmann and the American Century.* Boston: Little, Brown and Co.

Trillin, Calvin (1984) 'A Reporter at Large: Harvard Law School', *The New Yorker* 26 March.

US Cabinet Committee on Cable Communications (1974) *Cable: Report to the President.* Washington, DC: US Government Printing Office.

US House of Representatives (1976) *Cable Television: Promise versus Regulatory Performance.* Staff Report. Committee on Interstate and Foreign Commerce, Subcommittee on Communications (94, 2), January.

US House of Representatives (1977) *Options Papers.* Staff Report. Committee on Interstate and Foreign Commerce. Subcommittee on Communications (95, 1) May.

US President's Task Force on Communications Policy (1968) *Final Report.* Washington, DC: US Government Printing Office.

Yale Law Journal (1981) 'Papers from the Yale Law Journal Symposium on Legal Scholarship: Its Nature and Purpose', 90 (5): 955–1296.

PART III

CULTURAL HISTORY
Technology and Change

INTRODUCTION

Steve M. Barkin

This section of the yearbook contains selections that examine communications in the framework of broad cultural change. In choosing the five selections that appear here, the editors of the yearbook were struck with the originality and scope of researchers' concerns. Unlike traditional approaches to "media history" and "journalism history" that focus narrowly on communications institutions, and, to a somewhat lesser extent, on their products and audiences, these authors address the impact of new media technologies and behaviors on a society's shared values and sense of itself, on its changing perceptions of time and space. In placing technology in the most global of contexts, the authors present a form of historical analysis more holistic—and more challenging—than conventional media chronologies.

Nord opens the section with an analysis of readers and the nature of reading in late nineteenth-century America. Using a sample of working-class family budgets from an 1889-1890 federal survey, the author relates developing patterns of reading to a set of cultural variables including region, nationality, and community life. The data lend some support to the view that popular reading helped establish new communities and a semblance of community life in a newly industrialized, increasingly urban society.

Hartley and O'Regan examine television as an agent of physical and cultural change. With the introduction of television to Western Australia in 1959, the home itself was transformed, first into a sort of public place, a "theatrette." TV watching eventually changed the arrangement of furniture, spurred the innovation of the "family room," and contributed to a redefinition of public and private space, as popular culture became geared to private consumption. The authors observe that new video technologies have continued that pattern, "colonizing" and "domesticating" spaces that once had been demarcated as public.

Frith discusses developments in the technology of popular music in the context of the historical debate over the authenticity of mass culture. The author argues that the innovations of recording itself, the electrical microphone, and magnetic tape were liberating influences for musicians and audiences alike, and represented the assertion of consumer preference in music over more centralized forms of corporate control. Punk electronics, rapping, and the "ghetto blaster" are thus viewed as populist weapons against the cultural power of capital and the state.

Marvin relates the late nineteenth-century introduction of the electric light to a set of social and cultural transformations. The illumination of public places changed the nature of outdoor events. Electric-light messages became the centerpiece of patriotic and political gatherings, and the sky a palette for illuminated advertising. Correspondingly, electricity meant that many large outdoor community gatherings could move indoors and become private.

Winston examines the cultural implications of an aesthetic that emerged from the development of color film. Technologies of lighting, processing, and the new film stocks, Winston argues, evolved in culturally specific patterns so that desirable "flesh tones" became equated with a Caucasian standard. Later, the film and television industries adopted studio production techniques related to color film that also served ideological as well as technical ends: Capital-intensive methods served to "professionalize" film making, reinforcing the power of visual media and making them less accessible to their publics.

Throughout this section, the authors' emphasis is on developments in popular media, from working-class reading fare to "street music" to the now-ubiquitous electric light, not merely as artifacts or signposts of deeper cultural change, but as a direct ideological expression of shifting societal ideals and expectations. Technological innovation is regarded by the authors as inherently ideological, tied to questions of power and the maintenance of social order, and to the cultural processes by which reality is collectively defined and interpreted.

9

WORKING-CLASS READERS
Family, Community, and Reading in Late Nineteenth-Century America

David Paul Nord

This article argues that a genuine social history of reading in the nineteenth century requires more direct attention to audiences in addition to the traditional attention to producers and product. It suggests that historians of literacy have been more creative than mass media historians in using individual-level historical data (such as censuses, deeds, wills, government surveys) to study past reading behavior. One type of individual-level data that may be of use to mass communication historians is the series of family cost-of-living surveys conducted by state and federal bureaus of labor statistics in the late nineteenth and early twentieth centuries. These studies of working-class family budgets, some of which were published in nonaggregated form, include detailed information on family structure, income, and expenditures, including expenditures on newspapers and books. Through an analysis of a sample of cotton textile worker budgets from an 1889-1890 federal survey, this study found that expenditures for newspapers and books were associated in interesting ways with family income patterns, region of residence, and ethnicity. The study also found some evidence that reading among working-class families may have been related to the changing nature of community life in the new industrial society of late nineteenth-century America.

Who read newspapers, magazines, and books in the nineteenth century? Were readers different from nonreaders? Were avid readers different from moderate readers? Was reading associated with differences in income, ethnicity, region of residence, schooling, or other family characteristics? Was reading linked to the life-

AUTHOR'S NOTE: *Thanks to the staff of the Summer Institute in Quantitative History at the Newberry Library, Chicago, who helped me get started on this project. Thanks also to my research assistant, Jo Ellen Fair, who coded and keypunched the data. That task was supported by a Grant-in-Aid of Research from the Office of Research and Graduate Development at Indiana University.*

style of readers? These kinds of questions are central to an understanding of reading as a social institution during the early years of mass media in America. Yet we still do not know the answers. Historians in recent years have made marvelous contributions to our understanding of the extent and characteristics of simple literacy in eighteenth- and nineteenth-century America (Lockridge, 1974; Graff, 1979; Soltow and Stevens, 1981; Graff, 1981). But we still have much to learn about the history of reading among the majority of people who could read, particularly in the late nineteenth century, at the dawn of the era of mass communication. Nearly all of the research in the history of newspapers and magazines—and much of the research in the history of the popular book—has centered on the production, not the consumption, of reading materials. We know a lot about Joseph Pulitzer, Edward Bok, and Horatio Alger; we know very little about the readers of the *New York World,* the *Ladies' Home Journal,* and *Ragged Dick.*

The central assumption of this article is that scholars ought to look more carefully at the history of readers and reading as well as the history of literacy and the publishing trade. Carl Kaestle has recently made the same point. In a detailed review of the literature in the field, he concluded that the history of literacy and reading is at a turning point. Kaestle (1985: 43-44) wrote that:

> Historians of literacy have taught us a great deal in the past twenty years about the consequences of literacy and of print in the early modern West, and they have assiduously charted trends in signature-writing and self-reported literacy for later centuries. Many generalizations have been tested and refined. We can say, indeed, that we know a lot about these matters. Although some historians have also done imaginative work on the uses of literacy in everyday life, we know much less about this important aspect of the subject. Consequently, we need research on the functions of printed matter among different reading publics.

The purpose of this article is to suggest one way that this task might be done. Specifically, I will offer a description and an analysis of a collection of nineteenth-century data on working-class families that may suggest some partial answers to that deceptively simple question: Who read newspapers and books in the late nineteenth century?

HISTORICAL READERSHIP STUDIES

Of course, some historians have already made remarkable progress in the historical study of book readership. For many years, book and library historians have conducted studies that infer the characteristics and tastes of readers from book sales, from circulation records of libraries, and from the mere existence of libraries and the book trade in particular regions (Hart, 1950; Marshall, 1966; Harris and Davis, 1978). More recently, historians in this field have studied book ownership and reading behavior more directly through the analysis of probate records and other personal documents left behind by individual readers. Typically, readership studies in this new social history of the book review hundreds, sometimes thousands, of seemingly unrelated estate inventories and then use these individual-level data to generalize about who read what at a particular place and time (Harris, 1972; Darnton, 1982; Kett and McClung, 1984). Like other practitioners of the "new social history," they have in a sense learned to conduct surveys among the dead.

But these, of course, are mainly the well-to-do dead. What about the readership of popular books, magazines, and newspapers? This is an important question for the history of reading, but it is a much more difficult one to answer. Subscriber lists for mass magazines and daily newspapers are virtually nonexistent. Moreover, the reading of mass media has always been a much more ephemeral enterprise than the reading of quality books; people do not usually leave bundles of newspapers or paperbacks in their estates to be inventoried and probated. Yet newspaper and other popular reading is a behavior that has been recorded in some individual-level historical records. One such record is the family cost-of-living budget—a favored form of statistical survey conducted by the newly created bureaus of labor statistics on both the state and national levels in the late nineteenth and early twentieth centuries.

HISTORICAL LABOR STATISTICS

The creation of bureaus of labor statistics, beginning with Massachusetts in 1869, was part of the passion of late-nineteenth-century reformers for "facts." The transformation of America from an agrarian and commercial nation to an industrial nation brought with it an avalanche of immensely complicated economic and social problems. In their efforts to understand this strange new world, reformers and politicians sought help from the fledgling social sciences. Resolute in their faith in a scientific, factual basis for reform, they hoped to answer the great economic questions of the day through empirical investigations. No question was of greater concern than the so-called "Labor Question"—the interlocking problems of labor productivity, unemployment, pay, hours, child labor, labor organization, and social unrest. The first bureau of labor statistics was set up in Massachusetts in 1869, the Federal Bureau of Labor was established in 1884, and by 1891, 27 state bureaus had been organized across the United States (MacDonald, 1972).

Carroll D. Wright, who became the first U.S. commissioner of labor after his service as chief of the Massachusetts bureau, was the leading figure in the development of labor statistics from 1873 until his death in 1909. One of Wright's most important contributions to labor statistics was his effort to study empirically the cost of living of working-class families (Leiby, 1960; North, 1908-1909). Wright's cost-of-living surveys gathered detailed information on family size, age, ethnicity, and work patterns; on family income from all sources; and on family expenditures of every sort, from potatoes to life insurance. The original purpose of these surveys was to study consumption and its relation to income, taking into account a variety of other family, industrial, and regional variables. Several of the federal studies were also designed to provide Congress with information during tariff debates (Stigler, 1965; Williams and Zimmerman, 1935). Happily for historians, some of the studies were published in non-aggregated form, thus preserving the raw survey data for secondary analysis by posterity and posterity's computers. Happily for historians of literacy and reading, a variable commonly surveyed was expenditures for newspapers and books.

The most important cost-of-living surveys reported in nonaggre-gated form were published by Carroll Wright's bureaus in 1875 and in 1890 and 1891. The 1875 study, conducted when Wright was Massachusetts commissioner, was a survey of 397 working-class families in that state (Massachusetts Bureau of Labor Statistics, 1875). Wright's agents purposely selected the sample to represent a range of occupations; within each occupation the individuals interviewed were selected more or less at random.[1] The interviewers for all of Wright's surveys were persistent and meticulous, though the exact procedures they followed are not fully specified (Wright, 1890-1891). After he became U.S. commis-sioner of labor, Wright conducted a monumental replication of the Massachusetts survey—a study of the budgets of more than 8,500 families all over the United States and in several foreign countries in selected industries (U.S. Commissioner of Labor, 1890, 1991). Though these surveys may be the best sources for historical cost-of-living data, they are by no means the only such sources. Wright conducted other studies, as did several state bureaus (see, for example, Illinois Bureau of Labor Statistics, 1884).

A few social and economic historians have made use of these historical surveys. Econometric historian Jeffrey Williamson (1966-1967) used the data to study income elasticity in the nineteenth century. Economic historians Peter Lindert (1980) and Michael Haines (1979) used the surveys in studies of fertility, child costs, and family life cycles. Social historian John Modell (1978) looked into the consumption patterns of native workers compared to Irish immigrants. So far as I know, no one working in the history of literacy or mass communication has used these cost-of-living surveys to study reading behavior.

THE ERA OF MASS MEDIA

Wright's 1890-1891 survey falls in the midst of one of the most extraordinary periods in American economic history. It was an extraordinary era in media history as well.

First, this era is aptly remembered as the genesis of the modern, mass-circulation newspaper in America. Nationwide, the number of daily newspapers increased 78% in the 1880s, and the percentage growth of evening papers—the workingman's paper—was even greater, 112%. Over the same decade, the circulation of all dailies jumped 135%, from 3.6 million to 8.4 million per day. Altogether more than 4.5 billion copies of newspapers and periodicals were issued in 1890, a ten-fold increase from midcentury (U.S. Census Office, 1895). Second, the decades of the 1880s and 1890s saw the birth of the modern, mass-circulation national magazine. Lured by the development of cheap paper, the rise of national advertising, and a favorable postal act of 1879, magazine publishers were able for the first time in the 1880s and 1890s to establish a truly national mass medium (Mott, 1957). Third, the post-Civil War decades constitute the era in which book publishing—including the publication of enormous numbers of cheap books and paperbacks—"came to full flower in the New World" (Tebbel, 1975: 1). Fourth, this was an era of great growth in the foreign-language press in America. Between 1880 and 1890, the number of newspapers printed in foreign languages increased 45%—from 799 to 1,159 (U.S. Census Office, 1895).

Who was reading these newspapers, magazines, and books in 1890? To find out, I turned to the nonaggregated cost-of-living data in the *Seventh Annual Report* of the U.S. Commissioner of Labor (1891).

WORKING-CLASS READERS

My study of working-class readers is based upon a stratified random sample of 300 cases drawn from the 1891 report. In their original form, the data were already stratified by industry and state or country of residence. Because the surveys were designed to generate a factual basis for the congressional tariff debates, the industries studied were major protected industries of the time: bar iron, pig iron, steel, bituminous coal, coke, iron ore, cotton textiles, woolens, and glass. My sample consisted of 100 families in the cotton textile industry from the leading manufacturing states in each of the three major cotton-milling regions of the United States: *New England* (Massachusetts and New Hampshire), *Mid-Atlantic* (New York and Pennsylvania), and *South* (Georgia and North Carolina).[2] After a preliminary analysis of three industrial groups, I decided to work only with cotton textile workers. Of the industries surveyed by Wright, cotton milling was the *only* industry well represented across regions and ethnic groups. Because my interest lay with regional, ethnic, and family variations, rather than industry variations, it seemed logical to limit the analysis to one industry.

Before turning to regional, ethnic, and family variations in reading behavior, it is important to note the overall ubiquity of reading as a working-class activity in this era. About 77% of the families in the sample reported at least some spending on newspapers and books, a higher proportion than for any other discretionary expenditure included in Wright's survey.[3] The average annual expenditure for reading materials was $4.23. By comparison, families spent on the average about half this much for organization activities, about one and one-half times this much for amusements, and about twice this much for liquor. This raw figure of $4.23 amounts to about 2.4% of the average family's discretionary spending and about .75% of the family's total expenditures. Interestingly, these proportions do not seem very much less than comparable media expenditures in the twentieth century. Maxwell McCombs (1972) found that expenditures for printed media made up about 1.15% of consumer spending by all Americans during the period 1929-1968. In short, reading was a very widespread (though not universal) activity among these working-class families in the late nineteenth century.

Who were these working-class readers? What were they like? To seek answers to these questions, I looked at the relationships between expenditures for newspapers and books and four categories of family attributes: (1) income; (2) region of residence; (3) nationality of birth; and (4) family-community ties. I will explore each of these four categories in turn—though, as I will try to show, the real significance lies in their interconnections.

INCOME

The average annual family income from all sources for the cotton workers in my sample was $667, with 90% earning less than $1,000. Wages in cotton manufacturing were low for unskilled and semi-skilled operatives, especially women and children; but total family incomes were comparable to the other industries surveyed by Wright. The average pay of the husbands in my sample was $354—ranging from $31 to $978 per year. Although the husband was usually the principal wage earner, the children worked in about 52% of the families, often earning more, collectively, than their fathers. Only about 18% of the wives worked for wages, and their contribution to family income was considerably less than that of either husbands or children. Overall, it seems fair to say that individual wages were low in cotton textile work, but family earnings could range from bare subsistence to a modestly comfortable standard of living.

Income, not surprisingly, was a significant determinant of spending on newspapers and books. Then, as now, when people had more money., they tended to spend it. When the families in the sample are divided into equal thirds according to family income rank (low, middle, and high income), the high-income families spent nearly twice as much on reading materials as the low-income families (see Table 1).

This apparently simple linear relationship, however, was neither simple nor linear. The simple correlation coefficient between reading expenditures and total family income is only .15, a statistically significant, but weak, relationship. The weak relationship stems in part from the fact that spending on reading materials did not rise proportionally with family income. In other words, high-income families allotted a somewhat smaller proportion of their discretionary expenditures to reading compared with either low- or middle-income families, as Table 1 shows. Though interesting in some ways, a focus on total family income and reading tends to obscure more than it reveals. Family income patterns mask the influence of other family variables, including region of residence, nationality, and—perhaps most important— who earned the family's income, the father or the children.

REGION

On the surface, it would seem that region of residence would affect reading expenditures largely through differences in family income. Income in cotton textile manufacturing in the South was much lower than in either New England or the Mid-Atlantic states. Expenditures on books and newspapers by the southern workers were very low as well. But the influence of region was not purely an income effect. At every level of income, the Southerners were low spenders on books and newspapers.[4] Overall, the New Englanders in the sample allotted more than 3% of their discretionary spending for reading materials; the Southerners, by contrast, spent less than half that proportion (see Table 2).

TABLE 1
Average Expenditure for Newspapers and Books and Average Proportion of Discretionary Spending for Newspapers and Books Broken Down by the Income Status of the Family

Income Status	$ for Newspapers and Books	% for Newspapers and Books
Low Income	$ 2.93	2.7 %
Middle Income	$ 4.59	2.6 %
High Income	$ 5.17	2.0 %
Overall	$ 4.23	2.4 %

NOTE: Differences in mean expenditures among income groups significant, p < .01; differences in proportions not significant.

TABLE 2

Average Family Income, Average Expenditure for Newspapers
and Books, and Average Proportion of Discretionary Spending for
Newspapers and Books Broken Down by Region of Residence

Region	Family Income	$ for Newspapers and books	% for Newspapers and books
New England	$ 692	$ 5.32	3.4 %
Mid-Atlantic	$ 805	$ 5.08	2.6 %
South	$ 504	$ 2.30	1.4 %
Overall	$ 667	$ 4.23	2.4 %

NOTE: Differences in means among regions significant, p < .01.

Another way of getting at the effect of "Southernness" on
reading behavior among these mill workers is to compare readers
with nonreaders. For the purpose of this comparison (and some
other comparisons described later), I divided the families into
three groups: "nonreaders," those who spent nothing on books
and newspapers; "low readers," those who spent below the sample
median in the proportion of their discretionary income devoted to
reading materials; and "high readers," those who spent above the
median on that measure. (The median was about 2.5% of
discretionary spending for newspapers and books.) Table 3
displays the result. First, the South shows a significantly higher
proportion of nonreaders. But more important than this, few
Southerners were high readers. That is, few spent a large
proportion of their discretionary income on reading. And this
holds across income levels. For example, among the fourteen
high-income Southerners in my sample, only one family fell into
the category of high reader, compared with more than 40% of the
48 high-income families in the Mid-Atlantic states.

These figures on family reading *consumption* coincide with
what has long been known about the *production* of reading
materials in late-nineteenth-century America. The 1890 census
reported that per capita production of newspapers and periodicals
was much higher in the North than in the South. For the states in
my sample, the number of residents per copy of all newspapers

TABLE 3
Cross-Tabulation of Families by Reading Status
and Region of Residence

Reading Status	New England	Mid-Atlantic	South
Non-Readers	26 %	9 %	35 %
Low Readers	35 %	43 %	44 %
High Readers	40 %	48 %	21 %
Total % (N)	101% (98)	100% (100)	100% (100)

NOTE: Chi-square significant, p < .01.

and periodicals published was 0.41 for the Mid-Atlantic states, 0.53 for New England, and 3.79 for the South. In other words, the North had more copies of newspapers and magazines than people, and the South had nearly four people for each copy (U.S. Census Office, 1895). Of course, these are production figures, not circulation figures. But my data on spending suggest that circulation also was much lower among working-class readers in the South.

Though Table 3 shows most clearly the differences between North and South, it also suggests something about the working-class families in New England as well. More than one-fourth of the New England families in the sample were nonreaders. In other words, though New England had nearly twice as many high readers as the South, it also had—like the South—a large proportion of people who spent nothing at all on books and newspapers. And, in fact, many of these nonreading families fell into the high-income category. (Nearly 30% of the high-income families in New England were nonreaders, compared to only 6% in the Mid-Atlantic states.) Who were these people? Was their reading behavior similar to that of the Southerners? Might their experience shed some light on reading in the South as well as in the North? The answers to these questions are linked to another broad family variable—nationality of birth.

NATIONALITY

At first glance, nationality of birth appears to have been unrelated to reading behavior. When all three regions are lumped together, the data show no significant difference in the reading behavior of immigrants versus native-born Americans. Overall, immigrant families earned more income and spent a little more for books and newspapers, but both groups spent about the same proportion of their discretionary incomes: Immigrants spent about 2.4% for reading materials; native-born Americans about 2.5%. Table 4, however, tells a more subtle story. With regional effects controlled, it seems clear that nationality of birth did make a difference. In the North, native-born Americans were bigger spenders on reading, despite the fact that their family incomes were less. (This effect is not apparent when all three regions are considered together, because of the contradictory influence of the South, where all the workers were native-born Americans but were low spenders on reading nonetheless.) The difference between immigrants and native-born Americans was sharpest in New England. Here immigrant families earned substantially more than native Americans, but they spent less than one-half as much on reading—measured both in raw dollars *and* in proportion of discretionary spending. Why this striking difference? To answer this question, we need to look inside the families themselves.

Total family income is a poor predictor of reading expenditures, because it mattered very much *who* earned the income of the family. The simple correlation between reading expenditures and family income is only .15, but the correlation between reading expenditure and *husband's* income is nearly .40, a fairly strong correlation in this data set. The reason for the difference is that children's income is *negatively* correlated with reading expenditures; and the higher the family income, the larger the contribution from the children. In low-income families, about one-third of the school-age children worked, and the father's pay made up about two-thirds of the family's income. In high-income families, on the other hand, nearly three-fourths of the children worked,

TABLE 4

Average Family Income, Average Expenditure for Newspapers and Books,
and Average Proportion of Discretionary Spending for Newspapers and
Books Broken Down by Region of Residence and Nationality of Birth

Region and Nationality	Family Income	$ for Newspapers and Books	% for Newspapers and Books
New England			
--Native	$ 641	$ 9.04	5.9 %
--Immigrant	$ 709	$ 4.05	2.5 %
Mid-Atlantic			
--Native	$ 738	$ 5.48	2.8 %
--Immigrant	$ 852	$ 4.79	2.3 %
South			
--Native	$ 504	$ 2.30	1.4 %

NOTE: Differences in means among regions and among nationalities within New England significant, p < .01.

and the father's pay made up less than one-half of the family's income. High income usually meant children at work. And it was the children of immigrants and Southerners who seemed to work the hardest.

Table 5 shows how the composition of family income affected spending on books and newspapers. In general, the higher the proportion of family income supplied by the husband's earnings, the higher the proportion of discretionary spending on reading materials.[5]

In short, an important determinant of family expenditures on reading was the role that the children played in earning the family's income. Table 6 shows this relationship rather vividly. Families with children working were half as likely to be high readers as families who did not have their children at work.

To some extent, the importance of children working helps to explain regional and ethnic differences in reading behavior. As Tables 4 and 5 suggest, the groups that rank low on proportion of discretionary spending devoted to reading are also the groups that depended most on their children's incomes: southern natives and northern immigrants. But child labor is only part of the

TABLE 5

Average Income from Father, Average Income from Children, Proportion of Income from Father, and Proportion of Discretionary Spending for Newspapers and Books Broken Down by Region of Residence and Nationality of Birth

Region and Nationality	Father's Income	Children's Income	% from Father	% for Newspapers and Books
New England				
--Native	$ 479	$ 49	78 %	5.9 %
--Immigrant	$ 396	$ 190	63 %	2.5 %
Mid-Atlantic				
--Native	$ 471	$ 189	70 %	2.8 %
--Immigrant	$ 367	$ 280	52 %	2.3 %
South				
--Native	$ 235	$ 197	48 %	1.4 %

NOTE: Differences in means among regions and among nationalities within regions significant, p < .01.

TABLE 6

Cross-Tabulation of Families by Reading Status and Whether They Have Children at Work

Reading Status	No Children Working	Child Working
Non-Readers	23 %	24 %
Low Readers	28 %	52 %
High Readers	49 %	25 %
Total % (N)	100% (140)	100% (158)

NOTE: Chi-square significant, p < .01.

story, as Table 7 makes clear. Even when the children-at-work factor is controlled, the North-South difference and the native-immigrant difference are still apparent. Perhaps the most interesting of these groups are the native Southerners and the New England immigrants.

The reading behavior of Southerners was related to a variety of historical forces that made the South a distinctive region in America, even after Civil War. Southern cotton manufacturing,

TABLE 7

**Average Expenditure for Newspapers and Books and Average
Proportion of Discretionary Spending for Newspapers and
Books Broken Down by Region of Residence, by Nationality
of Birth, and by Whether the Family has Children at Work**

Region and Nationality	No Child Working		Child Working	
	$ for N & B	% for N & B	$ for N & B	% for N & B
New England				
--Native	$ 9.17	6.6 %	$ 8.71	4.1 %
--Immigrant	$ 4.65	3.4 %	$ 3.18	1.2 %
Mid-Atlantic				
--Native	$ 5.26	3.0 %	$ 5.77	2.7 %
--Immigrant	$ 6.61	3.5 %	$ 4.00	1.8 %
South				
--Native	$ 2.46	1.6 %	$ 2.20	1.3 %
Overall	$ 4.97	3.3 %	$ 3.56	1.7 %

NOTE: Differences in means among regions, within New England, and overall between child working and no child working significant, $p < .01$.

for example, was a major industry in the "New South" by 1890, but it stood apart from manufacturing in other regions. The mills were much smaller, much more widely scattered, and much more likely to be staffed by native-born American workers, including children (U.S. Census Office, 1895; Copeland, 1912; Mitchell, 1921). In general, manufacturing was not as closely associated with urbanization in the South as it was in the North. This in itself surely had some impact on reading behavior, because in nineteenth-century America both the production of reading materials and basic literacy were closely correlated with population concentration. And illiteracy was much more prevalent in the South than in the North (U.S. Census Office, 1895; Soltow and Stevens, 1981). But population concentration does not fully explain the disparity between the North and the South in either literacy rates or in the consumption of reading materials. Another factor strongly emphasized by Soltow and Stevens (1981) is schooling. They argue that school attendance, even in rural areas, was strikingly different between regions and was closely associated with differences in literacy.

On the basis of such aggregate regional comparisons, one might easily suppose that school attendance was closely related to reading behavior. My individual-level data, however, suggest otherwise. Certainly, the Southerners in my sample were much less likely than the Northerners to send their children to school. But nowhere did the fact that people had their children in school make much difference in their expenditures on reading materials. I found no correlations between reading expenditures and proportion of school-age children in school in any region, even when controlling for family income or income of the father.[6] Southern families remained significantly different from Northern families, regardless of whether they had their school-age children in school or not (see Table 8).

Perhaps some light can be shed on the reading habits of southern mill workers by comparing them with the most similar group in the North: New England immigrants. As Table 3 shows, New England had a large proportion of nonreaders. Most of these were immigrants. Among the immigrant families of New England, about 32% spent nothing on reading materials—a nonreading rate comparable only to the South. Who were these nonreaders? Half of them, it turns out, were from one particular ethnic group:

TABLE 8

Average Expenditures for Newspapers and Books and Average Proportion of Discretionary Spending for Newspapers and Books Broken Down by Region of Residence and by Whether the Family Has School-Age Children in School

Region	No Child in School		Child in School	
	$ for N & B	% for N & B	$ for N & B	% for N & B
New England	$ 4.26	2.5 %	$ 4.03	2.1 %
Mid-Atlantic	$ 4.70	2.5 %	5.28	2.3 %
South	$ 2.21	1.4 %	2.81	1.1 %

NOTE: Differences in means among regions significant, $p < .01$.

French Canadians. Among the 21 French Canadian families in the New England sample (21%), fully two-thirds spent nothing at all on books or newspapers. This low spending behavior was not due to poverty. In my sample, the French Canadian families scored well above average on family income (mean = $859). But their reading expenditures were extraordinarily low—about $1.29 per year, compared to the overall average of $4.23. The proportion of discretionary spending on reading was also extremely low—about 0.7%. The issue here is not simply one of language. Foreign language materials, including French publications, were readily available. Yet French Canadians' spending figures are lower than those for any other ethnic group, including the other foreign-language groups. The French Canadians were low spenders on reading even when their incomes were high. In fact, more than half of the high-income French Canadians were nonreaders, by far the largest proportion for any ethnic group in the entire sample.

Part of the explanation for the reading behavior of the French Canadians lies in the composition of their family incomes. The French Canadians had larger than average families, but they also had more than the average proportion of their school-age children at work. Thus, the proportion of family income earned by the husband in French Canadian families was very low, about 45% (see Table 5; see also Copeland, 1912). At the high-income level, the father earned only about 31% of the family income, the lowest for any ethnic group in the sample. But the French Canadians were not the only nationality group to lean heavily on their children for family income. The Irish, who earned on the average the highest family income in the sample ($881), were the most dependent upon their children. Overall, Irish fathers earned only 38% of the family's income, even less than French Canadian fathers. Yet the Irish scored well above the French Canadians in expenditures for books and newspapers (see also Modell, 1978). In short, the reading behavior of the French Canadians, like that of the Southerners, cannot be explained solely in terms of income or family earning patterns.

The same might be said of schooling. As with Southerners, school attendance does not seem to have been the key factor. French Canadians with children in school spent a larger proportion of their discretionary incomes on reading materials than did those who did not have their school-age children in school. But in *both* categories (children in school or not in school), the French Canadians scored the lowest of all ethnic groups in the sample. Just as the Southerners maintain their distinctiveness even when school attendance is taken into account, so here too, children in school does not seem to have been a key determinant of reading behavior.

Other family structure variables also fail to explain the reading habits of Southerners or French Canadians. I tried to discover, for example, if reading behavior was related to family life cycle. Working with these same data, Haines (1979) found that the life cycle of a late nineteenth-century family unfolded into fairly regular income and consumption patterns. In my sample, however, age of the family (husband + wife) was not correlated with reading expenditures, with or without controls for income. On the measure of family age, moreover, neither the Southerners nor the French Canadians seemed strikingly different from other groups in the sample. The southern parents were a little younger; the French Canadians a little older. On other family life-cycle variables—such as home ownership or whether the wife worked outside the home—these two groups were not significantly different from their neighbors.

So why did they spend so much less for newspapers and books? I think a more subtle cultural influence was at work, an influence that touched Southerners and French Canadians in similar ways and that had to do with their new lives in the new industrial communities of late nineteenth-century America.

COMMUNITY

In the South in the 1880s, the poor white workers were new to an industrial system that had not yet acquired a permanent working-class culture. They were rural people, and they often expected to return to the land (Carlton, 1982). Many, in fact, maintained their farming roots, while working in nearby mills. They continued to mark time by the traditional seasons of "hog-killin'," "cotton-choppin'," and "'tween crops." Those without local roots often lived the same migratory lives they had lived as share croppers. This persistence of traditional life styles led progressive-era experts on cotton manufacturing to complain about the improvident, undisciplined, undependable ways of southern mill workers (Copeland, 1912). The historian C. Vann Woodward (1951: 223) put the case somewhat more sympathetically: "The whole of this rustic industrialism moved to a rural rhythm." In short, these families were cultural transients.

The French Canadians of New England were similar to the southern mill workers in several ways. Like the Southerners, the French Canadians held tenaciously to their traditional ways, adamantly refusing to become part of a larger working-class culture. By 1890, they were recognized as perhaps the most separate and distinctive of the many ethnic groups in the polyglot textile industry of New England (Copeland, 1912). They were extremely clannish about marriage, church, schools, and other group values and behaviors. Because of their proximity to Quebec, they were also able to maintain close ties to their homeland. Their aim was what they called *la survivance:* the perpetuation of their historic and traditional culture. And they were remarkably successful until well into the twentieth century—perhaps more successful than any other American ethnic group (Theriault, 1980). By the 1890s, they did support a French-language press in New England, but newspapers were never so important to their lives or to the survival of French Canadian culture as were the traditional institutions of clan, church, and family (Theriault, 1980; see also U.S. Census Office, 1895). In the expanding American textile industry, in other words, they were strangers— not unlike the native-born mill workers of the South.

Viewed together, the behavior of the Southerners and the French Canadians may suggest a connection between reading and a feeling of arrival in a new culture, of involvement with the surrounding community—whether native or immigrant. If this is true, and there is a connection between reading and community involvement, there should be some relationship between reading expenditures and expenditures on other community-related activities. Indeed, there is some evidence that this was the case.

The interplay between family and community during the process of industrialization and urbanization has long fascinated historians. In a classic essay, Herbert Gutman (1973) suggested that the American working class, both native and immigrant, was only gradually and with much travail brought into the clock-and-machine culture of the nineteenth century. Over many decades, as they adjusted to new work routines and to the life styles of industry and city, workingmen and their families clung to preindustrial habits and behaviors. Thomas Bender (1978) describes this process of adjustment in terms of "gemeinschaft" and "gesellschaft," Ferdinand Tonnies' terms for traditional interpersonal community and modern contractual society. Bender argues that gemeinschaft was not replaced by gesellschaft, but rather the two forms of social experience came to coexist in nineteenth-century America. Traditional family and community behaviors continued to flourish side by side with the institutions of the modern marketplace society.

Some family historians have used census records and other historical data to try to test ideas such as these about family responses to changing environments. John Modell (1978) for example, using data from Wright's 1875 and 1890-1891 surveys, found that both American and Irish families increased what he calls their "prudential" expenditures, for such things as organization memberships and insurance. Yet, at the same time, "indulgent" expenditures on liquor and tobacco, which he views as a preindustrial cultural response to crisis, also remained high. In this and other ways, individual families exhibited traits of both industrial and preindustrial cultures (see also Hareven and Langenbach, 1978).

My data offer some evidence that reading was an activity associated more with modern community activities (gesellschaft) than with traditional activities of family and clan (gemeinschaft). I studied four categories of expenditures that touch on the lifestyle of the family in the community: family amusements, church and charities, insurance, and organizations. It seems to me that the first two of these categories suggest more traditional family and clan (gemeinschaft) interests; the latter two suggest more of a connection with the formal, contractual (gesellschaft) community.

The relationship between these four categories of expenditures and spending on newspapers and books is not exactly overwhelming, but it is clear. The partial correlation (controlling for income) is .27 between reading and insurance expenses, and .21 between reading and organization expenses. This is not a terribly strong correlation, but it is a statistically significant one. On the other hand, the partial correlations between reading and amusements and reading and church and charity are negligible and insignificant. Table 9 shows these relationships somewhat more vividly than the partial correlations, because the relationships are not altogether linear. In spending on amusements and church (gemeinschaft expenditures), nonreaders were not significantly different from readers in my sample. In spending on insurance and organizations (gesellschaft expenditures), on the other hand, nonreaders were quite different indeed. On the average, they spent less than half of the amount spent by even the moderate readers. And these relationships between readers and nonreaders hold *within* regions as well.

Embedded within these figures, of course, are the Southerners and the French Canadians (see Table 10). Their experience suggests what the figures might mean. Of the four categories of discretionary spending that I studied, the Southerners' chief expenditure was for family amusements; the French Canadians' primary commitment was to church and charity.[7] In the more gesellschaft categories, on the other hand, both groups fell well below the sample means.

Historians of the mass media have speculated that the popular newspapers and periodicals of the late nineteenth century helped to integrate the newcomer into the brave new world of modern urban and industrial life (Barth, 1980; Schudson, 1978). These new mass media may have helped to build new communities among the ashes of the old (Nord, 1985). My data lend some

TABLE 9

Average Expenditures for Amusements, Church
and Charity, Organizations, and Insurance Broken
Down by Reading Status of the Family

Reading Status	$ for Amusements	$ for Church & Charity	$ for Organizations	$ for Insurance
Non-Readers	$ 5.08	$ 9.06	$ 1.03	$ 4.00
Low Readers	$ 5.54	$ 11.61	$ 2.71	$ 8.78
High Readers	$ 5.89	$ 11.45	$ 3.25	$ 9.68
Overall	$ 5.56	$ 11.60	$ 2.51	$ 8.00

NOTE: Differences in means among reading status groups significant for Organizations and Insurance, $p < .01$; insignificant for Amusements and Church and Charity.

TABLE 10

Average Expenditures for Amusements, Church and Charity,
Organizations Broken Down for Southerners and French Canadians

Ethnic Group	$ for Amusements	$ for Church & Charity	$ for Organizations	$ for Insurance
Southerners	$ 6.73	$ 6.18	$ 1.82	$ 1.74
French Canadians	$ 6.66	$ 14.24	$ 1.30	$ 5.09
Overall Sample	$ 5.56	$ 11.60	$ 2.51	$ 8.00

NOTE: Differences in means between each ethnic group and overall sample (except for Amusements) significant, $p < .01$.

support to this association of working-class reading and modern community life. Though reading was a common activity for all groups in my sample of working-class families, the more avid readers seem to have been more at home with the institutions of the modern industrial community.

SUMMARY

This study of the family budgets of cotton textile workers in 1890 mainly confirms the expected—that reading was related to income, region, nationality, and community life. But, I hope, it also contributes to an understanding of how these general categories of family life may have been interconnected.

First, the analyses suggest that reading expenditures were sensitive to who in the family earned the income. Regardless of family income, a very important factor in expenditures on books and newspapers was children at work. The more the family depended on children's income, the less they spent on reading. This might seem to be merely the negative side of commitment to schooling, but I did not find this to be the case. Although children at work was always related to low-level reading expenditures, children in school was not.

Second, my data clearly show the expected regional variations in reading expenditures, with the South scoring extremely low on actual dollars spent on books and newspapers and low on proportion of discretionary spending for reading materials. Though the southern workers were more likely than the northern workers to have their young children at work, and much less likely to have them in school, these variables did not seem to be the keys to Southernness. No matter what controls I introduced, southern reading expenditures remained low and quite distinctive.

Third, I looked at nationality, comparing the Southerners and the southern work experience to a northern ethnic group with similar reading behavior: the French Canadians. For both groups, family work patterns were important. Both depended heavily on income from their working children, and neither group showed much concern for schooling. Yet, even with these factors controlled, the distinctiveness remained.

To explain this distinctiveness I looked at the similar cultural experiences of the Southerners and the French Canadians. Though they were extraordinarily different in many ways, both groups shared a fundamental similarity. They were cultural sojourners—*in* but not *of* the emerging modern communities of industrial America. Their commitments lay more with gemeinschaft institutions, such as family and church, and less with gesellschaft institutions, such as organizations and insurance companies. And, finally, I argued that the consumption of newspapers and books seems to have been tied more to this latter gesellschaft world.

NOTES

1. Modell (1978) checked the internal consistency of Wright's methods and results and found them fairly sound. Haines (1979) tested Wright's survey data against data from the 1890 census. He found some differences in some areas, such as age distributions, but overall he found the survey data fairly representative.

2. In fact, the analysis is based upon a sample of 298. Because of a coding error, I ended up with only 98 cases in the New England subsample. The error did not affect the randomness of the sample, and therefore should not have affected the analysis.

3. "Discretionary expenditures" are those over which the family exercised some significant choice. Specifically, I defined (and computed) discretionary expenditures as total family spending minus expenditures for food, rent, utilities, taxes, and medical care.

4. This statement is based upon an analysis of covariance, with income as a covariate.

5. This relationship (shown in Table 5) also holds in partial correlation analysis, within regions and across regions, with and without controls for family income.

6. Unfortunately, this data set contains no information on *parents'* education. Proportion of school-age children in school was the only index of commitment to education and schooling that I could devise.

7. On southern mill workers and amusements, see Copeland (1912). On French Canadians and their close connection to church and parish life, see Theriault (1980).

REFERENCES

BARTH, G. (1980) City People: The Rise of Modern City Culture in Nineteenth-Century America. New York: Oxford Univ. Press.
BENDER, T. (1978) Community and Social Change in America. New Brunswick, NJ: Rutgers Univ. Press.
CARLTON, D. (1982) Mill and Town in South Carolina, 1880-1920. Baton Rouge: Louisiana State Univ. Press.
COPELAND, M. T. (1912) The Cotton Manufacturing Industry of the United States. Cambridge, MA: Harvard Univ. Press.
DARNTON, R. (1982) "What is the history of books?" Daedalus 111: 65-83.
GRAFF, H. (1979) The Literacy Myth: Literacy and Social Structure in the Nineteenth-Century City. New York: Academic Press.
———(1981) Literacy in History: An Interdisciplinary Research Bibliography. New York: Garland Press.

GUTMAN, H. G. (1973) "Work, culture, and society in industrializing America, 1815-1919." Amer. Historical Rev. 78: 531-88. (reprinted in Work, Culture, and Society in Industrializing America: Essays in American Working-Class and Social History. New York: Knopf, 1976).

HAINES, M. R. (1979) "Industrial work and the family life cycle, 1889-1890." Research in Econ. History 4: 289-356.

HAREVEN, T. K. and R. LANGENBACH (1978) Amoskeag: Life and Work in an American Factory-City. New York: Pantheon.

HARRIS, M. H. (1972) "Books on the frontier: the extent and nature of book ownership in southern Indiana, 1800-1850." Library Q. 42: 416-430.

————and D. G. DAVIS [eds.] (1978) American Library History: A Bibliography. Austin: Univ. of Texas Press.

HART, J. D. (1950) The Popular Book: A History of America's Literary Taste. New York: Oxford Univ. Press.

Illinois Bureau of Labor Statistics (1884) Third Biennial Report, part 2. Springfield, IL: Author.

KAESTLE, C. F. (1985) The History of Literacy and the History of Readers. (Program Report, 85-2) Madison: Wisconsin Center for Education Research.

KETT, J. F. and P. A. McCLUNG, (1984) Book Culture in Post-Revolutionary Virginia. Worcester, MA: American Antiquarian Society.

LEIBY, J. (1960) Carroll Wright and Labor Reform: The Origin of Labor Statistics. Cambridge, MA: Harvard Univ. Press.

LINDERT, P. (1980) "Child costs and economic development," in R. A. Easterlin (ed.) Population Change and Economic Growth in Developing Countries. Chicago: Univ. of Chicago Press.

LOCKRIDGE, L. (1974) Literacy in Colonial New England. New York: W. W. Norton.

MacDONALD, W. D. (1972) "The early history of labor statistics in the United States." Labor History 13: 267-278.

MARSHALL, J. D. [ed.] (1966) Approaches to Library History. Tallahassee: Journal of Library History.

Massachusetts Bureau of the Statistics of Labor (1875) Sixth Annual Report. Public Document No. 31. Boston, MA: Author.

McCOMBS, M. E. (1972) "Mass media in the marketplace." Journalism Monographs, 24.

MITCHELL, B. (1921) The Rise of Cotton Mills in the South. (Johns Hopkins University Studies in Historical and Political Science, series 39, no. 2) Baltimore: Johns Hopkins Univ. Press.

MODELL, J. (1978) "Patterns of consumption, acculturation, and family income strategies in late Nineteenth-Century America," in T. K. Hareven and M. A. Vinovskis (eds.) Family and Population in Nineteenth-Century America. Princeton, NJ: Princeton Univ. Press.

MOTT, F. L. (1957) A History of American Magazines, 1885-1905, Vol. 4. Cambridge, MA: Harvard Univ. Press.

NORD, D. P. (1985) "The public community: the urbanization of journalism in Chicago." J. of Urban History 11: 411-441.

NORTH, S.N.D. (1908-1909) "The life and work of Carroll Davidson Wright." Quarterly Publications of the American Statistical Association 11: 447-66.

SCHUDSON, M. (1978) Discovering the News: A Social History of American Newspapers. New York: Basic Books.

SOLTOW, L. and E. STEVENS (1981) The Rise of Literacy and the Common School in the United States. Chicago: Univ. of Chicago Press.

STIGLER, G. J. (1965) "The early history of empirical studies of consumer behavior," in Essays in the History of Economics. Chicago: Univ. of Chicago Press.

TEBBEL, J. (1975) A History of Book Publishing in the United States: The Expansion of an Industry, 1865-1919. New York: R. R. Bowker.

THERIAULT, G. F. (1980) The Franco-Americans in a New England Community: An Experiment in Survival. New York: Arno Press.

U.S. Census Office (1895) Report on manufacturing industries in the United States at the eleventh census—1890. Part 3: Selected Industries, "Printing and Publishing" and "Cotton Manufacture." Washington, DC: Government Printing Office.

U.S. Commissioner of Labor (1890) Sixth Annual Report. Washington, DC: Government Printing Office.

———(1891) Seventh Annual Report. Washington, DC: Government Printing Office.

WILLIAMS, F. M. and C. C. ZIMMERMAN (1935) "Studies of family living in the United States and other countries: an analysis of material and method. (Miscellaneous Publication No. 23, U.S. Department of Agriculture) Washington, DC: Government Printing Office.

WILLIAMSON, J. (1966-1967) "Consumer behavior in the nineteenth century: Carroll D. Wright's Massachusetts workers in 1875." Explorations in Entrepreneurial History 4: 125-129.

WOODWARD, C. V. (1951) Origins of the New South, 1877-1913. Baton Rouge: Louisiana State Univ. Press.

WRIGHT, C. D. (1890-1891) "A basis for statistics of cost of production." Proceedings of the American Statistical Association 2: 157-177.

David Paul Nord is Associate Professor in the School of Journalism at Indiana University—Bloomington. His main interest is the history of mass media in the life of the American city. His most recent article in this area is "The public community: the urbanization of journalism in Chicago," J. of Urban History 11 (August, 1985). He is also the author of Newspapers and New Politics: Midwestern Municipal Reform, 1890-1900, *Ann Arbor: UMI Research Press, 1981.*

10

QUOTING NOT SCIENCE
BUT SIDEBOARDS
Television in a New Way of Life

John Hartley and Tom O'Regan

Perth hath not anything to show more fair

Imagine the scene, one night in Spring. All over the city and suburbs groups of twenty or more people are crowding around, in homes and in public areas, and all eyes are fixed on a new blueish kind of light. Right here in Perth, that light signals the dawn of a new age. And like the mysterious bleeps of the recently launched Sputnik, new sounds travel through space to capture all ears, reminding Western Australians of their myriad links - personal, industrial, architectural and now audio-visual - with a future world that's theirs in the making.

Of course, it wasn't exactly like that. The public on whom television was launched in October 1959 was not entirely unsuspecting. Plenty of planning, promotion and practice had gone into the launch. There were only 3,300 TV sets operating on opening night, but all the same an estimated 70,000 people jostled and joked their way into the picture.

Afterwards, things did change. Perth grew, its dependence on a few primary industries both being masked and reduced by its own expanding infrastructure. Its modernity may have been masked by its deference to authority from over east or overseas, but that mask only conceals the source of Perth's power - bodily comforts. The Italian designer Ettore Sottsass - founder of the 'Memphis' movement - has spoken for Perth's well-kept secret without knowing it when he says:

> World culture today is concerned with the American vision of comfort. Today and for many hundreds of years to come humanity will pursue earthly comfort. Comfort means to possess warmth, coolness, softness, light, shade, air-travel, Polynesian spaces or Alaska. To have money means to possess sensory possibilities, not power. Sensoriality destroys ideology, it is anarchical, private; it takes account of consumerism and consumption, it is not moralistic, it opens up new avenues (*p.142*).

Perth has been living this way for decades, opening up new avenues literally and metaphorically as its suburbs, beaches and high-rises express physically the sensory possibilities that are being explored within them. Occasionally there are public demonstrations of its modernist knowledges - glimpses through the mask when the city beams skywards to the future, all its lights ablaze, joined by massed Kingswoods in King's Park flashing their headlights, just to say 'G'day, mate' to the ultimate air traveller, a passing astronaut. There's even a mild gesture of recognition when a Concorde or a QE2 passes through. But the same fervour for comfort and sensoriality turns to fury when the American vision of comfort is transformed into its opposite: the American vision of power. So Carl Vinsons and their nuclear fists are greeted not with deference but offence, and Perth opposes power with the only means it has - pleasure boats for the flotillas and inflated prices for the sailors.

For the most part, however, Perth has grown privately, non-moralistically, producing its new way of life in the everyday energy of peoples' activities. Another 'Memphis' designer, Andrea Branzi, has suggested how far the public, historical world of culture and knowledge is a product of physical, bodily qualities and sensations:

> Today we know - and the experience of body art has confirmed our knowledge - that our perception of the environment is substantially a physical process carried out to a great extent by our body, which is not a brute receptacle of sensations and stimuli (on which only the 'intelligent' mind is able to impose order and meaning), but an active instrument capable of processing environmental data and of transforming them into experience and culture, utilising them independently of their allegorical or ideological meaning (*p.142*).

What this suggests is that culture, knowledge and experience are themselves forms of communication, but communication based as much on spatial relations, tactile qualities and tensions as on sights, colours and sounds. In such a context, the arrival of television in Perth can be looked at physically, as it were, and its subsequent changes and developments can be traced in the ways that people consumed space and time; how they learnt, or were encouraged, to accommodate their bodies to the TV and the TV to their physical environment.

One thing seems certain. Television was recognised as an agent of physical changes very early on. In 1962, Guy Branchi was already able to claim categorically that:

> The advent of television in Western Australia has undoubtedly altered the social pattern of the lives of the people ... People have tended to make adjustments in their way of living and to alter their activities to suit the viewing of their favourite TV programs.

Indeed, television appears to have become more popular, more quickly, in Perth than in the other State capitals. Among the general reasons for television's easy assimilation into peoples' lives was the existence of media, especially radio and cinema, that had already 'trained' people in the necessary skills for watching and enjoying TV. Radio in particular had paved the way. Some TV programs were literally radio shows with pictures. Much of the TV that was produced through the 1960s - game shows, today shows, kids' shows - tended to use formats made familiar in radio. More fundamentally perhaps, television was the same kind of dual distribution/exhibition system as radio, which, for the cost of a set and a licence, you could enjoy for free at home. And the interaction between public broadcasting (supplied by commercial or public corporations) and the routines of domestic life had been well-practiced in radio. Thus, TV borrowed radio's scheduling habits, and continued the practice of carrying advertisements during shows.

However, television had the one attribute of cinema that radio lacked - vision. This had several consequences. One was the practice of scheduling movies on Fridays and weekends, during the times when people might ordinarily have gone to the cinema. But another was to produce in the early TV audience in Perth a form of watching that retained some of the public, social feel of 'going out' to the cinema. TV was watched with an intensity, concentration and lack of conversation that would be unfamiliar today. Often the lights were dimmed or turned off. It was placed in the formal (public) lounge room and frequently watched by large groups which included visiting relatives, neighbours or friends. The transformation of a person's house into the equivalent of a public place had its effect on social habits and protocols, as Eric Fisher recalls:

> In the early days of TV in Perth, a visit to someone's place meant just walking in and saying hello. Most of the lights would be turned off. Then you would sit down and watch TV. Someone would rush out and make a cup of tea and bring in some biscuits, and when you finished viewing for the night you went home. I can recall being quite shocked by what appeared to be rude behaviour. You would be invited over - but you'd be lucky if the host or hostess noticed you when you arrived. It was ... 'come over, bring a beer, come in' ... and then back to the box.

Meanwhile, Perth was continuing to grow, but it grew out, not up. Then, as now, Perth had the lowest housing density of any of the major State

Be ready for T.V. when it comes to the West

Start a **TELEVISION SAVINGS ACCOUNT**

NOW ... at A.N.Z. Savings Bank

Although the first general telecast in the West is little more than a year ahead, it's not too early to think about your television set.

Whether or not you intend now to own a set, experience in the Eastern States proves that when it comes you'll certainly want to enjoy the wonderful entertainment television brings into your home. It will save you money ... and save waiting if you open an A.N.Z. Television Savings Account and start saving for this special purpose NOW.

It's so much easier to save this way

When you open an A.N.Z. Television Savings Account you receive your own special Television Savings Account Pass Book. See how much easier it is to save when you keep this money separate from your ordinary savings and add to it regularly. Resolve to put something aside at every opportunity and you will be in the happy position of being able to pay the whole or a major portion of the purchase price of your set.

Whole families can join in the fun of regular saving by using the special A.N.Z. Television Money Box. Small amounts soon accumulate and it doesn't take long for the contents of your money box to swell the balance in your pass book.

Money in your Television Savings Account earns interest at current rates and may be withdrawn at any time as with a normal Savings Account.

How to Open Your A.N.Z. Television Savings Account

The staff of any branch of A.N.Z. Savings Bank in and around Perth will be pleased to open your account. You can readily identify A.N.Z. Bank branches by the familiar blue and gold shield ... you will remember them by the friendly, efficient service that is a feature of all A.N.Z. offices.

Outstanding Popularity in Sydney and Melbourne

Television has proved extremely popular in Sydney and Melbourne since it started almost two years ago.

Television brings you interesting discussions and interviews on all subjects. It appeals to all tastes with special shows for children, women's sessions, hand-y-man demonstrations, sport, musical recitals, plays, variety and news events from many parts of the world coming right into your home.

"A typical scene from a popular live variety show in Melbourne"

You are sure to want T.V. ... so open an A.N.Z. Television Savings Account NOW at A.N.Z. SAVINGS BANK

 A.N.Z. BANK

Australia and New Zealand Bank Limited
Australia and New Zealand Savings Bank Limited

'The West Australian'. 18 October 1958

capitals; and then, as now, its public transport systems were less frequent than those of other cities. The well-known but badly-lit suburban sprawl around Perth was fertile ground for television. Watching TV at home meant you did not have to go into the city itself or to suburban centres - it cut out dead travelling time, substituting the possibility of immediate access to entertainment instead. This was something the cinemas, live theatres and libraries could not provide. On top of that, if you didn't like the show you weren't stuck with it - you could switch off or go into another part of the house.

Domesticating Consumerism

Perth may have been fertile ground for TV, and extra fertilisation may have resulted from some of its citizens being familiar with it already, coming from places that already had it. But even fertile ground has to be tilled. As a consumer item, the television set itself wasn't cheap. The average price was 180 guineas (guineas made big purchases sound cheaper), or ten bob a week. The tillage was enthusiastically undertaken in the media themselves. National publications like the *Australian Women's Weekly* had been carrying TV stories from early on - and both Sydney and Melbourne had a three-year lead on Perth. Locally, there were bank advertisements in *The West Australian* a full year before television was introduced, highlighting the 'need' for Perth people to start putting away money in order to be able to get a TV set when the moment arrived. These particular ads made much of the enjoyment people in Melbourne and Sydney were getting from television.

Such blandishments were all very well, but you couldn't touch, feel, see or hear a television with them. To make it a tactile reality, the opening was presaged by so-called trade transmissions. The corporate planning behind trade transmissions was to get a sufficient audience, by selling a sufficient number of sets, to make the opening night a corporate success: that is, to convince advertisers of the new medium's viability. So TVW 7 went on air a full month before the official opening, showing documentaries culled from film libraries such as those of Shell, BP and the State Film Library. You could see these transmissions in electrical retail shops selling TV sets, and also at night as part of home demonstrations.

These public and private demonstrations of TV were not just marketing instruments, they were cultural events in themselves. Having been primed by the massive retail effort conducted on radio and in the press, people were prone to give television their undivided attention. So much so that when The Highway Hotel in Claremont installed a TV just after opening night they felt obliged to remind patrons not to let their beers get warm! As for home demonstrations, these immediately entered the realm of neighbourhood politics. Television involved a whole new distribution system, and one which required its consumers to pay for it (like radio, but unlike the press). Early TV sets were sold mainly on the basis of home demonstrations, so the TV salesman (it was always a man) and his van became important components of the process. Having the TV man come into your house was a visible way of signifying your transition into and participation in the new and marvellous world of home entertainment. This was even more true for poorer viewers - having an expensive material possession like a TV set was a means of demonstrating a degree of economic control over your environment; and as the TV cost more to such viewers, it tended to be featured more prominently

in their homes. Gratifyingly, after the TV salesman had left, the mark of your transition was there for all to see in the shape of the outdoor aerial he'd erected for you. At this point, your neighbours and family would, for a period, avail themselves of your exclusive theatrette, and you'd become an unwitting agent for the salemen. Everyone could see what the TV did for your home, and imagine it in their own. Talk would centre on how much it cost and whether it could be afforded, on who had one and who didn't, on how interesting it was (even the test pattern), on where to site the set in the house, and on the programs and people you had seen - sometimes you might even glimpse an acquaintance in the audience of a show. By this stage, some of your neighbours would be feeling socially outpaced, and the salesman's van would be seen drawing up to another house. As ownership or rental became more widespread, and as the novelty wore off, television viewing began to lose its quasi-cinematic, social aspect, and to take on its more recently characteristic patterns - it was a private, family activity, with just one family per set.

People were already adjusting the social patterns of their lives, but they were not acting as the brute receptacles of sensations and stimuli. On the contrary, TV's rapid assimilation into their experience and culture resulted from its congruence with long-term propensities and changes that can be traced across a number of quite different domains. Perhaps the most general of these changes has been the process by which public and private space has been redefined: from the city centre to suburban shopping centres and then to malls; from public swimming baths to backyard pools; from picnicking in parks to the B-B-Q in the backyard; from the pub to the home cocktail bar; from health clubs to home gyms, games rooms and saunas; from cinema to TV; from football to Wide World of Sports; from 'live' theatre to TV drama.

Over a long period, and throughout the advanced and industrialising world, cultural consumption patterns have been decentred from public, mass activities, fragmenting into myriad, decentralised consumer rites and pleasures in and around peoples' homes. Naturally, the previously established public forms of entertainment were obliged to adjust too. Cinema attendances fell, and the audience resolved itself into precisely those who were self-propelled out of the home environment - young people and teenagers. 'Live' theatre, already cosily dying, lost yet more bums from its seats, resulting in public meetings that were held to deplore the situation. Public sporting fixtures, like theatres, lost patrons, and they too had to content themselves with specialised constituencies of supporters. In future, it would take very special events to draw an indiscriminate public out all together, irrespective of class, gender, age, ethnicity, income-bracket or occupation - events like Royal shows, 12-metre yacht races, Australia Day fireworks (simulcast on television) or summer heatwaves, especially when these coincided with non-ratings periods. Otherwise, popular culture on a daily basis was organised around private consumption, and the market leader in popular entertainment was television.

Sites (and Sights) of Struggle

The redefinition of public and private spaces meant that new energies were released in peoples' homes: energies that began to change the way that houses were organised. But as the 'Memphis' writer Barbara Radice has pointed out, the changes attendant on consumerism, are not simply the result of corporate marketing strategies. People began to alter their ways of looking and cooking for their own reasons. Radice comments:

> Consumerism, besides being a necessity induced by the production system, is also a pleasure; and a pleasure is never completely controllable or without consequences. Putting new signs on the air means circulating new energies, producing new desires, anxieties, incentives, and conditions.

Perhaps the first uncontrolled consequence of television's sudden appearance on the Perth scene was, ironically, the effect on its own neighbour-medium, the radio. Television grabbed radio's night-time audience and crippled its night-time shows. Accommodating itself to television's dominance in its own erstwhile realm of the home, radio looked increasingly to daytime audiences for advertising revenues. And it found them in another echo of American consumerism; the constant rotation of records, fast talking DJs, commercials, news updates and frequent station ident. jingles. The lazy respectability of speech and variety-radio was progressively speeded up to higher pitches - producing top 100 then top 40 radio, ever more cheerfully dedicated to the circulation of new energies, desires, anxieties, incentives and conditions.

But radio was not only displaced as an institutional medium, it was also displaced, literally, in peoples' homes. Under the existing arrangements, radios were substantial items of furniture, filled with valves and as yet showing no sign of their future transistorisation, miniaturisation and micro-circuitry. But because they were listened to rather than looked at, radio sets were not the focal object of living spaces. Eric Fisher, a local radio and TV personality of the 1960s, remembers TV's disruptive entry:

> In the forties and fifties there was a lounge room which always had a radio set in it. If you were lucky you might have had a radio in the kitchen too. You might have had a dining room too - not all homes had dining rooms then - they were for some a luxury. You usually had an open fire in the lounge which seating tended to be grouped around. The radio was wherever it was most convenient to have it so long as the sound could be heard. But with the advent of TV all the furniture had to be rearranged so you could view it.

Such rearrangements of furniture were in fact more disruptive than may at first appear - it wasn't simply a matter of reorienting the three-piece suite.

The big problem was the fireplace. But even this immoveable object was no match for the irresistible force of television. Architects and builders, always mindful that rooms need focal points as well as occasional warming, had tended to make fireplaces very prominent and eye-catching, often in the centre of the longer wall. Television sets, being expensive and averse to heat and sparks, were often placed in the corner, away from the fireplace. This meant that fires were immediately displaced to the edge of one's field of vision, and the rearranged seating was now unevenly exposed to the fire. It now required looking round deliberately to see if the fire needed tending, and getting up to do it meant crossing someone's line of sight to the TV. The upshot was, of course, that the open fire fell into disfavour during the 1960s and 1970s, being replaced by less obtrusive mobile heaters, whilst fireplaces themselves were often boarded up or removed altogether. Nowadays, in older renovated houses such as those in Fremantle, the feature fireplace may be retained, but as likely as not it will be the chosen place for siting the television. Unlike the open fire itself, the TV set can be looked at all year round, instead of being an object of visual interest for the short winter months alone.

Since they were designed to be looked at all year round, TV sets had to look good in themselves, especially as they were so expensive to acquire. Despite their electrical and scientific contemporaneity, TV sets were never marketed with this aspect of their design on display. On the contrary, the chassis, tube and valves were regarded as unsightly and even dangerous, so television never went through a do-it-yourself, "cat's-whisker" phase as radio had. Instead, TV sets were sold as items of lounge-room furniture, masking the apparatus in boxes of wood or wood-veneer that quoted not science but sideboards in their design. This approach made television simultaneously familiar and exciting, intimate and mysterious. Moulded housings were used too, producing a look which allowed the TV set to express an image associated with other modern domestic appliances, from certain kinds of radiogram to fridges and washing machines. But television was never one of the 'white-goods' (even though both types of appliance may have been made by the same manufacturer). The TV set was designed for the imagination, not for working areas like the kitchen. If it quoted any outside reference, it was not the world of work and science but that of the prestige entertainment media, sometimes alluding to theatre and cinema in the shape of the frame round the screen or in the drape-like material used to cover the speaker. The naming of TV sets confirmed these up-market associations: Washington, Kreisler, Motorola.

Once installed, television could come into its own. Itself the quintessential image of modernity, it was used to promote the purchase of other things that would fit into the modern, TV home. It stimulated both consumption and production. E.M. Branchi, writing in 1961, noted:

> Television in Western Australia has also called for a market for such commodities as TV lamps, TV clothes, TV suppers and TV furniture (p.26).

NT   THE WEST AUSTRALIAN, MONDAY, AUGUST 31, 1959.   49

All TV Hostesses Should Know

In the Eastern States, and overseas, TV viewing has conditioned women's selection of leisure clothes. Long sessions of lounging in an arm-chair have been found to play havoc with formal day or evening wear.

Informality

And so, for extended TV viewing anyway, the accent is on informality. Women have developed a liking for tapered slacks in brilliant, solid colours, topped with overblouses in futuristic designs.

Come summer, slacks give way to shorts worn with a shortie version of the "muu-muu" for cool comfort. Some simple slip-on tops are reversible, with solid colour on one side to match the shorts, and in reverse a contrasting printed design.

Most of them come in time-saving drip-drys, and are worn with ballarina shoes. But for the more exotic hostess, velvet or lurex tapered slacks with a jersey knit embroidered or glitter-sprinkled top and oriental slippers, give a sophisticated air.

Men, of course, remain as consistently indiscriminate in their choice of clothes as they always were.

Don't Let The New TV Set Destroy Your Room Setting

"LOOK at me," a television set demands —and immediately creates a problem for most home owners.

Just as television can dominate your life, it can disorganise your home unless thought is given to room settings before the receiver is purchased.

Chairs which normally sit in conversational style will move to face one direction. This introduces the danger of the room assuming the air of a picture theatre and people should be careful to arrange the furniture so that everyone can see the screen without destroying the homely atmosphere of the room.

"Where?"

"Where will I put the set?" is the first question most TV owners will ask. Perth decorator Mrs. Joyce Walker has a practical answer: "Put it in the most uncomfortable place in the room," she says. "Put it in the draughty corner, so you do not have to sit there, or in the cold corner, so you can sit near the fire at the opposite end of the room."

Of course, other things must be considered. The set should be placed with subdued lighting facing it rather than behind it. West Australians may find themselves with a special problem in the summer, when TV sessions begin long before the sun has set. Venetian blinds will regain popularity because they shut out the light while letting in the cool afternoon breeze.

The size of the room is no longer important, because a 21in. screen can now be viewed from a distance of about 6ft.

Furniture designer David Foulkes Taylor offers a novel suggestion to people planning new homes. Why not make allowance for the TV in a built-in space, in the corner of a room, a section of the wall, or as a room divider?

This idea is in keeping with the modern trend of dividing dining and living rooms by a lattice screen or framework of shelves and cabinet. Mr. Taylor suggests that the TV be placed in this framework, preferably on a swivel so it can be turned to face either room.

But wherever you put it, make sure it does not stand out in the room like a postage stamp. Perth interior decorators agree that TV should not be over-emphasised in room decoration and if it strikes the eye the moment you walk into a room, it is definitely in the wrong place.

Not Feature

Mr. Taylor believes that a simple, well-designed set can be placed in al-

all chairs will move towards it. The furniture should thus be arranged to enable easy viewing while retaining the natural atmosphere of the room, which is in danger of being lost if the room is transformed into a small-scale picture theatre.

Mrs. Walker has worked out a simple plan for a modern living room, which can be turned into a TV room at a few seconds' notice.

Simple Plan

At the far end from the receiver she would place a divan, with comfortable chairs scattered in a semi-circle around the room. For unexpected guests she would keep a stack of thick rubber cushions in a corner, to be pulled off and used as individual seats for short sessions. These cushions always look attractive and can be dotted around the room without blanking anybody's view of the screen.

Lighting can make or mar a viewer's enjoyment of TV. It is generally accepted that it should be seen in neither bright light nor complete darkness, but with a soft, indirect light somewhere in the room to counteract flicker on the screen.

A lamp with a shade which throws the light up towards the ceiling not down towards the screen or out to the viewer's face) should be placed near the screen. Certain types of wall brackets are also quite suitable.

For the comfort of the eyes, the wall behind the set should be a pastel colour, with the deeper colours reserved for other parts of the room.

Antique

People who live in homes with antique furniture may be apprehensive about television (the height of modernity) entering their home. Most interior decorators have welcome advice for these antique lovers. Leave the room alone, they say. Do not try to change its atmosphere to fit the TV set.

Nedlands interior decorator Mrs. Maria Dent believes that TV cannot be incorporated aesthetically into antique surroundings unless the set is made of darker, quieter toned wood."

She advises people who live in old homes not to worry if they cannot find a TV set to match their settings. She suggests building a screen to hide the set if it jars too much with the surroundings.

If advice like this is followed and a little extra thought given before the set is purchased, television will enter your home with the minimum of confusion.

COLOUR TV A LONG WAY OFF

COLOUR TV is a reality —it is in use in many English and American hospitals—but it seems unlikely as a commercial proposition in Australia for many, many years.

The reason lies in the high cost and complexity of electronic equipment to pick-up and separate the three primary colours, red, blue and green, then transmit them separately, receive them and synthesise them into the one colour image on a screen.

The cost of a home colour TV receiver alone is far above the normal black and white receiver.

One of the top New York television networks, Columbia Broadcasting System, attempted to introduce commercial colour television several years ago, using a mechanical colour convertor—a whirling disk synchronised with the three colour signals—but it was rejected.

It is considered unlikely that either U.S.A. or Britain will have commercial colour TV before five years at least—and Australia would hardly be in a position to bear the heavy cost burden of such a system for many years after that time.

'The West Australian', 31 August 1959

Without speculating for too long on what TV clothes may have looked like, it is worth noting that television sets themselves were often dressed, usually with lamps, plants and photographs, in a further attempt to domesticate and customise the bulky, recalcitrant shape, suggesting that TV sets were indeed regarded as like sideboards.

Television entered and altered the rhythms of household activity. The need to look as well as to hear put pressure on meal preparation and consumption: pressure upon cooking, washing up and other household activities to contract in time; and pressure upon eating to take place simultaneously with watching. Thus the familiar lounge coffee-table became the meal-table proper, and fast, convenience foods requiring little preparation and few utensils became the vogue.

Meanwhile, television commercials and programs alike were promoting and displaying the modern lifestyle of domestic consumption. This may have played its part in longer-term changes that were taking place in house design. WAIT architect Peter Little suggests that the major change to Western Australian housing stock over the last thirty years has been the migration of the toilet and the laundry. Initially these were found in the backyard, often as far from the dwelling as possible. But they were moved progressively closer; first to the verandah area, then inside, and finally, in the case of the toilet, into en-suites by the 'master' bedroom. Such a migration to some extent mimicks peoples' own migrations from outside to inside the home, where increased time (including time spent watching TV) meant increased incentive to improve, embellish and modernise.

Television itself was used to promote cleansing practices and products which went along with changing attitudes to health and the toilet; and it also encouraged spending on decorating and equipping the newly interiorised areas. Similarly, people were encouraged to spend more on a range of products that consumerised activities they'd engaged in all along - activities like washing their houses, clothes and dishes, or themselves and their hair. And once those yukky wet areas were moved out of the yard, it too was available for home-entertainment, with pool, B-B-Q, pergola, patio and outside phone-bell. Eventually, the outside area can even become the site for television-watching (though not often for the TV itself). In the hot summer months, some Perth families have solved the problem simply by pointing the TV out of a window and watching it from the yard - a process helped by the characteristic one-storey Perth house style, where the yard is on the same level as the house, and often partly enclosed by it in an L-shape.

Sounds of Trouble and Strife

When television first arrived, it was welcomed into the house as a guest - it was put in the formal lounge. Here it could be shown to other guests, and treated by the family with the respect it deserved. But this situation didn't last. As TV watching became more taken for granted, and as it extended into daytime and morning viewing,

(courtesy of West Australian Newspapers)

Convert
that Open Verandah
INTO A
MODERN
TV Room
WITH
Naco
AIR CONTROL
LouvrE WINDOWS

Contrary to initial thinking, a Lounge Room is NOT the ideal spot for TV. Experience has proved in America and the Eastern States, that maximum enjoyment and comfort is obtained with a separate TV Room. This way, children have endless fun entertaining their friends without upsetting your main living area.

A Back Verandah or a Front Porch only needs enclosing to make you a fine TV Room. With NACO "WEATHERSEAL" LOUVRE WINDOWS, you can add this extra living comfort yourself and at less cost—the few pounds you spend today will add hundreds to the value of your home.

AVAILABLE AT ALL
LEADING HARDWARE STORES

W.A. DISTRIBUTORS
BARNETT BROS
203-209 HAY ST. (EAST) PERTH

'The West Australian'. 31 August 1959

people got used to doing more than one thing at a time. The productivity of the home environment increased as people dropped into the lounge to iron, sew, study, play, read, argue, make love and fall asleep in front of the television. Similarly, children could be sent in there for the TV to baby-sit them.

Since in many homes the lounge room is the space that is most protected from mess, these activities became a source of tension. So there was strife if the children spilt food and drink in there whilst watching, but tension also arose because of the privileged separation of space that was the hallmark of the lounge. On the one hand, whoever was preparing the meals was excluded both from the experience of watching TV and from sharing family activities that had abandoned the kitchen for the lounge. On the other hand, any attempt to entertain guests in the lounge was in direct competition with the family members - especially children - who were ensconced there to watch TV. Double resentments, at being banished and at missing favourite TV shows, put pressure on the organisation of household space. This pressure was intensified by the fact that dividing house-space into public (social entertainment) spaces like the lounge and private (family activity) spaces like the kitchen went against the grain of the long-term trend in which such distinctions were being broken down. In short, TV sets in the lounge eventually inhibited the very sensorial possibilities and consumerist home culture they were designed to promote.

During the 1960s new houses were built with a new room - the family room - in addition to the lounge. In the existing housing stock, a family room was often the first thing added in the same period's mania for extensions. Appropriately, at the same time, TV cabinet design changed introducing moulded plastic forms and less bulky sets that heralded a less formal role for the TV itself. It was time for televisions to migrate into the family room. In the family room, which was usually adjacent to the kitchen, might be found the sewing machine, ironing board, boxes of children's toys, piles of magazines and books, and games. The TV could be so positioned as to allow an eye to be kept on it whilst working in the kitchen, especially as walls separating the two areas tended increasingly to come down.

While these new arrangements solved the earlier problems of banishment and missing shows, they brought problems of their own. One was noise. Television sound came into direct conflict with kitchen sound. Kitchens are noisy places. Not only is there the clatter of crockery and cutlery, but mixers, blenders, dishwashers, exhaust fans and other gadgets all make their presence felt. And some people like to listen to the radio whilst working in the kitchen, too. Meanwhile, over in the family room, the favourite show keeps modulating in and out of audibility as the kitchen noises compete with the TV noises. So someone turns up the sound, and squabbling ensues.

Another problem with the family room, for children at least, was surveillance. The architect Peter Little has suggested that parents were content to put up with the noise problem because having the TV in the family room allowed them to walk in (or through) and pass comments on whatever was being watched. In this way parents

can retain some measure of control over both their children and their children's viewing habits. If the TV were given its own room, or put in the children's bedroom, such casual policing would be impossible. Perhaps this explains why the television set has tended to stay in the family room - it has been integrated into the process whereby parents instil their values into their children.

That parents have been prepared to put up with squabbling and noise in order to keep an eye on their children's TV habits is perhaps an indicator of the disquiet that various authoritarian bodies - teachers especially - have expressed about TV's so-called effects over the years. The permeation of this disquiet into popular consciousness can perhaps be seen in the way that TV became known as the Idiot Box. It might also be seen in the famous 'Life: Be In It' advertisements where the big step taken by Norm is to get out of his TV chair and walk around. 'TV addiction' became something you had actively to guard against, and an obsession with it was reckoned an embarrassment.

But the term 'idiot box' was never taken at face value. TV may have been much maligned, but maligning never took the place of viewing; rather it showed peoples' knowledge of the pitfalls and control over the process. It indicated a certain distance from TV, and from one's own viewing habits, and it signalled a different social role for television, where TV needed to be integrated into various activities and routines, both work and leisure based. However, it was clear that there was little popular support for the more stringent measures taken by some middle-class and educationally minded parents, who sought to enforce the duties and obligations of work over and above the pleasures of leisure and entertainment. In such households, television would be strictly rationed and restricted to approved shows or even an approved channel (the ABC). In extreme cases, or where children used their intellectual skills not to do homework but to develop stratagems to outwit their parents' dictates, the punishment took the form of sensory deprivation - removal of the TV set from the house entirely.

However, for most viewers the disquiet about television may have had more to do with its difference as a bodily activity from more traditional popular entertainment, partly by simply representing it on screen, partly because people had at least to dress up and move their bodies to and from the theatre. But television, especially after a while, reduces its viewers not to passivity but to immobility, which can be fine - in America there's a TV fan society called the Couch Potatoes, who revel in it - but it can also be aggravating - the mental equivalent of bed-sores.

The Butterfly Dreams
Recent developments in audio-visual technology, and in its incorporation into peoples' homes and activities, have stressed the contemporary virtues of mobility and interactiveness, or, as the 'Memphis' writer Barbara Radice puts it:

Contemporaneity means computers, electronics, video-games, science-fiction comics, Blade Runner, Space Shuttle, biogenetics, laser bombs, a new awareness of the body, exotic diets and banquets, mass exercise and tourism. Mobility is perhaps the most macroscopic novelty of this culture. Not only physical mobility but also and above all mobility of hierarchies and values; and mobility of interpretations ... What matters to us is not their substance but their appearance ... It is the world of TV screens ... where, as in Zen stories, it is never clear whether you dream you are the butterfly or the butterfly dreams it is you.

And there was colour television. This often entailed having two television sets; so there were TVs in the bedroom, kitchen, study or even back in the lounge - one colour, one monochrome. Mobility invested the television set itself with the introduction of portables. These could be placed in eccentric or semi-concealed positions, finding room even on the shelves of corner stores near the cash register, and in other workplaces where periods of enforced immobility and isolation gave a whole new meaning to the idea of 'night-watchman'. Portables could be toted around and beyond the home; but they could also be used ideologically, as it were. The small screen and appearance of not being permanently installed was just the right look for those who wished to register their superiority over TV - for them, the portable TV itself said that their owner didn't *really* watch that much, and watched it selectively. But, like everyone else, such people still placed themselves within reach of contemporary communications, despite their misgivings.

The migration and fragmentation of TV sets implied a new regime of watching which henceforth characterises television. No longer was it the fixed, solitary object of peoples' gaze or attention - people had already learnt to do many things at the same time. Now television, like radio before it, had to compete for small segments of people's time. Sometimes the screen would be mere visual display, holding little more interest than other home decorations; at other times it would draw, or be given, peoples' full intensity of looking and listening. People dipped in and out of TV, in an alternating current of concentration and distraction.

TV screens were poised not simply to migrate around and outside the home, but actively to colonise and domesticate further the spaces that had once been strictly demarcated as public. At the same time, entertainments which once had been seen as essentially public were ready to be captured for home consumption. The marker and perhaps agent of this new phase was the video cassette recorder (VCR). VCRs were launched and have remained as a way of bringing feature films into the home. Never mind the difference in screen size, which means that the image is not just smaller but frequently attenuated because of the difference between TV and cinema screen ratios. People had already learnt to put up with such differences through broadcast movies. VCRs

meant that you could choose which film to watch and when to watch it. They also recaptured several low-intensity user groups, bringing them back into touch with TV screens. Among these were teenagers, who'd go to the video hire shop in groups as they might to the usurped drive-in, and take a film or films back to watch collectively in each other's houses. Other groups were those speaking languages not catered for by broadcast TV - any language but English. Specialist video shops proliferated, offering European, Asian and Indian films imported and circulated entirely for the video market. Thus, for instance, the Italian, Yugoslav and Greek communities have achieved one of the highest per capita levels of VCR ownership in Australia, which as a whole has one of the highest levels in the world, second only, perhaps, to Saudi Arabia.

Thus the suburban shopping malls carried the mark of television in the form of specialist video shops and video stalls in newsagents, delis, petrol stations and department stores. At the same time, TV screens themselves began to colonise the malls, being used by banks, building societies and travel agents to promote their services with specially made tapes. The foyer of Cinema City represents physically the breakdown of the dividing line between video and cinema by offering a bank of six videos for waiting customers to enjoy. Fashion stores like Irene Whyte have introduced video monitors as an integral part of window display and shop fitting, a logical extension of their established use of pop music for an ambience of contemporaneity and fashion. The shops that sell TVs and monitors, from Vox Adeon to Parry's, display their wares in banked rows. Usually all the sets are switched on, often showing the same picture, but rarely with the sound turned up. In fact, the difference between domestic and commercial uses of TV screens is no longer a distinction between public and private spaces, but one of excess - commercial space is identified by the sheer exuberance and conspicuous redundancy of having twenty screens showing the same video clip. Meanwhile, the discerning consumer has no need to rely on chance encounters with TV screens whilst out and about. The recent release of pocket TV in Western Australia is promoted for use 'indoors or out, in bright light or at night' - you need never miss the news or your favourite show, and of course you can use it at sporting fixtures to umpire the umpire's decisions.

Back at home, it's now not just a matter of where to put the screen or how many to have, but what kind to have and what to put on them. There's a struggle for access to the monitor, between broadcast TV and video films, between video clips and time-shifted TV recordings, and between commercially and home produced tapes. The struggle is set to intensify with the development of computers that effectively exploit the screen.

Other technical changes have reduced the isolation of the TV set as an appliance. With hi-fi and stereo-television, it is now possible to design integrated systems, where the TV becomes a component function within a total hi-fi system that will also include phono, cassette player,

FM/AM radio and maybe compact disc. As a result, televisions are now being designed with their own internal functions separated: the first thing to go being the sideboard-like stand, so the set can be placed into the system it's part of. Then there's a move to separate sound from picture. In some versions the separation is physical, mimicking the hi-fi plus two speakers format already in wide use; in others the separation takes the form of disconnecting the set's internal speakers and patching it into an existing system. The migration of sound out of the TV set means that the screen is now properly a monitor, its subservience to a larger system symbolised by the latest remote control devices which govern not only the choice between broadcast and VCR input, but the audio-levels of the hi-fi component as well. In fact the remote control is the visible sign of peoples' control over not just their own equipment but over the act of looking too. It is no longer necessary to get what you're given: the practice known as 'slaloming' is worrying advertisers who have found that people use the remote control to slalom from channel to channel in an effort to avoid ads before returning to the next segment of a chosen show; and they are equally worried about 'zapping', where people record a program for time-shifting to a more convenient viewing period, and then use the shuttle-search function to zap through commercial breaks. Furthermore, the remote control can be used to select away from unwanted segments of the programs themselves, and this is a function that will gain in importance as Perth moves into the era of Channel 0-28 and a third commercial channel, predicted for launch by the end of 1986.

Using the remote control also adds a new dimension to the facilities on offer in VCRs. Without squatting by the set or getting up from the chair, it is now possible to use the pause and search facilities to stop a narrative in its tracks, not only to eliminate ads, but to go back over a shot to see how it was done or to relish it in slow-motion; or even to use the pause to hold and to fetishise an actor's body or a scene. The appropriation by viewers of a kind of authorship of the material they view can indeed be realised literally, by re-recording clips from different tapes to make a 'scrap-book' video; or by selecting images almost randomly and dubbing on music to make the latest art-form, scratch-videos. You may have seen them at Praxis Gallery in Fremantle. The upshot, of course, is that broadcast television's carefully constructed realism can be seen for the construction it is; and its carefully organised scheduling habits can simply be countermanded.

For the audio-visual adepts who have a mind to do more than consume ready-made material, the way is now open to consume self-made images and sound. With the help of Super Beta, compact VHS or 8mm video, and with the increasingly sophisticated domestic video cameras, enthusiasts can now integrate self-shot sequences to match pre-recorded ones, whether taken from videotape, broadcast TV, radio, record or even compact disc. In the offing are previously unthinkable domestic editing set-ups that may eventually be linked to computers and computer-generated graphics.

Not everyone can afford to avail themselves of all this potential, and those who do may be the minority who get a thrill from sheer technical wizardry (and expense) rather than those who have an interest in audio-visual representation as such. But the fascination of these developments is just as much in their potential as in the realisations of it by any one type of user. What these developments mean is that moving images and sounds have been emancipated from their producers' intentions, and that peoples' relationships with television screens is not fundamentally more sophisticated and interactive than it was in 1959.

It also means that there are yet more enticements to centre leisure and entertainment in the home, and that such leisure is increasingly under the control of consumers themselves. Among those who are adept in audio-visual culture are of course the numbers of young people who count among their repertoire of skills the ability to play video-games: an ability that includes erasing the traditional distinctions between playing and looking, between consuming a product and making their own, between being subject to others' intentions (both authorial and authoritarian) and using their bodies to process environmental data into independent experience and culture. In short, those who have been brought up on 'and by the new audio-visual institutions of pleasure and consumption are now poised to invert the image; to dream the butterfly.

The Brechtian vision of people exploiting the resources of modern technologies seems to be developing, however, with few of the social consequences hoped for by Utopian writers like Brecht. Since the period in which he lived, the redefinition of public and private space has also played a part in redefining the spaces on which political action is conducted. No longer is it possible to make easy connections between mass communication and mass action. Now that people have begun to learn how to control the means of audio-visual production, it is clear that there will be no 'big bang' social revolution in consequence. Instead, fundamental change - a social revolution perhaps - is centred on the spaces, resources and activities that occur within the broadly defined arena of domestic consumer culture. In the nineteenth century, Karl Marx despaired for the political future of the French peasantry. Noting that their conditions of existence were similar throughout the country, he also found that these similarities did not entail any unity or class consciousness - the French peasantry, he said, formed a class to the extent that potatoes in a sack form a sack of potatoes. What seems to have changed since those epic days is not that the potatoes have, as it were, been mashed together by the political ideology or that, but they have escaped from the sack. Now we're all Couch Potatoes.

References

Radice, Barbara (1985) *Memphis: Research, Experiences, Results, Failures and Successes of New Design*, London: Thames and Hudson (available through Lamella Books, 333 South Dowling Street, Darlinghurst 2010, Sydney, NSW [(02) 331 45011]).

Branchi, E.M. (1961) 'History of TV in Western Australia', Graylands Teachers College. Manuscript is available in the Battye Library.

We wish to thank Peter Little, Eric Fisher and Geoffrey London for invaluable help in defining the terrain of this article.

11

ART VERSUS TECHNOLOGY
The Strange Case of Popular Music

Simon Frith

In early 1936 Cecil Graves, controller of programmes at the BBC, instructed his Head of Variety, Eric Maschwitz, and Director of Entertainment, Roger Eckersly, to keep crooning, 'this particularly odious form of singing', off the air waves.[1] In his memoirs of life in the BBC, written in 1945, Eckersly comments that crooners,

> seem from my experience to rouse more evil passions in certain breasts than anything else. I should very much like to point out that not all who sing with bands are crooners. There is a lot of difference between straight singing and crooning. The latter is an art of its own. I can't confess I like it, but I admire the skill with which the singer seems to pause for a split second either on top or below the note he is aiming at. (Eckersly, 1946: 144)

Crooning was a style of singing made possible by the development of the electrical microphone — vocalists could now be heard singing softly — and the source of a new sort of male pop star (Rudy Valee, Bing Crosby, Al Bowlly) whom the BBC found sentimental and 'effeminate'. (The association of crooning and sexual decadence was to be celebrated many years later in Dennis Potter's *Pennies from Heaven*.) The problem for the programme controllers was to define crooning in the first place and then to distinguish between 'good' and 'bad' crooning. Even after the war the Ted Heath Band couldn't get BBC broadcasts because their singer, Lita Roza, was defined as a crooner and therefore 'slush' (Heath, 1957: 94–5).

Twenty years later, in 1966, Bob Dylan toured Britain with his new

From Simon Frith, "Art Versus Technology: The Strange Case of Popular Music," *Media Culture and Society*, Vol. 8, pp. 263-279. Copyright © 1986 by Sage Publications, Ltd.

electric band. The Albert Hall concert was bootlegged so it is still possible to hear the slow hand-clapping between each number, the abuse hurled at the stage, and the shouting arguments between members of the audience. At the end of 'Ballad of a Thin Man' a voice rings clearly out: 'Judas!', 'I don't believe you', mutters Dylan as the chords start for 'Like a Rolling Stone'.

Fifteen years later, the pace of technological change is quickening. I had a call from a young band in Coventry who had entered the local battle of the bands sponsored by the Musicians' Union (slogan: Keep Music Live!). Their entry had been rejected — they use a drum machine. Was this official union policy? The answer was yes (although, of course, such policy is always open to debate and change). In the words of Brian Blain, the MU's publicity and promotion officer:

> In the first instance I would make the comment that the Union does seek to limit the use of synthesizers where they would be used to deprive orchestras of work. To this extent, in media engagements particularly and with touring concerts by singers of the calibre of Andy Williams etc, we do have a certain amount of success.
>
> However, I think it is to the Union's credit that we see the essential difference between that use of the synthesizer where it is clearly taking work away from 'conventional' musicians and its use in a self-contained band where there would not normally be any question of another conventional musician being used. In coming to this admittedly pragmatic view, we are merely following on a problem that keyboard instruments have always set an organization like this. Even the acoustic piano could be seen, in the beginning, as a displacement for a number of musicians and this has certainly been the case since the advent of the Hammond Organ.
>
> It is hopeless to look for a totally consistent view but I must say that I see a big difference between a synthesizer in a band, which at least requires a musician to play it, and a machine which takes the place of a musician.[2]

Pop and authenticity

These disparate examples of the controversies caused by the changing techniques of music-making suggest three recurring issues. First, technology is opposed to nature. The essence of the BBC case against crooning was that it was 'unnatural'. 'Legitimate' music hall or opera singers reached their concert hall audiences with the power of their voices alone; the sound of the crooners, by contrast, was artificial. Microphones enabled intimate sounds to take on a pseudo-public presence, and, for the crooners' critics, technical dishonesty meant emotional dishonesty — hence terms like 'slushy'. Crooning men were particularly unnatural — their sexuality was in question and they were accused of 'emasculating' music. Even Eckersly contrasted crooning with 'straight' singing.

Second, technology is opposed to community. This argument, common on the folk scene in the early 1960s, proposes that electronic amplification alienates performers from their audiences. The democratic structure of the folk community was thus unable to survive a situation in which the singers came to monopolize the new means of communication — electrical power. By 'going electric' Bob Dylan embraced all those qualities of mass culture that the folk movement had rejected — stardom, commerce and manipulation.

Third, technology is opposed to art. The Musicians' Union's objection to drum machines is partly a conventional union position, defending members' job opportunities, but it reflects too a belief that the drummer is a musician in a way that the drum machine-programmer is not. One effect of technological change is to make problematic the usual distinction between 'musician' and 'sound engineer', with its implication that musicians are creative artists in a way that engineers are not. What matters here is not the difficult issue of creativity itself but, rather, the idea of self-expression. The argument that recurred in the pop press in the 1970s was that the production of electronic noises by synthesizers left no room for individual 'feel' or 'touch'. Gary Numan could tell readers of *Melody Maker*'s musicians' advice page exactly how to reproduce his sound in a way that Jeff Beck or even Keith Emerson could not. They could describe their techniques but not their final, on-the-spot judgement. All Numan had to do was write down the position of his various switches. This was the context in which synthesizers were heard as 'soul-less', and their most pointed use was on the soundtrack of *Clockwork Orange*. Beethoven's Ninth Symphony, as synthesized by Walter Carlos, was the musical symbol of the film's theme — the dehumanizing use of art as behaviour therapy — and the March from *Clockwork Orange* was later used, with effective irony, as the theme music for David Bowie's 1972 stage show.

What is at stake in all these arguments is the authenticity or truth of music; the implication is that technology is somehow false or falsifying. The origins of this argument lie, of course, in the mass culture criticism of the 1920s and 1930s, but what is interesting is the continuing resonance of the idea of authenticity within mass cultural ideology itself. The key disputes in the history of rock, for example, were all presented (even *sold*) in terms of authentic new stars replacing inauthentic old ones. On his first RCA LP Elvis Presley is pictured playing an acoustic guitar and the back sleeve blurb begins:

> Elvis Presley zoomed into big-time entertainment practically overnight. Born in Tupelo, Mississippi, Elvis began singing for friends and folk gatherings when he was barely five years old. All his training has been self-instruction and hard work. At an early age, with not enough money to buy a guitar, he practiced for his future stardom by strumming on a broomstick. He soon graduated to a $2.98 instrument and began picking out tunes and singing on street corners.

In the mid-1960s the by now conventional routines of teen pop were challenged, in turn, by the 'authentic' moves of white rhythm'n'blues. In the words of their official 1964 biography:

> The Stones picked up Rhythm'n'Blues, grappled with it, learned to 'feel' it. And once they'd made up their minds to stick with it, through the worst of times, nothing could shake them from their resolution. They were determined to express themselves freely, through their music.
>
> And they decided unanimously that they were going to make no concessions to the demands of the commercialism that they frankly, openly, despised. (The Rolling Stones, 1964: 13)

A dozen years later punk musicians shook the rock establishment with a similar, if more apocalyptic, attitude. In the words of Caroline Coon in *Melody Maker* in July 1976:

> There is a growing, almost desperate feeling that rock music should be stripped down to its bare bones again, taken by the scruff of its bloated neck and given a good shaking.
>
> It's no coincidence that the week the Stones were at Earls Court, the Sex Pistols were playing to their ever-increasing following at the 100 Club. The Pistols are the personification of the emerging British punk rock scene, a positive reaction to the complex equipment, technological sophistication and jaded alienation which has formed a barrier between fans and stars.
>
> Punk rock sounds basic and raw. It's meant to. (Coon, 1976: 14)

Each of these moments in rock history fused moral and aesthetic judgements: rock'n'roll, rhythm'n'blues and punk were all, in their turn, experienced as more truthful than the pop forms they disrupted. And in each case authenticity was described as an explicit reaction to technology, as a return to the 'roots' of music-making — the live excitement of voice/guitar/drum line-ups. The continuing core of rock ideology is that raw sounds are more authentic than cooked sounds.

This is a paradoxical belief for a technologically sophisticated

medium and rests on an old-fashioned model of direct communication
— A plays to B and the less technology lies between them the closer
they are, the more honest their relationship and the fewer the
opportunities for manipulation and falsehoods. This model rests in
turn on familiar aesthetic positions. From Romanticism rock fans
have inherited the belief that listening to someone's music means
getting to know them, getting access to their souls and sensibilities.
From the folk tradition they've adopted the argument that musicians
can represent them, articulating the immediate needs and experiences
of a group or cult or community. It follows that if good music is, by
either set of criteria, honest and sincere, bad music is false — and
technological changes increase the opportunities for fakery. Take this
typical newspaper story from 1985:

> When Frankie Goes to Hollywood take the stage in Newcastle tonight, midway
> through their first British tour, they will face a little technical problem: how to
> reproduce in a 90 minute live set the state-of-the-art sound of the hits that have
> taken them months to produce in the studio, using some of the most sophisticated
> hardware money can buy.
>   Many groups have this problem nowadays. Some of them don't even try to solve
> it. Two weeks ago another Liverpool group, Dead or Alive, whose 'You Spin Me
> Round' currently tops the British pop charts, cancelled an appearance on Channel
> Four's rock programme, The Tube. They refused to go on without backing tapes,
> which would have contravened The Tube's 'live only' performance policy.
>   This sorry tale will provide only a footnote in the long and quirkish history of
> fakery in pop music. There is a roll-call, stretching back 20 years, of groups who
> were packaged for their sex appeal and did little playing on their own 'hits'. Other
> groups were actually fabricated after the event, simply to put a marketable face on
> the honest but anonymous toil of session musicians and producers. (Brown, 1985)

What is intriguing here is the slide from 'fakery' in terms of
technology to 'fakery' in terms of commercial manipulation. Two
sorts of insincerity are confounded and we end up with only the
anonymous session men who can call their work 'honest'. The
muddle of critical terms involved in this sort of story, the implication
that we can't 'trust' what we are hearing, reflects the confluence of
three problems that technology now poses to the rock concept of
authenticity.

First, there is the problem of aura in a complex process of artistic
production: what or, rather, *who* is the source of a pop record's
authority? The history of rock'n'roll rests on as complicated a set of
assumptions about its authors as the history of film (and rock has its
own version of *auteur* theory). There is always a need for *someone* to
be the author of a sound, the artist, but the relative artistic

significance of writers/musicians/singers/producers/engineers/ arrangers keeps shifting. It is now possible for a publicist to be credited as a record's real author — think of Paul Morley's role in the selling of Frankie Goes to Hollywood. Frankie, the pop phenomenon of 1984, gained success with a gleeful celebration of their own artifice — Trevor Horn's production turned a plodding Liverpool group into a wrap-around, techno-flash disco sensation; the videos for 'Relax' and 'Two Tribes' offered camp versions of masculinity; the Frankie hype was delivered in wads of advertising copy. This was packaging as art and so pop theorist Paul Morley, who wrote the prose for Frankie and their label, ZTT, was credited as their real author. He even appeared on stage in the ZTT show, reading his copy over an Art of Noise backing tape.

Second, technological changes raise issues of power and manipulation: how does the ownership of the technical means of production relate to the control of what is produced? Do technical developments threaten or consolidate such control?

Third, technology is seen to undermine the pleasures of music-making (and watching music-making). One important strand of rock common sense is that playing an instrument is a physical exercise, visibly involves the body, and is, above all, a matter of effort. This is reflected in the routine contrast of 'live' performance and 'dead' studio activity, and even now rock's core beliefs in energy and community can only be celebrated in concert (hence the importance of Bruce Springsteen). The guitarist became the symbol of rock because he (masculinity is a necessary part of the argument) communicates physically on stage even more obviously than the singer — the link between sound and gesture has become so familiar that audiences have even developed the 'air guitar', a way of sharing the guitarist's physical emotions without needing an instrument at all.

One reason why synthesizers, drum machines, tape recorders and so on are regarded as 'unnatural' instruments in performance is simply because playing them takes little obvious effort. Programming a computerized sampling device like a Fairlight engages the mind not the body and is not a spectator event. (Art music audiences, used to the action of orchestras and conductors, feel similarly insulted by computer musicians.) The explicit argument is that live performances allow for spontaneity, for performers' direct responses to their audiences; programmed instruments can't do this. But what really matters is not whether a show *is* spontaneous but, rather, whether it seems to be (the most celebrated live performers often have the most rigidly stylized acts — go and see James Brown on successive nights and see exactly the same 'improvisations'). Rock bands' use of 'artificial' aids are, therefore, hidden entirely (for example, the now routine use of backing-tapes) or disguised (electronic instrument manufacturers are skilled at producing devices that can be played as if they are normal keyboards or percussion — it's not really necessary to design a rhythm machine like a Syndrum or the Simmons Kit as something to be hit!). If the deception is discovered audiences do, indeed, feel cheated. I once watched Vince Clarke of Yazoo pretend to play his Fairlight (all he was really doing was loading and unloading floppy discs). When at last he got bored and walked away, the music played on and he was booed even more loudly than Bob Dylan at the Albert Hall.

In praise of technology

For Yazoo's fans, as for Dylan's a couple of pop generations earlier, new technology meant a new means of crowd control; the direct line between star and fans was fatally disrupted. This is a familiar position in rock, as I've shown, but it is, in fact, a reversal of reality. A more dispassionate history of twentieth-century pop reveals two counter-theses.

I. Technological developments have made the rock concept of authenticity possible

I can illustrate this by reference to pop's three central inventions. First, recording itself, from its beginnings at the turn of the century, enabled previously unreproducible aspects of performance — spontaneity, improvisation, etc — to be reproduced exactly and so enabled Afro-American music to replace European art and folk musics at the heart of western popular culture. This affected not just what sort of music people listened to (and listened to more and more after the First World War) but also how they listened to it, how they registered the emotional meanings of sounds, on the one hand, the musical shape of their own emotions, on the other. Recording made available the physical impact of an unseen performer, giving access to singers' feelings without those feelings having to be coded via a written score.

One immediate consequence was that star performers began to take over from composers as popular music's 'authors' (this was true in classical music too — Caruso was the first international recording star) but, more importantly, recording gave a public means of emotionally complex communication to otherwise socially inarticulate people — performers and listeners. The blues and hillbilly singers of the 1920s and 1930s were just as stylized, as rule bound, as the romantic songsmiths of the European middle-class tradition, but their rules could be learned and understood without the education and cultural training necessary to appreciate how classical music carries its meanings. The profound statements of pride, dread and defiance in a Robert Johnson blues, the subtle twists of desire and pain in a Billie Holiday song could be heard as truthful by listeners remote from these singers geographically, socially and in terms of cultural roots. I can still remember the instant exhilaration of Little Richard's 'Long Tall Sally', which I heard for the first time when I was about ten years old, growing up in a small Yorkshire town, with no idea at all about who or what Little Richard was. That conversion to black music, similar to the experience of small town middle-class children before the war hearing Louis Armstrong for the first time, was being repeated, as a result of rock'n'roll, for teenagers all across Europe, and can't be explained away in terms of commercial cultural imperialism.

The second important invention, the electrical microphone, I have already discussed with reference to crooning, but its general effect was to extend the possibilities of the public expressions of private feelings in all pop genres. The microphone had the same function as the close-up in film history — it made stars knowable, by shifting the conventions of personality, making singers sound sexy in new ways, giving men a new prominence in big bands, and moving the focus from the song to the singer. The first pop singer to become a pin-up idol, Frank Sinatra, was well aware of the importance of amplification to his appeal. As John Rockwell writes:

> As a young singer, he consciously perfected his handling of the microphone. 'Many singers never learned to use one', he wrote later. 'They never understood, and still don't, that a microphone is their instrument.' A microphone must be deployed sparingly, he said, with the singer moving it in and out of range of the mouth and suppressing excessive sibilants and noisy intakes of air. But Sinatra's understanding of the microphone went deeper than this merely mechanical level. He knew better than almost anyone else just what Henry Pleasants has maintained: that the microphone changes the very way that modern singers sing. It was his mastery of this instrument, the way he let its existence help shape his vocal production and

singing style, that did much to make Sinatra the preeminent popular singer of our time. (Rockwell, 1984: 51–2)

Sinatra was to remain sensitive to technical developments — in the 1950s he pioneered the use of the LP to build up moods and atmospheres in ways impossible on three-minute singles. From his perspective, technology was a tool to be used and one which could easily be misused. Sinatra famously dismissed Elvis Presley and rock'n'roll, agreeing with *New York Times* jazz critic, John S. Wilson, that 'singing ability is one of the least essential qualifications for success' in this new pop form:

> Recording techniques have become so ingenious that almost anyone can seem to be a singer. A small, flat voice can be souped up by emphasizing the low frequencies and piping the result through an echo chamber. A slight speeding up of the recording tape can bring a brighter, happier sound to a naturally drab singer or clean the weariness out of a tired voice. Wrong notes can be snipped out of the tape and replaced by notes taken from other parts of the tape. (Levy, 1960: 111)

In fact, Elvis Presley neither corrupted nor transformed pop tradition — he was the culminating star of the technology of music-making made available by electrical recording and amplification. For Presley's fans he was much more immediately, *honestly* sexy than Frank Sinatra.

The third significant invention, magnetic tape, began to be used by record companies in the 1950s and eventually made possible the cutting/splicing/dubbing/multi-track recording of sounds, so that studio music became entirely 'artificial'. What for John S. Wilson was a form of fraud became, for 1960s rock musicians, a source of new creative ambitions. Most developments in recording technique — long players, hi-fidelity, magnetic tape, stereophonic sound, digital recording, compact discs, etc — have, in fact, been pioneered by the classical divisions of record companies, as producers and sound engineers have tried to find ways of capturing the audio-dynamics of live orchestral music. In pop, though, these techniques were soon used to the opposite effect: studios became the place to make music impossible to reproduce live, rather than to recreate the ideal concert experience. By the end of the 1960s the studio was, in itself, the most important rock instrument. The Beatles' 'Sergeant Pepper' LP symbolized the moment when rock musicians began to claim to be making complex artworks.

Progressive rock set a problem for the received ideas of authenticity:

the rock'n'roll ideals of spontaneity, energy and effort were faced by new emphases on sensitivity, care and control. 1970s rock offered two solutions. On the one hand, effort and control were combined in the spectacular technological displays of art-rock groups like Pink Floyd and stadium rockers like Led Zeppelin; on the other hand, singer/songwriters like Paul Simon, Joni Mitchell and even John Lennon used studio devices and sonic collages to reveal themselves more openly, making music a matter of individual sensibilities that couldn't be engaged in the crude, collective setting of the concert hall. Punk was to rebel against the excessess of both technological and artistic self-display, but punk's very moralism suggested how closely by now rock aesthetics were entangled with ideas of honesty and dishonesty.

Punk only briefly interrupted the development of pop technology (a development that had, by the 1980s, led to the complete collapse of creative distinctions between musicians, producers and engineers) but it does illustrate my second historical thesis.

II. Technological change has been a source of resistance to the corporate control of popular music

This proposal, again, argues against orthodox pop history, so first I need to clarify my position: if we look at the history of inventions in the music industry — in terms of both production and consumption — those that catch on and are successfully marketed are the ones that lead, at least in the short term, to the decentralization of music-making and listening. To give a recent example, video tapes have become popular — video discs have not. The usual argument is that technological change is inspired by and makes possible the increased capitalist control of the market but, on the whole, recording technology has not worked like this. The music industry is essentially conservative, and uses new instruments to do old things more efficiently or cheaply rather than to do new things. This is obvious in the development of musical equipment, for example. Some devices have been invented in response to musicians' specific requests (the electric bass guitar, Marshall amps) but musicians have quickly found unexpected uses for the new instruments, and many electronic tools have been developed without any clear idea of what they might be used for at all — except, that is, as substitutes for existing instruments. Hence the importance to synthesizer firms of musicians who'll play their instruments and sell them by revealing their new possibilities.

It is because musicians (and consumers) have been able to use machines for their own ends that the mechanization of popular music has not been a simple story of capitalist take-over (or state control — see Bright, this issue). This has been true at all stages of pop history. Electrical amplification, for example, and, in particular, the development of the electric guitar in the 1930s, gave American musicians the freedom to travel and perform to large audiences without the capital expense of big bands, while the parallel development of recording broke the power of Vaudeville promoters and dance-hall owners to decide who could hear whom. The new industry gate-keepers, radio disc jockeys and record company A&R departments, had much less tight control on who could make music for a living — this was especially important for black music and musicians, and for making black music available to white listeners. Even the original 'synthetic' keyboard, the Hammond Organ, was first marketed as a do-it-yourself instrument — sounds you too can make at home! — and it is arguable that the creative process in rock, from The Beatles on, has been inspired by musicians struggling to make for themselves, on whatever equipment they can cobble together, sounds that originated in expensive studios. Far from being oppressed by the unequal distribution of technological power, musicians have been made inventive by it. Rock invention, then, is inseparable from both the use of technology and from musicians' attempts to control their own sounds.

The most striking example of this was punk. Its ideology may have been anti-technology, but the late 1970s rush of home-made records and independent labels was dependent, in fact, on the lower cost of good quality recording equipment, on the availability of cheap but sophisticated electronic keyboards. The punk movement involved electronic musicians like Thomas Leer and Robert Rental, Cabaret Voltaire and the Human League; the most commercially successful independent label, Mute, has had, almost exclusively, an electro-pop roster.

Avant-garde music of all sorts has been made under the influence of punk electronics in the last decade. In the long term it turned out that the punk challenge to established modes of stardom and authority worked more clearly musically than sociologically. Punks did not replace the pop order of stars and followers, but post-punk musicians have challenged the idea of the finished product. In the

1980s, it has been commodity form rather than commodity status that has been under threat. Packaged songs, records and stars have all become the object of further play and manipulation.

One strand of such play has come from consumers themselves: home taping has given fans a new means of control over their sounds; they can compile LPs and radio shows for themselves; and use Walkmans to carry their soundscapes around with them. The record industry itself has treated home taping as the source of all its troubles. Behind the recurring campaigns for levies to be imposed on blank tapes is the suggestion that people are using them to acquire music illicitly, without paying for it, without even giving the musicians involved their just reward. Every blank tape sold, from this perspective, is a record not sold.

It is worth noting a couple of points about this argument. First, it rests on inadequate evidence. The effect of home taping is primarily deduced from record sales figures rather than from an investigation of the consumer choices that lie behind them. The patchy public research evidence there is (commissioned by Warners in the USA and by the Communist Party in Italy!) shows, not surprisingly, that home taping involves a particular commitment to music — it is done by the people who buy the most records, and the substitution effect (a tape bought means a record not bought) makes no sense to people spending as much money on music as they can. What emerges, rather, is the shifting significance of music within leisure. Records are being replaced not by tapes as such but by other leisure activities; music is being used differently and in different, more flexible forms (Warner Communications, 1982; Ala et al., 1985).

It's interesting too that the record industry's home taping fears emerged after the event. This is another example of the multi-nationals' ignorance of the implications of their own inventions. To repeat a point I've already made, record companies are essentially slow-thinking; research and development means devising ways of making more money out of people doing what they already do. No one in Britain anticipated the VTR boom — Thorn-EMI decided not to invest in its initial development — while companies regularly mistake passing fads for lasting habits (hence Warners' fateful over-investment in Atari computer games). There are enough differences between different countries' uses of new technologies (why the home-based VTR pattern in Britain, the teen craze for video arcades in the USA?) and enough examples of products that don't sell despite massive capital investment, from quadrophonic sound systems to video discs, to suggest that consumers are not entirely malleable. In the record business, at least, the increasingly oligopolistic control of musical media is continually countered by the consumer preference for devices that can, in some sense, increase their control over their own consumption.

In musical terms the most interesting and influential 'folk' uses of new technology have been developed by black musicians and audiences in Jamaica and the USA. Jamaica is, perhaps, the clearest example of a society in which the opposition 'folk vs technology' makes no sense. Reggae is a folk form with records, studios, session musicians, and disc jockeys at its centre rather than live shows or collective sing-alongs. Jamaican DJs, in particular, pioneered the use of the record as a musical instrument, something to talk to and over, slow down and speed up, cut into and across, rather than as a fixed, finished good.

In the 1970s disco DJs in New York and elsewhere echoed (and were directly influenced by) these ideas. The most dramatic consequence was Brooklyn's hip-hop scene. This culture of rapping, scratch-mixing, graffiti, break dancing, etc, was, in traditional sociological terms, a street culture:

> Hip hop was originally born of kids evolving their own social networks, from crews to karate clubs, making their own dances, poetry, and music, in an attempt to make a harsh, cruel, often incomprehensible city a liveable environment. . . . In hip hop, mainstream fashion, art, language, leisure culture — mainstream values — are subverted by those who have been cast out of the status quo. (George et al., 1985: xvii)

But the means of this cultural enterprise were technological — the ghetto blaster, the turn-table — and everything, the subway train, the body, the record, became an object on which the hip-hop artist could go to work. Hip-hop music meant montage and collage:

> To phone Tommy Boy Records in February '84 was a treat. For as long as you were kept on hold there was the legendary 'Payoff Mix' in your ear, taking hip-hop cutting one step further into the realm of endless potential. It used the irresistible base of 'Play That Beat' to cut in fragments of 'Adventures on the Wheels of Steel', some James Brown soul power, 'Buffalo Gals', Funky Four's 'That's the Joint', West Street Mob, The Supreme Team, Culture Club, Starski's 'Live at the Disco Fever', Little Richard's 'Tutti Frutti', exercise routines (heel-toe, heel-toe), Humphrey Bogart in *Casablanca*, 'Rockit', the Supremes' 'Stop in the Name of Love', 'Planet Rock', Indeep's 'Last Night a DJ Saved my Life' and more. (Toop, 1984: 154)

All sounds could be grist to this mill, whether politicians' speeches, police sirens, bugged conversations, or the accidental effects of electronic distortion itself. As David Toop goes on to say:

> The concurrent fashionability of scratch mixing and sampling keyboards like the Emulator and Fairlight has led to creative pillage on a grand scale and caused a crisis for pre-computer-age concepts of artistic property. (Toop, 1984: 154)

Many of the best hip-hop records are not legally available. Their use of 'found sound' is, in record company terms, a form of piracy. The refusal to accept records as finished products threatens the basic organization of the music business as a profit-making enterprise — hence the virulent objections to home taping (and the systematic attempt to classify home-tapers and professional bootleggers together). Electronic technology undermines the idea of fixed objects on which copyright, the essential legal safeguard of art as property, rests. And so Malcolm McClaren's LP 'Duck Rock', a montage of sounds plucked from New York radio, South African townships and urban streets, shaped in Trevor Horn's studio, has to have an identifiable 'author' both in order to sell it and in order to assign its proceeds.

And this is where the final irony of the relationship between art and technology in the record business lies: record company profits are defended against new technology in the language of individual creativity. As Jon Stratton (1983) has shown, record industry personnel have long explained their activities and the 'irrational rationality' of music as a business in the ideological terms of Romanticism. What is happening now is that technology is disrupting the implicit equation of artists' 'ownership' of their creative work and companies' ownership of the resulting commodities — the latter is being defended by reference to the former. Copyright has become both the legal, ideological weapon with which to attack the 'pirates' and, increasingly, the source of multi-national leisure corporations' income, as they exploit the rights in their productions by licensing them for use by smaller companies and other media.

As John Qualen (1985) points out, the 'crisis' of the music industry in the last decade has concealed three significant shifts in the organization of profit-making since the late 1960s rock record boom. First, recording and publishing companies are now integrated, and an increasing proportion of record company profits come, in fact, from their exploitation of their publishing copyrights via air play, the

Performing Rights Society, etc. Second, the major record companies are, increasingly, licensing material from their back catalogues for use by independent TV and specialist music packagers. Third, record companies have begun to treat radio and TV use of records and videos not as advertisements for which they provide new material cheaply, but as entertainment services which should pay competitive prices for the recordings they use:

> In many ways the record industry is facing very similar problems to the film industry. Its base market is being eroded and fragmented (pre-recorded music sales are down, as are cinema admissions), costs are spiralling and the traditional distribution system is threatened by the new technologies.
>
> Though there will always be box-office biggies like *ET* (or *Relax* and *Thriller*), for the most part the earnings of the producers of films (pre-recorded music) will come not from their physical sale but from the exploitation by the producers of the rights they hold in their productions to broadcast and cable TV. The double advantage of this strategy for the record industry (which is far more vertically integrated than the film industry) is that, for the majors, it could eliminate the high cost of manufacturing and distribution. (Qualen, 1985: 16).

Conclusion

The political claims of 1960s counter-culture used to be derided for the apparent contradiction between ideology and technology: how could the USA or Britain be 'greened' by Marshall amps and expensive stereo hi-fi systems? For the told-you-so school of mass cultural criticism the argument for technological progress doesn't amount to much. Look what happened, in the end, to Elvis Presley and the electric Bob Dylan, to punk and hip-hop — they were all, one way or another, *co-opted*. This is a familiar argument on the left but rests on its own dubious assumptions. Can musical truth, whether class or gender or ethnic or individual truth, really be guaranteed by acoustics? This seems to be a question that worries first world intellectuals, anxious, maybe, about the roots of their own culture, more than anyone else. Third world musicians, like black musicians in the USA, have rarely been reluctant to adapt their music to new technology (or new technology to their music) (see Laing, and Regev, this issue). Compare the intense American feminist debate about 'women's music'. Should feminists use folk and jazz forms, as more 'authentically' expressive? Or is punk and noise and electro-stridency the necessary source of a new voice?

The debate here turns on who musicians want to reach and how they want to reach them as well as on the implicit ideologies of musical forms themselves, and this means entering the fray of the music market and pop taste, the role of songs and sounds in everyday life. To assume that what happens to stars and movements in the long term — co-option — discredits their disruptive impact in the short term is to misunderstand the politics of culture (and there is no doubting the momentary disruptive impact of Elvis Presley or the Rolling Stones, the Sex Pistols and X-Ray Spex). Technology, the shifting possibility of mechanical reproduction, has certainly been the necessary condition for the rise of the multinational entertainment business, for ever more sophisticated techniques of ideological manipulation, but technology has also made possible new forms of cultural democracy and new opportunities of individual and collective expression. It's not just that the 'aura' of traditional culture has been destroyed, but also that technological devices have been musicians' and audiences' most effective weapons in their continuous guerilla war against the cultural power of capital and the state. Each new development in recording technology enables new voices to be heard and to be heard in new ways; and pop voices are systematically denied access to other public media. The history of pop is, in part, the history of different groups using the same means (records) for different ends (profits, art, the articulation of community, self-aggrandizement, protest, etc). Technology determines how the competition for a voice is organized but does not determine who will be heard or how what is heard is interpreted. My own belief is that capitalist control of popular music rests not on record company control of recording technology but on its recurring appropriation of fans' and musicians' ideology of art. That the economic arrangements of music production and consumption have not yet changed, despite their increasing lack of fit with the actual production and consumption process, reflects the continuing power of nineteenth-century ideas of creativity and truth.

Notes

1. Thanks to Paddy Scannell for details of this dispute.
2. Letter from Brian Blain, 12 March 1981.

References

Ala, N. et al. (1985) 'Patterns of Music Consumption in Milan and Reggio Emilia from April to May 1983', *Popular Music Perspectives*, 2.

Brown, M. (1985) 'Pop — How Live is Live?', *Sunday Times*, 17 March.

Coon, C. (1976) *1988: The New Wave Punk Rock Explosion*. London: Omnibus.

Eckersly, R. (1946) *The BBC And All That*. London: Sampson Low, Marston and Co.

George, N. et al. (1985) *Fresh*. New York: Random House.

Heath, T. (1957) *Listen To My Music*. London: Frederick Muller.

Levy, A. (1960) *Operation Elvis*. London: André Deutsch.

Qualen, J. (1985) *The Music Industry*. London: Comedia.

Rockwell, J. (1984) *Sinatra*. New York: Random House.

The Rolling Stones (1964) *Our Own Story*. London: Corgi.

Stratton, J. (1983) 'Capitalism and Romantic Ideology in the Record Business', *Popular Music*, 3.

Toop, D. (1984) *The Rap Attack*. London: Pluto Press.

Warner Communications (1982) *Home Taping – A Consumer Survey*.

12

DAZZLING THE MULTITUDE
Imagining the Electric Light
as a Communications Medium

Carolyn Marvin

Marshall McLuhan, a popular media prophet of the 1960s, believed that the history of Western culture should be rewritten so as to cast successive new technologies of communication in the role of the great levers that moved it. Not the message of communication, McLuhan argued, but the medium—the structural characteristics of the techniques and machines of information storage, retrieval, and transmission—had a semiotic eloquence that overshadowed the particular details of the content. The medium, McLuhan declared, "shapes and controls the scale and form of human association and action."[1] McLuhan's account of cultural evolution in the West has found little favor among historians, but his appreciation of the relationship between technology and culture and his colorful efforts to spotlight that relationship helped focus the problem for others.[2] That relationship is now a staple concern of scholarship in the history of technology.

McLuhan's definition of an information medium was very broad. He was fond of insisting that even the electric light is an information medium. That this example was intended to shock McLuhan's readers is a measure of the historical distance we have traveled, for this claim would not have seemed nearly as strange in the popular or the scientific culture of late-nineteenth-century Europe and the United States (albeit in a somewhat different sense than McLuhan intended). This chapter is an attempt to reconstruct that forgotten dimension of the social history of electricity by tracing some early contributions of the electric light to the complex transformation of communication that began with the telegraph, proceeded through the electronic mass media, and continues at the present moment in computing technology.

In the late nineteenth century, some prophets of the future imagined great banks of electric lights spelling out letters and pictures to astonish passersby, or mammoth searchlights projecting stenciled messages

From Carolyn Marvin, "Dazzling the Multitude: Imagining the Electric Light as a Communications Medium," in J. Corn (ed.) *Imagining Tomorrow: History, Technology and the American Future*, pp. 202-217. Copyright © 1986 by J. Corn. Reprinted by permission.

and images on the clouds for the pleasure and information of all in the surrounding countryside. What was imagined was also occasionally attempted.

The communicative utility of the electric light did manifest itself in some areas; traffic lights, movie marquees, and neon signs still testify to this. However, the principal legacy of the electric light to modern mass communications was something different, something not foreseen: The electric light (particularly the incandescent light) helped transform public spectacles from traditional outdoor community gatherings lit by candles, bonfires, or oil lamps into the glittering indoor mass-media spectacles familiar to us.

Throughout the United States and Western Europe the public introduction of the electric light excited interest and curiosity. In 1886 the editors of the *Electrical Review* recalled the first appearance of electric lighting in New York shop windows as follows:

It was looked upon as a mere experiment, the continuation of which would soon prove more trouble than it was worth, and the neighboring stores took no stock in it. Soon, however, it was discovered that it was attracting the attention of customers and the general public to such an extent that its users were compelled to enlarge the stock. Owing to the brilliancy of the light pedestrians could walk by stores of the same character lighted by gas without even seeing them, so attractive was the brilliant illumination further along. They clustered and fluttered about it as moths do about an oil lamp. That settled it. The neighboring stores must have it, and the inquiry and demand for the light spread apace until now, when, as soon as the electric light appears in one part of a locality in an American city it spreads from store to store and from street to street.[3]

The scientists, engineers, and entrepreneurs upon whose comments and predictions this study is mainly based framed their expectations of electricity in terms of the only technological revolution familiar to them: that brought about by steam power. Many thought the impact of electricity would exceed even that great leap, completing its promise and salvaging its disappointments. Abundant, easily distributed, versatile electricity would reverse the centralization of production in factories, lead to the rise of clean cottage industries, unify the home and the workplace, and lower the divorce rate. By decentralizing the population, it would make the cities green with parks and gardens. Some nineteenth-century observers believed that the concentration of labor around steam-powered urban factories had made the visible differences between the working life of the city and the leisure life of the country starker than ever. They looked to electrical manufacturing and transportation to create a homogeneous landscape that would heal the

breach between classes which steam had exacerbated. They also expected electricity to democratize luxury and eliminate conflict based
on competition for scarce resources by producing goods cheaply and
abundantly. Not all predictions were so optimistic, but a great many
were concerned with these possibilities.

As a purveyor of message content, the electric light was not much
of a novelty; it simply extended the earlier uses of signal lights to
transmit warnings and news. However, the illumination of public places
by electric filament lamps seemed much more dramatic, more colorful,
more elaborate, and more versatile than the village bonfire (which
predated the Middle Ages), the floating-wick oil lamp of the eighteenth-
century garden fête, or the carbon arc lamp. Like its traditional predecessors, electric lighting conveyed the message that the occasion of
its use was exciting and vivid. Unlike their traditional predecessors,
electrically lighted events were often commercially sponsored and
organized.

The most striking electric-light spectacles were the great industrial
exhibitions of the late nineteenth century. The Chicago World's Fair
and Columbian Exposition of 1893 was one of the most splendid and
one of the most self-consciously electric. By the time of this fair the
promise of electricity occupied a place near the center of popular
enthusiasm, as expressed in the popular and trade press. The fair had
an advanced telephone and telegraph system for internal and external
communication; electrically powered boats, rail cars, and moving side-
walks; great electric motors that operated machinery; exhibits of the
latest electrical inventions, and 90,000 electric lights mounted on buildings, walkways, and illuminated displays.[4] One of the most popular
attractions was the 82-foot-tall Edison Tower of Light, a pedestal
covered with multicolored incandescent bulbs.[5] Another was the evening show at the Court of Honor, where jets of water from electrically
powered fountains and flashing electric lights combined in fanciful
patterns. In the lights of the Court of Honor one observer saw "great
flowers, sheaves of wheat, fences of gold, showers of rubies, pearls
and amethysts." Another sensed a nearly evangelical power in the
nighttime illumination of the fair:

Under the cornices of the great buildings, and around the water's edge,
ran the spark that in an instant circled the Court with beads of fire. The
gleaming lights outlined the porticoes and roofs in constellations, studded
the lofty domes with fiery, falling drops, pinned the darkened sky to the
fairy white city, and fastened the city's base to the black lagoon with nails
of gold. And now, like great white suns in this firmament of yellow stars,
the search lights pierced the gloom with polished lances, and made silvern

paths as bright and straight as Jacob's ladder, sloping to the stars or shooting the beams in level lines across the darkness, effulgent milky ways were formed or again, turned upward to the zenith, the white stream flowed toward heaven until it seemed the holy light from the rapt gaze of a saint or Faith's white, pointing finger.[6]

The spectacular effect of electric light in public spaces was a subject of interested discussion long before such lighting became a staple of fairs and expositions. In 1884 *Electrical World* claimed that only the electric light was "considered worthy or suitable to illuminate conspicuous and beautiful public buildings," and that electric lighting was the only form of decoration being considered for the Statue of Liberty. *Electrical World* reported several plans to light the statue, including one to project vertical beams of light upward from the torch to stand as "a pillar of fire by night." A second plan was to place lights "like jewels around the diadem," and a third was to place them at the foot of the loggia to illuminate the entire statue, so that "the illumined face of Liberty [would] shine out upon the dark waste of waters and the incoming Atlantic voyagers."[7] An imaginative journalist had proposed that the statue should hold aloft the world's largest electric light "to illumine the lower bay and even to make Coney Island, which with its myriads of lights glistens on a summer's night like a huge diamond, pale and insignificant, and like the evening star when the moon is in full form."

In a world where electric lights are prosaically utilitarian and unremarkably plentiful, such descriptions may be understood as a reaction to something novel in the experience of enthusiastic observers: the introduction on a new scale of the grand illusion, the effect that also most clearly defines success in modern mass media. Accustomed as we are to electric lights and to more elaborate illusions, it is difficult for us to imagine the original impact of the electric-light spectacle. By reilluminating nature, the electric light offered some observers a way of rediscovering it. It offered others a novel means to manufacture and sell what they described as the improved experience of nature.

New York Harbor was the setting for a number of electric-light shows in the 1880s. From the shore of Staten Island, Manhattan at night was said to look like a "fairyland" during one such show, with "a thousand electric lights dancing from out a sea of inky gloom, with here and there a cross, and there a crown, near which fireflies of huge dimensions start here and there with phosphor fires aglow, the streets ashimmer with silver, with calcined towers lumined against the unfathomable gloom beyond."[8] On Staten Island in 1886 a colored fountain inspired applause from opening-night spectators as it was put through its paces: "At one moment it was crystal, the next roseate, then successively green, blue, purple, gold, and from time to time the tints would blend, harmonize, and contrast with new charms at every change. . . . Far out in the bay it could be seen, looking like a gigantic opal, illuminated by its internal fires."[9] After a visit to the United States, William Preece, soon to be Chief Engineer of the British Post Office, and an attentive observer of American ingenuity, described for lecture audiences the commercial potential in the splendid spectacle of Brooklyn Bridge lit by 82 arc lamps: "It is so beautiful, in a scenic sense, that one of the enterprising ferry companies contemplates having nightly excursions during the summer season, which it is intended to advertise as the 'Theater of New York Harbor by Electric Light; price of admission, 10 cents.' "[10]

Outdoors the electric lamp was safer, cheaper, and more versatile than carbon arc lighting. Indoors it eliminated the disagreeable fumes of low-candlepower gas lighting and the intense glare and uncertain safety of arc lighting. Gradually, some outdoor events began to move indoors to the smaller settings for which incandescent lights were ideally suited. Fancy lights were laid on for sumptuous balls, receptions, and banquets, and entertainers appropriated the electric light as a performance prop.

In 1884 the Electric Girl Lighting Company offered to supply "illuminated girls" for indoor occasions. Young women hired to perform the duties of hostesses and serving girls while decked out in filament lamps were advertised to prospective customers as "girls of fifty-candle power each in quantities to suit householders."[11] The women were fed and clothed by the company, and customers were "permitted to select at the company's warehouse whatever style of girl may please their fancy." In Kansas City, employees of the Missouri and Kansas Telephone Company organized a public entertainment in 1885 in Merchants' Exchange Hall which was graced by "an electric girl, placed on exhibition" along with a model switchboard and telephone exchange.[12] "Electric girls" embodied both the personal servant of a passing age, a potent symbol of social status, and the electric light as ornamental object, a dazzling and opulent display of social status in a new age. In time, impersonal electricity would help banish most personal servants, and would make electric lighting essential and functional for all classes instead of a badge of conspicuous consumption for one. Indeed, electric girls were already transitional, since they were not traditional family servants but were hired for the occasion.

Entertainers also began to use electric lights to adorn their bodies in public performance. Before an astonished audience in Sheldon,

Iowa, in 1891, Miss Ethyl J. Davis of the Ladies Band Concert and Broom Brigade rendered a tableau of the Statue of Liberty, which the local newspaper reported in detail:

Miss Davis stood on an elevated pedestal, her upraised right hand grasping a torch, capped with a cluster of lamps, which alone would have been sufficient to illuminate the entire room. A crown with a cluster of lamps, and covered with jewels, and her robes completely covered with incandescent lamps of various sizes and colors completed the costume. The lights in the hall were turned down and almost total darkness prevailed. As the contact was made bringing the electric lamps into circuit, the entire hall was illuminated with a flood of light which almost blinded the spectators, and Miss Davis, standing revealed in the glaring light, certainly presented a picture of unparalleled brilliance and beauty.[13]

"The Greatest Event in the history of Brookings, South Dakota" was the description given by a local newspaper to a Merchants' Carnival held in 1890 at the Brookings opera house at which various industrial enterprises were represented by appropriately costumed ladies. One of them was Mrs. E. E. Gaylord, wife of the manager and electrician of the Brookings Electric Light Company. To represent that flourishing branch of commerce, Mrs. Gaylord wore

a crown of incandescent lamps and her dress was decorated with the same ornaments. The lamps were all properly connected, the wires terminating in the heels of the shoes. On the floor of the stage were two small copper plates connected to a small dynamo. When Mrs. Gaylord touched the plates the 21 lamps of her crown, banner and costume instantly flashed up and she stood clad in "nature's resplendent robes without whose vesting beauty all were wrapt in unessential gloom."[14]

In 1893 George W. Patterson of Chicago created a special novelty act of "electrical spectacular effects" with lighted Indian clubs. By swinging these clubs in a darkened room, he created the illusion of circles and other designs of solid light. Describing his act in 1899, the *Western Electrician* detailed a "striking feature" of the entertainment, the "electrical storm":

. . . beginning with distant heat lightning, gradually increasing to the fiercest of chain or "zigzag" lightning, with corresponding graduation of thunder, the latter being produced in the usual manner by a "thundersheet" of iron. . . . The effect is very startling, especially as it is accompanied by the fiercest thunder, the sound of dashing rain and by Mr. Patterson's voice laughing and singing "The Lightning King" through a megaphone. The "Lightning King" is followed by the latter part of "Anchored," in which a

Figure 1
Mrs. E. E. Gaylord representing electrical enterprise at the Merchants' Carnival, Brookings, South Dakota, 1890.

perfect double rainbow gradually appears and is dissolved by a water rheostat, by sending the rays of a single-loop-filament incandescent lamp through a prism. The colors come out beautifully.[15]

The familiar dimensions of bodily experience have always provided a reference point for exploring the significance and utility of new and unfamiliar technologies. The social uncertainties created by the introduction of novel, various, and intellectually mysterious technologies are reduced and appropriated for a variety of purposes by recasting them in this familiar idiom. Electric lights even appeared in jewelry. A New York exhibition in 1885 of "flash" jewelry from Paris included hatpins and brooches studded with tiny glittering electric lights.[16] The use of electric lights and effects in the realm of fashion was described in detail by *Western Electrician* in 1891:

Electric jewelry usually takes the form of pins, which are made in various designs. One such trifle copies a daisy, and has an electric spark flashing from the center. Another is a model of a lantern in emerald glass, while a death's head in gold, with a ray gleaming from each eye, is a third. The wearing of electric jewelry necessitates the carrying about of an accumulator which resembles a spirit flash, and is generally stowed in a waistcoat pocket. Brooches are made occasionally for ladies' wear, but as women have no available pockets, a difficulty arises with regard to the battery.[17]

The impulse to dazzle an audience with electrical effects found expression not only in entertainments in which the spectacle itself was the message but also in the construction from electric lights of illuminated letters and simple figural representations. Antecedents for texts of light go back at least to the illuminated sign in St. James's Park, London, in 1814, in which a star and the words, "the Peace of Europe," were created from more than 1,300 spout-wick oil lamps attached to iron frames to celebrate (prematurely, as it turned out) the end of the Napoleonic Wars.[18] The electric filament lamp made such achievements simpler and inspired still more ambitious ones.

A wedding in Atlanta in 1899 featured illuminated textual decorations. The groom, an electrical contractor, had draped 200 incandescent lights from one side of the church to the other. Directly above the altar hung a wedding bell fashioned of foliage and 100 colored lights. Further details were reported:

An arc light suspended from the interior of the bell represented the clapper. To the right of the bell a letter N, the initial letter of the name of the bride, formed of white incandescents, set in pink flowers, was supported, on invisible wires. A letter L for the groom was on the left. . . . . As the bride with her brother entered the church by one aisle and the groom with his best man entered by the other the letters N and L flashed into view and sparkled with great splendor. A murmur of admiration arose from the auditorium at the superb effect.[19]

As the minister pronounced the pair man and wife, "a single letter L in pink incandescents appeared on the bell and burned with a soft brilliance."

Texts and figures constructed from electric lights became popular for advertising. A common device was the "sky sign," which spelled out the name of a firm or promotional slogan or outlined an image against the blank wall of a building. An especially ambitious sign was erected in 1892 on the side of the 22-story Flatiron Building at the confluence of Broadway and Fifth Avenue with 23rd Street in New York. This sign consisted of 1,500 incandescent lights, white, red, blue,

Figure 2
Electrically illuminated sky signs, 1892.

and green, arranged in seven sentences of letters 3–6 feet high. Each
of the seven sentences lit up in succession in a different color from
dusk until 11 o'clock each night and brought "to the attention of a
sweltering public the fact that Coney Island . . . is swept by ocean
breezes," reported *Western Electrician*.[20] "So long as the changes are
being run," the account continued, "the public is attracted and stands
watching the sign, but as soon as the whole seven sentences are lighted
and allowed to remain so, the people move on their way and the
crowd disperses. This illuminated sign is not only a commercial success,
but when all the lamps are lighted is really a magnificent sight. Its
splendor is visible from away up town."

To attract crowds on the streets of large cities, advertisers often
used incandescent lights and magic lanterns in combination. On "magic
lantern avenues" in Paris, commercial messages were projected on
shop windows high above the street. In London "diverting and artistic"
displays of the same kind were set up in the Strand and in Leicester
Square as early as 1890.[21] Magic lanterns also projected "living photograph" advertisements on billboards, on pavements, and even on
Nelson's Column (until the Office of Works prohibited this "desecration"
in 1895).[22] In Edinburgh, an electric signboard in front of the Empire
Palace Theatre flashed out in 130 colored lights the words *Empire* and

Palace alternately, so that "one word [appeared] in the position previously occupied by the other."[23]

Patriotic and political events were also occasions for electric-light messages. In 1891 the national convention of the Grand Army of the Republic at Detroit was illuminated by an outdoor electrical design, the principal feature of which was a badge of light 48 feet high and 16 feet wide, inscribed with an eagle, a flag, and a cannon. "The words 'Hail, Victorious Army' were shown in letters seven feet high, 600 16-candle power lamps being required for this alone. In addition the G. A. R. monogram was shown in 12-foot letters of red, white, and blue lights. This was visible, it was said, for ten miles down the Detroit river. There was also an anchor, representing the navy, and a horse's head, standing for the cavalry. These took about 100 lights each."[24] In addition, 2,000 lights mounted on and surrounding city hall created a glow that could be seen for 5 miles in every direction.

In 1897 the city of Berlin celebrated the ninetieth birthday of Emperor Wilhelm with a "grand illumination." Multicolored lights arranged in the initials of the emperor and the empress and the significant dates of their reign were strung across public buildings and private houses.[25]

In the United States, the intense feeling kindled by Admiral Dewey's return from the Philippines in 1899 was expressed in dramatic displays of public support all over the country. In New York, the scene of the admiral's triumphant homecoming, an enormous "Welcome Dewey" sign in lighted letters 36 feet high was stretched 370 feet across the Brooklyn Bridge. The letter W alone consisted of 1,000 lights.[26] Chicagoans mounted an electric light picture of Dewey's flagship, the *Olympia*, on scaffolding at the corner of State Street and Madison. "The ship itself was outlined by 720 eight-candle power lamps, 200 red-bulb and 150 blue-bulb lamps being used. A 10,000 candle power, 35-ampere searchlight was placed in the pilothouse of the ship. Portraits of Dewey and McKinley were outlined by incandescent lamps."[27]

With the development of a national telegraphic network in the United States during the second half of the nineteenth century, it became customary for crowds to gather in the streets of many towns and cities on presidential election nights, partly for entertainment and partly to keep track of late returns, which were posted outside local newspaper offices where the wires ran. In 1896, an estimated 250,000 New Yorkers celebrated McKinley's victory in the streets as incoming electoral tallies were projected by calcium light on buildings all across the city. Returns were projected on the outside of the *New York Times* building beneath the slogan "All the News That's Fit to Print," which was spelled out in electric lights next to a magic-lantern portrait of the president-elect.

In that news and entertainment were presented dramatically and in rapid sequence, this scene in Times Square can be said to have prefigured the electronic broadcasting of the twentieth century. The crowds swirling in the street were a prototype mass audience. *Harper's Weekly* took this rather lightly, although it did note that the crowds were "entertained as well as instructed."[28]

Upon such experiments and spectacles future schemes of communication by electric light were erected with great imaginative flourish. To a twentieth-century-accustomed vision, the most fanciful were the proposals to inscribe the night skies with powerful beams of light that could be seen by all inhabitants of the surrounding countryside. This proposal, which appeared in many variations, was a plausible and promising technological extrapolation from existing achievements. It extended both the familiar principle of magic-lantern projection and existing applications of electric-light technology, including some newly hatched attempts to improve the reliability and safety of shipping.

The fact that vessels sailing the coast could often see the locations of towns from the reflections of their night lights off overhanging clouds inspired a series of experiments in which brilliant Morse-code flashes were projected overhead from naval vesssels. In one experiment the flashes were decipherable at a distance of 60 miles.[29] In another, an astonished crowd filled the streets in the vicinity of the Siemens-Halske factory in Berlin, where a light-projecting apparatus strong enough to illuminate handwriting at the distance of a mile was aimed at the sky. With the help of a large mirror, signals placed in front of the light were "repeated, of course on a gigantic scale, on the clouds."[30]

The prospect of illuminated messages on the slate of the heavens fascinated experts and laymen alike. "Imagine the effect," said the *Electrical Review*, "if a million people saw in gigantic characters across the clouds such words as 'BEWARE OF PROTECTION' and 'FREE TRADE LEADS TO H—L!' The writing could be made to appear in letters of a fiery color."[31] According to one electrical expert, "You could have dissolving figures on the clouds, giants fighting each other in the sky, for instance, or put up election figures that can be read *twenty miles away*."[32]

Since such projects were usually undertaken for commercial ends, the popular term for celestial projection was "advertising on the clouds." In 1889 an American inventor claimed to be negotiating with several firms that wished to "display their cards" on the sky.[33] A few years later in England, an experimenter was said to have succeeded in producing the letters BUF upon the clouds, although his target was apparently too small to accommodate the rest of the message: FALO BILL'S WILD WEST.[34] Advertising on the clouds, explained E. H. Johnson, one of Edison's close associates, was "simply a stereopticon on a large scale" that required a light sufficiently powerful to project on the firmament and a method for focusing diffuse light on a "cloud canvas" constantly shifting its distance from the earth.[35] "Even portraits are said to have been 'placed' on the clouds," stated one account, "though the report does not say how great the resemblance was."[36]

While conducting experiments with a large searchlight atop Mount Washington in New Hampshire over a period of months, a General Electric engineer, one L. Rogers, received letters from viewers as far away as 140 miles. He marveled to think that "hundreds of thousands of eyes were centered on that one single spot, waiting for the flash or wink of the 'great luminous eye.' "[37] Reflecting on the Mount Washington experiment a year later, Amos Dolbear, one of the inventors of telephony, imagined the day when great stencil sheets of tin and iron would be prepared for projecting on the clouds an "advertising sheet" with letters more than 100 feet long that could be read a mile or more away, and when weather forecasts would be "given by a series of flashes of long and short duration, constituting a code of signals."[38] The eventual outcome of Rogers's experiments in casting "legible lines" on the clouds was a huge, electrically powered magic lantern erected in 1892 atop Joseph Pulitzer's *World* building, then the tallest building in New York. It had an illumination of some 1,500,000 candles, and it weighed well over 3,000 pounds. An 8-inch lens projected stencil-plate slides of figures, words, and advertisements upon the clouds or, on clear nights, on the buildings nearby.

Objections to the vulgarity of advertising on the sky were common. In 1892, *Answers*, the penny-journal flagship of the British publishing empire headed by Lord Northcliffe, called the possibility of sky signs the "newest horror" in an article that went on to say:

You will be able to advertise your wares in letters one hundred feet long on the skies, so that they will be visible over a dozen countries. As if this truly awful prospect were not enough, we are told that these sky-signs can be made luminous, so that they will blaze away all night! A poet, in one of his rhapsodies, said that he would like to snatch a burning pine from its Norway mountains and write with it the name of "Agnes" in letters of fire on the skies.

But he would probably not have cared to adorn the firmament with a blazing description of somebody's patent trouser-stretcher, or a glowing picture, as large as Bedford Square, of a lady viewing the latest thing in corsets.[39]

Another British journal decried "celestial advertising" as follows:

... the clouds are to be turned into hideous and gigantic hoardings. This awful invention deprives us of the last open space in the world on which the weary eye might rest in peace without being agonized by the glaring monstrosities wherewith the modern tradesman seeks to commend his wares.[40]

If the sky was one surface upon which to project messages for the millions, the moon was another. *Science Siftings* reported in 1895 that an American named Hawkins planned to send a flashlight message from London to New York by way of the moon. Using the only satellite available in 1895, Mr. Hawkins had conceived the intellectual principles of satellite relay. The value of his plan, he announced, lay in covering long distances, "but electricity would be required for local distribution from the receiving stations. If a flash of sufficient strength could be thrown upon the moon to be visible to the naked eye, every man, woman and child in all the world within its range could read its messages, as the code is simple and can be quickly committed to memory."[41]

Signaling schemes to strike up a wireless conversation with extra-terrestrial beings received wide publicity. "With our powerful search-lights it would be possible to communicate with the planet Mars," Amos Dolbear wrote in his regular science column in *Cosmopolitan* in 1892, "if it should chance to be peopled with intelligences as well equipped with lights and telescopes as we are."[42] Others proposed semaphoric arrangements of giant lights flashing in Morse-code sequence. *Live Wire*, a dime monthly whose title bore witness to the popular association between excitement, novelty, and electricity, reported that Sir Francis Galton had proposed the construction of 75-by-45-foot heliographic mirrors to flash a regularly pulsing ray of sunlight to Mars. Charles Cross thought the beam of a powerful electric light might be gathered and concentrated at a single point by huge parabolic reflectors.[43] There was a proposal that "incandescent lights be strung over the sides of the Great Pyramid, and thus it be made a great square of light." According to *Live Wire*, "When it was pointed out how inadequate this would be, the proposer replied by saying, 'Then illuminate all the pyramids.' "[44] The French science-fiction novelist Camille Flammarion suggested grouping immensely powerful lights in the pattern of the Big Dipper to catch the eyes of extraterrestrial observers. The lights could be placed at Bordeaux, Marseilles, Strasbourg, Paris, Amsterdam, Copenhagen, and Stockholm. "But no one has yet been found to build seven lights each of about three billion

candlepower," explained *Live Wire*. A suggestion to work out a geo-
metrical problem in lights for the amusement of galactically remote
viewers was impractical, *Live Wire* concluded, because the lines of
every figure would have to be at least 50 miles wide and "made of
solid light." E. W. Maunder, Great Britain's Assistant Astronomer
Royal, speculated that "if ten million arc-lights, each of one hundred
thousand candle-power were set up on Mars, we might see a dot."[45]

A repeated assumption in imaginative portrayals of mass audiences
of the future was that such audiences properly belonged outdoors,
and that twentieth-century media would provide regular occasions for
outdoor assemblies. In these speculations, familiar nineteenth-century
images of spectators clustered about terrestrial illumination were expanded to the grander scale deemed suitable for illuminated celestial
displays. As it has turned out, mass audiences do not collect outdoors
to view electric-light messages in the night sky. However, other elements
of these speculations and of the early illuminated gatherings prefigure
the most familiar of modern public spectacles: television broadcast
entertainment. The so-called television special and other broadcasting
genres still use dramatic arrangements of brightly colored lights to
create visual excitement.

Television's inheritance from the electric light is technological as
well as social. Though poorly understood at the time, the original
electronic effect, the Edison effect, was created in an electric lamp
whose vacuum bulb was the forerunner of the tube that would soon
become the principal vehicle of broadcasting. The development of
electronics out of this puzzle in a light bulb eventually helped make
many face-to-face public gatherings nearly superfluous as families
retreated indoors to watch on their private television sets the descendants of the public spectacles that once would have entertained
them in the town square. It is not uncommon for technological innovations intended to streamline, simplify, or enhance familiar social
routines to so reorganize them that they become new events. Incandescent lights not only inspired new outdoor gatherings, such as night
baseball games; they also transformed many large outdoor community
gatherings into indoor private ones the size of a single family.

Because communication at a distance was actually implemented in
other forms, our cultural memories no longer include predictions made
in nineteenth-century voices that the media of the future might be
messages of light splashed across the firmament by searchlights or
great banks of flashing incandescent lamps. Our amnesia is testimony
to the tendency to read history backward from the present—to see
it as the process by which our ancestors looked for and gradually

discovered us rather than as a succession of self-contained accounts of a moral order, each with its own focused concerns and its own peculiar sense of inhabiting the crucial if not the final stages of human history. If every present attempts to colonize the past with its own spirit, it also appropriates the future with equal enthusiasm. The nineteenth-century conviction that important twentieth-century media would look like nothing so much as the nineteenth-century electric light writ large betrays the companion tendencies to read the past as a less glamorous version, and the future as a more glamorous version, of the present. In the last analysis, the utility of social prediction stands least of all on its accuracy as a pointer to the future. It stands much more on what it communicates about the perceptions, values, and imaginative reactions of societies to changes which they not only must devise ways of coping with and adjusting to but which they in large part also shape.

Notes

1. Marshall McLuhan, *Understanding Media: The Extensions of Man* (New York: McGraw-Hill, 1964), p. 9.

2. Elizabeth Eisenstein, for example, has recently acknowledged her debt to McLuhan while repudiating many of his conclusions about the impact of printing. See *The Printing Press as an Agent of Change: Communications and Cultural Transformations in Early-Modern Europe* (Cambridge University Press, 1979), volume 1, pp. x–xvii, 16–17, 40–41.

3. "Turning Off the Gas in Paris," *Electrical Review*, September 18, 1886, p. 4.

4. Trumbull White and William Igelheart, *The World's Columbian Exposition, Chicago, 1893* (Philadelphia: International, 1893), p. 302.

5. Ibid., pp. 322–323. See also Ben C. Truman, *History of the World's Fair, Being a Complete Description of the World's Columbian Exposition From Its Inception* (Chicago: Cram Standard, 1893), pp. 358–359.

6. Rossiter Johnson (ed.), *A History of the World's Columbian Exposition* (New York: Appleton, 1897), volume 1, p. 510.

7. "Lighting the Statue of Liberty," *Electrical World*, April 26, 1884, p. 136.

8. *Electrical Review*, September 1, 1888, p. 4.

9. *Electrical Review*, July 10, 1886, p. 9.

10. Remarks by William Preece in a speech before the Society of Arts in London, quoted in "The Light That Will Extinguish Gas," *Electrical Review*, February 7, 1885, p. 2.

11. "The Use of Illuminated Girls," *Electrical World*, May 10, 1884, p. 151.

12. *Electrical Review*, February 7, 1885, p. 4.

13. "Electricity in Iowa," *Western Electrician*, June 27, 1891, p. 367.

14. "The Representative of the Electric Light," *Western Electrician*, April 12, 1890, p. 210.

15. "Electrical Spectacular Effects," *Western Electrician*, April 8, 1899, p. 196.

16. "Trouve's Jewelry," *Electrical Review*, June 27, 1885, p. 2.

17. *Western Electrician*, November 7, 1891, p. 1.

18. William T. O'Dea, *The Social History of Lighting* (London: Routledge and Kegan Paul, 1958), p. 178.

19. "A Wedding with Electrical Accessories," *Western Electrician*, December 30, 1899, p. 381.

20. "Electrically Illuminated Signs," *Western Electrician*, December 30, 1899, p. 381.

21. "Smart Advertising Booms," *Answers*, August 2, 1890, p. 150.

22. *Electrical Engineer*, April 26, 1895, p. 18.

23. "Electrical Advertising," *Electrical Engineer*, January 4, 1895, p. 30.

24. "Electrical Decorations at Detroit," *Western Electrician*, September 12, 1891, p. 153.

25. "Electricity and the Birthday of the German Emperor," *Electrical Review*, May 14, 1887, p. 3.

26. "Electrical Decorations in New York," *Western Electrician*, October 14, 1899, p. 217.

27. "Electrical Illumination at the Chicago Festival," *Western Electrician*, October 14, 1899, p. 217.

28. "Election Night in New York," *Harper's Weekly*, November 14, 1896, p. 1122.

29. "Cloud Telegraphy," *Electrical Review*, May 5, 1888, p. 5. Reprinted from *Youth's Companion*, no date. The two vessels were the *Orion* and the *Espoir* of the British Navy. "The *Orion*, having thrown upon the clouds a regular messsage by means of successful flashes, this message was read and understood on board the *Espoir*."

30. "The Electric Light as a Military Signal," *Scientific American*, October 30, 1875, p. 281.

31. *Electrical Review*, October 6, 1888, p. 4.

32. "Advertising in the Clouds: Its Practicability," *Electrical World*, December 31, 1892, p. 427.

33. *Electrical Review*, December 21, 1889, p. 4.

34. "Even the Clouds Don't Escape Him," *Electrical World*, November 26, 1892, p. 335.

35. "Advertising in the Clouds" (note 32).

36. "Even the Clouds Don't Escape Him" (note 34).

37. "Advertising on the Clouds," *Invention*, February 17, 1894, pp. 150–151.

38. Amos E. Dolbear, "The Electric Searchlight," *Cosmopolitan*, December 1893, p. 254.

39. "The Newest Horror," *Answers*, July 16, 1892, p. 129.

40. "Even the Clouds Don't Escape Him."

41. "A Message From the Moon," *Science Siftings*, November 16, 1895, p. 77.

42. Dolbear, "The Electric Searchlight" (note 38).

43. Arthur Bennington, "Some of the Plans of Science to Communicate with Mars, 40,000,000 Miles Away in the Depths of Infinite Space," *Live Wire*, February 1908, p. 6.

44. Ibid.

45. Ibid.

13

A WHOLE TECHNOLOGY OF DYEING
A Note on Ideology and the
Apparatus of the Chromatic Moving Image

Brian Winston

THE AESTHETIC HAS LOST its innocence. Today in critical discourse it is seen, often as not, as nothing but a willing tool of "the ideology of the dominant class":

The aesthetic is for a number of reasons a peculiarly effective ideological medium: it is graphic, immediate and economical, working at instinctual and emotional depths yet playing too on the very surfaces of perception, entwining itself with the stuff of spontaneous experience and the roots of language and gesture. Precisely on this account, it is able to naturalise itself, to proffer itself as ideologically innocent.[1]

As Roland Barthes has pointed out: "Bourgeois ideology is of the scientific or intuitive kind, it records facts or perceives values, but refuses explanations; the order of the world can be seen as sufficient or ineffable but it is never seen as significant."[2] What follows is by way of a case study, taken from the realm of the moving image, illustrative of the ways in which ideologically complicit cultural production takes place.

No means of representation is as "innocent," as "scientific," as the photograph. Yet "every time we look at a photograph, we are aware, however slightly, of the photographer selecting that sight from an infinity of other sights."[3] Moreover, there are factors that go beyond the predelictions of the person handling the photographic apparatus, to the ideologically charged nature of the apparatus itself. Photographs, cinema, and television do not merely express in texts the

Reprinted by permission of *Daedalus*, Journal of the American Academy of Arts and Sciences, "The Moving Image," Vol. 114, No. 4, Fall '85 Boston MA.

ideology of the culture that produces them, with the possibility that other ideologies could equally easily be signified in different texts; rather, the technologies are themselves an ideological expression of the culture. It is one such expression—color film that more readily photographs Caucasians than other human types—that is our concern in this piece.

At the end of the documentary *El Pueblo Vencera*,[4] in a mirror image of the opening scene of the film, a young Salvadoran gun-toting guerilla in full fatigues encounters an elderly peasant woman, covered basket on head, in a clearing. The woman places her burden on the ground, pulls back the cover and reveals an Arriflex BL 16mm professional film camera for which the guerilla triumphantly exchanges his gun. If the pen was once deemed mightier than the sword, then today the camera can no doubt be thought mightier than the machine gun. But for this proposition to hold up, a preconditional further point must be admitted, viz, that the camera, a product of West German high technology costing some $15,000, is a device that serves, despite its provenance, any communications purpose. Implicit is the idea that, in the context of the politics of El Salvador or in any other situation, the camera is in some sense neutral—just as the gun is neutral.

That the cinema is a child of science and exhibits the supposed objectivity and accuracy of its parent is well known. Cinematography, like photography (and like the camera obscura), was initially introduced to the public as a tool of science, and those who worked the new apparatus in each case were *non tanquam pictor, sed tanquam mathematicus*.[5] It is worth noting that these supposed objective qualities are seductive enough to convince many—even Diego de la Texera, director of *El Pueblo Vencera*, who in different circumstances would be more on the *qui vive* as to the ideological forces with which they are dealing. It is as if de la Texera and other radical film and video makers have not understood the ideologically imposed limitations of the apparatus.

The apparatus of film and television is indeed so limited. It is, as A.D. Coleman points out, a product of "the lens culture" finally inaugurated by Cardano, Maurolycus, and Digges in the early 1550s,[6] and the replication of Northern European "distant point construction" perspective is its primary design objective.[7] The photographic image accommodates the previously established codes of representation just as the social circumstances in which these new images are consumed conform to preexisting and culturally specific patterns. The apparatus is not neutral, and altering its purpose requires considerable deformation of its inherent (i.e., designed-in) capacities and capabilities.

Understanding of the ideological implications of the institution of the cinema, including its apparatus, began in earnest in the aftermath of the *evenments* of 1968 and has been conducted in the pages of the French film journals with recent useful contributions from American and British film historians and theoreticians on specific issues. The agenda of this debate has broadened from (comparatively) simple considerations of the ideological intentions or implications of this or that film text, to include psychologically inflected discussions of the unavoidable ideological effects of viewing films and, to a lesser degree, television,[8] as well as accounts and explanations of the development and implications of the entire technical apparatus and economic structure of the film and television industries.[9] The discussion that follows is part of this latter project.

II

We so often forget, for example, that when a color film is seen projected, the color is not in the Bazanian sense a direct . . . registration of color in the natural world . . . there is, in fact, no direct . . . link between the color of the natural world and the color of the projected color film—*a whole technology of dyeing has intervened.*[10](italics added)

The makers of *El Pueblo Vincera,* a color film, must have been aware of the limitations placed upon them by the use of color when filming black people. All professionals fully understand that such films, despite continuous improvements in performance, do not render black skin tones as easily as they do white; and that, when filming blacks, it is often necessary to augment lighting, by bouncing reflected light back into the face from a low angle, for instance, so as not to lose details. Were these stocks to offer "a direct . . . registration of color in the natural world," we could simply attribute the difficulties of representing blacks on film to a natural racial disadvantage— somewhat like sickle-cell anaemia. But color film does *not* directly register the world; "a whole technology of dyeing intervenes."

    As the comedian Godfrey Cambridge once hyperbolized—but only
slightly—blacks look green on American (NTSC; National Television
Standards Committee) television, no knob-twiddling changes their
color (unless one makes the white people orange), and he for one was
not surprised. It is the history and ideological implications of this
technology, a white technology that best reproduces Caucasian skin
tones, that I wish to explore.

    At one level it is "inevitable" that the bias of color film should be
the way it is. After all, according to Kodak, more than eight billion
color negative exposures were made in the U.S. alone in 1982, and the
vast majority of them were by and of whites.[11] But the rhetoric
surrounding color film, as much in the technical and scholarly
literature as in advertising and other popular accounts, implicitly
denies any such partiality in favor of a stress on naturalness, realism,
and verisimilitude—mathematics, as it were, rather than painting.
Even aware scholars slip easily into this language. Edward Branigan,
for instance, in an otherwise most illuminating account of how film
historians have represented the development of color cinematography, describes both additive and subtractive photographic methods
as "natural color processes":

It is enough to note, without exploring details, that *natural* color processes
are usually divided into two types—additive color systems (e.g.,
Kinemacolor, early Technicolor, and modern television) and subtractive
color systems (e.g., Technicolor, Eastman Color, and Kodachrome). . . . We
have considered the invention of color with respect to the photograph
(*natural* color), but a second line of development lies closer to painting.
Hand-painted daguerreotypes appeared around 1839 and hand-painted
films appeared with the very first films in 1894. . . .[12](italics added)

A survey of color processes written for a professional journal by an
official of Eastman Kodak highlights the supposed naturalness of the
company's subtractive systems in the language of impeccable scientific description:

All of the [additive] systems discussed . . . have resulted in a final picture
being put on the screen in color by superimposing or adding the lights of two
or three primary colors. In nature, however, colors of objects are viewed by
subtraction; they absorb or subtract certain component parts of the visible
spectrum of white light and reflect the remainder, which the eye sees as
color.[13]

(This analogy between human vision and the way Eastman Kodak's color films "view" nature is obviously anthropomorphic and tendentious.)

Thus, the cultural specificity of color film is systematically denied, and instead it is suggested that the stocks, true to their scientific heritage, reflect and re-present the natural world. This places the development of color squarely within that received view, theoretically legitimated by André Bazin, which holds that the entire technological development of cinema progressively seeks to possess the world iconically. And as Natalie Kalmus, wife of the "inventor" of Technicolor, Herbert Kalmus, expressed it half a century ago when addressing a meeting of technicians that was held under the rubric "Color Consciousness":

From a technical standpoint, motion pictures have been steadily tending toward more complete realism. In the early days, pictures were a mere mechanical process of imprinting light upon film and projecting that result upon a screen. Then came the perfection of detail—more accurate sets and costumes—more perfect photography. The advent of sound brought increased realism through the auditory senses. The last step, color, with the addition of the chromatic sensations, completed the process. Now motion pictures are able to duplicate faithfully all the auditory and visual sensations. This enhanced realism enables us to portray life and nature as it really is, and in this respect we have made definite strides forward.[14]

Within this claim of general faithful duplication, "flesh" always comes to mean Caucasian skin tones.[15] Only in the mid-fifties does a degree of what might be called sophistication begin to creep into the professional discourse: "Flesh-color, even of the so-called 'white' races, varies from light pink or almost white to various shades of tan and brown according to the type of skin and the amount of sunburn. . . ."[16] However, elsewhere in the standard work just quoted, "flesh" ranks between "yellow" or "sand" or proximate to "peach" and "white."[17] The cultural assumptions of those concerned with the development and applications of color film are those of the society at large. Natalie Kalmus, for instance, had these unsurprising things to say about "black" and "white":

Black is no color, but the absorption of all color. It has a distinctly negative and destructive aspect. Black instinctively recalls night, fear, darkness, crime. It suggests funerals, mourning. It is impenetrable, comfortless,

secretive. It flies at the masthead of the pirate's ship. Our language is replete
with references to this frightful power of black—black art, black despair,
blackguard, blackmail, black hand, the black hole of Calcutta, black death
(the devastating plague of medieval Europe), black list, black-hearted, etc.
. . . . White represents purity, cleanliness, peace and marriage. Its introduction into a color sublimates that color. For example, the red of love becomes
more refined and idealistic as white transforms the red to pink. White uplifts
and ennobles, while black lowers and renders more base and evil any
color.[18]

It is no sin that Kalmus and her peers were less sophisticated than,
say, Wittgenstein (or Eisenstein) about color. The sin is that they
claimed, both in practice and theory, to be doing what came
naturally, rather than recognizing the cultural influences that led
them, through complex optics and chemistry, to a most highly
mediated analogue of the natural world of color.

III

There are two methods currently available for capturing color
iconically on a photographic plate. In one—microdispersion, developed by F.W. Lanchester in 1895—a coarse grating, with some three
hundred slits to the inch, is interposed within the body of the camera
between the taking lens and the film. The grating breaks up the light,
which is then collected by a second field lens and passed through a
narrow angled prism. Lenses on either side of the prism, the third and
fourth needed for the system, focus the image of the slits (turned by
the prism into spectra) onto the photographic plate. By these means,
the image is broken down into its constituent color elements—
dominant wavelength, chroma, luminance, and value—that are then
recorded on the plate. After development, the plate can be viewed by
reversing the light path through the system so that the taking lens
becomes a projection lens, and all of the original chromaticities and
intensities are recreated.[19]

A second direct method was developed in 1891 by Gabriel
Lippmann, professor of physics at the Sorbonne from 1878 and a
Nobel laureate in 1908. It was a Lippmann "photochrome" made in
the summer of 1893 by the Lumière brothers that ranks as the first
color portrait. Unlike the microdispersion method, the Lippmann
system does not require a special camera, only a modified plate

holder. It depends on an emulsion of extremely fine grain, in which the individual photosensitive granules are physically shorter than the color wavelengths that are to be recorded. The plate is placed in the camera with the emulsion side away from the lens. After exposing the plate, Lippmann poured a film of pure mercury against the emulsion, thus mirroring it. The light-waves of the image are reflected in the mercury back against the incoming waves and the interference pattern thereby caused is recorded on the plate. This pattern of stationary waves in the emulsion can then be developed and contains all the information of the chromaticities and intensities of the original colors. The image can be reproduced by using reflected light passed through the plate.[20]

"Photochromes" are obsolete and have never enjoyed any degree of popularity. The fine grain required to record accurately all the color data needs emulsions that are so slow as apparently to require several minutes of exposure even in sunlight, and the images can be viewed only by carefully positioning the eye at a precise angle— otherwise no color can be seen at all. Similar difficulties attach to the microdispersion method. The special camera is bulky, and the additional optics as well as the fine grain necessitate strong illumination and long exposures. However real or otherwise these disadvantages,[21] the direct systems do seem to require considerable light and certainly yield no prints.

There was not enough demand for the "scientific" direct color image to overcome these difficulties and ensure a diffusion of the techniques. For all that "photochromes" record photographically the physical parameters of the original spectral phenomena, the human eye/brain mechanism does not require such a degree of fidelity since it normally simplifies the color information it processes. Artificial renditions of color, it turns out, need not represent reality as faithfully as direct methods do. Filters and dyes are psychologically effective, although the abandoned iconic processes remain the standard against which the limitations of the more-than-a-hundred filter- and dye-based systems must be measured.

It was known from 1722 that when three mezzotinted copper plates, one blue, one red, and one yellow, are superimposed, they produce a full-color plate. The laborious handwork on the stone this system required was superceded by lithography, another three-color process introduced commercially in 1812. In 1861, the great English physicist Clerk Maxwell, while discoursing on the nature of human color perception, offered a suggestion as to how it might be demonstrated:

Let it be required to ascertain the colors of a landscape by means of impressions taken on a preparation equally sensitive to rays of every color. Let a plate of red glass be placed before the camera, and an impression taken. The positive of this will be transparent wherever the red light has been abundant in the landscape, and opaque where it has been wanting. Let it now be put in a magic lantern with the red glass, and a red picture will be thrown on the screen. Let this operation be repeated with a green and a violet glass, and by means of three magic lanterns let the three images be superimposed on the screen. The color on any point on the screen will depend on that of the corresponding point of the landscape, and by properly adjusting the intensities of the lights, etc., a complete copy of the landscape, as far as visible color is concerned, will be thrown on the screen.[22]

Maxwell's three-color hypothesis is the basis for all current color reproductive methods, photographic and electronic, and at first it might seem as if it agrees with the physiology of the human eye.[23] As far as can be determined, the cones of the retina, those photoreceptors sensitive to color, are of three types: the ρ (responsive to red-orange-yellow), the γ (responsive to orange-yellow-green-blue/green), and the β (responsive to blue/green-blue-violet). If Maxwell's filters, or any dyes used in a photographic process, only triggered one of these cone-types as appropriate, then the pattern of stimulation caused by viewing the reproduction would agree exactly with the original stimulus—as occurs in Professor Lippmann's images, for instance. Unfortunately, no filter can be found that will activate only the γ-cones. Wherever green appears, there will be an excess of β and ρ-cone stimulus that will render greens paler and, although scarcely noticeable in the reds and blues, will also cause whites to acquire a magenta tinge. Increasing the intensity of the red and blue lights or dyes restores the white but at the cost of distortion in the relative chromaticities and intensities—which, as it happens, is psychologically (or, perhaps better, ideologically) less offensive than off-white. And here is opened a whole can of colored worms, especially close (chromatically speaking) to Caucasian skin tones.

This is not the place in which to outline the range of choices facing those chemists and physicists whose job it is to produce color-sensitive photographic and electronic materials. Suffice it only to point out that with trichromatic systems (contemporary color systems, that is) the opportunities for choice and the need for decisions are boundless; this is why one color film or color television system is easily distinguished from another, and none, it can fairly be claimed, is perfectly iconic.

IV

From the beginning, motion picture films were hand-colored and were very often, if not most of the time, printed on tinted stocks. With the introduction of sound, tinting at the developing stage was abandoned because the process interfered with the optical sound track. Kodak responded by introducing a range of seventeen tinted Sonochrome positive stocks that did not affect the audio track.

Kinemacolor, the earliest movie system to exploit the Maxwell additive approach, was in commercial operation by 1909. It was a two-color sequential process in which camera (and projector) alternately exposed frames through revolving filter disks, at an increased rate of 32 per second. The disks contained two filters, one cyan/blue, the other red/orange.[24] The Dowager Empress of Russia, after watching at Buckingham Palace the Kinemacolor film of George V's Delhi Durbar, pronounced that it "gives one the impression of having seen it all in reality."[25]

Other subsequent additive systems rang the changes on the basic method of superimposing discretely tinted images. These included squeezing the images onto one 35mm frame or, in a significant development, splitting the image so that it fell through a green or red filter onto two separate film strips. Apart from registration difficulties, the comparative darkness of the blue filter translated into a brightness flicker in the sequential variants of this approach, and there was always a tendency, whatever system was used, towards color fringing—i.e., chromaticities did not agree exactly with the outlines of objects, but bled. Eventually, these additive processes would encompass three color filters rather than two, as many as four filtered images per frame, and, always, extremely complex cameras and projectors. Yet although the last variant was proposed as late as 1950, additive color reproduction never took hold in the cinema. Kalmus, of Technicolor, in describing what drove him from additive to subtractive processes, graphically illustrates why:

During one terrible night in Buffalo, I decided that such special attachments on the projector required an operator who was a cross between a college professor and an acrobat, a phrase which I have since heard repeated many times. Technicolor then and there abandoned additive processes and special attachments on the projector.[24]

In 1922, after six years of effort, Kalmus thus quit the search for additive solutions.

Subtractive systems, the principles of which had been outlined by du Hauron and, independently, by Cros in 1869, could in theory produce a colored film that would simply be threaded through a standard projector. Subtractive processes also rely on a series of separate trichromatically filtered black-and-white images, but instead of remaining discrete, each image is dyed and then superimposed—as in lithography—upon the others to create the full-color picture.

The major problem lay in the difficulty of dyeing the negatives. "Imbibing"—or relief image—was the earliest system, patented in 1874, for achieving this.[27] The gelatin of a negative swells up in proportion to the intensity of the exposure (or becomes thinner where more exposed), allowing a developing procedure in which a colored dye solution adheres to those parts thus distinguished. The exposed gelatin imbibes the liquid dye. Sequential imbibings create a full trichromatic subtractive image on the one gelatine base. This dye-image is easily copied so that many prints can be run off.

The Technicolor subtractive process used two films (one sensitive to the red-yellow range, another to the green-blue) cemented back to back. In a 1928 refinement, Kalmus managed to get them on the same celluloid base—a "bipack"—using the imbibing method. By 1932, the Technicolor process involved not just stock and developing techniques, but also a special beam-splitter camera, of the sort first introduced to aid an additive process in 1918, which exposed a blue/red bipack film and, simultaneously, a separate green negative. This produced a three-color master.

The system, in all its various forms, privileged the laboratory, because that was where the color image—for all that it was indexically (i.e., photographically) bound to represent colors in the real world—was, in effect, created. Although neither the special camera nor the superiority of Technicolor's imbibing technique were of Kalmus's devising, they enabled him to demand and obtain considerable control over the films shot with this process. He had perfected the most effective exploitation of known methods, and exceptional craft in the laboratory, as much as any other factor, was the basis of Technicolor's hegemony over cinema color. The close control exercised by Kalmus's "color consultants"—often over the resistance of studio technicians who were under no illusions about Technicolor's "naturalness"—limited the circumstances in which the film was exposed. The result was that the stock established its own reference system consistent, not with nature, but only with itself, as in one of Tolkien's fairy-tale worlds.

By the late forties, Technicolor's hegemony also entailed a range of patent and antitrust problems,[28] but since 1953 the camera and the special negative stocks had been abandoned. Technicolor is now essentially only a multinational chain of laboratories that bring their special skills to Eastman Kodak materials

The original Kodachrome process was introduced in 1913 and in 1916 was adapted for movies by use of a beam-splitter camera. In 1928, under license from its French developers, Kodak began to manufacture a film it named Kodacolor—a lenticular 16mm stock. Twenty years before, Gabriel Lippmann had envisioned a film stock that had, in effect, a myriad of tiny lenses embedded in the emulsion—a monochrome extension, in some sense, of his previous direct system—that would allow for normal viewing. The following year, 1909, Rudolph Berthon thought to place a three-color filter before such a film, and in 1923 a successful demonstration of a color lenticular process was given in Paris. The method produced prints of great delicacy, but attempts by Kodak, Paramount, and the French to make a 35mm lenticular stock were fruitless; anyway, by that time, the mid-thirties, Kodak was ready with a new Kodachrome.[29]

The chemistry enabling subtraction to take place on a single negative was understood in the same year Berthon began developing the lenticular stock. Rudolf Fischer and his assistant Johann Siegrist noticed that paraphenylendiamine, a photographic developer, produced oxidations as it worked on the silver halides of the film. It "coupled" with the emulsion to form a color, in effect making an insoluble dye.[30] Fischer patented the idea of "color-formers" or "dye-couplers" in 1912 and publicized a growing list of compound substances in a series of patents and reports in the British, French, German, and American technical press before the First World War.[31] Other workers in the early twenties added to the number of known couplers, but it was two young American amateur chemists (and professional musicians) who were to create the first practical application of Fischer's breakthrough.

In 1924, Leopold Mannes and Leopold Godowsky, Jr., patented a reversal film stock where two emulsions were placed on a single base, the lower one faster and sensitized to red, the upper one slower and sensitized to green-blue/green.[32] Clearly, the combination of dye-couplers and multilayer variable speed emulsion had the potential of producing, on one base, an integral full-color image with the trichromatic filters and all the necessary dyes "built in," as it were. By 1930, Mannes and Godowsky, working privately, still remained a step ahead of the industrial laboratories. At this point, Kodak had the good sense to hire them, and they moved out of various hotel rooms and the bathrooms of their parents' New York apartments to Rochester. By 1933, they had perfected a bipack reversal system for 16mm use; then on April 15th, 1935, Kodak offered a new Kodachrome amateur movie stock, the "tripac" implied by Cros's vision nearly seventy years earlier.

For the first time, an easy-to-use color stock was available that required no special apparatus. A year later, a 35mm version for reversal transparencies was introduced. Kodak designed the films so that the couplers were added, not to the emulsion, but during the development process. This created a situation as privileged as the one into which Kalmus had steered Technicolor; anybody could *expose* Kodachrome, but only Kodak could *develop* it. It is not entirely inappropriate that Kodachrome's "inventors" were known in the Kodak Research Laboratory as "God and Man." They had not only broken through into a new world of color, but in so doing they had created a virtual processing monopoly. The German company Agfa, close on Kodak's heels, produced a comparable stock at the same time with the couplers *built into* the film so that it could be developed anywhere.

Because these solutions all produced approximations and involved trade-offs in color responsiveness, grain, and overall sensitivity, that was not the end of the matter. The tripack subtractive film has undergone immense development since Mannes and Godowski's day. Agfa introduced a color-negative system just before the Second World War. Kodak marketed Ektachrome, a tripack with built-in couplers that could be developed at home. Edwin Land adapted his instant monochrome system to Polacolor in 1962. In general, all these film stocks gained steadily over the years in both sensitivity (with no concomitant increase in grain) and overall responsiveness.

After the war, the differences between Agfacolor and the American color films assumed an overt ideological significance when the Russians adopted, or rather captured, the former. Agfacolor became a "socialist" stock: it had paler colors, muted edges, and increased sensitivity to pastels. This was in contrast to Technicolor, which was "purer than reality, needing strong artificial light, aggressive, almost whorish." These are the terms, Dudley Andrew suggests, in which the French perceived the ideological differences in this color "cold war" of the late forties.[33] After the Second World War, the French, lacking a domestic subtractive system, were faced with choosing between domestic-additive (and therefore obsolete) methods, including a revived lenticular stock, or importing foreign technology. The domestic systems failed, and the French chose Agfacolor—but disguised in a politically acceptable form because obtained from Agfa's pre-war Belgian partners, Gaevert. Technicolor lost out in France, not just because of French ambivalence ("a desire for, and a loathing of, American technology," in Andrew's phrase) but more important, because with only three laboratories—in Hollywood, New Jersey, and London—it simply could not handle any more business. By 1948, it demanded nine months lead-time on principle photography, and printing schedules were being planned three years in advance.

V

We have presented the history of the development of *filmstocks* as the locus of choice and decision, but the color image depends, as Technicolor's insistence on control of the filmic event reveals, on more than just the stock. As we have indicated, the image can be altered (within the parameters of the film) during processing, although with color these options are much reduced. There are other major factors involved. Technicolor's move onto the studio floor was motivated as much by the desire to maintain absolute control over lighting as to prohibit outsiders from loading the cameras. (This was done ostensibly to protect the patent, but since that was a matter of public record, other factors must also have been at work.) Control of lighting was crucial, and when coupled with the existing power of the laboratory, ensured the consistency of Technicolor's performance, especially as sets, costume, and makeup could also be bent to highlight the process' most responsive aspects.

Natural and manmade "white" unfiltered lights are actually colored. They range from, say, the blue of a northern sky, through sunlight, to projection bulbs, and the comparative red of ordinary incandescent household lamps. (As conventionally measured in degrees Kelvin, these examples run from 7500 for the northern sky to 2800 for the household lamp.) With monochrome film, the color of the illumination is significant, but not critical. With color film, of course, it assumes a far greater moment.

After the First World War, film lighting had settled its own artificial code, mixing, in the interests of maintaining a largely realist convention, a number of theatrical systems: basic flat lighting, lighting for effects, and spotlighting. Peter Baxter persuasively argues that as electricity was introduced into the studios in the years before the war, there was a desire to emulate the most advanced stage techniques: "the cinema was moving in the same direction as commercial American theatre, and a few paces behind it."[34] The combination of techniques resulted in the "three-point" (i.e., keylight, fill-light, and backlight) overhead system—with almost no floor-level sources except for special effects—that is still in use today. For Baxter, this application of the electric light expresses the dominant ideological assumptions of the studios in creating a style that operates by "revelation and expression."[35]

Monochrome stocks became ever more sensitive until, in the late thirties, general lighting levels could be reduced by 70 percent. The studios were now so dim, comparatively speaking, that cinematographers began to use photoelectric light meters to ensure proper exposure, something the mysterium of the craft did not previously allow.[36] A sequence of responses, ostensibly occasioned by changes in the technology (sound as well as color), can be traced in lighting, set and costume design, and makeup. These changes are more complex than a simple technological progression suggests, since they actually reflect the forces at work within the organization of the industry, the social positioning of Hollywood, as well as the underlying thrust towards an ever-more-transparent mode of representation.

As a prophylactic against widespread filmmaking in the society, the combined effect of all these complications could not be bettered.

Movie production became, like newspaper production a hundred years earlier, more and more capital-intensive and less and less accessible. This is the trajectory, a common one in media technology since it can be seen not only in newspaper history, that the cinema traces. Once established behind a "high-tech" bastion, cheaper monopack color systems were introduced without fear that the other elements of the process would be easily duplicated either by those seeking entry to the industry or even by rank outsiders. Similarly, the 16mm format was improved and professionalized for television use, that is, within a highly capital-intensive environment. The public was left for nearly forty years with 8mm, a film too grainy for large-scale exhibition. The ideological underpinnings of these technological developments are, comparatively speaking, clearer than the cinema's supposed drive towards "realism."

Color was more than unrealistic, in the sense of being a highly manufactured approximation of the real world, and it was, as Ed Buscombe points out,[37] not used in those sorts of movies that at first sight might have been thought to benefit most from additional "realism"—social dramas in the genres of war and crime films (insofar as these were "realistic") or newsreels and documentaries. (It should not be objected that the color stocks were too slow for non-fiction since much of it was shot outdoors. Color newsreels were certainly possible and could have appeared much earlier than they did.) Instead, the first trichromatic Technicolor film was Disney's Oscar-winning cartoon *Flowers and Trees*. Douglas Fairbanks, star of the bichromatic Technicolor feature *The Pirate*, complained that color could distract the eye, confuse the action, and, presumably worst of all, "take attention from acting and facial expression."[38] It was also more expensive, a further significant factor during the Depression. Buscombe argues that color came to denote luxury, spectacle, or fantasy, and a celebration of its own technological mastery. Thus, Kansas is black and white; Oz is technicolored. So much did color come to signify a lack of serious intent that a Pathe producer was able to announce in 1947: "The French don't go in for musicals or color."[39]

A confusion therefore exists about the signification of color in the Hollywood film, a confusion that simultaneously deems color real and fantastic; there is also a certain cognitive dissonance in the professional discourse. Even Natalie Kalmus realized that despite motion pictures' faithful duplication of "all the auditory and visual sensations," there is a distinction between "natural colors and lights" and "man-made colors and artificial lights."[40] It is a distinction she and her fellow workers devoted their lives to ignoring.

VI

In all this it should not be forgotten that "perhaps the most important single factor in dramatic cinematography is the relation between the color sensitivity of an emulsion and the reproduction of pleasing flesh tones."[41] The failure to find a direct color system requires not only chemical manipulation; it allows manipulation to accommodate the cultural prejudices of the users—to make, by careful chemistry, already pleasing (Caucasian) flesh tones more pleasing than they are in nature. Determining which prejudices might be at work in the culture became an agenda item for the research laboratory:

Series of color prints have been made from well-exposed color separation negatives of several typical scenes. The prints of each of these differ in tone reproduction, balance and in other ways subject to controlled variation. These series have been presented to numerous judges, and their judgments have been compared with results of measurements of various colors in the prints.

Central to this positivist social science enterprise undertaken by Kodak researchers in the early fifties was a series of prints of a portrait of "a young lady" which exhibited

variations of balance from too red or yellow to too blue, and from too green to too pink. These prints were submitted to a number of judges who were asked to accept or reject each on the basis of color alone. . . .
  Optimum reproduction of skin color is not "exact" reproduction . . . "exact reproduction" is rejected almost unanimously as "beefy." On the other hand, when the print of highest acceptance is masked and compared with the original subject, it seems quite pale. . . .
  The discrepancy between "exact" reproduction and preferred reproduction is partly due to distortions inherent in the process, such that a certain discrepancy of a particular color is necessary to permit the best over-all reproduction of all colors in the picture.
  Similar results have been obtained with other colors. The directions and amounts of difference between exact reproduction and optimum reproduction are different for every color tested.[42]

Kodak, faced with the physical inevitability of distortion, here establishes the potential superiority of its products to the real world. The subject of the photograph can be made to have skin tones *more* pleasing than she has in reality. Exact reproduction, a supposed goal of the photographic and cinematographic project, takes second place to inexact, culturally determined, "optimum" reproduction. Caucasian skin tones are not to be rendered as they are, but rather as they are preferred—a whiter shade of white. The results of such social investigations as well as the growing understanding of the physics of color, the physiology of perception, and the chemistry of dyes and films, can be translated into ever more culturally determined products.

All this is not to suggest some crude conspiracy on the part of the industrial chemists or physicists responsible for the color of the moving image. The above account draws attention to the existence of choices in the development of these processes and to suggest that in situations of choice, consciously or unconsciously, cultural determinants will operate—as much in the scientific environment as anywhere. The Kodak experiment cited above speaks eloquently to how research is redolent of a specific culture: its results do not produce a film stock that can be readily manipulated to give good black skin tones.

That this should warrant attention is only the result of the operations of media, technology, and, especially, media technology in the culture. These operations, in a sense hidden because transparent, conform perfectly to Barthes's explication of bourgeois ideology in general: that in such ideology, "the order of the world can be seen as sufficient or ineffable, it is never seen as significant."[43] Indeed, so insignificant is it, that Western color film can supposedly be used as a tool against itself, as if a whole technology of dyeing had not intervened.

ENDNOTES

This paper could not have been written without the guidance and advice of my colleague Janet Staeger.

[1] Terry Eagleton, *Criticism and Ideology* (London: Verso, 1978), p. 20.

[2] Roland Barthes, *Mythologies* (London: Paladin, 1973), p. 142.

[3] John Berger, *Ways of Seeing* (London: BBC, 1972), p. 10.

[4]Produced by The El Salvador Film and Video Project, directed by Diego de la Texera, El Salvador/Cuba 1981 (distributed by Cineguild).

[5]Johannes Kepler, quoted in Svetlana Alpers, *The Art of Describing* (Chicago: University of Chicago Press, 1983) p. 50.

[6]I wish to thank A.D. Coleman for letting me read and quote from his unpublished manuscript, "The Lens," p. 24, revised and published as "Lentil Soup," in *Etc.*, Spring 1985, p. 19.

[7]It is commonly asserted that Quattrocento Perspectiva Artificialis (a.k.a. "costruzione legittina") as theorized by Alberti is the ground upon which the camera obscura portabilis' lens sits, but as Conolli (see footnote 9) correctly points out, this dominance was not without exceptions. It seems rather that Albertian perspective is somewhat beside the point, and the apparatus, as refined by Kepler, replicates the effects of the major alternative Dutch system in that no Albertian "window" is suggested between the artist and/or viewer, and the unified vanishing point, although capable of being accommodated to this system, was not as privileged as it was in Italy. See Alpers, op.cit., pp. 53ff.

[8]See Jean-Louis Baudry, "Ideological Effects of the Basic Cinematographic Apparatus," trans. by Alan Williams in *Film Quarterly*, Winter, pp. 39–47.

[9]See Jean Louis Conolli, "Technique et ideologie," part 1, *Cashiers du Cinema* (Paris), May/June 1971, pp. 21.

[10]Peter Wollen, "Cinema And Technology: A Historical Overivew," in *The Cinematic Apparatus*, edited by Teresa de Lauretis and Stephen Heath (New York: St. Martin's Press, 1980), p. 24.

[11]Eastman Kodak Co. press release CPI 8357NR, Rochester, N.Y., Jan. 25, 1983, p. 1, quoted in Coleman, op.cit., p. 3.

[12]"Color and Cinema: Problems in the Writing of History," *Film Reader #4*, 1979 p. 22.

[13]Roderick T. Ryan, "Color in the Motion-Picture Industry," *Journal of the SMPTE*, July 1976, p. 499.

[14]Natalie Kalmus, "Colour Consciousness," *Journal of the SEMPE*, Aug. 1935, pp. 139ff. The meeting was held by the Technicians Branch of the Academy of Motion Picture Arts and Sciences in Hollywood on May 21, 1935.

[15]See, for example, Joseph Valentine, "Make-Up and Set Painting Aid New Film," *American Cinematographer*, Feb. 1939, p. 54.

[16]R.W.G. Hunt, *The Reproduction of Colour* (London: John Wiley and Sons, 1967), p. 62.

[17]Ibid, pp. 127,157.

[18]Kalmus, op.cit., p. 144.

[19]Hunt, op.cit., p. 26.

[20]Josef Maria Eder, *Geschichte der Photographie*, 1932, translated as *History of Photography*, by Edward Epstean (New York: Dover, 1978), pp. 668ff.

[21]The caveat is because all modern accounts in the photographic literature which consistently speak to the excellence of the Lippmann method also stress its limitations, but are written with no indication that modern materials have been used to duplicate the original experiments. Therefore it is possible that the difficulties, originally highlighted by the inventors of other more diffused systems, have simply become part of the received history of photography and are more apparent than real.

[22]E.J. Wall, *The History of Three-Color Photography* (Boston: American Photographic Publishing Company, 1925), p. 4.

[23]However, our knowledge is limited—which is attested to, for instance, by the illogical color constancy experiment, first demonstrated by Gaspard Monge in 1789.

[24]Ryan, op.cit., pp. 496ff.

[25]Jay Leyda, *Kino* (New York: Collier Books, 1968), p. 47 note (quoted in Branigan, op.cit., p. 27).

[26]Ryan, op.cit., p. 500. Additive processes persist in television. In the NTSC system, three electron guns, like Maxwell's three filtered cameras, scan the image by means of a system of mirrors. In the receiving cathode ray tube, clusters of red, blue, and green phosphor dots—a system suggested in Germany by Flechsig in 1938 but harking back to the Autochrome plate of the Lumière brothers marketed in 1907—are activated to reproduce the original.

[27]Wall, op.cit., p. 390.

[28]Branigan, op.cit., p. 24.

[29]In 1955, Eastman Kodak revived the 16mm lenticular film because it could be developed faster than conventional substractive stacks, and increasing the speed of development was suddenly of importance. Prime-time color programming was just starting and needed to be recorded for networking to the other coast. Kodak saw in lenticular color film an opportunity to stunt the development of videotape recording, at this point just emerging from the experimental stage. Between September 1956 and February 1958, the pioneering network in color, NBC, used Kodacolor film for making "hot" (i.e., fast) kinescopes; but in November of 1956 CBS transmitted the first videotaped program. Sixteen months later, NBC gave up and went to the videotape. There are no contemporary lenticular stocks.

[30]Wall, op.cit., p. 406.

[31]Ibid, p. 417.

[32]Ibid, p. 158.

[33]"Post War Struggle for Colour," in de Lauretis and Heath, eds., pp. 61ff.

[34]Peter Baxter, "On the History and Ideology of Film Lighting," *Screen*, Autumn 1975, p. 92.

[35]Ibid, p. 100.

[36]Valentine, loc.cit. Photoelectric cells had been in production since 1911, and various light meters had been available.

[37]Ed Buscambe, "Sound and Color," *Jumo Cut*, April 1978, p. 25.

[38]Ibid.

[39]Andrews, op.cit., p. 68.

[40]Kalmus, op.cit., p. 141.

[41]Valentine, loc.cit.

[42]David L. MacAdam, "Quality of Color Reproduction," *Journal of the SMPTE*, May 1951, pp. 501ff.

[43]Barthes, loc.cit.

PART IV

JOURNALISM
Ideologies and Roles

INTRODUCTION

Steve M. Barkin

By now there is a considerable research literature on journalistic practices concerned with how the news media, in Fishman's phrase, "transform an indeterminate world into a formulated set of events." The articles in this section proceed from the shared premise of that research that news is a constructed reality. The articles address, in specific detail in some instances, news processes. In a larger sense, though, they deal with the underlying justifications for news processes, both in societal, ideological terms and through the self-perceptions of those who do newswork. Taken together, these selections represent an effort to extend and interrelate the literature on news construction.

Hallin's essay begins with a theoretical and historical overview of the critical debate over the media's ability to legitimize the existing order. Noting that American media take technical knowledge as a model for reporting of news, the author discusses the media's tendency to frame events in terms of strategy and tactics, success and failure. This "scientization" of American journalism, Hallin argues, reflects the predominance of an objective stance adopted by the media for purposes of self-legitimation, the needs of which may conflict with the ideological imperative to legitimate the system.

Bennett, Gressett, and Haltom then offer a case study illustrating the behaviors of journalists caught up in just this sort of ideological-professional quandary. Faced with a problematic story that does not conform to acceptable formulae, journalists engage in a process of "repairing" the news, recasting the plot of the story so that it becomes an object lesson in journalistic responsibility, not the story of an individual driven to a desperate act. Official sources corroborate that theme, distancing the event's principal figure from his own story while reinforcing the bounds of permissible news coverage.

The question of what journalists regard as an acceptable basis for knowledge is the subject of Ettema and Glasser's study. The authors contrast the epistemology of the daily reporter, who is conditioned to accept bureaucratically credible facts and accounts, with that of the investigative reporter, whose role-perceptions suggest a different set of values and responsibilities. Whereas the reporter of routine events declines to accept responsibility for the quality or value of what is reported, the investigative reporter has a personal, moralistic stake in the story.

Köcher's comparative study of British and German journalists focuses on differences in self-perceptions and role definitions that reflect dissimilarities in social, political, and legal structures. British journalists interviewed in the study viewed their role as that of neutral reporters, were strongly oriented toward a norm of objectivity, and were drawn to the profession largely because of the excitement offered by a news career. By contrast, German journalists were more likely to assume the role of advocate, were less constrained by the requirements of objectivity, and placed more importance on professional opportunities for self-expression.

In the section's final article, Pritchard employs an organizational perspective in examining the extent to which the output of the press influences the behavior of the prosecutor's office in the disposition of felony cases. Few agenda-setting studies have looked specifically at the impact of patterns of news coverage on public officials. Pritchard finds support for his hypothesis that the more extensive the newspaper coverage of a criminal case, the more likely the district attorney's office is to forego a negotiated settlement in order to push the case to trial.

In sum, these authors relate the practices and products of journalism to ideologically based rationales for newswork, to the self-justifications of practitioners, and to the actions of other social institutions. Their research may point to a new level of theoretical interest in newsmaking, a more integrative thrust that seeks to establish linkages between the newsroom, other agencies of social action, and the political and ideological contours of the larger society.

14

THE AMERICAN NEWS MEDIA
A Critical Theory Perspective

Daniel C. Hallin

Critical theory is concerned with the ability of human beings to reflect on their social life for the purpose of discovering, as Tolstoy once put it, "what we should do and how we should live." For this reason it has devoted a good deal of attention to the institutions of what Habermas calls the public sphere: the arena, formed as the liberal political order was replacing the feudal, in which private individuals come together to discuss the public affairs of the community.[1] At the heart of the critique of contemporary capitalism advanced by Horkheimer, Adorno, Marcuse, Habermas, and others is the thesis that the capitalist form of social organization that brought the public sphere into being nevertheless distorts and limits its development to the point that the society is unable to establish the process of dialogue and collective self-reflection that the advent of liberal institutions seemed to promise.

From the beginning the newspaper was among the key institutions of the emerging public sphere. "We should underrate their importance," wrote Tocqueville, "if we thought [newspapers] just guaranteed liberty; they maintain civilization."[2] And the young Marx, in the wonderfully overblown style of German romanticism, called the fledgling press "the omnipresent open eye of the spirit of the people . . . the ruthless confession of a people to itself . . . the mind of the state that can be peddled in every cottage, cheaper than natural gas."[3] Both expected the newspaper to assist in the birth of a fundamentally new political order, to enable the society as a whole, for the first time in human history, to open a dialogue about itself and decide in a public way the direction of public life. But this, according to critical theory, is not how it has turned out. The public sphere has given way to the "consciousness industry," the press as a potential medium of public dialogue to the "mass media," deeply embedded in a structure of domination.

Critical theorists have offered two types of explanation for the distortion of political dialogue in liberal capitalist societies. The first and more familiar concerns the structure of power in a class society. Unequal distribution of political and economic power gives to some members of society greater access and control over the institutions of political communication and organization than others. All interests and perspectives are not equally represented. Power intrudes upon discourse, and the outcome of debate can neither be considered a genuine consensus or compromise, nor can it be expected to reflect an assessment of all the information or insight potentially available.

The second argument is less familiar but more original to critical theory, and I will take it as my primary focus here. This argument, summed up by Habermas's phrase the "scientization of politics," concerns the type of social action and discourse characteristic of capitalist society. There are, according to Habermas, two types of action fundamental to human life. First, human beings must interact with nature to produce their material means of subsistence. This type of action, involving the manipulation of nature and of human beings as "forces of production" to achieve established purposes, Habermas calls purposive-rational action. Second, human beings must interact with one another to produce the frameworks of reciprocal expectation that make it possible for them to live as members of collective social institutions. This Habermas calls communicative action. Habermas draws these concepts in part from Aristotle's distinction between techne— "the skillful production of artifacts and the expert mastery of objectified tasks"[4]—and praxis—action directed toward human education and the realization of human potential. He accordingly distinguishes between two types of knowledge, technical and practical, which correspond to the two types of human action. Capitalism, Habermas argues, develops the capacity for purposive-rational action to a degree never approached by any previous social order. But it also tends to universalize that form of action and the standards of discourse and knowledge that correspond to it. All questions come to be framed as essentially technical or strategic questions, questions of the most effective means by which a given end can be attained. As a result society is unable to develop a capacity for communicative action through which it could resolve practical questions, those that have to do not with means but ends, not with techniques but standards of human conduct.

This, then, is the perspective from which I will examine the American news media. I will begin by making the argument that modern American journalism does in fact take technical knowledge as a model for the reporting of news. This conception of news reporting, I will argue, is a relatively recent historical development, connected with the rise of commercial mass media—and thus with capitalist forms of social organization—and with the professionalization of journalism. I will conclude by discussing the political implications of this transformation of journalism. As we shall see critical theorists have taken two very different positions on the political role of mass media. Marcuse, Horkheimer, and Adorno, writing in the 1940s, 1950s, and early 1960s, argued that the media were capable of producing an ideological consensus tight enough that the possibility of opposition to the existing structure of society became extremely problematic. Habermas, on the other hand, has cast doubt in his recent writings on the possibility of any such centralized production of social values and in fact has argued that liberal capitalist societies are susceptible to conflict and crisis precisely in the sphere of ideology and culture.

In discussing this debate over the media's ability to legitimize the existing social order, I shall introduce Habermas's recent work on the pragmatics of human communication, which points toward important new ways of approaching the study of the mass media. For Habermas all forms of human communication, however asymmetrical the social relations may have become, are essentially derived from the basic form of dialogue and must be seen as relationships between active human subjects. This suggests that we must direct our attention not only to the content of media messages but also to the character of the relations established between communicator and audience and the message that relation implies about the nature of social relationships generally. The news tells us not only what happened in the world today but who we are in relation to that world. I shall argue that the crucial consequence of the scientization of journalism, the shift to a technical angle in the reporting of news, may well lie in the message this form of journalism conveys about the nature of politics and the citizen's relation to it. The grounding of mass communication in dialogue also suggests that there may be limits beyond which the process of communication may not be stretched without destroying the legitimacy of the communicator. This point is important to understanding the relation of the mass media to the structure of social power: the ability of the media to support that structure ideologically is limited by their need to maintain the integrity of the process of communication on which their own legitimacy depends.

This argument is very preliminary. One might think, given the centrality to critical theory of the problem of public dialogue, that critical theorists would by now have produced a substantial body of research on the institutions of political communication. In fact, critical theory, which has been preoccupied for most of its history with the philosophical critique of positivism and the effort to develop a nonpositivist conception of social inquiry, has so far produced relatively little in the way of extended analysis of concrete social institutions, and the news media are no exception.[6] What follows, therefore, should be taken not primarily as a report on research already undertaken but as a proposal for future work in an area where most of the interesting questions remain to be addressed.

Technical Angle in News Reporting

A few examples will illustrate how the modern journalist reports political events. In December 1968 *CBS Evening News* featured a two-part special report on "pacification" in Vietnam. The series, which totaled an unusually long thirteen minutes in length, reflected the growing maturity of the American news media. A couple of years earlier Vietnam coverage had been primarily a chronicle of daily battlefield events. By late 1968 the media were beginning to make a conscious effort, at least occasionally, to offer background, analysis, and perspective. CBS had chosen well the topic for this particular background report. Pacification involved the struggle for political support or hegemony in the villages of South Vietnam, which was what the war was ultimately about. By this time, too, the media were beginning to venture beyond official sources of information. The CBS pacification report included a lengthy interview with a critic of administration policy (John Tunney, a senator from California); a few years earlier use of information from critics had been extremely rare in foreign policy coverage.

How did CBS provide background on the complex and controversial struggle for South Vietnam's countryside? Here are Walter Cronkite's introduction to the report and correspondent Murray Fromson's wrap-ups to the two segments:

Cronkite: American officials in Saigon came out with their most optimistic pacification report of the war today. They said that almost three-fourths of South Vietnam's seventeen million people now live in relatively secure areas controlled by the Saigon government. According to those officials Vietcong control has dropped to just over thirteen percent of the population with the remaining South Vietnamese living in contested areas. Tonight we get a look at one of those contested areas. . . .

Fromson [concluding part I]: So pacification does not stand still. It moves forward, it moves back. But what is the balance? What is the trend. . . ? An effort is being made to measure this, and we'll look at the measurements in our next report.

Fromson [concluding part II]: Another offensive by the Communists would undermine the program. . . . But the momentum seems to be in the other direction. Since the November 1 bombing halt government and U.S. troops have taken over nearly 800 hamlets previously regarded as contested. The goal is to occupy another three hundred of these hamlets by the anniversary of the Tet offensive.[7]

The story, in short, was structured from beginning to end around the question of effectiveness; each element was explained within this framework. A U.S. tank, for instance, had recently fired into the village in response to small arms fire, killing two civilians. "What may be regarded as a military necessity," Fromson reported, "also creates problems for the pacification team." The whole of part II was devoted to the computerized Hamlet Evaluation System (HES), which produced the official figures on the progress of pacification. That was where Senator Tunney came in; he was not there to discuss the wisdom or justice of U.S. policy in Vietnam but to offer an opposing view on the accuracy of the figures produced by the HES.

The tendency to frame and analyze events in terms of strategy and tactics, success and failure is characteristic of modern U.S. journalism. In Vietnam coverage, even stories about the political debate at home were shaped to this pattern. Reports about the antiwar movement, when they were not preoccupied with the possibility of a violent disruption of social order (another common focus in coverage of political controversy), focused heavily on the issue of whether the movement was gaining or losing ground: would as many people participate in this year's demonstration as in last year's? Would the demonstration have any impact on the president's decision, or would the president be watching a football game? Indeed only 40 percent of television reports on the antiwar movement contained any discussion of the war in Vietnam.[8]

Studies of election coverage have shown a heavy preponderance of attention to the horse-race angle and the strategic battle of wits.[9] "The Presidential debate produced no knockout blow, no disastrous gaffe and no immediate, undisputed victor," wrote the *New York Times*'s Hedrick Smith, analyzing the Reagan-Carter debate. "It was a contest of content against style, of a President repeatedly on the attack to put his challenger on the defensive while Ronald Reagan used his calm demeanor to offset Jimmy Carter's contention that he was 'dangerous,' "[10] In November 1981, when President Reagan's budget director in a published interview termed the administration's budget policy trickle-down economics and conceded the numbers on which it was based were dubious, the media's handling of the affair was not surprising. "The question all day at the White House," reported Lesley Stahl of CBS, "was: Can Stockman survive? Will he be fired?" And from congressional reporter Phil Jones: "The question is: Can Stockman regain credibility in Congress? If today's Senate Budget Committee hearing is any indication, it will be difficult for Stockman to be effective again."[11]

What I have called here the technical angle in news reporting is by no means the only way contemporary journalists frame political events. Journalism, like any other long-standing cultural institution, is intricate in its complexity. But the technical angle does tend to dominate political coverage, particularly when background and analysis are offered.[12] It also serves well to illustrate what is distinctive about contemporary journalism as a form of political communication. In order to understand why this form of journalism has become dominant and to assess its implications, it is necessary to trace the transformation of the news media from the small-scale political press of the eighteenth and early nineteenth centuries to the large-scale commercial mass media of today.

Displacement of the Political Press by Commercial Mass Media

When Benjamin Franklin in 1749 outlined the curriculum for a proposed Pennsylvania Academy, he stressed the importance of political oratory, noting that this required a knowledge not only of the rhetoric of the ancients but of the craft of newspaper publishing, "Modern Political Oratory being chiefly performed by the Pen and the Press."[13] Alexis de Tocqueville, writing in the 1830s, saw the American newspaper as catalyst of collective political action, essential for maintaining an active political life under conditions of mass democracy. Tocqueville wrote,

The leading citizens living in an aristocratic country can see each other from afar, and if they want to unite their forces they go to meet one another, bringing a crowd in their train. But in democratic countries it often happens that a great many men who both want and need to get together cannot do so, for all being very small and lost in the crowd, they do not see one another at all and do not know where to find one another. Then a newspaper gives publicity to the feeling or idea that had occurred to them all simultaneously but separately. . . . The newspaper brought them together and continues to be necessary to hold them together.[14]

The U.S. newspaper of the eighteenth and early nineteenth centuries was a vehicle of political debate and action. Neither objectivity nor political neutrality, the key values of contemporary journalism, was considered a virtue.[15] The main purpose of a newspaper, to the extent that it concerned itself with public affairs (newspapers also provided entertainment, commercial information, and religious and moral edification), was to express a particular point of view as forcefully and eloquently as possible. In the early nineteenth century as political parties were established, the press became primarily partisan. Most newspapers were backed financially by parties or politicians whose politics they represented and whose followers they served to mobilize. The press of this period was also relatively decentralized. Newspapers were small, numerous, and, given the small amount of capital required, relatively easy to establish; Franklin began as a printer's apprentice. The early American newspaper was both public and political: public in the sense that it was neither an official agency of the state nor primarily a private business venture but an organ established by citizens to communicate with one another; political in that it took a stand on the issues of the day. It was a quintessential institution of the public sphere, a means by which the ordinary citizen could be involved in the discussion of political issues.

The public sphere in the eighteenth and early nineteenth centuries, however, was restricted to a relatively small segment of the population. It was not until the 1820s and 1830s that property qualifications were dropped and the franchise extended to the entire white male population, nor until then that the newspaper became fully accessible to the masses. The papers of the pre-1830 period cost six cents an issue, nearly 10 percent of a wage worker's average daily income. They were read primarily by commercial and political elites. It was the penny press of the 1830s, the forerunner of today's commercial mass media, that first put newspapers in the hands of the mass public on a regular basis. This transformation of the American press was to prove paradoxical: on the one hand it democratized the market for newspapers, but on the other it centralized the means of political communication in the hands of large corporations and caused the atrophy of the mobilizing and advocacy roles previously fulfilled by the newspaper.

The penny papers and their successors were commercial rather than political enterprises. Introducing newly developed steam-powered cylinder presses, they lowered prices and expanded circulations by an order of magnitude. This gave them a new but very valuable product to sell: the attention of a mass audience. Advertising became the solid economic foundation of the new mass circulation papers, and the newspaper became a major commercial undertaking, requiring substantial capital investment and promising handsome profits. These profits had important political implications; they meant that the mass circulation newspaper, unlike its less lucrative predecessor, had no need of political subsidies to stay afloat. The economics of advertising, in fact, not only made it possible for the newspaper to free itself from political entanglements but probably created substantial incentives for the abandonment of politically committed journalism, especially of the partisan variety. A paper intent on maximizing its circulation could not afford the restriction of its audience that would result from identification with a particular political position.[16] The penny papers for the most part broke with the political tradition of the early American press, proclaiming their independence and their distaste for "political discussions of a merely partisan character," turning from "oratory" to news in the modern sense of the term.[17]

After the rise of the penny papers, the commercial press consolidated its hold on journalism, and the political journalism of the pre-1830 period gradually died out. Partisan newspapers continued to play an important role in journalism into the latter half of the nineteenth century, but by about the 1870s most had folded or converted to non-partisanship. The demise of the partisan press was followed by a period when the press was nonpartisan but nevertheless often activist, presenting itself as a defender not of a partisan viewpoint but of "the public good" in general, and crusading for everything from municipal reform to war with Spain. The great muckrakers of the progressive era belonged to this period in American journalism, as did the sensationalism of Pulitzer and Hearst. The modern American news media, committed not only to nonpartisanship but to the ideal of a professional, "objective" journalism, began to take shape roughly in the 1920s, becoming fully entrenched by the 1950s or early 1960s.

It is the ideal of objectivity that explains the emphasis on technique and efficacy in the news stories cited. The rise of commercial mass media transformed not only the institutional structure of political communication but also the structure of discourse itself. Commercial or professional journalism employed standards of truth and of the writer's proper relation to the audience very different from those of the political journalism. It had entirely changed standards for what needed to be said in a newspaper and how it should be said.

At the heart of this conception was the respect for "facts," which the penny papers proclaimed along with their political independence and which grew in importance as the commercial media developed. Just as the changing organization of the press paralleled the central change taking place in the wider economy, the growth of large-scale capitalist organization, the changing conventions of journalism paralleled the rise of science as a cultural paradigm against which all forms of discourse came to be measured. "We shall endeavor to record facts on every public and proper subject, stripped of verbiage and coloring," wrote James Gordon Bennett in his 1835 prospectus for the *New York Herald*.[18] The *Herald* was by no means free of verbiage or coloring, but it did emphasize news and the gathering of information rather than the political "oratory" that had been the stock-in-trade of the "six-penny" papers. By the 1920s Walter Lippmann and others would be speaking explicitly of scientific method and "the habit of disinterested realism" as a model for journalism. The journalist of the late nineteenth century, despite a commitment to factual reporting, did not yet radically separate fact and value; one could be a realist and yet a moralist, a recorder of facts and yet a political crusader. But by the early twentieth century realism had become objectivity: "a faith in 'facts,' a distrust of 'values,' and a commitment to their segregation."[19] And journalists came to think of themselves not as participants in a process of political discussion, even of a nonpartisan character, but as professionals, standing above the political fray.

The precise meaning of objective journalism has changed considerably over the course of the twentieth century. From about World War II through the early 1960s, objectivity was assumed to require strict separation not only between fact and value but between fact and interpretation. This was the heyday of straight journalism; news analysis for the most part was restricted to the signed column, and the ordinary reporter was supposed to tell "who, what, when, where" and leave it at that. The naive realism of straight objective journalism was shattered by the political conflict of the 1960s and 1970s, which produced both a credibility gap (a questioning of traditional sources of political information) and a clash of interpretations unknown in the years of wartime and cold war consensus. The stories examined above represent a concern for analysis and investigation born of the disillusionment and confusion of the 1960s. They offer the audience not just facts, not just a record of latest press releases, but perspective and summation, an interpretation of how the facts fit together and what they mean. But the 1960s and 1970s did not produce a questioning of objectivity itself; the "new journalism," which harkened back to the committed journalism of earlier periods, never gained more than a slippery toehold in the commercial media. In some ways, in fact, the 1960s and 1970s, precisely because the interpretation of reality had become subject to political debate, increased the journalist's and the news organization's need to appear strictly objective. The journalist had to provide analysis without appearing to depart from disinterested professionalism. And the easiest way to accomplish this was to focus on questions of strategy, effectiveness, and technique, questions that did not touch directly on conflicts of interest or clashes over the ends and values of political life. The political future of David Stockman is easier to assess with an attitude of detached realism than the actual policy of trickle-down economics, which inevitably raises the issue of how the interests and values affected by economic policy are to be weighed.

One-Dimensionality or Legitimation Crisis?

What are the consequences of the commercialization of the press and the scientization of journalism? Critical theorists have given two very different answers. The prevailing view in the 1940s, 1950s, and early 1960s held that the mass media had become fully integrated into a form of welfare state capitalism, which was rapidly expanding technical rationalization from the sphere of production into all aspects of social life.[20] The media had been stripped of the independent position the early press had held regarding the dominant social interests and had become not merely policemen of the ideological realm but something more sinister than that (policemen, after all, are only necessary to the extent that people resist social control). The media had become producers of consciousness. The consciousness they produced, moreover, was what Marcuse called a "one-dimensional" consciousness; it accepted the existing social order as defining the limits of rationality and sought merely to reflect that order, rejecting any attempt to speak of values or possibilities beyond it as inherently meaningless.

Centralization of Control over the Production of News

This perspective was never developed within critical theory beyond a few provocative essays or applied very systematically to an analysis of news reporting. But clearly there is a good deal of truth to it. The rise of the commercial media reversed the decentralization that had prevailed in the early days of the press, placing political communication once more under the control of established institutions, albeit institutions very different from those that had regulated political discourse before the advent of the newspaper and the pamphlet. It is interesting to look at the rise of commercial media in Great Britain, where the political implications of that development were more directly evident than in the United States.[21] The British newspaper was burdened by onerous political restrictions until well into the nineteenth century, including heavy taxes designed to keep newspapers too expensive to be either published or purchased by the lower classes. But repression proved not only ineffective but possibly counterproductive. Working-class papers published illegally, and the taxes, which they therefore did not have to pay, gave them a competitive edge over the respectable papers. Repression, in other words, ensured that the working class would continue to control its own press. By 1836 the growing illegal press exceeded the legal press in circulation. The liberal campaign for repeal of the "taxes on knowledge," which triumphed in the 1850s, made use of all the familiar arguments for freedom of the press, but the reformers did not leave their case simply to noble sentiments. To these they added the argument that a free market in information would place the education of the masses in the hands of men of "wealth and character." Said one reformer in Parliament, quoted in a fascinating article by James Curran, "We have made a long and fruitless experiment with the gibbet and hulks. Is it not time to consider whether the printer and his types may not provide better for the peace and honor of a free state, than the gaoler and the hangman. Whether in one word, cheap knowledge may not be a better political agent than costly punishment."[22] Freedom of the press meant not merely the lifting of censorship but the transformation of knowledge into a commodity, and the small-scale political press, like the inde-pendent petty producer of the precapitalist era, soon had to face the devastating economic power of highly capitalized mass production.

The radical press never attained a political importance in the United States comparable to its importance in Britain in the 1830s.[23] Perhaps this was in part because the United States had for a long time given market forces free reign in the sphere of information; no doubt it was largely due to the differing political and economic structure of the two societies. But when the penny papers appeared in the 1830s, there was nevertheless a growing labor press in the United States, and the penny papers played precisely the role described by the English re-formers: they spoke to the cultural and political needs of the constituents of the labor press, artisans who in the 1830s were facing loss of economic independence. But they spoke to those needs from a consensual, re-formist, and often a relatively apolitical perspective, emphasizing what the artisans had in common with the other and probably the primary constituency of the new commercial press, the rising middle class. "An emerging American working class," writes Dan Schiller, " . . . confronted newspapers that accepted and amplified belief in individual property, the market and the state, and that simultaneously drew heavily on its own experience. . . . The American working class had barely begun to employ the press as an agency of class identity when the commercial penny papers began to enlist the interest and identification of the laboring men."[24]

The liberal conception of a free market in ideas rested on the principle that the exchange of ideas should be insulated from the structures of wealth and power. In fact the rise of a market in ideas tied the production and dissemination of political information closely to the centers of economic and political power. There is a deep historical irony here. The coming of mass production, which so democratized the market for news, making the newspaper, as Marx put it, "cheaper than natural gas," at the same time centralized the production of news, placing the press under the control—today, in fact, generally monopoly control—of the corporation.[25] The American news media, moreover, have also come to have an intimate institutional connection with the state, despite the absence of formal state control. Modern American news organizations are so strongly geared toward reporting the activities and perspectives of government officials that one journalist gave his influential book the ironic title, *The Fourth Branch of Government*.[26] The news generally reflects the views of political elites faithfully enough that in a period like the 1950s and early 1960s, when conflicts within that elite are relatively insignificant, the political discourse that filters through the media to the public does come very close to the one-dimensionality described by Marcuse. There has, incidently, been relatively little research on the reasons for this historical connection between the rise of a commercial mass media and the institutionalization of relations between the news media and the state.

The Role of Ideology

There is also another, more impersonal but perhaps ultimately more significant face of power: the power of ideology. This is where the technical angle on politics and the principle of objectivity enter the picture. The scientist model of political discourse is a deeply rooted element of modern capitalist culture, which imposes itself on political discourse without any direct or conscious political intervention for the most part. I introduce the qualification "for the most part" because there have been times when this model of journalism has been emphasized for directly political reasons, and these are revealing. Objectivity was stressed by editors and publishers during the 1930s, for instance, when the Newspaper Guild was strong and relatively political, and there was concern reporters would slant the news toward the interests of labor.[27]

What are the implications of this use of the technical angle? Again, they are not simple, and I shall discuss some of the complexities below. But certainly that model of journalism does have the effect that Marcuse decried; it tends to exclude from political discourse all discussion of the ends of public policy. It conveys, moreover, along with the news of particular events, a general conception of politics more or less compatible with the prevailing low level of popular mobilization. It portrays politics either as a matter of administration or as a more or less sordid personal struggle for power (as in the story on the Reagan-Carter debate), and not, to use Habermas's phrase, as a process of "collective will-formation" and not therefore as a process in which the average citizen need be involved. It conveys to citizens a message about their own role in politics, and that message is essentially one of exclusion.

The News Report as a Speech Act

This last point touches on a dimension of communication much neglected in the study of the media. It is a basic principle of pragmatics, stressed by Habermas, who borrows it from J. L. Austin and John Searle, that any "speech act" has a twofold structure: it contains both a propositional and a "performative" content. It makes a statement about the world and simultaneously invokes or solicits a relationship between speaker and hearer.[28]

Consider the contrast between a modern news broadcast and an eighteenth-century newspaper. Let me take as examples the CBS broadcast containing the special report on pacification and an edition of the *New-England Courant*, an early American newspaper published by James Franklin and later Benjamin Franklin. The CBS broadcast analyzes for the audience in a factual and authoritative tone the progress of the pacification program. It contains virtually no statements that address the audience members directly; they are treated as strictly anonymous. It ends with Walter Cronkite's famous sign-off, "And that's the way it is, Tuesday, Dec. 16, 1968."

The *New-England Courant* dealt with political material of entirely different kind. One fairly typical edition contained a tract on the philosophical basis of law: "Law is right Reason, commanding Things that are good, and forbidding Things that are bad. . . . The Violation therefore of the Law does not constitute a Crime when the Law is bad; but the violation of what ought to be a Law, is a Crime even where there is no Law."[29] Along with this different kind of content went a different way of addressing the audience. The political tract, which was reprinted from a London journal, was introduced to the readers by a letter to the editor, signed in the fashion of the time, "Your Humble Servant, &c." It may in fact have been a contribution sent in by a reader, or it may have been written by the publisher. Most major articles were presented in the form of open personal letters.

In the two cases, very different relationships are established between speaker and hearer. The *New-England Courant* speaks to its readers in a personal tone, at an equal level. It invites them to participate in political discussion. CBS speaks to its audience as a provider of authoritative information. It solicits nothing beyond their attention, solicits of them no active role regarding the political material reported; indeed the authoritative and detached style of the report and the finality of the sign-off leave the impression that the matters discussed are essentially closed, at least until the next broadcast.

The technical angle is only one element of the ideology that shapes modern U.S. journalism. The role of ideology in political communication is a subject that cries out for more systematic investigation. A number of recent studies of the media have addressed the question perceptively, but there is as yet little systematic theory in the area. Most discussions of the role of ideology tend, for lack of theory, to slip by default into functionalism. They tend, that is, to identify certain ideological assumptions, supportive of the capitalist social order, which seem generally to dominate the news, and sometimes to show how these assumptions are effective—how, for example, they are built into the routines of journalism. But they then generally default the question of why these particular ideological principles become dominant, why a congruence develops between the ideological structures of capitalism and its political and economic structures, assuming that the fact of congruence is explanation enough.[30]

Legitimation Crisis?

One reason functional assumptions can be dangerous in the study of the media and of ideology generally is that cultural institutions do not always develop in ways that are functional for the established social order. This brings us to Habermas's theory of legitimation crisis, which departs sharply from the picture of ideological integration painted by the critical theory of the 1940s, 1950s, and early 1960s. The critique of late capitalist society advanced by Horkheimer, Adorno, and Marcuse is based largely on the "closing of the universe of discourse," which they believed that society had produced. Habermas's critique of late capitalism rests on the impossibility of this very ideological closure, the impossibility of an "administrative production of meaning." This argument, which Habermas presents in an admittedly sketchy and preliminary form in his *Legitimation Crtisis*, runs essentially as follows.[31] Liberal capitalist societies have been able to maintain political stability largely because they have permitted the state to intervene increasingly in the workings of the market, softening the social disruptions it produces and ensuring a level of private satisfaction high enough that the mass public will remain generally uninterested in politics. But state action to maintain an orientation of civil privatism has an ironic consequence; it results in an increasing "politicization of the relations of production": more and more areas of social and economic life, previously regulated by the market or by traditional institutions like the family and the church (whose functions, threatened by the tradition-shattering rationality of capitalist production, the state often takes over), are drawn into the political arena. Politicization creates an increased need for legitimation, for justification of social decisions that had previously seemed inevitable products of the market mechanism or expressions of cultural tradition. But legitimation is becoming increasingly hard to come by, precisely because the institutions that have borne the burden of cultural "production," the family, the church, and to some extent the market itself, are on the decline. And the resulting deficit of legitimation cannot, at least ultimately, be made up by any sort of managed production of ideology, for the latter is incompatible with the communicative action essential to the creation of shared normative structures.

It might seem that the media would be the logical institution to fill the legitimation gap, especially in the United States where they are almost entirely independent of the state and enjoy a much higher level of public trust than most other institutions. Habermas himself does not address the role of the media in *Legitimation Crisis*. But I would like to outline here, in a preliminary way, several reasons why it seems unlikely that the media could be counted on to play this role adequately and consistently.[32]

The anarchy of ideological production

Corporate control of the mass media does not guarantee that the media's cultural products will consistently serve the interests of the capitalist system as a whole, any more than corporate control of energy guarantees against an energy crisis. Certainly no major news organization is ever likely to become an open critic of capitalism, but the purpose of a news organization is to make profit, not politics, and there is no reason to assume that the narrow economic interest of the corporation will always coincide with the political interest of the system. If the anarchy of production leaves the capitalist system vulnerable to economic crisis, why should the anarchy of ideological "production" not leave it similarly vulnerable to cultural crisis?

Tensions within the dominant ideology

Neither does the hold of ideology over the journalist seem likely to guarantee that the media will consistently serve to legitimate the dominant institutions of capitalist society, though here we run up against the primitive state of knowledge about the structure and dynamics of ideology. Ideologies are as fraught with contradiction as are any other historical phenomena. Certainly that is true of the ideology that dominates U.S. journalism. The ambivalence of U.S. journalism is especially acute with respect to the state. Modern journalism is characterized by a great reverence for political authority, expressed in explicit terms at times of ceremony or crisis (the transition of power from Nixon to Ford, for example), and, perhaps more important, manifested implicitly in the whole focus and organization of the news-gathering process, which revolves like a satellite around the center of political power. But the U.S. journalist is also traditionally cynical about the holders and seekers of power, and that tradition has been reawakened and perhaps deepened by the political conflicts of the 1960s and the drift and ineffectiveness of the 1970s. This cynicism may itself be functional for the system in that it demobilizes the public, lowering what political scientists call the sense of political efficacy.[33] But that does not mean it could not simultaneously be hollowing out the myths that have sustained the welfare-national security state of the postwar period. When it comes to the economic structure of modern capitalism, the journalist is much less likely to express doubts. But even here there are ideological tensions. The American journalist believes in "free enterprise" and the rationality of modern capitalist technology and social organization; at the same time she or he clings to an ideology of traditional individualism that predates the corporate era and coexists with it somewhat awkwardly.

Universal pragmatics and the limits of ideological manipulation
The media, finally, have a need for legitimation of their own, which may conflict with the legitimation of the system. Here it will be useful to return to Habermas's pragmatics. Critical theory is concerned with developing a form of social inquiry that will be able to bridge the gap between is and ought, enabling us to offer rational answers, grounded in the analysis of human experience, to practical questions, questions of how we should live and act. Habermas believes the solution to this puzzle is to be found in the analysis of communication. The effective use of language presupposes certain relations of reciprocity between human individuals; these conditions for the possibility of effective communication, which can be established by a reconstructive science of speech acts, provide a basis for both normative discourse and for empirical analysis of the dynamics of human history. It is this "universal pragmatics" that provides the justification for the central premise of *Legitimation Crisis*, the premise that there can be no "administrative production of meaning." The use of communication as an instrument of domination, Habermas argues, violates the conditions of trust and reciprocity essential to the achievement of shared meaning. This is not to say communication cannot be used successfully for manipulative purposes. On the contrary, what Habermas calls instrumental or strategic communication is a routine fact of social life and certainly a central characteristic of contemporary political history; one need only to recall the effectiveness of government management of the news in the early years of the Vietnam war.[35] But it follows from Habermas's theory that there are limits beyond which the basic structure of human communication cannot be stretched.[36]

The idea of a universal pragmatics is fraught with theoretical difficulties, far too numerous and fundamental to be discussed here. But Habermas does seem to have stated a simple but neglected truth crucial to the analysis of ideological institutions. Every process of communication involves a social relationship, in fact, a network of relationships, among active human subjects.[37] the maintenance of these relationships imposes demands on institutions like the media that may conflict with the need of the system for legitimation. The media have to attend to their own legitimacy. They must maintain the integrity of their relationship with their audience and also the integrity of their own self-image and of the social relationships that make up the profession of journalism.[38] Maintaining these relationships requires a certain minimum of honesty, which, especially in periods of political crisis, can lead to conflicts of considerable ferocity between the media and other major social institutions and may seriously conflict with the legitimation requirements of the system. To a limited extent, this did in fact occur in the United States during the 1960s and 1970s.[39] We do not yet know how substantial the ideological consequences have been. It has often been observed that the fact of conflict between the media and other institutions does not necessarily mean the media are playing a delegitimating role in relation to the political and socioeconomic system, and this is clearly true. Indeed the media often see themselves in such cases as upholders of that system and present the correction of abuse as the ultimate proof of its soundness.[40] One study of the impact of Watergate coverage found that those who followed Watergate on television were more likely than others to lay the blame on individuals rather than the political system.[41] There is, however, no theoretical reason to assume this will always be the case, and the potential for disjunctions between the needs of the media and the needs of other institutions deserves more attention than it has gotten from critical analysts of the media.

To the extent that the media do not maintain the integrity of their relationship with their audience, moreover, legitimation may break down in another way: the media may become ineffective ideological institutions. This may in fact be one important consequence of the scientization of journalism. The shift to an attitude of detached realism places the ends and values of political life outside the normal bounds of political communication; and this is functional for the system. But at the same time it may render the media incapable of contributing to the establishment of new legitimating values if the old ones are beginning to break down. The modern mass media and the professional journalist clearly have great power (subject to the many political, economic, and social constraints within which they operate) to set the agenda of political discussion and to determine the context within which day-to-day events will be perceived. As purveyors of authoritative information, their strength is great indeed. But their ability to establish positive social values and political commitments may be another matter altogether.

Concluding Comments

The rise of commercial mass media, which began in the United States in the 1830s, had paradoxical political consequences. It democratized the market for newspapers; at the same time it centralized the production of political information and ruptured the connection between the press and an active public. It led to the decline of politically committed journalism and its replacement by a professional journalism that claimed to stand above politics. Professionalization transforms the nature of political discourse. It narrows discussion to questions of technique and effectiveness that can be approached with detached realism. It also changes the performative content of journalism; it transforms the newspaper from a political message addressed from citizen to citizen, inviting the reader to participate in political debate or action, into an authoritative account of the state of the world, addressed to an audience whose own role in that world normally is not at issue. For these reasons, the modern news media do not produce the kind of active, critical public debate that the newspaper seemed to promise when it first emerged as an institution of the public sphere. The American news media may, in fact, communicate to the public a conception of politics and of their own political role that strongly discourages active political involvement. Beyond this the precise consequences of the commercialization and scientization of journalism are not easy to judge. There is no simple answer, in particular, to the much-debated question of whether a commercial-professional news media can be expected to serve as an effective ideological support for the power structure of advanced capitalism.

This argument I put forward simply as a research proposal; all the links in the chain of development I have outlined here need to be investigated more thoroughly. I have suggested, for example, that the technical angle in news reporting results from professionalization, which in turn results from commercialization. In fact little is known about the interconnections among these three aspects of American journalism, and these most likely are considerably more complex than I have presented them here. Professionalization, for instance, no doubt has cultural and political as well as economic roots; it is particularly advanced in the United States and much less so in other advanced capitalist states.[42] And the technical angle is no doubt to some extent a reflection of the general political culture of the twentieth-century United States, not a result purely of the structure and ideology of the news media. Little is known, similarly, about how the public actually responds to the underlying messages about politics, embedded in the form of news presentation, which I have stressed. And the problem of legitimation is still shrouded in ambiguity. We do not know, for example, to what extent a system of political and economic power actually needs a coherent legitimating ideology that penetrates the consciousness of the mass public. Perhaps passivity and pragmatic acceptance of power are sufficient; in that case Habermas's strictures about administrative production of meaning would be more or less irrelevant to assessing the role of mass media in the maintenance of structures of power.

The mass media are an institution with a dual social identity. They are both an economic (or in Western Europe, often political) and a cultural institution; they are a profit-making business and at the same time a producer of meaning, a creator of social consciousness. Much research has been done in recent years on the political economy of the news media, the structure of the media as economic institutions, and the impact of that structure on their cultural product. This, however, is only part of the story: the "production" of culture—to use a common but misleading metaphor—also surely has imperatives of its own, which must be understood if we are to capture in its full complexity the functioning of an instituion like the news media. It is for this reason that I have placed such heavy emphasis on Habermas. Habermas seems to offer at least the beginnings of a systematic approach to the dynamics of ideological production, conceptualized in such a way that those dynamics can be linked with the economic and other processes that also shape the news media.

Underlying Habermas's contribution to the understanding of political culture and communication is the concept of dialogue, which is crucial in two respects. First, it is the concern with dialogue that leads Habermas, like others in the critical theory tradition, to focus on the character of political debate, the fate of the public sphere in liberal capitalist societies. But Habermas also uses the concept of dialogue in a new and powerful way: as the heart of a method of analysis of communication and culture. For Habermas, all forms of human communication, even under conditions of mass dissemination, are essentially relationships between human subjects, derived ultimately from the elementary structure of dialogue. The structure of dialogue therefore provides a basis for a theory of communicative action and hence of the "production" of culture. Whether one accepts the idea that a universal structure of dialogue underlies all communication, communication is clearly a relationship, not merely a product. It is essential to grasp not only the effects of mass communication (the focus of the positivist tradition) and the economic and political constraints under which it operates but also the specifically communicative or interactive constraints involved in the creation of shared meanings.

Discussions of the media and public policy are traditionally closed with exhortations to the media to provide the public with more and better information, "an informed and active public being essential to a vigorous democracy" (as the phrase goes). This is sensible enough advice, subject of course to the problem of saying what is to count as better information about public affairs. But it is also insufficient. The problem with the American news media, if one does in fact value active public participation, lies not so much with the quality of the product being offered the consumer as with the fact that the major relation of political communication has indeed become a relation of seller and consumer.

The modern mass media are relatively good at collecting and disseminating information. When one compares them with the newsgathering efforts of the precommercial, premass press, the organizational, technological, and even cultural advances are staggering. The mass public today receives an unprecedented quantity of information. Even the scientism of contemporary journalism represents a significant—and in certain ways democratizing—cultural advance. The shift from the oratory of early political journalism to the commercial media's focus on news and "facts" meant a shift of attention from abstract principles (the "right Reason" of the *New-England Courant*'s discussion of law) to the real historical events and social conditions that touched the mass public in their daily lives.

What the modern mass media cannot do is to play the role of sparking active public participation in deciding the direction of public policy. I use the word *cannot* deliberately. Individual journalists working in established news organizations can certainly from time to time break out of the focus on technique and strategy to raise the direction of public policy as an issue; they can be sensitive to the underlying message their reporting conveys about politics and the citizen's relation to it; they can give a hearing to those who do seek to play a mobilizing role. But all of this must remain within relatively narrow limits; the antipolitical tendencies explored here are deeply rooted in the structure and the professional ideology of the American news media. Few of us, in fact, would want the established news media to presume to play the mobilizing role of the decentralized press of Tocqueville's day. It is not a role appropriate to institutions with such massive social power.

To the extent, then, that life is to be breathed into the public sphere of liberal capitalist societies, the initiative must come from outside the institutions now dominating that sphere. The "Habermasian" analysis I have stressed suggests reason for at least cautious optimism that citizens' organizations can make themselves heard despite the centralization of control over the channels of political communication. However powerful they may have become, the mass media must maintain some semblance of a dialogue with the public. There is always, therefore, some degree of openness, of two-dimensionality in the communication porcess: when an active public challenge to the limits of political discourse arises, the media can ignore it only at the peril of their own legitimacy.[43]

Notes

1. Jürgen Habermas, "The Public Sphere: An Encyclopedia Article (1964)," *New German Critique* 1 (Fall 1974).

2. Alexis de Tocqueville, *Democracy in America* (Garden City, N.Y.: Doubleday, 1969), p. 517.

3. Karl Marx, "Debates on Freedom of the Press and Publication" [1842], in Saul K. Padover, ed., *Karl Marx in Freedom of the Press and Censorship* (New York: McGraw-Hill, 1974), p. 31.

4. Jürgen Habermas, *Theory and Praxis* (Boston: Beacon Press, 1973), p. 42. See also his *Knowledge and Human Interests* (Boston: Beacon Press, 1971).

5. I will not be concerned here with presenting a critique of the positivist tradition in media research, which is focused on the effects of media messages, primarily on individual attitudes. For such a critique, see Todd Gitlin, "Media Sociology: The Dominant Paradigm," *Theory and Society* 6 (September 1978).

6. One work that does attempt an empirical analysis of political communication from a critical theory perspective is Claus Mueller, *The Politics of Communication* (New York: Oxford University Press, 1973). Mueller's work, though, contains relatively little discussion of the media.

7. CBS, December 11 and 16, 1968.

8. See my *The Uncensored War: The Media and Vietnam* (New York: Oxford University Press, forthcoming); also Todd Gitlin, *The Whole World Is Watching: Mass Media in the Making and Unmaking of the New Left* (Berkeley: University of California Press, 1980).

9. Thomas E. Patterson and Robert D. McClure, *The Unseeing Eye: The Myth of Television Power in National Politics* (New York: Putnam, 1976).

10. *New York Times*, October 29, 1980, p. 1.

11. CBS, November 12, 1981.

12. One might object: "What about the editorial, the 'op-ed' page and the specialized press of political opinion? Doesn't modern American journalism merely differentiate news and political commentary?" Political commentary certainly survives in the modern media, but it survives in a subordinate and restricted status. It is no longer considered the primary task of journalism. It is banished from the front page. It also tends to be restricted to the prestige press. The *New York Times*, the *Washington Post*, and a few other papers with relatively elite readerships have fairly substantial "op-ed" pages, most U.S. newspapers do not, and television, which is the major source of information for the mass public, places a particularly low value on political commentary. The "op-ed" page itself is not unaffected by the growing importance of the technical angle in news analysis.

13. Benjamin Franklin, *The Autobiography and Other Writings* (New York: Signet, 1961), p. 213.

14. Tocqueville, *Democracy*, p. 518.

15. In discussing the early American news media, I draw heavily on two fine studies: Michael Schudson, *Discovering the News* (New York: Basic Books, 1978), and Dan Schiller, *Objectivity and the News* (Philadelphia: University of Pennsylvania Press, 1981).

16. Political neutrality is a long-run tendency, not an immediate demand of commercialism. At certain times, when competition among newspapers was intense, political crusades were a good way to sell papers. Once a newspaper aspires to cover an entire market, however—as advertisers prefer and as most papers (and television) do today—identification with a particular political position becomes much more problematic.

17. *Baltimore Sun*, quoted in Schudson, *Discovering*, p. 22.

18. Quoted in Schiller, *Objectivity*, p. 87.

19. Schudson, *Discovering*, p. 6.

20. The most important statements of this perspective are Max Horkheimer and Theodor W. Adorno, "The Culture Industry: Enlightenment as Mass Deception," in *The Dialectic of Enlightenment* (New York: Seabury Press, 1972), and Herbert Marcuse, *One-Dimensional Man* (Boston: Beacon Press, 1964).

21. See James Curran, "Capitalism and Control of the Press, 1800–1975," in James Curran, Michael Gurevitch, and Janet Woollacott, eds., *Mass Communication and Society* (Beverly Hills: Sage Publications, 1979); and George Boyce, "The Fourth Estate: Reappraisal of a Concept," and James Curran, "The Press as an Agency of Social Control: An Historical Perspective," both in George Boyce, James Curran, and Pauline Wingate, eds., *Newspaper History: From the 17th Century to the Present Day* (Beverly Hills: Sage Publications, 1978).

22. Curran, "Press as an Agency," p. 55.

23. There has been relatively little research on the radical press in the United States. See Joseph R. Conlin, ed., *The American Radical Press, 1880–1960* (Westport, Conn.: Greenwood Press, 1974), and Robert Armstrong, *A Trumpet to Arms: Alternative Media in America* (Boston: Houghton Mifflin, 1981).

24. Schiller, *Objectivity*, p. 74.

25. By the late 1970s fewer than 4 percent of U.S. cities had competing newspapers. See Ernest C. Hynds, *American Newspapers in the 1980s* (New York: Hastings House, 1980), p. 139.

26. Douglass Cater, *The Fourth Branch of Government* (New York: Vintage, 1959). An enormous literature bears on this point. Two of the most important works are Bernard Cohen, *The Press and Foreign Policy* (Princeton: Princeton University Press, 1963), and Leon V. Sigal, *Reporters and Officials* (Lexington, Mass.: D. C. Heath, 1973).

27. Schudson, *Discovering*, pp. 156–157.

28. Jürgen Habermas, "What Is Universal Pragmatics?" in *Communication and the Evolution of Society* (Boston: Beacon Press, 1979). A similar point is made by a little-known but extremely important Russian philosopher of language, Bakhtin. Bakhtin published under the name of a friend: V. N. Volosinov, *Marxism and the Philosophy of Language* (New York: Seminar Press, 1973). A good introduction to his work is Michael Holquist, "The Politics of Representation," in Stephen J. Greenblatt, ed., *Allegory and Representation* (Baltimore: Johns Hopkins University Press, 1981).

29. *New-England Courant*, May 7–14, 1722.

30. The most glaring example of this kind of functionalism is Luis Althusser, "Ideology and Ideological State Apparatuses," in *Lenin and Philosophy* (New York: Monthly Review Press, 1971). The best work on ideology and the media makes use of Gramsci's concept of hegemony. See especially Stuart Hall, "Culture, the Media, and the 'Ideological Effect,'" in Curran et al., *Mass Communication*, and the concluding chapter of Gitlin, *Whole World*. For Gramsci's own discussion of hegemony, see *Selections from the Prison Notebooks* (New York: International Publishers, 1971).

31. Jürgen, Habermas, *Legitimation Crisis* (Boston: Beacon Press, 1975). See also "Legitimation Problems in the Modern State," in his *Communication and the Evolution of Society*.

32. Cf. Douglas Kellner, "Network Television and American Society: Introduction to a Critical Theory of Television," *Theory and Society* 10 (January 1981).

33. Political scientists have tried, without success, to demonstrate a connection between the media and the level of political efficacy. But no one has devised a way to assess long-term

media effects through the use of quantitative methods. See Michael J. Robinson, "Public Affairs Television and the Growth of Political Malaise: The Case of 'The Selling of the Pentagon,'" *American Political Science Review* (1976); Arthur H. Miller, Edie N. Goldenberg, and Lutz Erbring, "Type-set Politics: Impact of Newspapers on Public Confidence," *American Political Science Review* (1979); and my critique of both in "The Media, the War in Vietnam, and Political Support: A Critique of the Thesis of an Oppositional Media," *Journal of Politics* 46 (February 1984).

34. Much of the ideology of the modern American journalist can be traced back to the progressive era, when the journalistic profession was just beginning to take shape. It is, it seems to me, the ideology of an independent middle class absorbed into corporate capitalism but not entirely comfortable with the new order. This is a connection that deserves more attention than it has gotten. There is some discussion of the importance of progressivism in Herbert J. Gans, *Deciding What's News* (New York: Pantheon, 1979).

35. See Hallin, *The Uncensored War.*

36. There is considerable ambiguity in Habermas's writing on this point, as there is in general on the relation between the normative and the empirical sides of his argument about legitimation. When Habermas writes in "Legitimation Problems in the Modern State," "Only the rules and communicative presuppositions that make it possible to distinguish an accord or agreement among free and equals from a forced or contingent consensus have legitimating force today," he is falling into a purely normative concept of legitimation (or perhaps confusing intellectual history with the history of actual legitimation processes), for the actual process of legitimation is in fact much more complex, involving, for one thing, a continuing importance of tradition.

37. Again Bakhtin is also relevant.

38. On the possibility of disjunction between the media professional and the structure of power, see Alvin W. Gouldner, *The Dialectic of Ideology and Technology: The Origins, Grammar, and Future of Ideology* (New York: Seabury Press, 1976).

39. See my "The American News Media from Vietnam to El Salvador, A Study of Ideological Change and Its Limits," in David Paletz, ed., *Political Communication* (Norwood, N.J.: Ablex, forthcoming).

40. David L. Paletz and Robert Entman, *Media Power Politics* (New York: Free Press, 1981).

41. Jack McLeod, Jane D. Brown, Lee P. Becker, and Dean A. Zieke, "Decline and Fall: A Longitudinal Analysis of Communication Effects," *Communication Research* 4 (January 1977).

42. A number of European countries are trying to find ways to preserve a political press, despite strong economic tendencies toward the elimination of such a press. See Anthony Smith, ed., *Newspapers and Democracy: International Essays on a Changing Medium* (Cambridge: MIT Press, 1980).

43. Gitlin discusses the interaction of the media and citizen activists in *Whole World*, and "News as Ideology and Contested Area: Towards a Theory of Hegemony, Crisis and Opposition," *Socialist Review* 9 (November–December 1979). See also Paletz and Entman, *Media Power Politics*, chap. 8.

15

REPAIRING THE NEWS
A Case Study of the News Paradigm

W. Lance Bennett, Lynne A. Gressett, and William Haltom

*A case study of how the news media "repaired" an
ambiguous story that slipped through the journalistic
gates reveals the boundaries of "what is news
and what is not" and illustrates an underlying
logic about how the world should be reported.*

Growing numbers of scholars criticize journalism and the news media
for harboring an implicit "news logic" that narrows the selection and
politicizes the representation of news events. Instead of implementing
the professional ideals of competitive investigative journalism, political
independence, and objective analysis, it is claimed, the American press
has developed a system of standardized news based on pack journalism
in the field and organizational imitation in the office. Early attempts to
identify the origin of this implicit news logic pointed mainly to the
routinization of news production both within (2) and across (3, 5) news
organizations. Among more recent explanations is the citing of government and other "official" news sources as coparticipants with the media
in the creation of standard news themes (1, 4, 6, 8, 11, 12, 13). The news
network of "rationalized" mass media organizations operates most
efficiently when fed by the high volume of professionally produced,
ready-to-report news matter that is generated by governments and their
support systems of social institutions (church, corporation, union, pressure group, and party).

  According to this symbiotic theory of news, efficiency is only one of
the benefits journalists gain from their working relationship with offi-

  W. Lance Bennett is Professor of Political Science at the University of Washington,
where Lynne A. Gressett is a Ph.D. candidate. William Haltom is Assistant Professor of
Political Science at the University of Vermont.

From the *Journal of Communication*, 1985; 35(3): 50-68. © 1985 *Journal of Communication*.
Reprinted by permission.

cials. An even more important benefit is that, by centering the news around official actions and reactions, the media are provided a stable "window" on reality. Establishing an official reference point for news events solves the major practical problem of "objective" journalism: how to validate the selection and representation of the subset of news events that is drawn from the larger universe of actual world events and their possible representations. In place of an operational definition of objectivity, mass media journalism has substituted the popular myth that the pronouncements of government officials and institutional elites somehow represent the reality in which the majority of people live. This presumption that authority is objective makes the news as much a propaganda instrument as a critical analytical tool.

The symbiotic theory of news also identifies a clear benefit that the government derives from the objectification of the status quo. A major problem facing liberal democracies is how to maintain control without losing legitimacy. Since the press frames virtually all important stories around the actions and reactions of institutional officials, the key institutions of polity, economy, and society appear to be responsive to all legitimate issues and interests. The construction of legitimacy, like the creation of objectivity, becomes, in this system, a circular process based on unquestioned assumptions about authority rather than critical analysis of the causes and consequences of world affairs. This confusion of authority and legitimacy with objectivity makes the news an active agent in the construction of a narrow but compelling version of reality—a version that is communicated so broadly and filled with such familiar symbolism that other versions seem biased and distorted.

In the manner outlined above, the organizational imperatives—
efficiency, stability, profit, credibility—of the news industry and the
political imperatives of government and social institutions—access to
the public, message salience, and legitimacy—converge to create a mass
communication logic called news. Among the observed features of this
logic are the following:

- The news is dominated by a remarkably small number of familiar
  themes and plots (4, 7, 10).
- Official representatives of government and industry organizations
  receive the lion's share of coverage in news about serious social and
  political issues (8, 12, 13).
- People outside the establishment often must engage in deviant,
  negative forms of behavior in order to receive news coverage (8).
- Since authorities generate and/or confirm most of the information in
  the news, objectivity and authority become confused, with the
  result that political climates establish the terms of objectivity (1,
  13).

> *Our analysis is intended to expand the symbiotic theory
> of news and politics on the crucial question of how
> journalists participate in the production of routine news.*

One reading of the current literature (the most obvious reading, we
believe) finds journalists trapped within a series of paralyzing dilemmas.
These dilemmas would seem to dictate the reporting of formula news
even if reporters try to be independent chroniclers of the day's events.
   To begin with, events are cast in familiar or normalized story themes
by officials. Reporters then encounter a number of obstacles if they seek
critical representations of official versions: short deadlines and other
organizational constraints (5), trails of documentation that lead back
again to officials and institutions (13), and their fears that deviant story
lines may compromise working relations with official sources (12) and
fellow journalists (3). In this passive-dependent reading of symbiotic
news theory, journalists are, at most, gatekeepers who avoid nonconforming stories (6) while reporting conforming ones (7, 8). Most of the
factors that lead reporters to open and close the gates do not presuppose
an acceptance of or belief in the reality that is constructed in the process.
   We suggest a somewhat more active view of the symbiotic news
construction process—a view in which journalists, like the public
officials who initiate most news, possess and apply actively a set of basic
assumptions about the bounds of social and political normalcy. It is
undoubtedly true that the initiative for normalizing most news events
comes from officials and institutional sources. It is equally likely that
most reporters most of the time act like passive transmitters of prepared

information. However, we suspect that the symbiotic relationship can persist over time only if most journalists share the guidelines of normalcy that are reiterated daily by the spectrum of newsworthy officials and groups they cover. Moreover, we suspect that, in certain instances, the press will rise to take an active part in the news normalization process.

For example, there must be times when ambiguous or problematic stories slip through the reporting gates and invite interpretations that, if left unchallenged, would raise questions about who or what in the world is normal, credible, and authentic. These instances of faulty gatekeeping are bound to occur because no symbiotic social system can be so mechanical as to exclude errors of judgment and inadequate socialization in the ranks. When a problematic news story slips through a journalistic gate, the journalism community (if a binding news logic exists) would be expected to take an active role in normalizing the story. The resulting "repair work," to use Tuchman's (13) term, might involve rewriting the story in more familiar terms as new "facts" are disclosed, or it might entail the editorial condemnation of a troublesome story as an example of bad journalism.

The case study presented in this article explores these practices in detail. If reporters and journalistic elites (editors, news critics, executives) can be shown to take an active part in transforming troublesome stories, the way will be opened for a better understanding of how journalists and officials divide the responsibility for the production of routine news.

Moreover, the documentation of what this repair work entails will add a theoretical dimension to the already well documented passive-dependent behaviors of journalists. Yet another contribution of this investigation is to free the symbiotic perspective from the nagging, common-sense criticism that there is no bias in routine news because the real world *is* dominated by official actors saying familiar things. Our data suggest that journalists engage in a broadly, if implicitly, understood practice of rewriting and recategorizing certain kinds of news events. This intervention in the social world is guided by an elitist logic that determines who ought to be given public voice to say what kinds of things. Only in a hegemonic sense can such a logic be regarded as broadly representative of social reality.

Finally, the discovery of active repair work on the part of journalists points toward a more accurate theoretical statement of the news-politics process than the symbiosis metaphor provides. Symbiosis invites connotations of a blind coordination of activities for the separate purposes of the actors involved. While the sharing of means to different ends certainly goes on in the news business (cf. Tuchman's [13] discussion of "objectification"), we also find that public officials and journalists in our case study shared aspects of a "cognitive map" of the world. The evidence for the existence of these cognitive maps and the behavioral routines that organize the world in terms of them suggests that the idea of a "paradigm" is a useful theoretical framework for understanding the news production process.

> *Virtually all case studies of journalistic practice have produced findings consistent with the possibility that journalists, in concert with their news sources, have created a paradigmatic understanding of what is and what isn't news.*

A paradigm, as defined by Kuhn (9) and other sociologists of knowledge, is a set of broadly shared assumptions about how to gather and interpret information relevant to a particular sphere of activity. Paradigms operate in some, but not all, information-producing areas of society. These systems for gathering and organizing information are based on necessarily incomplete and, therefore, sometimes incorrect assumptions about the nature of reality. Complex systems of representation always risk the exclusion or misdefinition of certain relevant features of reality because there are no independent, objective maps of the universe. Since universal standards of truth are nonexistent, paradigms are evaluated against the next best available criterion—practical utility. When a particular system of representation advances desirable values and goals, people tend to regard the underlying assumptions and the formal means of applying them as a valid system of knowledge. When a group acquires near-universal faith in the validity of a system of representing and applying information, that system attains paradigmatic standing.

The problem with grounding knowledge systems in criteria of functionality is that a limited set of functional criteria can lead to the validation of overgeneralized claims about the nature of reality. Overgeneralization can occur either because people whose purposes are not served by a knowledge system are excluded from positions of authority in the field of knowledge, or because the practical applications that might test and expose contradictions in a knowledge system simply have not yet surfaced. During "normal" periods, in which paradigms operate with high levels of authoritative consensus on their validity, they function as objective windows on the world. During such a period, a paradigm may become a circular, self-fulfilling knowledge system based on the systematic exclusion or authoritative discrediting of contending claims about reality. Hence paradigms, once established, tend to perpetuate their objective status not by opening themselves up to radical scrutiny, but by closing themselves off to troublesome facts and criticisms.

Not all information-producing fields are organized around paradigms. However, paradigms are fairly common in knowledge-producing fields that display such characteristics as control over the training of practitioners, standardization of methods for gathering and representing information, and authoritative internal review of new claims and contributions. Journalism possesses many characteristics of a paradigm-based field. For example, there is a high degree of professional control over the training process through which journalists acquire a code of ethics and a standardized reporting methodology. This training process feeds practitioners into the well-established patterns of "normal reporting" (beats, pack journalism, wire service leads, formula reporting, etc.)—patterns that seem so well suited to accommodate the steady supply of news from government and social institutions. The combination of professional training and routinized practice corresponds to a high degree of consensus on story selection, reporting angles, and trends in the profession. Moreover, the practices of editorial review and professional self-scrutiny could reinforce the application of an implicit definition of news.

The general features of journalistic activity outlined above do not prove that the news is paradigmatic, nor do they reveal the logic of a news paradigm, if it exists. However, these and other journalism patterns are symptoms of a paradigmatic field, and they encourage us to look more closely for the social dynamic that brings a paradigm and its logic into full view. If a news paradigm exists, then, like all paradigms, it will be confronted with the occasional problem of how to handle anomalous or troublesome cases that fall partly within the defining logic of the paradigm, yet fail to conform to other defining characteristics of the paradigm. Such "anomalies," as Kuhn (9) calls them, threaten to expose the limits and biases of a paradigm by suggesting that important properties of the real world have been excluded from the representational system.

At times, anomalies become so troublesome that representational systems are redefined to accommodate them. However, such "paradigm shifts" are rare and tend to occur only after the repeated failure of routine attempts to dismiss, or, in our terms, "repair" the problematic case. Our case study is one of successful repair work.

> *The way in which anomalies are repaired can reveal a*
> *great deal about both the logic of a paradigm and the*
> *grounds on which the logic is defended as objective*
> *in the face of competing claims about reality.*

If the news is produced by a paradigmatic logic that systematically excludes some categories of events from the realm of social significance, we should discover occasional breaches in the fine line between what is and what isn't news. Most potential anomalies are probably weeded out before they become troublesome cases for the profession to explain; this is the normal gatekeeping function. However, some events may display enough conforming characteristics along with nonconforming ones to become reported and only then raise the difficult question of "is this really news?" Based on what we know about both paradigms and news reporting, we offer the following general predictions about how an anomaly might enter the news system and then become repaired. The case study follows this sequence of disruption and repair work:

1. *The initial assignment and coverage decisions* are likely to be disrupted by uncertainties about whether and how to cover the story. Reporters may encounter problems in determining the boundaries of the "scene" and who the relevant actors are in it. In extreme cases journalists may get caught up in the story.

2. *The process of writing the story* will be disrupted by difficulties in finding a satisfactory angle. The information gathered in the original coverage may need to be augmented by outside "facts" in order to "normalize" the story. Clues about the way the paradigm works should emerge as the story is reconstructed.

3. *The diffusion of the resulting story in the mass media* may be characterized by disruptions and further attempts to "normalize" the story. If the story cannot be redefined around a conventional news theme, special attention may be paid to alleged violations of journalism procedures that account for the troublesome case. In extreme cases, the reporting angle may adopt a quasi-editorial look at "what went wrong."

4. *Editorial commentary* will be devoted to those stories that have been flagged as examples of bad journalism. The standard repair work at this level will be to point out that the offending story would not have developed if proper reporting methods had been observed, the implication being that the event triggered a spurious story based on methodological error rather than on blind spots in the current professional understanding of news.

These general hypotheses can be used as guides for analyzing the ways in which ambiguous events might engage and display the logic of a possible news paradigm. While no single anomalous case can reveal the logic of an entire paradigm, it is possible to begin constructing the logic through a cumulative case study approach. Each anomalous case should reveal some unique elements of the paradigm; cases can be accumulated until a coherent news logic is constructed and the theoretical input from successive cases diminishes. The case study that follows is a first step toward demonstrating the existence and assessing the substance of a paradigm for news.

> *"If you want to see somebody set himself on fire,*
> *be at the square in Jackson in ten minutes. . . . "*

That is what Cecil Andrews reportedly said when he called WHMA-TV in Anniston, Alabama, on the evening of Friday, March 4, 1983. He added that his planned self-immolation in the nearby Jacksonville town square was to protest unemployment in the United States. At 10:15 that evening, the news crew at the station called the Jacksonville police department to inform them of Andrews' threats and of their uncertainty about whether the call was a hoax or an actual event in the making. The police assured the television crew that they would check the square and meet the news crew. Neither Andrews nor the news crew had arrived at the scene by 11:00, and the two police officers who responded to the call returned to the station (about 100 yards away) to submit their paperwork and end their shift.

After being delayed by car trouble, a camera crew from WHMA arrived at the square about 11:15. Andrews approached them immediately, dousing himself with lighter fluid as he came. A firefighter spotted the activity and ran to the nearby fire station for an extinguisher. Meanwhile, the camera crew set up their equipment and began to film Andrews' efforts to set himself on fire. At 11:18, Andrews' second match ignited a small flame near his knee. He sat down on the lawn and fanned the flame until it began to spread rapidly over his body. After 37 seconds of filming, one of the cameramen stepped in front of the camera (which the other crew member continued to operate) and tried to assist the burning man. Andrews, by then engulfed in flames, ran across the square, where he was intercepted by two firefighters who put out the fire with an extinguisher. The camera recorded all 82 seconds of the episode, from the first match to the final dousing of the flames.

Journalistic treatment of this incident spanned a three-week period in which the story was released on the Associated Press wire, the videotape (which was never used by WHMA) appeared on the nightly news broadcasts of all three national television networks, the *New York Times* ran a front-page story and an accompanying editorial, both *Time* and *Newsweek* covered it, and two in-depth news analysis programs (CNN's "Crossfire" and ABC's "Nightline") were devoted to the story. We draw the data for our analysis from these sources and from the record of local coverage provided by the articles and editorials published in the *Anniston Star*. In an interview, *Star* reporter Robin McDonald answered our questions about how the original story was written.

Despite the amount of attention it received, the Cecil Andrews incident was not a typical "big story." In fact, much of the news coverage contained implicit suggestions (reinforced by explicit editorial commentary) that it was not a legitimate story at all. It is puzzling that an illegitimate story would receive so much attention aimed at creating the impression that it didn't deserve so much attention. Perhaps some aspects of the event cued routine reporting responses, while other features violated the bounds of normal news. Such a contradiction could account for the vicious cycle in which a widely reported story was impugned by those who reported it. If the news is paradigmatic, we should be able to isolate the sequence of repair activities that resolved the disruption and deflected questions about the validity of news as a representational system. In fact, the journalistic reconstruction of the Cecil Andrews story is evident at every step of the way, from the initial coverage, to the production and national distribution of the story, to its final dismissal by the editorial community.

The initial assignment and coverage decisions of the WHMA-TV news crew were clearly disrupted by the failure of the event to conform to implicit expectations about how it should have developed.

The arrangement between the news crew and the police to meet at the scene is our first clue about how a "normal" news story would have unfolded. In part, the notification of the police was a proper citizen's response to the situation. However, the role of the police also looms large in the camera crew's expectations about how the event would be scripted. When cameramen Harris and Simmons arrived at the scene, they were sure they would encounter the police and record some sort of police work in action. Indeed, had they not suffered car trouble en route to the scene, Simmons and Harris would have found the police there, and they probably would have captured a routine police story on tape. Instead, the crew found themselves alone with a man setting himself on fire. So strong was the anticipated script, however, that the crew acted as if it were covering a routine news event. In the words of Simmons, the camera operator, he kept the camera rolling because "my job is to record events as they happen. . . . I thought, 'the police are going to arrive. I'm going to have video of them subduing this guy.' "

Despite the fact that reasonable journalistic expectations had been dashed, there was little to be gained from the excuse that reality simply failed to conform to the script. Paradigms seem painfully contrived when reality is subordinated to them. Lacking an acceptable excuse, the crew was vulnerable to the criticism (expressed in all subsequent editorial commentaries) that they triggered the tragic event and that they failed to prevent the tragedy. While these facile criticisms are true in a sense, they fail to consider two relevant facts. First, many news events are staged for the purpose of being reported, and they do not commence until the cameras begin rolling. Second, Andrews' efforts to secure news coverage for his planned event do not distinguish him from many newsmakers who try to use the news to transmit messages. Rather, what seems to set Andrews apart from the typical newsmaker is his unusual script. Had he been an elected official or a community leader, his concerns about unemployment probably would have been aired through the more conventional means of a speech or a press conference. Had he owned the status of a member of a religious sect, his self-immolation might have been respected as a sign of philosophical commitment.

(Recall the self-immolations of Buddhist monks aired on the national news during the Vietnam war.)

Lacking an acceptable persona, Andrews was confined to the dramatic repertoire available to anonymous individuals who seek to make news. Findings from earlier news research (e.g., 8, 13) suggest that Andrews' best chance of making routine news would have been to create a dramatic scenario that pitted him directly against some authority who would oppose and, perhaps, prevent his actions. Had he taken hostages, barricaded himself in a building, or threatened property, Andrews' story would have presented no problems for news coverage. Instead of choosing a conventional script, Andrews acted like a person who did not want his message negated by direct conflict with a disapproving authority. He avoided the police and appeared alone in front of the camera. As a result, Andrews and the news crew were playing by different scripts. The result was a very awkward situation. Although the news crew acted as if guided by a well-established model of acceptable news, neither the public nor the journalism profession could accept this fact as an excuse for what happened without admitting that the news is rather narrowly contrived. In short, what began as a routine "officials respond to deviant behavior" story broke loose and entered the news world on its own terms. The problems created when this event slipped through the reporting gate are indicated by the way the story was reconstructed and rewritten during the first phase of the repair.

Writing the Andrews story should have proved troublesome if, indeed, its most obvious plot lines violated the news paradigm.

The way in which the story was presented, both by the television station that filmed it and by the local newspaper, indicates clearly that the event as recorded was not suitable as news. Both of the local news organizations presented marked reconstructions of the event. These reconstructions became the record of reality on which the national news media eventually based their paradigm-defending consensus that the event was unnewsworthy. Although both of the local news organizations were owned by the same family, the reconstructed story cannot be viewed as narrowly self-serving. In fact, H. Brandt Ayers, owner of WHMA-TV and the editor and publisher of the *Anniston Star*, followed his paper's front-page story with an editorial that defined the incident as an "avoidable tragedy" for which "the personnel of Channel 40 must bear some responsibility."

The reconstruction of the story at the local level relied on the paradigmatic theme of "official responses to actions that challenge the status quo." But how did an official become introduced into a situation that was notable primarily for the absence of an official in the first place?

The first move in this transformation was the decision by WHMA not to show its videotape. Station Manager Harry Mabry and News Director Phil Cox both cited "humanitarian reasons" for the decision, while station owner Ayers subsequently told an ABC "Nightline" audience that the tape was withheld because it was "tasteless." (Neither of these managerial pronouncements explains why Cox called the CBS Atlanta bureau shortly after WHMA broke the story to offer the network the tape—another indicator of the ambiguous character of the event that helped it slip through the gate in the first place.)

In place of the tape, WHMA aired a talking head of Jacksonville Police Chief Paul Locke describing what *he* saw on the tape. The importance of this twist in the story lies not so much with Locke's dry account of an unidentified man setting himself on fire as with the fact that an official had been introduced to interpret events. During the following week in which the story developed into a national news item, Locke became the interpreter of record. From his humble beginning as a surrogate viewer for the videotape, Locke ended up telling the press what the story was and wasn't about.

By the time Robin McDonald, reporter for the *Anniston Star*, concluded her series of articles on the incident, she was able to quote Locke as saying "It's definitely not a story of a man trying to burn himself up. It's not a story of unemployment. . . . " Locke presented this interpretation of what the event *wasn't* to the national and even the international media. He described his interview with *Pravda* in terms that sound like the clash of news paradigms. He reported that the first question the Russian news organization asked "was whether the man was black or white. Then, they asked me if he had to do with any political associations or any political parties. . . . They did not ask me if the man had any other reason than unemployment to do what he did. I made it a point to tell them that he did." Locke also provided the service of defining what the event *was* about. By the end of the week, news organizations were citing each others' confirmations of Locke's version of events. For example, McDonald was able to cite national corroboration of the local official version in the following interview with former CBS president and current NBC adviser Richard Salant on the CBS morning news:

> "The Police Chief has said it wouldn't have happened if the camera had not been there," Salant said. "That's a very tough issue. . . . If we ignored everything that was designed to attract our attention, we would only cover natural disasters." Should the two have intervened? "Of course they should," Salant said. "The only real issue is 'Did they do it fast enough?' "

The event had undergone a substantial transformation from Chief Locke's initial description of the videotape to his final pronouncements to the press about its significance. The resulting news story cast Cecil Andrews in a minor and decidedly apolitical role, while introducing a cast of officials who corroborated the more manageable theme of journalistic responsibility. This reconstruction fit easily into the conclusions of later commentary that the event itself was trivial and unnewsworthy and should have been dismissed as such by journalists familiar with professional reporting guidelines. The way in which this transformation of the event took place illustrates how paradigms operate on anomalous cases.

> *In order to understand how the story took shape, one of us interviewed Robin McDonald, the police beat reporter for the* Anniston Star *whose story angles shaped key themes in the national representation of the event.*

McDonald related that her first reaction upon hearing about the incident the morning after it happened was "My God, what a story!" Her initial thoughts about the substance and importance of the story were that "something so drastic as a suicide attempt over unemployment was sure to be big. The unemployment issue made the suicide potentially a national story." Her first efforts were to construct a persona for Andrews and a script for his behavior. In this process, McDonald said it became clear to her "almost immediately" that the unemployment situation was one of the "least pertinent reasons" for Andrews' self-immolation and, as a result, she "decided to play the unemployment issue very low."

McDonald's account makes it evident that she quickly ran up against the anomalous features of Andrews' case. She tried and failed to construct a suitable character for him. It is significant that she turned exclusively to town officials for her evaluation of Andrews. In the resulting story, the Andrews character was animated exclusively by the officials who spoke for him and interpreted his actions. Official reports of what Andrews said during the incident just didn't add up, in McDonald's estimation, to a story centered around Andrews. Even though Andrews' few reported utterances were issued while he was burning, McDonald searched them for evidence of philosophical consistency and found none. She noted, for example, that firemen at the scene heard Andrews shout "Put me out! Put me out!" McDonald concluded that his desire to be put out was inconsistent with his alleged intention of burning to death in the name of a higher cause. The firemen also reported that Andrews said he "didn't know" why he did it when they asked him for a reason. The camera crew noted that Andrews staggered and appeared drunk. The police chief reported that Andrews was chronically unemployed, but added, "I have been advised by the family that there were more problems involved than just unemployment."

Andrews' own story was never solicited. The deadline for the initial story may have made it impossible to contact Andrews, who had been removed to an intensive care unit in a Birmingham hospital where he was listed in poor condition with second- and third-degree burns over half of his body. However, McDonald's reconstruction of the event left no need to get Andrews' side of it later when he had recovered. In fact, the emerging story angle of "man manipulates media and journalists respond" provided McDonald with a good reason not to bring Andrews back into the story. She noted that he had "manipulated the media for his own purposes" and she did not want to reward his need for attention any further.

Thus, McDonald assigned Andrews a role in the story based on the few sketchy inputs of the officials noted above. Despite the paucity and ambiguity of the information on Andrews, McDonald expressed confidence that the real story had little to do with him. She noted that she could not tell his story directly because "nothing he has to say will reflect reality" and "I can't discern truth or reality in what he has to say."

The problem of discerning truth or reality to which McDonald referred is obviously not a straightforward empirical matter of gathering and evaluating a body of evidence. If independent interpretation based on the facts were the key issue in journalism, the hazy facts of the Andrews case would seem to support further investigation rather than speedy dismissal. After all, it isn't unreasonable to suppose that chronic unemployment is commonly correlated with "other" personal problems. Nor is it particularly surprising that a person experiencing the reality of burning to death might express the impulse to be put out, no matter how firm his resolve when he set himself ablaze. It also seems sensible to become intoxicated before enduring such intense and prolonged pain. Finally, it is hardly surprising that the victim would express confusion about his motives in the minutes after he had been extinguished.

The way in which McDonald went about "discerning truth or reality" displays the special nature of reality inside the news paradigm. Even if Andrews' private story had proved to be a revealing account of the tragedy of unemployment, it could not have been reported under the circumstances. All the available officials had joined the consensus that the story was about a poor, confused individual who successfully manipulated the media. For all practical purposes that was the news reality—a reality that depended less on the depth and clarity of facts than on the conclusions that officials drew from them. Presenting the "facts" of a story is one of the features that separates news from other forms of narrative. Collecting the facts enables news organizations to claim to have reported an event objectively. In the absence of some official corroboration, a competing account of Andrews' behavior would have no factual standing—particularly in a situation where journalistic tampering with reality was rapidly becoming the issue.

Considering the alternatives available to her, it is not surprising that McDonald solicited information from her normal roster of sources and produced a remarkably routine story written from the police angle. Andrews' motives were not introduced until paragraph 33 of the 37-paragraph article—and they were introduced in the form of the police chief's rejection of the unemployment motive.

McDonald's process of "discerning reality or truth" in the situation was based on competent, routine journalism that successfully restored the journalistic enterprise to its normal role of covering events from a distant vantage, mediated by official commentary. The return to normal journalism, however, had a slightly ironic effect in this case, since this was an abnormal story. The construction of an objective frame of reference on the incident had robbed the story of a central character who acted for reasons that made sense. The substitute story theme of "journalists create news" was developed to repair the gap that was left when the first step of the repair process divested the story of a credible "who, what, and why." This second step of substituting a paradigm-restoring story angle required some complicated moves by the national media covering the Andrews affair.

The national coverage of the story was marked from the outset by at least one disruption of the routine story development process: a week elapsed between the occurrence of the event and the appearance of the first national story on the front page of the **New York Times.**

Media critic Jeff Greenfield later reported this fact to the ABC "Nightline" audience in support of his argument that, whatever the Jacksonville story was about, it was too stale to qualify as news. Greenfield's assessment, while perhaps a paradigm-defending strategy, ignores the fact that the Jacksonville story really wasn't the same story a week later and that it took time to reassemble the pieces into a more suitable version of news.

CBS had been offered the footage earlier in the week, but Atlanta bureau executive Zeke Segal rejected it. Reacting only to the issue of whether the story had a credible actor committing a significant action, Segal explained, he rejected the story on the grounds that "he was simply a poor man who did something to himself. That itself is not news to a national audience."

At the time that Segal made this assessment, however, a different news theme was beginning to solidify. The issue of journalistic judgment was emerging as the documentable angle in Robin McDonald's local coverage. The headline on her story of Monday, March 7, read: "WHMA Holds Press Conference to Defend TV's Fire Response." By Thursday, this somewhat trickier theme of journalistic judgment was deemed newsworthy by the *New York Times.* Following the appearance of the reformulated story on the front page of the nation's leading newspaper, CBS's Segal revised his opinion of the story, saying that it had become "a totally different story. We had to investigate it."

Segal's revised opinion is rather perceptive. The story had become totally different both in the sense that the plot had been reconstructed and firmly anchored in objectifying news criteria, and in the sense that the *New York Times* broke it nationally on its front page. The rest of the key national media followed the lead of the *Times* and rushed to cover the story. All three networks sent camera crews and reporters to Jacksonville and ran stories containing varying amounts of the original WHMA videotape on their Thursday evening newscasts. The Associated Press issued a long story accompanied by a wirephoto of Andrews in flames. *Time, Newsweek,* and the in-depth analysis programs on ABC and CNN devoted special attention to the story. WHMA officials were besieged with requests to appear on public affairs shows in Canada, Australia, and the United States, including PBS's "Inside Story" and "The Phil Donahue Show." And, as mentioned earlier, Chief Locke was interviewed by *Pravda.*

> *The journalistic angle was complicated not only because of the story's incestuous "the news makes the news" qualities, but because it raised the delicate question of "what should journalists have done?"*

If journalism has a paradigm and a routine means of defending it, we would expect so central a question, once asked, to be steered directly to the "right answer"—something like, "Of course they should have intervened and stopped the situation. After all, the incident developed only because the journalists ignored normal reporting guidelines that exist to keep such unnewsworthy events out of the stream of truly significant news."

As if orchestrated by the same composer, the national coverage of the Jacksonville incident led the news audience to a paradigm-defending conclusion and in many cases imposed the conclusion, in an editorial fashion, in the text of the news stories themselves. The first element in common to all the national stories was the dismissal of Andrews as a credible actor. Andrews had been officially discredited in the process of repairing the story at the local level and that is where the national media left him. *Time,* for example, characterized Andrews as "an unemployed roofer and day laborer who had a history of instability" who was "staggering drunk on the night he telephoned his threat or plea to WHMA." The credibility of the journalistic angle, not to mention its satisfactory resolution, required a consensus among news experts that there was not a real news event anywhere in the background. Thus, Cecil Andrews became a stranger in his own story.

In addition to discrediting Andrews, the national media also united solidly behind the banner of journalistic responsibility as the theme for the story. The *New York Times* headline, for example, was "82 Seconds of Man Setting Himself Afire Haunt TV." *Newsweek* ran its article under the headline, "The Camera's Cold Eye." *Time* concluded its story at the beginning with the title: "When 'News' is Almost a Crime: In Alabama a TV Station Gets a Story that No One Should Want."

Even the stories that most resembled conventional "objective" news reports pushed obvious conclusions on the audience, as indicated by the concluding paragraphs of the Associated Press story:

> *"I'm not trying to condemn the news media," the police chief said, "But it's a fact when you have lights and camera that people are going to perform for the camera."*
>
> *H. Brandt Ayers, vice president of the Consolidated Publishing Company which is in the process of selling the television station to Jacksonville University, said he felt the incident could have been prevented and that some blame rests with the station.*

The majority of the national media were not content to leave room for speculation about what sort of "media responsibility" and blame these officials were talking about. In an unusual display of editorializing in the news, all of the network newscasts took pains to clarify the statements by Locke and Ayers so that there was no doubt that the media responsibility at issue was the failure of the camera crew to use good journalistic judgment. Dan Rather of CBS opened the story with these rather lofty lines: "Nothing is more objective than a television camera. Cameramen are trained observers. No matter what circumstances. No matter what dangers. But sometimes the rules must be broken." Rather's lines were the preface to a CBS correspondent's rhetorical question to Simmons and Harris: "You were two strapping men. You could have stopped him"—a question to which Simmons could only respond "Yeah." ABC noted that the "local and national press have roundly criticized WHMA, saying that WHMA created the event." NBC's Tom Brokaw set up the story this way: "Someone is in trouble. The camera crew is nearby. Do they just cover the scene or get involved?"

To make sure that the proper answer emerged to this question, many of those preparing news stories turned to journalism officials. As noted earlier, CBS interviewed its former president, Richard Salant, who said that "of course" the journalists should have put down the camera and stopped the incident. Fred Friendly, a Columbia Journalism School professor and another former CBS president, told *Time* that the story had so little redeeming social value that airing it amounted to "voyeurism." The current vice-president of CBS News, Edward Joyce, capped *Time*'s objectification of the right answer by noting the existence of guidelines that normally function to keep the news free of such unnewsworthy incidents: "This was a situation where one had to be human first and professional second. We have guidelines: where the presence of the camera could provoke danger, put the camera away."

All the national coverage converged on the same conclusion: the Andrews event was insignificant and unnewsworthy. It could have been prevented if the journalists had used good judgment: they didn't and it wasn't. Therefore, we have a news story that shouldn't have been. *Time* called for small television stations to make sure they understood that there were journalism guidelines that applied to such instances. WHMA held a journalism seminar on how journalists and officials should coordinate their responses to crisis situations. The seminar included 13 officials from various levels of the media and law enforcement. The story thus ended on an official consensus that there was a real world and that there were journalistic procedures designed to cover it. If the procedures were applied properly, the news would represent reality as we all understand it.

> *So conclusive and consensual was the ending to the national coverage that there was very little repair work left to be done at the editorial level.*

The editorial invocation of journalism ethics in the Andrews affair was a simple mop-up operation. The smooth assembly of the prior stages of repair work into a final pronouncement is illustrated nicely in an editorial in the *New York Times*. It is fitting that the nation's leading newspaper would produce such a definitive ending to this pesky incident. The editorial covers the full range of earlier repair work: from the opening claim that this was not a real event; to the easy inference that there was, therefore, no real story here; to the professional pronouncement that this was a case of bad journalism; to the implication that the profession had readily available ethical guidelines to prevent such occurrences. Q.E.D.: politics-as-usual was restored to the news, and the news-as-usual was returned to politics. The editorial, reprinted in its entirety here, illustrates how professional self-criticism can have the ironic effect of restoring the status quo.

The final line lays the issue to rest. The camera crew was creating the news, not reporting it. Everyone knows that a central tenet of journalism is that reporters cover the naturally occurring, "real" world. They don't aid in the presentation of artifice. This central tenet proclaims loudly that the issue did not involve the limits or contradictions of a paradigm. The issue was defined as the failure to apply properly a faithful and adequate representational system. The Andrews story was the artifact of methodological error.

The Double Fire

We've seen the brains blown from the skull of a Vietnamese and a truck overturn near the Washington Monument when its driver got a bullet in his head. We've seen the sad man leap and the drowning man lose hold of the life preserver. And last week, television viewers in Jacksonville, Ala., saw a drunken man set fire to himself. The scenes were alike in their horror, but the last was different in one particular. Those who filmed that blaze were not just witnesses to tragedy, they were also its stage managers.

Cecil Andrews, an unemployed roofer, called WHMA-TV four times on Friday, March 4, to say that to protest unemployment in America, he was going to set himself on fire in the town square. The station's news director notified the police, who said they'd handle it and that the station could send reporters along for a "free ride."

The police searched the square for nearly an hour, found no one and left. About 30 minutes later two TV cameramen arrived to find Mr. Andrews staggering from wherever he'd been and fumbling with a matchbook.

The TV crew said they tried to "delay" Mr. Andrews by turning the camera lights on and off, waving a hat and telling him the equipment needed time to warm up. Then, in the 37 seconds after the crew started filming, Mr. Andrews doused his jeans with lighter fluid, put a match to his knee and fanned the small flame. When engulfed by it, he yelled to the cameramen, "Put it out!" They couldn't. Mr. Andrews, aflame, ran across the square. He is now in a Birmingham hospital.

Asked why they didn't try to stop him sooner, the cameramen said they kept expecting the police to show up. If they had appeared, of course, it would have produced another kind of movie: a brief documentary on how to prevent a man from incinerating himself.

•

There was, however, a simpler way to prevent Cecil Andrews's act. The extent to which the often-solicited presence of journalists exacerbates any situation is in our business a matter of legitimate and intense concern and debate. But the question of whether that Alabama camera crew was reporting or creating the news is easily answered. Two devices lit that nearly fatal fire: Mr. Andrews's match and the switch that set the cameras whirring.

Whether we agree or disagree that the Andrews story should have been taken seriously as news is not the point here. The point is that a powerful system of logic underlies the news and provides implicit boundaries on the parts of the world that are newsworthy and the parts that are not. When ambiguous cases slip into the range of attention of this logic, a powerful system for organizing and representing information becomes engaged in the process of normalizing those cases. Normalized cases are either translated into routine news themes, or they are shown to be the unfortunate artifacts of a misapplied but normally reliable methodology.

Perhaps the reader's credulity still leans in the direction of agreeing with the media. Somehow Cecil Andrews just doesn't seem like a proper news story. That's precisely the point. How do things come to seem proper or improper? How do we form our conclusions about the limits of significant social reality? In order for the representational system of the news to work, we, the public, must share the logic of the paradigm. Part of this logic involves accepting the results of well-reasoned judgments about the standing of anomalies. The first question about a paradigm, then, is not whether one agrees with its output, but whether one agrees that it exists, as specified by a set of observable indicators. If the question is answered in the affirmative, as we feel the foregoing analysis warrants, then the question becomes whether the paradigm organizes the world of social values systematically in favor of certain values and groups and against others.

In order to imagine an alternative to the current news world, we would have to entertain instances in which officially presented views of things could be represented as unreasonable, unwarranted, or deviant. We would also have to imagine cases in which ordinary people might reasonably act in unusual or dramatic ways in response to life conditions they regard (despite the reassuring words of officials to the contrary) as insane or intolerable. The current lines drawn by the news paradigm make such reversals of perspective unlikely to occur until anomalous cases exceed the capacity of the news profession to repair them. It seems unlikely that the paradigm is currently under such threat.

So what can reporters do? Probably nothing. They are doing what they have been trained to do: report normal news and repair problematic stories that slip through the journalistic gate. Although we cannot expect well-socialized professionals to take the initiative to look critically at their own paradigm, standards for scholars are somewhat different. Since the news media take an active part in the selection, reconstruction, and evaluation of social life, scholars must pay critical attention to this process of turning problematic events into clear cases of news and not news. Cogent scholarly analyses of the news reconstruction process may provoke reform movements within journalism schools. With an eye toward establishing an agenda for such reform, we suggest that the occasional cases of problematic news may be worth more of our serious attention than all the formula news that's fit to print.

REFERENCES

1. Bennett, W. Lance. *News: The Politics of Illusion.* New York: Longman, 1983.
2. Breed, Warren. "Social Control in the Newsroom." *Social Forces* 33, 1955, pp. 326–335.
3. Crouse, Timothy. *The Boys on the Bus.* New York: Ballantine, 1973.
4. Darnton, Robert. "Writing News and Telling Stories." *Daedalus* 104, 1975, pp. 175–194.
5. Epstein, Edward Jay. *News from Nowhere: Television and the News.* New York: Vintage, 1973.
6. Fishman, Mark. *Manufacturing the News.* Austin: University of Texas Press, 1980.
7. Gans, Herbert J. *Deciding What's News: A Study of CBS Evening News, NBC Nightly News, Newsweek and Time.* New York: Vintage, 1979.
8. Gitlin, Todd. *The Whole World is Watching.* Berkeley: University of California Press, 1980.
9. Kuhn, Thomas S. *The Structure of Scientific Revolutions.* Chicago: University of Chicago Press, 1962.
10. Lapham, Lewis. "Gilding the News." *Harper's*, July 1981, pp. 31–39.
11. Molotch, Harvey and Marilyn Lester. "News as Purposive Behavior: On the Strategic Use of Routine Events, Accidents, and Scandals." *American Sociological Review* 39, 1974, pp. 101–112.
12. Sigal, Leon V. *Reporters and Officials: The Organization and Politics of Newsmaking.* Lexington, Mass.: D. C. Heath, 1973.
13. Tuchman, Gaye. *Making News: A Study in the Construction of Reality.* New York: Free Press, 1978.

16

ON THE EPISTEMOLOGY OF INVESTIGATIVE JOURNALISM

James S. Ettema and Theodore L. Glasser

In contrast to "muckraking," a term still used pejoratively to underscore the shady side of journalism, "investigative reporting" enjoys an unmistakably honorable connotation. At least since Bernstein and Woodward (1974) chronicled their now legendary efforts to expose corruption in the Nixon White House, investigative reporting has come to mean journalism of the highest order. Even when it falls short of its ideals, investigative reporting evokes the respect of journalists themselves because it signifies a special enterprise, an extraordinary confluence of time, talent, and resources.

While some data and considerable commentary exist on the status of investigative reporting (Dygert, 1976; Downie, 1976; Behrens, 1977), and while several text books endeavor to explain how reporters "do" investigative reporting (Anderson & Benjaminson, 1976; Williams, 1978; Bolch & Miller, 1978; Wier & Noyes, 1981;

This research was supported in part by The Graduate School of the University of Minnesota and the Gannett Foundation. An earlier version of this paper was presented to the Qualitative Studies Division of the Association for Education in Journalism and Mass Communication, Gainsville, Florida, August 1984.

Ullmann & Honeyman, 1983), little has been done to examine what is really distinctive about the "best" journalists doing the "best" journalism. In an effort to develop an appreciation for the peculiarities of investigative journalism, this study focuses on how reporters accomplish the fundamental and very practical task of knowing what they know. Our objective is twofold: (i) to review how daily reporters know what they know, and (ii) to contrast that with what we have learned about how investigative reporters accomplish that task. Ultimately, our goal is to contribute to a discussion that began in earnest nearly a half century ago when journalist-turned-sociologist Robert Park (1940) assessed news as a form of knowledge.

What we intend here is an aspect of the sociology of knowledge: a "sociology of epistemology." By sociology of *epistemology* we mean to limit ourselves to a study of how journalists know what they know.[1] And by *sociology* of epistemology we mean to differentiate between a philosophical examination of epistemology, for which we disclaim any pretension, and a phenomological examination of epistemology. Our study thus focuses on what journalists themselves regard as acceptable knowledge claims; it is not an effort to determine whether those knowledge claims are, in fact, valid.

We begin our pursuit of what qualifies as knowledge in the investigative journalism setting with several fundamental definitions and distinctions. Philosophers ordinarily define knowledge as a "justified true belief," where both the truth of the belief as well as its proper justification are regarded as the necessary conditions of knowledge (O'Connor and Carr, 1982). To justify a belief required that we identify the grounds for it—that is, the evidence in support of it and the reasons for accepting that evidence. It is important to understand that a true belief may not be justified—it may be, for example, just a lucky guess; and, conversely, a justified belief may not be true. In many practical matters, however, justification is very often the more useful criterion for judging beliefs because verification may be impractical or undesirable even if possible.[2] As Lewis (1946:255-257) points out, whether a belief can be defended as "rationally credible" is repeatedly a more impor-

tant issue than whether it has been (or can be) verified. Recognizing this, rhetoricians concerned with the role of argument in practical judgment insist upon standards of justification, not verification, when assessing the quality of an argument (McKerrow, 1977).
Phenomologists, of course, also bypass the obdurate question of
"genuine" knowledge and focus instead on the whatever passes
for "knowledge" in a particular setting, "regardless of the ultimate
validity or invalidity (by whatever criteria) of such 'knowledge' "
(Berger and Luckman, 1966:3). Their concern is, then, the practical, everyday justification of beliefs.

Our inquiry presupposes no absolute or objective standard of
justification; a justified belief is nothing more or less than belief
"that has been shown to be legitimate within a context of justification" (Lyune, 1981:148). We expect, therefore, the justification
of journalists' knowledge claims to depend upon—and vary according to—the context within which journalists operate. In the remainder of this article we seek to understand what journalists in
two different contexts do to create well founded, "rationally credible"—that is to say, justified—stories. We begin with an examination of the context of the daily reporter as that context might
reasonably be inferred from the work of Fishman (1980; 1982),
Tuchman (1973; 1978), Gans (1979), Sigal (1973) and others. This
context serves as a point of comparison for that of the investigative
reporter.

THE CONTEXT OF JUSTIFICATION FOR THE
DAILY REPORTER: A REVIEW

Although both daily reporters and investigative reporters concern
themselves with "hard" news, the characteristics of hard news are
very different in the daily reporting and investigative reporting settings. As Tuchman (1973:117) found in her study in the routines
of reporting, journalists organize themselves differently and allocate
resources differently as they move from one kind of story to another;
they "typify"[3] the work they do "along dimensions that reflect

practical tasks associated with their work.'' The hard news produced by the daily reporter tends to be more time-bound than the hard news produced by the investigative reporter, and the daily reporter is not able to utilize as many organizational resources as his or her investigative counterpart. Thus, the hard news of the two reporters are likely to be distinguished by the rigors of inquiry to which each is subjected.

But do the rigors of investigative journalism yield knowledge claims unlike the knowledge claims of daily journalism? Are the methods of investigative reporting a substantial departure from what Phillips (1977) describes as the primitive empiricism of daily reporting? The answer to the question of whether, in fact, daily and investigative reporters employ distinctive epistemologies must begin with an appreciation of what Fishman (1980:27-44) portrays as the principal objective of daily journalism: the beat system.

Fishman (1980:28) defines daily journalism's beat system as ''a complex object of reporting consisting of a domain of activities occurring outside the newsroom.'' As a resource for ''routinizing the unexpected,'' to borrow one of Tuchman's phrases, the beat system is essentially an organizing tool: it establishes a rationale for allocating editorial personnel and, by so doing, it identifies the most appropriate—and by inference, the least appropriate—sources of information (Sigal, 1973; Tuchman, 1973; Fishman, 1980). At least among American daily newspapers, the beat system flourishes as the dominant mode of news coverage. ''The beat system of news coverage is so widespread among established newspapers,'' Fishman argues, ''that not using beats is a distinctive feature of being an experimental, alternative, or underground newspaper'' (27).

In concept, beats fall into one of two broadly distinguishable categories: *locational*, such as city hall, the police department, and the courts, or *substantive*, such as law, medicine, and education (Gans, 1979:144). In practice, however, virtually all beats are locational, since only locations can offer daily reporters what they need most: ''a steady stream of timely information'' (Roshco, 1975:64). To be sure, these locations account for the spatial pattern to which Tuchman (1978) applies her ''news net'' metaphor:

There is a significant difference between the capacity of a blanket and that of a net to gather fodder for daily newspaper columns and television air time. Each arrangement may capture fresh information daily, thus confirming and reinforcing the old adage "old news is no news." (News grows stale like bread and cakes; it is a depletable consumer item.) But a net has holes. Its haul is dependent upon the amount invested in intersecting fiber and the tensile strength of that fiber. The narrower the intersections between the mesh—the more blanket-like the net— the more can be captured (21).

Daily reporters not only know where information can be found, as the news net metaphor suggests, but they know when to find it. The spatial pattern of the dispersion of reporters, Tuchman (1978:41-42) found, is augmented by the tempo or rhythm of the newsroom: "Just as reporters seek central spatial locations to find potential news events, so, too, reporters are temporally concentrated." Thus the production of news, particularly as news is produced on a daily basis, becomes spatially and temporally synchronized with the very beats to which reporters are assigned.

A well developed system of beats, then, is a remarkably efficient method for deploying personnel and gathering information: if reporters cannot know what will be news each day, they can at least know where and when to find it. As a practical matter, beats are efficient to the degree they can accommodate the exigencies of news by establishing standards for the selection of sources. Put another way, the efficiency of the beat system rests on its capacity to circumscribe *how* reporters will know what they know, an achievement inextricably wedded to *what* journalists will know. Sigal (1973:46) sums it up well: what journalists "know depends to a considerable extent on whom they know, which, in turn, depends on where they are."

For daily reporters, the empirical beliefs or propositions they glean from the beats they cover are ordinarily accepted at face value. As a practical matter, the scheduling characteristics of hard news— at least the hard news with which daily reporters must contend— leave reporters little time for verification. And as a matter of principle, the very idea of verification often implies conduct inimical to the canons of objective reporting (Tuchman, 1972; Roshco,

1975).[4] Accordingly, daily reporters strive for accuracy, not veracity: they will report propositions "fairly" and "accurately" but they will neither assess nor attest to the veracity of what is reported.

If the veracity of a proposition does not justify its publication, what standards of justification do daily reporters use? Following Fishman (1980), who provides a detailed and insightful examination of the news production process, the justification for a proposition is established by the very bureaucracy through which it appears:

Information which is bureaucractically organized, produced, and provided is hard fact; it is the stuff that makes up straight reporting. Any other kind of information . . . does not have the character of hard fact; it is stuff that makes up interpretive reports or news analysis (92).

Fishman offers two mutually auxiliary explanations for the acceptance these bureaucratic accounts find among daily reporters. One explanation focuses on what Fishman describes as the "socially sanctioned character of the bureaucrats' competence to know"(94-95); the other focuses on the performative character of bureaucratic documents and preceedings (95-100).

At least within the domain of their bureaucracy, bureaucrats appear to the daily reporter as self-evidently competent knowers. The daily reporter not only views bureaucrats "as having a special vantage point from which they can observe events" (Fishman, 1980:95), but the daily reporter also views bureaucrats as socially and politically "authorized" to know what they know. Moreover, bureaucrats are authorized to know what they know by virtue of their status or position in society, which no doubt enhances their appeal as "efficient" sources of information; "it always remains easier," Gouldner (1976:122-123) reminds us, "to publish accounts consonant with those offered by the managers of social institutions—accounts which thereby reinforce conventional definitions of social reality and the existent system of stratification."

Bureaucratic proceedings (e.g., a city council meeting) and bureaucratic documents (e.g., a deed) are similarly credible, due in large part to their "performative" nature. Following J. L. Austin (1961), 1962, 1971), Fishman defines performatives as utterances that "do something rather than merely say something"; performatives, it follows, "cannot be true or false because they are things in themselves and not statements about things" (1980:96-97). For the daily reporter, therefore, a bureaucratic account of something *becomes* something—just as "a lease *is* the leasing of property" or "an insurance policy *is* the insuring of valuables" (98).[5]

Bureaucratically credible accounts thus find acceptance among daily reporters not only because journalists ordinarily "participate in upholding a normative order of authorized knowers in the society," but because to treat bureaucratic accounts as factual "is also a position of convenience" (Fishman, 1980: 96). Daily reporters are therefore predisposed to accept bureaucratic accounts largely because the very organization and structure of newswork define bureaucracies—especially established public bureaucracies—as "the appropriate site at which information should be gathered" (Tuchman, 1978: 210); these are the very beats to which daily reporters are assigned.

The beat system is as efficient as it is, therefore, because it offers the daily reporter *pre-justified* accounts of "what is." The beat system not only reduces daily journalism to the coverage of mere appearances,[6] but it enables the reporter to operate within a context of justification that usually requires no independent anlaysis or evaluation of what passes as knowledge. Ultimately, this abiding faith in the authority of bureaucratically credible accounts allows the daily reporter to apply to the complex and ambiguous realm of public affairs the kind of empiricism Bernstein (1976: 112) calls "objectivism': "a substantive orientation that believes that in the final analysis there is a realm of basic, uninterpreted, hard facts that serves as the foundation for all empirical knowledge."[7]

The daily reporter's enduring commitment to the supremacy of bureaucratically credible facts—indeed, the very ethic of objectivity—rests on the belief that news is something journalists are compelled to report, not something journalists are responsible for creating. That is, because news presumably exists "out there"—apparently independent of the reporter—journalists are typically reluctant to accept responsibility for the quality or value of what is reported. The ideology of objective reporting, in short, accounts for what may be fairly termed the amorality of daily journalism (cf. Glasser, 1984).

THE CONTEXT OF JUSTIFICATION FOR THE INVESTIGATIVE REPORTER: A CASE STUDY

The daily reporter's knowledge claims, as we have argued, are usually immediately credible due to the context in which they arise—the news net composed of bureaucratically credible sources. The claims need not, then, be justified by the daily reporter because they are pre-justified. The investigative reporter, however, may not be so epistemologically fortunate. Indeed, as we attempt to show in the case study which follows, the investigative reporter not only shoulders the burden of justification, but also creates a method for doing so.

In this case study we focus on a particular investigative reporting team, a unit within a network-affiliated, major market television station composed of two reporters, a researcher and several clerical workers and student interns. Under the supervision of the station's director of public affairs, who also supervises a documentary production unit, the investigative unit produces four to six stories a year using the mini-documentary format (i.e., five segments each of about five minutes, running on five consecutive nightly newcasts). The topical focus of the investigative stories is wrong-doing of various sorts, what Gans (1979:56-57) calls "moral disorder" news. Indeed, the unit has clearly articulated its investigatory charge in the form of a "manifesto," which each member can recite with only slight variation. Here is one reporter's version:

The manifesto is, if I can remember it in its original language, "through standard and professional journalistic techniques to investigate and report (with the intention of gaining results) heretofore unknown facts regarding unsolved crime or political corruption which affects the community (and) which others seek to keep secret."

The format and the topical focus of the investigative unit distinguishes it from the documentary unit which produces hour-length programs on social issues, such as the rise of religious cults and the social status of children. The two units do, however, share a track record of outstanding broadcast journalism as recognized by a large number of regional and national citations including several du Pont/Columbia and Peabody awards.

Our method in the study of this investigative unit was the intensive interview. In these interviews we asked each of the members to outline the investigative process and to exemplify the process with one or two recent investigations. Members were asked to pay special attention to when in the course of an investigation they were required to decide whether or not information was true and to how they made that decision. In these interviews one reporter emerged as the most enthusiastic and articulate of the interviewees. This reporter is active in the Investigative Reporters and Editors (IRE) organization and had lobbied the station management for the formation of the investigative unit. Our study focuses on his thinking about this subject and thus attempts to interpret and appreciate the way in which one highly skilled and thoughtful practitioner makes sense of what he does. We do not seek, in other words, to merely describe the work of a random collection of news workers or a single typical worker but instead to learn from the ruminations of a master craftsman.

Justification as Process

While the knowledge claims of the daily reporter are pre-justified by the context in which they arise, the knowledge claims of the investigative reporter and his colleagues are not prejustified in this way. Indeed, their investigations into crime and corruption usually arise outside of the news net and may cite bureaucratically *incredible* sources. We find, however, that this investigative reporter has worked out for himself an elaborate process which justifies to himself and his colleagues the knowledge claims embodied in his stories. This process underscores the active stance of the investigative reporter, who must establish credibility, versus the passive stance of the daily reporter, who merely accepts credibility.

This process of justification is perhaps best conceptualized as a set of intellectual exercises which the reporter, often in concert with his colleagues, goes through at key points in the investigation. These are:

1. Screening the tips.
2. Weighing the evidence.
3. Fitting the pieces.
4. Evaluating the story.

These four points coincide with and reflect several of the steps identified by Bants *et al.* (1980) in the production of daily reportage by a local television station. What follows, however, are not descriptions of investigative production routines but rather of the phenomology of those routines. They are attempts to describe how a reporter thinks through and characterizes tasks which confront him.

Screening the Tips

For this reporter and his colleagues stories often begin with tips. A story about the fraudalent sales tactics and shoddy work of a basement waterproofing firm, for example, began with a call from an unhappy customer. The firm's refusal to deal with the complaint lead a brief story by the station's consumer affairs reporter which, in turn, generated a call from a former salesman for the firm who was willing to discuss the sales tactics. The researcher who is responsible for handling the unsolicited tips estimates that he handles about 25 such tips a week. Of these, he opens a file on one or two of them for further inspection by the unit's reporters.

The researcher and then a reporter screen the tips on several criteria and select those to be ''pitched'' to the entire unit at one of its regular meetings. Here is the reporter's description of the process.

(You) get a phone call and someone lays out an incredible story for you on the phone. You have absolutely no substantiation for the story, but you may run in the next room and say, "Hey, just got a call and if this thing is right we've got September. Let's pitch it Monday morning at nine in the meantime, this weekend, I'll work to get some more stuff sourced out on this thing to see if it's real."

By Monday you may find out it was not real, or you may find that it is real but impossible to do. You may find out that it's real, perfectly do-able, but will have no effect and doesn't matter to anyone whatsoever.

There are a million things you could find out between your initial idea or the initial discussion and the point you pitch it. But generally you'd give it a week I guess. A week of work before you'd mention it to anyone in a formal way. What usually happens (then) is some table talk in the conference room in a staff meeting. You go around the table and say, "What are your ideas? What have you got?"

In "pitching" the story to his supervisor and colleagues the investigative reporter must be able to show that the tip can meet three criteria. The tip must be (1) "real", and (2) "do-able", as well as (3) promise to result in a story which has an "effect." In practice, meeting the criterion of "real" does not require proof that the story implied by the tip is, in fact, true but merely the display of some additional evidence to that effect. There are indeed "a million things" the report could do, but at this point he need do only enough to show his colleagues that the tip *could be* real. Meeting the criterion of "do-able" requires the display of some plan for collecting enough additional evidence to make a case for the truth of the implied story. The reporter must convince his colleagues that the tip could be *shown* to be real. Finally the criterion of "effect" is akin to the daily journalist's judgment of news value. The story must be not only "real" and "do-able" but promise to make a difference in the community. In this first justificatory exercise, then, the reporter seeks little verification of the tip and the story implied by it. Rather he seeks justification for continuing, for converting the tip into a full-fledged investigation.

Weighing the Evidence

The tips which meet these criteria to the satisfaction of the investigative reporter and his colleagues become active investigations.

So begins the "legwork" of journalistic legend. Textbook authors have made much of this activity with chapters on the sifting through government records, conducting adversarial interviews and other such investigative tasks. For this investigative reporter, however, such tasks are certainly a good deal of work but not very intellectually problematic:

There are some things that are just standard in the trade. . . . Paper, documents, signatures, recordings, anything that captures the fact, that certifies the fact. So, always the first question I ask after some preliminary stuff is there any paper on this? . . . If there's not, I've got a lot more work to do. I would have to skip the paperwork and go directly to interviews.

This collection of evidence does follow a plan; the reporter, after the preliminary "table talk," must produce a "blue sheet" or plan confirming the "do-ability" of the investigation. The reporter, however, does not emphasize planfulness in his accounts of the collection of evidence. Indeed, he likens the collection of evidence to building "a mound."

The collected evidence, if not *dis*organized, is as yet *unorganiz*-ed. However, each item of evidence collected together into the mound possesses a property which is critical to the completion of the next exercise in justification—an exercise which yields justification for accepting the evidence as *sufficient* even if unorganized. The critical property is that of weight:

The heaviest evidence would be the act itself captured on videotape. The act itself. ABSCAM. Undeniably these people met with these other people and discussed bribes and money changed hands and went into the pocket. That's a big heavy piece of evidence. There's very little more you have to do to substantiate that the thing happened. You can put facts with it, like what time did it happen, what date did it happen, names of the participants, but the act itself happened. That would be what I would call the number one. Secondarily to that kind of video document would be a paper document that outlined the suspected act which was attested to by the parties involved.

The investigative reporter thus outlines a hierachy of evidence based on the notion of weight, a metaphor which, in turn, reflects the journalist's presumptions about its veracity. Highest in the hierachy are the artifacts produced in the course of the criminal or corrupt act; things which are accepted by the reporter as some aspect of the act itself. The heaviest evidence is a highly iconic representation of the act in the form of videotape. In the case of the waterproofing investigation the sales tactics were recorded by hidden cameras. Of somewhat less weight is "paper." In the waterproofing investigation this included training manuals outlining the tactics.

Lower in the hierarchy are the post-hoc accounts of the act. Accounts by "participatory witnesses," including confessions, are the heavier sort of account. In the waterproofing investigation these included the statements of the former salesmen. Of somewhat less weight are the accounts by the "non participatory witnesses." The statements of experts attesting to the shoddiness of the workmanship of the waterproofer is an example of this sort of evidence.

Below such accounts in the hierarchy is material which could best be described as pre-evidentiary—material which is not itself evidence but may lead to evidence. This includes hunches or "presumptions" as the reporter himself calls them. Of the least weight is the "anonymous phone call—as light as you can get."

Thus the investigative reporter's list of information to be gathered is distinguished from the daily reporter's list less by what is on it than by the hierarchical organization of the list based on "weight." For the daily reporter, weight is an irrelevant concept. When propositions originate in the news net and are embodied in bureaucratically credible "paper" and accounts, they are not more credible or less credible; they are credible—period! The daily reporter is always completely justified in citing such propositions. For the investigative reporter, however, weight is a critical concept because propositions often originate outside of the news net (indeed, they begin with the lowly hunch or phone call) and are embodied in the accounts of alleged criminals and other suspect accounts. The investigative reporter must himself provide justification for citing such propositions. "Heavier" evidence is more credible, more justifiable.

One other property of the evidence is central to the completion of this exercise in justification. This is whether the item of evidence tends to support the charges to be made in the story; whether the evidence is, in the words of the reporter, "inculpatory" or "exculpatory." Like the daily reporter, the investigative reporter feels he must faithfully seek "both sides." Unlike the daily reporter, however, the investigative reporter does not merely repeat both sides. Rather, the investigative reporter proceeds to *weigh* both sides and eventually comes to a judgment:

> It's simply the scales. You take inculpatory evidence and stack it up and you take the exculpatory evidence and stack it up and you have to be very truthful to yourself. You have to be as vigorous in seeking the exculpatory information as you are in seeking the suff that's damning. And once gathered, you watch the way it falls. And you say the preponderance of evidence is that this thing occurs in a damning way (but) sometimes there's perfect balance and your investigation continues. You keep going and going and going . . . It's simply the weight of the evidence.

Using the law as an intellectual resource, the reporter refers to this process of weighing evidence as the "preponderance test," the test used to decide the outcome of civil cases. The reporter uses legal metaphor and imagery often and here the image of the scales of justice is quite real to him. Indeed, he can precisely specify the psycho-physics of evidentiary weight:

> As you go down (the hierarchy of evidence) you need more of each . . . One non-participatory witness, one piece of material evidence, one document weighs as much as the videotape act.

It would be both an oversimplification and an exaggeration to suggest that all of the available evidence is collected and then weighed as would be the goal in a trial. Collecting and weighing evidence is an interative process which in any particular investigation may be repeated many times. If in this weighing exercise, the scale tips decisively toward the exculpatory evidence or if, after much effort, the scale cannot be made to tip, the investigation is abandoned. If, however, the scale tips decisively toward the inculpatory evidence, the investigation finally becomes a story.

What remains elusive, to us, and apparently even to the reporter himself without recourse to examples from specific investigations, is the weight necessary to make the scale tip decisively. It is clear, however, that the reporter expects to find conflicting evidence. Indeed, he must honestly seek out such evidence. If, however, the preponderence—the weight—of evidence does tend to support the charges of wrong-doing, then the reporter is justified at last in making the investigation into a story.

Fitting the Pieces

The collected evidence must be assembled into a television news story. While the reporter *weighed the evidence* in the course of the investigation now he *fits the pieces* into a story. The reporter invokes the metaphor of the jigsaw picture puzzle and explains some of the ways in which pieces are assembled.

> Reporter: I use chronology. Number the pieces one through a thousand by date and time and put them together starting with piece one. What happens is often you don't have the full sequence. You have one, two, nine and fourteen, eighty-five and that helps you put it together because you or your boss says you really do need pieces seven and eight here in order to even get the full idea . . . So you go out and get seven and eight and put that together. Then you may have 85 through 100 over here which makes another separate picture within the picture itself. It's the mast and you can put that all together and . . . just move the section over the hull that I have already put in place. I think it fits about there. I group chronologically and try to build the piece from the very first piece of information I have going back as far as I can and bring it forward then it gives me a time perspective on how things happen . . .

> Questioner: What other rules for fitting can you give us?

> Reporter: What we call the interlocking directorate schematic. Most stories have them. Those are the relationships of the individuals to each other and to the events. The two together, the chronology and the interlocking directorate analogy gives you a pretty good understanding of who knew what when, who did what when, with whom . . . It is simply done by doing a flow chart or a bunch of boxes with lines.

It may be necessary to cycle through the collection of evidence and the weighing exercise again and again before the necessary pieces are present, but eventually the puzzle is complete—or at least complete enough to present a coherent and credible picture. This notion of interlocking pieces of a puzzle is, then, quite necessary to the process of justification because the fit of each piece enhances the credibility of each of the others and, in turn, the whole picture assembled from them (cf. Tuchman, 1978:82-103). Accepting the story as true is increasingly justified as more pieces fit and the story becomes more complete and coherent.

Fitting the pieces into a picture is a point at which the reporter explicitly acknowledges that he must convince his boss of the credibility of what he has discovered. It is also the point at which he expresses the greatest concern for the credibility of the story to the television news audience. He is concerned that the fit of the pieces—the coherence of the story—shine through the completed mini-documentary segments.

He also recognizes, however, that because of broadcast time constraints, only some of the completed puzzle can be shown to the audience:

Mike [the investigative unit's supervisor] takes a look at your completed puzzle and says what is the most definite aspect of this puzzle; what is the most interesting aspect of this puzzle. And now let's take [a frame] and lay it over different portions of your puzzle and see which one is best. We'll just take a frame and move it around until we find a picture that has the most detail and then we will reshape [the picture] maybe. Then we will take your puzzle and we will paint a picture from your puzzle. I like your island but it is not in the [frame]. Let's, in this picture, move the island a little closer. You have well established the island. Let's move it in right behind the boat.

The reporter does, then, recognize that when he and his colleagues produce the story for broadcast, they frame a picture within the larger puzzle which they have assembled. There is even an acknowledgment that the picture can be manipulated—the island can be moved—for best effect. There is however, no hint that meaning is created, that reality is constructed. The meaning of the story—the pieces of the puzzle and the way each fits with the others—exists quite independently of the reporter and the picture he finally paints. Meaning is there to be discovered and assembled in the most credible way possible within the constraints of the mini-documentary television format.

Evaluating the Story

With the puzzle pieces found and assembled, the picture/story is subject to a final, sometimes dramatic, exercise in justification. The exercise begins by attempting to generate alternative explanations or additional exculpatory evidence which could disconfirm the story:

You turn yourself into a defense attorney and we do that a lot . . . And it's a lot of fun. We take the facts and turn them around on ourselves. We take our techniques and turn them around on ourselves. We see how it plays. What can they say to disprove them. They'll say, "The guy's out-of-town"
    And I'll say, "Well, have you found out whether he was in town or not?"
    "I haven't."
    "Well, get on your horse and find out whether he was in town."

In this attempt to develop disconfirmatory material the reporter may subject the story to the "moral certainty test."

I like some of the things that they go through in juries. You know, they struck moral certainty from jury instruction a long time ago because it was just too tough a test. Defense attorneys would say, "You have to be more convinced of this individual's guilt than you are convinced that there is a God." And people couldn't do it . . . We have to be morally certain that what we're saying is true.

A dramatic example of this test occurred in an investigation of a judge who was alledged to have paid children (i.e. underaged male prostitutes) for sex:

Tuesday afternoon I made a phone call to one of the boys that was going to be on the air Thursday, and I said, "I'm coming out to get you."
    And he said "what for?"
    And I said, "I'll tell you later."

Now I had lie detectored these guys, I had them ID (the judge) out of six very difficult photographs of gray-haired, heavyweight, middle-aged men. I had them describe artifacts in the house (bronze and ducks, titles of books on the bedstead), draw maps of the house, and then compare it with people who have been in the house . . .

I'm getting ready to go there in two days and accuse the judge of some pretty bad things. These kids are going to accuse him. I brought the kid in. It was 8:00 at night. I drove him to the station, and then I said, "take me to (the judge's) house."

He said, "Why?"

I said, "I just want you to drive me to (the judge's) house. Do you know where it is?" I said, "you described it, that it's on (a particular street), that it's yellow, that you entered through the back door with a three-car garage. You've given me all that stuff. I want you to take me there."

He says, "OK." Drove right to the house. He's fifteen, the fifteen-year-old. I said, "thanks," and I took him home.

In the course of the investigation of the judge, this witness' story had been corroborated by other boys. Further, this boy had been examined and cross-examined several times by the reporters to assess the internal consistency of his story. This late night ride to the judge's residence was, however, not merely one more cross-examination. Rather, it is best understood as an exercise in self persuasion—a final attempt to achieve moral certainty made imperative by a tip that the judge was contemplating suicide. This was, then, an attempt to justify the story simultaneously on both epistemological and moral grounds. The term "moral certainty" is, it turns out, very well chosen indeed for it captures the fundamental fusion of epistemological and ethical concerns which the investigative journalist must confront.

Justification and Equivocation

A justified story is, then, one in which the evidence is so "heavy" and the pieces "fit" so well that the reporter has become "morally certain" that he cannot disconfirm it. Despite this painstaking process, however, the reporter does not altogether abandon the rituals of balanced reporting. specifically, he still feels he must "cover the other side"—i.e., repeat the denial of the wrong-doer even though he is morally certain, presumably, that it is untrue:

Questioner: Why did (the judge) have the right to defend himself on the air?

Reporter: That's the American way. Balance . . . What I'm concerned
             about is whether I'm true to some real basic ethical considera-
             tions. That's just decency . . .

We do not doubt the sincerity of the reporter's decency rationale
for the right of response for the accused, but we also find at least
one other consideration in his insistence upon that right. While
the reporter does not, of course, accept the denial itself as true,
he does accept the existence of the denial as one sort of "conflicting fact"—a fact which does not fit well with all of the other puzzle pieces. Significantly, this conflict—this lack of fit—is sufficient
to cause the reporter to equivocate about the truth of the story:

The truth is general thing out there. I can have a view of the truth but I'm one
person. I can say, "my investigation, my finite abilities, my limited number of
questions asked, my examination of the facts indicate to me that this is the truth."
What I now have just rendered is an opinion . . . When you reach a conclusion
in an investigation where you have conflicting fact, what you have arrived at,
what you believe to be the truth, is an opinion.

Thus, even after the elaborate exercises reviewed here, the
reporter is reluctant to claim that his story faithfully reproduces
the truth as it exists "out there." The story is still only his opinion
concerning that truth and he is obligated, therefore, to cite the opinion of the accused as well. There is in this feeling of obligation,
we suspect, an intuitive sense of the distinction between justification and verification. The reporter has painstakingly developed the
grounds, the good reasons, for accepting the story as true. He is,
in our terms, willing to claim justification. And yet, in the face
of conflicting facts such as the denial of the accused, the reporter
wishes to stop short of saying that the story is more than opinion
about the truth. The reporter, in other words, is reluctant to claim
verification. There is too much at stake to claim certainty and abandon the strategies of objectivity.

THE PRODUCTION OF JUSTIFICATION:
CONCLUSION

Whereas the objectivism of daily journalism rests on bureaucratically credible facts that are immediately and uncritically accepted
as legitimate knowledge claims, the epistemology of investigative
journalism underscores what Schudson (1978:192) describes as the
investigative reporter's "mature subjectivity," a subjectivity "aged
by encounters with, and regard for, the facts of the world."
Specifically, the knowledge claims of the investigative reporter
studied here are firmly grounded in the process of screening tips,
assembling and weighing evidence, fitting facts and attempting to
disconfirm the resulting story. In the end, these exercises yield a
degree of "moral certainty" about the convergence of facts into
a truthful report. Taken together these activities constitute what
may be called the "production of justification," an achievement
generally antithetical to the ideals of daily reporting.

The epistemology of the investigative journalist thus distinguishes
itself from that of the daily journalist in three important ways. First,
the investigative reporter accommodates a variety of types of fact,
including facts dismissed by the daily reporter as bureaucratically
*in*credible. Second, the investigative reporter assesses the relative
quality of facts, an essentially rational—even if imprecise—process
from which facts emerge as more credible or less credible. And third,
the investigative reporter seeks to justify the larger truth of the story,
a truth often greater than the sum of the story's facts.

The investigative reporter is thus less burdened by—though not
unmindful of—the routines of objective reporting. The reporter,
however, has acquired a different, perhaps far heavier, burden:
responsibility for the quality of the facts reported as well as a defense
of the broader value judgments that effectively define the story's
theme. Still, as Gans (1979:183) reminds us, this does not render
investigative journalism—at least from the practitioner's
perspective—biased or partial: the quintessential investigation—
the expose—"typically judges the exposed against their own expressed values, and these can be determined empirically by the

reporter; as a result, even his or her value judgment is considered objective."

Investigative reporting is, in short, unabashedly moralistic. It is also highly personalized—even idiosyncratic. The process of justification reviewed here is the creative achievement of a single individual acting in concert with a few colleagues. We fully expect to find other reporters with different backgrounds, interests and assignments to have created different solutions to the epistemological problems of their craft. What we offer here, then, is by no means a model of how, in general, investigative reporters *do* know what they know, but rather an illustration of how investigative reporters *can* come to know what they know. It illustrates what one textbook (Williams, 1978:xi) describes as the investigative reporter's "conscious aversion" to the accepted methods of daily reporting and the standard definitions of news. And, more positively, it illustrates how investigative reporters can—indeed must—move beyond objectivism to develop criteria for assessing the quality and value of what is reported, which in the end translates into a heightened sense of responsibility for the consequences of their conduct.

NOTES

1. Our task, then, is far less ambitious than the recent studies by Gans (1979), Tuchman (1978), Gitlin (1980), Fishman (1980), Roshco (1975), and others whose work takes a broad sweep across, as Gitlin (1980: 15) puts it, "the nature, sources, and consequences of news."
2. From the "Correspondence theory" perspective, which is most sympathetic to journalistic objectivity, an empirical belief is either true or false, depending on whether its denotation or extension is actual or existent and ultimately testable by experience (Lewis, 1946: 35-70). For example, to say "the stove is hot" expresses a belief independent of the proposition itself; it *denotes* a "hot stove." To verify the proposition—to determine, that is, whether it is true or false—requires that we experience the "hot stove." But to *justify* our belief by determining what, if any, *credible evidence* exists in support of the proposition "the stove is hot." We note, for instance, a kettle of boiling water and take that as evidence of a hot stove, *credible* evidence because experience has taught us that kettles of water boil on when stoves are hot. We have thus justified—not verified—an empirical belief.

3. By "typify" Tuchman means to underscore the importance of the distinction between "typification" and "category": "Category" denotes a "classification of objects according to one or more relevant characteristics ruled salient by the classifiers" but "typification" implies a phenomenological orientation, a classification in which relevant characteristics are central to the solution of practical tasks or problems at hand and are constituted and grounded in everyday activity" (1973:116-117).

4. Verification is especially problematic for journalists because it involves their own experiences. For no matter how reliable the journalist may be as an observer, when the journalist may be as an observer, when the journalist's observations or experiences conflict with the "official" pronouncements of a presumably authoritative source, the tenets of objective reporting require the journalist to disseminate only the source's version. Molotch and Lester (1975), in a case study of what is probably one of the most extreme examples of the ethic of objectivity interferring with verification, report that journalists could see and smell a beach polluted by a massive oil spill and yet proclaimed the beach clean because President Nixon arrived at the beach and announced that it had fully recovered from the oil spill.

5. The term "performative" is derived from "perform;" and "indicates that the issuing of the utterance is the performing of an action" (Austin, 1962: 6). Performatives are especially prevalent in law—when, for example, a court declares a contract void or rules that a statute is unconstitutional. For an interesting examination of the importance of performatives in legal discourse, see Fletcher (1981).

6. As Gans (1967: 323) found when he studied the nature of the news media's coverage of local government, reporters were inclined "to cover the performing rather than the actual government." Often ignorant of the intricacies of government, reporters' stories tended to be limited to the government's "decisions and the performances that accompany them."

7. It is the realm of daily public affairs reporting that the routines of objectivity are most widely and consistently practiced. The literature on daily public affairs reporting which we have reviewed here thus contributes to the definition of an ideal type of daily reporting—a conceptualization we have sought to distill in our description of the daily reportorial setting.

Bibliography

Anderson, D. & Benjaminson, P. *Investigative reporting*. Bloomington: Indiana University Press, 1976.

Austin, J. L. Performative-constative. In J. R. Searle (ed.), *The Philosophy of language*. New York: Oxford University Press, 1971.

Austin, J. L. *How to do things with words*. J. O. Urmson, ed. New York: Oxford University Press, 1962.

Austin, J. L. *Philosophical papers*. New York: Oxford University Press, 1961.

Bantz, C. R., McCorkle, S., & Baade, R. C. The news factory. *Communication Research*, 1980, 7, 45-58.

Behrens, J. C. *The typewriter guerillas.* Chicago: Nelson-Hall, 19771.

Berstein, C. & Woodward, B. *All the President's Men.* New York: Warner Books, 1974.

Berstein, R. J. *The restructuring of social and political theory.* New York: Harcourt Brace Jovanovich, 1976.

Berger, P. L. & Luckmann, T. *The social construction of reality.* Garden City, N.Y.: Doubleday, 1966.

Bolch, J. & Miller, K. *Investigative and in-depth reporting.* New York: Hastings House, 1978.

Downie, L. *The new muckrakers.* New York; New American Library, 1976.

Dygert, J. H. *The investigative journalist.* Englewood Cliffs, N.J.: Prentice Hall, 1976.

Fishman, M. *Manufacturing the news.* Austin: University of Texas Press, 1980.

_____, News and nonevents: Making the Visible Invisible. In Ettema, J. S. & Whitney, D. C. (eds.) *Individuals in Mass Media Organizations.* Beverly Hills, CA: Sage, 1982.

Fletcher, G. P. Two modes of legal thought. *Yale Law Journal,* 1981, 90, 970-1003.

Gans, H. *The Levittowners.* New York: Random House, 1967.

_____. *Deciding what's news.* New York: Pantheon, 1979.

Gitlin, T. *The whole world is watching.* Berkeley: University of California Press, 1980.

Glasser, T. L. Objectivity precludes responsibility. *Quill,* pp. 13-16 (February, 1984).

Gouldner, A. *The dialect of ideology and technology.* New York; Seabury, 1976.

Lewis, C. I. *An analysis of knowledge and valuation.* La Salle, Ill.: Open Court, 1946.

Lyne, J. R. Rhetoric and everyday knowledge. *Central States Speech Journal.* 1981, 32, 145-152.

McKerrow, R. E. Rhetorical validity: An analysis of three perspectives on the justification of rhetorical argument. *Journal of the American Forensic Association,* 1977, 13, 133-141.

Mollenhoff, C. R. *Investigative Reporting.* New York: Macmillan, 1981.

Molotch, H. L. & Lester, M. Accidental news: the great oil spill. *American Jurnal of Sociology,* 1975, 81, 235-260.

O'Connor, D. J. & Carr, B. *Introduction to the theory of knowledge.* Minneapolis: University of Minnesota Press, 1982.

Park, R. E. News as form of knowledge. *American Journal of Sociology,* 1940, 45, 669-686.

Phillips, E. B. Approaches to objectivity: journalistic vs. social science perspectives. In P. M. Hirsch, P. V. Miller, & F. G. Kline (eds.), *Strategies for communication research.* Beverly Hills: Sage, 1977.

Roshco, B. *Newsmaking.* Chicago: University of Chicago Press, 1975.

Schudson, M. *Discovering the news.* New York: Basic Books, 1978.

Sigal, L. V. *Reporters and officials.* Lexington, Mass.: D. C. Heath, 1973.

Tuchman, G. Objectivity as strategic ritual. *American Journal of Sociology,* 1972, 77, 660-679.

_____. Making new by doing work: Routinizing the unexpected. *American Journal of Sociology,* 1973, 79, 110-131.

_____. *Making News: A Study in the Construction of Reality.* New York: Free Press, 1978.
Ullmann, J. & Honeyman, S. *The reporter's handbook.* New York: St. Martin's Press, 1983.
Weir, D. & Noyes, D. *Raising hell.* Reading, Mass.: Addison-Wesley, 1983.
Williams, P. N. *Investigative reporting and editing.* Englewood Cliffs, N.J.: Prentice-Hall, 1978.

17

BLOODHOUNDS OR MISSIONARIES
Role Definitions of
German and British Journalists

*Renate Köcher**

A comparative study of British and German journalists has brought to light extensive differences in their perception of their role, their professional motivations and their evaluation of the norm of objectivity. Even in countries with freedom of the press, therefore, journalism can develop in completely different directions, dependent upon the political, legal and historical settings. German journalism follows the traditional role of a species of political and intellectual career, which tends to place a lot of value on opinion and less on news. British journalism, in contrast, particularly sees itself in the role of transmitter of facts, a neutral reporter of current affairs.

Introduction

Communication researchers of many different nationalities seem to communicate effortlessly about journalism as they draw upon the wealth of theoretical and empirical national research results to put together little by little a comprehensive view of the profession: its goals and view of its role, the working conditions and methods, its ethical norms and the importance of journalism in a democratic state. The clearly defined task of providing information, the great and, in fact, increasing similarity of the technical conditions of production and the international network of mass communication, promote the image of a pan-cultural profession. Admittedly, Siebert, Peterson and Schramm (1963: 1) base their theory of the media on the main thesis '. . . that the press always takes on the form and coloration of the social and political structures within which it operates'. O.J. Hale (1964) saw an even closer relationship between society and the media; it was his conviction that there is no other social institution where national distinctions show up as clearly as in the organization and practice of the media. The empirical attention devoted to national peculiarities in the media scene, however, is essentially limited to comparisons of ownership and organizational

*Institut für Demoskopie Allensbach, 7753 Allensbach am Bodensee, West Germany.

structure, of the training available for occupations in communications and of quantitative measurements of the diversity of journalism; while we lack systematic comparisons of the level of journalists, their view of their role and their professional ethics, as well as comparative content analyses of reporting.[1] Comparative studies address themselves to the different conditions that prevail rather than to those who practice their profession under these conditions. It is only in recent years that a German and a British research group have jointly begun trying to establish to what extent different forms of journalism develop within different settings, varying in demographic structure and personality structure, ruled by different kinds of motives and taking distinct views of their role and of the ethics of the profession.[2]

This study is based on face-to-face interviews with 450 German and 405 British journalists with the print and broadcasting media, using standardized, structured questionnaires. The questionnaires of both countries were adapted to each other as far as possible so as to minimize limitations on comparability arising from differences in the way questions were formulated. Of the 450 German journalists interviewed, 276 worked (primarily) for the print media, with 155 working for the broadcasting media and 19 for agencies; the British sample comprises 271 journalists with the print media, 117 in broadcasting and 17 with the agencies. In the area of the print media, the investigation is based on journalists with daily papers and weeklies as well as with weekly news magazines; in the broadcasting area it is based on contributing editors in radio and television in the fields of politics, business, local news, culture and sports. The sample was designed disproportionately, with leading journalists over-represented — editors-in-chief, senior editors, directors and heads of department with the radio — so as to have an adequate statistical base for a comparative analysis of the view high-ranking journalists take of their role.[3] We dispensed with weighting, which reduces the influence of the responses of high-ranking journalists on the total results in line with their share of the universe. Owing to the data on the universes being insufficient in both countries, it could only have been conducted as an approximation and not as a precise adjustment. Instead, the results are always additionally presented here by relevant sub-groups, so as to demonstrate the range of responses when there are significant differences between groups.

Journalism and Traditions

Great Britain and the Federal Republic are two countries where extensive freedom of the press exists at present but which are characterized by basic differences in the historical, legal and structural setting within which journalism operates. Even freedom of the press, which journalists in both countries today take for granted as a prerequisite for their work, has a different quality in Great Britain from that in the Federal Republic, different as to its historic roots and providing different legal guarantees and limitations.

While the struggle for freedom of the press erupted in Great Britain as early as the mid-seventeenth century and its proponents steadily gained ground — the most important dates to mention are the abolition of censorship in 1695 and the complete decontrol of parliamentary reporting in 1771 — in Germany the confrontation did not begin until more than a century later, taking place under very much less favourable conditions. Rather than just having *one* powerful state as their opponent, those who fought for freedom of the press in Germany wore themselves out in confrontations with a great number of autonomous German small states, as if battling a hydra. It was not until 1848 that the right to freedom of the press was recognized, though this did not represent the final breakthrough, namely the end of government censorship. After brief periods of extensive freedom, which were also characterized by setbacks, a new phase of government pressure began in 1922; finally, in 1933 a twelve-year period of complete repression began, with the German press becoming a propaganda instrument of the national socialist regime.[4]

While freedom of the press thus had the strength of a tradition which has developed over the course of centuries in Great Britain, for German journalism it represented a new kind of freedom, which was quite unfamiliar, historically speaking. At the same time, however, this new freedom is accompanied by legal guarantees, which do not exist in Great Britain. This legal protective shield is a consequence of experiences during the Nazi period and of the desire to exclude the possibility once and for all that the press could ever be totally crippled again; at the same time it indicates a very different view of individual interests and of centralized government claims, with the latter given preference over the former, as well as a different view of the law. The difference between the legal conditions which journalists are confronted with in Great Britain and the Federal

Republic shows a consistent pattern, pointing to a different view of government and individual interests. There is more willingness to limit freedom of the press in favour of government interests in Great Britain than in the Federal Republic, while there is less willingness to limit it in favour of private and individual interests.

In contrast to the Federal Republic, Great Britain does not have press legislation, a legal guarantee of freedom of the press, in line with the English legal tradition of protecting freedom by keeping certain areas free of the law rather than by means of regulations (Löffler, 1969: 130; Report of the Commission on Privacy, 1972: para. 16). The guarantee of a privileged position for the press, as represented by German press legislation (Stammler, 1971: 209-10; see also Donsbach, 1982), was most recently considered by the Third Royal Commission on the Press in Great Britain in 1977 and then rejected. While German press legislation, as well as the jurisdiction of the German Federal Constitutional Court, ascribes a different quality to freedom of the press from that it ascribes to individual freedom of speech, the Third Royal Commission on the Press concluded its statement by saying '. . . we believe that, as a general rule, the press should stand on the same footing before the law as other institutions and all citizens' (Royal Commission on the Press, 1977: 185). This rejection of a legally privileged status for the press also characterizes labour law in Great Britain, which, in contrast to the German situation, does not allow for special regulations on the media or for limits on the influence the trade unions may exert.

This rejection of a legally privileged status weakens the British press in dealing with governmental interests. Though freedom of the press developed at an early stage in England, this should not obscure the fact that the English government has always been able to protect its interests vis-à-vis the press, in part by means of rigorous laws. Thus the importance of the libel laws has been underestimated by many of the envious admirers of early British freedom of the press; in the beginning, under Elizabeth I, they strictly served to protect government interests against undesirable publicity and criticism and even today are viewed as a really serious limitation on freedom of journalism, having a more serious effect than comparable laws, for example in the United States (Siebert, 1965: 55-6; Murphy, 1976: 168; and Rothman, 1979: 350). The Official Secrets Act, which makes the transmission and use of secret state documents punishable by law, is also considered by many to represent a threat to the freedom of journalism. While the Committee on the Official Secrets

Act arrived at this conclusion, it also rejected the view that Great
Britain's strategy of secrecy is excessive compared with other
democratic states (Report of the Committee on the Official Secrets
Act, 1972: para. 25/26). The Third Royal Commission on the Press,
however, expressed the conviction that accessibility to information
of public interest is subject to unjustified limitations in Great
Britain, resulting particularly from the over-classification or non-
classification of information (Royal Commission on the Press, 1977:
189-90). In the conflict with government claims to protection,
German journalists are in a more favourable legal position than their
British colleagues, since the German press receives privileged
treatment even according to criminal law; the special regulations on
'state treason by journalists' basically require protection of the state
and freedom of the press to be weighed against each other (Löffler,
1969: 254–5).

While legal guarantees of freedom of the press are subordinated to
government interests and the influence of pressure groups to a
greater degree in Great Britain than in the Federal Republic of
Germany, German journalists are subject to more restrictive
regulations when it comes to individual claims to protection. Thus,
in contrast to the Federal Republic, Great Britain does not have a
legally established right to privacy.

There is a temptation to interpret the different importance
ascribed to government and private claims to protection vis-à-vis the
press as a corollary of the way the political structures of the two
countries have developed historically: between a central English
nation-state, essentially unchanged in its structure for centuries, and
German 'particularism', initially integrated into a nation-state in
1866/67, through the provisional device of the North German
Federation, and definitively in 1870 with the founding of the Reich,
but which continues to exist in the federal structure of the Federal
Republic.

While the assumption that legal regulation of the press and the
political structure are related remains on the level of speculation,
there can be no doubt about either the relationship between the
centralized structure of Great Britain and the structure of the British
press or between German 'particularism' and the German press
scene. German 'particularism' favours the development of an
extraordinarily diversified regional press. In Great Britain, the local
and regional press has never had the importance it does in Germany;
instead, the country's centralized structure is also reflected in the

press, in 'London's domination of British journalism' (Hale, 1964: 43). In the late 1970s, two-thirds of the German population were in a position to choose between at least two regional newspapers and the regional press makes up 65 percent of the total circulation of the daily press.[5] During the same time period there were only two cities in Great Britain where independent provincial morning papers were in competition with each other and only one city with two provincial evening papers; in contrast, nine papers published in London and distributed throughout the entire country made up 90 percent of the total morning press sold (Royal Commission on the Press, 1977: 13–14; 51–2; 270).

It is not our concern, however, to consider the diversity of journalism (which has been analysed repeatedly by investigative commissions in both countries since the Second World War, with the British commissions tending to reach a more favourable conclusion), but the influence of the political structure, which has encouraged a different kind of diversity in journalism and a different view thereof. Diversity of journalism in a centralized setting not only implies that national and regional topics are weighted differently; it also encourages the tendency to seek diversity within one organ of the press rather than by competition between many different organs, each of which is homogeneous in itself.

In Germany the relaxation of censorship in 1848 led to the development of a press aimed at influencing and directing public opinion and with a commitment to a particular point of view. The great majority of newspapers were committed to a political party. Their own view of themselves as the standard bearers of a political camp essentially obviated the need to be objective. The consequence was *uniformity within a particular organ*, while the pointedness in the content and wording at the same time made the German press appear to possess extraordinary diversity (Hale 1964: 44).

This diversity and heterogeneity of the individual organs distinguished the German press from the English press. The popular mass press, which became established earlier in Great Britain and achieved success more quickly than in the other European countries, saw its main job as providing entertainment and information on a level geared to finding the widest possible readership (Ascherson and Wolter, 1977: 77–8). Neither a high level nor partisanship were considered compatible with this goal, as they were considered barriers to maximizing readership. Like the centralized orientation, this goal contributed to seeking *diversity within a particular organ*; it was the norm not only to reflect the spectrum of opinion by means of contributions from different points of view but also by considering different points of view within each contribution — an indication of an effort to reflect reality in comprehensive fashion, something which the missionary stance of the German press essentially precluded at the time.

In addition to the different structure of the press, a different concept of freedom had the effect of encouraging journalists to view themselves as serving the neutral function of a neutral reporter in Great Britain but as being committed to a journalism of opinion in Germany. The English Liberals' struggle for freedom of the press and freedom of speech originated in a concept of freedom, which, 'in contrast to continental philosophy, rather than taking the autonomous and separate individual as its point of departure, always focused as well on the position of the individual in society' (Stammler, 1971: 89). As a consequence, freedom of the press was interpreted as 'freedom of social communication from the very beginning in England' while on the continent — including Germany — there was a tendency to view it as a natural right of the individual to develop freely (ibid). The latter view encourages conscious subjective evaluation while the former impedes it.

Some Preliminary Hypotheses
Journalism has had a different course of development in Great Britain and in Germany, amidst a different intellectual and political climate and in a different political and media structure and with different legal privileges and limitations. Taking the difference in the historical and contemporary settings — which we have only been able to sketch in a general sense here — as a point of departure, the German–British journalism project posited the existence of a clear distinction between German and British journalists, as regards their demographic structure, their motivation and their view of their role, specifically:

— In Great Britain the view of their function is defined by the role of a neutral reporter, while in the Federal Republic journalism is primarily viewed as a 'species of a political career' (Weber, 1919: 28).
— As a consequence, the attraction of the profession resides in different phases of professional activity, for British journalists in

the research phase and for German journalists, in contrast, in the analytical phase, in the subjective-creative processing of the material.
— The requirement of objectivity does not basically conflict with the way British journalists view their role and thus is essentially accepted by them, while it conflicts with the German journalists' view of their role and is thus rejected by them.

Interpreting the Evidence

There are striking differences in the demographic structure of British and German journalism, which indicate that journalism as a career attracts different kinds of people in the two countries. The age composition makes British journalism a considerably 'younger' profession, which, in comparison to German journalism particularly, shows almost twice as large a proportion of journalists under thirty years of age.

The high percentage of very young journalists in Great Britain also means that the educational level is lower in terms of formal education. The Third Royal Commission on the Press set the proportion of British journalists with a university degree at 10 percent, with a gradually increasing tendency (Royal Commission on the Press, 1977: 178). During the same time period, studies in the Federal Republic show a far above average educational level for journalists compared with the general population: approximately 80 percent of German journalists have fulfilled the requirements for entering the university, two-thirds have at least begun university and one-third have a university degree (AfK, 1977: 33). These findings were confirmed by the present investigation. The extraordinarily great difference in levels of education between the German and British journalists is expressed in their view of themselves. Forty-two percent of the German journalists, as opposed to only 14 percent of the British journalists, categorize themselves as 'intellectuals'. The obligatory route via the provincial press in Great Britain may — as the Royal Commission suspected — contribute to the difference in levels of education between German and British journalists. The extent of the difference, however, suggests that in Great Britain journalism is a career which is less attractive to intellectuals to begin with or — to use a more objective definition — to persons with a higher level of education than in the Federal Republic.

The demographic differences indicate that there are different mechanisms of selection for the profession of journalism. We must distinguish between two processes of selection: selection by the profession, based on the application of its standards, rules of admission and recruitment mechanisms; and self-selection, which is essentially determined by the particular expectations of a career in journalism and by the specific motives of those concerned. What motivates the individual to choose a career in journalism? With the aid of factor analysis in both countries, the following attractive features of work in journalism were deduced as constituting the motivation for choosing a career in the field:[6]

— The *attraction of dealing with news*; this cluster of motives includes the variety of the profession as well as the chance to impart knowledge to others, to present the news.
— The excitement of the profession, the race against time.
—The professional freedom.
— *Self-expression, stimulating situations and opportunities for development*, resulting from meeting interesting people, pursuing one's interests, and the chance to work with language. In contrast to German journalists, British journalists also include contacts with interesting colleagues here.
— *The desire to have an influence.* In both countries this aspect includes criticizing abuses and publicizing grievances and the chance to influence political decisions. Among German journalists, these motives are related to the desire to have a broad forum for one's own convictions. Among British journalists — in contrast to their German colleagues — the chance to champion values and ideals and to impart knowledge are aspects of this desire to have an influence.
— *Material aspects* such as good pay and prospects for the future and *social prestige* constitute a separate cluster of motives *only* for German journalists.

Thus, the most important motives for German journalists are those relating to the need for self-expression and for developing one's potential as well as to the attraction of dealing with news and imparting information, followed by the motive of professional freedom. Limited importance is assigned to material motives and to social prestige. Among the majority of German journalists, the desire to have an influence is essentially limited to the urge to criticize abuses and publicize grievances, with only a minority listing the chance to express one's convictions or to directly influence political decisions as attractions of journalism as a career. The dominant motives for British journalists are those related to the excitement of the profession, such as working under time pressure, the eventful nature of the work and the attraction of dealing with news. Among British journalists the desire to have an influence is again expressed primarily by the urge to criticize abuses rather than by wanting to directly influence political decisions.

Since the individual factors in the motivation of German and British journalists in part show a different composition, the results are presented in Table 1, item by item, so as to facilitate a direct comparison. This direct comparison between German and British journalists shows that great differences exist in the importance attributed to the opportunity for self-expression and for development of one's potential, to imparting knowledge, to the eventful nature of the work, as well as to the potential for influencing society. British journalists much more frequently mention the exciting, eventful nature of the work as well as the appeal of working under time pressure as advantages of their profession. German journalists, on the other hand, more frequently name the chance to criticize and to express themselves. German journalists do, in fact, appreciate the eventful nature of their work; however, they essentially do not see themselves as passionate researchers who want to be the first to have the news and feel that they are constantly in a race against time. Only 20 percent of the German journalists, as opposed to 62 percent of the British journalists, like the quality of working under time pressure; only barely one out of three Germans as opposed to 55 percent of the British journalists finds the profession's lead in information appealing. German journalists, however, assign considerably more importance than their British colleagues to the chance to pursue their own interests further and to influence political decisions, as well as to the role of critic and to opportunities for self-expression. The differences support the thesis that British journalists concentrate more on the research phase than their German colleagues as well as the assumption that German journalists are more concerned with having an effect on society.

Older and younger journalists essentially view the attractions of the profession similarly, as the analysis by age groups again shows the homogeneity of this profession. Only two motives are mentioned in both countries significantly more often by younger journalists: the chance to criticize abuses and publicize grievances, and the opportunity to pursue one's own interests further. Only a time-series investigation can clarify whether the deviant responses of young

TABLE 1
Attractive Features of Journalism Identified by German and British Journalists

Question:
'What aspects of your present job do you particularly like? Please pick out all the cards that apply!'
(Presentation of cards)

Responses	German Journalists Total %	British Journalists Total %	Difference
The chance of uncovering and criticizing grievances	70	57	+ 13
The chance to express oneself	68	54	+ 14
The exciting, eventful nature of the job	64	70	− 6
The professional freedom to choose one's own tasks and subjects	64	59	+ 5
That one meets interesting people	55	56	− 1
The chance of imparting knowledge to others, to expand their horizon	46	60	− 14
The chance of championing values and ideas	42	44	− 2
The chance of pursuing one's interests further	38	25	+ 13
That there is so little routine	37	49	− 12
The chance of passing on my convictions to a lot of other people	34	—	—
To be among the first to know what's going on	32	55	− 23
The chance of influencing political decisions	29	18	+ 11
The interesting people one works with	22	42	− 20
Having to work under time pressure	20	62	− 42
Because it is fun to see one's name and work published .	17	27	− 10
Good pay and prospects	13	36	− 23
The high regard people have for journalists	2	6	− 4
The good prospects for the future	1	—	—
No answer	1	1	—

journalists indicate a change in professional motives and in their view of their role, a trend toward journalism with an increased interest in muckraking. The age correlation in the Federal Republic as well as in Great Britain tends to point to a difference by generations rather than to a long-term change in journalism.

There are also significant differences between British and German journalists in the view they take of their role, as is shown in Table 2. The study examined the degree of acceptance of channel roles among journalists, that is the extent to which the reporter sees himself or herself as a neutral reporter of events and a mirror of the public's thinking. Definite advocacy roles were also included in the study, specifically the roles of 'a spokesman for the underdog', 'a proponent of new ideas', 'a guardian of democracy', 'someone who exerts political influence', and 'someone who takes up grievances', as well as the roles of entertainer, instructor, and advisor.

The expectation was confirmed that channel roles meet with less acceptance from German journalists than from their British colleagues; German and British journalists differ more with respect to the mirroring function than in the view of their role as a neutral reporter of events. Interestingly, factor analyses show that the two channel roles — the neutral reporter of events and the mirror of the public's thinking — are viewed as part of one and the same dimension only by British journalists. In the responses of German journalists, however, the mirroring function is part of the same dimension as the view of oneself as 'a spokesman for the underdog', a helper and an advisor. This would indicate that German journalists not only accept this instrumental role of neutral reporter to a lesser extent than their British colleagues but that they also in part interpret it differently, as a really active role of advocacy.

Again in line with the hypotheses, the roles of criticizing abuses and of spokesman for the underdog, which stand for value judgments and advocacy, tend to be accepted by German journalists more than by their British colleagues. On the other hand, there is no significant difference in their view of the journalist's function as a guardian of the democratic system. When it comes to explicitly claiming a political influence, British journalists outdo their German colleagues, a finding which initially runs counter to expectations.

The greatest difference in the respective views of their roles taken by British and German journalists, initially comes as a surprise. It shows up in the claim to be an instructor or educator, a role included in the study as an aspect of opinion journalism, which is geared to having an effect. Only 16 percent of the German journalists make this claim in contrast to 74 percent of their British colleagues.

As Table 3 shows, by testing abstract descriptions of roles using concrete professional decision-making situations, it is possible to draw conclusions about how abstract concepts of roles are interpreted, for example the view of one's role as an 'instructor or educator' (Donsbach, 1982: 185). The apparent contradiction is resolved if the claim to act as an educator is not simply seen as representing a desire to provide guidance and, instead, the aspect of imparting knowledge is also taken into consideration.

The differences between German and British journalists in their acceptance of the educator role only fit in with the other findings of the study if we assume that imparting knowledge is the most important aspect of the claim to be an educator. In actual fact, there is a limited connection between the view of oneself as an educator and the inclination to educate and direct, both as regards British and German journalists. On the other hand, journalists in both countries who accept the role of an educator term the chance to impart knowledge and information an advantage of their profession far more frequently than their other colleagues. Thus the stronger emphasis on the educational role characterizing British journalists in fact fits into the overall view of British journalism as being oriented toward acquiring and imparting information.

TABLE 2
Perceptions among British and German Journalists of their Roles

Question:
'How do you view the job you do as a journalist? Please tell me whether you agree or disagree with the following descriptions. A journalist should see himself as. . .

Responses	German Journalists Total %	British Journalists Total %	Difference
Taking up grievances	95	76	+ 19
A neutral reporter of events	81	90	− 9
A guardian of democracy	79	82	− 3
A proponent of new ideas	72	76	− 4
A spokesman for the underdog	70	60	+ 10
Someone who advises and helps people	58	61	− 3
Someone who entertains the public	54	76	− 22
Mirroring what the public thinks	47	61	− 14
An instructor or educator	16	74	− 58
Someone who exerts political influence	12	24	− 12

TABLE 3

Interpretation of their Instructive Role by British and German Journalists

Question:

"Two journalists were sent by different editorial offices to attend the annual congress of a major political party. Both of them find the policy of this political party dangerous, but have different views on how to write their reports. Here you can read their comments. Which of them says what you also think?' (Presentation of an illustration)

Responses	German Journalists		British Journalists	
	Who See their Role as to Educate, Instruct %	Who do not See their Role as to Educate, Instruct %	Who See their Role as to Educate, Instruct %	Who do not See their Role as to Educate, Instruct %
'I regard this policy as dangerous. But in the account I write I shall simply report the discussions and decisions and leave my readers to see the danger for themselves'	32	33	69	77
'I regard this policy as dangerous too and in my account I shall select and emphasize the dangerous aspects. My readers should be in no doubt that I am giving them a warning'	54	51	23	17
Other answer	—	—	3	5
No opinion	14	16	5	1
Follow-up Survey:				
Number of journalists who named as an aspect of their job that they like: the chance of imparting knowledge to others, to expand their horizon	68	41	64	44

375

Despite differences in the way British and German journalists interpret their roles, the hypotheses are initially only confirmed in general terms; the extent to which abstractly formulated professional roles meet with acceptance, however, certainly does not allow for a strict distinction between British journalism, which is oriented toward channel roles, and German journalism, which is geared to advocacy. Instead, the way German and British journalists interpret their roles is a conglomerate of neutrality and advocacy. More than two-thirds of the journalists in both countries include the roles of a neutral reporter of events, a guardian of democracy, and a critic of abuses among their jobs. Neutral journalism and participant journalism are theoretical constructs, but it is almost exclusively mixed forms which exist in reality. This was the conclusion reached by Johnstone, Slawski and Bowman (1976: 120) when they tried to put American journalists into one of these categories: 'Despite the fact that neutral and participant values tend to be antithetical . . . it can be concluded that most newsmen do in fact hold patterns of beliefs which combine elements from each perspective.' In line with this, the view of their role taken by British and German journalists, rather than dividing them into supporters of a neutral role, on the one hand, and of a spokesperson's role, on the other, tends to show that there is greater emphasis on the spokesperson's role in German journalism.

Simultaneous support for the neutral role and the spokesperson's role does not permit us to reach any conclusions about the order in which they are ranked. The rank order of competing roles and norms is decided on a day-to-day basis, most clearly when there is a direct conflict between competing norms. While the level of acceptance of abstract roles appears to confirm the notion that German journalism barely shows traces of the traditional journalism of opinion and that it has essentially adjusted the British notion of the 'professionalized reporter', there are striking differences when everyday professional decisions are taken as indicators (Fabris, 1971: 360). As is shown in Table 4, faced with a situation where an extremist party is to be founded which would represent a threat to society, 90 percent of the German journalists consider it their job to fight this party, in constrast to only 53 percent of British journalists.

This view of the journalist's political role does not necessarily predetermine the strategy for fighting points of view that are thought to be wrong and dangerous. To the journalist who believes that facts, events and opinions speak for themselves, detailed reporting

TABLE 4
Interpretation of their Political Role by British and German Journalists

Question:
'Assuming an extreme political party was founded whose policy you thought
dangerous to society, would you consider it part of your job to oppose it?'

	German Journalists Total %	British Journalists Total %
Yes	90	53
No	10	47

Follow-up Question:
(put to journalists who consider it part of their job to oppose such a party): 'How do
you think this would best be done? By treating it according to news value, or by
reporting it to show your opposition or by refusing to give the party publicity?'

	German Journalists Total %	British Journalists Total %
Would best be done by —		
Reporting it and showing opposition	56	22
Treating it according to news value	29	59
Refusing to give publicity	11	9
Don't know	4	10

on the goals and activities of a political party thought to be
dangerous will represent a promising strategy for fighting it; to
others, this will merely seem a preliminary stage which needs to be
followed by criticism of the political party and by emphasis on the
threat it represents. The importance of publicity for the
dissemination of opinions and attitudes, finally, can make
withholding access to the media and remaining silent the only
effective strategy.

As Table 4 shows, British and German journalists who consider it
their job to oppose strongly points of view they consider wrong were
then asked which strategy was the most promising. The responses to
this follow-up question widen the gap between German and British
journalists, with the latter favouring the strategy of reporting strictly
'according to news value', neither very critically nor selectively. The

majority of German journalists, however, consider emphasizing the danger the most effective form of opposition.

In both countries, only a minority of journalists believes that keeping silent is a promising strategy. Whether journalists in this case basically consider the withholding of publicity to be a relatively useless means of fighting political positions or whether their opinion is premised on a free media system is an interesting question, though one which cannot be pursued in this investigation. The withholding of publicity is effective only as a unified or at least a widespread strategy, but not if it is only the isolated response of one journalist. The failure among journalists to take seriously the possible strategy of withholding access or publicity may thus result simply from the conviction that this is not really a promising strategy, given the media systems of the Federal Republic and Great Britain.

The question as to the most effective strategy was not directly related to the journalist's own practices on the job. Nonetheless, the responses indicate that German and British journalists tend to act differently. This disposition to act differently was then measured using a situational question, in order to determine how the journalist decides what kind of reporting to engage in. The setting was a party conference attended by two journalists as reporters; the two agree that the policy of this political party is dangerous, but they have different views on how to write their reports of the conference. The desire to describe the events in neutral fashion is contrasted with the determination to report in line with one's own perspective.

Journalists were given two options to choose from to respond to this situational question. The first, more impartial, option was: 'I regard this policy as dangerous. But in the account I write I shall simply report the discussions and decisions and leave my readers to see the dangers for themselves.' While 70 percent of British journalists agreed with this view, only 32 percent of their German colleagues agreed. Conversely, German journalists were more inclined to agree with the second, more committed option: 'I regard this policy as dangerous too, and in my account I shall select and emphasize the dangerous aspects. My readers should be in no doubt that I am giving them a warning.' Whereas 53 percent of German journalists agreed with this view, only 22 percent of British journalists chose this option. When these responses are broken down by age, a generation gap emerges among British journalists in contrast to their German colleagues. While both younger and older German journalists are equally inclined toward a more committed or partisan journalism, young British journalists are more definitely shaped by the neutral reporting model than their older colleagues. Among British journalists, a preference for the more neutral first option decreased with age: it was the preferred response of 77 percent under the age of 35, 67 percent between the ages of 35–44, and finally, 62 percent of those aged 45 and over.

The extraordinary differences between British and German journalists in their respective preferences for partisan and neutral reporting initially comes as a surprise, in view of the relatively similar interpretations of their professional role; in particular, this is inconsistent with the high percentage of German journalists who accept the role of a neutral reporter of events. The effect of this function is more limited for German journalists, however, having less influence on their decisions when there is a conflict between the claim of neutrality and the desire to take sides. These findings demonstrate the need to test the meaning of norms and roles using situational conflicts rather than just abstractly.

The concrete indicators provided by everyday decisions show that German and British journalists are part of a tradition, with a neutral role traditionally having greater importance in British journalism and a pronounced commitment to journalism-of-opinion characterizing German journalism. But what do these behaviour patterns imply when we consider how closely the reports received by readers, listeners and viewers in Great Britian and the Federal Republic approximate reality? Does this evidence mean that the British public is better and more completely informed?

The evidence from content analyses of German media reporting suggests that a definite selection of news based on the convictions of the selecting journalist takes place, that there is an indistinguishable mix of news and opinion and, in addition, that the news is selected and presented in a way which supports the editorial line discernible in the commentaries (see Noelle-Neumann and Kepplinger 1978: 51ff; and Schönbach, 1977). In order to compare the respective quality of British and German reporting, a comparative content analysis of the treatment of selected topics would be required. There has been a lack of such analyses to date,[7] and therefore these German findings can only be compared with independent British investigations dealing with a similar question. The Third Royal Commission on the Press concluded from a content analysis of reporting on three selected topics 'that the news coverage of the three selected subjects is highly factual in the sense of being both directly attributed and devoid of any overt bias. . .' (Royal Commission on the Press, 1977: para. 1071). This optimistic view of the success of efforts to be objective is contradicted by the case study of Halloran, Elliott and Murdock (1970), in which the media presentation of a demonstration against the Vietnam war is analysed in comparison with on-the-spot observation of the event (by participants). The study shows the extent to which the journalists' expectations shaped the coverage of the demonstration; when there was essentially no sign of the violence the journalists had expected, coverage by all the media focused on violent groups on the fringes of the demonstration, thus artificially making the 'reality' they were describing agree with their own expectations.

A stronger orientation towards the norm of objectivity cannot completely protect British journalism from 'self-censorship', or from being influenced by one's own perspective and knowledge. The goal of objectivity does not necessarily mean that reporting will be truer to reality and more complete if it is not accompanied by a recognition of the lack of impartiality in one's own work and if a high level of objectivity is taken for granted. It is Rothman's (1979: 349) view that in the Anglo-Saxon sphere the great importance placed on objectivity as a norm in journalism rests on this illusion, among others. The general acceptance of certain premises of *weltanschauung* has a long tradition, causing these assumptions to be taken for granted, particularly in the United States, and thus lending them an aura of unadulterated, unassailable truth. The consequence has been that the consciousness of the bias inherent in one's own observations and judgments has increasingly been lost sight of. Tunstall (1970) has also observed a highly uncritical relationship to objectivity, with hardly any doubt being cast on the assumptions that are made.

Conclusion

A final significant contrast between journalists in these two countries is presented by way of conclusion. British and German journalists differ greatly in their views on acceptable methods for obtaining information, as is shown in Table 5. It has already been noted that while German journalists focus on the processing and utilization of materials, British journalists focus on the research phase. This different emphasis placed on the different phases of work in journalism already showed up in their professional motives; the reactions of journalists to the conflict between the 'public's right to know' and the observation of ethical norms for research show the immense ambition of British journalists to get information — almost at any price. British journalists are marked by the conviction that the highest goal is satisfying the public's need for information, and that this by all means justifies the use of dishonest research methods. The overwhelming majority thinks that under some circumstances it is justified to gain inside information by becoming employed in a firm or organization or to badger unwilling informants to get a story, or to pay people for confidential information. The only thing the majority objected to was using a false identity; nonetheless, one out of three British journalists still consider this method acceptable. Investigations in the United States have shown that British and American journalists agree to a great extent in their willingness to disregard the norms of honest research methods (Gray and Wilhoit, 1983). The opinion of German journalists is completely different; the majority reject each of these methods and do not approve of them under any circumstance.

TABLE 5
Methods for Obtaining Information

Question:
'Journalists have to use various methods to get information. Given an important story, which of the following methods do you think may be justified on occasion and which would you not approve under any circumstances?'

Methods	German Journalists				British Journalists			
	Total %	18–34 %	35–44 %	45 + %	Total %	18–34 %	35–44 %	45 + %
Paying people for confidential information	25	39	23	16	69	74	75	56
Claiming to be somebody else	22	36	25	11	33	45	32	16
Badgering unwilling informants to get a story	8	15	9	4	72	78	75	60
Getting employed in a firm or organization to gain inside information	36	53	41	21	73	87	73	52

The preliminary hypotheses of the investigation have thus been confirmed with unexpected clarity: German and British journalists differ in their perception of their roles, their professional motivation and their evaluation of the norms connected with work in journalism. While British journalists see themselves as bloodhounds — as hunters of news — their German colleagues see themselves as missionaries.

Notes

1. An exception is provided by Brigitte Auth's master's thesis: 'Nationales Selbstbewusstsein in England und Deutschland: Eine Inhaltsanalyse der Sportberichterstattung beider Länder' (1983), University of Mainz.

2. The project funded by the Thyssen foundation was conducted by resarch groups at the Institut für Publizistik, Mainz and the Institut für Demoskopie Allensbach, directed by Professor Elisabeth Noelle-Neumann and at the Centre for Mass Communication Research, Leicester, directed by James Halloran.

3. For the details of the sampling design see Renate Köcher, 'Spürhund und Missionar: Eine vergleichende Untersuchung über Berufsethik und Aufgabenverständis britischer und deutscher Journalisten' (1985), dissertation, Munich.

4. On the different historical developments of freedom of the press see also: Frederick S. Siebert (1965) *Freedom of the Press in England 1476–1776*, 2nd ed. Urbana: University of Illinois Press; Kurt Koszyk (1966) *Deutsche Presse im 19. Jahrhundert: Geschichte der deutschen Press*. Berlin: Colloquium; and Martin Löffler (1969) *Kommentar zum Presserecht*, vol. 1, 2nd ed., Munich: C.H. Beck.

5. Percentage of subscription newspapers which are for the most part distributed locally/regionally as part of the total sales of daily newspapers in the Federal Republic. Walter Schütz (1983) 'Deutsche Tagespresse 1983', *Media Perspektiven*, 3: 190, 201. See also: *Bericht der Bundesregierung über die Lage von Presse und Rundfunk* (1978), 14.

6. An overview of the current status of motivation research was dispensed with since other writers have already treated this topic in detail. See Donsbach, *Legitimationsprobleme des Journalismus*, 111–130. The factors described in this study were produced by a cluster analysis of the items listed in Table 1.

7. A first step in this direction was made recently at the Institut für Publizistik of the University of Mainz with the master's thesis by Brigitte Auth: 'Nationales Selbstbewusstsein in England und Deutschland', op. cit.

References

Arbeitsgemeinschaft für Kommunikationsforschung (AfK) (1977) 'Journalismus als Beruf', internal research report, Munich.

Ascherson, Neal and Hans Wolfgang Wolter (1977) 'Journalistenausbildung in Grossbritannien', in Fischer, Heinz-Dietrich and Otto B. Roegele, *Ausbildung für Kommunikationsberufe in Europa, Journalismus* vol. 9. Düsseldorf: Droste.

Auth, Brigitte (1983) 'Nationales Selbstbewusstsein in England und Deutschland: Eine Inhaltsanalyse der Sportberichterstattung beider Länder', unpublished master's thesis, University of Mainz.

Bericht der Bundesregierung über die Lage von Presse und Rundfunk in der Bundesrepublik Deutschland (1978), print no. 8/2264 of the German Budestag, 8th legislative period.

Donsbach, Wolfgang (1982) *Legitimationsprobleme des Journalismus*. Frieburg and Munich: Alber.

Fabris, Hans Heinz (1971) 'Das Selbstbild des Kommunikators bei Tageszeitungen', *Publizistik*, 16: 357–68.

Gray, Richard G. and G. Cleveland Wilhoit (1983) 'Portrait of the US Journalist 1982–1983', Manuscript of lecture to American Society of Newspaper Editors, 9 May 1983.

Hale, O.J. (1964) *Publicity and Diplomacy, with Special Reference to England and Germany 1890–1914*, 2nd ed., Gloucester: Peter Smith.

Halloran, James D., Philip Elliott and Graham Murdock (1970) *Demonstrations and Communication: A Case Study*. Harmondsworth: Penguin Books Ltd.

Johnstone, John W.C., Edward J. Slawski and William W. Bowman (1976) *The News People*. Urbana, Chicago and London: University of Illinois Press.

Köcher, Renate (1985) 'Spürhund und Missionar: Eine vergleichende Untersuchung über Berufsethik und Aufgabenverständis britischer und deutscher Journalisten', dissertation, Munich.

Koszyk, Kurt (1966) *Deutsche Press im 19. Jarhhundert: Geschichte der deutschen Presse*, part 2, Berlin: Colloquium.

Löffler, Martin (1969) *Kommentar zum Presserecht*, vol. 1, 2nd ed. Munich: C.H. Beck.

Murphy, David (1976) *The Silent Watchdog: The Press in Local Politics*. London: Constable.

Noelle-Neumann, Elisabeth and Hans Mathias Kepplinger (1978) 'Journalistenmeinungen, Medieninhalte und Medienwirkungen', in *Publizistik aus Profession: Festschrift für Johannes Binkowski*, Journalismus vol. 12, Düsseldorf: Droste, pp. 41–68.

Report of the Commission on Privacy (1972) Cmnd. 5012, Paragraph 16, London: HMSO.

Report of the Committee on the Official Secrets Act (1972) Cmnd. 5104, Paragraph 25/26, London: HMSO.

Rothman, Stanley (1979) 'The Mass Media in Post-Industrial Society', pp. 346–499 in Seymour Martin Lipset (ed.), *The Third Century: America as a Post-Industrial Society*. Stanford: Hoover Institution Press.

Royal Commission on the Press (1977) *Final Report*, Cmnd. 6810, London: HMSO.

Schönbach, Klaus (1977) *Trennung von Nachricht und Meinung*. Freiburg and Munich: Alber.

Schütz, Walter (1983) 'Deutsche Tagespresse 1983', *Media Perspektiven*, 3: 181–203.

Siebert, Frederick Seaton (1965) *Freedom of the Press in England 1476–1776*, 2nd ed. Urbana: University of Illinois Press.

Siebert, Frederick Seaton, Theodore Peterson and Wilbur Schramm (1963) *Four Theories of the Press*. Urbana: University of Illinois Press.

Stammler, Dieter (1971) *Die Presse als soziale und verfassungsrechtliche Institution*. Berlin: Duncker and Humblot.

Tunstall, Jeremy (1970) *The Westminster Lobby Correspondents*, London: Routledge and Kegan Paul.

Weber, Max (1919) *Politik als Beruf*. Munich: Duncker and Humblot.

18

HOMICIDE AND BARGAINED JUSTICE
The Agenda-Setting Effect
of Crime News on Prosecutors

David Pritchard

THE EFFECT of publicity upon the adversary system of criminal justice has received an enormous amount of attention in recent years. The Supreme Court of the United States has addressed the fair trial/free press issue several times, and many social scientists have studied the effect of publicity on potential jurors (for reviews of the empirical research see Bush, 1970; Connors, 1975; Simon, 1977; Buddenbaum et al., 1981).

Generally overlooked in the fair trial/free press debate, however, is the fact that as many as 90 percent of all criminal convictions in the United States are the result of plea bargaining rather than full-blown adversary trials (Heumann, 1978; Brosi, 1979). The defendant admits guilt in return for some implicit or explicit concession from the prosecution. Because there is no jury, there is no chance that press coverage will prejudice the jury.

Nonetheless, it is possible that press coverage will taint the *process*. This study addresses that issue by examining the relationship between

Abstract This article reports the findings of research into the possibility that differences in newspaper coverage of individual criminal cases may influence the behavior of key justice-system officials with respect to those cases. The study analyzed police and court records regarding all people arrested for homicide over an 18-month period in Milwaukee County, Wisconsin. Newspaper coverage of those cases also was analyzed. The results suggest that the amount of space newspapers devote to a criminal case helps set the agenda of at least one class of public officials—prosecutors who must decide which criminal cases to plea-bargain, and which to take to trial.

David Pritchard is Assistant Professor at the Indiana University School of Journalism, Bloomington, Indiana 47405. An earlier version of this article was presented to the Annual Meeting of the Law and Society Association, San Diego, California, in June 1985. The author wishes to thank Professors William A. Hachten, Robert E. Drechsel, Sharon Dunwoody, and Stewart Macaulay for insightful comments on previous drafts.

From David Pritchard, "Homicide and Bargained Justice: The Agenda-Setting Effect of Crime News on Prosecutors," *Public Opinion Quarterly*, Vol. 50: 143-159 © 1986 by the American Association for Public Opinion Research. Published by The University of Chicago Press. Reprinted by permission.

newspaper coverage of individual cases and whether prosecutors engage in plea bargaining in those cases.

It is an important issue to consider, because the results of the consensual process epitomized by plea bargaining are quite different from those of the adversarial process epitomized by jury trials. For example, defendants found guilty by a jury are more likely to be sentenced to a period of incarceration, and can expect to receive substantially longer sentences than those whose cases are plea bargained, everything else being equal (Uhlman and Walker, 1980; Shane-DuBow et al., 1981; Brereton and Casper, 1982; Pruitt and Wilson, 1983).

Previous Work

Prosecutors are avid readers of newspaper stories about their cases, and most say that the news media are good indicators of the public image of the criminal justice system (Drechsel, 1983). So it is not entirely surprising that some prosecutors acknowledge that they take press coverage of a case into consideration in deciding whether to engage in plea negotiations.

For example, a study of plea bargaining in two California jurisdictions found that prosecutors and defense lawyers were less likely to agree in negotiations if a case had received news coverage (Utz, 1978). Surveys of prosecutors and public defenders in Cook County, Illinois, also suggested that a substantial number of prosecutors would not plea bargain in cases that had received news coverage (Jones, 1978). One Cook County prosecutor said: "I'd be crazy to bargain in any case that received a lot of news coverage. The public will demand justice, which means that I usually go to trial" (Jones, 1978:200). A Cook County public defender claimed that prosecutors refused to negotiate in publicized cases because they are "afraid of being considered soft on criminals" (Jones, 1978:202; see also Kaplan, 1965; Miller, 1970; and Eisenstein and Jacob, 1977).

Why might publicity make a prosecutor unwilling to plea bargain a case? Alschuler (1968) studied prosecutors in a dozen large American cities, and found that they were motivated more by what they perceived to be their self-interest than by considerations of justice or fairness for the defendant.

It is politically embarrassing for a prosecutor to consent to a light sentence for a serious offender, even as part of a plea agreement. It is usually easier, in fact, for a prosecutor to explain an acquittal than it is for him to explain a plea agreement in a publicized case; an acquittal can be attributed to the finder of fact. In routine cases, by contrast, there is little danger that sentencing will attract public attention. A prosecutor can maximize the political value of these cases by securing the maximum number of convictions, regardless of the price he pays in sentencing concessions (Alschuler, 1968:107).

In other words, prosecution is a political process, and prosecutors have a political stake in how their actions are perceived. Maintaining a public image as a crime-fighter is important to the prosecutor, perhaps to the extent of stressing adversary dispositions in publicized cases, regardless of the strength of evidence against the defendant. That way, if something "good" (like a conviction) happens, the prosecutor can take the credit. If something "bad" (like an acquittal or dismissal of charges) happens, the prosecutor can implicitly or explicitly shift the responsibility to the judge or to the jury. The result is that the blame is transferred (Newman, 1966; Galanter, 1983). Prosecutors may be especially likely to act this way in homicide cases (Alschuler, 1968).

In some cases, however, prosecutorial self-interest can lead to negotiations. This is most likely to happen when the prosecutor feels a need to get a conviction—any kind of conviction—despite weak evidence against the defendant. Alschuler writes: "Political considerations may, on occasion, make it important for a prosecutor to secure a conviction for a particular crime, and plea negotiations may provide the only practical means of achieving this objective" (Alschuler, 1968:109).

However, prosecutors' most common reaction to publicity, the existing research makes clear, is a desire to avoid being perceived as soft on criminals.

The notion that the press may influence prosecutorial decision making has clear parallels with the familiar agenda-setting hypothesis, which suggests that the relative prominence of an issue in the news media will influence how salient that issue is to members of the audience (McCombs and Shaw, 1972; McLeod et al., 1974; Becker et al., 1975; Shaw and McCombs, 1977).

Most agenda-setting research has focused on possible effects on ordinary citizens. Only a few studies have explicitly tested the hypothesis that the press may help set the agendas of public officials. Gormley (1975) found mixed evidence for an agenda-setting effect of newspapers on state legislators. Lambeth (1978) concluded that the press helped set energy policy makers' agendas. In a study notable for the fact that it used a direct, rather than a self-reported measure of public-official behavior, Gilberg et al. (1980) found that press content set the agenda for Jimmy Carter's 1978 State of the Union speech. Swank et al. (1982) suggested, but did not test, the hypothesis that newspapers contribute to the salience of crime on local political agendas. Cook et al. (1983) found that a televised investigative report changed the agenda not only of citizens but also of elected officials.

On the other hand, Walker (1977) concluded that for three safety-related issues, the agenda of the U.S. Senate set the agenda for the *New York Times*. And Protess et al. (1985) found that the only agenda affected by a newspaper investigative series was future press coverage of the subject of the series.

In addition to the agenda-setting literature, research into reporter-source interactions contains considerable speculation (and some anecdotal evidence) suggesting that journalists' decisions about which stories to play up can influence the behavior of public officials (see, e.g., Matthews, 1960; Cohen, 1963; Dunn, 1969; Sigal, 1973; Weiss, 1974; Miller, 1978; and Peters, 1980).

Despite these occasional forays, how the news media affect the behavior of public officials is an "inadequately researched area" (Rivers et al., 1975:223). Rivers et al. suggested that research should attempt to determine under what conditions publicity alters "personal and departmental resources in ways that affect the decision-making process" (1975:231).

Such research is especially important in the criminal justice area. Stanga noted that "the influence the press has, if any, on the prosecutor is a neglected area of inquiry" (1971:264). More recently, Buddenbaum et al. came to a similar conclusion, suggesting that "a study of the effects of pretrial publicity on the disposition of cases might also be useful, to establish how much influence pretrial publicity has on the way cases are handled and on the amount of time and money spent for similar cases that receive varying publicity" (1981:7).

The Context of the Study

This study focuses on prosecutors in the district attorney's office in Milwaukee County, Wisconsin. The basic business of prosecutorial organizations is prosecuting criminal cases. In Milwaukee, as elsewhere in the United States, such cases are processed primarily by plea bargaining, which serves the cause of conserving relatively scarce organizational resources (Brosi, 1979). At the same time, however, it is not a popular way of settling cases (Hearst Corporation, 1983). In Milwaukee, for example, less than a quarter of the population favors plea bargaining (Metropolitan Milwaukee Criminal Justice Council, 1980). In addition, one of the city's newspapers flatly opposes the practice (Wills, 1977), while the other is merely skeptical (Milwaukee Journal, 1981).

Although in theory defendants decide whether to plead guilty or to exercise their constitutional right to a jury trial, in practice the prosecutor generally controls whether a case is plea bargained (Blumberg, 1967; Alschuler, 1968; Casper, 1972; Alschuler, 1975; Heumann, 1978; Gifford, 1981; Gifford, 1983). On the one hand, limited resources compel prosecutors to use plea bargaining as the normal mode of settling criminal cases. On the other hand, the public's anger about crime suggests that the electorate may not respond warmly to a prosecutor who plea bargains a visible case.

Clearly, then, not all cases can go to full-blown adversarial trial (resource constraints), but some trials are necessary (the influence of public opinion).

This study hypothesizes that newspaper coverage of a criminal case influences whether prosecutors engage in plea bargaining in a given case, and that the more extensive the newspaper coverage of a case, the less likely the district attorney's office is to negotiate in the case.

Data

Data to test this study's hypothesis were extracted from police and court records and from news stories. Information was obtained on every nonvehicular homicide case presented to the district attorney's office for possible prosecution during the 18-month period between January 1, 1981 and June 30, 1982. The study focuses on homicides because lesser crimes seldom receive press coverage in a major metropolitan community like Milwaukee. Three homicides that had not been disposed of by May 31, 1983 were eliminated from the analysis. Prosecutors filed homicide charges against every suspect arrested for homicide during the study period. In all, the cases of 90 homicide defendants were included in this study.

To find out how the cases were processed, every publicly available document on each case was scrutinized. Included were the inmate registration log at the Milwaukee County Jail; case files at the office of the Milwaukee County Clerk of Courts, Felony Division, which contained copies of criminal complaints, autopsy reports and other pieces of documentary evidence, summaries (and sometimes transcripts) of hearings, and memos from the prosecution and defense; and all news items about the cases published by Milwaukee's daily newspapers, both owned by the Journal Company, which granted full access to its files of clippings. The editions of the morning *Sentinel* and the evening and Sunday *Journal* that circulate in Milwaukee County carried 744 staff-written items—news stories, editorials, and columns of staff opinion—about the homicides in this study.

Measures

The independent variable in this study is the level of newspaper interest in the defendant's case. The dependent variable is the behavior of the prosecutor's office with respect to the case.

LEVEL OF NEWSPAPER INTEREST IN A CASE

Conceptually, this variable is a function of the resources the newspaper organization is willing to devote to a case. Although newspapers have at their disposal several kinds of resources, the two that are most visible to outsiders like prosecutors are space in the paper and staff effort.

The amount of space a newspaper devotes to a case can be measured in a straightforward manner. The number of news items about a case is an interval-level variable. So is the number of paragraphs written about a case. This study divides total number of paragraphs by total number of stories to come up with a measure of the level of newspaper interest in the case: the average length of news items about the case, excluding editorials (which tend to be quite short) and excluding stories published after the prosecutor's discretionary period.

That discretionary period is defined as lasting from the date of the homicide until the mode of disposition was known, generally at the beginning of a trial or the acceptance of a guilty plea by a judge. Ending the discretionary period any earlier would skew the results of the analysis, because plea agreements can be—and in several cases were— made or unmade at the last minute. Cases that seem irrevocably headed toward adversary dispositions sometimes are negotiated on the eve of a scheduled trial. Similarly, defendants may accept plea bargains, but then change their minds at the hearing and refuse to plead guilty.

Average story length, rather than total number of stories or paragraphs, is used because average story length in theory is not a function of how long a case lingers in the felony disposition process. The total number of stories or paragraphs the press devotes to a case, on the other hand, can be more a function of how many pretrial hearings take place than of how interested the press is in the case.

Number of paragraphs, rather than number of column inches, is used to measure story length because varying column sizes in both newspapers made computing standardized column inches very difficult. Standardized column inches and number of paragraphs are highly correlated, however (Budd, 1964).

Both Milwaukee newspapers covered homicides similarly (Pritchard, 1985). For that reason, this study combines the newspapers' coverage to form a single variable: the average length of the stories the Milwaukee newspapers published about a defendant's case. Separate analyses were conducted for each newspaper's coverage, with results virtually identical to the result produced by the combined coverage variable.

The newspapers published no stories at all about 5 of the 90 homicide prosecutions in this study. Those cases are coded as having an average story length of 0.

The amount of newspaper staff effort devoted to a given case was measured by analyzing newspaper content. The typical piece of crime news comes directly from routine law enforcement or judicial sources, often documentary sources such as police blotters, jail logs, and criminal complaints (Stanga, 1971; Cohen, 1975; Sherizen, 1978; Drechsel et al., 1980). Reporters who cover police and court beats can gather such news with relatively little effort.

On some cases, however, reporters do more. They may use nonroutine sources such as witnesses to the crime, friends and relatives of the suspect and/or victim, or not-for-attribution comments from law enforcement officials. Editorials and staff-written columns of opinion also represent nonroutine kinds of coverage.

Accordingly, stories about homicide cases can be categorized either as "routine" (if only routine sources were used) or "nonroutine" (if at least one nonroutine source was used). Of the 744 news items in this study, 13.4 percent were nonroutine by this definition.[1] The variable created using the routine/nonroutine dichotomy is the proportion of nonroutine stories in the newspapers' coverage of a case.

This study did not attempt to determine whether predisposition coverage of individual cases was fair or accurate, however those terms might be defined. The independent variables attempt only to operationalize the level of press interest in a case, measured by the amount of organizational resources newspapers devoted to covering the case.

PROSECUTOR'S PLEA BARGAINING BEHAVIOR

Plea bargaining in this study is measured not by whether a case was settled consensually, but by whether the prosecutor actually engaged in plea negotiations. This "negotiated/did-not-negotiate" variable measures the prosecutor's actual behavior, not whether that behavior led

---

[1] All coding was done by the author. To test intercoder reliability, a colleague coded a 10 percent sample of the 744 news items. There was agreement on 96 percent of the items, resulting in a reliability coefficient (Scott's pi) of .85 (Scott, 1955).

to a consensual outcome. In theory, the negotiated/did-not-negotiate variable is untainted by the behavior of other actors in the criminal justice system. For example, although negotiations cannot succeed without the participation of the prosecutor, a willing prosecutor can be stymied by a defense lawyer or defendant unwilling to accept the prosecutor's terms. Such cases would be disposed of adversarially, but not because the prosecutor failed to negotiate.

Court records and/or news items contained explicit evidence that prosecutors engaged in negotiations in 45 of the 90 cases in this study. In 35 of the cases in which prosecutors negotiated, the result was a consensual settlement, in which the prosecutor and the defense agreed on the appropriate disposition of the case. In the remaining 10 cases, defendants refused plea bargains offered by prosecutors. Those cases either went to jury trial or were dismissed over the objection of the prosecution.

CONTROL VARIABLES

One of the most challenging tasks in a study of this nature is to hold constant factors that may affect both the independent and the dependent variables. In an attempt to achieve that goal, this study uses an extensive set of control variables. Much of the variation in crime seriousness, a factor that could influence both newspaper interest and prosecutors' plea bargaining behavior, is implicitly controlled by this study's exclusive focus on homicides.

Homicides themselves can vary in a number of ways, however, so additional control variables are used. They include personal attributes (race, age, and sex) of the homicide suspect and victim; whether the suspect and the victim knew each other; the suspect's prior record; the initial charge against the defendant (first-degree murder or a lesser homicide charge, such as manslaughter); whether the defendant was charged with crimes beyond the first homicide count; and the number of suspects alleged to have been involved in the homicide.

Some factors, such as the prominence of the homicide suspect and victim or the bizarreness of the incident, are difficult to quantify. In most cases, however, court records and news stories contain enough details of the incident and of the people involved in it to permit a qualitative evaluation of such aspects of the case.

Results

Discriminant analysis (Cohen and Cohen, 1975; Klecka, 1975) was used to test the hypothesis concerning the influence of newspaper coverage on plea bargaining behavior. The analysis supported the hy-

Table 1. Results of Discriminant Analysis, with Whether the Prosecution Negotiated as the Dependent Variable

Canonical correlation squared	.238
Improvement in ability to predict	53.3%
Relative contribution of significant discriminating variables:	
Average story length	34.8%
Suspect knew victim	26.9%
Prior record	19.5%
Initial charge	12.4%
Multiple charges	6.5%

pothesis: press behavior—specifically, the average length of stories about a case—was the strongest predictor of whether prosecutors engaged in negotiations. The proportion of stories about a case that relied partly or entirely on nonroutine sources, however, was not a significant predictor of negotiations.

Table 1 shows the results of the analysis. Of all the variables, five proved to be statistically significant (at $p = .05$) predictors: average story length (the shorter the average story, the more likely the prosecutor would negotiate); whether the defendant and the victim knew each other (negotiations were more likely if the defendant and victim had been acquainted); the defendant's prior record (negotiations were more likely if the defendant had no prior record); the seriousness of the initial charge (negotiations were more likely when charges were less serious); and whether the defendant faced multiple charges stemming from the incident (negotiations were more likely when there was only one charge).

The canonical correlation for the discriminant function is .4883, which means that the variables in the function account for 23.8 percent of the total variance in whether the prosecution engaged in plea negotiations. Average story length is the strongest predictor of prosecutorial behavior, contributing more than a third of the variance accounted for by the function, 34.8 percent, which is 8.3 percent of the entire variance.

Easier to understand, perhaps, is the fact that the discriminant function correctly predicts the prosecutor's negotiating behavior in 69 of the 90 cases (76.7 percent). Without the information contributed by the variables in the function, successful predictions could be made only half of the time. In other words, knowing the values of the variables in the function provides a 53.3 percent improvement in predictive ability over chance guessing. The function is statistically significant at the .0003 level.

Despite the statistically significant results of the quantitative analysis, the cases in which the discriminant function makes an incorrect prediction merit some attention. In 5 of those 21 cases, the discriminant function computes a case's probability of membership in a given category (negotiated or not negotiated) at more than 80 percent.[2]

There was no explicit evidence of negotiations in two of these extreme outlier cases (*Wisconsin* v. *Reynosa, Wisconsin* v. *Shelton*), despite circumstances in both—minimal press attention, previous relationship with victim, no prior criminal record, etc.—that strongly predict bargaining. Both cases went to trial, and both defendants were convicted.

The striking fact about the cases, however, is that both defendants may sincerely have believed they were innocent. Virginia Reynosa, for example, did not actually stab the person whose death led to her first-degree murder conviction; she merely urged her son on as he wielded the knife. In addition, there was some evidence of provocation on the part of the victim. The son was convicted of murder for the stabbing; the mother was convicted under a portion of Wisconsin law that makes parties to a crime as guilty as the actual perpetrators. The charges are legally equivalent, however, and in Wisconsin a first-degree murder conviction carries a mandatory life prison sentence.

Jessie Shelton said that she had been the victim of domestic violence, and shot her husband in self-defense. The prosecutor who took her to trial for manslaughter and the jury that convicted her may have been skeptical of that claim; Jessie Shelton weighed 290 pounds, and her husband was blind. The judge, however, was more sympathetic. Saying he found an element of self-defense in the shooting, he placed Shelton on five years' probation rather than sending her to prison.

Incidentally, Shelton's husband was the most prominent defendant or victim in this study. He owned a taxi company serving Milwaukee's black community, and he had been active in community affairs. A measure of his prominence is that he was the only defendant or victim who had been the subject of non-crime-related news coverage before the homicide. Despite that—and despite Jessie Shelton's potentially newsworthy claim that she killed her husband in self-defense—pretrial press coverage of the case was minimal (a total of three relatively short routine stories.)

At least from a social point of view, Reynosa and Shelton may have believed, rightly or wrongly, that they were innocent. If so, it is not surprising they would be unlikely to be receptive to negotiations that would lead to guilty pleas and prison terms, as almost always is the case when a homicide case is plea bargained.

---

[2] It should be noted, of course, that in 19 other cases the discriminant function's 80 percent-or-better predictions were correct.

In the other three extreme cases (*Wisconsin* v. *Fraser, Wisconsin* v. *Crosley,* and *Wisconsin* v. *Murray*), prosecutors engaged in negotiations despite circumstances—intense press attention, extensive prior criminal record, multiple charges stemming from the incident, etc.— that strongly predict no negotiations. All three homicides were fairly routine. The press attention to the cases resulted from chance occurrences unrelated to the nature of the crime or of the people involved in it.

The Fraser and Crosley cases were fairly typical inner-city homicides; both began with holdups at all-night gas stations and ended with the shooting of the gas station attendants. In each case, the prosecution bargained with the defendant because it needed his testimony against an accomplice.

Those evidence-related considerations apparently outweighed the influence of extensive press coverage in the cases. But the press focused on the cases for reasons having little to do with the crimes themselves. Fraser's lawyer, for example, asked the judge to bar the press and public from the courtroom. The request, a relatively unusual one in Wisconsin, and the judge's denial of it inspired some press attention. The newspapers also singled out the Fraser case for exceptional feature coverage. The robbery and shooting took place around midnight Saturday, too late for more than a one-paragraph story in the final edition of Sunday morning's *Journal.* That gave reporters all day Sunday to interview nonroutine sources for substantial stories that would be published on Monday, typically a "slow" news day because governmental beats rarely generate news on Sunday.

In addition, five months after the incident, the *Journal* interviewed friends and family of the victim, and published a 51-paragraph Sunday feature titled "Last Day of Work—and Life." Before the suspects were arrested, the victim's family received a series of terrifying telephone calls. The *Journal* ran an 18-paragraph story ("Chilling Calls Taunted Victim's Kin").

In short, Fraser's crime was fairly routine; the coverage of it was not. It is a case that may have been plea bargained only because prosecutors had evidence problems that forced them to seek Fraser's agreement to testify against his accomplice.

The prosecution offered a similar bargain to Sylvania Crosley, charged with first-degree murder and armed robbery in connection with a crime similar to Fraser's. Crosley's crime took place in 1976, but no arrests were made until 1981, when an informant told police who had done it. By that time Crosley was in prison on unrelated charges; without his testimony, his alleged accomplice would go free.

Crosley initially agreed to the deal. But when it was time for him to testify, he refused and charges against his alleged accomplice in the gas-station holdup had to be dismissed. Defendants who renege on deals make prosecutors and judges unhappy. Crosley was convicted at trial of first-degree murder and armed robbery, and the judge imposed the maximum sentence—life plus 20 years.

Crosley's crime, like Fraser's, was fairly routine. The press coverage was routine, too, until allegations were made that money had been paid to Crosley's lawyer to buy Crosley's silence. The possibility of corruption sparked a 50-paragraph *Sentinel* story, "Probe of Payment to Lawyer Urged," and a 15-paragraph story a week later noting that authorities were probing ("Allegations on Payment of Lawyer's Fees Probed"). No other stories about the case were as many as 10 paragraphs long.

The final case that was negotiated despite intense press coverage stemmed from a tavern shooting that was routine in all but one respect—a group of Milwaukee *Sentinel* staffers was at the bar when the shooting started. Two of the journalists were seriously injured by stray bullets.

Because of weak and contradictory evidence, no arrests were made for more than a year after the shooting. Before any arrests were made, the *Sentinel* gave the case extensive publicity, including two lengthy first-person stories by one of the journalists who had been wounded. Other unusual stories during that period included a 63-paragraph story detailing victims' and witnesses' disappointment with the police department's failure to make arrests in the case and a 33-paragraph feature about the widow of the man who was killed in the shooting.

Fifteen months after the homicide, two suspects were arrested. The evidence was so weak that charges against one were dismissed outright. The other defendant, Regan Murray, faced first-degree murder and four nonhomicide charges, but agreed to plead guilty to reduced charges.

Why were the charges reduced when publicity had been so extensive? The available evidence gives no definite answer to that question, but it appears likely that the prosecution realized that the shaky evidence made conviction at trial problematic. The public pressure from the *Sentinel* made some kind of conviction imperative: thus the negotiations (Alschuler, 1968).

Discussion

This study's findings suggest that newspapers help set the plea bargaining agendas of Milwaukee prosecutors, at least in homicide cases. The amount of space newspapers were willing to devote to the typical story about a case was a stronger predictor than any other variable in this study of whether the prosecutor would negotiate.

This research found evidence suggesting an agenda-setting effect of ordinary crime news, the kind produced day in and day out by beat reporters. Recent studies from Northwestern University's Center for Urban Affairs and Policy Research, on the other hand, have examined possible agenda-setting effects only of investigative news reports (Cook et al., 1983; Protess et al., 1985).

In addition, this study did not use self-reported data. Most other research in this area has relied on public officials' own estimations of whether they have been influenced by the media (Gormley, 1975; Lambeth, 1978; Cook et al., 1983; Protess et al., 1985). Virtually all the measures of prosecutorial behavior used in this study, however, came directly from court records. The data came from cases that were already completed, ensuring that the participants were not aware that their behavior would become part of a research project. In addition, the data were recorded by court employees as part of the normal routine of the criminal courts, with no hint that the data would provide the raw material for an academic study. Unless the raw data contain a systematic bias that is not immediately apparent, they are unobtrusive measures (Webb, et al., 1966), unlike the self-reported data used as dependent measures in much of the research into the possibility that the news media may set the agenda for public officials.

That said, it must be acknowledged that documentary records are far from perfect. The facts of certain cases, such as the Reynosa and Shelton cases, strongly imply that the prosecution offered a deal that was turned down, despite the fact that court records and newspaper coverage contain no explicit evidence of negotiations.

Similarly, the examination of the five "outlier" cases revealed that the strength of evidence against a defendant (or a defendant's accomplice) could influence whether the prosecution negotiated a case. Evidence strength was not included as a quantitative variable in this study because it is extremely difficult to measure in any systematic way (Eisenstein and Jacob, 1977:182–183). In addition, evidence strength may well be a socially defined construct greatly dependent upon attributes of the relationships between the prosecutor and the defense lawyer, and between the defense lawyer and the defendant.

Finally, it is difficult to predict what effect a strength-of-evidence variable would have on plea bargaining. If evidence is weak, the prosecutor has an incentive not only to negotiate but to offer a good deal. If the evidence is strong, however, the defendant has an incentive to plead guilty even if not offered a good deal to avoid the so-called trial penalty (Uhlman and Walker, 1980; Shane-DuBow et al., 1981; Brereton and Casper, 1982; Pruitt and Wilson, 1983). Guilty pleas in cases where there is no evidence of negotiations often are implicit plea bargains (Heumann, 1978).

Related to the issue of evidence strength are questions involving the content of negotiations. Do prosecutors offer the same bargains to all similarly situated defendants, or does the defendant's race, how his or her case was covered, or other factors influence the content of the actual negotiations? This study did not have access to information about the offers and counter-offers that are a normal part of negotiations, but researchers should attempt to gain access to such information (see, e.g. Maynard, 1984).

Future research should also examine in detail the extent to which prosecutors (or other law-enforcement personnel) influence newspapers' decisions about which cases to cover and how to cover them (see, e.g., Drechsel, 1983). This study found no evidence of such an influence, but then court records and news coverage are not the best places to look for such an effect. Researchers need to get into newsrooms, prosecutors' offices, courthouse hallways, and courtrooms to find the answers to such questions.

This study focused on a narrow class of public officials—prosecutors handling homicide cases—in one community. As such, it offers no conclusions about whether the press sets the agenda for public officials in other situations and other places. Ideally, future studies will address such issues.

References

Alschuler, A.
  1968 "The prosecutor's role in plea bargaining." University of Chicago Law Review 36:50–112.
  1975 "The defense attorney's role in plea bargaining." Yale Law Journal 84:1179–1314.
Becker, L. B., M. E. McCombs, and J. M. McLeod
  1975 "The development of political cognitions." In S. H. Chaffee, ed., Political Communication: Issues and Strategies for Research. Beverly Hills, Calif.: Sage Publications.
Blumberg, A.
  1967 Criminal Justice. Chicago: Quadrangle Books.
Brereton, D. and J. D. Casper
  1982 "Does it pay to plead guilty? Differential sentencing and the functioning of criminal courts." Law & Society Review 16:45–70.
Brosi, K. B.
  1979 A Cross-City Comparison of Felony Case Processing. Washington, D.C.: U.S. Department of Justice.
Budd, R.
  1964 "Attention score: a device for measuring news 'play'." Journalism Quarterly 41:259–262.

Buddenbaum, J. M., D. H. Weaver, R. L. Holsinger, and C. J. Brown
    1981   Pretrial Publicity and Juries: A Review of Research. Bloomington, Ind.: Indiana
           University School of Journalism.
Bush, C. R.
    1970   Free Press and Fair Trial: Some Dimensions of the Problem. Athens, Ga.:
           University of Georgia Press.
Casper, J.
    1972   American Criminal Justice: The Defendant's Perspective. Englewood Cliffs,
           N.J.: Prentice-Hall.
Cohen, B. C.
    1963   The Press and Foreign Policy. Princeton, N.J.: Princeton University Press.
Cohen, J., and P. Cohen
    1975   Applied Multiple Regression/Correlation Analysis for the Behavioral Sciences.
           New York: John Wiley & Sons.
Cohen, S.
    1975   "A comparison of crime coverage in Detroit and Atlanta newspapers." Jour-
           nalism Quarterly 52:726–730.
Connors, M. M.
    1975   "Prejudicial publicity: an assessment." Journalism Monographs 41.
Cook, F. L., et al.
    1983   "Media and agenda setting: effects on the public, interest group leaders, policy
           makers, and policy." Public Opinion Quarterly 47:16–35.
Drechsel, R. E.
    1983   News Making in the Trial Courts. New York: Longman.
Drechsel, R. E., K. Netteburg, and B. Aborisade
    1980   "Community size and newspaper reporting of local courts." Journalism
           Quarterly 57:71–78.
Dunn, D.
    1969   Public Officials and the Press. Reading, Mass.: Addison-Wesley.
Eisenstein, J., and H. Jacob
    1977   Felony Justice: An Organizational Analysis of Criminal Courts. Boston: Little,
           Brown and Co.
Galanter, M.
    1983   "Reading the landscape of disputes: what we know and don't know (and
           think we know) about our allegedly contentious and litigious society." UCLA
           Law Review 31:4–71.
Gifford, D. G.
    1981   "Equal protection and the prosecutor's charging decision: enforcing an ideal."
           George Washington Law Review 49:659–719.
    1983   "Meaningful reform of plea bargaining: control of prosecutorial discretion."
           University of Illinois Law Review 1983:37–98.
Gilberg, S., C. Eyal, M. McCombs, and D. Nicholas
    1980   "The State of the Union Address and the press agenda." Journalism Quarterly
           57:584–588.
Gormley, W. T., Jr.
    1975   "Newspaper agendas and political elites." Journalism Quarterly 52:304–308.
Hearst Corporation
    1983   The American Public, the Media & the Judicial System: A National Survey on
           Public Awareness and Personal Experience. New York: The Hearst Cor-
           poration.
Heumann, M.
    1978   Plea Bargaining: The Experiences of Prosecutors, Judges, and Defense Attor-
           neys. Chicago: University of Chicago Press.
Jones, J. B.
    1978   "Prosecutors and the disposition of criminal cases: an analysis of plea bargain-
           ing rates." Journal of Criminal Law & Criminology 69:402–412.

Kaplan, J.
1965 "The prosecutorial discretion—a comment." Northwestern University Law Review 60:174–193.
Klecka, W. R.
1975 "Discriminant analysis." In Nie, N., et al. Statistical Package for the Social Sciences, second ed. New York: McGraw-Hill.
Lambeth, E. B.
1978 "Perceived influence of the press on energy policy making." Journalism Quarterly 55:11–18, 72.
Matthews, D. R.
1960 U.S. Senators and Their World. Chapel Hill: University of North Carolina Press.
Maynard, D. W.
1984 "The structure of discourse in misdemeanor plea bargaining." Law & Society Review 18:75–104.
McCombs, M., and D. L. Shaw
1972 "The agenda-setting function of mass media." Public Opinion Quarterly 36:176–187.
McLeod, J. M., L. B. Becker, and J. E. Byrnes
1974 "Another look at the agenda-setting function of the press." Communication Research 1:131–166.
Metropolitan Milwaukee Criminal Justice Council
1980 Public Opinion Survey 600.
Miller, F. W.
1970 Prosecution: The Decision to Charge a Suspect with a Crime. Boston: Little, Brown and Co.
Miller, S.
1978 "Reporters and congressmen: living in symbiosis." Journalism Monographs 53.
Milwaukee Journal
1981 "A deeper look at plea bargains." Editorial, January 11.
Newman, D. J.
1966 Conviction: The Determination of Guilt or Innocence Without Trial. Boston: Little, Brown and Co.
Peters, C.
1980 How Washington Really Works. Reading, Mass.: Addison-Wesley.
Pritchard, D.
1985 "Race, homicide and newspapers." Journalism Quarterly 62:500–7.
Protess, D. L., D. R. Leff, S. C. Brooks, and M. T. Gordon
1985 "Uncovering rape: the watchdog press and the limits of agenda setting." Public Opinion Quarterly 49:19–37.
Pruitt, C. R., and J. Q. Wilson
1983 "A longitudinal study of the effect of race on sentencing." Law & Society Review 17:613–635.
Rivers, W. L., S. Miller, and O. Grady
1975 "Government and the media." In S. H. Chaffee, ed., Political Communication: Issues and Strategies for Research. Beverly Hills, Calif.: Sage Publications.
Scott, W. A.
1955 "Reliability of content analysis: the case of nominal scale coding." Public Opinion Quarterly 19:321–325.
Shane-DuBow, S., et al.
1981 Wisconsin Felony Sentencing Guidelines: Phase I of Research and Development. Madison: Wisconsin Center for Public Policy.
Shaw, D. L., and M. E. McCombs
1977 The Emergence of American Political Issues: The Agenda-Setting Function of the Press. St. Paul: West Publishing.

Sherizen, S.
  1978   "Social creation of crime news: all the news fitted to print." In C. Winick, ed.,
         Deviance and Mass Media. Beverly Hills, Calif.: Sage Publications.
Sigal, L. V.
  1973   Reporters and Officials: The Organization and Politics of Newsmaking. Lexing-
         ton, Mass.: D. C. Heath.
Simon, R.
  1977   "Does the court's decision in Nebraska Press Association fit the research evi-
         dence on the impact on jurors of news coverage?" Stanford Law Review
         29:515–528.
Stanga, J. E.
  1971   "The press and the criminal defendant: newsmen and criminal justice in three
         Wisconsin cities." Unpublished Ph.D. dissertation, University of Wisconsin.
Swank, D. H., H. Jacob, and J. Moran
  1982   "Newspaper attentiveness to crime." In H. Jacob and R. L. Lineberry, eds.,
         Governmental Responses to Crime: Crime on Urban Agendas. Washington,
         D.C.: National Institute of Justice.
Uhlman, T. M., and N. D. Walker
  1980   " 'He takes some of my time, I take some of his': an analysis of sentencing
         patterns in jury cases." Law & Society Review 14:323–341.
Utz, P. J.
  1976   Settling the Facts: Discretion and Negotiation in Criminal Court. Lexington,
         Mass.: Lexington Books.
Walker, J.
  1977   "Setting the agenda in the U.S. Senate: a theory of problem selection." British
         Journal of Political Science 7:423–445.
Webb, E. J., D. T. Campbell, R. D. Schwartz, and L. Sechrest
  1966   Unobtrusive Measures: Nonreactive Research in the Social Sciences. Chicago:
         Rand McNally & Co.
Weiss, C. H.
  1974   "What America's leaders read." Public Opinion Quarterly 38:1–22.
Wills, R. H.
  1977   Milwaukee Sentinel Editorial Policy.

PART V

ASPECTS OF MEDIA EFFECTS

INTRODUCTION: COMMUNICATION EFFECTS AND THE TWO CULTURES OF COMMUNICATION RESEARCH

Edward L. Fink

> Literary intellectuals at one pole . . . at the other scientists. . . . Between the two a gulf of mutual incomprehension—sometimes (particularly among the young) hostility and dislike, but most of all lack of understanding [C. P. Snow, *The Two Cultures: And a Second Look* (pp. 11-12). New York: Mentor, 1963].

Communication effects involve the interplay of human sensory and cognitive capacities, the sociological networks in which individuals are embedded, and the cultural apparatus for structuring, producing, and receiving information. There are two broad traditions in research on these effects, each with its own practitioners. On the one hand, there are those who title themselves "scientists." On the other hand, there are those for whom the notion of a social scientist is an oxymoron. C. P. Snow refers to this latter group (at least the literary among them) as intellectuals, since "while no one was looking [they] took to referring to themselves as 'intellectuals,' as though there were no others." Consistent with C. P. Snow's usage, we will refer to the nonscientists in communication as "intellectuals," with the understanding that this designation is merely a convenience.

In this section of the *MCRY*, we have examples of both cultural traditions, the scientific and the intellectual. It is revealing to see how each poses the question of communication effects. The two cultures can be distinguished not only in what they study, but also in how they choose to study it. Let us first examine the "ideal type" of each mode of inquiry.

The "scientific" mode of research poses questions that appear outside of history: The issues concern human capacities and fundamental processes that should (if the scientific theory is correct) be panhuman. Such theories are deterministic, even if their authors acknowledge the incompleteness of the current instantiation of their theories. Few variables are likely to be employed in a given investigation, and the causal structure of such a theory is acknowledged to be, in principle, simple. The experiment is the desired research design, and other designs are evaluated as good to the extent that they approximate the experimental model. Within this mode of investigation, there is likely to be explicit testing of a priori hypotheses using statistically based decision rules. (This last idea is embodied in communication research, even though it is not an essential aspect in many other scientific quarters.) The preferred mode of expressing theoretical relations in this mode is as mathematical equations.

The researcher from the "intellectual" culture of communication research sees the research enterprise as revealing the workings of history and culture. To this school, most knowledge is historically and culturally specific, including, to a great extent, the metaknowledge that parades as universal knowledge—the "laws" pronounced by the scientist. The idea that people are interpreters of and participants in their worlds is used to argue against any simple determinism. Thus, when those of this school engage in empirical research, many variables are likely to be employed. Since the social context is what provides meaning to the individual or group being investigated, investigators in this school are likely to study people in their natural habitats (as *homines socialia animalia*) and rely heavily on the artifacts created by their culture. Thus surveys, observation, and content analysis are the preferred data-gathering techniques. Theoretical statements here posit complex causal structures, which are likely to be presented in verbal form with an eye toward nuance and qualification.

The distinction made here is not the one commonly made between quantitative versus qualitative research. A highly quantitative study that describes a given historical or cultural period may not have, as a goal, laws or general theories of human behavior (see, e.g., R. W. Fogel and S. L. Engerman, *Time on the Cross*. Boston: Little, Brown, 1974). In this *MCRY*, note that the paper by Robinson and Levy, while quantitative, fits into the intellectual mode. On the other hand, a nonquantitative work may indeed form the basis of scientific analysis, as, for example, is true of much of Simmel's work (e.g., *Conflict and the Web of Group-Affiliations*. Glencoe: Free Press, 1955). In this section, the paper by Hawkins and Pingree, while not quantitative, presents a typology of variables which serves to place research on media effects in a scientific framework.

The study of media effects reflects both cultures. In the first part of this section ("Cognitive Effects"), the emphasis is clearly on what I have labeled the scientific. Thorson, Reeves, and Schleuder examine how cognitive capacity is affected by the number of channels to which the individual attends, and the complexity of the information provided by each channel; the research is experimental. Finn reports how the predictability of a text, in both its semantic and syntactic aspects, affects the enjoyment obtained from the text; his is a correlational study based on information-theoretic measures. Hawkins and Pingree present a typology of cognitive activity and cognitive effort variables, which, they argue, is useful for studying media effects on children. While they treat the receiver as an active constructor of meaning, they assume that "prediction is still possible." Finally, the study by Smith, Anderson, and Fischer looks at the development of children's ability to understand montage (camera techniques and editing manipulations presented in film and television). They show that the interpretive skills of young children evolve systematically, and that these skills are more highly developed than was previously believed. If we are concerned with how individuals come to understand their world, including the world provided by media, this careful investigation shows how a program of research on children can be an important beginning.

The second part of the section on media effects ("Audience Decodings") presents pieces that, to varying extents, are closer to the "intellectual" pole of research. The first, by Liebes and Katz, looks at the cultural influences that affect the "reading" of the TV drama "Dallas." The authors find that viewers with a more modern ("Western") orientation seem to employ interpretive mechanisms which distance themselves from the didactic or moralistic implications of the program.

Sigman and Fry's study in this section is similar to that of Liebes and Katz; in both, the media are considered to provide information and context for events which must be interpreted. Sigman and Fry demonstrate that both the provision of information (encoding) and its interpretation (decoding) are ideological acts, which rely on subtle and not-so-subtle linguistic practices.

Robinson and Levy, in the last article in this section, show that the comprehension of news correlates with the extent to which audience members talk about the news. Comprehension is indicated by the *correspondence* of two reports of the "facts": those provided by the decoders (the audience members) with those provided by the encoders (the media producers). While conversations about the news could result in views antithetical to those provided by Big Media, in fact, such conversations tend to enhance the media's message.

The seven articles in this section have been described as representative of the scientific and intellectual cultures. The authors of these articles may disagree with my characterization of their articles (even keeping in mind my special use of these terms). In fact, since many attributes differentiate these two approaches, none of these studies may be considered a pure exemplar of either.

As we study these articles, it is not clear whether we should rejoice at the pluralism they celebrate, or be dismayed at the lack of coherence of approach that they exhibit. In our field (and in this volume), we tend to value such heterogeneity, without carefully considering the consequences of this view. The norm is to suggest that we all benefit from the interaction of disparate views and a multiplicity of methods. Unlike Carey (this volume), I suggest that we consider the contrary idea, that such a collection of voices may result in a disruptive cacophony rather than a constructive harmony. Why might this be the case?

The division of communication research into two camps implies that the goals, as well as the means, of the two camps are different. Often a single article attempts to combine the two cultures in a product which fails to be good scholarship of either sort. To applaud diversity all too often fails to recognize this fact. Employing scientific trappings for "intellectual" work may mean ignoring the idiosyncratic, which should be at the heart of idiegraphic research. Employing "intellectual" tools to do "scientific" work may mean choosing a level of analysis which is inappropriate: We may attempt to do "science" using variables and relations which are, even at first blush, obviously culturally specific. It is one thing to be informed by scholarship different from one's own, and quite another to confuse these two cultures in a given work. If we recognize the great divide between the two types of scholarship, perhaps we can understand how to focus our research, and then base our research on a careful consideration of our research goals. Rather than celebrating diversity, the best that can be said is that we must be cognizant of the different assumptions and biases of our schools of research; this should be done before we can appreciate the contributions of the research itself.

19

MESSAGE COMPLEXITY AND
ATTENTION TO TELEVISION

Esther Thorson, Byron Reeves, and Joan Schleuder

Three experiments investigated the processing costs of watching television messages. Processing costs were indexed with a secondary task reaction time measure in which subjects were asked to pay attention to commercial messages while responding with button presses to randomly occurring tones or flashes. Response time to the secondary tasks was used as a measure of attention to the primary task (watching the messages). Audio and video complexity of the messages were within-subject variables, and the channels presented to subjects (audio-only, video-only, or both) was a between-subjects variable. Results indicated that: (1) for a tone secondary task, multiple-channel presentations demanded more capacity than single-channel presentations (video or audio channel only); (2) more capacity was required to process simple video and auditory information than complex information; and (3) complexity of information in an absent channel (e.g., visual information in the audio-only condition) produced the same slowed reaction times as those occurring when the channel was present.

Viewing television requires mental effort. Presumably, the expenditure of effort is controlled by discretionary processing strategies of viewers and by fixed properties of the stimulus. We watch what we want, but some messages are more compelling than others. Surprisingly little is known, however, about *how* difficult

AUTHORS' NOTE: *This article was presented as a paper at the Mass Communication Division of the 1985 International Communication Association Annual Meeting, Honolulu, Hawaii, May 23-26. The authors thank Brian Deith, Noreen Salzman, Nancy Jursik, and Alison Hodges for their aid in testing subjects.*

television is to process and about how processing changes as a function of the complexity of televised information.

This article discusses the psychological "cost" of viewing television. Two main questions are addressed: (1) Do the video and audio channels of television require equal processing capacity? and (2) Does increased complexity in one channel affect processing of the other? Additionally, the article introduces a measure of covert mental processing that does not depend on self-reports by viewers or inferences made from the ability to recall content.

Attention to television has been defined traditionally as the *selection* of programs—news, public affairs, comedy, violence, action-adventure—and the measures of selection have usually been questions about which programs people watched. Attempts to study processing *during* television watching have usually relied on viewer's ability to recall messages. This has been true for child audiences (Anderson and Levin, 1976; Lesser, 1974; Welch and Watt, 1982; Alwitt, Anderson, Lorch, and Levin, 1980; Anderson, Lorch, Field, and Sanders, 1981), and for adults viewing news (Chaffee and Choe, 1980), advertising (Calder and Sternthal, 1980; Madden and Weinberger, 1982), entertainment and special programs (Greenberg and Gantz, 1976; Howard, Rothbart, and Sloan, 1978), and political debates (McLeod, Durall, Ziemke, and Bybee, 1979; Miller and MacKuen, 1979; Carter, 1962).

Although postviewing recall measures can indicate comprehension, the information provided about moment-to-moment processing is limited. For example, questions about complexity in one channel interfering with processing in the other depend on finding less accurate recall in one channel after viewing. This information can indicate between-channel effects but cannot be used to identify the locus of the effect. Understanding, attending, remembering, and other processes could be involved.

In fact, few television studies have compared audio and video effects. Of those that have, most have relied on post-viewing performance measures (Hartman, 1961; Hsia, 1971; Borton, Belasco, and Echewa, 1974; Nasser and McEwen, 1976). The research on children's processing of television, however, has analyzed processing and learning from the individual audio and video channels (Pezdek, 1977, 1978, 1980a, 1980b; Hayes and Birnbaum, 1980; Watkins, Calvert, Huston-Stein, and Wright, 1980; Hayes, Chemelski, and Birnbaum, 1981; Duncan, Whitney, and Rinnen, 1982). These studies have gone beyond dependence on performance criteria and have used measures of attention during watching. Visual orientation ("eyes on screen") has been used to examine audio and video elements and their effect on children's understanding and recall (Huston, Wright, Wartella, Rice, Watkins, Campbell, and Potts, 1981; Krull, 1983; Watt and Welch, 1983). There are few adult studies with analogous measures (see Webb and Ray, 1979, for an exception) probably because this type of assessment of overt orientation would tell us little about the *processing* of televised messages. Measuring processing has been a formidable undertaking.

Although television research has not been concerned with adult ongoing processing of television, psychological research on attention has seen extensive development in the last thirty years, and a number of these experimental paradigms for studying attention have been suggested for television (see Reeves, Thorson, and Schleuder, forthcoming, for a brief review relevant to communication research). One of those paradigms, the reaction time secondary task procedure, was adopted in this research. This technique relies on psychological assumptions about processing capacity.

PSYCHOLOGICAL THEORIES OF PROCESSING CAPACITY

Undoubtedly, the most basic attribute of mental capacity is that it is limited (Broadbent, 1958). In an integrative review of the area, Posner (1982) suggested that limited capacity can be characterized by four specific ideas that are consistent with all major theories and measures of processing capacity. First, processing takes time. Even split-second differences represent significant elements of thinking. Second, many processing tasks are processed successively and the amount of interference one produces for another can be used as a measure of processing demands. Third, processing in the nervous system involves both facilitation and inhibition between levels of the system. Fourth, attentional processing favors stimulus change. These four notions suggest that processing capacity can be studied by pitting different tasks of known difficulty against each other and observing the costs, in time required, of combining them. A popular experimental procedure used since the late 1800s (Welch, 1898) for combining tasks is the reaction time secondary task. Here, subjects must perform a primary task quickly and accurately. At randomly occurring times, a second task is signaled and a response is required.

An everyday example of how the secondary task affects attention would be driving and periodically answering questions posed by a passenger. It is more difficult to answer the questions (a secondary task) when heavy traffic demands more attention to driving (the primary task). In an experimental example, a subject would be asked to keep a pointer on top of a moving spot (primary task) and also press a reaction time key in response to a periodic tone (secondary task). In any secondary task paradigm, it is critical to guarantee that the primary task remains primary in spite of the presence of the secondary task. This is accomplished by requiring that subjects retain high performance accuracy on the primary task.

Many recent elaborated models have suggested that capacity is not homogeneous, but rather depends on the type of tasks involved (Navon and Gopher, 1979, 1980). It has also been suggested that some processing is accomplished automatically, without cost to the primary task (Shiffrin and Schneider, 1977; Kahneman and Treisman, 1983). In general, the research on processing capacity using the secondary-task method suggests that people have a collection of processing resources that can be flexibly applied depending upon the tasks. It also suggests that subject variables, such as arousal level during the task and past experience with the task, contribute to response latency.

APPLICATION OF THE SECONDARY TASK TO COMPLEX PRIMARY TASKS

Most research on processing capacity has used simple primary task stimuli. However, a group of psychologists studying reading has recently examined secondary task effects with a complex primary task similar to television. Britton and his associates (Britton, Westbrook, and Holdredge, 1978; Britton, Holdredge, Curry, and Westbrook, 1979; Britton, 1980; Britton, Zieglar, and Westbrook, 1980; Britton, Glynn, Meyer, and Penland, 1982; Britton and Tesser, 1982; Britton, Graesser, Glynn, Hamilton, and Penland, 1983) have varied the difficulty of text passages along three dimensions: structure (word choice and syntax), semantics (meaningful versus meaningless), and the amount of prior knowledge about the texts. Reaction time to a secondary task (usually the detection of clicks) has consistently shown that conditions filling "cognitive capacity" produce slower responses. Capacity-filling tasks were those with difficult syntax, (Britton et al.,

1982), more meaning (Britton et al., 1979), and those involving more use of prior knowledge (Britton and Tesser, 1982). A particularly interesting aspect of Britton's results is that unless content is held constant and only syntax is varied, text materials judged to be "simple" produce longer reaction times to a secondary task than do those judged "difficult." Britton has concluded (Britton and Tesser, 1982) that this is because simple materials are more meaningful and engage cognitive capacity more extensively.

Our study used the secondary-task procedure to study similar characteristics of television viewing. Instead of manipulating text difficulty, we varied message complexity in two ways. First, unlike reading, television viewing is both visual and auditory. If the number of channels affects cognitive capacity, then television may require greater mental effort than single-channel presentations. Although it is possible that just hearing or seeing is not "television watching," the two single-channel conditions do require different mental effort. Corresponding reaction time differences would further validate application of the method to television viewing. Consequently, the experiments here used three channel conditions: audio and visual, audio-only, and video-only.

A second definition of complexity relates to the content and structure of messages in both channels. Britton measured text complexity in terms of grammatical simplicity and subjects' ability to guess missing words from the text (the Cloze test). A similar linguistic analysis was used in this study. Variations in grammatical simplicity and the number of ideas present defined audio anchor points for pretest subjects to use in judging audio complexity. A number of complexity indices have been developed for television pictures (Watt and Krull, 1974; Rice, Huston & Wright, 1982; Watt & Welch, 1983), and this study used these to define anchor points for subjects to use in rating complexity, and in selecting messages for a pretest. The main elements of visual complexity were cuts, dissolves, zoom-ins and -outs, pans, person and object movement, and scene changes.

Three experiments were conducted to assess the psychological cost of viewing television. Experiment 1 involved a 2 (audio complexity) × 2 (video complexity) × 3 (audio-visual, audio-only, and video-only) factorial design. It was expected that reaction times to a secondary task (detection of a tone) would be slower for simple audio and video messages than for complex audio and video messages, and slowest when both channels were present. Finally, because the secondary task was auditory and would be expected to interfere more with listening than with watching, it was expected that the audio-only condition would have slower secondary task reaction times than the video-only condition.

EXPERIMENT 1

METHOD

Subjects. Sixty University of Wisconsin students enrolled in an introductory advertising course participated for course credit during Fall Semester, 1983.

Stimulus materials. The stimulus set consisted of sixteen 30-second television commercials representing the factorial combination of simple and complex auditory information and two levels of visual complexity (simple visual-simple audio, simple visual-complex audio, complex video-simple audio, and complex video-complex audio).

The selection method for these 16 message units was a two-step process. First, 436 commercials were subjected to preliminary coding for visual and audio complexity. Video complex messages were those that contained many edits, scene changes, superimposed images, zooms, pans, central person or object movement, or background person or object movement (Reeves et al., forthcoming). Audio complex messages were those that contained many idea units as indexed by a count of linguistic propositions (Kintsch, 1974; Thorson and Snyder, 1984).

Next, the eight commercials judged to be most representative of the four complexity categories were presented in random order to 53 pretest subjects. Of the subjects, 18 only watched the 32 commercials, 19 only listened, and 16 both watched and listened. For each ad, subjects estimated on a 100-point scale the magnitude (Stevens, 1972) of complexity of the audio, video, or both channels. Before rating the 40 messages, subjects viewed or listened to anchors. A commercial depicting a man sitting in a chair and talking animatedly about frozen vegetables was the video simple-audio complex anchor. Subjects were told that the video portion of this message unit would be rated 10 and the audio portion 100. Three other messages representing simple-simple, complex-simple, and complex-complex ratings were shown. On the basis of the subject ratings, four message units per complexity level were selected for the experiment.

Four randomized orders of the 16 message units, each preceded by two practice commercials, were dubbed onto videotape. On the second audio channel, cues that generated four clearly audible tones were placed in randomly selected locations in each message. Tones were not placed during the first four seconds of the commercial, and no two tones were placed closer than four seconds.

Design and Dependent Measures. Audio and video complexity were within-subject variables, and the number of channels present (both, AV; audio only, AO; and video only, VO) was a between-subjects variable. Again, in the secondary-task paradigm, it is critical to establish that the primary task, (watching the messages), is not ignored in favor of the periodic interruptions. Here, this was accomplished by giving performance tests on information in the two channels after each commercial. Each test included six recognition questions. AO subjects, who only heard the commercials, were given six sets of four phrases. They were asked to identify the phrase that had occurred in a commercial. VO subjects, who only saw the commercials, were given six sets of four individual video frames and had to identify those that had appeared in a commercial. The AV subjects received both the phrases and pictures.

Procedure. A total of 60 subjects were assigned at random to the tape orders and channel conditions; 20 subjects were individually tested in each of the three channel conditions. In all conditions, subjects were presented with two practice commercials followed by 16 experimental messages. Subjects were instructed to attend closely to the messages, because they would be given a recognition test immediately after each commercial. They were also instructed to press a reaction-time button as quickly as possible whenever they heard a tone during each commercial.

Apparatus. Responses were made on a hand-held game paddle with reaction time button. Presentation, timing, and recording of the responses was controlled by an Apple II + microcomputer. Tones were generated by a model 2000 CDK Hewlett-Packard oscillator. Subjects viewed the commercials and the frame recognition test on a 19-inch Sony Trinitron television set.

RESULTS

Because the performance measures are a manipulation check on subject attention to the primary task, it
was important to establish performance equivalence
among conditions. The .05 level of significance was the
criterion level for all statistics. Figure 1 shows there
were no differences between subjects in the AV and VO
conditions on the video recognition test. Audio complexity had no significant effects in either condition,
but video-simple commercials showed higher video recognition than video complex commercials ($F(1,38) =$
66.40, $p < .01$).Similarly, the audio recognition tests
showed no significant differences between AV and AO
subjects as a function of video complexity, but audio
simple commercials resulted in higher audio recognition scores than audio-complex commercials ($F(1,38) =$
83.60, $p < .01$). In addition, there was a significant interaction between condition and audio complexity ($F(1,38)$
$= 19.21$, $p < .01$), such that subjects in the AO condition performed better than those in the AV condition for
audio-simple commercials. AO and AV were not different for audio complex commercials. Except for this interaction, condition did not influence performance on
the recognition tests, and the reaction times across
conditions could be directly compared.

Next, the reaction times to the secondary task were
examined (Figure 2). In a $3 \times 2 \times 2$ mixed factors analysis of variance with individual subjects' reaction times
as the unit of analysis, channel condition and audio
complexity showed no significant effects. Video complexity had a significant main effect in the predicted direction, for instance, reaction time to simple video
messages was slower ($F(1,57) = 9.10$, $p < .01$).

Visual inspection of the mean reaction times for the
three channel conditions (Figure 2) indicated a strong

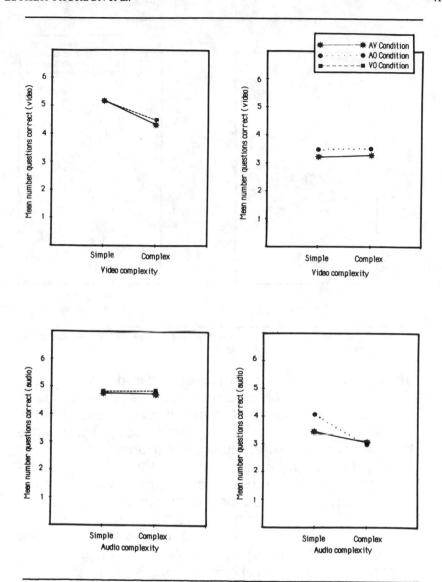

Figure 1: Video and Audio Recognition in Experiment 1 as a Function of Channel
Condition, Audio, and Video Complexity

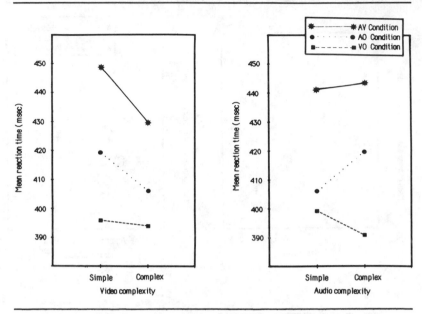

Figure 2: Reaction Time in Experiment 1 as a Function of Channel Condition, Video, and Audio Complexity

effect of condition, for both video and audio complexity. We suspected that high between-subject variations in each condition masked the statistical differences between the conditions. This could result from large between-subject differences in response latency that are attributable to idiosyncratic motor differences. Examination of the variation across subjects verified this, and consequently a second analysis of variance was done in which the unit of analysis was mean reaction time per message unit for each of the three channel conditions. This analysis showed a main effect for channel condition ($F(2,12) = 16.03, p < .01$).

The individual subjects analysis of variance produced an orderly progression in slopes for video complexity as a function of channel condition (first graph of Figure 2). Mean reaction time to the secondary task was significantly slower for the video simple messages in the AV ($F(1,19) = 4.08$, $p < .05$) and AO ($F(1,19) = 6.09$, $p < .05$) conditions. Video complexity had no effect in the VO condition. It is noteworthy that the main effect for video complexity was found for AO condition subjects who did not watch the messages. Because the factorial design ensured that the audio complexities in the video-simple and video-complex messages were not different, this result implies that AO subjects were reconstructing—through imagery, imagination or some other process—the visual channel.

Discussion. The video-complexity effects in Experiment 1 were consistent with Britton's finding that simple text passages produced slower reaction times to a secondary task. Britton would explain this result by suggesting video-simple commercials more fully fill cognitive capacity than do video-complex commercials.

Audio complexity, however, failed to show an analogous effect. Two explanations seem particularly plausible. First, the performance task interaction between audio complexity and channel condition meant that reaction times from AV and AO subjects were not directly comparable. People in the two conditions could have been differentially trading reaction time speed for performance accuracy, and this trade-off may have masked the effect for audio complexity. This possibility required a control experiment (Experiment 2) in which recognition performance was measured without the presence of a secondary task. If this manipulation were to produce the same interaction between audio complexity and channel condition, the reaction times in Experiment 1 would then be interpretable and a reaction time speed-performance trade-off would not explain why audio complexity had no effect on latency.

Second, because the secondary task in Experiment 1 involved responding to a tone, more attentional pressure could have been placed on the auditory processing system. This could have interacted with the processing of audio portions of the commercials so as to mask the differences between audio-simple and complex messages. To examine this possibility, Experiment 3 was designed to use a light flash rather than a tone as the secondary task. This manipulation was expected to reverse the complexity effects, such that audio complexity would have a main effect on reaction time, and video complexity effects would disappear.

Experiment 1 also produced an interesting and unexpected finding for the 20 subjects who did not see the video channel and yet reacted to its complexity as though it was present. This result could be explained by subject reconstruction of the missing channel or by a lack of independence between the factorial cells in the design. In Experiment 3, subjects were asked to rate the "imagined" complexity of the unseen channel in the AO condition and the analogous unheard channel in the VO condition. Accurate ratings would indicate that imaging might account for the results in Experiment 1, or that given one channel, subjects are able to predict the complexity of the absent channel.

Finally, the channel effects on processing capacity in Experiment 1 are easier to interpret than are the complexity effects. The AV condition placed greatest pressure, AO placed second greatest, and VO the least pressure on processing capacity. This would appear to be a simple result; more inputs required more processing capacity. AO was slower than VO as predicted, possibly because with a tone secondary task, the system had more difficulty processing a cue in the same channel as the primary task (AO condition). It may be easier to process the primary and secondary tasks in different channels (VO condition).

EXPERIMENT 2

METHOD

Subjects. Again, 60 University of Wisconsin students enrolled in an introductory advertising course participated for course credit during Fall and Spring Semesters, 1983-1984.

Stimulus materials. The 16 commercials and 2 practice commercials used in Experiment 1 served as the stimuli.

Design and dependent measures. Audio and video complexity were within-subject variables, and the number of channels present was a between-subjects variable (AV, AO, and VO). There was, however, no reaction time dependent measure, nor were there tones appearing during the commercials. Only the performance tests were administered, as before, immediately after each commercial was viewed.

Procedure. A total of 60 subjects were assigned at random to tape orders and conditions, with 20 people in each channel condition. Subjects were instructed to attend closely to the commercials, because they would be given a recognition test after each.

Apparatus. Except for omission of the tones, the apparatus was identical to Experiment 1.

RESULTS

The pattern of effects on the performance measures were identical to those of Experiment 1. On the video test, there were no differences between the AV and VO condition. Audio complexity had no effect, but video-simple commercials had higher accuracy scores than did video-complex commercials ($F(1,38) = 82.58$, $p <$ .01). Analogously, on the audio test, there were no significant differences between the AV and AO subjects, but the same audio complexity/channel condition interaction occurred ($F(1,38) = 23.54$, $p < .01$). AO subjects were more accurate for the audio-simple commercials than the complex ones, but AV subjects showed no difference.

Discussion. The results of control condition performance tests demonstrated that the primary task of processing the commercials was indeed a primary task. For audio performance, the interaction of audio complexity and channel condition (AV and AO only) was apparently a function of the primary task itself, rather than of differential effects of the secondary task on those two conditions of the primary task. This suggests that the results of Experiment 1 indicate that video complexity and viewing condition indeed affect processing capacity.

The next question concerned whether audio and video complexity effects depend on the channel in which the secondary task is given. This problem was examined in Experiment 3.

EXPERIMENT 3

METHOD

Subjects. A total of 60 University of Wisconsin students enrolled in an introductory advertising course participated for course credit during Spring Semester, 1984.

Stimulus materials. The same 16 commercials and 2 practice commercials used in Experiments 1 and 2 served as the stimuli.

The four randomly placed cues on the second audio track triggered light flashes rather than tones. The flash appeared behind and above the subjects' heads, creating an ambient light change rather than one centered on the television screen. Again, because the same cues were used, the flashes did not occur during the first 4 seconds of each commercial, and no two flashes were placed closer than 4 seconds apart.

Design and dependent measures. As in Experiment 1, audio and video complexity were within-subject variables, and the number of channels present (AV, AO, and VO) was a between-subjects variable. The recognition tests were administered as before, with AO subjects given the phrase recognition test; VO subjects given the picture recognition test, and the AV subjects receiving both tests. AO subjects were asked after viewing all 16 units to rate on two 10-point scales the complexity of what they "imagined" in the unseen video channel. VO subjects were asked to rate the complexity of what they "imagined" in the unheard audio channel.

Procedure. The testing procedure and instructions given to the subjects was identical to that given in Experiment 1.

Apparatus. Button-press responses to the flashes were made as before, under computer control. Subjects viewed the commercials on the same Sony Trinitron. The flash was generated by a photo stimulator connected to a strobe light mounted two feet behind and five feet above the seated subject.

RESULTS AND DISCUSSION

Again, performance measures were examined first to establish that the subjects treated the primary task as they did in the previous two experiments. The pattern of results was identical to those of Experiments 1 and 2. On the video recognition test, there were no differences between subjects in the AV and AO conditions. Audio complexity had no significant effects, but video-simple commercials showed higher recognition scores than video-complex commercials (F(1,38) = 68.36, p < .01). On the audio recognition tests, there were no significant differences between AV and AO subjects, but audio-simple commercials showed higher recognition scores than audio-complex messages (F(1,38) = 72.23, p < .01). Finally, there was again a significant interaction between condition and audio complexity (F(1,38) = 3.99, p < .05) such that subjects in the AO condition performed slightly better than those in the AV condition for audio-simple commercials, with no differences in the audio-complex commercials.

As can be seen in the cross-hatched line in Figure 3, using flash rather than tone as the secondary task stimulus eliminated the effect of channel condition. Whether analyzed with individual commercials as the unit of analysis (F(2,12) = .39, n.s.) or with subjects (F(2,57) = .02, n.s.), there were no significant effects of condition. Because the performance results of Experiments 1 and 3 were identical, it was appropriate to compare the slopes of the two lines in Figure 3 statistically. As expected, when the unit of analysis was message units (F(2,90) = 6.09, p < .01), there was a significant interaction between viewing condition and secondary task.

Figure 4 shows that video- and audio-complexity effects also changed with the secondary task stimulus. Here, video complexity produced no significant main effects, and audio-simple commercials were processed more slowly than were audio-complex ones (F(1,57) = 7.78, p < .01). There were no significant interactions between condition and either of the complexity measures. Analogously to the "absent channel" effect in Experiment 1, subjects who only saw the video (VO condition) reacted significantly more slowly to the simple level of

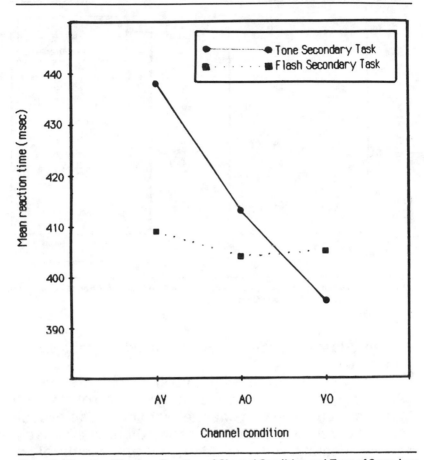

Figure 3: Reaction Time as a Function of Channel Condition and Type of Secondary Task

audio complexity (F(1,19) = 5.49, p < .05) than to the complex level.

Experiment 3 again replicated Britton's findings that simple materials (this time as measured on the audio track) slowed reaction time to the secondary task more than did complex materials. As predicted, the channel producing the complexity effect depended on the channel of the secondary task. When a tone secondary task was used, video complexity affected reaction times.

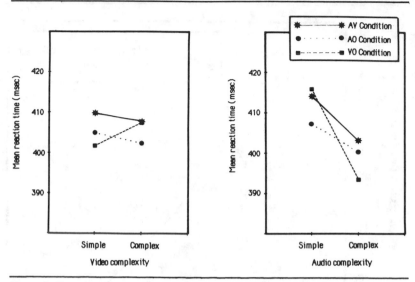

Figure 4: Reaction Time in Experiment 3 as a Function of Channel Condition, Video, and Auditory Complexity

When a flash was used, audio complexity affected reaction times.

The symmetry of these results may indicate that the secondary task is processed along with the other multiple occurrences in that channel, with no capacity costs to that channel. However, because there is a capacity cost in dealing with the additional processing of the tone or flash, the burden of that cost is shifted to the opposite channel, and as a result, the complexity of that channel shows a significant effect on reaction times. If this is the case, it argues for both flexibility in the allocation of processing capacity during television watching, and for a general equality of capacity allocation between the audio and video channels.

Also consistent with Experiment 1, Experiment 3 demonstrated another "absent channel" effect. VO subjects, who did not hear the messages, nevertheless showed a significant effect of audio complexity. Again, this is a critical result because it may mean that sub-

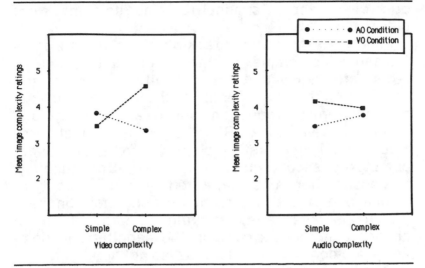

Figure 5: Image Complexity Ratings in Experiment 3 as a Function of Channel Condition, Audio, and Video Complexity

jects reconstruct events in the absent channel and are able to predict the complexity of the unattended channel.

The subject complexity ratings for the unattended channel can be seen in Figure 5. AO subjects rated the audio-complex messages significantly higher than the audio-simple messages. There was no significant difference, however, in their rating of the unseen video-simple and complex messages. The inverse held for the VO subjects. They rated the video-complex messages significantly higher than the video-simple messages, but showed no rating differences for the unheard audio-simple and complex messages.

These results indicate there was not sufficient information in either of the single-channel conditions to allow the prediction of the complexity level of the absent channel. This is verification that the complexity of the two channels of television was manipulated independently in the study. Although it seems reasonable and possibly even necessary to hypothesize that some "residue" of the absent channel remains, its form is not clear.

Finally, it is interesting to ask whether the costs of audio and video complexity in terms of reaction time effects are equivalent in magnitude. Under the assumption that the modality of the secondary task is not important, this question could be answered by summing the overall mean RT changes as a function of video complexity (first graph of Figure 2) and audio complexity (second graph of Figure 4). Unfortunately, this assumption is not warranted because modality of the secondary task interacts with channel condition (Figure 3). This means that summing across the three channel conditions to compare the magnitude of audio- and video-complexity effects is also not appropriate. In fact, these data do not allow evaluation of comparative magnitudes of the video- and audio-complexity effects.

GENERAL DISCUSSION

The basic finding that multiple-channel presentations required more mental effort than single-channel versions is straightforward: More information required greater processing cost. In contrast, the results for message complexity, although consistent with Britton's work on text, were counterintuitive with respect to television research. Why should simple messages require more attention?

Two explanations have been offered (Britton, Westbrook, and Holdredge, 1978). One is that complex material increases arousal, which in turn decreases response time to other tasks. This suggests that there is no less attention to complex material. The cognitive system is merely activated to a higher degree by complex messages and processes information more efficiently. A second explanation is that simple material is more engaging and involving, thus filling available cognitive capacity more fully and slowing reaction time to the secondary task. Distinguishing between these two possible explanations awaits research in which message complexity and subject arousal are manipulated independently.

These experiments also provided some evidence for the argument that complexity of both the audio and video channels influences attention. Instead of supporting the traditional psychological notion of visual dominance (Pick and Hay, 1964, 1965), these studies found that viewers, when faced with a secondary task, were able to "borrow" capacity from visual processing (Experiment 1) or from auditory processing (Experiment 3). Thus, visual processing does not appear to dominate the audio channel, although for certain content either could be prominent.

The secondary task procedure used in this study proved useful for assessing covert responses to television. The technique discriminated presentations that differed as a function of channel and message complexity—differences that would not be apparent from introspective questioning, from recall measures taken after viewing, or from obvious behaviors or orientations during viewing. Further, the unnatural imposition of the secondary task did not jeopardize the primary-viewing assignment. This was indicated by equivalent performance between experimental and control subjects on recognition measures.

In spite of the apparent complexity of television, researchers have constrained the scope of research about attention to television, primarily through reliance on self-reports about conscious attention and inferences drawn from recall measures. The recent development of observation procedures to measure visual orientation (Anderson and Levin, 1976) was important because it advanced the study of attention beyond a verbal ability to express a cognitive process. But even these procedures depended on counting overt responses. Apart from popular discussion of subliminal persuasion and hypnotic trances, mass communication researchers have been reluctant to acknowledge covert and unconscious features of attention to the screen. This research indicated the feasibility of examining attention at this level.

This study also provided further evidence that an experimental method used primarily with simple and often pure stimuli can be applied to the study of a complex stimulus such as television. The secondary-task procedure not only discriminated responses to a complex stimulus, it actually helped confirm that television presentations are themselves complex in at least two important ways. Processing information in two channels (audio and video) taxes capacity more than one; and thus two channels are more complex than one. In addition, television's complexity, or the properties that make it a psychological stimulus, can be defined in a number of ways. Different studies suggest that single attributes are dominant. Form and structure, semantic content, and physical properties have all been nominated as the most crucial elements for understanding how television is processed. Unfortunately, these attributes are often mentioned as competitors in a hierarchy of influence: Pictures dominate words; meaning is more important than structure; the medium is the message, and so on. It is perhaps most appropriate to view these characteristics together as single dimensions of a complex stimulus, important in different ways and at different times. Only two properties were examined in this study, and both produced psychological costs. Others are no doubt possible and should be studied. In fact, a method sensitive to change in covert mental activity may suggest attributes that have not been studied before because of the difficulty in designing criterion measures of effects.

A key question in the future study of television as a psychological stimulus is the possibility of stimulus reduction. To what extent can the elements of a television presentation be separated and experimentally manipulated without degrading the stimulus beyond recognition? This study, for example, relied in part on single-channel presentations that had no counterpart in the real world of media. So although it seems reasonable to suggest that multiple-channel presentations require more capacity to process than single-channel ones, it is difficult to translate the result to real media. The influence of information in the absent channel further highlights the difficulty in stimulus decomposition.

REFERENCES

ALWITT, L. F., D. R. ANDERSON, E. P. LORCH, and S. R. LEVIN (1980) "Preschool children's visual attention to attributes of television." Human Communication Research 7: 52-67.

ANDERSON, D. R. and S. R. LEVIN (1976) "Young children's attention to Sesame Street." Child Development 47: 806-811.

ANDERSON, D. R., E. P. LORCH, D. E. FIELD, and J. SANDERS (1981) "The effects of TV program comprehensibility on preschool children's visual attention to television." Child Development 52: 151-157.

BORTON, T., L. BELASCO, and T. ECHEWA (1974) "Dual audio TV instruction—a mass broadcast simulation." AV Communication Rev. 22: 133-152.

BRITTON, B. K. (1980) "Use of cognitive capacity in reading: effects of processing information from text for immediate recall and retention." J. of Reading Behavior 7: 129-137.

BRITTON, B. K., S. M. GLYNN, B.J.F. MEYER, and M. J. PENLAND (1982) "Effects of text structure on use of cognitive capacity during reading." J. of Educ. Psychology 74: 51-61.

BRITTON, B. K., A. C. GRAESSER, S. M. GLYNN, T. HAMILTON, and M. PENLAND (1983) Use of cognitive capacity in reading: effects of some content features of text." Discourse Processes 6: 39-57.

BRITTON, B. K., T. S. HOLDREDGE, C. CURRY, and R. D. WESTBROOK (1979) "Use of cognitive capacity in reading identical texts with different amounts of discourse level meaning." J. of Experimental Psychology: Human Learning and Memory 5: 262-270.

BRITTON, B. K. and A. TESSER (1982) "Effects of prior knowledge on use of cognitive capacity in three complex cognitive tasks." J. of Verbal Learning and Verbal Behavior 21: 421-436.

BRITTON, B. K., R. D. WESTBROOK, and T. S. HOLDREDGE (1978) "Reading and cognitive capacity usage: effects of text difficulty." J. of Experimental Psychology: Human Learning and Performance 4: 582-591.

BRITTON, B. K., R. ZIEGLAR, and R. WESTBROOK (1980) "Use of cognitive capacity in reading easy and difficult text: two tests of an allocation of attention hypothesis." J. of Reading Behavior 7: 23-28.

BROADBENT, D. E. (1958) Perception and Communication. London: Pergamon Press.

CALDER, B. F. and B. STERNTHAL (1980) "Television commercial wearout: an information processing view." J. of Marketing Research 17: 173-186.

CARTER, R. F. (1962) "Some effects of the debates," in S. Kraus (ed.) The Great Debates. Bloomington: Indiana University Press.

CHAFFEE, S. H. and S. Y. CHOE (1980) "Time of decision in the Ford-Carter campaign." Public Opinion Q. (Spring): 53-69.

DUNCAN, E. M., P. WHITNEY, and S. RINNEN (1982) "Integration of visual and verbal information in children's memories." Child Development 53: 1215-1223.

GREENBERG, B. S. and W. GANTZ (1976) "Public television and taboo topics: the impact of VD blues." Public Telecommunications Rev. 4: 59-64.

HARTMAN, F. R. (1961) Single- and multiple-channel communications: a review of research and a proposed model." AV Communication Rev. 9: 235-263.

HAYES, D. S. and D. W. BIRNBAUM (1980) "Preschooler's retention of televised events: is a picture worth a thousand words?" Developmental Psychology 16: 410-416.

HAYES, D. S., B. E. CHEMELSKI, and D. W. BIRNBAUM (1981) "Young children's incidental and intentional retention of televised events." Developmental Psychology 17: 230-232.

HOWARD, J., G. ROTHBART, and L. SLOAN (1978) "The response to 'Roots': a national survey." J. of Broadcasting 22: 279-287.

HSIA, H. J. (1971) "The information processing capacity of modality and channel performance." AV Communication Rev. 19: 51-75.

HUSTON, A. C., J. C. WRIGHT, E. WARTELLA, M. L. RICE, B. A. WATKINS, T. CAMPBELL, and R. POTTS (1981) "Communicating more than content: formal features on children's television programs." J. of Communication 31: 32-48.

KAHNEMAN, D. and A. TREISMAN (1983) "Changing views of attention and automaticity," in R. Parasuraman and R. Davies (eds.) Varieties of Attention. New York: Academic Press.

KINTSCH, W. (1974) The Representation of Meaning in Memory. Hillsdale, NJ: Erlbaum.

KRULL, R. (1983) "Children learning to watch television," in J. Bryant and D. R. Anderson (eds.) Children's Understanding of Television. New York: Academic Press.

LESSER, G. S. (1974) Children and Television. New York: Vintage Books.

MADDEN, T. J. and M. G. WEINBERGER (1982) "The effects of humor on attention in magazine advertising." J. of Advertising 11: 8-14.

McLEOD, J. M., J. A. DURALL, D. A. ZIEMKE, and C. R. BYBEE (1979) "Reactions of young and older voters: expanding the context of effects," in S. Kraus (ed.) The Great Debates. Bloomington: Indiana University Press.

MILLER, A. H. and M. MacKUEN (1979) "Informing the electorate: a national study," in S. Kraus (ed.) The Great Debates. Bloomington: Indiana University Press.

NASSER, D. L. and W. J. McEWEN (1976) "The impact of alternative media channels: recall and involvement with messages." AV Communication Rev. 24: 263-272.

NAVON, D. and D. GOPHER (1979) "On the economy of the human processing system." Psychological Rev. 86: 214-255.

NAVON, D. and D. GOPHER (1980) "Task difficulty, and dual-task performance," in R. S. Nickerson (ed.) Attention and Performance. Hillsdale, NJ: LEA.

PEZDEK, K. (1977) "Cross modality semantic integration of sentence and picture memory." J. of Experimental Psychology: Human Learning and Memory 3: 515-524.

PEZDEK, K. (1978) "Recognition memory for related pictures." Memory and Cognition 6: 64-69.

PEZDEK, K. (1980a) "Arguments for a constructive approach to comprehension and memory," in F. B. Murray (ed.) Reading and Understanding. International Reading Assn.

PEZDEK, K. (1980b) "Life-span differences in semantic integration of pictures and sentences in memory." Child Development 51: 720-729.

PICK, H. L. and J. C. HAY (1964) "Adaption to prismatic distortion." Psychonomic Science 1: 199-200.

PICK, H. L. and J. C. HAY (1965) "A passive test of the Held reafference hypothesis." Perceptual and Motor Skills 20: 1070-1072.

POSNER, M. I. (1982) "Cumulative development of attentional theory." Amer. Psychologist 37: 168-179.

REEVES, B., E. THORSON, M. L. ROTHSCHILD, D. McDONALD, J. HIRSCH, and R. GOLDSTEIN (forthcoming) "Attention to television: intrastimulus effects of movement and scene changes on alpha variation over time." Int. J. of Neuroscience.

REEVES, B., E. THORSON, and J. SCHLEUDER (forthcoming) "Attention to television: psychological theories and chronometric measures," in J. Bryant and D. Zillman (eds.) Perspectives on Media Effects. Hillsdale, NJ: Erlbaum.

RICE, M. L., A. C. HUSTON, and J. C. WRIGHT (1982) "The forms of television: effects on children's attention, comprehension, and social behavior," in D. Pearl, L. Bouthilet, and J. Lazar (eds.) Television and Behavior:

Ten Years of Scientific Progress and Implications for the Eighties. Washington, DC: Government Printing Office.

SHIFFRIN, R. M. and W. SCHNEIDER (1977) "Controlled and automatic human information processing: perceptual learning, automatic attending, and a general theory." Psychological Rev. 84: 127-190.

STEVENS, S. S. (1972) Psychophysics and Social Scaling. Morristown, NJ: General Learning Press.

THORSON, E. and R. SNYDER (1984) Viewer recall of television commercials: prediction from the propositional structure of commercial scripts. J. of Marketing Research 21: 127-136.

WATKINS, B., S. CALVERT, A. HUSTON-STEIN, and J. C. WRIGHT (1980) "Children's recall of television material: effects of presentation mode and adult labeling." Developmental Psychology 16: 672-674.

WATT, J. H. and R. KRULL (1974) "An information theory measure for television programming." Communication Research (January): 44-68.

WATT, J. H. and A. J. WELCH (1983) "Effects of static and dynamic complexity on children's attention and recall of televised instruction, " in J. Bryant and D. R. Anderson (eds.) Children's Understanding of Television. New York: Academic Press.

WEBB, P. H. and M. L. RAY (1979) "Effects of TV clutter." J. of Advertising Research 19(3): 7-65.

WELCH, A. and J. H. WATT "Visual complexity and young children's learning from television." Human Communication Research 8: 133-145.

WELCH, J. (1898) "On the measurement of verbal activity through muscular activity and the determination of a constant attention." Amer. J. of Psychology 1: 288-306.

Esther Thorson is Assistant Professor in the School of Journalism and Mass Communication at the University of Wisconsin—Madison. Her research interests focus on emotional, cognitive, and attentional processing of persuasive messages.

Byron Reeves is Professor in the School of Journalism and Mass Communication at the University of Wisconsin—Madison. His research interests are the psychological effects of mass communication.

Joan Schleuder is a graduate student at the University of Wisconsin—Madison. Her major research interest is the cognitive processing of television messages.

20

INFORMATION-THEORETIC MEASURES OF READER ENJOYMENT

Seth Finn

Two studies based on an information theory model of reader enjoyment investigated the role of syntactic and semantic unpredictability in determining readers' evaluations of journalistic prose. In each study, reader enjoyment ratings for a set of articles reporting a single news event were compared with cloze procedure results in which function-word and content-word responses were analyzed separately using entropy and cloze scoring techniques. Both studies revealed a statistically significant correlation between function-word predictability and reader enjoyment. In addition, a strong correlation between content-word unpredictability and reader enjoyment in one study supported the notion that readers prefer texts that are characterized by a high degree of semantic unpredictability.

Although Shannon (1949; 1951) himself experimented with entropy measures to characterize the redundancy of printed English, it was Taylor (1953; 1955; 1956) who first developed an information theory based methodology for rating the readability of English prose. The methodology he called cloze procedure was basically a guessing game in which readers attempted to restore texts that had been mutilated by deleting words at specified intervals. Taylor (1953) introduced the procedure as an alternative to reading-ease formulas that relied upon element-counting routines. In a clever example, Taylor showed how cloze procedure was superior to the Flesch

Author's Note: This investigation was supported in part by a grant from the University Research Council of the University of North Carolina at Chapel Hill. Requests for reprints should be sent to Seth Finn, Department of Radio, Television, and Motion Pictures, Swain Hall 044A, University of North Carolina, Chapel Hill, NC 27514.

(1948) and the Dale and Chall (1948) formulas, which rated a sample of Erskine Caldwell's fiction—difficult because of its long sentences—and Gertrude Stein's writing—easy because of her use of short words and short sentences.

Cloze procedure provided a more sensitive estimate of reading ease because it probed two important dimensions in reading comprehension: the degree of redundant information within the text and the amount of information shared by author and reader at the outset. Inasmuch as both these factors contributed to intelligibility, the proportion of deleted words that readers were able to guess correctly (usually expressed as a percentage score) provided a subtle measure of the text's readability for similar audiences.

Taken to its extreme, however, cloze procedure's approach to readability suggested that the most readable texts would be generally redundant and uninformative. Although the adoption of cloze procedure as a readability formula made explicit the traditional information-theoretic conflict between intelligible form and informative output (Moles, 1966, p. 77), researchers generally ignored the problem. Like the element-counting formulas that preceded it, cloze procedure reflected a very narrow definition of readability and a frustratingly simple model of the relationship between writers and their audiences (Kintsch & Vipond, 1979; Finn, 1983; in press).

AN INFORMATION-THEORETIC MODEL
OF READER ENJOYMENT

The model of reader enjoyment presented in Figure 1 attempts to redress some of cloze procedure's deficiencies in depicting the writer-reader relationship. In particular, it is designed to illustrate how journalistic prose and other forms of nonfiction writing function as sources of entertainment (Donohew, Nair, & Finn, 1984; Finn, 1983) as well as information. Its innovations stem from the integration of psychological theories of physiological arousal with contemporary models of reading as a multilevel, information-processing task.

The model presumes a stepwise progression in the processing of information beginning at the Decoding Level where words are recognized and placed into an intelligible syntactic structure. At this

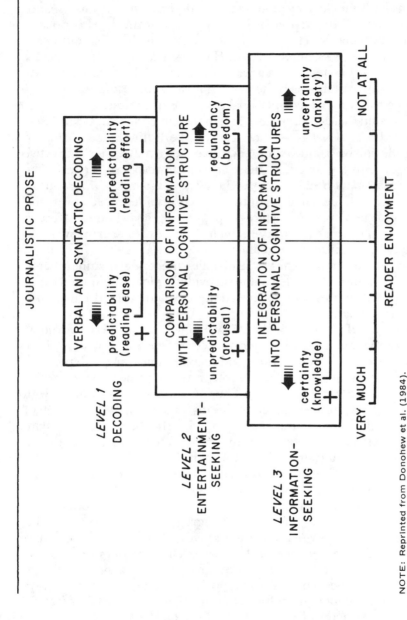

NOTE: Reprinted from Donohew et al. (1984).

Figure 1: An Information-Theoretic Model of Reader Enjoyment

435

basic perceptual level, the model assumes, as does cloze procedure, that predictability contributes to reading ease and, in turn, reader enjoyment. Indeed, predictability is crucial at this level because it permits many aspects of verbal decoding to be handled automatically (LaBerge & Samuels, 1974; Haber & Haber, 1981; Samuels & Eisenberg, 1981), so the reader can focus attention on higher level cognitive tasks in which the intelligible content of the text is compared with the reader's personal cognitive structures.

Beyond the Decoding Level, then, the model specifies two closely related tasks, which nevertheless need to be distinguished because of the distinctive contribution each makes to the reader's affective response to the text. The most immediate response occurs at the Entertainment-Seeking Level, where the comparison of new information with personal cognitive structures identifies novel and unpredictable content, which—up to an optimal point—effects a pleasurable sense of arousal (Hebb, 1955; Cofer & Appley, 1967; Madsen, 1968; Donohew, Palmgreen & Duncan, 1980). In contrast to traditional approaches to readability, the model assumes that at this level, unpredictable content provides a pleasurable stimulative effect that compensates for the additional mental effort it demands from the reader.

At the Information-Seeking Level, however, the model acknowledges the ambiguous long-term effects of new information. New information can both reduce and increase uncertainty depending upon how well the reader can integrate it into personal cognitive structures (Berlo, 1977, p. 26). Thus, information that conflicts with the reader's attitudes, beliefs, opinions, or any other expectation of reality can increase uncertainty, thereby effecting anxiety (Atkin, 1973) that diminishes reading enjoyment. By contrast, positive affect most likely results only when information can be comfortably integrated into existing cognitive structures, thereby adding to the reader's store of personal knowledge.

As the model suggests, novel semantic content can produce conflicting affective responses whose aggregate result is heavily influenced by the relative weight readers give to their entertainment- and information-related needs. But inasmuch as readers often select texts to accommodate their perceptions of the world, one should not assume that these conflicts routinely arise or that readers are always so serious-minded that information-seeking criteria predominate in their assessments of written texts (Donohew, Nair, & Finn, 1984). Ultimately the model allows for the possibility that much of a text is evaluated at the Information-Seeking Level in a strictly passive fashion, especially when the reader is driven by a physiological need for arousal rather than the reduction of cognitive uncertainty.

TWO TESTS OF THE CLOZE PROCEDURE MODEL

Whereas Taylor's cloze procedure was designed to measure only one dimension of the text—redundancy—the information-theoretic model presented above recognizes the need to account for three levels of textual (un)predictability. As one might anticipate, the most vexing measurement problems occur at the Information-Seeking Level where individual differences among readers may have a major impact on assessments of reader enjoyment. Rather than attempt to measure such differences among readers, however, this research proceeded on the assumption that the selection of noncontroversial texts would dampen idiosyncratic responses to the extent that they would then constitute an acceptably small source of random error.

Two correlational studies are reported here: The first used a sample of nine newspaper and magazine articles reporting the Apollo 11 moonwalk of July 20, 1968. The second used a sample of nine articles describing the aftermath of a moderate earthquake that hit Coalinga, California on May 9, 1983. In both cases, the news events were noncontroversial and widely reported. As noted above, noncontroversial stories were desired in order to mitigate the impact of personal opinion on reader enjoyment, and the broad coverage given these events assured a wide range of print sources from which to choose articles that would effect distinctive levels of reader enjoyment despite their factually similar content. These conditions provided the most favorable opportunity for exploring the associations between reader enjoyment and measures of unpredictability at the Decoding and Entertainment-Seeking Levels of the model (Figure 1). In particular, two hypotheses about reader enjoyment were tested: First, at the Decoding Level, that reader enjoyment is negatively correlated with unpredictable syntactic forms, and second, at the Entertainment-Seeking level, that reader enjoyment is positively correlated with unpredictable semantic content.

Testing these two hypotheses, however, required two innovations in traditional cloze procedure. First a method had to be devised to discriminate between deleted words associated with the syntactic

and the semantic dimensions of the text. Here current psycholin-
guistic theory suggested an appropriate solution. The commonly
used distinction between function words and content words
provided the basis for a reasonable partition of syntactic and semantic elements:

> Content words are those that carry the principal meaning of a sen-
> tence. They name objects, events, and characteristics that lie at the
> heart of the message the sentence is meant to convey. They include
> nouns, main verbs, adjectives, and most adverbs. Function words, in
> contrast, are those needed by the surface structure to glue the content
> words together, to indicate what goes with what and how. They in-
> clude articles, pronouns, conjunctions, auxiliary verbs, and pre-
> positions.[1] (Clark & Clark, 1977, p. 21).

The second innovation—one that Taylor (1955) had previously
investigated—was to use Shannon's entropy formula,

$$H = \Sigma p_i \log_2 1/p_i$$

rather than cloze procedure's customary percentage scores, in order
to derive an estimate of the degree of unpredictability represented
by each blank. Aside from the obvious ties between cloze procedure
and information theory, Shannon's entropy formula recommends
itself as a peculiarly useful statistic for characterizing variance in
categorical data (Finn & Roberts, 1984). Although cloze scoring
routinely groups all wrong answers into a single category, Shannon's
entropy formula weighs the contribution of each unique response to
generate an aggregate unpredictability score. Briefly, the formula
denotes that entropy (H) is equal to the sum of the logarithmically
transformed probabilities (p_i) of each unique response. The precise
manner in which these calculations are performed is described in the
Method section.

THE APOLLO 11 MOONWALK STUDY

Method

To derive reader enjoyment scores for the nine sample articles,
144 junior college and state university students in the San Francisco

Bay Area rated 800-word prose passages using a questionnaire devised by Funkhouser and Maccoby (1971). Each student, after reading a randomly assigned article, indicated how much he or she enjoyed reading that specific article by marking a seven-point scale ranging from "Enjoyed Very Much" to "Enjoyed Not At All." They then indicated on two additional scales how much they generally enjoyed reading articles about history and science. A one-way analysis of variance revealed a statistically significant difference between groups on the first question ($F(8, 135) = 2.49$, $p < .02$), but not on the two control items. The reader enjoyment measure was further validated using a set of 16 semantic differential scales. Reader enjoyment scores exhibited a strong correlation with such descriptors as "entertaining," "pleasing," and "interesting" ($r > .71$), and nonsignificant relationships with such terms as "heavy," "complex," and "serious" ($|r| < .09$).

In the second phase of the study, a comparable group of 144 participants completed cloze procedure tests prepared from the nine sample articles. Every eighth word had been deleted resulting in approximately 100 blanks per article. The cloze instruments (like the sample articles rated in the first phase) were administered randomly in various classroom settings. Each cloze-form article was completed satisfactorily by 16 students. None of the students in phase one took part in phase two. No student was ever administered more than one cloze test.

An excerpt from the cloze procedure test for one sample article—the *Reader's Digest* account of the Apollo 11 moonwalk—is presented in Figure 2. The entropy score for each blank was computed by comparing the guesses of the 16 participants who completed each cloze form. In the last paragraph, one can note the relative degree of difficulty in predicting function words and content words. "AT" and "AS" are the deleted function words. "POETIC" is the deleted content word.

Table 1 illustrates how the responses were scored using Shannon's entropy function. Because there were 16 responses per blank, the maximum entropy score was 4.0 bits. In the lefthand column are the various guesses students filled in for the function word "AT" and the content word "POETIC." Thirteen students guessed "AT" correctly, and only three had other unique answers. The entropy score is .994 bits.

By contrast, the guesses evoked by the blank for the deleted word "POETIC" are considerably more varied. No student correctly guessed "POETIC," although seven did fill in the blank with the word

EXCERPT FROM CLOZE PROCEDURE TEST

Suddenly everything changes. We see the surface

_____OF_____ the moon pierced by craters, sown

with _SMALL_ and large rocks that shine white

as _SNOW_ . And then in this empty and

inhuman _LANDSCAPE_ we see the mooncraft,

comforting and human, _THOUGH_ it resembles

an awesome spider.

One marvels _AT_ the fantasy this

picture radiates, as plain _AS_ it is. In

a word, it is _POETIC_ .

Figure 2: An Excerpt from the Cloze Test for the *Reader's Digest* Article Reporting the Apollo 11 Moonwalk

"AWESOME." Three readers guessed "FANTASTIC," and six others gave uniquely different responses. The distribution of guesses in this case results in an entropy score of 2.475 bits.

Results

The summary data in Table 2 allow for the comparison of each article's reader enjoyment score with its average function- and content-word entropy scores. (Corresponding cloze scores for each article are also included.) The reader enjoyment scores range from a high of 5.69 for the *Time* story to a low of 4.19 for the San Francisco *Examiner* story. The function-word entropy scores range from a low of .98 bits for the New York *Times* to a high of 1.54 bits for the San

TABLE 1
Computation of Function and Content Word Entropy Scores

Cloze responses	Probability of word choice (p_i)	$p_i \log_2 1/p_i$
AT	.8125	.2439
of	.0625	.25
over	.0625	.25
[blank]	.0625	.25
	$\sum$ =	.994 bits
POETIC	--	--
awesome	.4375	.5217
fantastic	.1875	.4528
beautiful	.0625	.25
breathtaking	.0625	.25
fascinating	.0625	.25
magnificent	.0625	.25
picturesque	.0625	.25
spectacular	.0625	.25
	$\sum$ =	2.475 bits

NOTE: Maximum entropy score per word is 4.0 bits.

Francisco *Examiner.* The content-word entropy scores range from a high of 2.42 bits for the *Time* article to a low of 1.88 bits for the St. Louis *Post-Dispatch* story.

Pearson product-moment correlation coefficients (Table 3) provide a statistical measure of the hypothesized relationships between reader enjoyment and function- and content-word unpredictability. As predicted, there is a strong negative correlation ($r = -.70$, $p < .05$) between reader enjoyment scores and function-word

TABLE 2
Average Entropy and Cloze Scores for Deleted
Function- and Content-Words in Nine Moonwalk Articles

Articles	Enjoyment	Function-Word		Content-Word	
		Entropy	Cloze	Entropy	Cloze
Time	5.69	1.08	73.2	2.42	29.6
Sacramento Bee[a]	5.38	1.05	69.2	1.89	37.1
New York Times	5.25	.98	72.7	2.00	38.8
Reader's Digest	5.19	1.04	73.0	2.12	38.2
Newsweek	5.19	1.11	73.2	2.29	31.2
Life[b]	5.13	1.32	64.0	2.28	29.5
Life[c]	4.38	1.17	67.9	2.00	39.4
St. Louis Post- Dispatch	4.25	1.25	62.8	1.88	41.4
San Francisco Examiner	4.19	1.54	58.9	2.31	30.4

NOTE: Each score is based on the responses of 16 different readers or cloze procedure participants.
a. Primary source is Associated Press.
b. First person article by astronaut Edwin Aldrin.
c. First person article by astronaut Neil Armstrong.

entropy. In addition, a positive correlation ($r = .28$, n.s.) between reader enjoyment and content-word entropy is obtained as hypothesized, and when function-word entropy is controlled, the partial correlation ($r = .74$, $p < .05$) accounts for more than half the variance in the nine reader enjoyment scores.

Discussion

These results provide a substantial degree of support for the argument that novel semantic content plays a significant role in making journalistic prose enjoyable to read. But Table 3 reveals unexpected results also. At the zero-order level, the correlation coefficients derived by using simple cloze scores as measures of function- and content-word unpredictability exhibit slightly higher values than the corresponding entropy scores.[2] Even more remarkable, however, is the correlation between reader enjoyment and cloze content scores when controlled for function-word entropy. This hybrid approach to estimating the unpredictability of function and content words results in a partial correlation coefficient ($r = -.91$, $p < .01$) that explains more than 82% of the variance among the reader enjoyment scores for the nine moonwalk articles.[3]

THE COALINGA EARTHQUAKE STUDY

Method

These promising and yet curious results from the moonwalk study prompted a replication using a sample of nine articles reporting a more recent and less monumental news event: the earthquake that hit Coalinga, California in May 1983. The procedures used were substantially identical except: (a) The sample articles were approximately 500 words long, (b) the cloze deletion scheme eliminated every fifth word, and (c) the participants were primarily sophomores and juniors at a major state university in the southeastern United States. Moreover, a larger group of participants (N = 195) was available to rate the nine sample articles in the first phase of the study.

As in the moonwalk study, a one-way analysis of variance revealed a statistically significant difference between the reader enjoyment scores ($F (8, 186) = 3.559$, $p < .001$), but not the two control questions. Responses to a set of 15 semantic differential scales revealed strong correlations between reader enjoyment scores and descriptors such as "entertaining," "interesting," and "exciting" ($r > .67$), but nonsignificant relationships with such terms as "familiar," "complex," and "heavy" ($|r| < .12$)

Results

Table 4 presents the reader enjoyment scores as well as the function- and the content-word entropy scores for the nine Coalinga

TABLE 3
Correlations Between Reader Enjoyment and Entropy
and Cloze Scores for Nine Moonwalk Articles

| | Reader Enjoyment | | |
| | Zero-Order | Controlling for Function-Word | |
		Entropy	Cloze
Function-Word			
Entropy	-.70*		
Cloze	.78*		
Content-Word			
Entropy	.28	.74**	.38
Cloze	-.32	-.91***	-.62

*p < .05, df = 7; **p < .05, df = 6; ***p < .01, df = 6.

earthquake articles. The reader enjoyment scores range from a high of 4.55 for the *Newsweek* story to a low of 3.14 for the Los Angeles *Times* article. The function-word entropy scores range from a low of .65 bits for the lead story in the San Francisco *Chronicle* to a high of 1.33 bits for the Los Angeles *Times* lead article. The content-word entropy scores range from a high of 2.20 bits for the *Guardian* to a low of 1.51 for the San Francisco *Chronicle* lead.

Discussion

Although the negative relationship between reader enjoyment and function-word entropy is readily apparent, even a cursory comparison of the earthquake results (Table 4) with the moonwalk results (Table 2) reveals a decline in the values of all three variables. As the correlation coefficients in Table 5 suggest, the most significant result of these lower function- and content-word entropy scores

TABLE 4
Average Entropy and Cloze Scores for Deleted
Function- and Content-Words in Nine Earthquake Articles

Articles	Enjoyment	Function-Word		Content-Word	
		Entropy	Cloze	Entropy	Cloze
Newsweek	4.55	.69	79.6	1.66	49.7
San Francisco Chronicle (Lead)	4.48	.65	76.2	1.51	52.5
New York Post	4.45	.71	83.5	1.83	40.6
San Francisco Chronicle (Color)	4.45	.79	78.7	1.76	39.3
Christian Science Monitor	4.38	1.06	69.2	1.80	33.0
Chicago Tribune	4.14	.96	74.8	2.10	37.3
Arkansas Gazette[a]	3.64	.92	68.8	1.98	36.9
The Guardian (UK)	3.57	1.24	64.6	2.20	35.6
Los Angeles Times	3.14	1.33	63.2	1.64	43.1

NOTE: Each enjoyment score is based on the responses of 21 or 22 readers (N = 195). Each unpredictability score is based on the responses of 16 cloze procedure participants.
a. Primary source is United Press International.

appears to be a major shift in the relative impact of the two types of unpredictability on reader enjoyment. Not only is function-word entropy more highly correlated with reader enjoyment (r = −.84, p < .01) in this second study, but as the signs of the zero-order correlations indicate, content-word unpredictability and reader enjoyment exhibit a negative association. The signs of the correlation coefficients change from moderately negative to positive only when one controls for function-word entropy.[4]

TABLE 5
Correlations Between Reader Enjoyment and Entropy
and Cloze Scores for Nine Earthquake Articles

| | Reader Enjoyment | | |
| | Zero-Order | Controlling for Function-Word | |
		Entropy	Cloze
Function-Word			
Entropy	-.84*		
Cloze	.86*		
Content-Word			
Entropy	-.33	.04	-.15
Cloze	.29	-.37	-.10

*p < .01, df = 7.

GENERAL DISCUSSION

Although the results of the earthquake study reveal an unanticipated relationship between content-word unpredictability and
reader enjoyment, these new data do not necessarily conflict with the
evidence provided by the moonwalk study. First, it is important to
note that across both studies the most enjoyable articles are generally
those with the highest content-word unpredictability scores. In fact,
the moonwalk articles exhibit higher reader enjoyment scores despite their higher function-word entropy scores. Such an outcome
tentatively suggests that function-word predictability may contribute to increased reader enjoyment only within a limited domain
and that one journalistic topic may be intrinsically more enjoyable to
read about than another, because the subject matter affords the
author more opportunities to enhance semantic unpredictability
without critically increasing reading effort.

Second, the manipulation of unpredictability measures when computing partial correlation coefficients reveals a shift of statistical values in the earthquake study (Table 5) that is strikingly similar to the pattern exhibited by the moonwalk study (Table 3). In both instances, it appears that (a) function-word entropy scores operate as an effective control for disclosing the association between reader enjoyment and content-word unpredictability, and (b) content-word cloze scores better reflect the degree of semantic unpredictability in the text than entropy scores do—a finding that should be of more than passing interest to information-theorists.[5]

CONCLUSIONS

Although these information-theoretic measures of reader enjoyment require further experimental refinement, their implementation in these two studies are noteworthy from both a methodological and theoretical point of view. With the adoption of new scoring techniques, cloze procedure has once again proved itself to be an especially sensitive device for probing the relationship between text and reader. The information-theoretic measures reported here are more than descriptive statistics reflecting the form, structure, or complexity of social artifacts. They are subjective measures of information achieved by intervening and disrupting the communication process itself.

In particular, function-word entropy appears to operate very efficiently as a relative measure of the mental effort a text demands at the Decoding Level. By comparison, the measures of content-word unpredictability presented here are rudimentary at best, but their predictive power could well be enhanced by the development of a scoring method that would more accurately reflect the intersection of the writer's and the readers' intellectual domains (see Figure 3).

Theory and method are curiously intertwined as well in another aspect of this research. The two studies reported here confront a traditional problem in the practical application of information-theoretic measures: the receptor's ability to shift from one mental level to another in the course of processing information. As Moles (1966, p. 125) notes,

the first rational extension of information theory is to consider successively several levels on which the receptor grasps the message.

These levels give rise to superposed messages, all different, in principle, from each other. Each level has its own signs, its code, its repertoire, hence its rate of information per sign.

The model of reader enjoyment proposed here explicitly recognizes that the reader responds to unpredictability on at least three levels. The studies have reflected this multilevel approach by attempting to operationalize the concept of unpredictability at two levels while controlling for it at a third. Admittedly the empirical results are sometimes equivocal, but at a minimum they suggest that information-theoretic measures may be useful not only in their customary role as estimates of reading ease, but also in revealing the links between individual needs for physiological arousal and the attraction of novel content in written communication.

NOTES

1. For the purposes of the studies reported here, I have adopted a convention first devised by Funkhouser and Maccoby (1971), who defined function words as the 50 most commonly used words in English prose, a convention that in practice is surprisingly faithful to the definition above.

2. Because cloze scores reflect the number of correct guesses, the signs of the correlation coefficients are reversed.

3. Due to the small number of articles in the sample, the correlational analysis was checked to assure that no single article had an undue effect on the overall results. In addition to plotting the values used in the correlations, the data were reanalyzed using Spearman transformations (Conover & Iman, 1981) and a jackknife procedure in which partial correlation coefficients were recomputed with each of the articles deleted from the sample (Anscombe, 1973). The nine partial correlation coefficients computed using only eight articles at a time produced highly stable results. The minimum and maximum r-values fell between −.87 and −.95.

4. A check of the correlational analysis in this study revealed more variance in the partial correlation coefficients when individual articles were systematically deleted. Although in six cases the partial r-values fell between −.33 and −.39, the r-value dropped to −.09 when the *Christian Science Monitor* article was deleted and −.12 when the Los Angeles *Times* article was deleted. By contrast the partial r-value jumped to −.75 when the Arkansas *Gazette* article was deleted.

5. Although from a statistical viewpoint the use of Taylor's cloze scoring technique requires one to forfeit considerable information regarding the variety of guesses collected for each blank, routine entropy scoring can misrepresent the degree of contrast between the readers' guesses and the word actually deleted. If one represents the relationship between author and audience (or in information-theoretic terms between source and destination) with a Venn diagram (Figure 3), then

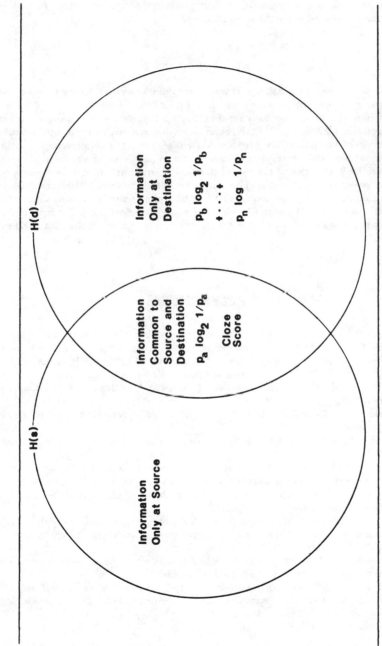

Figure 3: Venn Diagram Illustrating the Difference Between Entropy and Cloze Procedure Scoring Techniques

449

it is evident that the entropy scores computed from cloze responses are almost exclusively measures of entropy at the destination.

The relationship is revealed even more precisely if Shannon's entropy formula is written without the aid of the summation sign.

$$H = p_a \log_2 1/p_a +$$
$$p_b \log_2 1/p_b + \ldots + p_n \log_2 1/p_n$$

Only the expression $p_a \log_2 1/p_a$ characterizes the intersection between source and destination—the term pa being identical to Taylor's cloze score.

Given Shannon's essentially semiotic conceptualization of the communication process (Finn & Roberts, 1984), this observation does not invalidate entropy scores as estimates of unpredictability in the text, but it does suggest that refinements should be explored—especially in regard to measures of semantic unpredictability—that better reflect the intersection of the mental domains of writer and reader. In the case of function-word unpredictability, however, it may be that the set of possible responses is so small (due to linguistic constraints) that Shannon's entropy measure accurately reflects the degree of contrast between the readers' guesses and the writer's intentions, providing a significantly more sensitive measure of variance than normal cloze scores do.

REFERENCES

Anscombe, F.J. (1973). Graphs in statistical analysis. *American Statistician, 27,* 17-21.

Atkin, C. (1973). Instrumental utilities and information seeking. In P. Clark (Ed.), *New models for mass communication research* (pp. 205-239). Beverly Hills, CA: Sage.

Berlo, D.K. (1977). Communication as process: Review and commentary. In B.D. Ruben (Ed.), *Communication yearbook 1* (pp. 11-28). New Brunswick, NJ: Transaction Books.

Clark, H. H., & Clark, E. V. (1977). *Psychology and language.* New York: Harcourt Brace Jovanovich.

Cofer, C. N., & Appley, M. H. (1967). *Motivation: Theory and research.* New York: John Wiley.

Conover, W.J., & Iman, R.L. (1981). Rank transformations as a bridge between parametric and nonparametric statistics. *American Statistician, 35,* 124-133.

Dale, E., and Chall, J.S. (1948, January). A formula for predicting readability. *Educational Research Bulletin, 27,* 11-20, 28.

Donohew, R.L., Nair, M., & Finn, S. (1984). Automaticity, arousal, and information exposure. In R. N. Bostrom (Ed.), *Communication yearbook 8.* (pp. 267-284). Beverly Hills, CA: Sage.

Donohew, L., Palmgreen, P., & Duncan, J. (1980). An activation model of information exposure. *Communication Monographs, 37,* 225-303.

Finn, H.S. (1983). An information theory approach to reader enjoyment of print journalism (Doctoral dissertation, Stanford University, 1982). *Dissertation Abstracts International, 43,* 2481A-2482A.

Finn, S. (1985). Unpredictability as correlate of reader enjoyment of news articles. *Journalism Quarterly, 62,* 334-339, 345.

Finn, S., & Roberts, D. F. (1984). Source, destination, and entropy: Reassessing the role of information theory in communication research. *Communication Research, 11,* 453-476.

Flesch, R. (1948). *The art of readable writing.* New York: Harper & Row.

Funkhouser, G. R., & Maccoby, N. (1971). Communicating specialized science information to a lay audience. *Journal of Communication, 21,* 58-71.

Haber, L. R., & Haber, R. N. (1981). Perceptual processes in reading: An analysis by synthesis approach. In F. J. Pirozzolo & M. C. Wittrock (Eds.), *Neuropsychological and cognitive processes in reading* (pp. 167-200). New York: Academic Press.

Hebb, D. O. (1955). Drives and the CNS (conceptual nervous system). *Psychological Review, 62,* 243-254.

Kintsch, W., & Vipond, D. (1979). Reading comprehension and readability in educational practice and psychological theory. In L-G Nilsson (Ed.), *Perspectives on memory research* (pp. 329-365). Hillsdale, NJ: Erlbaum.

LaBerge, D., & Samuels, S. J. (1974). Toward a theory of automatic information processing in reading. *Cognitive Psychology, 6,* 293-323.

Madsen, K. B. (1968). *Theories of motivation.* Kent, OH: Kent State University Press.

Moles, A. (1966). *Information theory and esthetic perception* (J. Cohen, Trans.), Urbana. University of Illinois Press. (Original work published 1958)

Samuels, S. J., & P. Eisenberg (1981) A framework for understanding the reading process. In F. J. Pirozzolo & M. C. Wittrock (Eds.), *Neuropsychological and cognitive processes in reading* (pp. 31-67). New York: Academic Press.

Shannon, C. E. (1949). The mathematical theory of communication. In C. E. Shannon & W. Weaver (Eds.), *The mathematical theory of communication* (pp. 29-125). Urbana. University of Illinois Press.

Shannon, C. E. (1951). Prediction and entropy of printed English. *Bell System Technical Journal, 30,* 50-64.

Taylor, W. L. (1953). 'Cloze procedure': A new tool for measuring readability. *Journalism Quarterly, 30,* 415-433.

Taylor, W. L. (1955). Application of 'cloze' and entropy measures to the study of contextual constraint in samples of continuous prose. *Dissertation Abstracts, 15,* 464-465. (University Microfilms No. 10,554)

Taylor, W. L. (1956). Recent developments in the use of cloze procedure. *Journalism Quarterly, 33,* 42-48.

Seth Finn is Assistant Professor in the Department of Radio, Television, and Motion Pictures at the University of North Carolina. He earned his Ph.D. in Communication Theory and Research from Stanford University (1982). Prior to his return to academic life, he was a senior news producer at KRON-TV, San Francisco.

21

ACTIVITY IN THE EFFECTS OF TELEVISION ON CHILDREN

Robert P. Hawkins and Suzanne Pingree

Television effects research since the mid 1970s has increasingly recognized the child viewer as an active rather than passive participant. The notion that children are active in their use of television is now so widespread that it is tempting to consider it the base assumption of a new dominant paradigm in effects research (Pingree & Hawkins, 1982). Unfortunately, researchers mean so many different things by "active" that it is not clear what this dominant paradigm is. For example, active viewer can denote the locus of control in the communication transaction, as in Anderson and Lorch's (1983) work on active monitoring of television by preschool children. The activity of viewers as they approach television with various purposes and needs is also central to the theoretical perspectives of the uses and gratifications approach (cf. Blumler, 1979; Levy & Windahl, 1984). Or activity can refer to comprehension strategies such as learning to focus on central instead of incidental events (Collins, 1982). For Salomon (1983), in contrast, activity refers to the amount of mental effort invested during viewing. Dervin (1982) intends a much more substantial shift of paradigms from sender centered to receiver centered, in which "effects" is a misnomer for subjectively defined and controlled construction of meaning. The same recognition of the possibility of systematically different responses to the same message is present in research motivated by cognitive developmental theories proposing qualitative developmental differences in cognition (cf. Wartella, 1979).

These meanings for activity have very different implications for television effects. Some merely posit variability between individuals, others reject the idea of effects altogether, and still others are initially tangential to effects. In this chapter, we propose to elaborate on meanings of activity as they are applied to television use and suggest how these different meanings imply different kinds of effects.

We first make a key distinction in the various meanings of activity, namely, between those meanings that center around different kinds of cognitive activities employed while processing television and those meanings that refer to the overall amount of cognitive effort that viewers apply to processing television. There is sufficient research to show that both are important in cognitive effects of television, but the research also suggests that they are important in quite different ways.

However, neither the kinds of cognitive activities employed nor the amount of effort applied can be examined separately. Cognitive effort makes sense only as applied to some processing activity; cognitive processing activities make a difference in the effects of television depending on how much effort is applied. Thus, our model of individual cognitive processing in television effects on children (Fig. 12.1) shows cognitive activities as affecting children's attention to television, information constructed as a result of that attention, and meanings constructed from that information. Cognitive effort is applied to those cognitive activities and is hypothesized to determine the amount they affect attention, retention, and construction. We return to this model in more detail later, but first we elaborate on cognitive activities and effort.

COGNITIVE ACTIVITIES

Much of our knowledge about the kinds of cognitive activities that are involved in message processing comes from studies of how and how much children comprehend the television they watch. Researchers have been very active in this

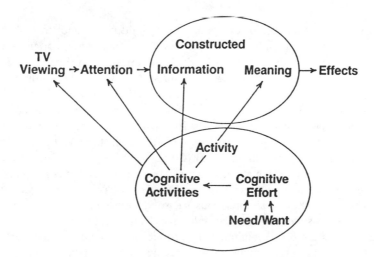

FIG. 12.1 A model of activity in television use and effects.

area (see reviews by Collins, 1982; Pingree & Hawkins, 1982), and recent work
has also given young children credit for more abilities than previous research
by reducing the task demands for comprehension and processing measures (e.g.,
Smith, Anderson, & Fischer, 1985). This research also allows us to break cognitive activities during viewing down into a number of components children (and
presumably adults as well) employ in processing television messages. A list of
such activities follows, along with a brief summary of evidence for the necessity
and use of each.

Segmenting

Television presents sounds and images continuously, although adult viewers are
accustomed to using a variety of cinematic devices and dramatic conventions to
break action into meaningful chunks of related actions. In one study comparing
break points placed in the same film by respondents of different ages, adults and
ninth-grade children segmented by combining scenes. Third-grade children generally made use of these adult break points, but also broke the program at many
other points, including breaking within a scene (Wartella, 1978). Breaking a
program into many segments should tend to produce memory and processing
overloads because the larger number of discrete units may make relating scenes
more difficult.

Focusing

Because the sheer number of things a viewer could notice and remember is so
very large, another logically necessary activity is to focus on important or useful
information and to ignore most of the incidental information. Even if effects are
not defined from a sender's perspective, some sort of focusing seems inescapable,
although the definition of what is important or unimportant may vary.

There are a number of studies showing that after 8–10 years, the mix of
central and incidental items learned shifts so that a decreasing share of total
learning is incidental to following the plot (Calvert, Huston, Watkins, & Wright,
1982; Collins, 1970; Hawkins, 1973). Some of the tests of alternative explanations in these and other studies suggest that young children lack strategies
favoring the selection and encoding of plot-relevant content while filtering out
irrelevant detail. Young children thus seem equally open to all that television
presents, whereas older children are selective. However, given some recent work
suggesting that preschool children can reproduce more of a television story using
dolls than they are given credit for with recognition tests (Pingree et al., 1983;
Smith et al., 1985) this conclusion bears reexamination.

Reading Formal Features

In recent years there has been a great deal of attention to what several researchers have called the "formal features" of television—visual effects, movement, and editing; audio compression, sound effects, and music; and formally defined information content or entropy (cf. Rice, Huston, & Wright, 1982; Watt & Welch, 1983). Huston and Wright (1983) propose that formal features can play three roles in young children's television viewing: (a) maintenance of attention through the orienting response to change, (b) marking significant content for children's monitoring strategies through learned associations between features and content, and (c) signifiers of some of the meaning gained from the television program. In the third case, formal features require a cognitive activity that might be called *reading*, that is, applying learned or constructed interpretations to the formal features.

We are beginning to gain some idea of the range and types of features that can be assigned meaning as one processes television (Huston & Wright, 1983; see also Anderson & Smith, 1984, on "montage"), but we have as yet only a vague understanding of the extent to which each of these different features is used or how they are integrated into an overall meaning when they complement or contradict each other. More important for the study of children and television, we need considerable work on how children learn that formal features are potentially meaningful and then learn particular meanings for individual features or combinations of features. Experience with television seems important, but we do not know how much experience, at what ages, and with what relationship to nontelevision experience. Smith et al. (1985) showed even preschool children assigning meaning to formal features in very short animations.

Using Time

In a sense, the time order of events in a program is just another formal feature, and children's use of time in processing television and making sense of it is again the reading of formal features. However, time order seems especially difficult for children and thus deserves some special consideration. For example, Leifer et al. (1971) found that preschool children could not sequence even three central scenes from a 20-min film of a familiar fairy tale they had just seen, and 7-year-olds did very poorly when the sequence contained five or more central events. Even when children are old enough to begin integrating motives for and consequences of aggressive acts (third grade), the additional temporal distance provided by inserting an intervening commercial seriously disrupted their abilities (Collins, 1973).

Part of this poor performance with time may be due to problems of memory overload in long sequences and testing that is too demanding, as suggested by studies in which young children were able to keep events in order (Smith et al.,

1985). However, there are also some indications that young children's difficulties with time may be a more fundamental disinclination to use time, even if not an inability. Collins, Wellman, Keniston, and Westby (1978) found that second graders' comprehension was essentially unaffected by editing that jumbled the order of scenes within a television program, and fifth and eighth graders were less able to draw the inferences, many of which depended on the time order of events.

Drawing Inferences

Much that is crucial to gaining adultlike comprehension of a television program is never presented explicitly, but instead requires the viewer to draw inferences based on what is available in the program. Thus, we might observe two actions and draw a connection such as causation or motivation between them. Often these meanings are intended by the sender and are only implied for reasons of narrative economy and because the producer can safely assume that all adults will draw the intended inference. Thus, we are left to infer spatial relationships, the passage of time, character perspective and motivation, causation, and consequences throughout television programming.

With children, however, such assumptions seem questionable. Collins in particular has done a number of studies showing that children do less well with implicit than explicit central content (Collins et al., 1978; Collins, Sobol, & Westby, 1981; see Collins, 1983, for a fuller review). That the ability (or inclination) to draw inferences is the root of some of this difficulty is revealed by analyses showing that second graders did not draw the expected inference even when they knew the relevant explicit information; fifth and especially eighth graders will draw the appropriate inferences as long as they have learned the necessary explicit information.

On the other hand, preschool children were able to reconstruct implicit material using dolls (Smith et al., 1985). Filling in events not shown was fairly easy for 4- and 7-year-olds, and inferring the passage of time from camera techniques was most difficult (with character perspective and location intermediate), but even for time inferences, more than a third of the youngest children reconstructed the action correctly. Several factors could be responsible for the very different results. First, the poor inference results were with recognition tests, and the good results were with doll reconstructions. Second, many of Collins' inferences were about relatively abstract things such as motives, goals, and consequences of action, whereas the inferences in Smith et al. were very concrete. Third, the inferences children drew in the Smith study seemed to be based largely on the formal features presented, while Collins' inferences tended to draw more on general world and television knowledge. Thus, we see no contradiction from these very different results. In fact, what they make clear is that the number and range of inferences useful in comprehending television are very great indeed and that this cognitive activity is very central.

Drawing on Other Knowledge

Although some inferences require drawing conclusions based on formal features, others require the application of one's knowledge about television and the world in general. A number of researchers have proposed that this application of knowledge often proceeds via scripts or schemata, that is, organized prototypic expectations of individuals, objects, and event sequences (Bower, Black, & Turner, 1979; Schank & Abelson, 1977; Wyer & Srull, 1981). These schemata are hypothesized to serve as a framework for new information, as mnemonic aids, and as guides to the interpolation of missing actions, motivations, and plans. Scripts and schemata seem to be very handy tools for organizing experience, but they can also be a source of error, as when Collins and Wellman's 7-year-olds were judged to make schema-driven or stereotypic errors (1983).

All these activities seem necessary in one form or another to achieve comprehension of television as the sender intended it. Of course, comprehending artificially simplified television might not require each one, but regularly broadcast television watched by children seems to need them all. But what about meanings not intended by the sender? By "constructed information and meaning" in our model, we endorse the receiver perspective of granting independence and subjectivity to viewers in constructing meanings that may be quite different from what the sender intended.

For the cognitive activities listed, this distinction between sender-intended meaning and individually defined variations in meanings seems irrelevant. All of the activities seem necessary to attend to television, acquire facts, and construct meanings, regardless of what those meanings are. But several other activities are part of processing television subjectively, which have nothing to do with achieving adult-defined comprehension. We propose three, largely without evidence, because their role in adult-defined comprehension research is only as intervening variables enhancing or inhibiting effects, not as processing activities in their own right.

Evaluating Information

One viewer activity that probably has considerable impact on the meanings they construct is assigning values and affect to bits of information taken from the television content. These values then form part of the meaning constructed and may also influence application of other cognitive activities.

Making Connections

Another activity in assigning meaning to television is making comparisons between the television content being viewed and past real-life and television experience. This activity is more general, subjective, and less tied to regularities than the application of schemata. That is, although schema application deals with recognizing the immediate as representative of some generalization, making connections refers to an activity such as distinguishing between reality and fantasy portrayals, but it could also include connections that are much more isolated and unpredictable. Nevertheless, such associations are a potential starting point for considerable analytic thought.

Stimulation

Finally, an activity in response to television may be independent or creative thought. Such thought may begin with connections and continue to create meanings and relations that seem to an outside observer to be entirely independent of the television viewing experience. Including them here is thus rather far from comprehending television in the usual (adult-defined) sense, but because we are discussing cognitive activities in processing television, the inclusion seems appropriate.

This list is not exhaustive; there probably are some other cognitive activities in processing television, especially in the latter group of subjective activities. Nonetheless, the number and variety of activities used in processing television are large, and the activities are interrelated in complex ways, such that the interactions are themselves as important for understanding television as any activity alone.

COGNITIVE EFFORT

In addition to the cognitive activities used in processing television messages, activity has meant the amount of effort applied to processing. Thus, we can describe more or less effort applied to focusing processes, more or less effort applied to comparison processes or evaluative processes, and so on. Recently, researchers have made some serious attempts to measure amount of cognitive effort, using operationalizations centering around attention, brain waves, reported amount of thinking while viewing, and results of cognitive effort.

Attention

Attention probably has been used more than other operationalizations of cognitive effort, especially as an intervening variable that locates cognitive processes between message reception and effect. For example, two studies show that survey attention measures (questions such as "How much attention do you pay to television news?" which can be answered "a great deal," "some attention," or "don't pay much attention") contribute their own predictive power beyond that of exposure measures for political effects of mass media (Chaffee & Choe, 1979; McLeod, Leutscher, & McDonald, 1980).

However, self-report measures of attention may not be a particularly accurate way to measure cognitive effort. In the first place, they assume that people are self-aware or that their attentiveness is salient enough to answer such questions meaningfully. But more problematic, survey questions about attention may be asking for traitlike responses, when effort is likely to be much more situational. That is, the assumption that effort is applied consistently across viewing situations (whether these situations are conceptualized as different kinds of television content or different personal contexts for the viewer) may provide a misleading average.

Researchers have also operationalized attention as visual orientation to the television screen. Much of this research began by focusing on attributes of television content that would capture and maintain children's attention so that maximum learning would take place (Anderson & Levin, 1976; Lesser, 1974; Rice et al., 1982), but this approach has little to do with what we mean by cognitive effort.

More recent work by Anderson and his colleagues, however, begins to make an argument for visual attention as an indicator of cognitive activity. Their research suggests that even very young children strategically direct their visual attention to content that is comprehensible (Anderson, Lorch, Field, & Sanders, 1981; Lorch, Anderson, & Levin, 1979). From these results and others (Anderson & Lorch, 1983), they argue that children learn that some formal features of television signal significant messages and that comprehensibility is a prime factor in determining significance for young children. It is not clear at present what proportion of children's attention is passively captured by salient formal features of television and what proportion is actively directed the the child. But to the extent that attention reflects the child's monitoring, it also provides an indirect indicator of the amount of prior cognitive activity directing that visual attention.

The problem with visual attention as a measure of cognitive effort is that although it is sometimes necessary to watch carefully while applying effort, it may often be equally or more useful to look away. For example, if some aspect of television content stimulates viewers to think about the relationships between ideas, very hard thinking about these ideas might be better accomplished if viewers divert their attention from television either physically (moving their eyes away) or psychologically (putting their eyes out of focus and "clicking out"). Thus, amount of visual attention by itself may partially capture what we mean by cognitive effort, but it could also represent no effort at all.

Brain Waves

The use of electroencephalographic (EEG) recordings made while viewing television constitutes another major attempt to measure cognitive activity. This approach is based on research suggesting that the alpha portion of EEG is an inverse indicator of the amount of cognitive activity (Greenfield & Sternbach,

1972). EEG has the advantage of being measured continuously in both amplitude and duration so that the researcher can associate variations in activity with variations in content; in contrast, dichotomous visual attention measures may indicate nothing more active than an orienting response. It also has the advantage of measuring activity within the brain rather than using some exterior indicator that may or may not be related to cognitive activity.

However, it is not clear at present exactly what EEG means (it probably is also sensitive to the orienting response) or how variations in EEG relate to reasonable outcomes of cognitive effort. Although some researchers appear to be finding EEG patterns that are potentially exciting (see, e.g., Reeves, Thorson, & Schleuder, chapter 13 in this volume), research linking EEG with effort and other indicators of activity is just beginning.

Thinking While Viewing

Some researchers have attempted to measure quantity of cognitive effort during viewing by asking about it directly. Salomon (1983) has suggested the construct of amount of invested mental effort (AIME) in nonautomatic elaboration of material as a measure of the amount of mindful or deep processing of television content. For example, he argues that AIME increases "when a unit of material cannot be easily fitted into existing schemata" (p. 187). When respondents are questioned about the amount of AIME they generally expend with media and with various types of media content (adventure, news, science, etc.), it has been found to be associated with greater learning (Kane & Anderson, 1978; Salomon, 1983).

Results of Cognitive Effort

As with visual attention, it may be possible to infer amount of cognitive effort from the results of effort. That is, for some kinds of cognitive activities (e.g., focusing, segmenting, inferring, etc.), those children whose performance is superior most likely devoted more effort to those activities at some previous point. For example, Pingree (1983) studied fifth, sixth, and seventh graders' ability to infer television content that was not explicitly presented in the program. She predicted that children who scored high on this ability would also be the most affected by implicit social reality messages on television because of their greater ability to draw inferences.

Surprisingly, the children who did less well at the inference task seemed most affected. High scoring children were consistently unaffected by social reality messages. Pingree suggests that what was measured as inference-making ability may have reflected the results of prior cognitive effort. A similar argument can be used to explain Pingree's (1978) and Reeves' (1978) results with children's perceptions of reality. For both studies, perceptions were directly related to beliefs, although perceived reality had been hypothesized to work only as an intervening variable. What had been conceived of as an indicator of children's beliefs about television's portrayal of reality might also have located prior cognitive effort of other sorts.

Most of these measures of cognitive effort are fairly unsatisfactory. Self-report measures are likely to be unreliable, are likely to elicit responses about usual behaviors when responses in specific situations and contexts would be more valuable, have tended thus far to measure activity while viewing and to ignore activity related to television content during nonviewing periods, and have assumed that subjects are aware of their cognitive effort level so that they can report those levels accurately. Unobtrusive measures (e.g., visual orientation and EEG) probably measure much more and much less than cognitive effort. What looks like effort may be effort, or it may be something less rich and interesting. In addition, for visual orientation at least, some effort is almost certainly taking place where that measure would suggest no effort, that is, when people aren't looking.

Finally, no measure is specific enough for precise predictions about outcomes. All of these are measures of effort in a general sense: "How hard were you thinking just then?" We need measures of cognitive effort applied to each type of cognitive activity so that some sense can be made of how this effort and activity are being used by children (and adults). We also need measures of whether effort is being applied to several activities simultaneously and/or to the integration or mastery of these activities. In other words, cognitive activity and cognitive effort will be more useful as explanatory variables to the extent that measures of both activities are specific.

IMPLICATIONS FOR EFFECTS

We began this chapter by suggesting that researchers have been using activity to mean many things, thus leading to some confusion about whether contradictory results represent true conflicts or just unfortunate disagreements over definitions. Now that we have distinguished between cognitive activities and cognitive effort and suggested many specific activities, the semantic disagreements are less troublesome, but trying to describe and predict the effects of television is still complex. We begin by returning to our model of individual cognitive processing in television effects (Fig. 12.1) and explaining our intentions in more detail.

One usage of activity has not been dealt with directly so far, although we think it is implied throughout. This is the general philosophical approach of emphasizing the relative power and independence of receivers of mass communications. It does not necessarily mean discarding traditional conceptualizations of effects as changes or differences (or the lack of change or difference) in learning, attitudes, or behavior resulting from using television. What it does require, however, is not making the assumptions of determinism about effects and of isomorphism of messages and effects. That is, one should avoid the magic bullet assumption that message reception will necessarily produce change, but one should also avoid the more subtle assumption that any given message will produce a particular sort of effect (e.g., assuming violent content produces aggressive behavior rather than fear, desensitization, or revulsion).

We do not want to argue that messages have no influence or that there is no predictable relationshp between television messages and the changes that result. Our models of television effects need to predict subjectivity and audience independence while still allowing for substantial similarity of effects on occasion. For television effects on children (and perhaps for adults as well), we propose a model of individual cognitive processing in such effects (Fig. 12.1) that bases variability largely on the intermediate result of comprehension, that is, information and meaning constructed from viewing.

We show these as two separate intermediate products for simplicity, but label them both as constructed to suggest a continuum of multiple levels of depth. One might be tempted to separate the facts retained from the meanings constructed, but this would bias toward an objectivist assumption about just what facts are there and tend to ignore individuality in selecting and interpreting these facts. Still, there is a real sense in which construction can vary from relatively unprocessed segmentation, selection, and reading formal features to constructions that are highly processed by multiple activities and far removed from the original perceptions. We want these intermediate products to express a continuum of levels or amount of construction in which individual variation is possible from the beginning, but in which subjective variability in interpretation becomes successively more probable with greater processing.

The placement of television viewing at the left of Fig. 12.1 (i.e., at the beginning of the model) does not reflect causal priority; it is simply the beginning of a cognitive processing model. Actually, the amount and kind of television viewing a child does are themselves the product of many antecedents, including most of the other elements in our model (see also Rubin, Chapter 14 in this volume).

Activities, Effort, and Effects

In applying this model for research on effects, we see two broad research agendas. The first concerns the ways in which cognitive effort applied to these various activities changes the intermediate and traditional effects of viewing television. Because cognitive activities work in different ways for viewers' processing of television, the application of more or less effort to them may have different outcomes. Some cognitive effort while viewing may increase learning, comprehension, or the isomorphism between television content and viewer beliefs or behaviors. In other cases, cognitive effort may decrease learning from television or increase the likelihood of beliefs opposed to those presented on television.

Alternatively, active thinking while viewing may sometimes lead to creative and diverse beliefs that would seem to have little to do with television content (see Hawkins & Pingree, 1982, and Pingree, 1983, for fuller discussion of these ideas as applied to social reality effects). With the distinction between cognitive activity and cognitive effort, we should be ready to specify programs, outcomes, and populations for which we are willing to make each of these kinds of predictions.

Individual hypotheses can be thought of as residing at intersections of a matrix in which the rows are the various kinds of cognitive activities and the columns are various effects of viewing television, including predictions about intermediate products such as getting the meaning the sender intended or constructing one with considerable variation. One might then predict that as greater effort is applied to such processes as segmenting, focusing, drawing inferences, reading formal features, or using real-world knowledge, the likelihood of constructing the sender's intended meaning increases. This could be elaborated by restricting such a prediction to early, less-processed constructions and predicting greater likelihood of variation from the sender's intention with increased effort for higher level constructions, and for the application of effort to activities such as evaluation, making connections, or stimulation. Or one might predict that individualistic meanings are more likely a result of some types of activity than others, such as applying real-world knowledge, and less so from reading formal features.

Or one could predict, although it would be difficult to test, the level to which construction proceeds based on the activities brought into play and the amount of effort devoted to them. Predictions could also be made about the effects of energy expended regardless of activity or, in some cases, of activities regardless of the amount of energy expended (i.e., hypothesizing that the effects of an activity are dichotomously present or not). All such predictions should then move to more traditional effects on attitudes, behavior, social agendas, and so on, with the intermediate products themselves still tested and treated as intervening variables.

Competence and Performance

A second broad research agenda needs to deal with factors that determine children's application of effort and activities to processing television. Here we see three subagendas. One deals with the ability to perform and coordinate cognitive activities, and the other two appear in the model as factors influencing the amount of cognitive effort applied. To discuss these, we would first like to distinguish between competence and performance in processing television. Chomsky was very careful to point out that his phrase-structure and transformational grammars were theories of linguistic competence, describing what people knew about language and not theories of linguistic performance, describing how people actually behave in producing and decoding language (1965). A similar distinction may be crucial in describing people's real-life processing of television because what people actually do may often be less than they could do optimally.

Coordinating Abilities

One problem for children lies in the distinction between individual competencies and the competence to coordinate a variety of activities. Research on children's comprehension has for years cataloged the abilities young children do not have that lead to their difficulties with television. However, recent research on comprehension (Pingree et al., 1983; Smith et al., in press) suggests that even preschool children have many abilities they were thought to lack and can do many of the cognitive activities we outlined. At the minimum, these studies show that preschoolers can focus, segment, use time, and draw inferences (at least in some fashion). However, for a period of years thereafter, children's application of these abilities is uncertain and uneven, probably reflecting other limitations on their abilities.

Processing television requires children or adults to apply, not just a few, but many different cognitive activities, all of which seem necessary and useful. Thus, one major problem for children processing television, and an important topic for research, is just how one coordinates all the different activities that go into processing television, and how one integrates and organizes the products of these various activities.

What Viewers Need to Do

Problems in coordinating and using cognitive activities may also influence competence-performance by changing the amount of effort viewers need to apply. While children are learning to coordinate their cognitive activities, they need to deal with information overload, a problem that is familiar from studies of distraction and division of attention.

Commercial television shows provide a fairly rich stimulus environment, and several varieties of overload could thus limit cognitive effort applied to various comprehension activities. The richness of the stimulus—many things happening at once—provides many distracting features that can lead to dead ends, during which crucial features have been ignored (e.g., is that car in the background going to turn this way and enter the plot or go on past and out of view forever?). With sufficient processing capacity, both foreground and background action can be monitored, but if capacity is exceeded and if the wrong choice is made, comprehension (adultlike meanings) will be downgraded.

A related overload may have to do with capacities of working memory and may operate in studies where children as old as 8 comprehend less when related facts are separated by a commercial instead of immediately following one another

(Collins, 1982). Full-length television programs may simply separate facts needing integration too far apart in time.

In addition, although recent studies were able to show that very young children could do a number of the cognitive activities we posited, they do not tell us about the cognitive capacity implications of having to do many of them more or less simultaneously. The constant switching between activities and integration of these cognitive activities may provide the overload for children.

A key idea here is *automaticity*. With experience, processing cinematic conventions becomes highly automatic and makes very little demand on cognitive resources. Thus, as processing television becomes more automatic, the demands of each individual interpretation become reduced, and cognitive resources are available for parallel processing and other aspects of comprehension.

Another factor that may be related to automaticity is the concept of schema or scripts as organized, prototypic expectations of individuals, objects, and event sequences. Earlier, we discussed how applying schema may be an important cognitive activity in processing television, but in addition, their application to the problem of processing television is expected to reduce the cognitive demands of that processing, both by allowing low-effort, top-down interpretation of the television stimulus and by allowing high-probability predictions that make focusing and segmenting more efficient. Context cues and schema for television programs probably give adult viewers the advantage of predicting whether to attend or not. Thus, schema application can make it easier for effort to be applied to other cognitive activities.

Schank and Abelson (1977) suggest that children younger than 4 years are basically in the process of acquiring scripts. Thereafter, they argue that scripts and schemata become more elaborated, easier to instantiate, and more flexible each time they are instantiated. Although subsequent research has demonstrated that even younger children have scripts for familiar event sequences such as eating dinner (Adams & Worden, 1983; Nelson & Gruendel, 1981), it is clear that they have some difficulties manipulating and applying them. Thus, we would expect relatively little benefit to cognitive capacity of script use early in their acquisition, but progressively greater reductions in processing demands through their use with continued experience.

What Viewers Want to Do

A third set of factors that can affect performance has to do with motivations or orientations toward the viewing task. Children (or adults) may approach their viewing situation with more or less interest, involvement, intent, or something like a cognitive set that motivates them to put forth more or less effort than they would otherwise apply. In research with children and adults, Salomon (1983) found evidence that stereotyping of television affects effort invested. He found less variance in his respondents' feelings about their own abilities, in the amount of energy they said they invested in processing, and in the depth they attributed to their response to television compared to the same material in print form. His results also suggest that the more stereotyped the perception of the medium, the less effort was invested in it.

Other factors in the viewing situation can change effort expended. Reasons for viewing and the viewer's relative effort in approaching the choice of what to view may contribute to more or less effort in processing. When "to relax" or "I just like it" are important reasons for viewing, for example, we suggest that cognitive activity will be lower. In a study of the relationship between effort in the decisions to view and what to view and active television processing while viewing, Rouner (1983) found partial support for this hypothesis. Rouner used college students' self-reports of decisional effort and found some relationships between this effort and a set of measures that would seem to locate cognitive effort while viewing.

Both formal and content features of the television program being watched will be more or less easy to process, but we hypothesize that such features may also be more or less motivating as well. For example, one can argue that some television genres, primarily soap operas and mysteries, inherently motivate more effort in solving their puzzles, keeping track of secrets and clues, and making predictions about character actions (Cantor & Pingree, 1983). Similarly, sports fans may devote exceptional energy to some sports viewing in comparing athletes' performances statistically and in predicting plays.

We also suggest that some situations are motivating for greater expenditure of energy in and of themselves. These situations actually act on individual expectations and reasons for viewing, but we mention situations separately to emphasize that the process begins externally to the individual. For example, viewing with others (e.g., parents) instead of alone could lead to greater effort through mechanisms such as modeling of interest and attention, instantiation of family values (Atkin & Greenberg, 1977), or to less effort through diffusion of the need to keep up with the plot. Or, viewing in competition with other activities could lead to less effort in viewing, although there is some reason to believe that dividing attention actually calls up more effort (Turnure, 1970).

CONCLUSION

The concept of activity is generating a great deal of activity in research on television effects on children (and for effects research generally). To alleviate some of the resulting confusion, we have differentiated between the cognitive activities applied in processing television and the cognitive effort applied to these activities. In so doing, we have also presented a model of how these various elements play a part in the effects of television, and we have proposed several research agendas implied by the combination of concept distinctions and their places in the model.

We want to reemphasize the need to keep distinct the different types of cognitive activity in processing television, as well as to keep clear the difference between effort and activities. This is not to say that these concepts can only be studied individually and in isolation. On the contrary, a large part of our research problem is to deal with a real multiplication of concepts theoretically and operationally.

Finally, we want to reemphasize the receiver-oriented perspective, which gives receivers credit for independence and the ability to construct meanings. In adopting such a perspective, one need not give up all similarity of meanings and effects. Prediction is still possible. But prediction does need a sensitivity to the receiver, and that means increasingly greater care in conceptualizing and operationalizing the products or effects of mass communication. In so doing, we need to distinguish in fairly detailed ways between products at different stages or levels of construction.

All of this multiplication and specification of concepts necessarily multiplies the number of testable hypotheses as well. Our hope is that these more specific hypotheses will also be more powerful.

REFERENCES

Adams, L. T., & Worden, P. E. (1983, April). *Script development and memory organization.* Paper presented at the meeting of the Society for Research in Child Development, Detroit, MI.

Anderson, D. R., & Levin, S. R. (1976). Young children's visual attention to attributes of television. *Child Development, 47,* 806–811.

Anderson, D. R., & Lorch, E. P. (1983). Looking at television: Action or reaction? In J. Bryant & D. R. Anderson (Eds.), *Children's understanding of television* (pp. 1–33). New York: Academic.

Anderson, D. R., Lorch, E. P., Field, D. E., & Sanders, J. (1981). The effects of TV program comprehensibility on preschool children's visual attention to television. *Child Development, 52,* 151–157.

Anderson, D. R., & Smith, R. (1984). Young children's TV viewing: The problem of cognitive continuity. In F. J. Morrison, C. Lord, D. F. Keating (Eds.), *Advances in applied developmental psychology,* (Vol. 1, pp. 115–163). New York: Academic.

Atkin, C. K., & Greenberg, B. S. (1977). *Parental mediation of children's social behavior learned from television.* Unpublished manuscript, Michigan State University, Department of Communication, East Lansing.

Blumler, J. (1979). The role of theory in uses and gratifications research. *Communication Research, 6,* 9–36.

Bower, G., Black, J. B., & Turner, T. J. (1979). Scripts in memory for text. *Cognitive Psychology, 11,* 177–220.

Calvert, S. L., Huston, A. C., Watkins, B. A., & Wright, J. C. (1982). The relation between selective attention to television forms and children's comprehension of content. *Child Development, 53,* 601–610.

Cantor, M. R., & Pingree, S. (1983). *The soap opera.* Beverly Hills, CA: Sage.

Chaffee, S. H., & Choe, S. Y. (1979, April). *Communication measurement in the March 1979 NES pilot study*. Paper presented at the meeting of the American Political Science Association, Washington, DC.

Chomsky, N. Y. (1965). *Aspects of the theory of syntax*. Cambridge, MA: MIT Press.

Collins, W. A. (1970). Learning of media content: A developmental study. *Child Development, 41,* 1133–1142.

Collins, W. A. (1973). The effect of temporal separation between motivation, aggression and consequences: A developmental study. *Developmental Psychology, 8,* 215–221.

Collins, W. A. (1982). Cognitive processing in television viewing. In D. Pearl, L. Bouthilet, & J. Lazar (Eds.), *Television and behavior: Ten years of scientific progress and implications for the eighties* (Vol. 2, pp. 9–23). Washington, DC: U.S. Government Printing Office.

Collins, W. A. (1983). Interpretation and inference in children's television viewing. In J. Bryant & D. R. Anderson (Eds.), *Children's understanding of television* (pp. 125–150). New York: Academic.

Collins, W. A., Sobol, B. L., & Westby, S. (1981). Effects of adult commentary on children's comprehension and inferences about a televised aggressive portrayal. *Child Development, 52,* 158–163.

Collins, W. A., & Wellman, H. (1983). Social scripts and developmental changes in representations of televised narratives. *Communication Research, 9,* 380–398.

Collins, W. A., Wellman, H., Keniston, A., & Westby, S. (1978). Age-related aspects of comprehension and inference from a televised dramatic narrative. *Child Development, 49,* 389–399.

Dervin, B. (1982). Mass media: Changing conceptions of the audience. In R. E. Rice & W. J. Paisley (Eds.), *Public communication campaigns* (pp. 71–88). Beverly Hills, CA: Sage.

Greenfield, N. S., & Sternbach, R. A. (1972). *Handbook of psycho-physiology*. New York: Holt, Rinehart & Winston.

Hawkins, R. P. (1973). Learning of peripheral content in films: A developmental study. *Child Development, 44,* 214–217.

Hawkins, R. P., & Pingree, S. (1982). Television influence on constructions of social reality. In D. Pearl, L. Bouthilet, & J. Lazar (Eds.), *Television and behavior: Ten years of scientific progress and implications for the eighties* (Vol. 2, pp. 224–247). Washington, DC: U.S. Government Printing Office.

Huston, A. C., & Wright, J. C. (1983). Children's processing of television: The informative functions of formal features. In J. Bryant & D. R. Anderson (Eds.), *Children's understanding of television* (pp. 35–68). New York: Academic.

Kane, J. M., & Anderson, R. C. (1978). Depth of processing and interference effects in the learning and remembering of sentences. *Journal of Educational Psychology, 70,* 626–635.

Leifer, A. D., Collins, W. A., Gross, B. M., Taylor, P. H., Andrews, L., & Blackmer, E. R. (1971). Developmental aspects of variables relevant to observational learning. *Child Development, 42,* 1509–1516.

Lesser, G. (1974). *Children and television: Lessons from Sesame Street*. New York: Random House.

Levy, M. R., & Windahl, S. (1984). Audience activity and gratifications: A conceptual clarification and exploration. *Communication Research, 11,* 51–78.

Lorch, E. P., Anderson, D. R., & Levin, S. R. (1979). The relationship of visual attention to children's comprehension of television. *Child Development, 50,* 722–727.

McLeod, J., Leutscher, W., & McDonald, D. (1980, August). *Beyond mere exposure: Media orientations and their impact on political processes*. Paper presented at the meeting of the Association for Education in Journalism, Boston, MA.

Nelson, K., & Gruendel, J. (1981). Generalized event representations: Basic building blocks of cognitive development. In M. Lamb & A. Brown (Eds.), *Advances in developmental psychology* (Vol. 1, pp. 131–158). Hillsdale, NJ: Lawrence Erlbaum Associates.

Pingree, S. (1978). The effects of nonsexist television commercials and perceptions of reality on children's attitudes about women. *Psychology of Women Quarterly, 2,* 262–277.

Pingree, S. (1983). Cognitive processes in constructing social reality. *Journalism Quarterly, 60,* 415–422.

Pingree, S., & Hawkins, R. P. (1982). What children do with television: Implications for communication research. In B. Dervin & M. Voigt (Eds.), *Progress in communication sciences* (Vol. 3, pp. 225–244). Norwood, NJ: Ablex.

Pingree, S., Hawkins, R. P., Rouner, D., Burns, J., Gikonyo, W., & Neuwirth, C. (1984). Children's reconstruction of a television narrative. *Communication Research, 11,* 477–496.

Reeves, B. (1978). Perceived TV reality as a predictor of children's social behavior. *Journalism Quarterly, 55,* 682–689, 695.

Rice, M. L., Huston, A. C., & Wright, J. C. (1982). The forms and codes of television: Effects on children's attention, comprehension, and social behavior. In D. Pearl, L. Bouthilet, & J. Lazar (Eds.), *Television and behavior: Ten years of scientific progress and implications for the eighties* (Vol. 2, pp. 24–38). Washington, DC: U.S. Government Printing Office.

Rouner, D. L. (1983). *Individual and environmental determinants of television viewing behavior.* Unpublished doctoral dissertation, University of Wisconsin, Madison.

Salomon, G. (1979). *Interaction of media, cognition, and learning.* San Francisco: Jossey-Bass.

Salomon, G. (1983). Television watching and mental effort: A social psychological view. In J. Bryant & D. R. Anderson (Eds.), *Children's understanding of television* (pp. 181–198). New York: Academic.

Schank, R., & Abelson, R. (1977). *Scripts, plans, goals, and understanding.* Hillsdale, NJ: Lawrence Erlbaum Associates.

Smith, R., Anderson, D. R., & Fischer, C. (1985). Young children's comprehension of montage. *Child Development, 55.*

Turnure, J. E. (1970). Children's reactions to distractors in a learning situation. *Developmental Psychology, 2,* 115–122.

Wartella, E. (1978, August). *Children's perceptual unitizing of a televised behavior sequence.* Paper presented at the meeting of the Association for Education in Journalism, Seattle, WA.

Wartella, E. (1979). Children and television: The development of the child's understanding of the medium. In D. Wilhoit & M. de Bock (Eds.), *Mass communication review yearbook* (Vol. 1, pp. 516–553). Beverly Hills, CA: Sage.

Watt, J. H., & Welch, A. J. (1983). Effects of static and dynamic complexity on children's attention and recall of televised instruction. In J. Bryant & D. R. Anderson (Eds.), *Children's understanding of television* (pp. 69–102). New York: Academic.

Wyer, R., & Srull, T. (1981). The processing of social stimulus information: A conceptual integration. In R. Hastie, T. Ostrom, E. Ebbesen, R. Wyer, D. Hamilton, & D. Carlston (Eds.), *Person memory: The cognitive basis of social perception* (pp. 227–300). Hillsdale, NJ: Lawrence Erlbaum Associates.

22

YOUNG CHILDREN'S COMPREHENSION
OF MONTAGE

Robin Smith, Daniel R. Anderson, and Catherine Fischer

SMITH, ROBIN; ANDERSON, DANIEL R.; and FISCHER, CATHERINE. *Young Children's Comprehension of Montage.* CHILD DEVELOPMENT, 1985, **56**, 962–971. 2 studies examined children's comprehension of brief stop-animation televised segments incorporating elements of cinematic montage such as pans, zooms, and cuts. Children reconstructed the action and dialogue in these segments using the same dolls and settings depicted. In Study 1, there was no effect of cinematic techniques on reconstruction performance of 3- and 5-year-olds as compared to control segments filmed without these techniques. The results challenged the assumption that the use of such techniques per se contributes to young children's poor comprehension of television shows. In Study 2, 12 new segments were produced in which comprehending the montage required inferences of character perspective, implied action sequences, spatial relationships, and simultaneity of different actions. Averaging across all segments, 62% of the 4-year-olds and 88% of the 7-year-olds demonstrated clear comprehension of the montage. Inferences concerning implied action sequences were easiest for both ages. Inferences of simultaneity were most difficult for 4-year-olds, whereas inferences of character perspective were most difficult for 7-year-olds. Preschool children are thus capable of understanding cinematic events conveyed through camera techniques and film editing, despite previous assertions to the contrary. This ability nevertheless substantially increases with age.

Young children's comprehension of film and television has been a topic of considerable recent interest (see Bryant & Anderson, 1983, and Collins, 1983, for reviews). A common research finding is that young children's comprehension of film and television is poor. Often this is attributed to children's inability to comprehend events portrayed through the use of camera techniques and editing manipulations, known generally as *montage.* Yet no previous studies have directly examined this assertion.

The principles of montage have been regarded by film theorists as the "real and only code of the film" (Kjorup, 1977). However, montage has been defined differently in different contexts. Broadly, it refers to the juxtaposition of shots in a film. Monaco (1981) lists two more specific definitions: (1) a dialectical process in which a third meaning is created from the juxtaposition of shots with two independent meanings, and (2) a process of economically conveying information by using a number of short shots to communicate the essential elements of events. The use of the term montage in the present context refers to the broadest definition.

Most prime-time family TV programs incorporate a remarkable amount of montage. In one randomly selected episode of "Little House on the Prairie," we counted 311 cuts, 56 pans, 10 zooms, and 4 fades. There was thus a density of about 8.1 cinematic techniques per minute. Another popular program—the "Dukes of Hazzard"—used approximately twice as many in one randomly selected episode. We counted 556 cuts, 118 pans, 38 zooms, 6 freeze frames, and 63 dolly or truck shots (e.g., as if the camera were on top of a car in a chase scene), for a total of 781

This report was written while R. Smith held a National Research Service Award from the National Institute of Mental Health. The research described here was supported by grants from the National Science Foundation and by a Research Scientist Development Award to D. R. Anderson from the National Institute of Mental Health. Portions of this paper were presented at the biennial meetings of the Society for Research in Child Development in Boston in April 1981 and at Detroit in April 1983. Preliminary analyses of the data were discussed in a chapter by Anderson and Smith. We are grateful to our mentor and colleague, Dr. Nancy Myers, for sharing her wisdom and support throughout this project. We thank John Lee for his assistance in the film-to-tape transfer and Sharon Davenport for her assistance in gathering and coding data. Requests for reprints should be addressed to Robin Smith, Institute of Child Development, University of Minnesota, 51 E. River Road, Minneapolis, MN 55455.

techniques, or about 16.7 per minute. Given the frequency of such techniques, their use and interpretation must be central to the young child's processing of TV content. Many changes of scene and action must be integrated across these perceptual transformations to achieve a unified representation of the narrative (Anderson & Smith, 1984; Huston & Wright, 1983).

One possibility is that the use of such techniques *enhances* children's comprehension of the story. In research with adults, Carroll and Bever (1976) reported that viewers used cinematic techniques to help parse film sequences. Cuts that coincided with true event boundaries furthered "segmentation," but cuts that did not indicate an event change were not perceived as such. In other research with adults, Kraft (1981) found that short filmed sequences with cuts were preferred over uncut sequences and were judged to be significantly more interesting, more active, stronger, quicker (in pace), and longer than sequences without cuts. The use of cuts, however, did not facilitate the recall of activities in the sequences. Further, recall of cuts was quite poor, suggesting that adults process such techniques quite automatically.

The notion that adults quite automatically process cinematic techniques accords with intuition and research findings. There is a common belief, however, that such "film literacy" is gradually acquired. One source of such belief is the anecdotal data from anthropologists reporting instances of lack of integration across cuts among cinema-naive non-Western populations (e.g., Forsdale & Forsdale, 1966). Also, film theorists have claimed that increasing film literacy among Westerners has led to increased cinematic pacing. Harrington (1973) reports that the average number of shots per hour has risen steadily since the 1940s and 1950s, and that the length of fades has shortened.

The gradual acquisition of film literacy is also a common assumption in the research and theoretical literature on children's comprehension of TV. This literature has indicated that preschoolers' representations of such content may be fragmentary and incomplete. Early research on film comprehension, for example, reported that even 6-year-old children did not understand the relationship between film sequences and perceived them as a series of unrelated events (Flapan, 1965; Franck, 1955; Zazzo, 1956). Leifer, Collins, Gross, Taylor, Andrews, and Blackmer (1971) found that 4-year-olds poorly ordered the three most central scenes from a 20-min film.

Noble (1975) reported that young children were poor at sequencing events within a film and suggested that they perceive television narratives as separate and fragmentary incidents rather than as a story. In fact, Collins, Wellman, Keniston, and Westby (1978) reported that second-grade boys showed no evidence of being able to distinguish a normally presented detective show from the same story edited so that the major component scenes were presented in random sequence.

From such evidence, it is often claimed that young children are unable to comprehend the cinematic techniques used on TV. For example, Baron (1980) claimed that "eight appears to be the average age when understanding concepts related to TV technique appear. Such techniques as zoom and editing are not well understood by younger children" (p. 11). Also, Tada (1969) suggested that "to couple two shots of different camera angles is an intellectual task too difficult for a child of four, who just acquired the topological concept of space" (p. 125). The clear implication of the developmental research is that rather than enhancing comprehension, the use of editing techniques disrupts the construction of a unified representation of TV narratives. According to this point of view, the preschooler perceives an edited event sequence as a succession of states with little meaningful relationship to each other.

Research on such issues has been hampered by the difficulty in testing young children's comprehension. Particularly problematic is reliance on verbal recall, given the lack of expository skills in preschoolers (see Brown, 1976). In addition, research on the effects of cinematic techniques has been hampered by the necessity of using already existing program material in which the use of such techniques is confounded with familiarity of contextual variables such as setting and characters and with the complexity of the narrative structure of the program. Rice (1979) rated the use of formal features (including such techniques) and linguistic features in six popular children's shows and found that the distribution of formal features was related to patterns of linguistic features within the show. For example, the shows with a moderate amount of verbal complexity also demonstrated a moderate use of formal features. Furthermore, TV program genres such as children's programs are characterized by particular constellations of formal features (Huston et al., 1981). Due to the nature of the medium, then, it has been impossible to directly assess the effects cinematic techniques have on comprehension independent of the familiarity of content and complexity of narrative structure.

Study 1 avoids these problems by making use of original stop-animation television segments that present the same content with and without the use of cinematic techniques. In addition, rather than employing verbal recall procedures, the children are asked to reconstruct the action and dialogue using the same dolls and sets depicted in the segments. Preliminary pilot work indicated that this technique is ideally suited for assessing young children's comprehension of TV content. The major question addressed by the study is whether young children's comprehension of television is enhanced or diminished by the use of montage.

Study 1

Method

Materials.—Original program material was created by filming stop-animation stories of Fisher-Price dolls enacting scenes in three different sets—the Fisher-Price playhouse, school, and "Sesame Street" replica. The films were shot using a Super 8 film camera with single-frame and automatic zoom capabilities (the Chinon XL555 Macro lens model) and Kodak Ektachrome 160 movie film, Type A. The camera was mounted on a tripod before a table illuminated with four 500-watt photoflood lamps. On the table was a nonreflecting gray mat upon which the dolls and sets were placed. Animation was accomplished by moving the doll a short distance and shooting several frames, the distance and number of frames depending on speed and action requirements. For example, average "walking" speed for our purposes required five frames per quarter-inch (.37 cm) distance. Pans and zooms are readily accomplished even as the action apparently continues. Before actual filming began, each story was carefully blocked out with each shot determined in terms of lens setting, light level, character action, camera technique, and number of frames per movement distance.

Once the films were developed, they were transferred from color Super 8 film to three-quarter-inch color videocassette format by means of a Kodak VP-X film videoplayer. Subsequent editing was done using a professional videotape editing system. Dialogue and sound effects were added in the editing process.

Each of the three scripts was filmed in three different editing conditions. In the first condition, the action unfolded in front of a stationary camera. No cinematic techniques were used. In the second condition, the camera panned and zoomed in at various points in the story. In the third condition, pans and zooms were combined with cuts. The cuts either provided closeups of conversational referents or deleted portions of ongoing actions (e.g., cutting from a scene of a character at the top of a staircase to a scene of the character walking away from the bottom of the staircase). The scripts were three simple stories, each consisting of nine simple actions and utterances.

To illustrate, the nine units in the script entitled "At Billy's House" are (1) [Billy says] "Mom, can I go out to play with Susie?" (2) [Mother says] "Yes you may." (3) Billy walks to the steps. (4) Billy walks down the steps. (5) Billy walks to the swing set. (6) [Billy says] "Hi Susie. Want to go on the other swing?" (7) [Susie says] "OK." (8) Both walk to the other swing. (9) [Susie says] "Gee this is fun." In the second condition, the camera zoomed in from an establishment shot of the whole scene to a closeup of Billy and Mom before they started speaking. The camera then panned, following Billy as he moved through the set. The third condition included the above as well as a cut to a shot of Susie (as the referent of the conversation) between units 1 and 2, and a cut from Billy at the top of the stairs to the bottom, deleting unit 4. In scoring the children's reconstructions, the same nine units were used in all conditions, having been judged as those units that were representative of the "canonical" story. Any other actions were noted as well.

Subjects.—Seventy-one preschool children, 17 males and 18 females at age 3 and 18 males and 18 females at age 5, participated in the study. Subjects were within 1 month of their birthday.

Procedure.—Children were brought to the University of Massachusetts Child Study Center by a parent. After a few minutes of playing with toys in the waiting room, the experimenter escorted the child to the viewing room. Another brief warm-up session was conducted in which the experimenter asked the child to replicate some actions she performed with the Fisher-Price dolls. Parents completed a questionnaire on the child's TV viewing habits while their children were being tested.

Each child viewed each of the three segments in one of the three conditions.[1] Order of presentation was randomized. After presenting a segment on a color monitor, the experimenter put the Fisher-Price set and dolls that were portrayed in that story on a table in front of the child and asked him or her to reconstruct the story "as if you were making the same TV show." The entire session was videotaped for later coding.

For prompting and analysis purposes, the scripts were divided into action or dialogue units. Each unit consisted of either a discrete action or a discrete utterance. The unit boundaries were determined prior to producing the segments by consensus among three judges. Children were given a chance to reconstruct the entire narrative without prompts first, and some did. After the first attempt, the experimenter then began with the first script unit and probed for those units that had not been reconstructed by enacting or stating (depending on whether it was action or dialogue) the previous unit. For example, if the child spontaneously reconstructed unit 1 but not unit 2 in the script entitled "At Billy's House," the experimenter waited until the child was finished with the first run-through and then said "Good! OK, I have a few questions about that story. Remember, Billy said, 'Mom, can I go out to play with Susie?' What was next?" Only those units that were left out in the previous run-through were probed by the experimenter's statement or enactment of the prior unit. Protocols were scored such that the child received two points for each unprompted unit, one point for each prompted unit, and none if the unit was not reconstructed. Two observers independently coded all three protocols for 10 of the children and achieved an interobserver agreement of 98.2%, calculated as total number of agreements divided by total number of agreements and disagreements.

Results and Discussion

A mixed-model ANOVA with three between-subjects variables—age (2), sex (2), and story-condition combination (6)—and one within-subject variable-condition (3)—was performed on total reconstruction scores. The analysis revealed no effect of cinematic technique on reconstruction scores. There were also no main effects of sex or interactions with sex. There was, however, a main effect of age, $F(1,47) = 80.17$, $p < .001$, such that 5-year-olds reproduced more story units than 3-year-olds. The mean total reconstruction scores for children at each age are presented in Table 1.

The results of the first study indicated that, relative to the unedited segments, the use of cinematic techniques such as cuts, zooms, and pans did not disrupt the reconstruction of the televised event sequences for preschoolers. It must be kept in mind, however, that these sequences were much shorter than those used in most studies of children's comprehension of television, and that the cinematic manipulations were mild.

Study 2

In contrast to assertions in the literature on children's film and TV comprehension, Study 1 found no deleterious effects of montage on young children's reconstruction performance. Study 2 employed longer event sequences incorporating more challenging cinematic manipulations. Such manipulations are implied by discussions of montage as a filmic code whereby new meaning emerges through the juxtaposition of shots. A classic example is provided by Whitaker (1970) in which a scene of a cabin in the forest is suc-

TABLE 1

MEAN TOTAL RECONSTRUCTION SCORES IN EXPERIMENT 1

	AGE	
CONDITION	3	5
1	4.71	11.24
2	5.06	11.71
3	4.61	10.83

NOTE.—The maximum possible score is 18.

---

[1] For example, a child might view the segment entitled "At Billy's House" in condition 1, the segment entitled "At School" in condition 2, and the segment entitled "Sesame Street" in condition 3. These were six possible story-condition *combinations* (not permutations, since order of presentation was randomized). If 1, 2, and 3 represent the conditions and A, B, and C represent the stories, the combinations are (1) 1A, 2B, 3C; (2) 1B, 2A, 3C; (3) 1C, 2A, 3B; (4) 1A, 2C, 3B; (5) 1B, 2C, 3A; (6) 1C, 2B, 3A. At both ages, subjects were distributed equally across these combinations. Thus story-condition combination was a between-subjects variable in the ANOVA model. Since there were no effects of that variable, it will not be discussed further. Editing condition was a within-subjects variable with three levels.

ceeded by an indoor scene of a man reading a book while sitting in a chair before a fire. The viewer of this sequence is expected to infer that the man is inside the cabin. Reversing the sequence of shots, on the other hand, leads to the inference that the man is reading about a cabin in the forest. In the first case the inference is primarily spatial in nature, and in the second case the inference concerns character perspective—the mental images of the man while reading.

Study 2 was designed to assess children's comprehension of such filmic codes. Twelve new segments were produced that each incorporated elements of montage requiring inferences of space, simultaneity of action, implied action (called "ellipsis" in film theory), and character perspective. Preschoolers were compared with school-age children, since it was possible that these films would be considerably more difficult to comprehend than the films in Study 1. Analyses examined reconstructions of the critical units of action and character placement deemed indicative of comprehension of the montage.

Method

Materials.—The 12 new segments each incorporated techniques that conveyed either very simple or somewhat more complex changes in space (five segments), simultaneity (two segments), ellipsis (three segments), or character perspective (two segments). Filming methods were identical to those in Study 1. Several new sets manufactured by Fisher-Price were used. Brief sample descriptions of the four types of segments are provided below in the discussion of the results.

Subjects.—Eighty-two children, 40 4-year-olds and 42 7-year-olds, were tested. Of the 4-year-olds there were 20 males and 20 females; of the 7-year-olds, 19 were male and 23 female. All children were within 1 month of their birthday.

Procedure.—The procedure was similar to that used in Study 1 except that order of presentation of the segments was not randomized. Instead, half of the children at each age viewed and were first tested on segments 1–6 followed by segments 7–12, and the other half first viewed and were tested on segments 7–12 followed by segments 1–6. Also, a warm-up session included viewing and reconstructing the three stories used in Study 1 in the still-camera, no-cuts condition. If the child did not reconstruct most of the action and at least one dialogue unit from these unedited segments, testing was terminated. Six

4-year-olds and no 7-year-olds were eliminated under this criterion. Finally, the Peabody Picture Vocabulary Test was administered before the viewing session began.

Results and Discussion

The average score on the Peabody Picture Vocabulary Test was 108 for the 4-year-olds and 115 for the 7-year-olds. There were no significant relationships between PPVT scores and performance on the montage testing. The reconstruction performances were scored in terms of the sequences of actions and character placements that were judged (on an a priori basis) to reveal clear comprehension of the montage. Each reconstruction was assigned a score of 1 (complete reconstruction of all critical units) or 0 (partial or no reconstruction). It is our judgment that these scoring criteria were quite conservative but appropriate to the descriptive question of young children's comprehension of montage. The analyses treated each segment individually in an age × sex design or combined the segments into the four classes of segments (space, simultaneity, ellipsis, character perspective) in an age × sex × segment class design. In addition, an analysis was performed comparing explicitly depicted action units to implicitly depicted action units in an age × sex × explicitness design.

Ellipsis.—Three segments were designed to imply actions that were not explicitly depicted. The actions were implied by both visual cues and character dialogue, as is the common practice in film and television productions.

One of these segments was entitled "Helping Dr. Bill." The segment begins with Joe standing next to a stretcher and an ambulance. He says that he needs to deliver the stretcher to Dr. Bill. The camera cuts to Dr. Bill standing outside the hospital set and saying that he needs the stretcher. We then see a shot of Joe loading the stretcher into the ambulance. The last shot shows Dr. Bill standing next to the stretcher and then pushing it into the hospital. Deleted are explicit shots showing Joe getting into the ambulance, driving to the hospital, and unloading the stretcher (three critical units). A child was given credit for comprehending the ellipsis if he or she loaded the stretcher into the ambulance, placed Joe in the truck, rolled the truck over to the hospital, and unloaded the stretcher, *or* had Dr. Bill unload the stretcher, since either character could have done it. An age × sex analysis was performed on this and each of the segments using Myers's (1958) multiple classification extension of Fisher's exact prob-

TABLE 2

MEAN PERCENT OF CHILDREN RECONSTRUCTING ALL CRITICAL UNITS FROM
TELEVISED STORIES IN EXPERIMENT 2

STORY (Number of Critical Units)	AGE		SIGNIFICANCE
	4	7	
Space:			
Time to Go (3)	25	86	<.001
Susie Takes a Nap (1)	83	80	...
It's Going to Rain (1)	68	91	<.01
Susie Arrives at School (4)	65	93	<.01
Susie's New Dog (3)	55	79	<.05
Ellipsis:			
Visiting Oscar (3)	65	100	<.001
School's Almost Out (1)	100	100	...
Helping Dr. Bill (3)	70	95	<.01
Simultaneity:			
Driving Too Fast (3)	38	91	<.001
Taking a Walk (3)	55	98	<.001
Character perspective:			
Things to Do (1)	93	95	...
Susie at the Airport (3)	30	38	...

ability test (alpha level = .05). The results are indicated in Table 2. There were no sex main effects or interactions with sex, but in two ellipsis segments 7-year-olds performed significantly better than 4-year-olds.

Given the relatively high levels of performance by both ages in reconstructing implied actions, it was of interest to compare this performance to reconstructions of explicitly depicted actions.

Across all 12 segments, there were 28 explicitly portrayed actions that were tested for reconstruction and 16 implicit (deleted by script and cinematic technique) actions. Each child was scored for the percentage of correctly reconstructed actions of each type. The results are shown in Table 3. An analysis of variance indicated a main effect of age, $F(1,80) = 23.40$, $p < .001$, such that 4-year-olds reconstructed fewer actions of both types (74%) than 7-year-olds (82%). In addition, there was main effect of action type, $F(1,80) = 173.37$, $p < .001$, such that explicit actions were more likely to be reconstructed (85%) than implicit actions (71%). There was no interaction of age × explicitness of action, and there was no main effect or interaction with sex. This analysis indicates that while implied actions were less likely to be reproduced than explicit actions in general, the poorer performance of younger children was not specific to implied actions. Relative to their baseline reproduction performance, 4-year-olds reproduced implied actions nearly as well as 7-year-olds. The majority of children at both

TABLE 3

MEAN PERCENT ACTION RECONSTRUCTION
PERFORMANCE IN EXPERIMENT 2

ACTION TYPE	AGE		MEAN
	4	7	
Explicit	82	89	85
Implicit	66	76	71
Mean	74	82	...

ages obtained a coherent representation of these stories by correctly filling in the essential missing action implied by the cinematic techniques and the dialogue.

Space.—Almost all video action takes place in some kind of space shown directly, revealed by a succession of shots or movements of the camera, or simply implied by showing a part of the space. Within the cinematic space, objects and characters have locations relative to the space as a whole and also relative to each other. It is apparent, therefore, that spatial inferences are a central aspect of film and TV comprehension.

Five segments were designed to test the children's ability to represent the cinematic space and place the depicted objects and characters correctly within that space. One such segment was entitled "Susie Takes a Nap." In this story, an establishment shot of two buildings (an "establishment shot" identifies the location of subsequent action) is followed by a zoom to Susie looking out one of the four windows. There is a cut to an interior shot of Susie, from behind, looking out the window. After a brief monologue, Susie gets into her bed.

The children were asked to reconstruct this sequence, placing Susie in the correct room and reenacting the story. A child was given credit for comprehension of the montage if he or she placed the doll in the correct room without hesitation. We used the criterion of "without hesitation" in this segment because a few children seemed to search for the correct room, perhaps looking for distinctive features of the room rather than relying on their knowledge of its location. The results for this and the other space segments are shown in Table 2. In four of the five segments, the 7-year-olds performed significantly better than the 4-year-olds. There were no main effects or interactions of sex. Two of the 4-year-olds and one of the 7-year-olds placed the doll in the wrong room. All chose the *other* upstairs room of the four possible rooms in the set (two upstairs and two downstairs). The age difference in committing this error was not significant.

In general, across these segments, we found that while the children only sometimes replicated the exact placement of characters and objects, they were generally quite good at placing them correctly relative to each other, to the setting as a whole, and to the camera. In the one segment that the 4-year-olds reconstructed poorly ("Time to Go"), the most common error was a right-left reversal of the characters. Four-year-olds were significantly more likely to commit this error than 7-year-olds, $t(80) = 2.315, p < .01$.

Character perspective.—A fairly common cinematic technique is to show what a particular character is seeing or thinking. For example, in the *"Dukes of Hazzard"* show that we analyzed, one shot portrayed an automobile side-view mirror that was reflecting the image of the sheriff's patrol car as it was pursuing the boys. From the preceding shot, which shows one of the boys looking out the window as he is driving, we are to infer that we are looking through his eyes and seeing the sheriff in the mirror. In that episode, there were 24 instances of character perspective shots. "Things to Do," portrayed a doll considering several alternative activities. The segment was filmed as if the alternatives were seen through the doll's eyes. This was done by panning over a toy TV, an easel, an arts and crafts table, and a magazine rack. A voice-over simultaneously represented a child considering each of these activities, as they appeared on camera, as "things to do." The doll was never actually shown on screen. After viewing, the children were handed a doll and asked, "What did Susie do in this show?" Ninety-three percent of the 4-year-olds and 95% of the 7-year-olds always held the doll so as to face the object the way the camera had portrayed the doll's perspective while walking the doll past the items and repeating the voice-over.

The other character perspective segment ("Susie at the Airport") was considerably more complex. It depicted Susie going for an airplane ride as seen through her eyes looking through the window of the airplane as it taxied, took off, and landed. Both age groups performed relatively poorly with respect to indicating character perspective, insofar as the majority did not place Susie in her plane seat facing out of the window. Nevertheless, 85% of the 4-year-olds put the doll in the correct airplane (out of three), which they then flew away from the airport. A common error was to put the doll in the wrong airplane (one the doll "saw" through her window). Anomalously, more 7-year-olds than 4-year-olds committed this error, although the difference was not significant. In neither character perspective segment was there a significant age or sex effect or interaction.

Simultaneity.—Two segments presented parallel simultaneous actions conveyed by rapid intercutting. In "Driving Too Fast," two trucks proceeded down converging roads toward an intersection, as a pedestrian observed them. The action was conveyed by a rapid series of cuts from one truck to the other and to the pedestrian. Truck direction and the implication of an impending collision were conveyed by the angle of the truck's movement with respect to the camera. The other segment, "Taking a Walk," involved a similar depiction, except that the segment represented two characters walking on converging paths with the implication that they would meet at the intersection. In both segments, 7-year-olds performed nearly perfectly and significantly better than the 4-year-olds. There were no effects of sex.

Comparisons across Classes of Montage

Reconstruction data within each class of montage (ellipsis, space, character perspective, simultaneity) were combined so that each child was assigned a percent correct score for each class. The data were subjected to an age × sex × class analysis of variance, where class was a within-subjects variable. Table 4 indicates the results. There was a

TABLE 4

MEAN PERCENT OF CHILDREN RECONSTRUCTING ALL CRITICAL UNITS FROM
TELEVISED STORIES IN EXPERIMENT 2 AVERAGED OVER STORIES IN EACH CATEGORY

	AGE		
STORY CATEGORY (Number of Stories in Category)	4	7	SIGNIFICANCE
Ellipsis (3)	78	98	<.001
Space (5)	58.5	88.5	<.001
Character perspective (2)	56	65	N.S.
Simultaneity (2)	48.7	94	<.001

main effect of age, $F(1,78) = 79.94$, $p < .001$, due to better performance by the 7-year-olds. There was also a main effect of class, $F(3,234) = 24.75$, $p < .001$, and a class × age interaction, $F(3,234) = 11.47$, $p < .001$. Bonferroni t tests (see Table 5) indicated significant age differences in ellipsis, simultaneity, and space reconstructions, but not in reconstruction of character perspective. The 4-year-olds' performance on space, simultaneity, and character perspective did not differ, but each of these was worse than performance on ellipsis. The 7-year-olds were worse on character perspective than on the other three classes; space and simultaneity did not differ, but each was worse than ellipsis.

General Discussion

In Study 1, cinematic montage neither enhanced nor diminished reconstruction performances of 3- and 5-year-olds. In study 2, using a range of techniques requiring a variety of inferences of space, simultaneity, ellipsis, and character perspective, 4-year-olds were correct on an average of 62% of the key inferences, and 7-year-olds were correct on 88%. Inferences concerning implied action sequences were easiest for both ages, and inferences of simultaneity were most difficult for 4-year-olds, while inferences of character perspective were most difficult for 7-year-olds. Overall, these results indicate that preschool children comprehend more information conveyed through montage than had been previously estimated. Nevertheless, this comprehension improves for those classes of techniques that appear to require coordination of perspectives (space, simultaneity, and character perspective).

These findings of good comprehension of montage must be reconciled with the many reports of poor comprehension of film and television by young children. Part of the difference must lie in the task used to test chil-

TABLE 5

RESULTS OF BONFERRONI t TESTS

	t Values (80 df)		Significance	
Age differences in category scores:				
Ellipsis	7.28		<.001	
Space	7.55		<.001	
Character perspective	1.79		N.S.	
Simultaneity	5.08		<.001	
	39 df, for 4-year-olds		41 df, for 7-year-olds	
	t Value	Significance	t Value	Significance
Within-age differences in category scores:				
Space-simultaneity	1.74	N.S.	1.67	N.S.
Space-ellipsis	4.71	<.001	3.72	<.001
Space-character perspective	.59	N.S.	5.25	<.001
Simultaneity-ellipsis	4.37	<.001	1.54	N.S.
Simultaneity-character perspective	1.14	N.S.	6.27	<.001
Ellipsis-character perspective	4.76	<.001	8.50	<.001

dren's comprehension. Previous studies have used testing methods that are heavily dependent on children's language, which may lead to underestimations of their knowledge. The reconstruction task appears to be particularly well suited for young children. In fact, in a follow-up study in which verbal recall was compared with reconstruction, we found that the reconstruction task is indeed a more sensitive indicator of comprehension in 7-year-olds as well as 4-year-olds (Gibbons, Anderson, Smith, Fischer, & Field, in preparation). It is possible that recognition measures would reveal even better comprehension, especially among the younger children.

Another significant difference lies in the program material. These segments were short and minimally challenged the children's world knowledge. The segments, furthermore, were specifically constructed to test for certain aspects of children's comprehension. The programs used in other studies, while representative of broadcast television, are more complex, with potentially large confounds between world knowledge required to interpret actions and the complexity of cinematic techniques used to convey those actions (see Rice, 1979). Over a lengthy and relatively complex TV program, then, our results suggest that enough cinematic transitions may not be comprehended that overall program comprehension could indeed be fragmented. Our findings of good comprehension with these short segments and other researchers' findings of poor comprehension of full-length dramatic programs are not, therefore, inconsistent.

We view these findings on early comprehension of montage as a starting point for future theoretical and experimental explication. There should be little doubt that as children's knowledge of the world increases, their comprehension of montage continues to develop, eventually encompassing appreciation of sophisticated symbolism and aesthetic devices. The extent to which such growth is dependent on learning the conventions of the medium, increasingly sophisticated conceptual knowledge, or sensitivity to the invariant relations between events remains to be determined. One approach to disentangling these possible sources of developmental differences is suggested by the research method described here. For example, in order to determine the extent of children's sensitivity to the information that specifies continuity and coherence, it should be possible to manipulate the spatial, temporal, and linguistically specified relations between film events and to

identify points at which the reconstruction of the unified event breaks down.

Given the extraordinary amount and variety of audiovisual media, a systematic and verifiable theoretical account of comprehension of montage would have considerable applicability. Such a theoretical account requires further empirical description and analysis of the actual use of montage as well as its comprehension. In any case, the present findings indicate that some substantial comprehension of montage is already established in the preschool years.

References

Anderson, D. R., & Smith, R. (1984). Young children's TV viewing: The problem of cognitive continuity. In F. J. Morrison, C. Lord, & D. F. Keating (Eds.), *Advances in applied developmental psychology* (pp. 115–163). New York: Academic Press.

Baron, L. J. (1980). *What do children really see on television?* Paper presented at the annual meeting of the American Educational Research Association, Boston.

Brown, A. L. (1976). The construction of temporal succession by preoperational children. In A. Pick (Ed.), *Minnesota Symposia on Child Psychology* (Vol. 10, pp. 28–83). Minneapolis: University of Minnesota Press.

Bryant, J., & Anderson, D. R. (Eds.). (1983). *Children's understanding of television: Research on attention and comprehension.* New York: Academic Press.

Carroll, J. M., & Bever, T. G. (1976). Segmentation in cinema perception. *Science, 191,* 1053–1055.

Collins, W. A. (1983). Interpretation and inference in children's television viewing. In J. Bryant & D. R. Anderson (Eds.), *Children's understanding of television: Research on attention and comprehension* (pp. 125–150). New York: Academic Press.

Collins, W. A., Wellman, H., Keniston, A. H., & Westby, S. D. (1978). Age-related aspects of comprehension and inference from a televised dramatic narrative. *Child Development, 49,* 389–399.

Flapan, D. P. (1965). *Children's understanding of social interaction.* Unpublished doctoral dissertation, Columbia University, New York.

Forsdale, J., & Forsdale, L. (1966). Film literacy. *Teacher's College Record, 67,* 608–617.

Franck, G. J. (1955). *Uber Geschehensgestaltungen in der Auffasung von Filmen durch Kinder.* Leipzig: Barth.

Harrington, J. (1973). *The rhetoric of film.* New York: Holt, Rinehart & Winston.

Huston, A., & Wright, J. C. (1983). Children's processing of television: The informative functions of formal features. In J. Bryant & D. R. Anderson (Eds.), *Children's understanding of television: Research on attention and comprehension* (pp. 35–68). New York: Academic Press.

Huston, A. C., Wright, J. C., Wartella, E., Rice, M., Watkins, B. A., Campbell, T., & Potts, R. (1981). Communicating more than content: Formal features of children's television programs. *Journal of Communication*, 31, 32–48.

Kjorup, S. (1977). Film as a meeting place of multiple codes. In D. Perkins & B. Leondar (Eds.), *The arts and cognition*. Baltimore: Johns Hopkins Press.

Kraft, R. N. (1981). *The psychological reality of cinematographic principles: Camera angle and cutting*. Unpublished doctoral dissertation, University of Minnesota, Minneapolis.

Leifer, A. D., Collins, W. A., Gross, B. M., Taylor, P. H., Andrews, L., & Blackmer, E. R. (1971). Developmental aspects of variables relevant to observational learning. *Child Development*, 42, 1509–1516.

Monaco, J. (1981). *How to read a film*. New York: Oxford University Press.

Myers, J. (1958). Exact probability treatments of factorial designs. *Psychological Bulletin*, 55, 59–61.

Noble, G. (1975). *Children in front of the small screen*. London: Constable.

Rice, M. (1979). *Television as a medium of verbal communication*. Paper presented at the annual meeting of the American Psychological Association, New York.

Tada, T. (1969). Image-cognition: A developmental approach. In *Studies of broadcasting* (pp. 105–177). Tokyo: Nippon Hoso Kyokai.

Whitaker, R. (1970). *The language of film*. Garden City, NJ: Prentice-Hall.

Zazzo, R. (1956). L'influence du cinéma sur le développement de la pensée de l'enfant. *L'Ecole des Parents* (Paris).

23

PATTERNS OF INVOLVEMENT IN TELEVISION FICTION
A Comparative Analysis

Tamar Liebes and Elihu Katz*

This article analyses discussions of an episode of *Dallas* by focus groups of different ethnic origins in Israel and the United States. It identifies four rhetorical mechanisms by which viewers may 'involve' themselves in or 'distance' themselves from the story: referential *v*. critical framings; real *v*. play keyings; collective or universal *v*. personal referents; and normative *v*. value-free evaluations. Use of these mechanisms varied across the groups, and when the cultures were arrayed along a multidimensional involvement scale overseas viewers appeared to be more involved in the programme than Americans. Possible roles for involvement in the process of viewer susceptibility to programme messages are then discussed.

Introduction[1]

To study the effects of television, says Gerbner, don't ask people about television, ask them about life. In their famous series of studies, Gerbner et al. (1979) attempt to infer the influence of television from the correspondence between what heavy viewers say about life and what television says about it. Whether one agrees with Gerbner's method or not (Hirsch, 1980), it is an important step beyond inferring effects from content analysis alone, or from individual self-reports alone.

For the same reason, one cannot accept content analysis as a basis for statements about cultural imperialism. To study the effects of the widespread diffusion of US television programmes abroad, one must examine both the message and its incorporation into the consciousness of viewers. Neither intent nor effect need be witting, but the message must be shown to be self-serving in some way from the point of view of US interests, and its incorporation must be found to create or increase dependence on the message and/or its

---

* Tamar Liebes is a lecturer in the Department of Cinema at Tel Aviv University and a Research Associate at the Communications Institute of the Hebrew University. Elihu Katz is Professor of Sociology and Communication at the Hebrew University and at the Annenberg School of Communications, University of Southern California.

From Tamar Liebes and Elihu Katz, "Patterns of Involvement in Television Fiction: A Comparative Analysis," *European Journal of Communication*, Vol. 1, pp. 151-171. Copyright © 1986 by Sage Publications, Ltd.

supplier, and to have debilitating consequences for the self-interest of viewers from other cultures.

Unlike Gerbner, we are not satisfied with inferring effects, but would like to get closer to the process of influence in action. As far as US television overseas is concerned, we are not even certain that people understand the programmes. Perhaps they may only look at the pictures, or weave their own story into what they are offered.

This paper, then, is about the ways in which people are engaged by television fiction. It is a study *not* of effects but rather of the processes that might lead to effects. Specifically, it is a study of patterns of *involvement* in an episode of the world-wide hit *Dallas*, focusing on how viewers discuss the programme in nearly natural settings. These discussions reveal several different types of involvement; and involvement, we believe, may hold the key to effect.

Method

Ideally, we should like to have empirical data on how people talk naturally about television: whether they refer to the medium or to specific programmes; how they decode what they see and hear; how they help each other to do so; whether and how they weave the experience of viewing into their social and political roles; whether they have categories for criticism, and if so, what these are. The only data we know come from several quasi-anthropological studies of family interaction (Bryce and Leichter, 1983; Lull, 1981); two analyses of peer group discussion of film (Custen, 1982; Laulan, 1983) focus group discussions of a news programme (Morley, 1980) and a radio marathon (Merton, 1946);[2] and two questionnaire studies attempting to clarify the critical ability and vocabulary of television audiences (Neumann, 1982; Himmelweit, 1983).

We tried to combine these methods in our own study, although what we have done does not pretend to solve the problem of truly unobtrusive observation of natural conversations concerning television. We organized some 50 small groups of viewers of *Dallas* by asking an initial couple to invite two other couples from among their friends. The group viewed an installment of *Dallas* in a living room setting, together with others who might have joined them anyway.[3] Following the programme, our observer switched on his tape recorder and put a series of open questions to the group; in some cases recording was begun during the viewing period to catch spontaneous conversation.

First, the group was asked to retell the episode in their own words, then to describe the attributes and motivations of the three leading characters, following which we introduced a series of somewhat more specific queries such as 'How would you end the series?' 'Is the programme real?' 'Are they trying to tell us something?' 'What does the programme say about America?' etc. In short, we were interested not so much in effect, not even in gratifications, but rather in what is understood and how it is talked about.

We applied this method to five ethnic communities, four of them in Israel (Israeli Arabs, veteran Moroccan Jews, Russian Jews only recently arrived, and kibbutz members, mostly second-generation Israelis) and to groups of second-generation Americans in Los Angeles. The Israeli groups represent a naive attempt to simulate the diverse cultures that have made *Dallas* a world-wide hit, while the US groups are the audience for whom the programme was presumably intended in the first place. An effort was made to make groups comparable as to age and education, but we did not have full control over the invitations, and certainly not over the correlation between ethnicity and education in the general population. We wanted to see whether the American readings differed from those of the Israelis and whether the Israelis differed among themselves. We chose *Dallas* not only because of its popularity, but because of its dependence on words, because it is so American in form and content. The puzzle of how most of the world manages to understand it all may thereby be revealed.

The generic problem of the study, then, is addressed through analysis of how viewers use the narrative to discuss their own lives. Our object is to discover the mechanisms through which the viewer interacts with the programme, becoming involved with it, and perhaps affected by it, in different ways and to different degrees.

A major indicator of involvement — or, better, a measure of the viewer's ability to distance himself from the reality of the programme — is the extent to which he or she invokes the 'meta-linguistic' rather than the 'referential' frame in responding to the programme. The 'referential' (Jakobson, 1980) connects the programme and real life, as if the viewers were relating to the characters as real people and in turn relating these real people to their own real worlds.

The 'critical' (Jakobson's 'meta-linguistic') frames discussions of the programme as a fictional construction with aesthetic rules. Referential readings are probably more emotionally involving;

critical readings are more distant, dealing as they do with genres, dynamics of plot, thematics of the story and so on. We shall see, however, that certain uses of the critical may betray an effort at self-protection, a refusal to admit emotional involvement.

About What? The Subjects of the Referential Statements

All referential statements that figure in the interaction within the discussion groups were coded by topic, and the 23 resulting topics were then reduced to 4. These are: (1) motivations for action; (2) kinship/relations and norms; (3) moral dilemmas, having to do with (mainly) with the price of success; and (4) business relations. There is substantial similarity among the ethnic groups in the rank-order of attention given to each of the topics. With the exception of the Arabs, motivation was the most discussed topic in all groups; in other words, reference to the motivation of the characters in the story led to talk of motivations in real life, and vice versa.

The Arabs focused their referential statements, first of all, on the subject of kinship roles and norms; for the other groups, this was the second most frequent referential category. Thus, relations among story spouses, generations, siblings and so on were frequently used to discuss kinship relations in real life, and vice versa. Moral dilemmas occupied the kibbutz groups and the Arabs disproportionately; only Americans make frequent reference to business relations in story and life.

The large measure of agreement over the rank-order of the topics discussed referentially suggests that programmes such as *Dallas* may be able to impose an agenda on diverse communities of viewers. It seems a better bet, however, that the social agenda proposed by the programme coincides, with pervasive and pre-existing concern, with the primordial human motivations and inter-personal relations, particularly within the family. This is a clue to the ease with which a programme like *Dallas* crosses cultural frontiers and engages participation.

Within these broadly defined topics, however, the different groups display different tendencies in their interpretations. In explaining motivation, for example, the Americans and the kibbutz members invoke a sort of Freudian theory, perceiving individuals as governed by irrational drives and connecting these with childhood events. Thus, JR's personality is thought to derive from his having been second to Bobby in his mother's favour. Interpretations of this kind, of course, relieve individuals of much moral responsibility. In contrast, a large proportion of the Russian statements invoke 'determinism' of another form, as if people behaved in a particular way because their roles impelled them to; as if businessmen, for example, or women, were programmed by society. The Moroccans, also 'blame' society, but invoke a Hobbesian model in which the world is a jungle in which individuals must fend for themselves. In this, they come close to the 'Mafia principle', which at least one analyst (Mander, 1983) finds in the programme. Only the Arabs — who focus not on motivation but on family interrelations and moral dilemmas — find the individual free and responsible enough to struggle against temptation and constraint.

When asked explicitly — late in the focus interview — about the message of *Dallas*, respondents said that the predominant message they perceived is that 'the rich' or 'the Americans' are 'unhappy' or 'immoral'. There follows an implicit, sometimes explicit, 'and we are happier', or 'we are more moral'. In the more spontaneous referential statements coded here, however, emphasis shifts from a moralistic mood to a pragmatic one. Indeed, when discussing the programme informally, the groups which were most moralistic in their replies to the formal question — the Arabs and Moroccans — say that it teaches that one has little choice but to act immorally; in effect, the message they perceive is that immorality pays.

Relating to *Dallas*: Referential and Critical Frames

But rather than focus on the *what* of viewer's statements, this article focuses on the *how*.[4]

The first thing we shall do, therefore, is to calculate the ratio of use of 'critical' and 'referential' *frames* by ethnicity. Having done so, we shall focus on the 'referential' only, that is, on those statements that associate television fiction and real life. We shall also analyse these statements in terms that will permit description and measurement of the ways in which viewers involve themselves in, or distance themselves from, the programme. Thus, within the world of the referential, we shall distinguish two kinds of *keyings* ('Real' and 'Play'), three kinds of *referents* ('I', 'We', 'They') and two kinds of *value orientations* (interpretive or 'value-free', and evaluational or 'normative').

We extracted from the 54 group discussions every statement that connects an observation about the programme with an observation about real life or about the programme as 'text' or artistic construction. The overall ratio of the two types of statements is better than

3:1 in favour of the referential. For every 18 statements about life, the average group makes 6 'critical' statements. This finding itself is of interest, though it is hard to judge without comparison to reactions by similar populations to other media, such as books or the theatre. A question of interest is whether the naturalism of television, in both content and viewing context, makes difficult the distance required for critical thought.

Here are several examples. The first is critical, the second referential:

Example One (Kibbutz group 81)

Reuven: It's impossible to achieve one's goal in this series; I'll tell you why. It's what they call a 'soap opera' in the States. Are you familiar with this term? It's a series that goes on for years on end, and in order to get the audience to stay with it, it ends in the middle. The audience hopes the missing end will be told next week, but it never is. They always manage to get to another scene that won't be completed either. That's the way they hold the audience for years, endlessly. If they get to some ending, if everybody gets what he wants the following week, nobody will view
. . . .
Avi: The series will end.

By contrast, the following example refers directly to real life:

Example Two (Russian group 66)

Lara: It's not clear to me why he wants so much to get his son back.
Natasha: As somebody explained to me, in the United States family status — whatever is going on behind the curtains — is very important for one's career. Every big manager has a family picture on his desk, his wife and children. That's why all the flirting is unconnected with the career. That's why his family status is so important, from the point of view of his career.

Comparing ethnic communities in this way, we find that the groups differ significantly in the ratio of referential to critical utterances. The highest ratios (the most critical utterances relative to the referential) were made by the Russians, followed by Americans and kibbutzniks, followed by Moroccan Jews and Arabs (see Table 1). Higher education also increases the proportion of critical statements, but even when education is held constant, the rank-order of ethnic differences remains unchanged.

That the Western groups make more statements in the critical frame invites speculation. The obvious inference is that Western culture inculcates critical distance. If so, this may be related to

TABLE 1
Statements in Referential and Critical Frames, by Ethnicity
(percentages)

	Americans	Moroccans	Arabs	Russians	Kibbutz
Critical (meta-linguistic) frame	27	10	11	37	28
Referential frame	72	90	88	62	72
No. of statements (100%)	(293)	(264)	(167)	(251)	(187)

greater experience with dramatic forms; or it may be that a Western story invites Western-educated viewers to take a more critical stance. It is of particular interest to note that the cutting point of ethnic differences in this respect is not between the American and non-American groups — even if the latter are handicapped by subtitles — but between Russians, Americans and Israeli-educated kibbutzniks on the one hand, and Arabs and Moroccan Jews on the other. That the newly arrived immigrants from Russia — rather than the Americans — are so meta-linguistic, even though they are probably as unfamiliar with American popular culture as are Moroccan immigrants and Arabs, suggests that there may be something to cultural distance after all, but from *within* a Western tradition of textual criticism which is applicable to other media and genres.

A high ratio of critical to referential does not necessarily mean that the absolute number of statements about life is low. The kibbutz groups, for example, were high in both types of statements. On the other hand, the very high number of statements about life of the Arab group is inverse to the number of their critical statements.

The Keying of Referential Statements: 'Real' and 'Play'
Not only do the ethnic groups vary in the relative frequency of their statements about real life and fiction; they also formulate these statements differently. Most statements have a straightforward, 'serious' character; they are indicative in form. When they relate the story to life, they do so *realistically*. By contrast with these stands another set of statements that take a more *playful* form; they are more 'poetic', in Jakobson's sense, relating the story to imagined situations in life in a subjunctive mood.[5] They involved the 'trying on' of characters by imagining how wonderful or awful it would be

to be like them. Following Goffman, we call these forms *keyings*, the one 'real' and the other 'play'. (It is noteworthy that most of the 'play' utterances come in the first, more open, portion of the group discussion, and decline sharply as the questions become more closed.)

Consider the following examples. The first is a realistic keying, from a Russian group:

Example Three (Russian group 65)

Sima: Pam feels that Bobby neglects her; he's never home.
Misha: It's true, but what can he do? What's a man busy with? To be occupied only with family is not practical; it's not realistic. Either he has to stop worrying about money and tend to his family all day long, or he has to be busy with something else — that is, with work. In fact, if a man works 12 hours a day, he can't be occupied with his family the way a woman can.

Here is an example of a ludic keying, illustrating how viewers take an idea from the programme and play with it subjunctively in their minds or in interaction with others:

Example Four (American group 07)

Beverly: I think you have to be a scuzzy person to be able to act like that to begin with. I mean, if I had a million dollars (he's talking about 50 million dollars for just a place to store his damn oil), if I had 50 million dollars I would give it to all my friends, all my kids; I wouldn't connive and cheat just to get more.
Don: Give her a hundred bucks and she splits five ways (ha, ha). Twenty to each kid.

The American and kibbutz groups specialize in this kind of ludic keying (though, as we shall see, even they make many more serious than playful statements). Thus, in discussing the almost-collusion between Miss Ellie and her son JR in his diabolical plot to kidnap his son away from his estranged wife, an American woman said, 'If my son robbed a bank, would I drive the getaway car?' The subjunctive and ludic character of this kind of 'trying on of roles' fictionalizes life, almost making the speaker a character in a story.

Example Five (Kibbutz group 84)

Noah: He (Bobby) seems to me the most balanced, the most considerate of the lot.
Yigal: It reminds me of our kibbutz Admissions Committee. Truly, I swear (laughs).

Noah: I'm the Admissions Committee. It's OK.
Dina: In short — you'd accept him.
Noah: He might not achieve what he wants but . . . in stages, what's called
          slowly but surely, he gets there somehow.
Gila: Zehava, what do you think of Bobby?
Yehudit: When her husband is in the army — then she thinks about him . . .
          (laughter).
Zehava: I'll compromise on him too. (To Yehudit) You're disgusting.

The statistical summary of the proportion of the two kinds of
keying is presented in Table 2, which makes clear that the
Americans and the kibbutzniks engage in ludic keyings more than
the others. The Russians, who make critical statements more often
than the Americans and kibbutzniks (Table 1), do not distance
themselves when it comes to keyings. Their statements about the
relationship of the story to life are as serious as those of Moroccans
and Arabs. From other data, not presented here, we know they
treat the programme more didactically, as if it contained teaching
materials, however manipulative. Even when they speak critically,
they are more likely to be concerned with the ideological implications of the programme than the other groups.[6]

About Whom: The Referents

More light can be shed on ethnic differences by examining the sociolinguistic patterns in which the subjects of these utterances reside.
We classified each statement by referent, or in other words by the
pronoun employed by speakers in transferring a story reference to
real persons. The Referent categories divide into 'primary references' to self and family; references to ethnic group and the nation;
and 'universal' references — distant from self — to abstract social
categories such as 'businessmen' or 'women'. We call these 'I', 'We'
and 'They'. As Table 3 shows, the universal 'they' is the dominant
referent for all groups, but the Russians far exceed the others in

TABLE 2
'Real' and 'Play' Keyings in Referential Statements, by Ethnicity
(percentages)

	Americans	Moroccans	Arabs	Russians	Kibbutz
Real keyings	79	87	87	92	75
Play keyings	21	13	13	8	25
No. of referential statements (100%)	(213)	(236)	(147)	(145)	(135)

reference to universals: three-fourths of their referential statements are of this more abstract kind. To continue an example (Example Three) referred to earlier.

Example Six: (Russian Group 65)

Marik: Woman was created for the family, and I think that for her, 'child, kitchen and church' as the Germans say, is the most important thing,

Marik: A woman who has a lot of leisure and doesn't use it as is necessary, that is, it's important to find her some specific occupation. I don't mean she has to have a job, but something specific for her.

Misha: Something to fill the free time, otherwise she has a real problem. Why do they write about Princess Diana who also has a tough problem. Her husband is occupied with sport, government affairs, and is very little at home.

Marik: Let's compare her (Sue Ellen) with Princess Diana.

Misha: Same thing.

Marik: I think that, when a woman marries somebody like JR, she ought to know how a man like that occupies himself, what he can give the family and what he can't give the family. That is, can he give time to the family as Sue Ellen imagines?

By contrast, the American and kibbutz groups are lower in 'they' references and high in references to self and family. For example:

Example Seven: (Kibbutz group 81)

Sarah A: The funniest was when they tried to kill him. Her (Sue Ellen's) behaviour was simply . . . . How could she suddenly . . .? True, you feel guilty; then you worry about a person, but to suddenly love him . . . .

Daughter: It was because she was feeling guilty she was afraid.

Sarah A: What, then, because I think I'm guilty I should suddenly sell myself my personality . . . . In the beginning when what's his name, the father, got a heart attack she looked at the house as if it would be hers and then her mother-in-law said, 'Don't worry, you will not be here.'

Sarah B: But that's how people are.

Sarah A: It's not true. You hated her for this behaviour . . . . The way she used to despise her sister-in-law . . . . Now you feel sorry for her.

Amalia: Because she was jealous.

Sarah A: What did she have to be jealous about?

Shaul: If they would have shown the good things about her in the beginning . . . .

Sarah A: Then I have to be nasty! I can be jealous inside myself.

Amalia: Situations in life can cause you to be nasty, frustrated.

Aharon: No, no, I don't accept that.

Sarah A: I don't accept it.

Aharon: I believe that if you would be in her situation and were living with someone like JR you might have behaved in the same way. You forget she's living with someone I would not be prepared to live with for one minute and she lives with him. And she was watching all the time him being unfaithful. It isn't *her* who started being unfaithful. It's *him* who did.

Sarah A: No, I don't have to descend to the other person's level. I have to rise above it. Why didn't she run off?

Aharon: Where would she run off to? Did she have anywhere to go . . .

Sarah A: To live all this luxury. I would throw everything behind me and become a servant in someone's house in order not to have to live that kind of life.

Aharon: You have not been in such a house yet. Don't say you would throw it all away.

Sarah A: I think so.

Far more than the other groups, the Arabs use 'Arab society' as a frequent reference.

Example Eight: (Arab group 42)

Ravia: Sue Ellen as well — I agree she's rebellious and stubborn. Tries to get revenge against her husband. In all the ways he was unfaithful to her, she's unfaithful to him. In our Arab society it's different. In our society the man will do anything and the woman wouldn't (laughter). Because that's the way we were brought up. It's difficult to change.

Moged: (to Ravia) You think all men in our society are JRs?

Ravia: Almost, yes (laughter).

Moged: A small JR.

Ravia: JR's sons.

Kibbutzniks and Moroccans sometimes invoke Israelis and Jews as referents.

Example Nine (Moroccan group 20)

Yossi: The same story all the time. He (JR) feels himself strong with his money. I can tell you, who in Israel could get away with that?

Elihu: Can I do it?

Machluf: Akiva Nof, the member of Knesset, had a similar story with his wife. The journalists have shaken the whole country with Akiva Nof until now. In Israel he (JR) could not possibly behave in such a way. He and his money. He would be put in prison. He and his money. They would confiscate it.

Table 3 summarizes the distribution of referents by ethnic groups, showing, indeed, that the Americans and kibbutzniks are highest in

TABLE 3
Referents of Referential Statements, by Ethnicity
(percentages)

	Americans	Moroccans	Arabs	Russians	Kibbutz
Primary ('I') referents	44	24	18	14	38
'We' referents (ethnicity, nation)	2	13	18	10	11
'They' (abstract)	54	63	64	75	51
No. of referential statements (=100%)	(213)	(236)	(147)	(145)	(135)

the use of personal and primary references ('I'); the Russians are highest in the use of abstract referents ('they'); while the Arabs are the only group to make substantial use of 'we' categories referring to ethnic or national identification.

Comparing these different uses of the referent form suggests that the abstract referents of the Russians ostensibly reiterate the kind of distance from direct personal involvement in the story which we observed in their predilection for the critical over the referential. Here we see that, within the referential, the Russians again choose to distance themselves by alluding to general social categories rather than to themselves. On the other hand, such abstract generalization betrays an almost believing attitude in the 'truth value' of the programme, of the sort we have seen in the Russian use of 'real' keyings. They are less likely to say, 'I have an uncle who is like JR' than to say 'capitalists have to act that way'.

If abstract categories imply distance, then the Americans and the kibbutzniks may be said to be more involved in the programme because their references are personal. There is room for a counter-argument, however. It might be argued that the abstract generalizations of the Russians — 'women belong in the kitchen' — leave no room for distance between story and behaviour, while the personal references of the Americans and kibbutzniks may create distance at least in the sense of leaving room for myriad other possibilities. Thus, it is possible that, by bringing story and themselves closer together in this way, the Americans and kibbutzniks may be distancing the truth value of the story, while the Russians, in their universal truisms, may be bringing it closer.

Even if this counter-argument is correct, however, it should be made clear that it is *our* argument, not theirs. From the speakers' point of view, surely 'they' is more distant than 'I' or 'we'. It is only from the observers' point of view that the question can be raised as to whether this is not simply rigid stereotypization. Since this article deals with referential statements from the viewers' vantage point, we shall rank 'they' as more distant than 'I' or 'we'. Proceeding on this line, we will also maintain that 'we' is more committed than 'I' because the 'we' invokes a role, a public persona, taking an official stance on behalf of a group, whereas 'I' is lighter, less committed, less consistent.

The Arab groups, we would say, are most engaged. They do not simply analyse the programme, as do the Russian users of 'they', or simply personalize, as do the Americans and the kibbutzniks: they actively argue. They read the programme as a challenge to their own values and experience the need to dissociate themselves. They reassert their own opposing values.[7]

Value Orientations

Continuing this exploration of the rhetoric of the referential, we distinguish between statements that are interpretive without being judgemental (which we call 'value-free') and statements that are both (which we call 'normative'). The latter include interpretation but go on to take a stand in favour or against the behaviour being interpreted. We apply this distinction to all statements that were keyed as 'real'.[8]

Consider an example of an interpretive value-free statement:

Example Ten (American group 04)

Jus: I would imagine that some of those wealthy families are kinda like that; I bet the Kennedys were.

N: No, they went East.

J: I don't think you have to be wealthy to be like that; you can have a stinker in any family.

Jus: Yeh, but look at the old man; he chased Gloria Swanson and all those girls.

J: Who are you talking about? The Kennedys or *Dallas*?

Jus: Kennedys.

W: Fitzgerald, the old man Kennedy.

N: Joseph Kennedy.

Jus: She just asked do you think they are real people.

J: Yes, of course, but I said you don't have to be a powerful, wealthy family to give birth and raise a stinker, a lot like JR or Kennedy.

Jus: That's true.

N: You may not be like that, if you didn't have that money.

J: C'mon.

All groups have far more value-free interpretations than normative utterances. The Arabs, however, differ from the others in their relatively high use of the evaluational:

Example Eleven (Arab group 43)

Anise:　Sue Ellen is JR's wife, but Arabs believe that she is a bad woman, she's too free and has gone astray.

Sherifa:　A bad woman. Considering the behaviour of her husband, there may be some justification for what she does, but I wouldn't behave that way.

Anise:　I think so too. According to our norms, she is forbidden both to drink and to smoke. In the final analysis, I pity her.

An examination of Table 4 makes clear that the Arabs are the only group that makes substantial use of the evaluational orientation. They are more likely than the others to add a 'normative' verdict — approving or condemning, often with some degree of passion — to their interpretations. The Moroccans, too, may be said to be slightly more normative than the three Western groups.

Patterns of Involvement in Television Fiction

Up to this point, we have analysed four rhetorical forms in which viewers of differing ethnicity couch their statements about *Dallas*. Implicitly, we have been arguing that each of these forms is a measure of involvement in, or 'distance' from, the programme. Let us now make this argument explicit by examining the four rhetorical forms typologically.

Table 5 positions each ethnic group on each of the four dimensions.[9] It will be recalled, for example, that Americans and kibbutz members tended towards 'play' keyings, while the other three groups tended towards the 'real'. Accordingly, in the 'Keyings' column, Americans and kibbutzniks are labelled B2 ('play'), while the others are labelled B1 ('real') because they take the reality of *Dallas* for granted. Similarly for the other three dimensions of rhetoric. A high proportion of 'we' statements (A1) is considered more involved, while a low proportion is ranked more distant.[10] The 'referential' frame (C1) is more involved than the 'critical' (C2); and the 'normative' orientation (D1) is more involved than the 'value-free' (D2).

The table makes clear that the Arabs and the Americans stand at opposite extremes of this scale of involvement/distance. Thus, the Arabs speak most 'referentially' (C1), hardly using the 'critical' frame at all (see Table 1). They talk 'real' (B1) rather than 'play'

TABLE 4
Value Orientations in Referential Statements, by Ethnicity
(percentages)

	Americans	Moroccans	Arabs	Russians	Kibbutz
Value-free: interpretation	90	85	60	92	90
Normative: inter- pretation and evaluation	10	15	40	8	10
No. of referential statements, 'Real' keyings only (= 100%)	(169)	(204)	(127)	(131)	(102)

(see Table 2). They speak for their group and their culture in the language of 'we' (A1; see Table 3). Their interpretations are also more engaged; they are the only group that speaks 'normative' evaluations (D1; see Table 4).

TABLE 5
Patterns of Involvement, by Ethnicity

	A Referent	B Keyings	C Frame	D Value Orientation
Arabs	1	1	1	1
Moroccans	1	1	1	2
Russians	1	1	2	2
Kibbutz	1	2	2	2
Americans	2	2	2	2

Notes

A = referent*: A1, more involved: high proportion of 'we'
              A2, more distant: high proportion of 'I'

B = keying: B1, more involved: low proportion of 'play' keyings
              B2, more distant: high proportion of 'play' keyings

C = frame: C1, more involved: low proportion of critical statements
              C2, more distant: high proportion of critical statements

D = value orientation: D1, more involved: high proportion 'normative'
                        D2, more distant: low proportion 'normative'

* See rationale for this order, pp. 162–164 and footnote 9.

The Americans and kibbutzniks are most 'distant'. They use the 'critical' or 'meta-linguistic' frame to a high degree (C2); their keyings are 'playful' (B2); their referents are to the less committed 'I' (A2); their value orientations are neutral (D2) rather than normative.

There are a variety of in-between patterns. In a sense, the Russians take even more distance than the Americans in that they use the 'they' referent most and the proportion of their 'critical' statements is highest of any group (see Table 1). On the other hand, they take the programme seriously; they use 'real' keyings (B1) rather than 'play' keyings.

The Moroccans are also in between, but they are more difficult to position. They are as involved as the Arabs in frame (C) and keyings (B), but they are not as normative (D) as the Arabs.

In sum, measuring the degree of involvement of the five ethnic groups in terms of use of rhetorical forms finds the 'Western' groups with the most complete set of distancing mechanisms, as if they were issued defensive equipment together with the remote control of their television sets. The Americans and the kibbutzniks — native-born, and most 'modern' of the Israelis — address *Dallas* more 'critically', personally and playfully. Although the Russians are even more 'critical', invoking most meta-textual references, they are not so lighthearted about the programme; they seem to take it very seriously, at both the referential and the meta-textual (critical) level. Indeed, we know — from data not presented here — that the Russians use 'normative' criteria not in the referential frame but in the critical frame.

Ironically, the groups whose cultures seem most remote from the culture of *Dallas* seem more involved in the programme. Perhaps traditional culture is not so remote, given its concern with extended family, which is also the locus of political and economic power! Indeed, this is implied in a study of *Dallas* in Algeria (Stolz, 1984). This argument suggests that the programme is more referential for the more traditional groups. More likely, however, is the probability that the Arabs and Moroccans are challenged by the programme to 'defend' themselves, to respond reflexively by examining their own values in the light of what they perceive to be the 'real' but threatening option of 'modernity'.

Conclusions
This article originates in discussions of an episode of the American

television series, *Dallas*, by small, quasi-natural groups from four ethnic communities in Israel and matched groups of second-generation Americans.

The article — part of a larger project — examines cultural differences in patterns of talk about the programme, with particular reference to the rhetorical mechanisms by means of which viewers 'involve' or 'distance' themselves from the story as depicted on the screen.

Four such mechanisms are analysed: (1) *framings*, the context to which viewers' statements about the programme are assigned: 'referential' (dealing with real life) and 'critical' (dealing with the story as an artistic construction); (2) *keyings*, the register in which referential statements are made: 'realistic' or 'playful'; (3) *referents*, the real-life object to which some element of the story is connected, defined in terms of the pronouns, 'I', 'we', 'they'; and (4) *value orientations*, the extent to which a 'realistic' statement is purely interpretive or evaluational as well: 'value-free' or 'normative'. The five ethnic communities were compared in terms of each of these rhetorical mechanisms separately, and then an effort was made to discover patterned variations in 'involvement' or 'distance' by scoring the groups in terms of a single, multidimensional scale made up of all four mechanisms.

All this seems to add up as follows. First, most statements, in all groups, are based on perception of the programme as real. That is, there are far more referential than critical (meta-linguistic) statements, and, within the referential, far more keyings to the 'real' (serious, indicative, familiar) than to 'play' (fantasy, subjunctive, hypothetical). Moreover, most statements, in all groups, refer to people in general or general categories of people ('they') and fewer statement are in the 'I' or 'we' form. These statements are interpretive in character — observations and explanations of behaviour — without value judgements; evaluational ('normative') statements are far fewer. 'Pragmatic' may be a good name to describe this overall tendency to the 'real' and the 'value-free'.

Overall, then, one may say that discussion of *Dallas* — presuming that we have successfully simulated such discussion — accepts the programme as real and as morally unproblematic in spite of the back-stabbing and corruption which underlie the human relations that are the subject of the referential statements.

Second, the subjects of the statements are similar enough among the ethnic groups to suggest that a programme like *Dallas* may indeed set agendas for thinking and talking, not so much by imposing these subjects, but by evoking primordial concerns and perhaps even by offering opportunities for discussing them. This may be a clue to the world-wide comprehensibility of such programmes and their popularity. Ostensibly, it would seem likely that the social world of *Dallas* would be more readily recognizable in the modern Western societies, where 'immorality pays'. This, however, may be incorrect, both because Western viewers may discount the programme as unreal, and because some of the characteristics of the Ewing family may indeed be more traditional than modern.

Patterned deviations from the dominant pragmatic pattern ('real' and 'value-free') are the concern of this paper. On the one hand, we are interested in use of the 'critical' (meta-linguistic) at the expense of the 'referential' and in use of 'play' keyings at the expense of 'real' keyings. That is, we are interested in identifying those groups, and those situations, in which the viewer distances himself from the reality by using meta-linguistic frames and ludic keyings. On the other hand, we are equally interested in the move from the abstract 'they' and the 'value-free' in the direction of more intimate referents ('I' and 'we') and more evaluative, therefore more emotionally loaded, orientations.

Examining cultural differences in these terms, a third conclusion can be drawn. We find the Arabs at the one extreme that appears to maximize involvement: they talk in referential frames, with real keyings, and make moral judgements about the programme in terms of the opposing norms of their own society ('we'). At the other extreme stand the second-generation Americans who appear to have all of the mechanisms of distancing and discount at hand. They speak 'critically' of genres and production problems; they speak playfully and pragmatically of the real-life implications of the programme for themselves ('I') and each other. The Russians differ from the native Americans and Israelis in generalizing the programme to 'they', but balance this distancing with a belief that the programme is 'real' and, consequently, dangerous.

Fourth, arraying the cultures on the multidimensional scale of 'involvement' or 'distancing', the ostensible conclusion must be that the more 'modern' groups are less involved in the programme, knowing the mechanisms of distancing and discount, while the more traditional groups are more 'involved'. If this is indeed so, as the data strongly suggest, the explanation is easy: the Western groups,

certainly the native Americans and kibbutzniks, have been
socialized in the genres of television (Hall, 1980), have good reason
to question its reality, and know how to relate to it lightheartedly
(Stephenson, 1967), not considering it worthy of moral outrage.
(Only the Russians indicate concern for the possibility of ideological
manipulation.)

Two caveats need mention here. There is the possibility that the
ludic may be no less involving than the real — more distant and
more serious — keyings. Once entered, play can be very absorbing,
of course, and one's only protection is to remember that it is a game.
Some of the ludic interactions we have analysed end in intimate
revelations of the real. The other caveat is that the generalizations
that follow the referent 'they' may be so all-embracing to those who
speak them that the lesser involvement which we attribute to 'they'
may be incorrect. If this is the case, the Russians, who specialize in
interpreting the 'they' almost as participant observers, may be more
enveloped than those who speak of 'I' and 'we'. Both these caveats
need to be borne in mind.

Finally, presuming, nevertheless, that we have successfully
arrayed the several cultures in terms of their distance from the
equation of story and real, we must push harder on the central
question of this article and ask whether the mechanisms of distance
innoculate against the influence of the programme. The answer
appears to be 'yes'. The more traditional groups, lacking the
rhetorical mechanisms of defence, seem to be more vulnerable. In
the absence of discounting mechanisms, the admission of the
agenda of the programme to the most intimate circles — even
women are gradually infiltrating the traditionally male audience,
sometimes even sitting together — poses a competing paradigm
which cannot but shake the system.

But again, we must propose a caveat in that the Western groups
lack a *normative* defence. Along with the variety of mechanisms for
cognitive discounting of television fiction, the fact is that their moral
defences are down. Even in 'play', moral nihilism may have an
effect. In the absence of the Arab moral shock, and the Russians'
ideological suspiciousness, exposure to a steady stream of
programmes, each one of which pushes the boundaries of conventional morality one step further back, may, in the last analysis, make
Western audiences as vulnerable as the others.[11]

These conclusions, we repeat, are based on two sorts of assumptions which must be borne in mind: (1) that we are correct in our

decisions about what is 'high' and 'low' involvement; and (2) that the more highly involved are more likely to be affected. Thus, we believe we are correct in assigning 'ludic' and 'they' keyings to low involvement and 'real' and 'we/I' keyings to high involvement, but we may be wrong.

We also may be wrong in assuming that involvement makes for vulnerability. 'Normative' rebuttals, as we have said, may make Arab viewers *less* vulnerable by virtue of their higher involvement. By the same token, 'ludic' viewers — if they are properly coded as less involved — may be more influenced by virtue of their lowered defences. These are the points at which mass communications research has need of a psychology of drama.

Notes

1. This is a revised version of a paper presented at the International Television Studies Conference, British Film Institute, in London, July 1984. The article is part of a project on cross-cultural diffusion and decoding of US television fiction. Data and analysis are from the doctoral dissertation of Tamar Liebes for the Communications Institute of the Hebrew University of Jerusalem, 1986. The Annenberg School of Communications at the University of Southern California provided funding for the research.

2. The focus group method is widely used in the commercial pre-testing of films, programmes and products by marketing and communications research organizations. It would be very useful to have academic access to these data.

3. Questionnaires were administered to group members following the discussion. It is quite clear from the response that the programme is typically watched in a social setting, and typically talked about afterwards. The protocols of the discussions themselves contain references to conversations about *Dallas* that took place prior to the meetings organized by us. It is safe to say that viewers of *Dallas* discuss the programme and that our constructed groups often coincide with natural groupings of viewers and discussants.

4. The subjects of the referential and critical statements were coded twice: once as abstracted statements, and again as subjects of interaction within the group. We refer to the latter coding in this paper. For details see the PhD dissertation of Tamar Liebes, The Communications Institute, Hebrew University of Jerusalem.

5. These keyings are applicable also to the 'critical' frame. One can speak of genre, for example, seriously or playfully. One of our respondents defined *Dallas*, poetically, as 'Big House on the Prairie', alluding to another popular American soap.

6. The 'messages' perceived by viewers are discussed in Liebes and Katz (1985).

7. This is not quite Hall's (1980) 'oppositional' reading, in that the message is decoded as intended even if disagreement follows.

8. Statements keyed as 'play' are omitted. They may be assumed to be value-free, and their inclusion does not affect the analysis.

9. The columns have been arranged to display the scalar patterns. A more 'logical' order, of course, would show 'Frame' as the first column, since it makes the major distinction between referential and critical.

10. Since the majority of all groups spoke in 'they' statements, we here drop the more universal 'they' and compute the ratio of 'We': 'I'. Thus a high proportion of 'We' will be labelled A1, and a high proportion of 'I' A2.

11. The creator of *Dallas*, David Jacobs, told us that escalating immorality, and proposing its acceptability, is one of the secrets of the success of the series.

References

Bryce, Jennifer W. and Leichter Hope Jensen (1983) 'The Family and Television: Forms of Meditation', *Journal of Family Issues*, 4: 309–28.

Custen, G.F. (1982) *Film Talk: Viewers Responses to a Film as a Socially Situated Event*. PhD dissertation, University of Pennsylvania.

Gerbner, George et al. (1979) 'The Demonstration of Power', *Journal of Communication*, 29: 177–96.

Gross, Larry (1985) 'Life vs Art: The Interpretation of Visual Narratives', *Studies in Visual Communication*, 11: 2–11.

Hall, Stuart (1980) 'Encoding and Decoding of the Television Discourse', pp. 128–38 in S. Hall et al. (eds), *Culture, Media, Language*, London: Hutchinson.

Herzog-Manning, Herta (1983) Unpublished report on German viewers of Dallas, and private correspondence.

Himmelweit, H. (1983) 'The Audience as Critic', in Percy Tannenbaum (ed.), *Entertainment Functions of Television*. Hillsdale, NJ: Lawrence Erlbaum.

Hirsch, Paul (1980) 'The "Scary World" of the Non-viewer and Other Anomalies: A Reanalysis of Gerbner et al.'s Findings on Cultivation Analysis', *Communications Research*, 7: 403–56.

Jakobson, Roman (1980) 'Linguistics and Poetics', in K. DeGeorge and F. DeGeorge (eds), *The Structuralists From Marx to Lévi-Strauss*.

Kaboolian, L. and William Gamson (1983) 'New Strategies for Use of Focus Groups for Social Science and Survey Research', paper read at Annual meeting of American Association for Public Opinion Research.

Laulan, Anne-Marie (1983) *Le Role des mediateurs dans l'access a l'ouevre d'art filmique*, 2 vols. Doctoral thesis presented to University of Paris V. Lille: Atelier National de Reproduction des Theses, Universite de Lille III.

Liebes, Tamar and Elihu Katz (1985) 'Keys to the Forum: Mechanisms Through Which Television Fictions Triggers Talk of Social Issues', paper read at Annual Meeting of International Communications Association, Honolulu.

Lull, James (1981) 'Collective Ethnographic Data in Studies of Media Audience Behaviour', paper read in International Communications Association.

Mander, Mary (1983) '*Dallas*: The Mythology of Crime and the Moral Occult', *Journal of Popular Culture*, 17: 44–8.

Merton, Robert K. (1946) *Mass Persuasion*. New York: Harper.

Morley, Dave (1980) *The Nationwide Audience*. London: BFI.

Neuman, W. Russell (1982) 'Television and American Culture: The Mass Medium and the Pluralist Audience', *Public Opinion Quarterly*, 46: 471–87.

Stephenson, William (1967) *The Play Theory of Mass Communications*. Chicago: University of Chicago Press.

Stolz, Joelle (1984) '*Dallas* in Algeria', Geneva: Institute des Etudes Developmentelles (unpublished).

Thomas, Sari and Brian P. Callahan (1982) 'Allocating Happiness: TV Families and Social Class', *Journal of Communication*, 32: 184–90.

24

DIFFERENTIAL IDEOLOGY AND LANGUAGE USE
Readers' Reconstructions and Descriptions of News Events

Stuart J. Sigman and Donald L. Fry

□   *Building on the work of Trew and his associates, this essay analyzes qualitative questionnaire data on readers' perceptions and reconstructions of the events and ideologies presented in newspaper texts. The results bear directly on the* *interaction between the ideology "embedded" in texts and the readers who encounter those texts. A sociolinguistic and interactional perspective on the media/audience relationship is therefore developed.*

THE present essay derives from our dual concern for the social consequences and uses of linguistic forms, and for the impact of media content on audiences' perceptions and descriptions of news events. This essay reports the results of a study which was designed to compare two reader groups' understanding of a news event as a function of the newspaper source they were asked to read.

Linguistic form and linguistic content are inextricably bound in the production of communication messages; the meaning which one derives from a sentence, for example, is a function of the numerous phonological, morphological, syntactic and discourse rules from which selections are made. The various linguistic constraints and units which are associated with different languages carve out different categories of persons and relations (Whorf, 1956; Rosch, 1977). Similarly, the various resources available in a single language provide diverse classifications of people, objects, and processes. Referentially similar sentences, such as "John hit Mary" and "Mary was hit (by John)," may be distinguished on the basis of the relative prominence of the actors and activities depicted in each as a function of word and syntactic choice. Communication messages are in this sense multi-functional, conveying at a

Mr. Sigman is Assistant Professor of Communication, State University of New York at Buffalo. Mr. Fry is Assistant Professor of Speech Communication, Wichita State University.

From Stuart J. Sigman and Donald L. Fry, "Differential Ideology and Language Use: Readers' Reconstructions and Descriptions of News Events," *Critical Studies in Mass Communication*, Vol. 2, pp. 307-322. Copyright © 1985 by Speech Communication Association. Reprinted by permission.

minimum, both referential and social messages.

In a similar fashion, recent mass communication scholarship has begun to focus on the diverse formats available to media professionals for structuring mediated messages. These innovative studies have moved beyond the treatment of media messages as discrete bits of information, and, instead, evidence a concern for the overall organization of messages and for the impact that variations in structural characteristics may have on audience perceptions. For example, Greendale and Fredin (1977) concerned themselves with the interconnections between and among national issues in newspapers. They found clearly defined clusters of issues which seemed to group together both in newspapers and in the minds of audience members, but they also found differences in the cluster patterns between newspapers and their audience. Bybee (1981) has attempted to establish the relationship between structural characteristics of information presentation formats and the relative ease of audience decision-making. His results gave some support for the importance of matching information presentation formats and decision-making strategies to increase the ease of audience decision-making.

Trew (1979a, 1979b), a British sociolinguist, provides an interesting research report in this vein. Trew suggests that verbal descriptions invariably create and embed attitudes towards the events and activities that are portrayed through language. In specific, an individual's selections from the lexical and syntactic options provided by one's language can be used to communicate—in addition to "factual" information—differing assumptions or ideologies about persons, episodes, and/or relationships. Trew has chosen to study language use in newspaper reports as an indicator of differences in ideologies and attitudes towards the depicted news events.

Our combined interest in language functions and mass communication has led us to attempt an extension of Trew's analysis of the linguistically-mediated ideology in newspapers. In particular, we have attempted to address two related tasks which were left untouched by Trew's original report: (1) to consider readers' awareness of the implicit ideologies carved out of and embedded in the linguistic structures of the mass media; and (2) to question how the language employed in a discourse text (in this case, newspaper articles) serves to provide readers with particular "tools" for constructing a view of reality, for organizing events and the relations between them. After a somewhat more detailed description of the analyses provided by Trew and of the notion of ideology itself, we will present data which bear on these research questions.

LANGUAGE AND IDEOLOGY

Trew argues that "social ideology or theory involves the representation of the social in terms of social identities engaged in relations and processes of action and interaction" (1979b, p. 154). One way to study the nature of these relations and processes is to explore the various event and relationship categories which are provided by a given language. As Rosch writes: "Nature is, in reality, a kaleidoscopic continuum, but the units which form the basis of the grammar of each language serve both to classify reality into corresponding units and to define the fundamental nature of those units . . ." (1977, p. 501). Trew's ideology-directed linguistic analysis focuses on contrasting classification patterns for actors and actions, and on the varying degrees of prominence resulting from these patterns, which are employed by different linguistic texts. Such an analysis seems to be an attempt to study at the level of language structure what McGee (1980) calls "ideographs," devices which embody and transmit ideologies.

Trew's research explores two separate newspaper articles covering the same event, a civic disturbance during a carnival in London, England, and how various linguistic devices employed by each newspaper are related to differing conceptions of what actually occurred. That is, the newspapers embed in the "same" factual reports different perspectives on the salient actors and actions. The original articles were selected from two daily newspapers, the *Sun* and the *Morning Star,* and were published in 1977. At the time, the *Sun* was the largest circulation newspaper in Great Britain and had no formal political affiliations, while the *Morning Star* was the smallest circulation daily and was affiliated with the British Communist Party.

Trew's analysis points to several important similarities and differences between the *Morning Star* and the *Sun* reports.[1] First, there are a number of equivalent descriptions contained in the two articles, primarily in the total information provided and the specific incidents mentioned. For example, both articles refer to rioters, additional participants, and several of the same specific incidents (including a carnival interrupted by a riot). The factual information, then, does not clearly discriminate between the two newspapers' reports.

At the same time, Trew notes compelling differences in the distribution of references to the participants in each news account as either active or passive subjects in the various transactions. That is, there are differences in whether the

participants are depicted as *agents* of actions, or as *objects* who are affected by the agents' actions. Trew analyzes these distinctions by categorizing transactive (causal) and nontransactive (noncausal) clauses, and then by establishing agent and affected status for the participants mentioned within the former. An example of a transactive clause from the *Sun* article is: "The mob stoned them [police] and they used their riot shields to protect themselves." In this case, a process involving two participants, one active and causal and the other acted upon, is presented by the newspaper. An example of a nontransactive clause from the *Morning Star* is: "Dozens of police coaches were in the area and groups of police were standing on every corner." Here only one participant group is mentioned, and there are no (causal) transactions between participant groups. Trew demonstrates that the *Sun* report has more transactive clauses than the *Morning Star* report, presumably indicating a greater concern for causal interaction on the part of the former.

In addition to the above differences, Trew discusses certain variations with regard to the prominence given to the participants described by the two newspapers. Both articles isolate a minimum of three distinct groups involved in the situation: the police; groups of youths; and the general carnival attendants. In the *Sun* report, the groups of youths are treated as the most active participants, acting on each of the other groups. Action verbs such as "hurl," "burst through," and "stone" are used to describe the youths' behavior. The *Morning Star* mentions only one transaction between the youths and another group. Moreover, it treats the police as the most active group and implies that they are the initiators of (rather than reactors to) most actions. Verbs such as "clear," "charge," and "break into" are associated with the actions of the police.

The third major difference between the two articles resides in the classification of the youths. The *Morning Star* consistently describes the youths as "groups of youngsters." In contrast, the *Sun* employs a variety of terms, including "mobs of black youths," "gangs of youths," "thugs," and the like. This mode of classification in the *Sun* appears to be congruent with the newspaper's general concentration on the youths as the major force behind the violence. It should be noted that there is no lexical variation in the way the other participants in the riot are described by the two newspapers.

Trew summarizes the differences in the two articles in the following manner. The *Sun* reports the event as a process having participants as its initiators, in this case gangs of youths. The article implicitly considers these youths the source of the violence by treating them as agents of action and by classifying them as gangs and as thugs. Such treatment leads to the conclusion that the youths present a problem of social order to which the police justifiably and appropriately respond. This attitude is made explicit in a subsequent *Sun* editorial. The *Morning Star* treats the situation and the participants quite differently. According to Trew, the carnival and its attendant violence are treated by the *Morning Star* as processes without participants. That is, due to the greater employment of nontransactive clauses, causal relationships seem to be deemphasized in this article. Attention in the *Morning Star* report is directed toward the implicit connection between violence and general social conditions, not to the specific actions of persons. Within this context, though, the police are treated as

the most active group and as the initiators of most actions.

Trew and his colleagues (Fowler & Kress, 1979) imply that the mass media organize audiences' perceptions of events, and that the different linguistic structures employed by various media structure perceptions in different ways. Kress and Hodge argue that the linguistic structures of a particular piece of discourse "act to alter the way in which a reader meets the material and tend to structure his interpretation in specific ways" (1979, p. 28). They would seem to agree with McGee's suggestion that the symbolic embodiments of ideology have a presumptuous and public quality to them, capable of "influencing ... the shape and texture of each individual's 'reality' " (1980, p. 5). However, Trew and his associates present no empirical test for this assertion other than the textual analyses; these authors do not study the process by which this influence occurs, that is, the *interaction* of audience members with media discourse. How do newspaper readers react to and employ the linguistic texts with which they are confronted?

An alternate way to phrase the present concern is to question the location of "ideology." A single definition of ideology itself is difficult to come by, for, as Williams points out, there are three main uses of the word:

(i) a system of beliefs characteristic of a particular class or group;

(ii) a system of illusory beliefs—false ideas or false consciousness—which can be contrasted with true or scientific knowledge;

(iii) the general process of the production of meanings and ideas. (1977, p. 55)

In subsequent discussions, Williams goes on to suggest that the "distinction between 'true' and 'false' consciousness (must be) effectively abandoned" (1977, p. 68), and that ideology is best conceived of as the process within which persons become conscious of their social condition, that is, as the dimension of social life in which meanings and values are produced. Thus, he argues against a static view of ideology: "We speak of a world-view or of a prevailing ideology or of a class outlook, often with adequate evidence, but in this regular slide towards a past tense and a fixed form suppose . . . that these exist and are lived specifically and definitively, in singular and developing forms" (1977, p. 129).

While recognizing the social structural functions and dynamics of ideology, Trew seems to use the term in the first sense outlined by Williams, to refer to a generalized orientation about the world, its constituent events, actors and relationships. Trew argues that ideology is "a system of concepts and images which are a way of seeing and grasping things, and of interpreting what is seen or heard or read" (1979a, p. 95). This position assumes that mediated texts contain and convey ideologies, that the ideologies transmitted by the mass media and interpreted by audiences are identical. Such an assumption is debatable:

Information . . . does not have an objective, univocal meaning apart from the universe of meanings held by sources and receivers, but takes on meaning for a source or a receiver depending on his or her situation.

Researchers sharing this perspective locate the process of communication in the attempts of individuals or groups to make sense out of a situation. (White, 1983, p. 282)

A definition of ideology and its symbolic embodiments which locates the power and influence of ideology solely in the text is problematical for mass communication (as opposed to linguistic) analysis because of the interactive nature of communication. The force of a synchronic structure of ideograph clusters (McGee, 1980), or of a set of causal syntactic relationships (Trew, 1979b), must be analyzed within the framework of the encoding/decoding situation of the source and of the receiver. It is clearly possible that what may be intended or encoded as ideological on the part of message "originators" may not be so perceived by message "recipients" (cf. Hall's [1980] notion of "oppositional codes" and Eco's [1972] "aberrant decoding"). In addition to this, message "originators" may employ linguistic conventions rhetorically to mask the ideological nature of a text from audiences, thereby claiming the existence of an objective or nonideological discourse. The basic question, then, is whether readers presented with a mediated text are able to detect its ideological position, or simply build up what they perceive to be a repertoire of (neutral) information related to world events.

METHOD

As noted above, our concern here is with the impact of various language structures studied by Trew on readers' own articulations of the events depicted in the newspapers. In order to generate data relevant to this concern, a questionnaire was constructed and administered to students in a communication course at a large state university ($n = 204$). Each questionnaire reproduced either the original *Sun* or *Morning Star* article, and posed a series of open- and closed-ended questions. Subjects were randomly assigned to read either the *Sun* or the *Morning Star* article. Completion time for the reading and the questionnaire ranged from 45 to 75 minutes.

Results of an analysis based on the closed-ended questions (consisting of 16 semantic differential and 42 Likert-type items) are reported in another paper (Fry and Sigman, 1984). The present essay is primarily concerned with the subjects' responses to the open-ended questions, which asked the readers to provide a paragraph paraphrasing the article presented, to describe the actions of the various participant actors, to indicate the responsible party (or parties), and to select one of two editorials which most closely approximated the spirit and intent of the original article. The editorials were actual discourse drawn from the *Sun* and the *Morning Star*. It should be reiterated that we did not intend the questionnaire data to serve as collaborative indices for Trew's content analysis. Rather, our goal was to gauge readers' responsiveness to and understanding of the content found in the two newspapers.

Because of the time-consuming and detailed nature of qualitative analysis, it was not possible to systematically study all 204 questionnaires for this report. Instead, 30 of the questionnaire sets were randomly selected (with equal representation of the two conditions) from the larger subject pool for detailed analysis here.

RESULTS

Perceptions of Responsibility for Rioting and Violence

Trew's analysis suggests certain variations in reader reconstructions of the rioting and carnival situation based on stimulus condition. Since the *Sun* article had a much greater frequency of transactive clauses and a greater concentration on active participants than the

Morning Star article, readers of the former should reconstruct the overall situation and the participants as more active and involved. Further, it was felt that *Sun* readers would isolate the groups of youths as significantly more responsible for the riot, while *Morning Star* readers would select the police. The following analysis generally supports these predictions, but also indicates a far more complex structuring of the news event on the part of the respondents.

The respondents were asked to assign responsibility for the event to a person or group of persons and to pinpoint aspects of the newspaper article which directed this choice. A number of individuals or groups were designated by *Sun* readers and a variety of reasons were supplied by the respondents for these selections. Two respondents named the "carnival stewards" (or "organizers of carnival") as the responsible party. These respondents seemed to have a clear sense of the overall sequencing of the reported events, and placed responsibility on those who apparently provided the first bit of provocation:

The riots might not have started if the stewards hadn't asked the disco to shut down while the carnival was still going on.

The article states this started the event (riot)—the organizers wanted to close the disco. The thugs did not want to close the disco.[2]

Ten of the respondents isolated the persons affiliated with the mobile disco as the responsible party (one of these respondents included the carnival organizers, and another the police, as dual responsible parties). Various names were used as labels for these participants, including "thugs," "blacks," "10 youths," "8 black youth," and "owners of disco." These persons were perceived by *Sun* readers as active and primary contributors to the event. However, their actions (albeit "violent" and "rebellious") were seen as reactions provoked by the carnival organizers:

The article states that the riots began when the black group was asked to close down— then the small group developed—and others. It was contagious?

Youths—they were obviously offended by the carnival organizers' insistence that they close.

Those individuals affiliated with the carnival were described by the *Sun* readers as "insensitive," "uncaring" and "unorganized."

Only one *Sun* respondent, who pinpointed "blacks" as the responsible persons, did not specify an interactive cause for the violent episodes:

[List the factors or conditions pinpointed in the newspaper story which lead you to believe that this is the responsible party/ parties.] (1) obvious initiation; (2) waiting to be provoked.

In general, and with this one exception in mind, it should be stressed that the readers did not see the rioters' actions occurring outside of a context; instead they appeared to be able to articulate a clear causal relationship between and among the carnival organizers, the disco owners, and the rioters. This sort of reconstruction is consistent with the structure present in the *Sun* article itself. It is also interesting to note the appearance of what might be considered a conservative ethos or attitude toward the event on the part of the *Sun* readers. Civilians (both carnival and disco operators) were depicted by the respondents as being in conflict with each other, while the authorities were not mentioned as either initiators of, or primary actors in, the disturbance. Only one *Sun* reader

mentioned "the police" as a responsible party, and then only because the police did not act quickly and decisively:

The police were partly responsible for continuing to allow the violence earlier in the day [to continue].

The lack of blame or responsibility attributed to the police by the *Sun* readers can be further seen in the responses to another series of questions. Respondents were asked to provide descriptions of each of the participants included in the newspaper story. The police were depicted by *Sun* readers as "restorers of peace," "anticipating trouble, assertive, prepared," "ineffective, brave, outfought," "inadequate," "trying to maintain crowd control," "helpless, passive," and "determined, brave, daring." Thus, the police were described as having attempted, though unsuccessfully at times, to carry out their authorized duties. Several respondents also made reference to an "injured policeman," who was "grateful, lucky, proud," and "brave, young, strong." Overall, *Sun* readers created and sustained a largely sympathetic view toward the police.

It should be pointed out that the terms "thugs" and/or "youths" are used by four *Sun* readers to refer to a different party of individuals from those already discussed above. The *Sun*'s use of the word "thugs" at the very end of the article seems to have prompted one respondent, in answer to the query as to what conditions pinpointed in the story led the respondent to select a particular responsible party, to write: "Because this is the only name I can think of at the end of the story." With the proliferation of characters (and the multiple names for certain characters) labeled by the *Sun*, this may not be a surprising reaction at all. Other respondents fingered "thugs" as the principal party, but clearly distinguished these individuals from the (black) disco owners:

The thugs are responsible for this event because they came to the carnival with knives and weapons of destruction to hurt people and rob them of their money. A carnival is a good opportunity for the thugs to attack because the people are having a good time and do not expect to be hurt.

The *Sun* article is itself somewhat ambiguous as to whether the "black youths running a mobile disco" who, when asked "to close down for the night," began "the riot," are the same "small group of youths" who "[started] violence . . . early in the afternoon," who "beat up people in lavatories for the small change they were carrying," and who "attacked a group of press photographers." The word "thugs" is used only once by the *Sun* to refer to the rioting individuals who refused to follow the carnival stewards' pleas for peace: "Everyone listened except the thugs." The use of the word "thugs" as a single summary label and the varied references to several rioting or violent groups earlier in the article seem to have led some readers to consider all the rioters as the same, or as parts of one violent entity, and to perceive rampant and indiscriminant violence on the part of various civilian groups.

We will now consider the *Morning Star* readers' attributions of responsibility. Of the 13 respondents who answered the responsibility question, 7 defined the responsible party in terms of actions without specifically labeling a person or persons: "a group that was attending the carnival; no names"; "persons involved in scuffle"; "those shooting from stores"; "the people starting the fighting"; "the people who started the scuffle in one of the streets."

One respondent who referred to two responsible parties was able to name only one of them: "It [the newspaper] did not identify the name—those who were fighting and throwing missiles. In part, the police." A second respondent who named two responsible parties also described the choices in terms of the participants' actions, leaving description of characteristics of the groups largely unspecified: "A group of people in a building. A group in the street." It is interesting to note that the two amorphous groups listed by the latter respondent as responsible for the event were subsequently described in nonactive terms. More specifically, the actions of the responsible parties were defined in relation to the behavior of the police. When asked the reason for selecting the two responsible parties, this respondent wrote: "The police kept moving in until they broke in the building and it seemed over. The police moved over the ones in the street, pushing with their truncheons."

The above data do not necessarily mean that the majority of the readers of the *Morning Star* article were unable to discern distinct actor groups, rather that certain of the participants (the "rioting youths" in particular) appeared to them as relatively nameless and faceless. In one question, subjects were asked to list all the individuals or groups which they felt had been involved in the event described by the newspaper. One subject, who was unable to determine a single *responsible* party, did list two involved parties: "police, youth." The latter's role was described as being that of "trouble makers"; they were also depicted as "riotous, uncontrollable, loud."

The remaining six *Morning Star* subjects listed a variety of participants or involved persons, including "spectators at carnival," "(crowd control) police," "families," and "children." Again, however, those individuals who might be said to have been the source of the rioting and/or looting were labeled with vague terminology:

Fighting crowd—they engaged the police in a street fight by throwing cans and things at them.

Certain group of the crowd turned to violence.

One interpretation of these data considers the kind of constructed reality about the depicted events to which the readers have access. While *Morning Star* readers seem to be aware of the existence of a carnival and a riot, and of spectators, police and rioters, they do not seem to be able to describe clearly the latter group or to depict its actions or characteristics. It may be suggested here that *Morning Star* readers have a sense of process or of activity, but not fully a sense of the individual contributions to this—a proposition which is in accord with Trew's analysis of the actual *Morning Star* report.

Of the remaining *Morning Star* readers who did name a specific responsible party (six in total), three listed "rioters," one "rioters, police," one "the youth," and one "the crowd." No background descriptions (e.g., racial or socioeconomic labels) were provided by the respondents. In a few instances, the responsible individuals named by readers were described in terms of the *police's* actions (i.e., in terms of what the police did to them):

The rioters who had been subdued by the police before.

These descriptions are consistent with Trew's contention that the *Morning Star*'s syntactic constructions provided readers with an "active" view of the police.

Unspecified youths and rioters were also placed in various active sentence constructions by *Morning Star* readers:

They were throwing things at the police.

They apparently were trying to get as many policemen as possible in retaliation for an earlier event.

Finally, the respondents' statements seem to indicate that there was some ambiguity as to whether the rioting individuals (our term) were part of the carnival goers or constituted a separate group:

First they [the crowd] were having a good time, and then they became militant.

If the crowd parted to let the youth thru it was more than horseing [sic] around—they were "running" for a reason.

In other words, some of the *Morning Star* readers were left with the impression that the individuals who turned violent were also people who had enjoyed the carnival earlier in the day; in contrast with the perceptions of the *Sun* readers, the two groups were not clearly distinguished for *Morning Star* readers.

To summarize, while *Morning Star* readers were apparently able to isolate agency or responsibility in at least one group of participants depicted by the newspaper, the actual characteristics and make-up of this group were left unclear, or, at least, unspecified. This contrasts with the situation depicted by *Sun* readers who placed responsibility squarely with an active group of youths. Interestingly, *Morning Star* readers did not clearly place responsibility on the police as would be suggested by Trew's analysis. While the police were not seen as the responsible party nor as the primary initiators, they were seen as a necessary element in the event process. This is most clearly seen in the consistent connection between the responsible parties and police behavior in the minds of the respondents. Such a connection is less explicitly articulated by *Sun* readers.

Editorial Selections

Trew argues that editorials make manifest the ideology or theory often implicitly embedded in news reports. His analysis of the editorials dealing with the carnival from both the *Sun* and the *Morning Star* suggests a strong correspondence between the explicit ideology of each editorial and the more tacit ideology of the matching article. Trew's analysis reveals the following differences: "The end of the 1977 Notting Hill carnival is presented [by the *Morning Star*] as a case of alienated young people disturbing the communal leisure activities of thousands of people" (1979b, p. 136). In contrast, the *Sun* describes the violence as a case of "disruption of lawful activity, a challenge to the rule of law and a threat to the rights of citizens" (pp. 136–137). Furthermore, the *Sun* employs multiple lexical items to refer to the rioters: "the small but dangerous thug element"; "hooligans"; "louts"; and "thugs" (pp. 132–134). The *Morning Star* uses the term "young people," except for one instance in which the editors apparently quote (and reject) the *Sun*'s employment of "thugs" (p. 133).

To generate an additional perspective on the impact each newspaper had on readers' reconstructions of the London event, subjects were asked to read each of the carnival-related editorials, and to judge which was most probably published by the newspaper whose original account they had already read.[3]

The initial tabulation shows that 10 of the 15 *Morning Star* readers correctly selected the matching editorial, while 9 of 14 *Sun* readers selected the appropri-

ate editorial (one *Sun* reader did not respond to this question). These findings suggest an ability on the part of the readers to discern the explicit ideology expressed in the editorial in the basic news article. In many respects, though, the explanations provided by the readers for their choices are more interesting than their accuracy of selection. It is these responses that provide us with further insights into the readers' understanding of the events surrounding the carnival and the rioting as a function of the information source and its linguistic organization.

In general, *Sun* readers who selected the *Sun* editorial pointed to the treatment and descriptions of the police, and to the specificity of details contained in the writing. This editorial (editorial "A") and the original *Sun* article were perceived as positively oriented to the police's actions and responsibilities:

Editorial "A" seems to support the police just as the newspaper story did.

Related to a generally supportive attitude toward the police, readers also perceived the *Sun* as holding a "hard line" *vis-à-vis* the rioters:

It [editorial "A"] seemed to rehash the same line of thinking and also suggest very stiff sentences for the thugs.

Editorial "A" blames the youths for their own actions and wants to make them pay for their crimes. Editorial "B" blames society for not being sensitive enough to the problems that exist.

It is interesting to note that several of these respondents labeled the first editorial as more "conservative," and the second as more "liberal." Moreover, they attended to the *Sun* editorial's frequent use of the term "thugs."

As noted, the first editorial (the *Sun*'s), was also perceived by *Sun* readers as presenting more details than the second one:

This editorial ["A"] was more specific about the details and .not as general as editorial "B."

[Editorial "A" is] more specific about riot.

This focus on editorial specificity should be related to the degree of emphasis on causal relationships prominent in the original *Sun* article. Inherent in this newspaper's concentration on causal relationships is the syntactic specification of *who did what to whom*. This apparently lends itself to more detail in reporting, particularly in terms of describing responsibility and relating actions between and among participants. Since the *Morning Star* article and its editorial provided somewhat vague descriptions of causal interactions, concentrating instead on social conditions and processes (e.g., "penny-pinching attitudes," "alienation"), the level of specificity was much less clear.

Morning Star readers who correctly selected the second editorial isolated certain implicit or explicit themes embedded in the news article which also appeared in the editorial:

It promoted the continuation of the carnival (as did the story highlight the success of the carnival).

It didn't back "tough" law. It was liberal.

Other *Morning Star* readers seemed to note a difference in overall tone between the two editorials and found the correct editorial more consistent with the original article:

Editorial "A" was exact to the point—very opinionatated [*sic*]. Editorial "B" was less threatening to me for some reason.

As can be seen, readers were generally able to connect the implicit ideology embedded in the article with the more explicitly stated positions in the associated editorial. *Sun* readers seem to have found a favorable treatment of the police and the police's actions in the original news account, and chose the editorial which explicitly supported the police and condemned the rioters. On the other hand, the majority of *Morning Star* readers selected the editorial which promoted the continuation and the importance of the carnival for future years, which did not label specific protagonists, and which advocated a "calm" solution, all positions perceived to have been included in the *Morning Star*'s reporting of the event.

It is worth noting at this point that the impact of the article read by the respondents was not complete in terms of structuring the respondents' perceptions and subsequent descriptions of the event. Several individuals read and made use of the terms found in the news texts, yet their usages clearly reflected their own life histories as well. For example, one *Sun* reader who correctly chose editorial "A" wrote:

It seemed to me that this one was more in line with my point of view than "B." Maybe I feel radical today.

A *Sun* reader who incorrectly selected editorial "B" similarly indicated:

The editorial "A" was written in a very condemning way. It advocates stopping all public activities—pleasures as well as political. This is not the way to be democratic and solve the problems evident.

Finally, a second *Sun* reader who made an incorrect editorial selection based the choice on apparent impartiality:

I chose this editorial because I believe it to be the most impartial appraisal of the situation.

The newspaper account of the carnival incident was as written also impartially [sic].

While the present data cannot be used to assess completely how this respondent is employing the term impartial, it is interesting that this respondent (as well as others) chose to interpret the *Sun* article in this manner. This, despite the fact that the *Sun* clearly assessed (at least in a linguistic sense) unilateral responsibility, and labeled the groups of youths in an extremely pejorative fashion. This perception may well be due to either an expectation of how an impartial news article should appear based on a history of reading such articles or an acceptance by the respondent of the apparent validity of the report in the *Sun* and labeling it as impartial, or both. Interestingly, other *Sun* readers suggested that this newspaper used an "unbiased," a "straightforward," and a "calm" writing style. One *Sun* reader incorrectly selected the *Morning Star* editorial for this reason:

It showed a calm approach to reporting a message or incident. This is the same attitude I received from the first article.

It may be that the original *Sun* article's use of active clauses detailing the actions of both the police and the rioters, and describing in depth both the riot and the disco, provides readers with the impression of an unbiased and balanced rendering of the facts.

CONCLUSIONS

The results bear directly on the interaction between the ideology "embedded" in texts and the readers who encounter those texts. According to the original linguistic analyses conducted by Trew (1979a, 1979b), the two texts used as stimuli in this study are ideological. The reporters who wrote the stories, as well as the organizations which employed

them, made use of particular linguistic structures, whether consciously or unconsciously, in order to place the depicted participants in certain relationships, to explain a particular situation, and to justify selected social actions. Nevertheless, the presence of these ideological positions might well be nothing more than a passing concern for communication scholars unless it were possible to establish the nature of the impact such texts have on readers.

We posit in the present context that various linguistic structures, such as transactive and nontransactive clauses, function as "tools" to aid in both making sense of a complex social situation *and* in expressing that sense to others. Newspaper articles report events in the world which are largely removed from the audience's daily experiences; thus, they provide readers with a particular view of the actors and actions which constitute the world, and a set of linguistic symbols (especially classificatory terms) for communicating that perspective to others. McGee similarly writes that "human beings are 'conditioned,' not directly to belief and behavior, but to a vocabulary of concepts that function as guides, warrants, reasons, or excuses for behavior and belief" (1980, p. 6).

In asking our respondents to comment on attributions of responsibility and to provide descriptions of the parties involved in the riot, we were able to access not only the respondents' perceptions of responsibility but also the means through which the information was provided to them. The different presentations of the event by the *Sun* and the *Morning Star* led to noticeably different reconstructions by the respondents. This, in and of itself, is by no means an insignificant finding since the structuring of responsibility for social acts can profoundly affect society's reaction to such acts. Of even more interest, though, are the linguistic differences between *Sun* and *Morning Star* respondents in how they reconstructed the situation. *Sun* respondents, on balance, provided reconstructions which articulated clear causal relationships among the participants. *Morning Star* respondents described the participants in noncausal terms and employed such nonspecific labels as "a group" and "persons."

The two respondent groups, then, have not only drawn differing conclusions about responsibility, but they have selected linguistic structures to express those conclusions which are similar to those used in the news article they read. Thus, the linguistic structure of the "message" becomes, in part, a tool to aid the reader in the reconstruction of the event. By taking on the linguistic structure the reader may also adopt some of the ideological characteristics carried by that structure, whether the reader is conscious of this or not.

While it is possible to demonstrate that variations in linguistic structure lead to differences in how readers reconstruct events, it is also important to consider whether audiences perceive and utilize news reports as "ideology" or as "information." This is a particularly crucial question since the meaning that is attributed to a text by readers is an interaction between what the text brings to readers, in terms of its structural characteristics and causal depictions, and the readers' own perceptions about causality in certain generic social encounters and their own attitudes and experiences.

A reader's encounter with a text is an extremely complex interaction. Certainly, variations in how individual readers attribute meaning to a text or parts of a text should be expected. In the present context, several subjects suggested that they had been presented with an objec-

tive, and, presumably, nonideological article. These readers perceived the article they read as factual and substantive. Their questionnaire responses were consistent with those provided by others reading the same newspaper, yet they did not seem to reveal any awareness that the "facts" may have been filtered through some linguistically-based ideological apparatus. Other readers recognized attempts by the reporter/newspaper to explain and justify certain situations and conditions, thus manifesting a level of consciousness of the embedded ideology.

The responses given by the subjects as to why they matched one of two editorials to the text they read can be used as rough markers for the depth of encounter the readers had with the text. Some of the subjects were quite clear in their perceptions of the ideology apparent in the text. Several labeled the text and the editorials as conservative or liberal, or noted the distinction between the assignment of blame on youths and that on society. Other respondents noted differences in partiality, in tone, and in policy recommendations of the two newspapers. These responses clearly focus on the ideological level. In contrast, several subjects made their discriminations between the editorials based on the amount of information or detail which was presented. These subjects seemed not to be assessing the differences in embedded ideology at all, apparently functioning strictly at the "informational" level.

It is premature to suggest here that most *Morning Star* readers absolutely believed they were presented with a "party line," while *Sun* readers considered their newspaper to be objective and primarily informative. Nevertheless, there is some indication that at least two processes may have been involved in some readers' dealings with the newspaper texts. First, some readers may have apportioned part of the text to the category of ideology; this material was often labeled by them as "biased" and was viewed critically and with some suspicion. Second, some additional parts of the text may have been viewed as objective and substantive information, and, therefore, judged on the basis of truth and accuracy. Which components of a text are so apportioned will depend upon each reader's previous attitudes toward the event or similar events, the reader's previous knowledge of this or similar events, the reader's experience with and expectations for the newspaper's overall style of presentation, and the structuring conventions used to convey the information and the ideology.

These observations raise a number of questions concerning the ideological status of the texts analyzed by Trew (and by implication of any message subjected to content analysis without informant data—cf. White, 1983). The present data seem to suggest that the ideological orientations of newspaper articles may be differentially attended to and judged as ideological, based on the presence of certain linguistic conventions (cf. Glasgow University Media Group, 1976; Tuchman, 1972). Moreover, the ideological match between a text's "initiators" and "recipients" may not always be coincident; therefore, it is important to uncover the interaction processes resulting in interpretive junctures and disjunctures.

At least three possible outcomes of these processes can be noted here (cf. Hall's [1980] three decoding situations): (1) readers may *detect* the ideological orientation of their news source and decide either to agree or disagree with it; (2) readers may *assimilate* the ideological position without being aware of this; and/or (3) readers may formulate opinions about events based on their *information exposure* without considering that the information source itself is providing an ideological message. It is likely that readers will make use of mediated texts differently depending upon their perceptions of each text as either "reportorial" or "editorial." It should be noted, therefore, that we have referred in this essay to readers' *reconstructions* of events and ideological depictions; the readers are neither passive recipients of media ideology nor independent judges. With regard to the presumed ideology of a medium or information source, researchers need to distinguish between consistent patterns of language usage on the part of the medium, and the perceptions of these on the part of audiences; the ideology of a text may be separately (re)constructed by mass media organizations and mass media audiences.

Such an analytic treatment of ideology expands upon the kind of diachronic and synchronic descriptions of ideographs advocated by McGee (1980). Ideographs must be understood in their historical context, and also in their use in clusters at any particular moment. The present study indicates that separate synchronic analyses may be necessary for different populations within a society; for example, that the linguistic tools for communicating an ideological position may be variously attended to and employed by media producers and audiences.

In summary, the present data suggest a set of related concerns which need further exploration. First, since news texts organize to some degree audience understanding of world events, there is need for systematic analysis of the structural characteristics of news coverage. Such an analysis needs to move beyond bits of informational data to focus on the structural features for conveying ideology. The linguistic approach used by

Trew (1979b) and the rhetorical concepts offered by McGee (1980) appear to hold great promise in this regard.

Second, there is a need to understand how the audience for news encounters news texts. We need to go beyond the tacit assumptions that measures of information gain adequately capture the outcomes of news encounters, and that interpretations of news items other than those intended by producers are indications of audience "confusion" or lack of basic communication skills. As outlined above, audience members will vary in the depth with which they confront texts and will vary in the meanings they attribute to described circumstances.

Finally, there is an ongoing need to face the issue of ideology as it relates to mass communication. As with any significant issue, exploring ideologically-related questions is frought with difficulties, not the least of which are definitional. In the present context, we have chosen to explore the "enactment" of ideology through an analysis of audience reconstructions of news texts. While we feel it is appropriate, given the nature of the present study, to continue seeing ideology along the lines developed by Trew, as a generalized orientation, ideology must nevertheless be studied in terms of specific contexts of application. More specifically, within this framework ideology is not simply a social/structural issue, but an interactional/interpretive one as well. In this regard, we have presented data related to the various interpretive outcomes of readers' encounters with media ideology. It would seem to be dangerously simplistic to position ideology solely at the macro-social/structural level without considering the possibility of changes or variations in ideology through society members' interactions with, for example, media texts. It would also appear to be naive to ignore those social/structural characteristics of ideology which are clearly significant in explicating the positioning of ideology in a social system. By taking an interactional/interpretive stance towards ideology the possibility of understanding how audience members differentially take up and use ideological content and "tools" in their attempts to explain, justify and guide their social lives can be opened.   □

NOTES

[1]Copies of the original newspaper reports can be secured by writing the authors.

[2]Parenthetical comments were provided by the subjects. Comments contained in brackets are those of the present researchers.

[3]Readers were also asked to select one of two headlines for the newspaper account presented to them. Their responses repeat the findings for the editorial selections, and so only the latter are reported here.

REFERENCES

Bybee, C. R. (1981). Fitting information presentation formats to decision-making: A study in strategies to facilitate decision-making. *Communication Research, 8*, 343–370.

Eco, U. (1972). Towards a semiotic inquiry into the television message. *Working Papers in Cultural Studies, 3*, 103–121.

Fowler, R., & Kress, G. (1979). Critical linguistics. In R. Fowler, B. Hodge, G. Kress, & T. Trew (Eds.), *Language and control* (pp. 185–213). London: Routledge & Kegan Paul.

Fry, D. L., & Sigman, S. J. (1984). Newspaper language and readers' perceptions of news events. *Newspaper Research Journal, 5,* 1-11.

Glasgow University Media Group. (1976). *Bad news.* London: Routledge & Kegan Paul.

Greendale, S. C., & Fredin, E. S. (1977). Exploring the structure of national issues: Newspaper content and reader perceptions. In P. Hirsch, P. Miller, & F. G. Kline (Eds.), *Strategies for communication research* (pp. 167-183). Beverly Hills: Sage.

Hall, S. (1980). Encoding/decoding. In S. Hall, D. Hobson, A. Lowe, & P. Willis (Eds.), *Culture, media, language* (pp. 128-138). London: Hutchinson.

Kress, G., & Hodge, R. (1979). *Language as ideology.* London: Routledge & Kegan Paul.

McGee, M. C. (1980). The "ideograph": A link between rhetoric and ideology. *Quarterly Journal of Speech, 66,* 1-16.

Rosch, E. (1977). Linguistic relativity. In P. N. Johnson-Laird & W. C. Wason (Eds.), *Thinking: Readings in cognitive science* (pp. 501-519). Cambridge, England: Cambridge University Press.

Trew, T. (1979a). Theory and ideology at work. In R. Fowler, B. Hodge, G. Kress, & T. Trew (Eds.), *Language and control* (pp. 94-116). London: Routledge & Kegan Paul.

Trew, T. (1979b). 'What the papers say': Linguistic variation and ideological difference. In R. Fowler, B. Hodge, G. Kress, & T. Trew (Eds.), *Language and control* (pp. 117-156). London: Routledge & Kegan Paul.

Tuchman, G. (1972). Objectivity as strategic ritual: An examination of newsmen's notions of objectivity. *American Journal of Sociology, 77,* 660-679.

White, R. A. (1983). Mass communication and culture: Transition to a new paradigm. *Journal of Communication, 33,* (3) 279-301.

Whorf, B. L. (1956). *Language, thought, and reality: Selected writings of Benjamin Lee Whorf.* Cambridge, MA: MIT Press.

Williams, R. (1977). *Marxism and literature.* Oxford, England: Oxford University Press.

25

INTERPERSONAL COMMUNICATION AND NEWS COMPREHENSION

John P. Robinson and Mark R. Levy

THE PERENNIAL survey finding that the American public obtains most of its information from television is widely cited and generally accepted. Indeed, almost two-thirds of all Americans now identify television as their "main source" of news and that proportion has grown steadily since the late 1950s (Roper, 1983, 1985). While numerous researchers have raised methodological cautions about this generalization (Carter and Greenberg, 1963; Stone, 1969–70; Robinson, 1971; Stevenson and White, 1980), the "debate" over where the public gets most of its news by and large has been conducted in a conceptual and theoretical vacuum.

First of all, "main source" studies are almost always based on self-reports of information gain. Such subjective measures indicate only where people *think* they find out the news. However, self-reports of

---

Abstract   This study examines the role of interpersonal and mass media channels in public awareness and comprehension of major news stories. Unlike previous research which asks about respondent perceptions of their "main source" for news, this study attempts to determine *actual* comprehension of stories that had been in the news during the previous week. On the basis of two separate probability samples, respondent awareness and comprehension of a week's news was measured and related to demographic, news media use, and interpersonal discussions variables. A Multiple Classification Analysis of the data indicates that conversation about the news is a major and often overlooked correlate of comprehension, and that interpersonal channels may play at least as important a role in the public's awareness and understanding of the news as exposure to the news media.

John P. Robinson is the Director of the Survey Research Center and a Professor of Sociology at the University of Maryland. Mark R. Levy is an Associate Professor of Journalism and a Research Associate of the Center for Research in Public Communication, University of Maryland. An earlier version of this article was presented to the 40th annual meeting of the American Association for Public Opinion Research, McAfee, NJ, May 1983. Support for this study was provided by the John and Mary Marke Foundation.

From John P. Robinson and Mark R. Levy, "Interpersonal Communication and News Comprehension," *Public Opinion Quarterly*, Vol. 50: 160-175 © 1986 by the American Association for Public Opinion Research. Published by The University of Chicago Press. Reprinted by permission.

channel influence measure neither *actual* information gain nor, perhaps more important, how well that information is comprehended. These shortcomings have hindered our ability to understand the role of the mass media in the opinion formation process and suggest the need for studies based on better measures of information gain and comprehension.

Second, when asked "main source" questions, fewer than 1 respondent in 20 typically points to interpersonal channels as their principal news source. This finding stands in marked contrast to several well-established paradigms of public opinion and mass communication research. For example, the importance of "people" as an information source has been demonstrated in numerous studies of political communication effects (e.g., Katz and Lazarsfeld, 1955; Tichenor et al., 1973; Robinson, 1976), diffusion of innovations (e.g, Mason, 1963; Rogers, 1983), and communication about "major" news stories (e.g., Troldahl and Van Dam, 1965; Greenberg, 1964; Gantz, 1983). On the basis of this literature, then, one might expect to find previously overlooked linkages between interpersonal communication, information gain, and news comprehension.

The study presented here examines the comprehension of news and relates levels of comprehension to the use of mass media and interpersonal communication channels by individuals. This study is informed by the revision of the two-step flow hypothesis outlined in Robinson (1976) and by the general literature on interpersonal communication (see, for example, Schramm, 1973; Chaffee, 1982). It assumes that information is often, but not always, characterized by a "horizontal" flow between reasonably well-informed and interested individuals, and that information exchange in interpersonal settings is facilitated by such factors as greater personal involvement, immediate feedback, tailoring of messages, and the like.

We further assume that interpersonal discussions may be an important and largely overlooked agent in what Gerbner et al. (1980) have hypothesized is a "mainstreaming" process. Given that much of what individuals know about "the world out there" comes to them from the mass media *and* through interpersonal channels, the interaction of media messages and interpersonal discussion becomes central in considering the mechanisms that create possible "mainstreaming" effects. It is, after all, well documented that interpersonal discussions sometimes exercise a social control function, pressuring individuals into conformity with generally accepted perceptions and understandings. If those attitudes, perceptions, and understandings originate even partly in media messages, then talking about the news may simultaneously produce audience understandings which are widely shared and which are highly similar to journalistically created accounts of social reality.

Method

Unlike previous studies of news comprehension which have experimentally manipulated message attributes (e.g., Findahl and Höijer, 1976; Katz et al., 1977; Gunter, 1980) or which have sought to determine recall and comprehension of a single evening's news (e.g., Neuman, 1976; Robinson et al., 1982), this study focuses on actual national and international news messages, published and broadcast over a week's time.

While there is nothing magical about a seven-day period, asking about news at the end of a week may more realistically reflect actual patterns of audience exposure. The chance, for instance, that an individual will have watched any given evening's network news may be as small as 1 in 20 (Robinson, 1971; Lichty, 1982). However, over the course of a week, the likelihood of any exposure to network news and its associated opportunity for information gain and comprehension rises substantially.

Additionally, over the course of a week, there is an accumulation of exposure to the news (Bogart, 1981). To the extent that coverage of "important" news within and across news channels is complementary or redundant, audiences are more likely to receive several accounts of the same news item—and that too might aid awareness and comprehension. Further, taking a week's worth of news virtually assures that a greater substantive variety of news will have time to unfold and develop. Increased story "maturity" may aid individuals seeking to integrate the news into semantic memory (Woodall et al., 1983). Finally, studying what people know about the news after a week may allow time for interpersonal discussion of the news. News stories sometimes serve as a "coin of social exchange" (Levy, 1978a, 1978b), and, as was suggested above, it is possible that the interpersonal utility of the news may enhance its recall and comprehension.

SAMPLES

Two separate probability surveys were conducted by telephone from the Survey Research Center at the University of Maryland using the random-digit-dialing method of household selection. In the first sample, 407 adults living in the greater Washington, DC metropolitan area were interviewed during May 1983. To maximize generalizability and to obtain a greater variety of news stories, a second set of interviews with 544 adults nationwide were carried out during June of 1983.

Most interviewing was done on weekends and was based on the stories that had received prominent media attention in the preceding seven days. Interviews were spread approximately equally throughout each month. Completion rates were 74 percent for the regional sample and 71 percent for the national sample, after 10 callbacks to establish whether the telephone numbers were actually of telephone households.[1] Data from both surveys were weighted by respondent sex, age, and education to ensure representativeness with 1980 Census Bureau figures for the region and the nation.

NEWS MEDIA USE QUESTIONS

In both surveys, respondents were asked the following media exposure questions: (1) "Over the past seven days, have you read any daily newspaper?" (2) "Over the past seven days, have you read any national news or commentary magazine?" (3) "Over the past seven days, have you listened to any news broadcasts on the radio?" (4) "Over the past seven days, have you watched any news programs on television?" Each "yes" response was coded "1"; each "no" was coded "0." Responses on these four items were summed for each respondent into an index of news exposure.

All respondents were also asked, "Did you talk with anyone about anything in the news last week?" If "yes," respondents were then asked, "About how many such conversations did you have?" and "Who did you talk with?" Additionally, respondents reporting conversations about the news were asked: "Can you remember any of the things you talked about?" and if so, "What was that?"

News stories discussed by respondents in the national sample were then coded by two trained research assistants and one of the authors to determine whether the item was "definitely," "maybe," or "not" one of the "most important" national or international stories of the preceding week. (A discussion of how the week's "most important" stories were identified follows below). Intercoder agreement on this measure was 87 percent.

While respondents were free to mention conversations about local, national, or international news items, our analysis focused on "cos-

---

[1] Estimates of public comprehension of the news presented below are, of course, subject to sample biases due to the elimination of nontelephone households and the nonresponse rate. Telephone interviewing may have excluded, for example, some poorer, older, and non-English-speaking respondents, while some people who are less interested in the news and less well informed about it may have disproportionately refused to be interviewed. Thus, although it should not affect our analysis of the *correlates* of news comprehension, it is likely that our point estimates of news comprehension may be marginally inflated, even though the data were weighted to match census figures for education, age, and sex distribution.

mopolitan'' news (Merton, 1949), that is, national and international stories of more than purely local interest. While knowledge of different types of news may have different correlates, and awareness and comprehension of local news may be even more influenced by word of mouth, at least one study that systematically examined *both* national and local news stories has found considerable similarity in the background and media use correlates associated with both types of news (Becker and Whitney, 1980).

In addition, to assess and control for individual interest in the news, respondents in the national sample were asked, "How closely do you follow national and international news in the media? Would you say very closely, somewhat closely, or not very closely." Respondents were also asked standard demographic items (e.g., sex, age, education, etc.).

SELECTION OF NEWS COMPREHENSION ITEMS

All respondents were asked "awareness" and "comprehension" questions about the "most important" stories from the week preceding the interview. The selection of "most important" news stories represented a collective judgment by a rotating panel of five or more high-ranking news professionals who worked for *The Washington Post*, *USA Today*, Associated Press, CBS News, and ABC News. (For a more general discussion of this technique, see Robinson et al., 1982.) Each week this panel of journalists was asked: (1) What have been the "big stories" of the past week? (2) What were the one or two most important things ("main points") that the audience should have learned from those stories?

Examples of "important stories" and their "main points" include: an earthquake in California with no fatalities; the nationwide outbreak of AIDS and its effect on homosexuals, Haitians, and others; Congress limiting the "tax cut" out of concern over the federal deficit; U.S. Senator John Glenn announcing his presidential candidacy; the Pope visiting Poland to support Solidarity; the reelection of British Prime Minister Margaret Thatcher by a landslide; and the expulsion of the U.S. ambassador from Nicaragua for "spying" and the subsequent reaction of the Reagan administration.[2]

In choosing the final list of stories for inclusion in the week's survey, every effort was made to include only items that had received extensive coverage in both print and broadcast news media. Finally, the wording of survey questions was checked with the panel to insure

---

[2] For a complete listing of news stories and their associated awareness and comprehension questions, see Robinson and Levy (1986).

appropriateness and accuracy. Audience awareness of any given news story was measured by a "yes–no" response to a question which took the generic form: "Did you hear or read anything last week about ——?" If "yes," the respondent was then asked a question, usually open-ended, which had been designed to test the degree to which the individual knew a given story's "main point" as defined by the panel of journalists.[3] Over the course of each four-week field period, we asked respondents in the regional sample about 23 different persons, events, or phenomena that had been in the news, and respondents in the national sample about 31 distinct persons, events, or phenomena.

SCORING OF NEWS COMPREHENSION ITEMS

Responses to the open-ended comprehension items were coded by the authors using a 9-point scale, developed in connection with earlier comprehension studies (Robinson and Sahin, 1984). Coding was by consensus, with initial intercoder agreement in excess of 90 percent. Scores on the comprehension scale ranged from 0 to 8. Responses which recalled either the "wrong" story or failed to give its "main point" were rated 0 or 1, while a failure to recall anything beyond the initial awareness of the story was coded 2. Vague recollections of the story were coded 3 or 4, depending on response specificity. The code of 4 was assigned if the respondent was able to recall correctly some detail about the story (e.g., the identity of a the principal person in the story), but not the story's "main point." A reply containing the correct "main point," however, was coded 5, with one point added to the basic score of 5 for any additional correct detail provided—up to a score of 8 if the respondent noted not only the "main point" but three additional, cogent story details.

Thus, for example, in stories about AIDS, respondents were asked, "Do you know about any particular group of people who have been affected (by AIDS) more the others?" A response of "homosexuals" was coded 5. If the respondent said "Homosexuals" and Haitians, drug addicts, and/or hemophiliacs, that response was scored as a 6, 7, or 8, depending on how many groups beyond the "main point" (homosexuals) were named.

A summary measure representing total news comprehension for the week was then constructed for each respondent.[4] For each answer to a

---

[3] Examples of "main point" comprehension questions include: "How many people were killed in the (California) earthquake?" "Why did Congress want to limit the tax cut?" "Why was Senator Glenn in the news?" "What do you think the purpose of the Pope's trip (to Poland) was?

[4] Obviously, two comprehension measures have been developed: the first gauges the "depth" of information on a single story; the second, the summary score, measures the

specific comprehension item scored 5, 6, 7 or 8, the respondent received one point. These points were then summed and normalized to equalize the total number of weekly news items which varied slightly from week to week. Scores on this summary measure of news comprehension ranged from 0 to 9 in the regional sample and from 0 to 14 in the national sample. A score of 0 indicated no stories comprehended, while a summary score of 9 in the regional sample or 14 in the national study indicated comprehension of all items for a given week.

Ideally for our research, we should have had a specially devised "information meter" that would have automatically registered when respondents understood a news story and that recorded the source from which the information came. Given the current unavailability of such a device, we simulated the process with surveys. Our simulation asked first about the news information that respondents did have and second about the news sources respondents used. If users of news medium A possessed information that users of news media B did not, we took that to be reasonable evidence that news medium A was the more important information source. While this is not causal evidence (if indeed such social science data can be definitively gathered at all), it is the closest *field* approximation that we believed could be devised.

Results

The mean "awareness" score was 68 percent in the regional sample and 62 percent in the national sample. That means that roughly two-thirds of respondents in each sample said they had heard or read about the story. Details of U.S. government actions, in both domestic and foreign policy, tended to rank near the bottom in terms of public awareness, while respondents were most aware of especially dramatic news of real or potential danger and "human interest" stories.[5]

Means news comprehension scores were 2.7 (out of 9 weekly stories) in the regional sample, and 4.6 (out of an average of 14 stories per week) in the national sample. Thus, on average, somewhat less than one-third of the major news stories examined each week were comprehended by respondents sampled. No respondents in the regional sample successfully understood the "main point" of more than five of the week's major news stories. Fewer than 4 percent of national re-

"breadth" of respondent comprehension *across* a number of news stories. Limited analysis to date has found that the media use and interpersonal communication correlates of the two comprehension measures are highly similar.

[5] A story-by-story listing of "awareness" and "comprehension" scores is available on request from the authors.

Table 1. Weekly Conversations About News

	Regional Sample (407)	National Sample (544)
No. of conversations		
None	35%	40%
1–2	10	14
3–5	25	23
6–9	16	12
10 or more	14	11
Discuss "big" news		
Yes	n.a.	18
Maybe	n.a.	15
No	n.a.	51
Can't recall topic(s)	20	16

spondents comprehended 12 or more items and none had a score of 14. In general, these results are consistent with earlier parallel studies conducted in Great Britain (Robinson and Sahin, 1984); and like the pattern reported above for the awareness measure, comprehension was often, but not exclusively, higher for stories with dramatic or "human interest" content.

Almost two-thirds (65 percent) of respondents in the regional sample and almost as many (60 percent) of national respondents said they had talked "about things in the news" during the week prior to their being interviewed (Table 1). In both samples, the largest proportion of conversations, two-thirds or more, were with "friends" or "colleagues at work," with family members making up the remainder of conversational partners.

Only 20 percent of regional respondents and 16 percent of the national sample who reported having news-oriented conversations were unable to recall the topic of those discussions. This is a rather low proportion, based as it is on an unaided recall question. Indeed, it suggests that news—be it local, national, international, or some mix— has a relatively high salience for most individuals.

Of respondents (national sample only) who could recall what they talked about, some 21 percent reported having at least one conversation which was coded as "definitely" dealing with one of the "most important" stories of the week. Another 18 percent of the national sample reported at least one conversation that was coded as "maybe" focusing on one of the week's major stories.

BIVARIATE CORRELATES OF NEWS COMPREHENSION

The average scores on the summary measure of news comprehension for each major background variable group are presented in Table

Table 2. Mean News Comprehension Scores by Demographic, Media Use, and
Communication Behavior Variables

	Regional Sample	National Sample
All respondents	2.7 (407)	4.6 (544)
Sex		
Male	3.3 (180)	5.7 (237)
Female	2.3 (226)	3.8 (307)
Age		
18–19	0.7 (9)	2.9 (17)
20–29	2.3 (97)	3.8 (127)
30–39	3.2 (90)	4.8 (113)
40–49	3.2 (63)	5.1 (82)
50–59	2.7 (68)	5.0 (63)
60–69	2.6 (49)	5.4 (76)
70 or older	2.7 (31)	4.2 (66)
Education		
< High school	1.7 (80)	3.1 (95)
H.S. grad	2.1 (119)	4.0 (278)
Some college	2.7 (71)	5.4 (94)
College grad	4.0 (137)	6.7 (49)
Graduate educ	—[a]	8.4 (28)
News exposure index		
0	0.5 (6)	1.2 (3)
1	1.0 (37)	2.8 (51)
2	2.1 (76)	3.6 (156)
3	2.8 (177)	5.0 (234)
4	3.6 (110)	6.2 (100)
How closely follow news		
Very closely	n.a.	6.4 (101)
Somewhat	n.a.	5.3 (266)
Not very	n.a.	2.5 (177)
Talks about news		
None	1.8 (143)	3.3 (219)
1–2	2.3 (38)	4.2 (74)
3–5	2.8 (101)	5.5 (127)
6–9	3.8 (66)	5.7 (64)
10 or more	3.9 (59)	6.8 (59)
Discuss "big" news		
Yes	n.a.	6.8 (98)
Maybe/no/DK	n.a.	4.1 (446)

[a] Respondents with post-college education included in college graduate category.

2. In general, there is considerable consistency between the regional and national samples with regard to these correlates of news comprehension. In both surveys, for example, there were fairly large differences in the comprehension scores of men and women, with men tending to have higher scores. Comprehension also increased with respondent age, although both sets of data showed some tendency for curvilinearity, with older respondents scoring lower than middle-aged respondents.

In both samples, level of formal education was the major predictor of news comprehension (see Robinson, 1967; Hyman et al., 1977 for similar results with other information survey questions). The average comprehension score of respondents with a college degree, for example, was more than double that of respondents who had graduated from high school.

Exposure to news media was also a clear but somewhat less powerful correlate of comprehension scores. For example, respondents in both samples with the least exposure to the news (i.e., 0 or 1 on the News Exposure Index) had mean scores that were less than half those achieved by those respondents reporting exposure to all four media news sources. However, because of the small size of this minimal exposure group, news exposure had less of a correlation with comprehension scores than did formal education. Interest in the news was another important correlate of comprehension scores, with respondents who claimed to follow the news "very closely" also scoring over twice as high as those who followed the news "not very closely."

Average news comprehension scores were also clearly correlated with the interpersonal communication variable. Talking about news with other people was related to considerably higher comprehension levels. As the number of conversations about news increased from none to 10 or more for the week, the average comprehension score more than doubled in both samples. Additionally, respondents in the national sample who reported talking about one or more major stories of the week had comprehension scores which were among the very highest in the study.

Table 2, then, links news comprehension scores with several possible predictor variables, considering each of those variables one at a time. The question naturally arises whether some of these correlates emerge as more powerful predictors after simultaneous adjustments are made for each of the other correlates in Table 2. For example, many of the correlates of comprehension examined here are also often linked with the strongest correlate of comprehension, namely, formal education. It could well be that controlling for the respondent's level of education would substantially reduce, or even eliminate, the correlations of news comprehension with news media exposure, interest in the news, or news-oriented conversations.

MULTIVARIATE ANALYSIS OF NEWS COMPREHENSION

News comprehension scores were next subjected to a Multiple Classification Analysis (Andrews et al., 1973) in order to determine the impact on comprehension of media use and communication behavior variables after controlling for demographic factors and the other media use questions. This MCA technique provides a combination multiple regression and analysis of variance adjustment on survey data.[6]

As Table 3 demonstrates, differences in the average comprehension scores for men and women in both samples are substantially reduced, after the other factors in Table 2 are taken into account. Statistical controls also reduce some of the curvilinearity of news comprehension and age in the regional sample, while educational differences and comprehension in both samples are also somewhat reduced.

Differences by levels of news media exposure are also considerably constricted by multivariate controls; and similarly, the gap is narrowed between respondents in the national sample who follow the news "very closely" and only "somewhat closely."

The interpersonal discussion variable is also affected by simultaneous controls for other variables, and several departures from the earlier pattern are found as well. Thus, in the regional sample, peak comprehension scores are reached in the 6–9 conversation group and then dip slightly in the 10 or more conversation category. In the national sample, peak comprehension scores are reached in the 10 + conversation group, while the mean comprehension score for respondents reporting 6–9 conversations dips below the score for the 3–5 conversation group.

The small sample sizes for the two groups reporting the largest number of conversations may account for some of the instability in the data. Indeed, if the data from the two samples in Table 3 were merged, the combined data would show clear monotonicity with number of conversations. The difference in average comprehension scores between the no-conversation group and the 10 + conversation group then would be 1.1 for the regional sample and 1.6 for the national sample, representing more than a 30 percent gain in news comprehension after MCA adjustments. For the national sample that is a larger difference than the 0.8 point gain between the four-media vs. 0–1 media use group combined (to obtain meaningful sample size); for the regional sample, the 1.4 point gain in mean comprehension scores across news media use is 0.3 points larger, but that is not a large difference.

---

[6] One advantage of MCA over other multiple regression techniques is that it provides straightforward adjusted averages for specific categorical groups in the sample (e.g., for men and women, or blacks, whites and other racial groups.) An MCA is also useful for ordered groups (e.g., high vs. middle vs. low education), since one can see whether relationships are linear and monotonic or have "peaks" and "valleys" in the middle categories. The principal drawback of MCA is that it does not provide error estimates that are necessary to conduct standard statistical tests on average difference scores between groups. However, certain "rules of thumb" have been developed for interpreting average group differences, and they are followed, where applicable, in this article.

Table 3. MCA Analysis of Comprehension Scores by Demographic, Media Use, and Communication Behavior Variables

	Regional Sample	National Sample
All respondents	2.7 (407)	4.6 (544)
Sex		
Male	3.0 (180)	5.3 (237)
Female	2.6 (226)	4.0 (307)
Age		
18–19	1.9 (9)	3.9 (17)
20–29	2.3 (97)	3.8 (127)
30–39	2.9 (90)	4.3 (113)
40–49	2.7 (63)	4.9 (82)
50–59	2.8 (68)	5.0 (63)
60–69	2.9 (49)	5.6 (76)
70 or older	3.7 (31)	4.8 (66)
Education		
< High school	2.0 (80)	3.4 (95)
H.S. grad	2.2 (119)	4.3 (278)
Some college	2.7 (71)	5.2 (94)
College grad	3.7 (137)	6.1 (49)
Graduate educ	—[a]	7.1 (28)
News exposure index		
0	2.0 (6)	3.3 (3)
1	1.6 (37)	4.1 (51)
2	2.4 (76)	4.3 (156)
3	2.9 (177)	4.8 (234)
4	3.1 (110)	4.8 (100)
How closely follow news		
Very closely	n.a.	5.6 (101)
Somewhat	n.a.	3.0 (266)
Not very	n.a.	3.5 (177)
Talks about news		
None	2.3 (143)	4.1 (219)
1–2	2.3 (38)	4.2 (74)
3–5	2.6 (101)	5.1 (127)
6–9	3.6 (66)	4.9 (64)
10 or more	3.4 (59)	5.7 (59)
Discuss "big" news		
Yes	n.a.	5.7 (98)
No	n.a.	4.4 (446)

[a] Respondents with post-college education included in college graduate category.

Thus, in both samples, the extent of discussion of the news seems to be at least as powerful a predictor of comprehension as the extent of news media exposure, and in the more generalizable national sample, such discussion was associated with almost twice as much spread in news comprehension as was media exposure.

A final insight into the importance of the interpersonal factor is given at the bottom of Table 3. If a respondent reported talking about even one of the week's "big news" stories, then, even after controlling for all other correlates reported in the table, that respondent was likely to score significantly higher on comprehension. Coupled with the findings reported above about comprehension and the number of news-oriented discussions, this result suggests that both the quantity *and* the quality of conversations are important factors in understanding the news.

Discussion

In summary, then, what can be said about the public's awareness and comprehension of national and international news over a week's time? First, and perhaps most obviously, it should be noted that there is a striking similarity between findings from the two surveys. Despite considerable geographic differences among respondents in the two samples and despite differences in the news stories examined each week, there is considerable overlap in the patterns within and the relative importance between key news comprehension correlates. This consistency across two independent samples points to a reassuring degree of generalizability in our findings.

Second, while education was found to be the single most important predictor of news comprehension, respondents who reported more conversations about the news were also more likely to score higher in news comprehension. Talking about the news, especially the week's "most important" national and international news, seems to have at least as powerful an effect on comprehension as mere exposure to the news media.

That finding, we believe, has serious implications for journalism, public understanding, and even the democratic process. While a full discussion of those implications is well beyond the scope of this article, we want to make one observation in passing. Journalists and politicians often complain that the public is not interested in the news and lacks the educational background to understand what gets reported (Robinson et al., 1982). Our study demonstrates, however, that controlling for news interest and education, public understanding of the news does increase as people talk about it. Journalists and others would do well, then, to consider ways to create and present news which stimulates or otherwise takes advantage of this powerful interpersonal "second stage" of the information flow.

Finally, the findings presented here bear directly on our general theories and models of the mass communication process. Two general paradigms inform most communication scholarship: one, the so-called dominant or American approach, is a fundamentally empirical and pluralistic model of relatively limited communication effects in which the power of the mass media is often mitigated by interpersonal influences; the other, the so-called critical or European perspective, finds major conceptual and empirical flaws in the dominant model and assumes often pervasive power for the media (Curran et al., 1982; Gitlin, 1978).

Our study, we believe, suggests a bridge between the two paradigms. On the one hand, our findings strongly suggest that interpersonal communication plays a crucial role in the reception, retransmission, and interpretation of mass media messages. That conclusion argues in support of the dominant theory and its continuing emphasis on the importance of social networks for the mass media process.

However, that same conclusion, namely that interpersonal communication increases the fidelity between the manifest content of mass media messages and the interpretations and meanings derived from those messages by audiences, can be interpreted to support the notion of a more powerful, "mainstreaming," or possibly even "ideological effect" of mass communication (Hall, 1983). From this perspective, interpersonal communication could be seen as helping to create audience "readings" of mass media messages that are closer in substance to "professional," and thereby ideologically "preferred," understandings of reality (Hall, 1980).

To substantiate such an assertion, of course, would require findings drawn from many different research sites in the mass communication process, and would necessarily involve both micro- and macro-studies of audiences, communicators, and culture more generally. This article obviously has a more limited scope, although our findings do have implications for such an investigation.

We have not, for example, offered *direct* evidence that the public interprets the news from any particular ideological standpoint; and we are aware that audiences are at least capable of creating "negotiated" or "oppositional" decodings of news messages (Morley, 1980). But we also have shown that public awareness and comprehension of the news, to the extent it occurs at all, often bears a striking similarity to journalistically encoded reality.

Similarly, the complex and often problematic relationship between journalistic encodings of the news and the more general phenomenon of ideology remains unexamined here. But other researchers have already shown that the ideological and thematic range of most news messages is fairly limited (Gans, 1979), and that represents an important precondition for demonstrating a linkage between audiences, communicators, and ideologies.

Taking these factors into account, and fully recognizing that much more work is needed, we still think it is plausible to speculate that conversations about the news will both increase the "accuracy" with which news messages are comprehended and the degree to which those messages may have ideological, essentially status quo consequences.

References

Andrews, F. M., J. N. Morgan, J. A. Sonquist, and L. Klem
  1973 Multiple Classification Analysis. Second Edition. Ann Arbor: Institute for So-
        cial Research, The University of Michigan.
Becker, Lee, and D. C. Whitney
  1980 "Effects of media dependencies." Communication Research 7:95–120.
Bogart, L.
  1981 Press and Public. Hillsdale, NJ: Lawrence Erlbaum Associates.
Carter, R., and B. Greenberg
  1965 "Newspapers or television: which do you believe?" Journalism Quarterly
        42:29–34.
Chaffee, S.
  1982 "Mass media and interpersonal channels: competitive, convergent, or com-
        plementary?" In G. Gumpert and R. Cathcart (eds.), Inter/media. Second Edi-
        tion. New York: Oxford University Press.
Curran, J., M. Gurevitch, and J. Woollacott
  1982 "The study of the media: theoretical approaches." In M. Gurevitch, T. Ben-
        nett, J. Curran, and J. Woollacot (eds.), Culture, Society and the Media. New
        York: Methuen.
Findahl, O., and B. Höijer
  1976 Fragments of Reality: An Experiment with News and TV Visuals. Stockholm:
        Sveriges Radio.
Gans, H.
  1979 Deciding What's News. New York: Pantheon.
Gantz, W.
  1983 "The diffusion of news about the attempted Reagan assassination." Journal of
        Communication 33 (Winter):56–66.
Gerbner, G., L. Gross, M. Morgan, and N. Signorielli
  1980 "The 'mainstreaming' of America: Violence Profile No. 11." Journal of Com-
        munication 30:10–29.
Gitlin, T.
  1978 "Media sociology: the dominant paradigm." Theory and Society 6:205–253.
Greenberg, B.
  1964 "Person to person communication in the diffusion of news events." Journalism
        Quarterly 41:489–494.
Gunter, B.
  1980 "Remembering the television news: effects of visual format on information
        gain." Journal of Educational Television 6:8–11.
Hall, S.
  1980 "Encoding and decoding." In S. Hall, D. Hobson, A. Lowe, and P. Willis
        (eds.), Culture, Media, Language. London: Hutchinson.
  1983 "The rediscovery of 'ideology': return of the repressed in media studies." In
        M. Gurevitch, et al. (eds.), Culture, Society and the Media. New York:
        Methuen.
Hyman, H., C. Wright, and J. Reed
  1977 The Enduring Effects of Education. Chicago: University of Chicago Press.
Katz, E., H. Adoni, and P. Parness
  1977 "Remembering the news: what the picture adds to recall." Journalism Quar-
        terly 54:231–239.
Katz, E., and P. Lazarsfeld
  1955 Personal Influence. New York: The Free Press.
Levy, M.
  1978a The Audience Experience with Television News. Association for Education in
        Journalism and Mass Communication, Journalism Monographs, Number 55.
  1978b "Opinion leadership and television news uses." Public Opinion Quarterly
        42:402–406.

Lichty, L.
 1982   "Video vs. print." The Wilson Quarterly, Special Issue.
Mason, R.
 1963   "The use of information sources by influentials in the adoption process." Public
        Opinion Quarterly 27:455–466.
Merton, R.
 1949   "Patterns of influence: a study of interpersonal influence and communication in
        a local community." In P. Lazarsfeld and F. Stanton (eds.), Communication
        Research 1948–1949. New York: Harper and Brothers.
Morley, D.
 1980   The 'Nationwide' Audience. London: British Film Institute.
Neuman, W. R.
 1976   "Patterns of recall among television viewers." Public Opinion Quarterly
        40:115–23.
Robinson, J.
 1967   "World affairs information and mass media exposure." Journalism Quarterly
        44:23–30.
 1971   "The audience for national TV news programs." Public Opinion Quarterly
        35:403–05.
 1976   "Interpersonal influence in election campaigns: two-step flow hypotheses."
        Public Opinion Quarterly 40:304–19.
Robinson, J., and M. Levy
 1986   The Main Source: Learning from Television News. Beverly Hills, CA: Sage
        Publications.
Robinson, J., and H. Sahin
 1984   Audience Comprehension of Television News: Results from Some Exploratory
        Research. London: BBC Audience Research Department.
Robinson, J., H. Sahin, and D. Davis
 1982   "Television journalists and their audiences." In J. Ettema and D.C. Whitney
        (eds.), Individuals in Mass Media Organizations. Beverly Hills: Sage Pub-
        lications.
Rogers, E.
 1983   Diffusion of Innovations. Third Edition. New York: Free Press.
The Roper Organization
 1983   Trends in Attitudes Toward Television and Other Media: A Twenty-Four Year
        Review. New York: Television Information Office.
 1985   Public Attitudes Toward Television and Other Media—A Time of Change. New
        York: Television Information Office.
Schramm, W.
 1973   "Channels and audiences." In I. de Sola Pool and W. Schramm (eds.), Hand-
        book of Communication. Chicago: Rand McNally.
Stevenson, R., and K. White
 1980   "The cumulative audience of network television news." Journalism Quarterly
        57:477–81.
Stone, V.
 1969– "Sources of most news: evidence and influence." Journal of Broadcasting
 1970   14:1–4.
Tichenor, P., J. Rodenkirchen, C. Olien, and G. Donohue
 1973   "Community issues, conflict, and public affairs knowledge." In P. Clarke (ed.),
        New Models for Communication Research. Beverly Hills, CA: Sage Pub-
        lications.
Troldahl, V., and R. Van Dam
 1965   "Face to face communication about major topics in the news." Public Opinion
        Quarterly 29:626–34.
Woodall, W., D. Davis, and H. Sahin
 1983   "From the boob tube to the black box: television news comprehension from an
        information processing perspective." Journal of Broadcasting 27 (Winter):1–
        23.

PART VI

MEDIA INSTITUTIONS, TECHNOLOGY, AND POLICY

INTRODUCTION

Mark R. Levy

The world of mass communication is changing. New communication technologies and organizations are challenging the media status quo. What are these new social and cultural forms? What are their consequences for individual and public life? Are we experiencing a communications "revolution"—a radical disjuncture in the mass communication process—or do the new technologies and organizations represent a dramatic but fundamentally *evolutionary* development in mass communication?

Answering those questions ought to be high on the mass communication research agenda, for the issues raised by the changing media environment are both scientifically compelling and socially and politically important. However, our review of materials for possible inclusion in this section suggests that much research on new technology and communication policy often appears to be relatively marginal to the concerns of most *mass* communication scholars.

Of course, basic and policy-relevant research is being done on the new communications technologies. Cable TV, VCRs, videotex, DBS, integrated services digital networks (ISDN), home computers, and so forth—all are the subject of research, sometimes by communications scholars, sometimes by economists, lawyers, or others. But much of this work, especially that with a telecommunications emphasis, is neither framed in terms of the long-running issues and controversies in *mass* communication research nor couched in the technical language of that tradition. And, for the moment at least, that means most of this often interesting and significant research on new technologies and/or policy will not find an "easy" home in a *Mass Communication Review Yearbook.*

Naturally, such a conclusion immediately raises troubling questions about not only the scope of *MCRY,* but, more important, about fundamental definitions of our field and its subject of study. Do the new technologies simply provide mass media researchers with a new research site for studying "old" theoretical controversies? Or is the mass communication process being altered so significantly that our "old" theories and preoccupations are becoming increasingly irrelevant? What, indeed, is the future of the mass media and how should it be studied?

In his article, "Is Media Theory Adequate to the Challenge of New Communications Technologies?" McQuail grapples with these key issues by assessing the utility of current mass communication theory for guiding new technology research and policy. Most implications of new communication technologies and institutions, McQuail concludes, "are not 'off the map' of current thinking," although emerging theory should pay closer attention to interactive aspects of the audience experience and to power relationships.

The "power" of the mass media is also the focus of two articles, both taken from a special issue of the *Journal of Communication,* focusing on "the marketplace of ideas." While some critics have argued that media concentration is antithetical to the free exchange of ideas and information, Compaine offers a counterposition in "The Expanding Base of Media Competition." New technologies, Compaine suggests, are blurring the boundaries between traditional media formats and contents, and this blurring is leading to a greater availability and diversity of information. Media structure in the United States, Compaine concludes, has never been "more open, diverse, and responsive to public needs."

Similarly concerned with the impact of media organization on the "marketplace of ideas," Hirsch focuses specifically on the book publishing industry. In "U.S. Cultural Productions: The Impact of Ownership," Hirsch rejects those "worst-case scenarios" in which the rise of media conglomerates necessarily reduces the outlets for creative and heterodox authors. Indeed, Hirsch observes, small publishers are thriving and the number of new books published yearly is at record levels.

The interplay of industry structure and economic forces is also examined by Blumler, Brynin, and Nossiter in "Broadcasting Finance and Programme Quality: An International Review." Drawing on a cross-national analysis prepared for the so-called Peacock Commission on Financing the BBC, the article evaluates the principal financing options open to public service broadcasters and concludes that while none is "perfect," some are less imperfect than others.

Finally, in "Property Rights in Information," Branscomb offers a wide-ranging review of "the laws of the Information Age." Specifically, Branscomb traces how courts and legislatures have wrestled with often conflicting claims over 10 different legal rights, ranging from the right to collect to the right to expunge information. The integrity of the individual, she insists, should be held no less dear "in a digital environment . . . than in a voice circuit or on a printed page."

Overall then, these articles suggest that our knowledge regarding media institutions, technology, and policy is growing, but that it also must be regarded as highly tentative and not especially well focused. The challenge for mass communication researchers is to decide, first, how our definitions of the field and our theoretical frameworks should be adapted to absorb, and benefit from, the research literature that has already developed in this area; and second, how most expeditiously and fruitfully to study the new communications technologies.

26

IS MEDIA THEORY ADEQUATE TO THE CHALLENGE OF NEW COMMUNICATIONS TECHNOLOGIES?

Denis McQuail

The 'old' media — of cinema, radio, recorded music and (even older) the newspaper and periodical — began life without benefit of much that is recognizable as theory, whether social or social scientific. The least old of the currently established media — broadcast television — was, through war-induced delay, established more consciously than its predecessors with an eye or ear to social and political considerations and with some awareness of potential consequences for society. Social scientific theory has been accumulated and worked out during the last 35 years or so to an extent that it may not unreasonably be characterized as the old, or established, theory for old media, even if these are still, for the most part, the only media we have. The new media will, in any case, have an extensive inheritance when they reach maturity and the question is whether they will have much value or be too linked to the older realities to serve for the emerging future.

To pose a question about adequacy is to presume some utility and relevance and also some criteria for assessment. There are two main potential areas of application for theory — one is research on communication and the other is policy making for the new media. Thus, what is being asked is, first, whether the existing body of theory helps give direction to relevant research and, second, whether it helps in locating problems for (social) policy in relation to new media. For either purpose, the requirements from theory are not so different. It should validly capture the reality of the applications, implications and consequences of new media. It should provide terms or concepts for describing this reality. It should help explain what is happening. It should have some predictive power — pointing at least to relevant possibilities of media development and effect. For policy application, the main emphasis should be on problem identification and the evaluation of alternative courses of action. For research what is needed from theory is, first of all, concepts, and secondly, hypotheses. Media theory is essentially an informed consciousness of what is happening when systems of public communication change. The title adopted for this chapter seems to presume that a fundamental change is at hand. One of the subsidiary functions of theory will be to help to decide whether this is so or not, aside from the more obvious changes in 'hardware' and behaviour.

Basic social values

Media, or mass communication, theory has itself deep roots in earlier, more fundamental, thought about society and, like all social theory, it has strong normative elements. Before examining what is specifically 'media-related' theory, it is worth identifying the most relevant basic social values which have influenced both the media themselves and thinking about mass communication.

The first is *freedom*, which has helped to legitimate the expansion and diversification of all kinds of media activity and has been the basis for opposition to paternalist, authoritarian and manipulative uses of media or to interference by state or church in communication. More specifically, freedom has meant ease of access to channels, resistance to monopoly or censorship, maximum freedom of expression consistent with safeguarding the rights of others and the ultimate security of the state. The second main relevant value is that of *equality*, which favours a fair distribution of the cultural and informational goods which communication offers, including access both as sender and receiver to the means of communication. In the 'first communications revolution', this value was invoked in favour of near-equal distribution of reception possibilities and a representative approach to access as senders for different groups and interests. The relative strength of the equality norm has helped to justify some interference with market forces and a degree of control inconsistent with complete freedom to send and receive. The third value of the classic trio is less easy to render by a single English word or to recognize as a direct influence on media arrangements. It is the value of 'togetherness' − favouring community, solidarity, cooperation, integration, against isolation, fragmentation, individuation, 'privatization'. It is likely to be invoked in defence of established patterns of life and culture, of the specificity of language and belief. It translates also into support for national, regional and local media forms and may also, less widely, be expressed in those forms of media which correspond to other bases of solidarity, such as class, religion or political allegiance. Related to this value (although sometimes viewed more as simply the reverse of freedom) is the value placed on *order*, in the sense of morality, tradition and continuity, as opposed to unregulated change and deviance from established standards.

These remarks may seem a diversion from the announced subject, but by naming these values and then considering the difficulty which one would have in adding to them, one already has a provisional answer to part of the question posed in the title. These will be necessary elements in any social theory relevant to new media and it is hard to imagine any significant additions, subtractions or alternatives.

Dimensions of media theory

What follows is an attempt to summarize conscious efforts to make sense of and predict the course of historical processes which have occurred and are occurring, as the means of communication have developed, especially in the 'first age' of mass communication, which extends from the start of this century to the present time. The theory discussed is not value-free, but it is more than a statement of preferences and has some claim to offer an objective account of mass media experience. The available 'old theory' can most economically be summarized in terms of three main dimensions or oppositions which, between them, map out the space occupied by different versions of the communication–society relationship and the likely social implications of developments and applications of communication technology. These dimensions can be related to each other and used to differentiate and compare possible positions in respect of the new media.

(i) Media or society as first mover?

The question indicates a choice between a 'media-centred' and a 'society-centred' view of the relationship. The former stresses the means of communication as a force for change, either through technology or the typical content carried. The latter emphasizes the dependence of both on other forces in society, especially those of politics and money. From this second point of view, the forms of mass media are an outcome of historical change – a reflection and consequence of political liberalization and industrialization and a response to demands for servicing from other social institutions. The media-centred view, which has found its advocates in the work of the 'Toronto school' (Innis, 1951, and McLuhan, 1962) and its best example in the case of the printing press, allots an independent causal role to the dominant communication technology of the epoch in question. If we deal with the immediate past and forget the niceties of inter-media differences, which really interested McLuhan, the dominant form underlying the first communications revolution has been one of large-scale distribution from central sources to many widely scattered individuals. There are strong and weak versions of media-centred theory and there are also possibilities for attributing causal influence to some media in some cases for some social institutions, without having to reject a view of media dependency 'in the last resort'.

A distinction between technology and content also allows some scope for negotiation between one or other global alternative. For instance, the 'cultivation' theories of Gerbner et al. (1980) seem to involve the view that 'dominant message systems' (i.e. content) owe more to the working of certain institutional forces in society than to the intrinsic properties of television as a medium — hence reconciling a 'sociological' with a 'communicative' perspective. The 'society-centred' view is also open to differentiation, since the forces of 'society' can either be formulated as matters of class, culture and social structure broadly and collectively conceived, or as individual differences of interest, motive, or social location which account for selective use of, and response to, communication and subordinate media to the needs of personal and micro-social life. The media are seen as dependent, in much more specific ways, but the same broad conclusion — that people and society are users rather than used — is reached.

The distinction between media and society goes with other relevant theoretical lines of division, which can really only be named: between base and superstructure explanations of social change; between more idealistic and more materialistic approaches; between an emphasis on communication as expression or consummation or a view of it as a means of transmission or an instrument for achieving some end. This last distinction also helps to differentiate 'culturalist' traditions of study from sociological ones, each with its characteristic aims and methods of enquiry. It directs attention also to a major issue which has to be faced in dealing with new media possibilities — that of weighing cultural against material consequences. In general, media-centred theory is more supportive of a view of powerful mass media, the power lying either in the consistency and repetition of messages reaching many people or in the inevitablility of adaptation by social institutions to the opportunities and pressures of communication forms, with consequences for the messages carried and the relations between senders and receivers.

(ii) 'Dominance' versus 'pluralism'

The second main dimension of theory is less easy to describe apart from its normative and ideological elements, separating as it does those who view media as an instrument of dominance in a class-divided society from those who accept the premise of pluralism — that in free societies media have developed so as to reflect and express a wide and representative range of views and interests. The objective aspect of this dimension lies in the different assessment of the actual condition of most media systems — they are more or less pluralistic according to measures which can be applied. Less open to objective assessment is the cause, nature and further tendency of trends towards 'dominance'. The normative component is readily apparent — most who subscribe to theories of dominant media are also critical of media for this reason, although not always espousing pluralistic alternatives. Most of those who see the media as pluralistic value them for being so and may also value the liberal society which, in most cases, provides the guarantee for pluralism. While pluralist theorists oppose trends towards media dominance, they do not always identify economic concentration, for instance, as inevitably inconsistent with a pluralistic media reality.

There are too many different views of society and pieces of theory underlying the simple opposition under discussion to be dealt with adequately, but it is relevant to the present purpose to mention some of the main sources of the 'dominance' attributed to the media. One is the location of ownership and control in a given class with other kinds of power. Another is the fact of economic concentration and integration and of semi-monopolies of public control in some cases. A third is the industrial basis of mass communication, with its associated mass production and dissemination, leading to homogeneity of content and monopolizing of attention. A fourth is the market economy in which media operate which tends to exclude or discourage minority or deviant products in a consistent way, thus helping to keep the system stable and unified. A fifth source is the prestige and status which the media tend to acquire and which rubs off on those with access to mass media.

Thus, the posited dominance has several sources — conscious efforts to use power in class interests, technological factors reducing diversity, economic arrangements favouring uniformity and the management of demand, social forces which ensure that some social power and influence go with access to mass media. The belief in the reality of media pluralism rests mainly on confidence that supply will be determined by demand and if this is allowed free expression by individuals and interest groups, pluralism will be ensured, given the capacity of media systems to increase and diversify. In addition, pluralistic theory tends to resist the view that the efforts of a single dominant class consciously seeking to use media for class ends provides the key to understanding the working of the media we now have.

(iii) Centrifugal versus centripetal effects of media

The third relevant dimension, which is closely related to the value of 'togetherness', distinguishes the view that mass communication contributes to change, fragmentation, diversity and mobility from the alternative view that it is a force for unity, stability, integration and homogeneity. In turn, this reflects the larger sociological dilemma of reconciling change with the maintenance of order. The picture is further complicated by differences in the relative value placed on order and change respectively and we can identify both a 'positive' and a 'negative' version at each pole of the dimension. The positive version of a centrifugal effect stresses modernization and individual freedom, while the negative version points to isolation, privatization, alienation and vulnerability to manipulation. The positive version of the centripetal effect stresses the potential for integrating and unifying, the negative version indicates centralized control, repression or manipulation. In one way or another, each of these four sub-versions of media effect derive from some key aspect of 'old' media – centralized production and dissemination to scattered individuals, high attractiveness and ubiquity, tendencies to homogeneity of content and unity of control.

There is an obvious relationship between this dimension and the previously summarized ideas of dominance and pluralism. For simplicity, this correspondence can be expressed by locating along with 'dominance' the two negative versions mentioned – media as promoting either isolation or centralized represive control – and with 'pluralism' the two positive versions – media as promoting freedom, choice and 'healthy' (because self-chosen) forms of social cohesion on the basis of group, place, politics or religion. The assimilation of these two dimensions helps to provide a fuller account of two opposed versions of media tendency – towards uniformity and repressive control or towards pluralism and voluntarism. The result of this discussion can be summarized by plotting the two main dimensions against each other, as in Figure 1.1. It is worth pointing out that the 'technology' variant of media-centred theory indicated in this figure corresponds with the 'structural' variant of society-centred theory (at the other end of the horizontal line), since both are in some sense 'materialist' notions and new technology is often an example, or a consequence, of structural change. So too does the 'content' aspect of media relate to the 'individualist' variant of society-centred theory, since, if content does have its own effects, it has them first of all on individuals and, in addition, individuals relate more directly or consciously to content than to technology.

FIGURE 1.1
Main dimensions of media theory

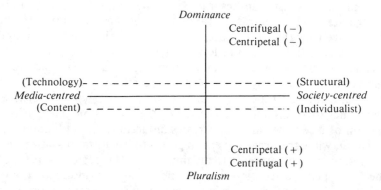

If this account of dimensions of media theory is reasonably complete and correct, it should be possible to locate in the space of Figure 1.1 most of the interpretations of, and attitudes to, the working of 'old' media, with some guidance from the values summarized at the outset. The most important amongst such ideas have already been noted in arriving at the dimensions and need not be repeated. However, it may be worth pointing out the following general guides to location. The more pessimistic views about media tend to belong to the upper quadrants, the more optimistic to the lower. Hence, questions of control belong above, and of freedom, below. Concerns about content and culture belong on the left-hand side, and about social structure, on the right. Correspondingly, questions of supply belong on the left and those about demand on the right. In the top left belong fears about cultural harm from dominant media, in the top right fears of political repression. In the bottom right belong functional theories about the positive contribution of media to social life at the level of group and community. In the lower left belong theories of individual need satisfaction through media content and its consumption or use.

The second communication revolution
So much has been said or written about the significance of new media that it would be tedious to repeat it, especially as so much is speculation. Nevertheless, an answer to the question posed in the title of this chapter needs some statement of what the challenge of new media is usually taken to involve. Some of the changes which are either expected or possible can be summarized in a few key terms, which are often held to differentiate the future of new media from the past (or present) of the old, especially: abundance of production and

supply; freedom of choice; interactivity; narrowcasting; loss of central control; decentralization; search and consultation. The new media seem, especially, to offer the potential of a shift in the balance of power, away from the sender and towards the receiver, making much more content of all kinds more accessible to users and choosers, without dependence on mediating and controlling systems of mass distribution. There is also likely to be much differentiation of available information services and a blurring of the institutional boundaries between 'mass' and individual communication as well as between private and public spheres of communication. One way of representing and comparing the key features of 'old' and 'new' media flow has been suggested by the work of two students of telecommunications, Bordewijk and van Kaam, who have tried to identify the main forms of 'information traffic'. For them, drawing on the analogy of the computer, the two main features of communication flows are storage of information on the one hand and access to, or use of, information on the other. They locate the key variables which differentiate information systems (not simply human communication) firstly in terms of the centrality or otherwise of the store of information and, secondly, the centrality or otherwise of control over access — in effect over choice of subject matter to be consulted or received and over the time at which this takes place. Their scheme, given below as Figure 1.2, assumes a set of participants arranged in the pattern of a wheel around a central hub. Communication flows (traffic) can take place between any set of participants at the rim or between the centre and any one or more of the participants at the rim. By considering each participant (including the centre) as having a store of information which is drawn on (accessed), or added to, in communication, a fuller picture of possible communication patterns can be arrived at.

By cross-tabulating 'information store' against 'control over choice of time and subject', in terms of whether each is 'central' or 'individual', a set of four categories of communication traffic is arrived at, as in Figure 1.2. The difference between a central and individual information store, while deriving from that between a large data bank and a single person, is also analogous with the difference between a mass media organization and a single audience member or that between a library and a reader. It can also correspond with the difference between 'information-rich' individuals or groups and those which are 'information-poor'. The difference between central and individual control of access to information, while it can be taken literally, also corresponds to that between constraint and freedom and low and high communication potential.

FIGURE 1.2
Four patterns of information traffic

	Information store	
	Central	*Individual*
Control of time and choice of subject: *Central*	Allocution	Registration
Control of time and choice of subject: *Individual*	Consultation	Conversation

Key:

Allocution The simultaneous transmission of a centrally constituted 'offer' of information intended for immediate attention, according to a centrally determined time scheme.

Conversation An exchange between individuals of information already available to them, according to a mutually convenient time scheme.

Consultation The selective consultation by individual participants of a central store of information at times determined by each individual.

Registration The collection in a central store of information available to, or about, individual participants, according to a centrally determined choice of subject and time.

Source: Adapted from Bordewijk and van Kaam (1982).

     For the most part, the entry labelled 'allocution' (derived from a Latin word meaning direct address from a leader to followers) stands for the typical 'old media' forms of communication – from a central source to many separated receivers and at times and on subjects determined by the sender. This is especially apposite for national broadcasting. The consultation pattern is also long established as a mode of communication (e.g. libraries) and newspapers can be considered as consultation as well as allocution media. The conversation pattern is currently represented, in media terms, mainly by telephone and postal services and the 'registration' pattern (of which more below) is hardly known as yet in public communication, although it is a long established element in many organizations for record-keeping, control and surveillance. In brief, the potential of new media is to increase the possibilities for consultation (telematics, multi-channel cable and video) and for conversation (via interactive cable, radio and linked computers) and for registration (central recording by computer of all uses of information media connected to a system). The general pattern which can be predicted from the potential of new media is of a shift away from the top left cell of Figure 1.2 and a redistribution of communication 'traffic' to the other three cells. This seems to indicate a general increase in individual freedom to gain information and a reduction in the dominance of centralized sources.

This seems to offer some qualitative guidance in handling those features mentioned above as characteristic of new media, especially in relation to control, narrowcasting and interaction. On the first of these, it suggests that individuals will acquire more control over what and when they receive and consult. Even so, what is available for consultation in central stores can still be centrally determined and much will depend on how diverse the central stores are in content and management. Further, it is possible to interpret the 'registration' pattern, as many have done, as significantly increasing the potential for central control through surveillance of information and information-related activities, which may often be politically sensitive. Lastly, it is possible for individual information stores to develop, so that much more extensive 'conversation' patterns could reduce dependence on central information stores, with diminished chances for surveillance. On the question of 'narrowcasting', besides multiplication of allocutive channels (via multi-channel cable and many satellites), the main implication of the scheme presented is that, by expressing demand through acts of consultation, users will stimulate specialist kinds of supply. In respect of interaction, two main developments open up − a wider range of conversational possibilities with other individuals and various kinds of interactive consultation with collective agencies, for the supply of goods and services. One further use of the scheme in Figure 1.2 is to note that the top row entries (allocution and registration) are associated with a need for regulation and the bottom row (consultation and conversation) with absence of regulation. The left-hand column indicates issues of property rights in information and the right-hand column identifies issues of privacy.

Assessment of media theory

The issues suggested by consideration of the media theory dimensions discussed above can serve as an agenda for the assessment and can be named as follows. The central question, we should recall, is whether the old theory alerts us to the problems of new media and provides us with relevant concepts, ideas and organizing principles. The issues are:

1. The degree of control which society has or can have over media development and the extent to which media independently shape societal developments.
2. The allocation of power over media between social actors and interests and the use of media in the exercise of power.
3. The contribution of communication to change and order in society and culture.
4. The pattern of social relationships as mediated by communications media.

On the question of the balance of control as between media and society, the values and dimensions named above do seem to identify the main problems and offer concepts and a framework for anticipating or evaluating alternative lines of development. In particular, we are alerted to aspects of the new media which seem to restrict the control which society can exercise: the increased flow across national frontiers; the very fact of abundance; the momentum behind technological change which can force the hands of policy makers; the fact that the expanding types of communication traffic and relationship, especially 'conversation' and 'consultation', are neither as easy nor as legitimate to control as 'allocution'. The case for media-centred theory in its technological variant is strengthened by the little experience already available, since the future is already being defined by governments and influential parties as an information society, with new information technology as driving force and its accumulation as a primary goal.

The main issue of power as formulated in old media theory is still very relevant to the emerging new media situation, although changes in the way in which informational power operates call for theoretical revision. The implications for power are fairly apparent: the power or competitive position of some actors will be strengthened by having more access to useful information than is available to others; it is quite likely that new media will widen overall differentials of knowledge between social groups, because of the unequal distribution of competence in using the new information tools and the relative decline in allocutive channels, which have until now tended to be distributive and equalizing in tendency. These remarks apply mainly to information for instrumental application in decision-making or opinion-forming (but also in the production and managing of exchange or control relationships). It is less clear what to expect in respect of the ideological function of information, which has been well performed by allocutive media in the past, according to current theory. It would seem, at first sight, that if 'allocution' declines, so will the possibility for hegemonic control of mass consciousness weaken. Much depends on the nature of the increased diversity made possible and on precisely where power over content and distribution will come to be concentrated. Media theory concerning power has mainly developed in relation to public opinion and the public sphere of politics and new media pose a broad challenge to both.

Change and order issues are unlikely to be very different in the new media situation, although we are promised more rapid change as a result of more information and threatened with some instability brought about by: greater freedom to choose from abundant messages; less uniformity of the audience or public; less consistency or predictability of behaviour by the audience. The new communication situation seems to suggest greater individuation and functional specification of audiences (user groups), greater disparities and lower degrees of collective consciousness. There are ideas for handling these matters in existing theory, but the latter is not very sensitive in the sense of helping to distinguish between the variety of conditions of knowledge differentiation which can be expected. Existing theory is also rather simple-minded in its implicit valuations: mainly against over-control and in favour of freedom; against isolation or anomie and for solidarity and integration. These terms seem rather more easy to apply to older, allocutive media situations than to the more complex pattern of offer and reception which characterizes new media. The issue of relationships belongs here as well, since in 'old theory' it goes mainly with ideas of solidarity and integration. According to the scheme presented in Figure 1.2, new media seem to have quite profound implications for patterns of relationships, promoting more symmetry, less dependence on central sources, more response and interaction, yet also threatening loss of visibility and openness, of stability and durability of ties between senders and receivers and therefore having a potential for weakening the moral ties between individuals and their societies, of the kind sustained by voluntary social institutions.

In the summary evaluation of the version of 'old media theory' presented above, it seems that most implications of new media and of the alternative futures being opened up are not 'off the map' of current thinking. We can provisionally identify what seem the most relevant questions, even if the working out of values and propositions for application to the new situation has yet to be done. Since these new situations are still more heralded than here, this is not a very negative judgement. The main attitudes to new media are also possible to account for according to the scheme presented. The horizontal dimension (in Figure 1.1) still differentiates a belief in the capacity of new media to change society from a belief in the primacy of societal arrangements and of individuals in determining the shape of any communications revolution and thus of any attendant change in society. For the most part, appropriate values and preferences go with these alternative assumptions, in a predictable way. The vertical dimension still separates those who see the new media as strengthening the hand of political and economic elites from those whose pluralistic assumptions and values make them optimistic about the future in an information society, which they generally welcome. On the crucial question of whether the changes in prospect really do constitute a revolution, theory still offers alternative positions.

Media theory and public policy for new media

One strand in the evaluation promised at the outset relates to media policy: does existing theory offer guidance in choices which have to be made now or in the near future? The question is much too large to deal with adequately, but it can be opened up for attention by summarizing what appear at the moment to be the main dilemmas of policy. These are given in Figure 1.3, on the assumption that there is a more or less agreed version of the potential of new media.

FIGURE 1.3
Dilemmas of media policy

New media potential

First choice	Discourage	Encourage
Second choice	Public	Private
Third choice	Monopoly	Diversity
Fourth choice	Content regulation	Technical regulation

The choices are arranged so that there is a fair amount of consistency between the items in each column, although each choice has a certain independence from the others and a 'right-hand' choice at one option, for instance the encouragement of new media, does not preclude the option of public institutional means for achieving this. There is however some tension between the options listed on the left and those on the right and, for the most part, one would not expect them to be associated with each other. It is a feature of the current political reality, in Europe at least, that the climate of decision-making favours industrial and economy policy, which gives more weight to the set of right-hand options, which happen generally to be those of the political right. The alternative, 'cultural policy', which has tended to dominate media policy in the past in Europe, is mainly associated with caution over, if not actual discouragement of, rapid new media growth and generally goes with the options on the left-hand side in Figure 1.3.

Not surprisingly, there are links between these choices and media theory. To begin with, 'cultural policy' has tended to go with a position in the upper left quadrant of Figure 1.1 – a combination of awareness of media power and sensitivity to the content of what is made available. Industrial policy, as usually formulated, belongs more to the lower right cell – going with a belief in pluralism and the individual and a confidence in societal mechanisms as levers of change (the structural variant, with its link to technology). Encouragement of new media rests on a belief in pluralism, positive views of change, individualistic theories of media and society and probably a technological version of media-centred theory. Discouragement generally goes with dominance theory, societal pessimism and (possibly) the content version of media-centred theory. The option of private (financially and institutionally) frameworks for development is more consistent with pluralism than with dominance theory and the latter would favour public control in the wider general interest and so as to limit the commercial exploitation of media by large monopolistic corporations. The diversity–monopoly choice may not seem like a very real dilemma, but there is often a practical issue of retaining or weakening existing public monopolies or quasi-monopolies and there is a real concern that commercial development can strengthen the monopoly control of private business over sectors of the media. Attitudes and preferences in these matters are distributed in fairly obvious ways along the vertical dimension of Figure 1.1. On the fourth choice, aside from the direction given by cultural policy (towards the regulation of content) or by industrial policy (technical regulation only), the differences are to be accounted for in terms of varying positions on the horizontal dimension. The more media-centred one's theory, the more attention one gives to control of content, and the more society-centred, the greater is one's inclination to attend only to technical regulation.

This discussion suggests that theory is still adequate for describing and classifying policy positions and probably also for justifying them. This does not, however, say a great deal and it is relevant to point out that so far the most significant choices which have been faced in the context of the development of new media have mainly been decisions about old media. In a sense, therefore, the true issues of new media have not yet really entered into the policy-making debate, except as issues of property, area of competence (as between private and public sector) or as matters of moral standards.

Gaps and deficiencies

Some inadequacies of theory have already been suggested. They derive, in the main, from concentration on the allocutive mode of communication which has been and remains the dominant form. This shows, first of all, in the analysis of power. Current theory seems to offer a very unnuanced view — a choice between monolithic media in the hands of a class or state or a neutral arena in which power struggles are played out between more or less equal competitors. The first view attributes great powers of persuasion, mobilization and 'cultivation' to the media over a passive and dependent audience, the second offers a power vacuum in which individuals choose freely and resist unwanted influence. The new media are likely to be less monolithic, but they are still likely to be relevant for the exercise of power, as sources and carriers of information of potential value for instrumental uses and rational calculation. Direct persuasion and mobilization of a large mass following is both less easy and less possible in a very differentiated society. Not everything will change, but media theory has not been sufficiently sensitive in the past in its handling of matters to do with power and this lack of sensitivity is likely to be an increasing liability, if not made good.

Secondly, there are deficiencies in matters to do with media systems and organizations. The main problems likely to emerge fall under two headings, one to do with relations to society and the other concerning relations between media and their own audiences. On the first it can be argued that existing media, growing up relatively slowly in relation to society, have acquired adequate institutionalized arrangements for handling many rights and responsibilities. Some of these belong to the sphere of professional self-regulation, as in matters of information quality, moral and cultural standards, respect (or not) for privacy, editorial responsibility. Others concern matters of the media system as a whole, for instance diversity, representativeness, access, equal availability, obligation to carry channels, service to other institutions or to society in general. With the rapid emergence of new media, there is a risk of some deprofessionalization and destabilizing of institutional control. The rapid growth of new media, often fragmentary and functionally specific in what they do, is quite likely to undermine, or at least challenge, a whole network of norms, understandings, arrangements and interdependencies which are rooted in social theory and are taken for granted as part of the media scene. They also happen to be somewhat taken for granted by media theory and the study of media will not be made easier by the lack of a well-developed framework of ideas in this area of social theory.

On the second matter — concerning relations between media and public — 'old theory' does provide a framework in which to place the notion of solidary and moral relations between a communication source and its own public, even if the emphasis has tended to be somewhat negative. Thus, there is more theorizing about the absence of this kind of relationship than about its positive character — pointing, for instance, to manipulation from above or calculative choice-making from below. While this emphasis is not so mistaken in the case of much mass communication, there do still exist possibilities for moral ties to form and endure between mass media and their publics and the media still play a not unimportant part in the public sphere of social life and in democratic politics, as platform, critic, watchdog and mobilizer. While new media promise more interaction and smallness of scale, they may also entail a new kind and degree of social atomization and an impoverishment of the arena of public life, even an increase in the degree of depoliticization, which has already been remarked upon as a feature of the television age. It is unclear what the future holds in store for the audience which is neither a target mass, nor a set of freely choosing individuals, but a public in the classic sense of a dispersed but self-aware set of persons with similar interests and aims. New interactive media benefit such communities of interest, but there are also counter-forces towards fragmentation. The area of intra-organizational communication based on expert knowledge will extend, on the one hand, and, on the other, the network of more or less private, individual or intra-group contacts is also likely to grow. This is not necessarily bad, but it does not seem fully accounted for by theory, which is mainly based on the notion of large-scale communication of rather similar content to many people. It is not really a task for theory to imagine futures or to moralize about them, but it is a task of theory to identify questions of this kind and provide tools for handling them.

In respect of the audience, existing theory offers two main alternative conceptualizations — either as object for assault and capture or as a set of individuals choosing actively according to needs and circumstances. Until more is known of how new media will develop it is hard to judge the adequacy of one or the other version. There may actually be more of the 'old' allocutive media traffic, by way of broadcast satellites and seeking to increase total audiences. There may also be more selectivity as a result of more supply and more flexibility in control and access for users. Where existing theory may be deficient is in its dependence on, or derivation from, a view of audiences as selectively reacting to a flow or stream of material, rather than choosing consciously according to individual needs and tastes. The difference is one of degree of activity since the latter, the pattern encouraged by the new media, presupposes a goal-directed and less habit-determined set of behaviours. In the future, audiences are also less likely to be aggregates open to characterization in terms of a set of choices of content. Some development of theory of choice-making under varying conditions is likely to be needed. These brief remarks about gaps and deficiencies can also serve as a source for a research agenda.

References

Bordewijk, J.L. and B. van Kaam (1982) *Allocutie*. Baarn, Netherlands: Bosch and Keuning, n.v.

Gerbner, G., L. Gross, M. Morgan and N. Signorielli (1980) 'The Mainstreaming of America', *Journal of Communication*, 30: 10–27.

Innis, H. (1951) *The Bias of Communication*. Toronto: University of Toronto Press.

McLuhan, M. (1962) *The Gutenberg Galaxy*. Toronto: University of Toronto Press.

27

THE EXPANDING BASE
OF MEDIA COMPETITION

Benjamin M. Compaine

*New technologies have blurred the boundaries
of traditional media formats and content,
offering new configurations and options for
accessing and distributing a diversity of ideas.*

Competition has traditionally been a feature of the media environment. Often, some new technology or technologies have fostered this competition, in general adding to the alternatives rather than replacing older ones. Still, life is complicated for anyone interested in the subject of competition in media, as compared to competition in almost any other sphere. In virtually all literate societies, the mass media—newpapers, magazines, books, television, radio, records, films, electronically accessible data bases—are regarded as more than commodities. They are charged with conveying the messages of that society. And, as a tenet of democratic theory, those media are also charged with maximizing a diversity of ideas, opinions, and information of all sorts. This article focuses on competition in pluralistic societies that hold dear the diversity of information sources.

Economists who specialize in measuring the extent of competition—or its obverse, concentration—tend to treat each of the media the same as any other industry, counting up who owns what, calculating percentages, devising indices of pricing power. But the technology of recent

Benjamin M. Compaine is Executive Director of the Program on Information Resources Policy at Harvard University. Portions of this article are drawn from "New Competition and New Media," a speech to the 6th International Congress, Institut pour le Développement et l'Aménagement des Télécommunications et de l'Economie, Montpellier, France, October 25, 1984, and published in *Bulletin de l'IDATE*, No. 17, October 1984; and in a speech at the University of Missouri, April 28, 1983, as part of the Dr. Scholl Foundation Forum on "Private Enterprise and the Media: Interpreting the Economy of the 1980s."

Compaine, Benjamin M., *New Competition and New Media*, Program on Information Resources Policy, Harvard University, 1985, as reprinted in *Journal of Communication*, summer 1985, vol. 35 #3. Reprinted by permission.

years has made the definition of the appropriate divisor for concentration indices debatable. What is the appropriate market? Should one look at the market for newspapers isolated from that for magazines? To what extent are broadcast television and even radio fungible for the substance of the print media? The economists' approach of looking at a specific medium, such as newspapers, is becoming less valid—if it ever was valid—as the technologies of the alternative media forms merge into one another.[1] The shaded area of Figure 1 highlights the portion of the information business that is generally considered as the "mass media."[2]

Also relevant to the problem of defining the market is the problem of defining the user of the medium. Some media, such as newspapers and magazines, and (in the United States to a degree more than almost anywhere else) broadcast television and radio, are paid for in total or large measure by advertisers. Thus, an appropriate measure of economic concentration for these media may not be how much consumers pay to receive them but to what extent the pricing of advertisements creates market power. On the other hand, media forms such as books, records, and theatrical films are funded mostly or totally by their users, in which case the economic consideration is the ability of suppliers to charge nonmarket prices to consumers.

In addition to competition within a particular media segment and competition among media industries, competition can also be defined geographically. Newspapers in the United States and Canada, and to lesser degrees elsewhere, are largely local media. Although the United States has about 1,700 daily papers and no more than about seven percent of total daily circulation is controlled by any one firm, only about 30 central cities have fully competitive newspapers and only one, New York, has three alternatives.[3] By comparison, according to the 1985 *Broadcasting Cablecasting Yearbook,* the New York metropolitan area had 39 radio stations in 1984 and, depending on where one lived, 12–14 over-the-air television channels. Even the fiftieth-ranked market, Dayton, had 7 over-the-air TV channels and 12 radio stations. Thus, most people have more choice in the number of television signals they

---

[1] Similar technology is being used to produce media that are called by different names. National newpapers such as *USA Today* and the *Wall Street Journal* are sending facsimiles of their composed pages to remote printing sites using data transmission and satellites similar to the way that programmers send their materials to cable operators. Internally, the electronic newspaper is a reality, as computers and video displays have replaced typewriters and copy paper. Videotex and teletext use broadcast, cable, or telephone transmission to video displays for text and graphics that otherwise would be at home printed on paper.

[2] For a complete discussion of the construction and application of the information business map, see (7).

[3] This move toward one-newspaper cities is not quite as bleak as it may sound. Accompanying the demise of competition in central cities has been the development of newspapers in suburban areas that have grown up around the central city in the past 35 years. Thus, many people and advertisers still do have a choice of newspapers—the metropolitan daily or the local daily.

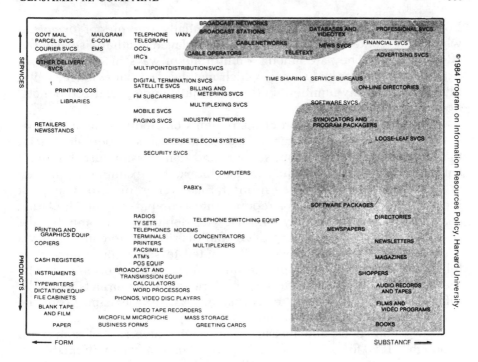

SERVICES				
GOVT MAIL	MAILGRAM	TELEPHONE VAN's		BROADCAST NETWORKS
PARCEL SVCS	E-COM	TELEGRAPH		BROADCAST STATIONS

©1984 Program on Information Resources Policy, Harvard University.

Figure 1: The mass media on the information business map

receive, even though there are fewer television stations nationally than there are newspapers. Book and magazine publishers, relying as they do on large regional and national markets, compete in a larger geographical context. Cable operators, while providing a dizzying array of channels, for the most part are monopoly providers within their highly restricted franchise territories and are subject to a decreasing amount of government control over their pricing. Finally, there is a new factor of potential global competition, as videocassette player/recorders proliferate and as direct broadcast satellite systems, perhaps out of the control of the nation to which their programming is receivable, start beaming signals in competition with land-based—and often government-controlled—television. In effect, the traditional market boundaries with which so many were so comfortable are receding toward the horizon.

> *A second problem in discussing competition*
> *arises from a blurring of the distinction among*
> *what had been well-understood media formats.*

Today, "television" can be delivered not only over the air, but via cable, discs, or directly from a satellite. The picture on the screen can be the type of text and graphics typically associated with magazines, books, and newspapers. Thus, the conventional labels are less useful than ever.

For example, "print" and "video" are essentially examples of *formats* in which some content or substance can be displayed or otherwise manipulated by users. They are among a multitude of ways in which we can express *information substance*, which may be data, knowledge, news, intelligence, or any number of other colloquial and specialized denotations and connotations.

Process is the application of instruments or products, such as typewriters, computers, printing presses, telephone wires, or delivery trucks, to the creation, manipulation, storage, and transmission/distribution of substance, in some intermediate or final format. For example, a traditional newspaper, an ink-on-newsprint format, relies on processes that include entering thoughts of a reporter into a computer by manipulating a keyboard of a video display terminal with storage in the computer, the eventual creation of a printing plate, and distribution to consumers via trucks. If the same article were distributed to some consumers via a telephone link to a video display terminal, some of the process would be the same (the entering and storing of information), the formats would be different for the end user (text on screen vs. ink on paper), but the substance might remain constant.

How, then, does one measure how much diversity of sources is "enough"? If 20 firms account for 50 percent of newspaper circulation in the United States, is that too few firms, just enough, or too many firms creating too much fragmentation in society? If not this number, then what? An even stickier question is, what are the adequate ground rules for ensuring that any person's or institution's ideas—political, social, commercial—have some opportunity for access to the media? And more difficult still, how does one measure which formats should have what conditions for access? For example, it may be relatively easy to provide access to a print newspaper because of its space flexibility. And as authoritarian societies know, the photocopying machine has become Everyman's printing press. On the other hand, what about access to prime-time broadcast television? Up to now there has been limited spectrum available, particularly in the major metropolitan areas, and prime time cannot be expanded by more minutes than nature has provided for us. Cable television, a newer process for a familiar format, alleviates the spectrum problem, but it can never eliminate the fact that a handful of channels will likely get the bulk of the viewing audience at any given time. Thus, even as technology provides us with more conduits for distributing information, there is no guarantee that the mass audience will want to receive much more than what traditionally has been mass entertainment. Indeed, in the United States, dozens of cable networks have been struggling to achieve even a one or two percent market share, as the bulk of the audience with access to dozens of stations persists in viewing the commercial and public broadcast networks, plus three or four of the newer offerings, the most successful of which—the pay television networks—are showing other forms of mass audience fare.

> *In exploring the dimensions of the question of*
> *media competition, newspapers and books, as the*
> *oldest formats and a continued focus of the media*
> *concentration issue, warrant an extended discussion.*

There are fewer directly competitive newspapers today than 50 years ago. In part the reason for this involves both the essential role of the newspaper and demographic trends.

The daily newspaper in the United States has always been an intensely local medium, covering local events and providing an advertising base for local advertisers. National advertising provides only about 15 percent of advertising revenue. However, as is well documented, since 1946 the population of the cities has been moving to the suburbs and beyond, and newspapers sprang up or expanded to meet the growing local market. Newspapers in older cities such as Philadelphia, New York, and Boston found themselves competing for circulation with thriving newspapers in nearby Doylestown, Long Island, and Quincy. Retailers, following the population to the suburbs, found that their budgets were being stretched thin and increasingly concentrated their center city advertising in the paper with the larger circulation so that they might also advertise in the suburban papers. Herein lies one reason for the demise of competing city newspapers.

Second, newspapers, especially evening newspapers in the cities, have had to compete for readers' time with other and newer media. Since the heyday of daily newspaper penetration in the 1920s, first radio and then television have been introduced into the daily media mix. With television, in particular, newspapers have been competing not directly for consumer or advertising dollars but for audience attention.

Newspapers, after all, are not just news. They are filled with entertainment items, human interest articles, and commercial information. Nor is television just entertainment. Although media elitists disparage local television news in particular, the fact remains that the evening hour of news, weather, sports, and fluff is not all that different than the content of most daily newspapers. Local television news also represents time taken away from the newspaper. At the very least, it helped speed the end of the two-newspaper family.

These two compelling factors (among others) that have changed the structure of the newspaper industry are not insidious. Instead, they suggest something of a zero-sum game. For the residents of the suburbs, there continues to be a real choice of newspapers. For everyone, there is a net gain in the number of media choices. Individuals can get news, information, and entertainment from the daily paper, from a variety of weekly newspapers, from three or more similar (although not identical) television stations; they can get national news from at least three major magazines—another factor that was in little evidence 60 years ago. For much of the population, all-news radio stations are another alternative. The development of locally based cable and the as-yet-unknown potential creative uses of computer-based services may also enhance this diversity. The variety and number of outlets in many markets today, representing almost as many separate owners in each market, contrasts sharply with the fewer total number of outlets—virtually all newspapers—in any comparable group of cities in 1920.

A related issue is that of newspaper chain ownership. While no one seriously worries about chains of supermarkets or retail stores, newspaper chains are an issue because newspapers—and the rest of the media for that matter—are conveyors of ideas and information rather than commodities. Therefore, this argument goes, they must be judged by a different standard than other commerce. Chain ownership may mean that control is in the hands of a publisher and editor who might have no ties to the community or that a single individual might dictate the editorial policy of many newspapers, and thus is bad for society.

Among the pertinent facts are that two-thirds of all daily newspapers are owned by about 160 groups. They are concentrated in the larger newspapers, accounting for about 75 percent of daily circulation. Almost one-third of these chains actually consist of six or fewer newspapers (3, p. 41, Table 2.15). As recently as 1960, there were 109 groups, owning less than a third of the daily papers (although they still accounted for close to 50 percent of daily circulation). Thus the trend toward chains, though slowed considerably in the 1980s by a reduced number of newspapers available for sale, is indisputable.

There are at least two reasons for this trend. First, the introduction of new technology into the production of newspapers in the 1970s resulted in substantial cost reductions and an increase in profit, which had been sagging terribly before then. Some family-owned newspapers could not afford the investment in the technology, however, and their newspapers thus were more valuable to firms that could afford them and quickly bolster profits to a greater level. Hence, the price offered for newspapers escalated dramatically; in fact, the restoration of reasonable profit margins to newspapers made them an attractive investment for the first time in years. And although newspapers that were fighting head to head with a local competitor had problems, those papers that did not have direct competition at least had greater room to adjust their price and expenditures to earn an attractive return on investment. (Despite the term "monopoly newspaper," these papers could not derive what economists recognize as true monopoly profits. They did face competition from other media, including weekly and all-advertising "shopper" papers, as well as suburban papers in the case of central city papers.)

A second reason for the growth of chains was federal tax policy. According to a study by the Rand Corporation, public policy, in the form of tax regulations, explains most of the reason for independent publishers selling out, most often to chains (4, pp. 4–8). On the death of the owner of the family-owned newspaper, the estate tax laws require setting the value of the newspaper at its market value—that is, what it would be worth if sold. This might be many times its book value and frequently created a tax liability well in excess of the heirs' ability to pay the tax. Thus, the property was sold—at an appropriate market value— either after the owner's death or in anticipation of it. On the acquirer's side, another tax law requires a very high tax on corporate-retained earnings, unless they are being held for necessary business purposes, such as expansion. Thus, profits had to be spent, and acquisitions were one way to do so.

Have the trend toward one-newspaper cities and the growth of chains been bad or good for society?

Here, of course, facts take a back seat to evaluation. In general, one argument holds that society is probably no worse off, and perhaps better off, than it was 30 or 50 years ago. There is nothing inherent in either the one-newspaper city or the chain trends to warrant alarm with regard to media diversity or to the role of newspapers in the practice of democracy.

In the first place, the demise of direct competition is a function of economics, technology, and social patterns; not much that is practical can be done about it. Corporations cannot be forced to start businesses or to stay in business if they don't want to. Nor can business be told where to operate (except for zoning-type regulations) or what markets to serve. Some might argue that society could provide tax breaks to corporations that start newspapers in places that already have them. That alone is not likely to compensate for the risk, however, and any direct subsidy would run into First Amendment barriers.

The chain ownership question is more complex. Given that, in traditional economic terms, there is nothing approaching a national newspaper monopoly in the United States, the only restriction to date has been in preventing common ownership of newspapers that had been competing in adjacent communities. For that reason the Times Mirror Company, owner of the *Los Angeles Times,* had to sell the newspapers it bought in nearby San Bernardino. But it was permissible for Gannett, another chain, to purchase them. The alternative to chain ownership would require establishment of a standard for unacceptable concentration of newspaper ownership that differed from standards for other private-sector business. Both the justification and standard would have to be quite subjective. And here, too, the First Amendment would come into play. The result might be more long-term damage that would follow from leaving things alone.

Indeed, there is no compelling evidence that newspaper readers have been ill served by the trend toward groups. There are at least as many documented cases in which a paper purchased by a group was substantially improved as there are cases in which a paper was weakened (3, pp. 42–46). As in any other business, owners have different styles and priorities. The good ones or poorer ones are not necessarily determined by chain ownership.

The matter of local versus absentee ownership is another issue in which the pluses and minuses probably get canceled out. On the negative side of absentee ownership, the publisher and top editors put in by the major chain owner hope to distinguish themselves and get promoted to a larger newspaper and their long-term ties to the community may be minimal. But this can be balanced by the negative aspect of the family-owned small-city newspaper. When the owning family has long been part of the local establishment, one might ask how much crusading such publishers will allow their papers to do or to what extent they will question the local bank's practices when the president is a childhood chum of the publisher or criticize friends on the school board. Excessive local boosterism may prevail. None of this is inevitable, but, just as with chain ownership, nothing automatically makes local ownership more beneficial.

Finally, an evaluation of the quality of chain-owned newspapers risks falling into the trap in which journalists and media critics judge all newspapers by the *New York Times*. The fact is that small-town newspapers were never very good. If we fault them today for their front-page news capsules and reliance on wire service copy, we should also analyze what they were like in the supposedly good old days. Did they have a reporter in Washington doing occasional local pieces, as the chain papers can order from the chain's own bureau? How many column inches was the newshole compared to total inches today? How large was the full-time staff? How well were they trained? How objective was the reporting by today's standards? How much did the paper cost in constant dollars compared to today? An unscientific eyeballing of newspapers around the United States today and some understanding of newspapers in days passed suggest that the typical chain-owned paper today is probably much better than the locally owned paper of 50 years ago.

> *Newspapers, along with other print industries,*
> *have talked more about their "mission" than their*
> *"business," but there are signs that this is changing.*

As recently as 1973, the only solid material available on the commercial side of the newspaper business was in a few unpublished doctoral dissertations. For magazine publishing there was not even that. There were only two books on the book publishing business; the findings of one of these, written in 1931, could have been reprinted almost verbatim because so little had changed in the conduct of this "gentleman's" business. But the term "business" increasingly is being applied to book publishing, and most signs indicate that this has been an overall positive development for the universe of potential book purchasers. In the book publishing industry there were 635 publishing companies in 1947. Today, there are about two and a half times that number. Between 1970 and 1980, an average of 50 new publishers emerged annually, replacing some of the firms that failed or merged and each bringing out a minimum of three titles a year (3, pp. 452–453, Table 8-1). Between 45,000 and 55,000 new book titles and editions are published annually, adding to the more than 550,000 in print faster than old titles are taken out of print (9, p. 225, Table 379)—a rate of growth greater than that of the U.S. population.

Most publishers specialize in textbooks, professional books, and reference works, rather than literature or trade nonfiction. It is the latter categories that are typically thought of as the contribution of book publishing to culture. Still, 5,470 new fiction titles were published in 1983, well over twice the number in 1960. There was an even greater increase in literature and an 85 percent increase in juvenile titles (9, p. 225, Table 379; cf. p. 593, Table 997).

The number of bookstores also has shown a sharp increase. For years, bookselling was primarily a trade dominated by "mom and pop" stores in big cities. Book clubs grew because of the notoriously poor distribution of books (2), particularly outside the Northeast. Booksellers, like many publishers, were often in business because they enjoyed books themselves; they stocked what they liked, not what would necessarily sell well to the nonliterati. Into this void came two multibillion-dollar retail chains, Dayton Hudson Corp. and Carter Hawley Hale Stores, which in the 1970s began opening B. Dalton and Waldenbooks outlets, respectively. Most of these initially went into suburban shopping malls outside the Northeast, for the first time bringing books to where the people were. Still, they have been criticized by media elitists for stocking "only" the most popular eight or ten thousand book titles and for having undue influence on what gets published due to their sizable orders for publishers.[4]

In 1958, the retail trade census counted only 1,675 bookstores large enough to have a payroll (and only 2,885 including the "mom and pop"

---

[4] Such criticisms are reminiscent of the nineteenth-century English literati's concerns about the masses "reading the wrong thing, for the wrong reason, in the wrong way" (1, p. 368)—that is, reading fiction rather than self-help books. A respected trade editor who recently complained that people are reading too many how-to and similar "light" books at the expense of literature (8) might find ironic the comment of a British librarian in 1879 that "schoolboys or students who took to novel reading to any great extent never made much progress in after life" (1, p. 233).

stores). In the 1982 tally, the number had grown to 9,300 with a payroll (9, p. 786, Table 1406).

Book publishing is a business that lends itself to boom and bust, for every book published has to be sold as a separate product. Consider the implications if Pillsbury had to introduce a new cake mix every week, pay for the research and development, promote it, get distribution on crowded supermarket shelves, and then move on to develop and promote the next cake mix, while the competition does the same thing. The economics of publishing are such that most of the cost is fixed first-copy cost. That means that on a best seller there is a very high marginal profit. But such successes must be balanced with the many other books that never recover even the advance paid the author.

Book publishing, like its magazine cousin, is a business that has a very low entry cost (except for a few segments, such as mass market paperback and school textbooks) but a fairly high failure ratio. Considering also the nonbusinesslike approach that typified much of the industry until the past decade, one begins to understand the forces that lead to the mergers of the Harpers with the Rows—they were for survival. But there is a constant stream of new entries, like Workman Press or David Godine, looking for publishing niches and hoping to grow with them. Perhaps they too will be acquired, opening new opportunities for others.

With the dispersion of substance available via common carrier satellite and telephone, access by more sources to more sources is likely to increase further, not diminish.

Some commentators are in fact now concerned about fragmentation of society and information overload as the result of the overwhelming variety of formats for substance. The proliferation of new communication processes over the years has made it increasingly difficult for any single entity or small cabal, even governments that have the will and power, to have total control over the mass media.

One of the most dramatic pieces of evidence that technology is moving faster than the ability of governments or business to control the media is the competition that videocassette recordings are providing for broadcasters and movie house operators. As might be expected, the penetration of VCRs has been greatest in those countries that already had the largest number of television sets. But as Table 1 indicates, the United States and Canada lag well behind Western Europe in their use. Moreover, these figures likely understate penetration in Europe in that they cover only machines exported by Japan. Although these account for almost all sales in the United States and Canada, the tabulation does not count the sizable number of the machines manufactured and sold in Europe. But even with those counted, leading the world in VCR ownership are the oil-rich Middle Eastern nations. It has been reported

Table 1: Videocassette recorder penetration in selected regions, 1983[a]

	No. of TV sets in use	No. of VCRs imported	VCRs as % of TV sets	Medium no. of broadcast networks
	n	n	%	n
Western Europe[b]	119,222,000	16,844,000	14.1	2
United States and Canada	189,280,000	14,426,000	7.6	5
Middle East[c]	2,470,000	1,938,000	78.5	2
Australia and New Zealand	6,422,000	1,561,000	24.3	2

Source: Calculated from compilation by CBS Inc. from *Table & Television Factbook*, 1984; Japan Tariff Association, *Japan Exports & Imports*, 1976–1983 editions.

[a] Videocassette recorders exported from Japan to indicated destination, 1976–1983. Does not take into account transhipments once in destination country or non-Japanese-made VCRs, primarily those made by Thomson in Europe.

[b] Belgium, Denmark, Finland, France, Greece, Iceland, Ireland, Italy, Luxembourg, Malta, Monaco, Netherlands, Norway, Portugal, Spain, Sweden, Switzerland, United Kingdom, West Germany.

[c] Major oil-producing or -supported countries: Bahrain, Iran, Kuwait, Qatar, Saudi Arabia, United Arab Emirates.

that bootlegged copies of the controversial program "Death of a Princess" were being shown in living rooms in Saudi Arabia at the same time it was being broadcast—over that government's protests—in Great Britain and the United States (10, p. 39).

What determines the penetration of VCRs? It appears that where there are not significant government-imposed barriers, a substantial factor is competition from other forms of television. In Western European nations, where there are typically two government-controlled or highly regulated television networks, VCRs gave viewers their first opportunity to become their own programmers, through renting or buying tapes. In England, where the tradition of renting televisions has carried over to VCRs, there is a booming tape rental market, with prices as low as 50p per night. A cynic might conclude that, when it has the chance, the mass audience demonstrates that it is not being fulfilled by the fare that the broadcasters are providing—at least not enough of the time. (The other side of this coin is that viewers may find the quality of programming so compelling that they record one program for later viewing while watching the other in "real" time.) In the United States, which has four over-the-air networks and a growing number of cable-supplied networks, VCRs have seen healthy growth only since about 1982, and overall penetration is still relatively low.

If the need to foster diversity is a positive and cherished value in democracies, then the degree to which various media processes are fungible is of import.

The manufacturers of steel cans learned quite a while ago that their ability to set prices and gain market share was determined not only by their relatively few steel can competitors, but by others who made aluminum, glass, and even cardboard containers. Similarly, broadcast-ers, whether private or government-controlled, must recognize that they are no longer the only rooster in the video barnyard and that it will likely get more competitive rather than less so.

A statistical study by two economists at the Federal Communications Commission has found "strong support [for] the proposition that VCRs and cable [television] are substitutes." It also reported "some support to the conclusion that VCRs and broadcast television are complements" (6, p. 27). While noting some paradoxes and data problems, the authors believe that their statistical evidence "tends to support the proposition that the video product market should be broadly defined—to include (at least) broadcast television, cable and VCRs" (6, p. 31).

It is much too early to make any judgments about the impact of direct broadcast satellites. For all practical purposes, a DBS service does not exist as a mass market service anywhere in the world, although bits and pieces are starting to become available. More than one million (mostly rural) households in the United States are the largest identifiable market for *de facto* DBS to date, having purchased large antenna dishes to capture the signals intended as raw feeds to cable headends and broadcasters. For this constituency, DBS is a substitute for a lack of broadcast television.

Print publishers have felt the heat of competition longer than their newer electronic brethren. Before radio made its way into the mass media mix in the 1930s, the newspaper industry in the United States held 45 percent of media advertising; consumer magazines held about 8 percent (see Figure 2). While magazines held their share through the

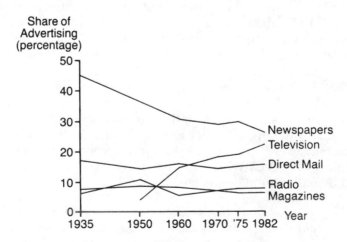

Figure 2: Media shares of advertising expenditures, 1935–1982

1950s, radio and, to a lesser extent, television eroded newspaper share to 31 percent by 1960. Newspapers have lost a small amount of market share to television in the past 25 years, with newspapers' share now down to about 27 percent and magazines' near 6 percent. In large measure, this erosion accounts for the inability of cities to support the competing newspapers that existed before there was electronic media competition for consumer attention and advertiser expenditures.

Newspaper publishing companies in the United States did not sit idly while their franchises deteriorated. In 1983, one-third of the 447 television stations in the 100 largest markets were owned by firms that also published newspapers. However, as the result of an FCC policy discouraging newspaper-television affiliations in the same market, by 1983 only 8 percent of the stations in the 100 largest markets were owned by the local newspaper (5, p. 3). They also owned about 600 out of about 9,500 radio stations. Companies that own newspapers have been a diversified group, as the holdings of seven companies in Figure 3 indicate. They are Dow Jones, Gannett, Harte-Hanks Communications, Lee Enterprises, New York Times Co., Times Mirror Co., and the Washington Post Co.

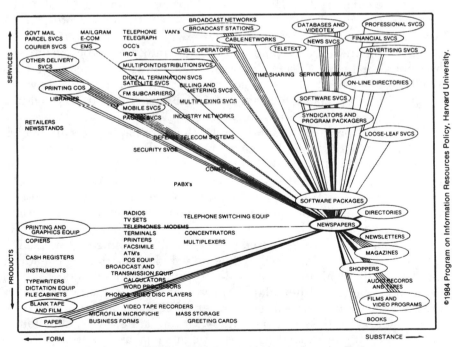

Figure 3: Holdings of seven newspaper-owning companies

Today, publishers of newspapers face two forms of real and potential competition. As far as most publishers are concerned, their real competitors are the U.S. Postal Service and the highly computerized firms that have grown to take advantage of postal rates for mailing printed circulars that the publishers themselves compete to deliver as part of the newspaper. The direct mail business has thrived through the years. Before television, direct mail accounted for about 14 percent of advertising expenditures. With no dramatic shifts over the years, it now has about a 16 percent share. The ability of direct mailers to compete with newspapers is purely a function of price, which in turn is determined by several layers of postal agencies. The mailing companies, like the publishers themselves, have taken full advantage of computer technology to improve their product but still depend on physical handling and delivery for reaching the consumer.

The potential competitor for newspapers goes under the name of videotex or electronic publishing. It is much too soon to know when, if at all, these computer- and telecommunications-based services will have an effect on local newspapers because such services still require hardware in the home that costs hundreds of dollars at a minimum and ongoing telecommunications costs that alone could be greater than the current price of a printed newspaper. Advertisers, who provide about 80 percent of the revenue for daily newspapers in the United States, are far from certain as to how they could use the videotex systems.

One of the most feared potential entrants into the media business in the United States is A.T.&T., now about one-third its December 1983 size in revenue but still a major player. The court overseeing the A.T.&T. break-up mandated that A.T.&T. be excluded from providing substance over its own lines at least until 1990. This action was the direct result of political intervention by the newspaper industry, which feared that A.T.&T. could have gotten into the electronic classified business, thereby threatening the most profitable piece of the print newspaper. However, A.T.&T. has joined with Bank of America, Chemical Bank, and Time Inc. to form Covidea, for the announced purpose of providing telecommunications-based financial transactions and presumably information as well.

In the meantime, an industrial power, IBM, has teamed up with CBS, with its broadcast and publishing interests, and Sears, the merchandiser and (lately) financial services provider, to put together a videotex system a few years hence. Other players in videotex include Knight-Ridder, already one of the largest newspaper publishers and an owner of broadcaster properties; Times Mirror, with similar holdings; Dow Jones, a publisher with an expanding electronic financial and general information service; Gannett, the largest newspaper publisher, with its USA Today update service; CompuServe, originally a computer time-sharing company; Reader's Digest, owner of The Source electronic information data base; RCA, in a joint venture with Citibank; and Chase Manhattan, E. F. Hutton, Merrill, Lynch, and several other financial concerns interested in providing customers with value-added services and at the same time cutting down on the paper flow for financial transactions. More firms are expected to get involved, despite the uncertainties.

What do these developments and potential developments say about concentration and competition in the media?

Clearly, many of the players involved with the newer media services are the same ones we know in the older media. But still others are from territory that seems light years away. In that sense, the number of competitors is increasing as the interests of the players blur and merge. This may add to the already growing confusion over the appropriate boundaries for identifying the relevant industry to investigate or regulate.

We might look to the old print business for some hint of the future of the electronic one. One reason that the print business has had more freedom to operate is that it was not constrained by the limits of the technology, as was broadcasting. Printing presses might be expensive, but there was no technological limit to the number that could be made available, unlike 6 MHz frequencies, for example. Moreover, publishers rarely had to depend on owning their network for distribution. The existence of a government-supported common carrier postal system that reached every household and business, from the top of the Cascades to the bottom of the Grand Canyon, ensured publishers access to customers.

The parallel institutions in electronics have been the telegraph and telephone networks. Until recently, however, these were largely restricted to point-to-point carriage of voice or low-volume analogue signals. Today, the harnessing of computers to the telecommunications networks makes possible the economic transmission of a vast volume of data. The twisted copper wire pair goes nearly everywhere the postal carrier goes. As long as the telephone system is a common carrier, virtually anyone will be able to become an electronic publisher with a far lower capital investment than was necessary when one also had to own—or pay for the use of—a printing press.

The empirical evidence indicates that the media structure in the United States is by far more open, diverse, and responsive to public needs and wants than at any time in history, notwithstanding the contrary sense that is suggested by the headlines created when media companies merge. There are no headlines proclaiming arrival of a new journal or the growth of phenomena such as a Cable News Network. Independent *ad hoc* television networks are another subtle but substantial change in the balance of media competitiveness.

Ownership in the aggregate is constantly shifting but is far from concentrated, except in a very few specific geographic locations. Since the days of the old media barons like Greeley, Pulitzer, and Hearst, few owners of media groups have sought to manipulate the editorial thrust of their properties. At best, their objectives have been to produce quality editorial publications and programs; at worst, simply to make a profit. But this motive can be consistent with acceptable, if not always outstanding, substance.

In general, however, as time goes on, any entity or small groups of entities will likely have more difficulty attempting to control the substance or process of delivery of that substance, short of implementing a totalitarian regime. And even totalitarian societies will find their job of control more challenging. Over the centuries technology has helped expand competition for the creation and distribution of ideas, information, and entertainment. We are not at the beginning of an era, but in the midst of that long-term trend.

REFERENCES

1. Altick, Richard D. *The English Common Reader: A Social History of the Mass Reading Public, 1800–1900*. Chicago: University of Chicago Press, 1974.
2. Cheney, O. H. *Economic Survey of the Book Industry 1930–1931*. New York: Bowker, 1931.
3. Compaine, Benjamin M. et al. *Who Owns the Media? Concentration of Ownership in the Mass Communications Industry* (2d ed.). White Plains, N.Y.: Knowledge Industry, 1982.
4. Dertouzos, James M. and Kenneth E. Thorpe. "Newspaper Groups: Economies of Scale, Tax Laws and Merger Incentives." Report for the Rand Corporation, Santa Monica, Cal., 1982.
5. Howard, Herbert H. "Group and Cross-Media Ownership of Television Stations, 1984." National Association of Broadcasters, Washington, D.C., June 1984.
6. Levy, Jonathan D. and Peter K. Pitsch. "Statistical Evidence of Substitutability Among Video Delivery Systems." Federal Communications Commission, Washington, D.C., April 1984.
7. McLaughlin, John F. "Mapping the Information Business." In Benjamin M. Compaine (Ed.) *Understanding New Media*. Cambridge, Mass.: Ballinger, 1984.
8. "Reading and the Book." A meeting convened at the American Academy of Arts and Science, June 25, 1982.
9. U.S. Bureau of the Census. *Statistical Abstract of the United States, 1985*.
10. White, Thomas and Gladys Ganley. *The "Death of a Princess" Controversy*. Cambridge, Mass.: Program on Information Resources Policy, Harvard University, P-83-9, 1983.

28

U.S. CULTURAL PRODUCTIONS
The Impact of Ownership

Paul M. Hirsch

**A discussion of the book publishing industry
suggests that the "profit or perish" motive
and the rise of communications conglomerates
have not necessarily diminished the vitality
or number of ideas in the marketplace.**

Mankind's first mass-produced item was surely the brick, the second probably the book. . . . A fistful of [rejection] letters, not all of them troubling to get his name right, may reinforce a novelist's suspicion that most publishers' first readers are chimpanzees, reporting to editorial directors who lie on the floor and hiccup. In less-paranoid moments. . . , he may recognize the voices assumed by human beings trying to pretend they aren't serving a venture in mass production, a theme concerning which it behooves us to be less naive than they'd like.

—Hugh Kenner, *Harper's* (17)

Bridging the gap between creative artists and their audience is a well-known phalanx of organizational middlemen and women: art galleries, book publishers, agents, personal managers, concert promoters, record producers, movie studios, newspaper reviewers, radio talk shows, television networks. Periodic upheavals occur among these mediators concerning the legal limits and content of their business relationships with

Paul M. Hirsch is Professor of Sociology and Business Policy, Graduate School of Business, University of Chicago. Funds for the research on which this article is based were generously provided by grants from the John and Mary R. Markle Foundation and Yale University's Program on Nonprofit Organizations. The author is grateful to Steven Struhl and David Wilford for assistance and has benefited greatly from discussions with John Cawelti, Paul DiMaggio, and Woody Powell.

From the *Journal of Communication*, 1985; 35(3): 110-21. © 1985 *Journal of Communication*. Reprinted by permission.

VALERRY

one another. Recent examples include changes in U.S. tax laws governing movie financing; a movement by nearly all large firms in the book
publishing and record industries away from distribution by independent
jobbers; a major revision of U.S. copyright law; and relaxation of consent
decrees or orders by the Federal Communications Commission enabling
major television networks to participate in the production of TV shows
and in the ownership of cable television franchises.

Where cultural productions are concerned, the referent for "ownership" is nearly always these organizational mediators, rather than either
the artists they deal with or the audiences to which they link creators.[1]
How such changes in the corporate world of these mediators affect art
and culture is a perennial and often-debated question. One reason is the
sheer difficulty of demonstrating that the two are related at all—or, if so,
how much.

As the dollar amounts involved in all of these activities continue to
rise, many of the firms already involved in or newly entering these fields
are unquestionably large. A growing number of these corporations have
divisions engaged in other lines of business entirely unrelated to any
phase of fine art, popular culture, or mass communication. These
economic facts remind us that the term "cultural product" connotes an
industrial setting, in which analogues to research and development,
production, wholesaling, and retailing can be developed. These analogous activities have been variously described as impeding the creative

---

[1] As we shall see, this need not always be the case. Some performers today are under
exclusive contract to a specific television network, much like movie stars were virtually the
exclusive "property" (a trade term) of their employers in the heyday of the studio system
and its stable of "contract players."

enterprise, as being (at best) necessary evils, or as actually making a positive contribution to art—by freeing the artist to be more creative, for example, rather than becoming bogged down in having to personally produce, publish, promote, or distribute his or her own work.

In this article, I lay out some of the issues underlying the more simple and rhetorical question of whether changes in ownership matter, issues such as "for whom?" and "under what conditions?" I cover different cultural and communication media, types of ownership, organizational goals and strategies, and (inevitably) models of human nature.

For many years—long antedating the recent waves of corporate mergers and acquisitions among some organizational middlemen of culture—participants and observers of the "cultural production process" have enjoyed or more often bemoaned the need for producers and distributors, artists and promoters, having to live together. Further, all share the fate of being at the mercy of audiences whom they collectively view as usually unappreciative or stupid and as either too predictable or too capricious.

Before launching into the question of recent changes in ownership, it is therefore important to consider (a) just what sets and types of owners are being replaced by or are selling out to (b) what other types and sets of owners, (c) whether or how much these overlap, and (d) what are the working relationships between them, if any. In so doing, we can begin to estimate if, and to what extent, there are any differences between these owners and in the values and policies they represent. Where differences are found, there is good reason to expect these will show up as matters of degree rather than kind.

Obviously, the quality of our answers will depend on the means of assessment available, and here we encounter several interesting problems of measurement. When seeking to assess artistic quality or to obtain an economic analysis of the markets for cultural products, we are blessed or damned by two facts. First, what constitutes artistic quality is usually hard for even experts to agree upon (7). Second, economic models of markets are deliberately indifferent to the intrinsic quality of the products concerned or the uses for which they are purchased. Within the broad categories of entertainment, leisure, and art, for example, most products will be seen as substitutable for one another: whether one prefers rock concerts, ballet, or snowmobiling is simply "a matter of taste." While both economic and sociological approaches to fiction would count the number of first novels published annually, neither would be comfortable estimating how many of these were above average, typical, or god-awful.

To illustrate some of the ironies and general complexity involved in assessing the impact of ownership changes on the vitality of our culture, consider the concluding sentence of a *Publishers Weekly* feature (8, p. 47) on the reaction of authors and agents to mergers and larger firm size in the book publishing industry. Their "fervent wishes" for "changes

they hope large corporations with business expertise will bring to pass"
are reported to be (a) bigger sales for all books, (b) better merchandising
and distribution, and (c) salvation of the middle book and the first novel.
The paradox inherent in these three wishes is their mutual incompatibil-
ity. Better merchandising and distribution (which all agree are needed
for the book industry) entail larger sales for fewer books and very likely
no change for the better concerning middle books and first novels. Of
course, the reason such incompatible wishes can appear together is that,
while each author is doubtless individually aware of this contradiction,
the fervent hope is that his or her book will be one of those selected as
the beneficiary of better merchandising, rather than being merely
published and left to die. Note that it is hardly a new phenomenon to see
books advertised and promoted; the hope expressed is for more expenditures and better forms of marketing. A shift in this direction, then,
represents a matter of degree.

> *To understand what it would take for a shift in this
> direction to become a qualitative change as well, let us
> consider a few "worst-case" scenarios for book publishing.*

Scenario 1. The publishing of trade books will become dominated by
three large firms. Like television networks, they will succeed in controlling 80 percent of the market. In consequence, they also adopt the policy
of (a) producing bigger profits by the selection of "surefire" moneymak-
ers; (b) weeding out truly excellent, unusual, or bizarre fare in favor of
the "cheap shot," which is violence, surefire formula comedy, and sex;
(c) going for books or authors that are either inflammatory but profitable
or safe, established, and profitable; and finally, (d) taking a direct
interest in editorial policy, such that "most of the books in the rack a few
years hence may be chosen for you, like television programs, by Mobil,
Exxon and the rest."

The first three of these strategies were suggested by John Hersey,
Herman Wouk (both in support of an Authors Guild submission to bar
further mergers in the industry; see 1), and columnist Kevin Phillips
(21), respectively; each anticipates that, if the industry became highly
concentrated, it would act as we expect any oligopoly or monopoly to
behave within a capitalist economy (8).[2] The fourth strategy, fearing a
more political than economic approach to book publishing, is taken from
an article by Leonard Lewin (18, p. 570) in the *Nation*. Of special
interest in the first and third strategies above are the casual assumptions
that one can easily distinguish at first blush a "surefire moneymaker"
from a "dog" or a "sleeper" and a profitable inflammatory work from one
that will lose money. We will return to this problem shortly.

---

[2] The last year in which *Publishers Weekly* devoted an in-depth feature to this topic, or
reported serious public concern over it, was 1978.

Scenario 2. All of the major paperback lines are corporately controlled by firms with additional holdings in the publishing business (trade books in hard cover), the entertainment media (movies, television), or both. Before long, they will buy and distribute only books with wide mass market potential. Standardized, less original works will be favored; preferential treatment may be given to books from hard-cover affiliates; authors, agents, and independent publishers will be at a disadvantage when trying to negotiate terms for subsidiary rights.

Scenario 3. With the ascendance of accountants and finance people to the top of the industry, (a) it will be harder for good books to get published; (b) independent firms will not be able to offer terms to authors as attractive as those offered by more cash-rich subsidiaries of big, integrated firms; (c) independent firms will be squeezed out, distribution will be locked up by the large firms, and fewer new firms will enter the industry; (d) in short, good books will go unpublished, independent publishers will leave the industry, and fewer new firms will enter.

These "worst-case" scenarios all express fear that before long publishing will be run in a more businesslike fashion, to the advantage of the corporate mediators involved but at a high cost to both authors and society. Despite the three wishes cited earlier—particularly the one for better merchandising and promotion—there is a more fervent desire, shared by many authors and readers, for change to be held to a bare minimum.

The facts as I see them strongly suggest this has indeed been the case. The cause for such good cheer, however, is not that conglomerate firms have abandoned their stockholders nor that traditional publishers accept books solely out of love for good literature. Rather, it is because the market for ideas remains unpredictable, ideas are difficult to prejudge, and the cost of printing, offsetting, or photocopying a manuscript remains low enough that virtually anyone can "publish" anything. As the director of MCA, Inc.'s, publishing division tried to explain (before Japanese imports achieved a 20 percent share of U.S. auto sales) to Kevin Phillips (21, p. 33): "Everyone would like total control of an idea, but the book business isn't like the car business. You can't control the market."

> *Precisely because it is so difficult to control*
> *the book market, an entire culture, with nuances*
> *and complex sets of mutual expectations, has*
> *grown up around our knowledge of this industry.*

This culture of book publishing holds that the market is uncertain; that publishers "always" produce more titles than they can sell (usually because they can't predict which ones will fall into each category); and that consequently there will "always" be, in terms of sales, a high ratio of published losers to winners. Also, most books will not receive reviews, and only a small percent of those published will appear in retail outlets. The "worst-case" scenarios above assume an unlikely world in which the market for new titles suddenly becomes predictable and the entry of newcomers into the field is curtailed. Many fear such developments because the attendant rationalization of the publishing industry would transform the present web of contractual and intuitively understood business and social relationships.

Parts of the book industry already exhibit such alien cultural forms. At Time-Life Books, for example, market projections of mail-order sales are accurate enough that the titles in *every* series offered to date have been profitable. Writers are hired to produce these books to their editors' specifications and paid a flat fee, not a royalty (13; see also 14). Similar though less successful efforts to produce Edi-texts, or "assembly line"– written college texts, were met with high levels of protest by academic writers and their colleagues. The indignation these inspired, I suspect, stems as much from their violation of the informal nuances of the more traditional author-editor relationship than from concerns over how the editing was done or about whether the fees were fair. For those adversely affected by these changes, the writing process appears cheapened and author-editor ties loosened.

In scholarly book publishing, and to a lesser extent for first novelists, the question of which house publishes one's work matters less for the anticipated financial return (nil) than for the reputation of the house. Here, the motives and career-related needs of the author often form a fragile intersection with those of the publisher. In many such instances, *who* publishes the work is of greater interest to authors than the question of whether it will be possible to get the manuscript into print at all.

Publishers' different approaches to authors addressing different cultural markets illustrate my contention that by and large many traditional publishers have behaved like "gentlemen," as will those buying into this field now, because the book market is generally unpredictable and rewards such behavior. When market conditions change, so will the policies of firms in the publishing industry, whose own organizational needs now require that they "profit or perish" (18, p. 569). Conglomerate middlemen do not have the capacity to transform diverse readers of books into a controllable market with an oligopolistic or monopolistic structure. While they may succeed in inching slightly in that general direction, such trends are reduced by the entry of a thousand new firms a year (2) and the continuing uncertainty involved in depending on editors to locate and attract potentially best-selling authors. Most new entrants are small and may well economically complement whatever degree of economic concentration has been achieved (3). I emphasize my belief that if publishers (or anyone else) *could* succeed in exerting such control, they would—regardless of whether they entered the field in 1905 or 1985. In fact, publishers have sought to market fewer books in larger quantities for well over a hundred years, during which time virtually every house of any size today engaged in the very practice of mergers and acquisitions that has alarmed so many contemporary critics (22). As Coser, Kadushin, and Powell (5, p. 30) put it: "[Such blockbusters] are a conservative approach to the problem of coping with uncertain market demand."

On a more general level, there seems to be little question that in all areas of life people prefer to exercise more rather than less control and to be more certain than less certain about how things will turn out. Hence, where we find high levels of uncertainty and low levels of control, it is reasonable to assume this is not a state chosen by the participants but rather one thrust upon them by the external conditions of their environment. Neither fine art nor popular culture constitute exceptions to this generalization. Where creators, producers, or distributors have been able to control their market—be they the French Academy or major Hollywood studios—they have done so tenaciously. Where they cannot, the situation usually is described as more competitive, democratic, and/or chaotic.

In measurement terms, economists derive the nature of an industry's internal decisions—on product lines, prices, and overall strategy—from what is known about the market environment in which the industry operates. For example, we expect prices to fluctuate more for agricultural commodities than for electricity partly because the former industry functions in a competitive market while the latter is a regulated monopoly. Applied to cultural industries, this leads us to expect that a change in market structure would make particular strategies, and types of cultural products, more or less attractive (6).

For example, when commercial television took large chunks of their audience away from movies, radio networks, and mass circulation magazines, each adapted by (a) acting far more competitively; (b) reducing the per capita investment in most new units (movies, programs/formats, or new magazines) produced; (c) cutting overhead by putting more people on commission, flat fees, or royalty contracts; and (d) directing their offerings to newly defined audience segments (e.g., "youth") in place of the mass, heterogeneous audience lost to the new medium (14, 15).

Where new ownership can alter a whole industry's market structure, changes of equally great magnitude may be expected. But such large-scale shifts in audience and technology are nearly always beyond the control of any single firm or even group of firms. Rather, to the extent that a change in ownership per se can effect cultural change, it will revolve around issues in each organization's internal administration. Two examples in publishing would be a new owner selling off the backlist or insisting that final decisions on contracts for all new acquisitions be left to the sales manager and staff.[3]

> *In sum, if we assume that any owner will prefer control to chaos, questions concerning cultural organizations are reframed from issues about motives to an inquiry into one's power to reduce market uncertainty.*

From this it follows in broad brushstrokes that (a) if new owners can move the surrounding market structure from an uncertain to a more controlled state, they will, and (b) if they cannot, either their policies will then continue to follow in the traditions of their predecessors, or they will sell off the acquisition to someone else, who will begin the process again. Events in the second of these categories make for stories of colorful business deals and personalities but have little measurable effect on our culture. More substantial changes can be anticipated only if there are any significant alterations in the surrounding market structure. Much talk about changes in publishing fails to make this distinction and so contributes instead to confounding the two categories. Additional issues of some bearing on the market for book publishing include the following.

First, between 1960 and 1980, industry sales jumped from one to four billion dollars. These kinds of numbers attracted new entrants, large and small (and are still doing so, if recent corporate takeovers of Prentice-Hall and Scott, Foresman are bellwethers for the 1980s). Describing the 1960s to researcher Walter Powell (22), one editor-in-chief remarked: "I remember one day when a salesman came in and said quite earnestly that we should accept every proposal as received for publication because he felt he could sell anything." Into this setting came outside investors. Mergers and acquisitions continued in the 1970s but occurred more between firms *already* engaged in the publishing field; college and textbook sales leveled off, with sales in dollars growing at about the same pace as inflation.

Second, the number of small book publishers has skyrocketed since 1974.[4] At the editorial end, large size brings few special advantages;

---

[3] Two extreme and atypical examples of ownership changes affecting single firms are the exits by Bobbs-Merrill and Free Press from publishing fiction and scholarly social science, respectively.

[4] Baker's (2) estimate of 1,000 new entrants a year represents a substantial jump over Noble's (19) earlier figure of 100 a year, also in *Publishers Weekly*.

small publishers carry lower overheads and obtain gross margins equal to or above those of their larger counterparts on professional and trade books. (For textbooks, small size is a disadvantage.)

Third, most concerns expressed about changes in ownership are future- rather than present-oriented. They address the possibility, and somewhat increased potential, for abuses to occur, rather than point to actual events or patterns being put into effect.

Finally, the numbers of titles released annually remain at record highs. The consensus about the worst that can happen to a "quality" fiction writer seems to be that (a) the book will still be accepted for publication but may go to a smaller press or be produced by a scholarly imprint division rather than as a trade book; (b) it may be less widely distributed, remaining available for the knowledgeable audience but less so for others; (c) the book may (in the exceptional case) be not only selected by the trade book division but declared a "blockbuster." Here, a John Irving can become Mario Puzo's equal. In this vein, trade editors do not discriminate actively against quality; rather, there are limits to the number of works that can be tapped for such heavy promotion and hype.

All of the issues discussed so far in connection with book publishing also have arisen concerning every other art and communication medium.

In broadcasting and motion pictures, where the dollars invested per production dwarf those in publishing and involve many more creative personnel, it has long been accepted that the organizational middlemen call the tune (11). For recordings, where the major firms periodically lose and regain control of their market, the process of bypassing independent distributors appears to have entered a terminal phase (12, 20).

Such commercial decisions and internal tugs-of-war among these mediators between artist and audience generate far less public discussion than the objectively smaller changes that have occurred in publishing over the last two decades. One reason for this, I think, is that we accord different institutional roles to different cultural industries. Authors of books, in this context, are producers of original ideas and works, which later provide the materials picked up, diluted, and mass-merchandised by the larger mass media. In this transformed guise, the author's original work is subjected more to the standards of box office, ticket sales, or ratings, rather than to the more reasoned and critical assessment he or she would otherwise expect from reviewers, readers, or peers. The differences in expectation that an artist's work are permitted by "producer" as distinct from "distributor" media are substantial. Whereas the former service a smaller audience and reward originality and the breaking of molds, the latter cater to a mass audience, demand more formulaic writing, and provide stylized genres.

Stated in these extreme forms, it is not surprising (nor as inappropriate culturally) to find that the distributor media are the more centrally administered and oligopolistic. If we expect them to "retail" cultural developments to many millions of people, their prospects for delivering originality and complex ideas are clouded from the outset (see 16). To be sure, a Norman Lear or Steven Bochco can produce artful and innovative television, but it is our knowledge of the parameters within which they work and the built-in constraints that enable us to appreciate their accomplishments. (Similarly, it is a knowledge of the constraints inherent in making B-movies, or working within the structure of the sonata form, that enables audiences to appreciate what their favorite directors or composers have achieved.)

On the other hand, we expect serious authors to be freer from the tyranny of formulas. A market structure within which they retain a high degree of autonomy is an effective facilitator of this state. The prospect of unbridled mergers, acquisitions, and the rise of new and insensitive owners upsetting the structure that has so long put up with authors' autonomy, market uncertainty, and the confusion engendered by competitive markets was (and remains) sufficient to produce a high state of vague, generalized discomfort.

Interestingly, it is the business of mass market paperbacks that could become more like an oligopoly in the near future. Yet there is more ambivalence and ambiguity in our culture over this form of book than probably any other. Is it elite or mass culture? Do these books represent the origination or retailing of ideas? Have they "cheapened" the word? These kinds of questions, perhaps holdovers from earlier controversies, suggest that public discussion about publishing will treat paperbacks as midway between a producer and distributor medium. This would occur in spite (or in anticipation?) of the paperback book business becoming more like an oligopoly.[5]

Such a development also would be compatible with formulations by Herbert Gans and John Cawelti about the nature of linkages between artist and audience. In his 1975 book *Popular Culture and High Culture* (10), Gans suggests that the high culture audience is creator-oriented, whereas most other audiences and types of culture exhibit a consumer orientation. Similarly, Cawelti's (4) discussion of communal and reflexive matrices, where the distance between creator and audience is very short, distinguishes both from the "professional" matrix, in which there are more middlemen and the audience is more anonymous and hetero-

---

[5] Trade paperbacks, the so-called "aristocrats" of paperbacks, have a mixed financial record, but it is too early to call them either a wild success or a failure.

geneous. I see the institutional role assigned to producer media by our culture as one in which the artist-audience relationship is close. Scholarly book publishing approaches Cawelti's communal matrix, insofar as the author often knows most of his or her readers personally. Much book publishing—of both high culture and certain genres (detective stories, science fiction)—also has communal elements and is oriented to the writer-creator.

The distributor media, best exemplified by network television, are just the opposite. Nielsen ratings are consummately consumer-oriented; the appropriate matrix is that of the professional. Between these different poles and distinctions falls the paperback.

It is a commonplace in most lines of economic endeavor that those who process raw materials, transform them, and merchandise the finished product receive the lion's share of economic rewards. The field of cultural endeavors is relatively unusual in that we strongly desire to reward our creators and to commune with their audiences, but avoid or ignore the organizational mediators linking each to the other.

In this article I have compared the economic and organizational settings of several cultural industries. Changes in ownership were shown to play a role subsidiary to each industry's market structure. Without significant changes in the structure, there is little room for new owners to maneuver in seeking to bring about any changes at all. Examples from book publishing were taken to illustrate these points, for book publishing is widely valued as a producer medium and has been the focus of recent concern about the impact on culture of changes in ownership of organizational mediators between artist and audience.

Our discussion of book publishing suggests a number of points. First, few adverse or long-range consequences, in terms of what gets published, can be found to have followed any of the merger activity in this industry since 1960. Second, book publishing remains highly competitive in its market structure, with the result that changes in ownership can have little impact on the market structure within which these firms must operate. Third, small publishers are thriving and the number of new titles released remains at record levels. Under these circumstances, it remains unlikely that worthy books are going unpublished. Fourth, if public policy considerations are to be drawn from the above, an important one is that it is far more sensible for private and public agencies to subsidize authors to write than to interfere in the publishing process—the current policy of the National Endowment for the Arts (9). Finally, paperback and textbook publishing, and book distribution in general, may become (even) more oligopolistic in the future.

Overall, then, a sober consideration of the economic and organizational changes that have taken place in the book publishing industry suggests that their impact on the quantity of elite cultural products is less than critics would have us believe and may in fact belie a conflict of desires on the part of the "creators" of culture to benefit from the consumer orientation of the mass marketplace.

REFERENCES

1. "Authors Guild Asks U.S. to Halt 'Sinister' Merger Trend." *Publishers Weekly*, June 20, 1977, pp. 21–22.
2. Baker, John. Editor-in-chief of *Publishers Weekly* and *Small Press*. Personal communication, 1983.
3. Carroll, Glenn R. *Publish and Perish: A Dynamic Analysis of Organizational Mortality in the American Local Newspaper Industry from 1880 to 1975*. Greenwich, Conn.: JAI Press, in press.
4. Cawelti, John. "The Concept of Artistic Matrices." *Communication Research* 5(3), July 1978, pp. 283–304.
5. Coser, Lewis, Charles Kadushin, and Walter Powell. *The Culture and Commerce of Publishing.* New York: Basic Books, 1983.
6. DiMaggio, Paul. "Market Structure, The Creative Process, and Popular Culture." *Journal of Popular Culture* 11(2), Fall 1977, pp. 436–452.
7. Einhorn, Hillel J. and Clayton T. Koelb. "A Psychometric Study of Literary-Critical Judgment." *Modern Language Studies* 12(3), 1982, pp. 59–82.
8. Evans, Nancy. "How Authors Are Affected." *Publishers Weekly*, July 31, 1978, pp. 45–47.
9. Fields, Howard. "Giving Money Away." *Small Press* 1(1), September–October 1983, p. 4.
10. Gans, Herbert. *Popular Culture and High Culture*. New York: Basic Books, 1975.
11. Gordon, David. "Why the Movie Majors Are Major." *Sight and Sound* 42, Autumn 1973, pp. 194–196. Reprinted in Tino Balio (Ed.) *The American Film Industry*. Madison: University of Wisconsin Press, 1976.
12. Grover, Stephen. "Record Industry May Be in Groove Again After One of Worst Slumps in Its History." *Wall Street Journal*, September 5, 1979, p. 8.
13. Grover, Stephen. "How an Ex-Secretary Climbed to the Top in Publishing Field." *Wall Street Journal*, September 17, 1979, pp. 1, 19.
14. Hirsch, Paul. "Processing Fads and Fashions: An Organization-Set Analysis of Cultural Industry Systems." *American Journal of Sociology* 77, January 1972, pp. 639–659.
15. Hirsch, Paul. "Public Policy Toward Television: Mass Media and Education in American Society." *School Review* 84, Summer 1977, pp. 481–512.
16. Hirsch, Paul. "Production and Distribution Roles among Cultural Organizations: On the Division of Labor Across Intellectual Disciplines." *Social Research* 45(2), Summer 1978, pp. 315–330.
17. Kenner, Hugh. "No Place for the Avant-Garde." Review of *Mulligan Stew* by Gilbert Sorrentino. *Harper's*, June 1979, pp. 83–90.
18. Lewin, Leonard. "Publishing Goes Multinational." *Nation*, May 13, 1978, pp. 567–570.
19. Noble, J. Kendrick, Jr. "Assessing the Merger Trend: Signs Point to Growth for Small Companies and Increasing Diversification in Large Firms." *Publishers Weekly*, July 31, 1978, pp. 35–42.
20. Peterson, Richard and David Berger. "Cycles in Symbol Production: The Case of Popular Music." *American Sociological Review* 40, April 1975, pp. 158–173.
21. Phillips, Kevin. "Busting the Media Trusts." *Harper's*, July 1977, pp. 27–34.
22. Powell, Walter. *Getting into Print*. Chicago: University of Chicago Press, 1985.

29

BROADCASTING FINANCE AND PROGRAMME QUALITY
An International Review

Jay G. Blumler, Malcolm Brynin, and T. J. Nossiter*

This article was originally a report for the British government's Peacock Committee on Financing the BBC. Comparative conclusions concerning the impact of different funding arrangements for the range and quality of television programming are drawn from analyses of broadcasting systems in Britain, the United States, France, Italy, the Netherlands, Sweden and West Germany. Common trends and pressures are identified. Prime-time television schedules are compared. British programme performance is evaluated. A purpose for public service broadcasting in a period of telecommunications change is proposed. The principal options of broadcasting finance are reviewed in the light of international experience: full advertising; limited advertising; sponsorship; co-production finance; and the licence fee.

In March 1985, the British government appointed a committee under the chairmanship of Professor Alan Peacock to assess future financial options for the BBC, including advertising and sponsorship. In September 1985, the Committee on Financing the BBC commissioned a series of enquiries from the Centre for Television Research at the University of Leeds into the implications of alternative funding arrangements for 'the range and quality of existing broadcasting services' in Britain. These included:

1. A comparative content analysis of the range of programmes available to prime-time audiences in the UK and six other countries, each with a different broadcasting structure;
2. Commentaries from academic experts on issues of finance and programme quality as they have arisen in five West European countries: France, Italy, the Netherlands, Sweden and West Germany;
3. Interviews with a cross-section of 120 programme makers in the

*Professor Blumler is Director and Dr Brynin a Research Fellow at the Centre for Television Research, University of Leeds, Leeds, LS2 9JT, where Dr. Nossiter, a Reader in Government at the London School of Economics, is also a Visiting Fellow.

From Jay G. Blumer, Malcolm Brynin, and T. J. Nossiter, "Broadcasting Finance and Programme Quality: An International Review," *European Journal of Communication*, Vol. 1, pp. 343-364. Copyright © 1986 by Sage Publications, Ltd.

United Kingdom, securing their views on a) how their work is commissioned, funded, scheduled and controlled, b) the kind of creative climate that results, c) how broadcasting finance impinges on that climate and d) any significant developments perceived in the role of such factors in recent years;

4. Interviews with a cross-section of seventy-five executives and producers working in American television a) to identify the impact of competition for advertising on the range and quality of commercial network programming, b) to assess the financial problems (and proposed solutions) facing American public television and c) to consider whether any lessons can be drawn from the American experience for British broadcasting.

The results were submitted to the committee in January 1986 in the form of seven reports:

'British Television: a Mixed Economy' by T.J. Nossiter, with a separate report on news and current affairs by Malcolm Brynin.

'Television in the United States: Funding Sources and Programming Consequences' by Jay G. Blumler.

'Problems of Structure, Finance and Programme Quality in the French Audiovisual System' by Roland Cayrol.

'Broadcasting Structure and Finance: the Case of the Netherlands' by Denis McQuail.

'Broadcasting in Italy' by Gianpietro Mazzoleni.

'Television in Sweden 1985: Position and Prospects' by Kjell Nowak.

'Public Broadcasting Services in the Federal Republic of Germany: Organization, Finance, Programmes' by Winfried Schulz.

In addition, the investigators were asked to draw a set of comparative conclusions from all branches of the research. The international evidence is accordingly reviewed from three standpoints below:

1. The pressures that are transforming the environment in which broadcasting organisations virtually everywhere must compete for audiences, funds and status.

2. The comparative performance of British broadcasting in terms of the range and quality of its programming.

3. An assessment of the possible impact of the main options for financing the BBC in the future on the range and quality of British television.

Before offering our conclusions, however, it is important to consider how far the experience of other countries may be applicable to British broadcasting policy.

The Validity of International Comparisons

It should be stressed at the outset that the study of comparative broadcasting finance is in its infancy and cannot be expected to yield entirely straightforward or definitive conclusions. At this stage its pursuit is necessarily more a matter of drawing reasonable inferences from a range of evidence than of firmly demonstrating the unequivocal effects of adopting certain funding arrangements.

In a variety of ways the histories, structures, economies and cultures of national broadcasting systems are unique. It is easy to see how this statement applies to virtually all the countries covered in our work. In Britain there has been the legacy of Reith, in France a tradition of state control, in Italy a dominance of major parties that has latterly been outflanked by commercial entrepreneurs, in Germany a postwar reconstruction of broadcasting along federal lines allied to a *proporz* principle of representation in the main governing bodies, in Sweden a long-standing social-democratic ethos, in Holland the peculiarities of 'pillarization' and in the United States an unabashed business spirit (alongside a public television 'ghetto').

Moreover, the degree to which any broadcasting system can produce a range and quality of programming, protect and develop its domestic output and compete in the world communication market must partly be a function of its country's size, population, wealth, geographical location and even the language its people speak. For example, direct broadcasting by satellite (DBS) is an imminent competitive threat to the public service systems of continental Europe, still only a prospect in the UK and a non-starter in the United States. Thinking of dimensions of size and other resources, Sweden and the Netherlands have small populations (eight million and fourteen million respectively), and the speaking of Swedish and Dutch is chiefly confined to those countries. France (fifty-four million), Germany (sixty-one million), Italy (fifty-seven million) and the UK (fifty-six million) all have more substantial populations — though even in toto they are exceeded by the United States (234 million). French and German are spoken outside the national borders, while Britain and the United States use the current world language. And although all the countries studied are advanced industrial societies, the per capita GNP of the poorest (Italy) is only 35 percent of the richest (Sweden), while the British per capita GNP is 46 percent of Sweden's and 51 percent of that of the United States. The cumulative advantages enjoyed by broadcasters in the United States are highlighted by the huge advertising revenues (at ever-rising rates) that are paid, sometimes lavishly, for its commercial television (totalling $15 billion in 1984). In the British case specificially, it would be prudent, it seems to the authors, to bear in mind that, despite our relative advantages of language and programming traditions, rapid economic growth remains an uncertain prospect for the future.

Despite the cultural uniqueness of each society and the numerous factors that may determine the character of television provision, the Peacock Committee should find it worthwhile to consult foreign experience. Since certain funding options that might be contemplated for the BBC have been adopted elsewhere, it only makes sense to consider how they appear to have worked out. Several of the national reports do quite convincingly trace certain programming consequences back to the manner in which the broadcasting organizations concerned have been financed, suggesting that, amidst all the determinants of programme range and quality, funding arrangements may be a key influence. In certain cases, such consequences stand out particularly clearly because financial changes have recently been introduced with noticeable effects already on broadcasting policies and schedules.

In a spirit of cautious confidence, then, we ask: What comparative lessons and conclusions may be drawn from the recent experience of seven broadcasting systems?

Common International Developments
Three broad trends, impinging to a greater or lesser degree on television in all western societies, emerge from the national reports.

First, all the broadcasting systems are under pressures of environmental change, posing challenges to the established providers and their traditional policies. According to the several national report authors, the German broadcasting system is 'undergoing a fundamental change', the French audiovisual system 'a profound change', and Swedish broadcasting is 'entering a new era'. American television was described by one informant as experiencing, if not a revolution, then 'a damn fast evolution'. A social process of 'depillarization' is unsettling Dutch reliance on pluralistic 'confessional broadcasting';

and a massive dose of unregulated private television is transforming Italian broadcasting.

The principal agents of change are clear:

The spread of new communication technologies.

Multiplication of TV channels with associated prospects of audience fragmentation.

Intensified competition for audiences and revenues, some of the rivalry stemming from swashbuckling entrepreneurs, who are uninhibited by public service groundrules and standards.

Prospective internationalization of the audience with simultaneous transmission of programmes into more than one national system.

Erosion of the previously unrivalled position of over-air broadcasting organizations, though they are likely to remain as significant originators of domestic programme production and sources of audience satisfaction.

Second, to date, the politicians, who are ultimately responsible for broadcasting policy and finance, have not measured up coherently and far-seeingly to the resulting challenges. According to the authors of the several national reports, in Italy, they have allowed broadcasting to lapse into 'a state of lawlessness' without 'clear-cut policies', while in France, contradictory policies for public and private television have been adopted. In Sweden, 'raising the licence fee is considered politically risky among the majority in Parliament, in spite of the fact that increases from licence fees in real terms have declined by about 30% . . . from 1972–3 to 1983–4.' Public service broadcasters in Holland have to cope with a tendency 'from on high to will cultural goals that will not be adequately funded'.

Third, there are signs of a drift across most systems towards more avid competition for large audiences (even among public service broadcasters) and the provision of more mass-appeal programming. According to the authors of the several national reports, in Germany, 'marketing criteria are increasingly determining the broadcasters' decisions on programme structure and content', while the schedules for RAI in Italy show big increases in entertainment programming from 1980 to 1983. In Holland, broadcasting has become more ' "commercial" in spirit if not in structure and finance', with 'more entertainment and films, . . . more show-business styles and formats, . . . more quizzes, chat shows and game shows'. In Britain, the 'new BBC' is pursuing more aggressive scheduling strategies, and arts and current affairs funds have recently been cut in favour of entertainment and daytime television. French television has moved 'closer to matching, without totally imitating, the recipes for success and programming schedules of American and European commercial television networks'. (The commercial networks in the United States have also resolved to 'concentrate their contributions more determinedly and exclusively on mass entertainment provision' than they have in the past.)

Poltrak (1985), a CBS researcher, would not have been surprised. Writing in a recent issue of the *EBU Review*, he predicts that 'competition [for viewers will] be greater in Europe than it has been in the US'. 'Free of any constraints', he continues, 'the most successful video marketplace competitors will be those that give the viewers what they want', while 'programme services less directed towards maximising audience size will be more vulnerable to new competition.' His analysis usefully crystallizes a policy choice to be weighed in broadcasting finance: should public service broadcasting organizations be allowed to take advertising on the assumption that this will enable them to compete more vigorously and effectively with their proliferating rivals for maximum viewership? Or should public service broadcasting be expected to fulfil a different function from that pursued by single-minded market entrepreneurs, depending on non-commercial sources of funding compatible with it?

British Broadcasting Performance:
a Comparative Assessment
Two overall conclusions can be drawn from comparisons of British television with broadcasting provision in other countries. They apply to the criteria of programme range and quality, respectively.

Programme Range
First, the range of programming available to *all* the population in the UK is among the most extensive, if not actually *the* most extensive, provided by the major broadcasting systems studied. We put this contingently, because the only way in which a more definitive statement could be made would be through an unacceptably expensive, time-consuming and multi-lingual viewing of video tapes over substantial periods of time. It is also highly probable that the range of choice available at any point in time on the different UK channels is greater than in most other countries (in contrast, for example, to the tendency documented in the report on 'Television in the United States' for all three commercial networks to show the same

types of programmes at the same times). The range of choice at *peak* viewing times is also very likely most extensive in the UK, although the British report points out, on the basis of a comparison of schedules in 1976 and 1985, that this may have narrowed somewhat over the last ten years.

Some empirical support for these judgements may be consulted in Table 1, which shows the results of a modest comparative content analysis of prime-time television schedules in the countries studied. It represents only a limited sample — three midweek days in mid-October 1985 and only the output from 6.00 pm to 11.00 pm. Nevertheless, it gives some indication of the range of programmes at peak viewing time on various channels in these countries. It also shows the impact of advertising on programme transmissions. The following points stand out from the analysis:

1. The three commercial networks in the United States rely heavily in peak time on series, serials and soaps — about half the total output of NBC and ABC. The CBS figure was somewhat lower, because on one of the days a movie was shown. No other national channel provided so much programming of this kind. Also distinctive of the American commercial pattern is an above-average amount of local news. But the figures for national news on the American networks are lower than anywhere else except for the Italian commercial channel.

2. American public television also shows a distinctive profile — but of a totally opposite kind. It concentrates on the provision of news, current affairs, documentaries and cultural programming. Documentary material is tolerably well represented in the samples from Australian ABC, France, Germany and ITV in Britain as well. Swedish television was the only other source of much arts programming in the period covered.

3. A fair number of single plays or films appeared in the television output of Germany, Sweden and France, but not, on the days recorded, on BBC or ITV.

4. The commercial channel in Italy presented a very considerable amount of light entertainment (but no news). A smattering of light entertainment programmes appeared in most other schedules as well, particularly in the French output — but there was very little on Swedish television and none on Australian ABC.

5. A sizable amount of sports coverage was provided by the Australian commercial channel. Had other days in October been

TABLE 1
Comparison of Peak-Time Schedules of Thirteen Television Channels in Seven Countries
Percentage of Content in Various Categories on Three Weekday Evenings in October 1985

	UK BBC 1	ITV 1	France TF1	Germany ZDF	Italy RAI 1	Canale 5	Sweden TV. 1	Australia Ten	ABC	ABC	CBS	US NBC	PBS
1. National News	20	9	13	15	16	—	15	16	14	8	8	8	29
2. Local News	8	11	—	—	—	—	—	—	—	15	16	15	—
3. Current Affairs	10	9	—	10	6	—	8	—	21	—	—	—	13
4. Light entertainment, Domestic	17	14	27	8	12	41	3	10	—	7	8	8	—
5. Light entertainment, Foreign	—	—	—	—	—	—	—	—	—	—	—	—	—
6. Series, Domestic	18	30	—	6	1	—	3	—	2	49	33	46	—
7. Series, Foreign	9	—	7	15	10	16	9	12	16	—	—	—	—
8. Plays/films, Domestic	—	—	15	11	—	—	11	—	—	—	15	—	—
9. Plays/films, Foreign	7	—	—	—	19	11	16	21	5	—	—	—	—
10. Music	—	—	—	5	—	—	—	—	—	—	—	—	—
11. Minority	—	—	—	—	—	—	24	—	—	—	—	—	29
12. Arts, etc.*	—	—	9	—	4	—	—	—	5	—	—	—	29
13. Children	5	9	16	15	6	—	7	—	8	—	—	—	3
14. Documentary	5	3	—	5	4	3	2	17	16	—	—	—	23
15. Sport, Domestic	—	—	—	—	3	—	—	—	5	—	—	—	—
16. Sport, Foreign	1	2	3	3	3	—	2	3	6	—	—	3	—
17. Continuity, etc.	—	13	7	7	11	3	—	20	3	3	2	3	3
18. Advertisements	—	—	3	—	—	27	—	—	—	17	18	20	—
19. Other	—	—	—	—	4	—	—	—	—	—	—	—	—
	100%	100%	100%	100%	99%	101%	100%	99%	101%	99%	100%	100%	100%

*Arts, religion, education, public access programmes.

included, this category would have been strongly represented in the figures for the American commercial networks as well.

6. Far and away the largest amount of advertising appeared in Italian Canale 5 — 241 minutes out of 900 or eighteen minutes to the average hour. The next highest amounts were found on the American commercial networks and on the Australian Channel Ten (approximately twelve minutes to the hour). By contrast, advertising on ITV averaged but eight minutes to the hour. Of the other public service systems with restricted advertising, RAI carried about seven minutes per hour and the French and German channels four minutes hourly. Australia's Channel Ten is particularly ruthless in how it interrupts programmes, regardless of content. But no breaking up of programmes is allowed in the German, French and Italian RAI channels — except in foreign programmes with built-in natural breaks.

7. In terms of overall range, the greatest variety was provided by BBC 1, ZDF in Germany, RAI in Italy, Sweden's TV 1 and Australian ABC. The narrowest range came from NBC and ABC in the United States and Italy's commercial Canale 5. The ITV profile for programme range was superior to most of the other purely commercial channels (i.e., the three American networks and Canale 5), though on a par with Australia's Channel Ten.

More generally, this evidence suggests that broadcasting systems which are most dependent on advertising also schedule the narrowest range of programming.

Programme Quality

A second major conclusion of this study must be that for programme quality British television stands up very well to international comparison. This does not mean that we are blind to the shortcomings of BBC and ITV (some of which explain the decision to create Channel 4 with an innovative brief), though an attempt to list them will necessarily reflect our personal judgements. For example, there are some rather lightweight series in the mainstream BBC-1 and ITV schedules at present, while pressure to move less diverting fare to later hours or to other channels has not always been resisted. There may be some justice in an American producer's charge that makers of British television drama tend to seek inspiration in literary classics and recent history, while neglecting the dramatic potential of many contemporary social problems. Sometimes the more aggressive scheduling practices described in the British report seem designed to black the rival channel's eye without evident public benefit. Other troubling straws in the wind include recent resource and responsibility shifts (reduced BBC budgets for the arts and current affairs; delegation of more responsibility for non-peak programming in ITV to the smaller programme companies to allow the Big Five to concentrate more of their own effort on network entertainment). Even so, on most scales of good television organization and provision, British broadcasting must be awarded a high rank among the best.

Of course qualitative judgements of cultural goods are difficult to make and establish. It was interesting to find in this connection that most authors of the national reports had independently concurred (1) that for a mass medium, such as television, elitist and narrowly high-cultural criteria of quality were inappropriate and (2) that there were several *sorts* of quality by which television provision might be judged. It is in the spirit of this latter proviso that we now sum up the qualitative record of British television.

One tolerably objective criterion of quality might be found in indicators of international peer recognition. If the winning of awards for outstanding programmes is anything to go by, then British television is far and away the best in the world. The point is illustrated by Table 2, which shows how British television has fared over the last ten years in the two most prestigious international competitions — Prix Italia and Montreux. Out of the sixty Prix Italia awards that could have been captured, British television alone took seventeen (27 percent), many more than the next most successful national performer — Sweden's Sveriges Radio with seven. At Montreux the record has been virtually identical — nine out of twenty-nine prizes for Britain (31 percent).

Another relevant criterion might concern producer motivation. Other factors being equal, a strong commitment among programme-makers to high standards should encourage the production of good-quality work. Certainly the British report graphically illustrates the ability of many BBC and ITV producers to articulate with conviction and example what good programme-making means to them in their spheres. This is in marked contrast to the inability of many American broadcasters to say much at all on this theme. The contrast in standards upheld in the two systems we studied in greatest detail shows up in other ways as well. Whereas in American network television, audience maximization is the test that almost all

TABLE 2
Prizes Won at International Television Festivals
1976–85

	Montreux (Light Entertainment and Comedy)	Prix Italia			
		Drama	Documentary	Cultural	Total
Britain	9	5	4	8	17
Sweden	1	3	2	2	7
France	—	—	3	1	4
West Germany	1	1	1	2	4
Italy	2	—	1	—	1
Netherlands	—	2	—	1	3
USA	3	1	4	1	6
Australia	—	—	—	—	—
Other	13	8	5	5	18
Total	29	20	20	20	60

programmes must pass sooner or later (and more often sooner), British broadcasters tend to see it more as a matter of building an audience and retaining its allegiance for a varied provision. As soon as such lines are blurred and different programme types are pitted against each other, as in American commercial television, audience maximization becomes the sole principle, a narrowing of programme range ensues and considerations of quality become vulnerable. Again, British programme-makers felt that it was possible to have good-quality programmes in all genres. There were good and bad documentaries, there was good and bad light entertainment. 'Good' in such cases implies an attempt to add something to sheer audience-holding ingredients, an important distinction in support of programme quality that seems much fainter in the United States.

The clarity and nature of broadcasting purpose, supported by appropriate constitutional arrangements, is another condition that should favour good-quality programming. Regarded in this light, Sweden and the Netherlands have had distinct aims in structuring broadcasting and — despite their small size and limited economic bases — have until recently appeared to perform tolerably well. Italy, however, has latterly been at sixes and sevens over broadcasting organization, as what was formerly a state monopoly has been forced to compete against an essentially unregulated set of commercial rivals. In France, the imposition of state control has weakened the legitimacy of public broadcasting and been countered by periodic but incomplete attempts to confer greater freedom on television producers and journalists. German broadcasting policy has been an object of increasingly contentious partisan conflict and has suffered from much political and administrative fragmentation. In contrast, the structure of British broadcasting, combining safeguards for editorial independence with accountability through public authorities, has fostered an impressive clarity of purpose, shared broadly throughout BBC and ITV alike. No other system among those we have studied has such a strong and clear sense of what it is about.

Moreover, the British system is unique among those we have examined for its wide-ranging conception of public service broadcasting. It is therefore less likely arbitrarily to limit the sorts of qualitative achievements to which its producers can aspire. Although all foreign examples included notions of public service, none exhibited it in the more comprehensive form it takes in Britain, including:

1. Universal availability of a satisfactory signal for all four extant broadcasting channels;
2. Programming serving three objectives of equal importance: range, quality *and* popularity;
3. Obligations to provide entertainment as well as information and education;
4. Supervision of all broadcast output for conformity to standards of impartiality, decency, taste, etc.;
5. Balanced scheduling, taking account of the days of the week and the time of day at which programmes are presented;
6. Accountability to Parliament in 'arms-length' forms;
7. Responsiveness to the audience mediated through professional values.

This last point introduces yet another possible criterion – the degree to which a broadcasting system enables the mass public to appreciate good-quality programming. Despite a lingering Reithian legacy, a great strength of public service broadcasting, as practised in Britain, has been how it has carried the mass audience along with it: often catering for popular tastes with high-quality production standards and offering diversity to stretch interests and horizons without creating an impression that uplift was being imposed. This is in contrast to certain European systems, which, originally predicated on a more-or-less direct representation of specific social and political groups inside broadcasting councils (as in Holland, Germany and Italy), seem to have had particular difficulty in adjusting to the shock of recent commercial rivalry. Possibly because the broadcasting organizations were less attuned to the needs of the general audience, the new entrepreneurs have been able to present themselves as the people's champions against entrenched and stuffy elites. The Italian report implies, for example, that competition jolted RAI out of its monopolistic 'inertia' and made it aware that 'the public demanded modifications of programmes in terms of quantity, novelty and service', precipitating a 'conversion from a heavy cultural perspective to a more commercial one'. The report on the Netherlands also suggests that traditional cultural policies for Dutch television are now perceived as 'somewhat elitist' and are at odds 'with populist tendencies, which the times seem to favour' there. In Britain, however, the different and characteristic stress on the principle of independence — that broadcasting should not be under the thumb of any social or political group — may have made it easier for programme-makers to get closer to their audiences through a range of mechanisms that are detailed in the British report.

Finally, British broadcasting has maintained production conditions that by-and-large encourage programme-makers to offer and realize their best. A comparison of the two substantial pieces of research that were commissioned clearly shows that in the British system, producers, including writers, enjoy more autonomy and are less subject to day-to-day bureaucratic interference and control than are their American counterparts and that their production routines are less rigid and more hospitable to creativity.

Options for Financing the BBC

The advantages and disadvantages of the means contemplated for financing a broadcasting organization must depend to some extent on the ends they are expected to support. Although we have expressed our respect for the traditions of public service that have imbued British broadcasting, not to reconsider them would be to ignore the inexorable pressures of telecommunication change at work throughout Europe and in the United States. In the present situation we discern two opposite dangers. One is that public service will be equated in practice with a virtually 'imperialist' attempt to be involved in as many areas of broadcasting as possible, contesting every possible source of competition for viewers' attention but risking the dilution and loss of any distinctive purpose (Burgelman, 1986). The opposite danger — of equating public service simply with those programmes that are unable to pull their weight in the marketplace — is underlined by the limited part that public television plays in

American broadcasting and by the great difficulty it has had in trying to break through to some more substantial role.

In our view, however, there is a vital function for public service broadcasting to fulfil in the fluid communication scene that is emerging, the performance of which should not be utterly dependent on audience-maximizing strategies. The coming period is likely to witness: more fragmentation and segmentation of audiences; more transnational programming; more isolated viewing patterns. In that context, public service broadcasting should be a force for cultural integrity, helping society in all its parts to bind, re-connect and commune with itself amidst all the fragmenting distractions. This requires institutions that can provide strong national programming services in the fields of news and current affairs, drama (from soap to culture), sports, popular music, the arts and the coverage of major events of national and symbolic importance.

Complete Reliance on Competitive Advertising
On this option, the international lessons are full and unambiguous. They warn that competition for advertising on any scale would be quite destructive of programme range and a threat to many facets of programme quality. The evidence for this conclusion may be summarized from four standpoints.

First, there is the experience of those systems that have adopted or moved towards this option, whether by design or by default. The American report traces 'pervasive' effects to the three networks' competitive dependence on advertising, impinging on both the production process and on the types of programmes that emerge from it. Advertisers come to have 'rights', to which the system becomes increasingly amenable. The creative community is co-opted to its goals of delivering maximum audiences via programmes that will not disturb or upset. In particular, such a system tends 'to be inimical to broadcasting range — of programme form, of *sorts* of quality favoured, of viewer affect and experience stimulated' (as the American report concludes). Put differently, such a television system tends to cater for a much narrower set of satisfactions (chiefly those of passing time, relaxation and escape) than the full range of communication gratifications, interests and needs to which programming could respond.

The cases of two of the larger European countries also clearly demonstrate that the introduction of competition for advertising into television systems that were previously free of such competition can affect both policy and programming dramatically. Thus, just as the Italian report quotes the President of RAI as stating that 'any public service working in a competitive environment cannot help defending and enlarging its market shares as a *top priority*' (our emphasis), so too has the head of one of the French public channels urged his colleagues to adopt 'the mental attitude of the private sector'. The effect on the range and quality of programming, especially in Italy, has been startling: it has been significantly reduced. There is also some evidence of the manipulation of programme content for the benefit of advertisers.

Second, as argued in the conclusion to the American report, the introduction of advertising to the BBC would disrupt for the worse the internal dynamics of British broadcasting. From the British research a picture emerges of a system that delicately balances incentives to attract large audiences with genuine though vulnerable commitments to programme range and quality. In that context, competition for advertising would be bound to tilt the scales toward mass-audience television and against many of the varieties of quality to which British broadcasters still aspire, including the provision of a balanced and occasionally challenging schedule.

Third, there are many reasons of principle why maximum-audience demand for programmes should not become virtually the sole determinant of supply:

1. There is a wide variety of audience tastes, and it is up to those who provide programmes not to let one sector of the audience, even if large, dictate to others. Marginalization of those tastes to less popular viewing times is unfair. This is not just a matter of 'high' and 'low' culture but of how a range of tastes is to be catered for in policy and schedules.
2. Ratings say nothing about the intensity of audience appreciation. A programme with a fifteen million audience may have fifteen million tolerably contented viewers, while a programme with a five million audience may command a deeply loyal following whose satisfaction is far more intense. Systems committed to 'quality' and financed by methods supportive of it are more likely to do justice to the latter as well as the former. Sometimes the most widely viewed programmes may be popular simply because they displease least.
3. When audience maximization reigns, it is tempting for programme-makers to package their products with superficial appeals

calculated to hold attention. But if the emphasis is on the quality of the content rather than the packaging, a deeper level of satisfaction and a more positive awareness of the value of the programme is possible.

4. In the area of factual programming especially, it is possible to please the audience and raise viewing figures at the cost of distortion and superficiality. It is the duty of news and current affairs production teams to question and to report what happens, not to tell people what they want to hear.

5. The audience cannot actually demand a programme. It can only accept or reject a programme after it has been shown. Any system which gives 'more of the same' because the same is highly popular is failing in its duty to the audience, since the latter is not given the chance to accept or reject something new.

Fourth, the underlying assumption (often part and parcel of the full advertising option) that television could become like a politics-free market — to which producers, unconstrained, would bring and display their wares, and at which viewers would freely make their choices — is naive. Due to its very large audiences and its assumed-to-be potent images, television will always be surrounded by a host of socially- and politically-based expectations, pressures and constraints. This feature emerged in an unexpected guise from the American enquiry, which discovered how various 'political' pressures could even seep into a thoroughly market-oriented broadcasting system through advertisers' sensitive, blame-shunning pores. Insofar as television is an inescapably 'political' medium, then, it may be preferable to continue to define its purposes through public bodies, which must periodically account for how they have served society and used the resources they were granted.

Limited Advertising

This might seem a more attractive option, particularly if (1) advertising could significantly augment BBC resources without (2) diminishing licence fee revenues and (3) be suitably regulated. Mutual strains inhere in these conditions, however, and it could be difficult to keep them in balance. For example, the conclusion to the American report lists various safeguards that might be adopted to limit the encroachment of advertising influences on the range and quality of BBC programming:

No programme-specific pricing of commercials.
Limitations on the amount of advertising time for sale, relative to total BBC
revenues.
A separate agency to sell commercial time.

But if fewer commercials are sold and their rates are not directly
dependent on the audience sizes of the individual programmes in
which they are inserted, less income may be earned. With advertising-
based incentives to fashion an audience-maximizing schedule for the
BBC as a whole, many of the less popular programmes might be
relegated to off-peak viewing times. And no safeguards of the
integrity of BBC output could mitigate the potentially stiff pressures
that would be exerted on ITV programming, threatening *its* range
and quality, since at present it sells commercial time according to the
audiences drawn for specific programmes, a mechanism that it could
hardly be expected to abandon.

Moreover, as the American report concludes:

> once advertisers are granted footholds throughout a television system, they are
> likely to become a political force within it, so that no regulatory deal which is
> struck at a particular moment of policy decision will necessarily remain durable
> afterwards.

The warnings of a number of American informants that it can be
difficult to make controls on advertising stick (whether on amount,
content or placement) are confirmed by developments elsewhere. In
Italy, both RAI and private television aired many more commercials
in 1985 than the law in force allowed. Private television also evaded a
law forbidding cigarette advertising. Even the report from more
strictly controlled Germany mentions 'a tendency to by-pass the
restrictions for TV advertising, including the principle of separating
advertising from programmes'.

Some of the foreign case studies also illustrate the insecurity that
can result from mixed funding arrangements, whereby a broadcasting organization significantly depends on more than one source
of revenue. The experience of American public television indicates
that when public funds are short and unreliable, the mounting
pressures to attract more commercial support are difficult to hold in
check. In several systems of continental Europe, the short-term
interests of politicians have discouraged governments from maintaining licence fee shares of total funding and forced channel
managers to make ends meet through a combination of more
advertising, cheap programme imports and formula television.

Could British politicians be expected to react differently?

A variant on the mixed funding option would divide the licence fee between the BBC and ITV, while permitting both to compete for the pool of advertising income. The licence fee component could be destined to provided core finance or to support informational, educational and cultural forms of programming on the assumption that these constitute 'public service' proper. Either version would, of course, entail a fundamental restructuring of British broadcasting with unforeseeable consequences. That apart, however, the international evidence does not suggest that such a radical scheme could avoid the deleterious effects commonly associated with mixed funding arrangements. If the licence fee was used to provide base finance, then the effects on programme range and quality would be essentially similar to those found in fully competitive advertising systems. If the licence fee was assigned to a more narrow range of programming, tendencies to schedule for audience maximization would not be significantly diminished, while the informational and cultural output might be singularly vulnerable to political pressure since exclusively dependent for funding on authorization by the government of the day of any licence fee increases that might from time to time be required.

Sponsorship
Among the foreign systems covered by the research, only American public television depended substantially on commercial sponsorship of programme projects (termed 'underwriting' by PBS). According to its experience of this source:

1. Business sponsorship can sustain a significant amount of cultural programming, but only a small number of firms are interested in being modestly credited for their association with prestige ventures.
2. Although sponsorship tends to bias provision towards non-controversial projects and programmes, such pressures can be countered with suitable commissioning and scheduling policies, so long as sufficient funds are available from other sources. Sponsorship as such is not risky, but near-exclusive reliance on it could be.
3. Such a system does create difficulties for producers, who may have to spend a great deal of time and effort soliciting backing from would-be sponsors.
4. To broaden the circle and increase the contributions of corporate

supporters, there is pressure to relax controls on how they are acknowledged and to cross the line between underwriting and spot advertising.

Limited sponsorship, conceived as a modest supplement to BBC funds, if closely controlled to prevent editorial interference and commercialism, is unlikely seriously to jeopardize its programme range and quality. It might even ease the entry into the schedules of high-quality and often expensive programmes which are at risk when other funds are tight. Dangers of distortion could arise, however, if certain specified types of programmes (say, arts programmes, single plays and documentaries) were designated, as a matter of policy, as requiring sponsorship in order to stand a chance of being made at all.

Co-production Finance

This appears to be an inescapable and growing feature of international broadcasting. It potentially threatens programme quality in two ways: (1) through pressures to adapt stories, stars, production styles and treatment to standards of foreign audiences, and (2) through loss of editorial control to foreign producers. The ability of the BBC to withstand such dangers could depend crucially on whether, when embarking on co-financing deals, it is tending to beg for outside money or tending instead to offer a distinctive asset (its reputation for high-quality production), with which other broadcasting organizations would wish to be associated. We conclude that to the degree that the *other* main funding sources of the BBC serve to safeguard its reputation for high programme quality, the stronger will be its chance of defending its own editorial standards when entering into this international marketplace.

Subscription

Among the foreign systems studied, experience of this source of finance was confined to Canal Plus in France, recently created as a fourth-channel supplement to the three public networks. Cayrol reports in his paper on the French audiovisual system that, in order to attract broader support, the channel's controllers have largely abandoned their original intention to specialize in cultural programming (classical films, first-run movies and quality documentaries) in favour of more 'popular television'.

Setting aside technical factors and confining ourselves to programme-related considerations, we see both advantages and disadvantages in subscription as a prime source of BBC revenue. The main possible benefits are first, that it would reduce the financial dependence of the BBC on the government of the day, from which it must seek authority to increase the licence fee; and second, that it would strengthen the BBC's incentive to ensure that its distinctive menu (much broad-appeal programming, combined with a host of commitments to range and quality) remains in line with public expectations. In the short run at least, subscription would also preserve the long-established principle of British broadcasting that each major provider of television should be able to count on its own distinctive source of revenue, not having to compete with rivals for it. The main disadvantages of subscription are first, that as cable television becomes more widely available, competitive pressures on the Corporation to narrow programme range and to limit its commitment to quality might grow; second, the tendency to push smaller-audience programmes into scheduling ghettoes might be hastened; and third (and more insidiously), the *public* character of public service broadcasting might be diluted, to the degree that only certain definable portions of the population decide to subscribe to the BBC service.

The Licence Fee

It is unnecessary to add a great deal to what is already known and has been written about this familiar option. We will therefore limit ourselves to a few comments on how this method of financing the BBC now appears at the end of our comparative research journey through seven broadcasting systems.

In our view, of all the available options, the licence fee causes fewest problems and is most compatible with commitments to programme range and quality, as well as with fulfilment of that function of promoting cultural integrity, which we have proposed above as a distinctive mission for public service broadcasting in the years ahead. Its outstanding merit is that it frees broadcasters to allocate the resources they receive as they see fit towards realization of that multiplicity of purposes by which the mixed economy of British television has been guided. Moreover, as the bulk of our analyses have demonstrated, its actual track record in support of British programme range and quality is quite unassailable.

Admittedly, the licence fee is not a problem-free option, but we wonder whether all the difficulties are really insurmountable. Although it exposes the BBC to political pressures, with courage and reassertion of the principle of broadcasting independence these can be effectively resisted, as the final outcome of the *Real Lives* episode showed. Not all the politicians' fears about voters' reluctance to accept licence fee increases have a firm grounding in public-opinion evidence, and different methods of collection could help. It is true that if nevertheless the fee was to be kept below the level of rising costs, the range and quality of BBC programming could suffer. But if the licence fee was to fall short of what Corporation managers thought they needed in a given period, the safest course (safer certainly than taking advertising) would be to limit the growth of the BBC to the natural growth of the licence fee.

One further conclusion is incontestable: No method of financing broadcasting is perfect. Our research, however, has uncovered a certain amount of envy of the British system of television finance among broadcasters elsewhere. The principle of allocating different funding resources to different broadcasting organizations has played some part in debates in Sweden and Germany. According to Cayrol, 'the *present* British television system is considered by French audiovisual professionals and experts to be one of the most enviable models'. And American public broadcasters, long suffering from the lack of an assured and ample supply of public funds, have also advised us not to trade in our 'jewels' for something less worthwhile.

Apart from such unsolicited testimonials, it seems to us that it may not be in the interests of government, viewers or broadcasters to make significant changes in the financing of the BBC: not in the interest of government, because the responsibility of television to pay serious attention to political and parliamentary affairs could be weakened in a more commercial system; not in the interest of viewers, because the range and quality of programmes available to them might deteriorate; and not in the interest of broadcasters, because the system might be less supportive of their desire to make the best possible programmes across the spectrum for the largest audiences consistent with quality of content and technique. Neither do the many changes that are transforming the terms of broadcasting competition abroad dictate a different view. British television cannot be insulated from such pressures, but it should be financed in ways that safeguard and strengthen its distinctive asset in the international market: its reputation for serious drama, thoughtful documentaries and high-quality programming generally.

References

Burgelman, Jean-Claude (1986) 'The Future of Public Service Broadcasting: A Case Study for a "New" Communications Policy', *European Journal of Communication*, 1(2): 173–201.

Poltrak, David (1985) 'What Happens When Competition Comes – the American Experience', *EBU Review* 36(6): 14–20.

30

PROPERTY RIGHTS IN INFORMATION

Anne Wells Branscomb

The subject of this paper—the laws of the Information Age and, more specifically, property rights in information—is a difficult one, but it is absolutely essential to pursue if we are to enter the Information Age knowledgeably and with an understanding of the consequences.

After an introductory section which presents definitions of property and historical background on information protection, the paper reviews recent developments with respect to property rights in information, analyzes several of the major areas of concern, and develops some general principles to guide us in the application of the law to the new technologies. For almost every right in this area there is an opposing claim or an adversarial relationship. Therefore, in each individual case it is a matter of balancing equities and sensibilities that often defy codification. As discussed in individual sections below, the rights include:

1. the right to know information about ourselves and the world we live in
2. the right to collect information—the investigative function
3. the right to acquire information—archived by others
4. the right to withhold information—about ourselves, personal, corporate, or national
5. the right to control the release of information
6. the right to receive compensation for information
7. the right to protect information—the security function
8. the right to destroy or expunge information
9. the right to correct or alter information

10. the right to publish or disseminate information—access to the marketplace of ideas

INTRODUCTION

Many scholars, including Colin Cherry,[1] Fritz Machlup,[2] and Harlan
Cleveland,[3] rightfully argue that information has characteristics different from those of natural resources and manufactured goods upon the
exchange of which our economic system rests. However, if we are to
transform our economy into one that relies primarily upon the economic
value of gathering, storing, processing, and distributing information,
we must develop principles from which we can derive economic value
for such activities. Therefore, it is not very helpful to the public debate
to insist that information must by its nature be shared or that it is
naturally leaky or uncontainable.

In civilized societies, especially in information societies that are
firmly rooted in an educated citizenry and intellectual prowess, we
will not tolerate the unnecessary spilling of proprietary information
any more than we will tolerate oil spills polluting our oceans. Neither
will we tolerate exclusivity with respect to information upon which
our livelihood as a nation depends. Inevitably we must turn to our
legal system to develop and to sustain those rights that we consider
inalienable and equitable and to delineate the boundaries between what
is considered public and what is to be protected by the law as private.

Definitions of Property

Property is a legal concept that dates back to the earliest history of
civilization and that is central to the efficient functioning of market
economies. The word deals with the boundary line between what is
yours and what is mine, or between what belongs to everybody and
what belongs to nobody.

Property, according to *Black's Law Dictionary*, is "that which is
peculiar or proper to any person; that which belongs exclusively to
one; in the strict legal sense, an aggregate of rights which are guaranteed
and protected by the government." The word is derived from the Latin
word *proprio* meaning to "own." The verb *appropriate* means "to
make a thing one's own; to make a thing the subject of property, to
exercise dominion over an object to the extent, and for the purpose,
of making it subserve one's own proper use or pleasure."

According to *Webster's*, the word *property* means, for tangible
objects, "something to which a person has legal title," and for intangible
rights, that "in which a person has a right protected by law." The

word *proper* itself is the root from which *property* is derived. *Webster's* defines *proper* as that "which is socially appropriate: according with established traditions and feelings of rightness and appropriateness," or that which is "sanctioned as according with equity, justice, ethics, or rationale," or that which is "marked by rightness, correctness, or rectitude . . . entirely in accordance with authority, observed facts, or other sanction."

Our Founding Fathers followed John Locke's definition of property as including "that property which men have in their persons as well as goods," and James Madison concluded: "In a word, as a man is said to have a right to his property, he may be equally said to have a property in his rights."[4]

In Spanish law the *propios* or *proprios* were certain plots of land reserved as the unalienable property of the town, for the purpose of erecting public buildings, markets, and so forth, or to be used in any other way, under the direction of the municipality, for the advancement of the revenues or the prosperity of the place.

In recent years international lawyers have become enmeshed in defining the ownership of international public spaces. Antarctica is the world's only landmass not territorially designated by proprietary ownership. However, the ocean seabed and outer space have been subject to much debate over what constitutes the "common heritage of mankind" or "the province of all mankind."[5]

Information is neither naturally proprietary nor naturally shared any more than the earth, or ocean seabed, or space is naturally the province of mankind or the property of individuals, nation-states, or other legal entities.

Although we have lagged behind the Japanese in our research and study of the social impacts of the Johoka Shakai (the Japanese term for information society),[6] we have led the world in litigation, legislation, and judicial interpretation of legal rights and obligations with respect to information. Public discourse for many years to come will concentrate on defining property rights in information that are marked by rightness and in accord with equity, justice, ethics, or reason, and will focus especially on defining those rights that are subject to an effective sanction.

History of Information Protection

The conflict between public and private information is as deeply rooted in our historical documents as is the protection of both private and public real estate. New England villages were built around a "common," or public area, in which villagers gathered on public occasions, much as the Spaniards promenaded around their central parks in the cool of evenings. In both cases the open spaces were essential to the exchange of information in communities that depended upon face-to-face voice communications. Counterparts of such places include the ancient Greek agora, or marketplace, and London's Hyde Park Corner.

We have protected our seacoasts for public access up to the high-water mark and have developed a great national park system for the protection of animals and for recreational activities. The concept of public ownership of airwaves arose at the time of Teapot Dome scandals when the public was outraged about the private exploitation of our great natural resources. There was no natural obligation to make the airwaves a public asset, as lawyers could map out private rights in spectrum resources just as easily as they have in land masses. It was considered the right and proper way of handling the Tower of Babel that existed on the airwaves and prohibited anyone from using that resource efficiently.

The Constitution provides for Congress to protect patents and copyrights, whereas the Bill of Rights in the First Amendment establishes an unregulated marketplace of ideas. Thus the Founding Fathers pursued the contradictory goals of protecting the work products of inventors and writers while at the same time preserving the public interest in the availability of information. We have tried to walk a tightrope between providing too much or too little protection for information. Cases abound in the law with regard to what constitutes "fair use" of information generated by another without his or her permission. The basic philosophy was that facts and ideas could not be protected, but only the composition (in the case of authors) and the embodiment of an idea in a product or process (in the case of patents).[7] Consequently, we have preserved the open access to laws of nature and to mathematical formulas that can be easily replicated. At the same time we have attempted to provide authors and inventors with legal protection for their expertise in order to compensate them for their efforts, to encourage greater productivity, and to increase the body of knowledge upon which human progress depends.

This concept of protection of intellectual property is not shared by all the nations of the world, nor is it derived from any natural law. Other cultures have their own concepts of propriety with respect to intellectual output. There is nothing universal about copyright, patents, or trade secrets. These are devices for reconciling the interests of society with those of the individual and of linking intellectual productivity with commercial gain. Their origins are in Western cultural history and are deeply rooted in the development of the printing press and industrial manufacturing societies. These are legal concepts designed to encourage a positive attitude toward innovation and social change. These concepts began to develop in the late Middle Ages; they have no logical counterpart in early civilizations where the products of intellectual expertise belonged to the community and not to their creators.[8]

All societies have developed an information policy, the most stringent of which is exemplified by the burning of books in China in 213 B.C. and the burying alive of some 460 scholars who were thought to be able to teach their contents from memory. Throughout history knowledge has been closely guarded, usually by a priesthood whose continuity depended on the maintenance of secrecy concerning rituals, herbs, hieroglyphs, or, in the case of American Indians, secrecy of the sand paintings used to heal the sick and bless newlyweds.

Thus we can consider computer hackers a *new* breed of priests, whose primary motive has been to disseminate information about new computer software as widely as possible rather than to keep their expertise closely guarded. It is a startlingly new concept, therefore—that of considering information as a natural resource which in its natural state will tend to permeate the society. Such dissemination has always depended upon skills that must be acquired, nurtured, and supported by social sanctions.

Knowledge can only be acquired by developing one's intellectual skills. Thus, the protection of intellectual activity developed alongside the rise of a class of individuals who had the leisure to produce artistic, literary, or useful inventions. There is substantial evidence that early Greeks recognized the rights of artists to be identified with their works and to have them performed or presented as created.[9] The first adjudication of a copyright issue seems to have taken place in the Middle Ages when a zealous clergyman visited his former teacher long enough to make a hurried copy of his Book of Psalms, the copying of which was not sanctioned by the king.[10] The elaborate rules that we are attempting to follow today awaited the advent of the printing press in 1436 and the rapid industrialization of Western Europe.[11]

The Constitution of the United States[12] endows the federal government with the power to regulate copyrights and patents as a device to "promote the progress of Science and useful Arts by securing for limited Times to Authors and Inventors the exclusive Right to their respective Writings and Discoveries." Thereby authors and inventors were encouraged to share their output with the nation. Surprisingly, there was little debate concerning this clause. The *Federalist* papers merely reflect that "the utility of this power will scarcely be questioned. The copyright of authors has been solemnly adjudged in Great Britain to be a right of common law. The right to useful inventions seems with equal reason to belong to the inventors. The public good fully coincides in both cases with the claims of individuals. . . ."[13]

In both cases it was assumed that it was in the public interest to encourage the widespread dissemination of knowledge and to nurture native intellect. Interestingly enough, the copyright law that was enacted gave protection only to American authors, denying any protection to imported works, which led to widespread copying of English publications.[14] This had the opposite effect from that of encouraging native talent allegedly intended by the legislation. As the piracy and copying of English information products were far cheaper than acquiring the original works of American authors, a flourishing publishing industry developed primarily for textbooks copied from English sources. Thus the Copyright Act of 1790, a high priority on the calendar of the First Congress, was a cornerstone in the philosophy of the new nation to encourage literacy and widespread dissemination of useful knowledge—an early development of technology transfer. It took another century to amend the act to recognize international copyright arrangements that gave mutual protection to American authors from unauthorized reprints by foreign publishers.[15]

Despite the long and complex historical experience with copyrights and patents developing protection for the production of information, it was only late in the last century that we began to build a body of law limiting the use of personal information.[16] In the last 90 years we have made great progress in accommodating ourselves to the intrusion into our personal and political lives of an independent press, both print and electronic media, and we are beginning to forge a new law with respect to computer communications as well.

THE RIGHT TO KNOW

The right to know can involve either simple or complex matters, e.g., the simple matter of the right of individuals to know of their origins and who their true parents are, or the more complicated matter of the right of the public to information that provides the basis for public decisions. However, no such right is absolute. For example, with the advent of amniocentesis, which permits identification of the sex of an unborn child during periods of pregnancy when an abortion can still be legally performed, it has become a controversial issue whether or not the couple should be told the sex of the child. Relatives and doctors withhold the information that a patient has a terminal disease where, in their judgment, it would be psychologically damaging to the patient.

Geraldine Ferraro and her husband confronted a difficult decision with respect to the release of information that Mr. Zaccaro considered would be damaging to his business interests. His tax returns were not legally required by the strictest interpretation of the campaign disclosure laws, but the public believed it had a right to know the facts in order to pass judgment on Ms. Ferraro's qualifications to be vice-president.[17]

"Anatomy of a Libel Suit," an excellent two-hour program produced for public television by the Columbia School of Journalism, dramatized the dilemma between the public's right to know and the private right to control personal information. It contrasted the role of the press in acting as surrogate for the public with the right of individuals to maintain secrecy about their personal affairs and the right of corporations to protect internal memoranda and documents that may prove embarrassing or damaging to their business. The rule of law that has evolved, as enunciated in *Times* v. *Sullivan*[18] two decades ago, is that the public's right to know takes precedence over the personal right to privacy. If one is a "public figure" (e.g., a public official—even a policeman on the beat) or a quasi or limited public figure (e.g., one who is well known in the press already with respect to the controversy in question), then the press can be held liable for misstating facts only where malice (e.g., intentional lying or flagrant disregard for the facts) can be shown.[19]

THE RIGHT TO COLLECT INFORMATION

The right to collect information is vested primarily in the government and is differentiated from the right of journalists to investigate the facts. Many businesses and institutions collect information—banks, insurance companies, credit institutions, hospitals, universities—but there is no legal right to do so. Most of the information is freely given or exchanged for services. In most cases there is a quid pro quo for the disclosure of the information based upon either an explicit or an implied contract. Having delivered sufficient consideration to legitimize a contract, the institutions consider the information proprietary and are loathe to release it even to the subjects of the information, be they patient, customer, or student. It has taken federal and state laws as well as court orders to require universities to make their records available to students and their parents,[20] and universities are still troubled about the consequences of having what they consider sensitive records open to inspection because it will inhibit professors and other staff from being candid about their observations. Also, a recent case holding that individuals have no inherent legal interest in records concerning themselves held by others is quite troubling.[21]

States as well as the federal government have been forging a new framework for privacy over the past several decades, and the effort has become more intense since the 1960s. The primary federal privacy legislation now in effect controls access of the public to government data banks in which information is collected and aggregated.[22] However, the right of the government to collect information is fundamental to the survival of the nation. Its economic health as well as its physical and political health is at stake. The census, which was started in 1890, is a fundamental function of the federal government. In order to collect demographic data and aggregate it for analysis, the government must have the power to compel citizens to respond. This is a very sensitive area, and many citizens do not agree that they should be compelled to release the necessary data. However, allocation of public funds is based upon percentages of identifiable groups, for example, children of the military living within a school district. Also, market information— important to a healthy private sector—is gleaned from the economic statistics that are collected by the Bureau of Economic Affairs in the Department of Commerce.

Stringent legislation exists to protect individuals from disclosure of information that is identifiable as specific to an individual or corporation. However, the access laws have made it extremely complicated to protect such anonymity for large enterprises, and many corporations feel that their trade secrets may be jeopardized even though one of the exceptions to the law is that such disclosure may occur.

A very disturbing decision was handed down recently by the New York State Court of Appeals. Under New York law domestic insurance companies are required to keep certain books and records, including minutes of their corporate board of directors' meetings. Such records have been voluntarily sent to the State Insurance Department under a promise of confidentiality. However, the court ruled that the agency must disclose the minutes of the directors' meetings to the *Washington Post* under New York's Freedom of Information Law, which defined "records" as "any information kept, held, filed, produced or reproduced by, with or for any agency . . ." and that an amendment to the act had eliminated any reference to an exemption for records "confidentially disclosed."[23]

THE RIGHT TO ACQUIRE INFORMATION

The right to acquire information is a public access issue that goes beyond the right of the press to investigate and/or the right of the government to collect information. It involves the right of citizens to acquire information already collected by others. James Madison observed that "a popular government without popular information, or the means of acquiring it, is but a prologue to a farce or a tragedy, or perhaps both." Based upon that verity, the United States has built its information policy upon a broad base of public education, public libraries, public subsidies for newspapers and other printed materials, and a government printing office that publishes the information gathered and processed by the federal government. Strictly speaking, public access may be difficult to conceive of as a property right. However, it is basically a legal entitlement to use public property, e.g., that information which is gathered and processed and published with federal funds and/or has become generally available to the public.

Patents and copyrights are the legal means by which authors and inventors are encouraged to share their creative endeavors with the public in exchange for the legally protected right to control the use of their intellectual products.[24] However, there has been considerable concern that many of these patents become buried in government archives and are never turned to productive use.

This concern is especially pertinent for patents owned by the government, where private enterprises have no incentive to develop the technology. Only 4 percent of the government's 30,000 patents have been developed and marketed.[25] In response to this concern, Congress amended the patent and trademark laws in 1980 to permit universities, small business firms, and nonprofit institutions to apply for patents on federally funded research and to retain exclusive licenses on these patents for as long as eight years.[26] Although this legislation has offered a cure for one problem—the loss of productivity from development of government patents—it has created another—the concern that the basic purposes of universities will be altered. In particular, there is concern that university efforts to sponsor research jointly with industry, in response to diminishing public funding of research, may change the public availability of information produced in universities.[27]

For the general purpose of making information available to the public, aside from the Government Printing Office (GPO), there are extensive federal libraries including the Library of Congress (LC), the National Library of Medicine (NLM), and the National Technical

Information Service (NTIS). These organizations collect and disseminate information developed with federal funds (as in the case of NTIS), registered with the Copyright Office (as in the case of the LC), or collected because it is pertinent to basic research being conducted by scientists and physicians both in federal employment and around the country (as in the case of NLM).

In recent years there has been much turmoil about the dissemination of information that has been processed by federally owned computers and is available in machine-readable form. The most recent policy enunciated by the present administration is that such information will be offered to private contractors for electronic dissemination. Users will pay for the direct cost of accessing the data from computer-based systems, but the federal government will exercise no influence over the fees that contractors or subcontractors may charge the public to access such on-line data.[28] Another pioneering project has been undertaken by the Trademark Office, which has entered into barter arrangements with private companies to exchange government data for services in designing the computer graphics software and entering the data to access trademark registrations on-line through an electronic data base. The ultimate goal is to produce the paperless office in which manual files will no longer be maintained.[29] This is a far cry from the previous practice of agricultural data being distributed freely and without charge by congressmen to their constituents and from that of county agents offering their consulting services to local farmers. Congressman Byron Rogers from Colorado's First Congressional District used to send baby books to all new parents with his compliments, and many useful publications are offered at a modest cost by the Government Printing Office.

Public libraries agonize over the high costs of distributing information on-line, as charges are not imposed on the the use of books unless they are overdue.[30] There is, of course, no natural rationale that requires public libraries to permit readers to read books in their collections without charge. Indeed, in former times libraries were very carefully guarded assets, access to which was strictly regulated. Neither is there a natural rationale which requires that access to computer-based information be subject to usage-sensitive charges. The main difference is that it is more convenient to measure and collect the marginal cost of computer access than it is for manual systems.

THE RIGHT TO WITHHOLD INFORMATION

The personal right to privacy is basically a right to withhold information from public dissemination or disclosure. It is quite limited in a society that believes in the free flow of information. In the United States the press is encouraged to serve as a watchdog and to seek out wrongdoing in public and private institutions.

As the press has become more and more diligent in its role and the means of surveillance and investigation have become more sophisticated, it is not surprising that public agitation with respect to the advent of new information technologies has sparked an interest in privacy laws. The most basic property right is the protection and integrity of one's own person—the right to withhold information about oneself that one considers to be one's own, the right to disclose information about oneself at such time and place and under such conditions as one chooses, and the complementary right to know of and to correct information about oneself that is inaccurate and damaging to one's pride or reputation.

Scholars of privacy insist that privacy is a natural instinct that has roots in the earliest of civilizations. However, when one visits the pueblos and cliff dwellings of the Southwest Indians it is difficult to believe that our early forebears on this continent enjoyed very much privacy. And those of us who grew up in small-town America also have serious doubts that privacy is so deeply rooted historically. Indeed, it seems a newly won privilege of urban civilization where the sheer numbers of citizens living together make it virtually impossible for everyone to keep track of everyone else. Therefore, it comes as something of a surprise that there is such commotion about information technologies that have the capability to reimpose the surveillance that was characteristic of small, tightly knit communities.

Nonetheless, it is a characteristic of our evolving civilization that we are developing an increasing respect for the individuality and privacy of every human being in addition to a recognition of proprietary rights in real estate and other material possessions. Therefore, it follows logically that we will also evolve a body of law to protect information about ourselves as well as information concerning our corporate enterprises and public institutions.

Some rights have become universally accepted and require no legal sanction. For example, many women in our society prefer not to tell their age, and that preference is usually respected. The privacy of other information, such as that about sexual behavior, is less universally accepted; e.g., we are only recently beginning to accept overt homosexuality among those in positions of power and influence such as the teaching profession and the judiciary. Consequently, there has been a strong incentive to protect such information from disclosure. Criminal activity, physical illness, psychiatric treatment, credit history, and sources of income are all areas in which we have developed concerns about disclosure if disclosure would be damaging to personal interests or if such information would be damaging to the public interest. A case in point was disclosure of the information concerning the psychiatric treatment of Senator Eagleton, which affected his viability as a candidate for the vice-presidency of the United States in 1972.

Trade secrets are protected under a very extensive body of law developed through state legislation and the common law. However, trade secrets law is full of contradictions and inconsistencies with the laws of copyrights and patents, particularly with respect to the protection of proprietary interests in computer software. The basic philosophy of both copyright and patents is to disclose information in order to expedite the public dissemination of information but to provide compensation to the authors or inventors, whereas trade secrets law rests upon nondisclosure to the public. Attorneys for computer software companies are in a great dilemma about whether to withhold, disclose, license, release, or rely upon royalties. To cover all bases is very difficult, since reliance upon one theory of law may foreclose use of another.[31]

Use of the social security number as a universal identifier has met with great opposition from proponents of privacy. Thus, many people refuse to disclose their social security number because they fear that the government will misuse the personal information referenced by social security number in many data banks. Nonetheless, social security numbers as identifiers have become widely used by both the government and private organizations. The majority of citizens seem to have no qualms about disclosing the number, and many feel that the advantages of cross-referencing data bases far outweigh the dangers.

Another area of the law that is very controversial and rapidly developing is the asserted right of journalists to withhold the identity of their sources. Here the right of the public to know is in conflict with the right of those accused of wrongdoing to know the source of the accusation. Investigative reporters claim that they will be unable to obtain information from those with knowledge, especially where their source's future may be jeopardized (e.g., by discharge from employment for "whistle-blowing" or by retribution at the hands of criminals for "squealing"). This area of the law is still very much in a state of flux.[32]

The Supreme Court, when reviewing a journalist's plea for a special privilege,[33] noted that Congress might elect to legislate a special privilege for those who inform the public, but it failed to restrict the category to journalists. The Court included lecturers, pollsters, novelists, academic researchers, and dramatists among those who might seek or merit the right to protect the confidentiality of their sources.

This right is greatly desired by most scientists, despite the seeming contradiction between the philosophical basis of an open exchange of information in the pursuit of knowledge and the closed system of individual sovereignty of the researcher over the management of the data, subject to a peer group review.[34] In 1971 Professor Samuel Popkin of Harvard University went to jail for a week for refusing to disclose the sources of his research related to issues in the Pentagon papers litigation.[35]

The only two areas in which scientific researchers can obtain protective orders to protect their sources are in cases of psychiatric illnesses or drug abuse.[36] Efforts to persuade Congress to enact the protection alleged to be required by scientific researchers in other areas have been unsuccessful.[37]

THE RIGHT TO CONTROL THE RELEASE OF INFORMATION

The corollary to the right to withhold information is the right to release information at a time or place of one's own choosing. This right is recognized for corporate products, and corporations carefully guard the release of information about new products. Similarly, news releases are dated, and publishers usually respect the embargo both as a matter of common practice and in order to preserve the relationship with the source of the information for future publication.

The right to control the release of information is particularly important to those engaged in scientific research. Traditionally (until recently), basic researchers neither sought nor received much financial reward for their discoveries, but they jealously guarded their rights of paternity. Dorothy Nelkin summarized their position as follows:

> Scientists resist external control as a threat to the quality and integrity of research and as an infringement on their right to control the production and dissemination of their work. From this perspective, the question of ownership is unambiguous: the concept of individual sovereignty guides scientific behavior.[38]

There is nothing more zealously guarded by scientists than the peer group recognition that comes from first publication of research results that may lead to an esteemed professorship or even a Nobel Prize. In his study of scientists, R. K. Merton concluded that a scientist's claim to intellectual property rights was limited to such recognition and esteem.[39] However, with the changing economic environment in which academic research is being conducted and with large profits to be claimed, especially in the field of genetic engineering, all this may be changing. The incentive to claim property rights in scientific research that extend beyond paternity is becoming more compelling.

Nelkin has astutely observed:

> This assumption [that scientific sovereignty is in the public interest] leads to a fundamental contradiction: the use of secrecy to maintain sovereignty within a community whose work is based on open communication of research findings.[40]

Interestingly enough, at the same time that the incentive to control research findings more efficiently has increased, the technological imperative is in the direction of making it easier and easier to share scientific research. Computer networking among scientists has become widespread, facilitating the cooperative efforts of scientists from many parts of the world in joint research projects. Such simultaneous and sequential exchanges in a dynamic electronic environment often make it difficult to determine paternity with any kind of legal validity,[41] and the bits and bytes flowing freely via satellite from laboratory to laboratory may make it difficult to trace what librarians call an "intellectual audit trail." Thus, the dilemma arises for scientists that the economic environment in which they now work impedes the optimum use of a technology that has the greatest promise for sharing their intellectual output with the rest of the world.

An additional problem has arisen with the public outcry to be able to see the information upon which the scientist's judgment is based rather than to rely upon the expert opinion of the research scientist as reviewed and validated by a peer group. This is the primary reason for controlling the release of scientific data. Research scientists check and recheck their data until there is reasonable assurance that it is reliable before sharing it with the court of peers who will judge its authenticity and validate it for public distribution. However, the data in a university computer may not be as easily protected from premature release as the research notebooks of a pre-computer period.

There are many other types of data bases where release of information provided by individuals is routinely made available to the public or even sold for profit by both private and public institutions. Have you noticed, for example, how quickly you receive solicitations from boating magazines and commercial houses after you have purchased a new boat and registered it with the state authorities or documented it with the Coast Guard? Direct mailers are notorious for the speed with which they sell your name to their colleagues after you purchase an item. All of this is expedited by the use of computers for recording and distributing addresses.

In most jurisdictions there is at present no legal right to require entities to which you disclose your name and address to protect that information. However, there seems to be a groundswell of increasing concern about such use.[42] A few states have acted to prohibit the use of motor vehicle registration lists for direct marketing without the consent of the registrant,[43] and a number of others have enacted legislation restricting the distribution of cable television subcription lists.[44] Most companies are able to acquire such information quite easily. Several companies specialize in the distribution of motor vehicle registration lists, which are considered to be the most valuable and up-to-date address lists. Some institutions, such as American Express, voluntarily inquire whether you wish to have your name distributed to other commercial enterprises, and the Direct Marketing Association promises to have your name removed from all mailing lists if you so request. However, a trial run of this system by the author merely precipitated a deluge of catalogs from many direct mail houses that had not previously known the address.

Perhaps in an open society whose economy rests upon commercial enterprise, some of us do not cherish the protection of our own names from disclosure to third parties without our permission. Indeed, the telephone company requires those who cherish privacy to pay extra for the privilege of an unlisted telephone number. However, it should be a prime tenet of the right to privacy that government agencies should not disclose personal information for commercial purposes without prior consent of the person.

Credit agencies freely exchange information about one's reliability. The legal status of such information within the care and within the files of another is not entirely clear. However, some recent cases are troubling. A bank was held legal owner of the information about a depositor, who had no right to enjoin release of that information.[45] Medical doctors are usually held to be the owner of their own files about patients, and attorneys are the custodian and rightful owner of their own files about their clients. The attorney-client privilege protects disclosure by the attorney of client information to third parties, and doctors operate under an ethical mandate not to disclose medical information about the contents of their files to outsiders. However, the ease with which electronic files are being invaded today suggests that the law is not yet in place that will protect such files in the Information Age and/or that neither public nor commercial enterprises are willing to pay the price of data protection by encryption.

The case of material obtained illegally is another instance in which the right to control release of information is important.   Where criminal liability is predicated upon such information, it has been a long-standing principle of U.S. law that information obtained by illegal search and seizure is not permitted to be used to convict.[46] However, recent Supreme Court cases suggests that this rule may be weakened.[47]

In the case of publication of illegally obtained information, the law is not so protective of the source, and the government was unable to obtain an injunction against the *New York Times* to prevent publication of the Pentagon papers.[48] However, the former—the case of material obtained illegally—rests upon a basic principle of fairness to defendants and the latter—that of publication of illegally obtained information—upon the overriding right of the public to know. Consequently, in each case there is a balancing of public against private interests in release of information. There is an implicit conflict between the interests of the First Amendment in open and uninhibited circulation of information and the rights of interested parties (whether individuals, corporations, or governments) to prevent the disclosure of information that they consider may be damaging to them.

The most interesting case to date in this area has been the Elizabeth Taylor action to enjoin ABC from televising a docudrama about her life in which she had enjoyed no participation nor had had any opportunity to review the contents. It was Miss Taylor's argument that the story of her life was hers to distribute.[49] As she was an actress of note whose family fortune rested upon her abilities as an actress and her resultant fame, it was a reasonable argument that she had not merely a personal right of privacy not to be invaded by publication of information about herself but that she had a commercial interest to be protected from exploitation by an unauthorized commercial enterprise.

Usually the legal claims in such cases are based upon libel, privacy, or false light, but Miss Taylor's claim was a more novel claim of misappropriation of information rightfully belonging to her. She based her claim upon statutory rights and the common law "right of publicity."[50]

Libel cases against producers of historical documentaries have been dismissed on the grounds that certain events are of such historical significance that the First Amendment confers "leeway" to permit the public to view the reconstructed portrayal.[51] The problem is more critical with living subjects, especially those like Miss Taylor whose livelihood is based upon the electronic presentation that is also the vehicle being used for the historical representation. Courts have held that the right to file suit for invasion of privacy would not be available to descendants, although "merchandising rights" have been held to be passed to subsequent generations.[52] Inevitably, in such cases there is a conflict of many interests: those of the authors to the integrity of their creative freedom, those of the public to view historical events in perspective and in the latest information technology, and those of the subject or the subject's heirs either to protect the integrity of information or to retain the right to receive compensation for distribution of information that was generated through the efforts of the subject. Rights of paternity and integrity have not traditionally been covered by U.S. copyright law, but are established by contract.[53]

THE RIGHT TO PROFIT FROM INFORMATION

There are many mechanisms for supporting the creation of intellectual products, such as the maintenance of monasteries, public universities, and venture-capital firms or the patronage of wealthy families, for example, in Italy during the Renaissance. Yet copyright and patent laws have been the mainstay of public policy in market economies since the Statute of Anne was enacted in 1709.[54] Basically, this first copyright law protected the right of authors to dispose of their works in return for financial remuneration rather than for public acclaim.[55]

As this system was designed for the print media and primarily for the protection of the financial interests of publishers rather than of authors, it has been the subject of much controversy in the electronic age. The law had great difficulty in accommodating itself to machines. Even as early as the days of the player piano, the courts had difficulty in finding that the instructions to the piano were a "copy" of the underlying work that could be perceived by the human mind rather than a machine.[56] The author John Hersey, a commissioner on the Commission on New Technological Uses of Copyrighted Works (CONTU), which advised the Congress on the applicability of copyright principles to computer software, wrote an anguished dissent to the CONTU recommendation that software be so considered:

> Works of authorship have always been intended to be circulated to human beings and to be used by them—to be read, heard, or seen, for either pleasurable or practical ends. Computer programs, in their mature phase, are addressed to machines. . . . The computer program communicates, if at all, only with a machine.[57]

Hersey's colleagues on CONTU did not have as much difficulty coping with computers as he did, and recommended to the Congress that computer software be absorbed within the rubric of copyright protection.[58] Indeed, even with doubts about the statutory protection, lawyers have shown great ingenuity in devising methods to protect the interests of their clients through licensing agreements, centralized royalty exchange programs, and contractual arrangements.

Computer Software—*Apple* v. *Franklin*

The arguments over legal protection for computer software have been extensive and have only temporarily been resolved with the enactment of a special amendment in 1980 to the Copyright Act of 1976. The amendment was specifically intended to authorize copyright law to cover computer programs,[59] although the Copyright Office had been accepting computer software for copyright registration since 1964.[60] The Copyright Office had, in fact, registered more than 2,000 such programs prior to the investigative hearings of CONTU, primarily offered by IBM and Burroughs, two of the largest developers of computer software.[61]

Much of the success of Apple in introducing the personal computer to the marketplace rested upon its successful efforts to encourage the free exchange of software programs by its users and the offer to facilitate the opportunity for circulation. However, when the Franklin Computer Company copied its operating program in order to facilitate the running of software designed for Apple computers on Franklin hardware, Apple went to court to enjoin the practice. There was no question about the source of the software, as the Franklin version even contained references to Applesoft. The basic legal argument was that object code, in which the Apple operating system was written, was not copyrightable. The lower court, in the spirit of John Hersey, was unable to cope with this "baffling" new technology and found no infringement. Where were the original "works of authorship" in this electronic gibberish? What was "fixed in a tangible medium of expression"?

The defendant also suggested that for the copyright laws to cover the situation there must be some representation of irreparable financial harm. Rather than harm to the plaintiff, the defendant argued that the irreparable harm would ensue upon issue of an injunction against Franklin, a fledgling personal computer manufacturer with only 1,000 machines sold, compared with Apple, the then leader in the field, with 440,000 computers sold and sales of over $335 million in 1981. Franklin argued that equities and public interest were on its side to foster competition in the industry and to keep a balance between competition and protection. However, the appellate court disagreed. Although finding that the underlying interest of the copyright law required a presumption of irreparable harm to the plaintiff, the court said the copyright law required no such actual showing. The court had no difficulty in finding that the $740,000 invested by Apple in developing its operating system software represented a substantial investment in jeopardy, which would satisfy the underlying public policy considerations. It also found no difficulty in obviating the necessity of discriminating between object and source code,[62] since one is used to more readily get access to the other. In effect the two satisfy the same functional purposes—to tell the computer what routines it is to perform. The Supreme Court agreed, or at least refused to enter the argument.[63]

However, the debate about the appropriate protection for software continues.[64] Some software firms, such as Freeware, offer their programs for a contribution on the theory that wide dissemination is desirable and, at least in their judgment, profitable. Other software houses, while attempting to protect their intellectual efforts through licensing agreements to control unauthorized copying, nonetheless admit that staying ahead of the competition in innovative programs is what protects their financial investment. It remains doubtful whether or not this will be true in the more stable economic environment when software programs have matured and found their natural niches in the marketplace. Indeed, some of the young geniuses who started their careers as computer hackers have admitted to being devastated by the piracy of their work product after hours and hours of labor expended in its creation. How public policy addresses this issue will remain of high priority in the Information Age, as economic interests become more and more tied directly to information products and services.

Videotape Piracy—*Sony Corp.* v. *Universal City Studios*

An even more difficult copyright issue, one that is no nearer resolution, is that of videotaping television programs off the air through the use of videocassette recorders (VCRs). As recently as the early 1970s, network programs did not carry a copyright notice, because the law presumed that broadcasting a program on television was not a "publication" but a private performance to be governed by the contract negotiations and agreements reached between the two parties—the network originator and the broadcasting station that aired the program. At the time there was no conceivable way a user could record and resell the performance. Consequently, there was no "copy" that could be the subject of copyright registration.

All that has changed with videotaping, which is flourishing. Some 4 to 5 million VCRs are now purchased annually[65] (13 percent of the

American public already owns VCRs[66]), and more than 14,000 videotape leasing outlets have cropped up all across America.[67] However, the receipt of royalties from the rentals of such recordings is prohibited by law under the doctrine of "first sale," which grants a copyright owner the right to transfer the ownership but not to control the secondary uses thereafter.[68] As a consequence, no royalties are collected on the millions of rentals of videotapes of popular motion pictures. The sale of such tapes has not been large, but the market is growing steadily. The release of *Raiders of the Lost Ark* just before Christmas in 1983 precipitated a record of 500,000 purchases in less than a month.[69] The rentals now reach close to a billion dollars annually and run about nine to one over purchases.[70]

Most of the litigation has involved the taping off the air of television distributed programming. The time to resolve the issue has taken almost a decade, as the initial suit was filed in 1976. Although the lower court did not see a violation of the Copyright Act in the at-home taping of television programs, the Ninth Circuit Court of Appeals agreed with the complainants that their rights had been infringed and that they deserved relief. The Supreme Court disagreed, admonishing the appellate court for enlarging the scope of "an article of commerce" that is not the subject of copyright protection and beyond the power authorized by Congress. In addition, the Court found that the widespread primary use of VCRs was for "time-shifting" or otherwise viewing a program that could not be seen at the time it was first televised. Thus, the respondent was unable to "show that the practice has impaired the value of their copyrights or has created any likelihood of future harm." Also, the Court determined that VCRs were used for other, quite legitimate purposes in addition to that of recording plaintiff's intellectual products.[71]

Taping of television programs for personal use appears to have become accepted as a fair use of copyrighted material. This is not in accord with the historical interpretation of fair use, since the programs are taped in their entirety. The use of the doctrine in the past has usually been restricted to copying portions of the work "for purposes such as criticism, comment, news reporting, teaching (including multiple copies for classroom use), scholarship, or research."[72] The rationale of the court must have been the unlikely efficacy of trying to put Pandora back into the box and the fact that no commercial use of the tapes was either alleged or documented. The case might go quite differently for the resale of programs taped off the air.

The holding was consistent with the photocopying case,[73] which had to reckon with the efficacy of trying to hold back a technology that had produced countless street-corner copying houses all over the country—a development that makes it possible for any citizen to become an information provider. Furthermore, the Williams & Wilkins case involved the photocopying by the National Library of Medicine and National Institutes of Health (NIH) of scientific articles (many of which were taken from the plaintiff's 37 professional journals) in single copies for distribution to the NIH staff of 12,000 plus satisfying thousands of requests from cooperating libraries around the country.

In each case the Court was concerned about dealing with a new technology in a judicial context rather than leaving the legislative function to Congress, but in both cases the justices were divided in their opinions.

The motion picture producers are now taking their case to Congress and seeking repeal of the first-sale doctrine. They are also pursuing their legal rights in the courts against all potential defendants in the videotaping industry but without any redress being sought against users whose only videotaping is for their personal use in the home.[74]

Insider Information—SEC v. Winans

Another concern of the public is that insiders not be permitted wrongful financial gain from the use of information prior to its disclosure to the public. The Securities and Exchange Commission (SEC) regulates the buying and trading of stock by the executives and owners of businesses who have available to them information that could affect the stock market price.[75] Historically, financial information has carried monetary value second only to that of military information. Indeed, the Rothschilds are supposed to have based their fortune upon advance information of the defeat of Napoleon at Waterloo brought to them by their fleet of carrier pigeons.

In an open society such as ours, there has been considerable ferment about manipulation of the stock market by those with sensitive jobs. The most recent case and the most innovative one is the indictment of R. Foster Winans, a former employee of the *Wall Street Journal* and columnist of "Heard on the Street," for using the advance information that he controlled for personal profit in stock market trading.[76] Indicted along with Winans were two others, another former *Journal* employee and a former stockbroker from Kidder, Peabody, & Company. Also expected to be indicted is an attorney who allegedly used the information and profited therefrom. Over a million dollars in profits were reputed to be gained by the four in the alleged conspiracy to defraud the readers of the *Journal* through a failure to disclose the financial interest of the writer in the outcome of his articles.

Although the indictment contains allegations of securities, mail, and wire fraud, it is this novel legal theory of a fiduciary obligation to his readers that has precipitated much speculation among legal scholars. Proponents of the First Amendment and defenders of the press such as Floyd Abrams deplore such disclosure of financial interest as a forced speech that is inherently abhorrent to the constitutional right of free speech. However, investors in the stock market who rely upon such reputable sources as the *Wall Street Journal* for their financial information must necessarily be concerned about the opportunity for manipulation of the data and the stock market. This case presents an interesting dichotomy for those who prefer an unregulated marketplace, since the integrity of the information must necessarily rely upon either the ethics of the profession or the rule of law. Certainly the dispatch with which Winans was released from his employment by the *Journal* underlines the concern of the paper for its reputation.

Clearly the SEC insider rules were not originally intended to anticipate such a situation. A basic sense of fairness to the stock-trading public suggests where the equities lie. However, the legal situation is not so clear. While the theory of a legally enforceable fiduciary duty has appeal to those concerned with fairness in the marketplace, it may not technically lie within the Supreme Court's restrictive definition of insider trading. Winans was not an officer of any of the companies in which he traded. He was in the position of gathering information about them and/or disclosing it at a time and place convenient to his trading posture. The most solid legal argument may be that he embezzled the information about the time of publication of his column from his employer and released it to his coconspirators, who became thereby participants in the alleged theft.

The most expansive exposition of the legal position of the courts was expressed in a 1968 case: "Anyone—corporate insider or not—who regularly receives material nonpublic information may not use that information to trade in securities without incurring an affirmative duty to disclose. . . . [Federal securities laws] created a system providing equal access to information necessary for reasoned and intelligent investment decisions."[77] Prior decisions have concluded that the fiduciary relationship necessary to bring the SEC rules into action required direct responsibilities to the stockholders.[78] Consequently, the government may lose the case on technical points. Nonetheless, the indictment itself is a major step forward in focusing public attention upon the problem of authenticating sources of information and protecting the integrity of information upon which the public must make decisions. Certainly, there will be amicus curiae briefs filed by representatives of the working press, and publishers will argue that government intrusion upon the self-regulation of the industry will do more harm than good. However, where financial interests affecting the buying public are concerned, I suspect that the scales will fall more heavily upon the side of regulation if the courts fail to protect the integrity of financial information. One caveat, however: When the state of Alabama enacted legislation requiring reporters covering state government to disclose their economic interests that might constitute a conflict, the reporters succeeded in obtaining an injunction against its use.[79] There was no presumption of wrongdoing as in the Winans case, since the dangers were prospective rather than retrospective. Certainly, this is one of the areas in which the divergent thrusts of the First Amendment draw a clear line of battle.

Other Cases

Another area for concern in the future is that of public officials commercializing their memoirs or using information from their official experiences for profit. However, public servants may argue that their "stock in trade" is their intellectual output during their incumbencies much as Elizabeth Taylor claimed a commercial interest in her professional persona and the right to exploit her name, image, and reputation. The difference, of course, is that public officials receive their financial support from public coffers, whereas performers are dependent upon commercial exploitation of their performances as the economic basis of their livelihood. The public policy question is whether news gatherers are derelict in their duties to the public when they pay their news sources for disclosure of information.

A more serious problem occurs in cases such as that of Watergate defendants Haldeman and Ehrlichman, who were paid for their appearances on television. Since Watergate, there is growing concern about the right of public servants to financial gain from their public service, or especially for their public disservice. However, there is very little case law on the subject. This is probably because there is no one to represent the public interest—no injured party to litigate the issue. Several decades ago litigation arose over the right of Admiral Rickover to claim a copyright in his speeches delivered during government service.[80] In another case, Richard Nixon was not permitted to claim executive privilege to block the subpoena of the special prosecutor for the famous incriminatory tape recordings.[81] More recently, the Ford memoirs became the subject of litigation when *The Nation* published excerpts or paraphrasings of some of Gerald Ford's observations about Watergate and its aftermath prior to the publication date scheduled and precipitating the cancellation of a contract with *Time* magazine to publish portions of the manuscript.[82] The court held that *The Nation*'s article—only 2,250 words, of which at most approximately 300 were copied—was a fair use of facts contained in the 200,000-word manuscript and were "the very essence of news and of history." After reviewing cases holding that neither news events, historical facts, nor biographical facts are copyrightable, the court summarized its view that public events cannot be monopolized by participants in them.[83]

> We have been asked to examine complex questions concerning the Copyright Act and the memoirs of a public official. Throughout our consideration, we have been guided by the conviction that the statute was not meant to obstruct the citizens' access to vital facts and historical observations about our nation's life. By far the greatest part of the article in The Nation was no more than the reporting of information concerning political decisions at the highest level of government. These facts were sown in and gathered from the shared ground of our country's history. They are the "property of all". . . .[84]

Inroads are also being made into the quite disreputable practice of some criminals committing their crimes for the purpose of gaining notoriety. Given the enthusiasm with which publishers pursue the right to publish such stories, it is not surprising that we have begun to think twice about the consequences of promoting financial gain from antisocial acts as we become more dependent upon information products for our economic health. A prudent and wise rule, it could be argued, would not permit a criminal to profit from his or her own wrongdoing. Proceeds should more equitably be allocated to the victims or their families or be used to reimburse the government for the cost of incarceration. The former has been addressed in the enactment of what are called the Son of Sam laws. These were precipitated by the chain of murders committed by David Berkowitz in New York several years ago.[85]

THE RIGHT TO PROTECT INFORMATION

There are many areas in which we have recognized a right to protect sensitive information that has already been gathered, processed, and archived. For example, the dockets of juvenile offenders are not available for public inspection in many jurisdictions. Medical records are not open to the public. Government documents are sometimes stamped TOP SECRET, SENSITIVE, or EYES ONLY. Yet all of these protected areas are suspect under the opposing theory of the public's right to know and the fear that activities that take place in secret and that are not recorded in publicly available documents will cover up actions that are not in the public interest or that reflect negligence or incompetence.

Sunshine Laws and Freedom of Information Laws

Sunshine laws and freedom of information laws[86] have wreaked havoc with the traditional practices of organizations to conduct their business in private and to disclose actions to the public after debate is over. Universities as well as industry smart under pressure to open up their inner circles to greater representation from the public. Seats on college and university governing boards now include student members as well as faculty and staff, and corporations seek board members with public constituencies.

All of this is a very healthy and inevitable trend in an open and vital information society. It may encumber decision making and render it more costly, but democratic governance demands broad participation in making public policy. Such participation necessarily requires widespread dissemination of information upon which public decisions are predicated.

Strategic Information

However, sunshine laws and freedom of information laws also present new obstacles to security agencies. Gathering of strategic intelligence by tradition is assumed to operate in seclusion beyond the reach of public surveillance. Many people are concerned that the new technologies make it even more difficult to protect information of a sensitive nature because of the ease with which invaders can break into the system. The movie *War Games* is a good example of the fear that has been engendered concerning the potential for harm by unauthorized entry into computerized defense systems. Yet advances in computer cryptography have swung to the side of those who encrypt, if they use sound methods. We are assured that breaking into the data bases of the Department of Defense and the Central Intelligence Agency and National Security Agency is far more difficult than is represented by Hollywood. Still, it is a worrisome problem both from a technical and from a legal standpoint. Recently officials were astonished to discover that wiretapping a voice line was prohibited by statute, yet tapping into a digital transmission was not.[87] The law lags far behind the technology.

Other countries are more concerned than ours is about the vulnerability of information that is gathered, processed, and/or maintained in data bases outside their own boundaries. This is not entirely a specious argument, as the assets of Iran were impounded during the Iranian hostage crisis. Also, the billions of dollars whirling daily through the SWIFT computerized network from bank to bank internationally are a good example of information of high value that cannot by its nature be controlled physically within the confines of a single nation. A country that tried to do so would become isolated from the international economy and would have to fall back upon its own resources.

This has not inhibited countries such as Sweden from elevating the question of national vulnerability to a high level of public anxiety.[88] In the case of Sweden the concern was prompted initially by discovery that the Malmö fire department processed its data in a computer time-sharing service in the United States. To be invaded by aliens and to discover that your strategic data were stored in an enemy computer would certainly put an end to a war prematurely. As a result of such fear, nation-states purchase and maintain computers for their own essential information rather than use the more expeditious and less costly route of time-sharing with other countries. However, this is the price of maintaining national sovereignty over critical information in the absence of any international protocols for such protection outside their own geographical boundaries, within which they are presumed to have absolute jurisdiction.

Export Control of Technical Data

The current argument over new legislation to replace the old Export Administration Act,[89] which has now expired, highlights the problems that ensue when technical data are treated as a controlled commodity. Despite the long-standing existence of the restrictive clauses contained in the earlier versions of the act, it has only recently come to the attention of scientists that much of their existing open practice concerning the exchange of unpublished scientific data, in person, by mail, by conference, and by computer, is permitted only by the notion of a General License by the Department of Commerce.

The Bucy Report of the Defense Science Board[90] recommended that the export control system should reduce the number of controlled items on the Controlled Commodities List and concentrate on the transfer of applied technologies, the mastery of which would permit hostile nations to replicate U.S. military manufacturing capability. Thus, they recommended restricting only "arrays of design and manufacturing knowledge," and "keystone" manufacturing equipment. However, although the Congress incorporated the board's definitions into the 1979 act, it had left no guidelines concerning how such determinations were to be made. The extensive proposals of the Department of Defense, such as the highly controversial and secret Militarily Critical Technologies List, have not yet been approved by Congress.

Because the proposed new legislation permits U.S. law to reach out and control companies in other friendly countries to which technology has been transferred, the European Economic Community (EEC) has filed formal complaints through diplomatic channels deploring this intrusion upon national sovereignty and noting that the economic sanctions of the U.S. government over the Soviet pipeline had led to considerable "political and commercial damage."[91]

Transborder Television—Protection of Cultural Identity

Another example of protective policies has been initiated in Canada, which is concerned more about cultural identity and its own economic independence than about strategic security, since the main threat it suffers from the United States is to its cultural and economic integrity. In certain respects Canada has been ahead of the United States in entering the Information Age. Marconi's first transatlantic radio transmission was from Nova Scotia rather than from Truro, Italy. Morse's telegraphy found uses in Canada before it came into use in the United States, and Canada orbited domestic communications satellites two years before the United States was able to "get off the ground." Furthermore, Canada has been years ahead of the United States in its anticipation of the social impact of the new technologies and in integrating public policy towards the use of new technologies into national priorities.

One of the primary concerns of the Canadian Department of Communications has been the spillover of U.S. television stations across the Canadian border and the widespread development of cable television to pick up such stations.[92] As a consequence of these nearby sources of prime-time entertainment, Canada is one of the most heavily cabled countries in the world. The first reaction of the Canadian authorities was to propose not licensing cable systems that undertook to retransmit foreign broadcasts.[93] However, the public response to this proposal was so overwhelming that it was never put into action. The next effort was intended to stop advertising dollars (estimated at $20 million to $25 million annually) from going to U.S. television stations rather than their going to the Canadian Broadcasting System. Canadian authorities in 1971 determined that Canadian cable systems should delete the U.S. advertising from their retransmissions of U.S.-originated television programs and substitute Canadian advertising instead.[94]

This brought an uproar from border broadcasters who took their fight into Canadian courts and began to agitate in the United States for retaliation. The Canadian Radio-Television Commission (CRTC) suspended further implementation of the commercial deletion policy, but initiated as an alternative a rule that Canadian companies could not deduct the cost of advertising on non-Canadian communications facilities.[95] This added fuel to the long-standing controversy between U.S. and Canadian authorities that has yet to be resolved. Variously, the U.S. Congress has tried to implement retaliatory measures that would prompt the Canadian authorities to relent. An effort has been made to enact reciprocal legislation, although there are no genuine economic sanctions that would be comparable. Efforts have been made to restrict the deductibility of U.S. attendance at conventions in Canada and to restrict the marketing of the Telidon videotex system in the United States. A complaint filed with the Special Trade Representative[96] resulted in a finding that the Canadian practice was unreasonable, burdensome, and restrictive to U.S. commerce. Although both Presidents Carter and Reagan have called for mirror-image legislation, no practical solution has yet been reached.

This Canadian border spillover problem is a good example of a nation-state's determination to protect information that it considers proprietary and to exclude information that it finds objectionable. However, it is also evident that the two countries have widely divergent philosophies underpinning their information policies—the United States is dedicated to a free marketplace for information as protected by the First Amendment and best achieved through an unregulated economy, whereas the Canadians look upon information policy as a means to an end—the promotion and protection of their own cultural identity and economic viability.

THE RIGHT TO DESTROY OR EXPUNGE INFORMATION

Just as the Chinese more than 2,000 years ago resorted to book burning to remove the collective memory of prior social systems, governments today use less stringent but similar methods of changing the course of history. It is usual to call attention to the Soviet practice of rewriting history with a Marxist interpretation, but we are not as aware of efforts within our own society to do the same thing. Frances Fitzgerald reports her findings that textbooks used in American schools have changed their views of history on the average every five years since the 1930s.[97] Little Black Sambo is no longer black, and the 1930s version of *King Kong* with its fearful monster finally overcome has turned into a 1970s version with the multinational oil company exploiting the beast and destroying the island culture by depriving the natives of their religious symbol. Each reflects the social concerns of its own generation, and such reinterpretation of fiction is accepted as literary license. Aside from a very real ethical concern about accuracy, objectivity, and reliability of information, every society will accommodate its information policy to its own political circumstances.

There are sound reasons for destroying some records when they have served their purposes. Shredding machines would not sell so well were it not so. In a society where the printed word is pervasive and copies abound, it is not so easy to destroy all copies. However, within a centralized data base where it may be more efficient to keep the source material on file and merely make copies at the convenience of the user, we may need to worry about what is to be expunged and when in order to avoid information overload or overspill and/or to get rid of redundancy. With computerized archives being so roomy and so cheap, it may become uneconomic to clean out the files. In addition, with so many coauthors and coinventors, it may be difficult to determine who has the right to expunge or delete.

THE RIGHT TO CORRECT OR ALTER INFORMATION

Public Records

As important as the right to acquire public information is the right of individual access to personal information. This was the consensus of data protection leaders from nine European countries attending a 1984 conference in Bellagio. The mere existence of such right, they concluded, is likely to have a salutary effect upon keepers of records.[98] Although many European countries have centralized governmental authorities who license data bases and act as ombudsmen to enforce the rights of citizens, the United States has no counterpart. Such rights as are available are left to the courts to enforce. These include the right to compel the correction of inaccurate or untrue data in government files.[99]

Broadcasting

The broadcasting counterpart of the right of the individual to access personal information in public records is the personal attack doctrine, which permits the subject of an attack to obtain a copy of the offensive audio or video broadcast and to reply.[100]

Newspapers

There is no right in the print media, comparable to the personal attack doctrine, that permits an individual to reply to material already published. In order not to chill the freedom of speech that the First Amendment seeks to protect, the appropriate recourse to an inaccurate or untrue statement is a libel action after the fact for money damages. However, in California, where many libel actions are filed by prominent entertainers, the libel action may not be pursued if the publication voluntarily published a retraction of the alleged inaccurate information.[101] Also under the rubric of privacy protection (a competing First Amendment right), an injunction may be obtained to prevent publication of material that will place the plaintiff in a "false light."[102]

Efforts to establish news councils to serve as watchdogs on such abuses and to urge offenders to publish replies have not been very successful, as some of the major news companies refuse to participate. The effort of the Florida legislature to enact a right of reply for newspapers was struck down by the Supreme Court as intrusive upon the editorial judgment of the news media.[103]

Consequently, the new technologies of both broadcast and computer have come under more stringent rules than the old media. However, it must be remembered that the abuses to be corrected at the time of the First Amendment were strong government intrusions into news content, whereas today the greater fear is the danger of private corporate control over the means of distributing information.

Many of the major newspapers and magazines regularly publish corrections of items from previous editions. They should continue to do so in their own interest and that of the public. As they enter the age of electronic publishing (and many, such as Gannett, Time, Inc., and Dow Jones, are already delivering their content via satellite or engaging in the delivery of videotex), they may become subject to the laws governing the electronic media. However, they may find that the public is more sympathetic with the later evolution of the law as a more equitable and workable solution to balancing property rights in information in the sophisticated technological environment. The First Amendment shield, with which they so vociferously assert their right

to be protected from public accountability, may not serve them well unless they have themselves conformed to the tenets of its underlying philosophy.

THE RIGHT TO DISSEMINATE INFORMATION

None of the other rights would be very meaningful if there were no right to send forth the information into the marketplace of ideas. However, such dissemination carries an economic cost when any technology other than the human voice is employed. Every community has some place that operates as a public forum. In small-town America it was around the steps of the county courthouse. Portuguese sailors who settled New Bedford met on street corners, and some New England villages meet at the town dump. Most societies have large squares in which great numbers of citizens can assemble for public festivals and pronouncements of policy—the Mall in Washington, D.C., Red Square next to the Kremlin in Moscow, St. Peter's Square in the Vatican, Red Square next to the Forbidden City in Beijing, and Marcos Square in Manila. Lafayette Square in Washington, D.C., may have once served that purpose, but it has long since been landscaped with gardens and walks that discourage protestors from marching near the White House.

However, the technologies of print, broadcast, and computer have made this method of disseminating information obsolete except as a backdrop for television versions that can be disseminated to many millions more than could ever be accommodated in one place.

In the United States we accommodated our policies very rapidly to the print media by establishing a system of post roads over which the mails and the newspapers could travel. We have provided preferential rates to books, newspapers, and magazines, and even to merchants' catalogs—and a special franking privilege to congressmen for expediting messages to their constituents. A nationwide penny postcard made it possible for the constituents to reply with low cost, and even to send their messages to each other.

The applicability of this principle of a public forum carries over into a concept of common carriage for voice messages on telephone and telegraph. The law has had great difficulty, however, in coping with the broadcasting industry because content decisions and carriage media are both under the control of a regulated broadcaster. Nonetheless, there is a limited public forum responsibility in the fairness doctrine which requires that broadcasters devote time to opposing viewpoints when issues of public importance are aired.[104] Numerous efforts have

failed to establish a right to communicate over the broadcast media for the purpose of responding to commercials on the basis that they were really "infomercials"[105] or to obtain a right of access to the electronic media for the initiation of public issues.[106]

The courts have been very protective of broadcasters and only recently reaffirmed the long-held view that television is not a public forum even if it is controlled by a public agency.[107] Viewers have no right to compel any particular kind of expression over the public airwaves. The Constitution requires content neutrality only with respect to an activity that has traditionally functioned as an open marketplace of ideas. However, the Supreme Court did not view public television as assuming this role.

In renouncing the Federal Communications Commission's (FCC's) aborted attempt to establish public-access channels on cable television, the Supreme Court concluded that the FCC was attempting, without legislative authorization, to create a public right that did not exist, and it commented that the right to speak does not include a right to an audience in a nonpublic forum such as newspapers, magazines, or on the Senate floor.[108]

However, the power of the press, as a surrogate of the people, is a powerful tool for reform. As the movie *Gandhi* so vividly portrayed, the presence of the *New York Times* reporter and that paper's publication of Gandhi's fight for India's independence gave international credibility to the separation movement, increasing its influence internally.

For the protection of human rights the exposure of violations to public view may be the only way to impose sanctions upon the wrongdoers. The student demonstrators and ghetto youth of the late 1960s understood this better than did public authorities. As Arthur Clarke so eloquently expounded concerning his brainchild, the geostationary orbital communications satellite:

> The very existence of the myriads of new information channels, operating in real-time, will be a powerful influence for civilized behavior. If you are arranging a massacre, it will be useless to shoot the cameraman who has so conveniently appeared on the scene. His pictures will already be safe in the studio five thousand kilometres away; and his final image may hang you.[109]

Certainly, both the access of the news gatherer or researcher to the subject matter and the availability of a means of distributing the information are essential to the health of the public enterprise in a democratic society. How to assure this access in an economy that puts high priority both on using private businesses to provide the

technological means of access and on noninterference with freedom of speech is a quandary of utmost importance to the legal profession and the public.

SOME OBSERVATIONS ON PRACTICAL PRECEDENTS AND PHILOSOPHICAL PRINCIPLES

The newer information technologies have created some options and opportunities that transform the environment for interactive communications. They have also precipitated much soul-searching concerning basic principles that should apply to their use. However, these technologies do not come to us in a legal vacuum. As a nation we have many legal theorems and practical precedents gleaned from a rich heritage of concern about basic rights in information in other media to guide us.

We can, with some assurance, make several observations:

1. We are reluctant to reward wrongdoers for their wrongdoing.
2. We prefer to encourage and reward innovation even through novel legal theories based upon notions of common sense, commercial fairness, and human justice.
3. The courts will not do a useless thing like trying to curtail the videotaping of broadcast material in private homes or to prohibit the photocopying of published copyright materials for personal use.
4. The courts will not try to expand a legal theory that is ridiculous in its application, e.g., attempting to differentiate between source and object code as a means for determining copyrightability of computer software.
5. The courts are reluctant to apply novel legal theories that have not received the sanction of the administrative agency which has jurisdiction over the subject matter, e.g., enunciate a judicial First Amendment right of access to the broadcast media.
6. The law must conform to public acceptance of what is right and equitable.
7. The concept of property rights, whether applied to material goods or to intangible information, is neither simple nor absolute. It reflects the values of a society that equally cherishes individual freedom of action and the sharing of information for the common good.

It is also possible to derive some basic principles that underpin our philosophy of property rights in information.

1. We must have a public medium through which information may be exchanged freely between information providers and information users. This may be a common-carrier channel (for telephone, telegraph, or electronic mail), a public-access channel for cable television, an op-ed page in newspapers, or a public bulletin board such as the Democracy Wall in the People's Republic of China. The village green or public

auditorium simply will not suffice in the age of electronic information highways.

2. Liability for content should rest upon the originators and producers of information, not on the carriers, unless they are one and the same.

3. The sources of information and the nature of their economic interest must be appropriately identified and authenticated in order to establish credibility and to permit those harmed by a message to seek redress, unless there is some overriding public interest in protecting the identity of the source who may be personally harmed or put in jeopardy by the disclosure.

4. Proprietary rights in information generated for commercial purposes should be recognized, legally protected, and compensation provided through justiciable means.

5. The piracy, embezzlement, misappropriation, or misuse of information should be punished.

6. Freedom of speech should not be impaired except in circumstances in which there is a clear and present danger that the health and safety of the nation is in question or that the health and safety of an individual is in serious jeopardy. This should be true whether or not the person in question is a public figure or private person.

CONCLUSIONS

The basic principles outlined above need not be circumvented in an electronic age any more than they have been in the past.[110] They are derived from a long legal history of concern about the integrity and independence of the individual in a free society. What is needed is a commitment to preserve the principles we hold dear in a digital environment no less than in a voice circuit or on a printed page. The late Ithiel de Sola Pool, who devoted his last intellectual effort to the preservation of First Amendment principles in the Information Age, wrote:

> The mystery is how the clear intent of the Constitution, so well and strictly enforced in the domain of print, has been so neglected in the electronic revolution. The answer lies partly in changes in the prevailing concerns and historical circumstances from the time of the founding fathers to the world of today; but it lies at least as much in the failure of Congress and the courts to understand the character of the new technologies. Judges and legislators have tried to fit technological innovations under conventional legal concepts. The errors of understanding by these scientific laymen, though honest, have been mammoth. They have sought to guide toward good purposes technologies they did not understand.[111]

These good and well-intentioned public servants need the sound judgment and sage guidance of scientists and engineers if the law is to make reasonable sense in the Information Age. It is important that there be mutual understanding among those involved in both legal and technological innovations as these developments clash at the crossroads of change.

NOTES

1. C. Cherry, *A Second Industrial Revolution?* (unpublished manuscript).
2. F. Machlup, *The Production and Distribution of Knowledge in the United States*, Princeton University Press, Princeton, N.J., 1962.
3. H. Cleveland, "Information as a Resource," *The Futurist*, pp. 34-39, December 1982.
4. "Legal Lore," *New York State Bar Journal*, pp. 49-50, May 1984.
5. *Compare* art. I of the *Treaty on Principles Governing the Activities of States in the Exploration and Use of Outer Space, Including the Moon and Other Celestial Bodies*, 18 U.S.T. 2410, T.I.A.S. 6347, 610 U.N.T.X. 205, signed at Washington, London, and Moscow on January 27, 1967, and entered into force on October 10, 1967, with the Preamble of the *Information Composite Negotiating Text of the United National Third Conference on the Law of the Sea*, A/Conf. 62/WP, 10 Rev. 2, done at Caracas on April 1, 1980, not yet in force and as yet unsigned by the United States.
6. Y. Ito and K. Ogawa, "Recent Trends in Johoka Shakai and Johoka Policy Studies," *Keio Communication Rev.* 5:15ff, March 1984.
7. A. R. Miller and M. H. Davis, *Intellectual Property: Patents, Trademarks and Copyright*, pp. 18-19, West Publishing Co., St. Paul, 1983.
8. E. W. Ploman and L. C. Hamilton, *Copyright: Intellectual Property in the Information Age*, pp. 4-9, Routledge & Kegan Paul, London, 1980.
9. These rights can be traced down to the so-called moral rights of "paternity" and "integrity" contained in art. 6 of the Paris Convention of 1971 (the latest version of the Berne Convention). U.S. copyright does not protect these rights, and the opposition of Hollywood producers to them may explain the failure of the United States to ratify the Berne Convention. *See generally* R. Brown, *Kaplan and Brown's Copyright*, p. 656, Foundation Press, Mineola, N.Y., 1978.
10. Ploman and Hamilton, *op. cit.*, *supra* note 8, at 8.
11. *Ibid.*, at 9.
12. Art. I, sec. 8, cl. 8.
13. B. Ringer, "Two Hundred Years of American Copyright Law," in *Twenty Years of English & American Patent, Trademark & Copyright Law*, p. 117, American Bar Association, Chicago, Ill., 1977.
14. *Ibid.*
15. Copyright Act of March 3, 1891, 26 Stat. 1106. *See generally* Ringer, *op. cit.*, *supra* note 13, at 127.
16. S. Warren and L. Brandeis, "The Right to Privacy," *Harvard L. Rev.* 4:193, 1890.
17. Dow Jones News Service documents 120827-0219, August 24, 1984; 120822-0348, August 21, 1984; 120821-0312, August 20, 1984.
18. 376 U.S. 254 (1964).
19. B. W. Sanford, "Twenty Years of Actual Malice," *2 Communications Lawyer* 1, Summer 1984. The definition of "public figure" has been greatly expanded beyond that of public officials by the recent reversal of the $2.05-million judgment awarded

by a jury in the libel suit of William Tavouleareas, president of Mobil Corporation. Tavouleareas unsuccessfully argued that if he had become a "public figure" it was because of notoriety brought about by the libel and was not due to any inherent public function of his position. In announcing his intent to appeal his case to the Supreme Court, he said, "I am appealing because I believe the law must not accord one institution in our society the unrestrained power to so damage our leaders that it jeopardizes our society's ability to function." *Communications Lawyer 1(3)*:10, Summer 1983.

20. *See, e.g.*, The Family Educational Rights and Privacy Act of 1974, P.L. 98-380 sec. 513, 20 U.S.C.A. sec. 1231g, and the Texas Open Records Act, sec. 7 of art. 6252-17a, V.T.C.S., and Office of the Attorney General of Texas, Open Records Decision nop. 229, October 26, 1979.

21. U.S. v. Miller, 425 U.S. 435 (1976).

22. The Privacy Act of 1974, P.L. 93-579, December 31, 1974, 88 Stat. 1896, Title 5 U.S.C. sec. 552a, as amended P.L. 94-394, September 3, 1976, 90 Stat. 1198, P.O. 95-38, June 1, 1977, 91 Stat. 179.

23. In the matter of the Washington Post Company v. State Insurance Department et al. No. 73, State of New York, Court of Appeals, March 29, 1984.

24. In the case of copyrights for a period of the lifetime of the author plus 50 years, 17 U.S.C. sec. 302(a); in the case of patents for a period of 17 years, 35 U.S.C. sec. 154.

25. "New Patent Bill Gathers Congressional Support," *Bioscience 29*:281, May 1979.

26. The Patent and Trademark Amendment Act, P.L. 96-517, December 12, 1980.

27. *See generally*, D. Nelkin, "Proprietary Secrecy Versus Open Communication in Science," *Science as Intellectual Property: Who Controls Scientific Research?*, pp. 9-30, Macmillan, London and New York, 1984.

28. Department of Agriculture RFP 84-00-R0-6, March 15, 1984. According to remarks reported in *Commerce Business Daily*, February 28, 1984, the Office of Management and Budget considers this RFP a prototype for distribution of electronic data by the federal government. Examples include *Market News Reports* from the Agricultural Marketing Service and *Situations Reports* from the Economic Research Service.

29. The authorization for this project contained in P.L. 96-517, sec. 9, requiring development of a comprehensive plan for transferring the files to an electronic data base, and P.L. 96-247, Title 35 U.S.C. sec. 6, authorizing "cooperative exchange ventures," are being challenged by the "cottage industry" of trademark searchers who use the hard-copy files without paying fees for access.

30. This was not always the case. The first public library in the United States was started by Benjamin Franklin in Philadelphia in 1731 as a subscription library. There were 50 original members, who paid 40 shillings to join and 10 shillings per annum. Subscribers paid double for books not returned. It was not until 1800 that the Library of Congress was started, and the New York Public Library opened in 1837. M. C. Tyler, "The Historic Evolution of the Free Public Library in America and Its True Function in the Community," in B. Taylor and R. J. Munro, eds., *American Law Publishing 1860-1900*, Glanville, Dobbs Ferry, N.Y., 1984.

31. D. M. Davidson, "Protecting Computer Software: A Comprehensive Analysis," *Jurimetrics Journal 23(4)*:339 at 400f, Summer 1983.

32. The leading Supreme Court case in this area is Branzburg v. Hayes, 408 U.S. 665 (1972), which recognized the necessity to compel disclosure to a grand jury when

criminal behavior is involved. *See also* 99 A.L.R. 3d 37 and P. L. Glenchur, *Hastings L. J. 33*:623-652. Courts will not countenance tortious behavior in the gathering of news. *See* Galella v. Onassis, 487 Fed. 986 (2d Cir. 1973) where defendant was enjoined from approaching the plaintiff closer than 25 feet.

33. Branzburg v. Hayes, *supra* note 32.
34. For an excellent discussion of this issue, *see* D. Nelkin, chap. 4, "Rights of Access Versus Obligations of Confidentiality," in *Science as Intellectual Property: Who Controls Scientific Research?* Macmillan, New York and London, 1984.
35. United States v. Doe (In re Popkin), 460 F. 2d 328 (1st Cir. 1972), *cert. denied, sub nom.* Popkin v. United States, 411 U.S. 909, 1973.
36. Public Health Service Act, as amended 1974, 42 U.S.C. sec. 242(a) and the Comprehensive Drug Abuse, Prevention, and Control Act of 1970, P.L. 95-633, 21 U.S.C. sec. 242a(b) and sec. 872(d).
37. *E.g.*, Privacy of Research Records Bill, S. 867 (April 4, 1979) and H.R. 3409 (April 3, 1979), 96th Cong. 1st Sess.
38. Nelkin, *op. cit., supra* note 27.
39. R. K. Merton, ed., *The Sociology of Science*, p. 273, University of Chicago Press, Chicago, Ill., 1973.
40. Nelkin, *op. cit., supra* note 27.
41. Pool & Solomon, "Intellectual Property and Transborder Data Flows," *Stan. J. Int'l. L. 16*:113, 1980.
42. The Direct Marketing Association has been monitoring some 80 pieces of proposed legislation during the last several years.
43. *E.g.*, New Jersey, Pennsylvania, Nevada, and Virginia.
44. *E.g.*, Illinois, California, Connecticut, and Wisconsin.
45. *Op. cit., supra* note 21.
46. Miranda v. Arizona, 384 U.S. 436 (1966); *see generally* 30 A.L.R. Fed. 824. For cases concerning illegal beepers, bugging, and wiretapping, *see* 57 A.L.R. Fed. 646, 59 A.L.R. Fed. 959, and 97 L. Ed. 237. *See also* M. Goldey, "Aspects of International Voice Communications to and from the United States," *Jurimetrics J. 24(1)*:8-12, Fall 1983, regarding electronic surveillance of international mts calls outside the United States and the admissibility of such evidence in courts.
47. Minnesota v. Marshall, ___U.S. ___, 79 L. Ed. 2d 409 (1984); New York v. Quarles, ___U.S. ___, 81 L. Ed. 2d 550 (1984); Berkemer v. McCarty, 468 U.S. ___, 82 L. Ed. 2d 317 (1984); Massachusetts v. Sheppard, 468 U.S. ___, 82 L. Ed. 2d 737 (1984).
48. U.S. v. New York Times, 403 U.S. 713 (1971).
49. Elizabeth Taylor v. American Broadcasting Companies, Inc., 82 Civ. 6977 (S.D.N.Y. 1982).
50. New York Civil Rights Law, sec. 50-51; the Lanham Act for damage to protectable service and trademarks, and unfair competition under New York General Business Law, sec. 368(d).
51. *See* Street v. NBC, 645 F. 2d 1227 (1981), *settled and cert. dismissed*, 70 L. Ed. 2d 636 (1981).
52. *Compare* Hicks v. Casablanca Records, 464 F. Supp. 426 (S.D.N.Y. 1978) and Maritote v. Desilu Productions, Inc., 345 F. 2d 418 (7th Cir. 1965) with Lugosi v. Universal Pictures Co., Inc., 172 U.S.P.Q. 541 (Cal. Super. 1972) and Price v. Hal Roach Studios, Inc., 400 F. Supp. 836 (S.D.N.Y.).

53. *See*, *e.g.*, Gilliam v. American Broadcasting Companies, Inc., 538 F. 2d 14 (2d Cir. 1976).
54. 8 Anne, c. 19, republished in R. S. Brown, *Copyright*, p. 851, Foundation Press, Mineola, N.Y., 1978.
55. Ploman and Hamilton, *op. cit.*, *supra* note 8, at 30.
56. White-Smith Music Publishing Co. v. Apollo Co., 209 U.S. 1 (1908). This inadequacy has been cured by the 1976 act, which defines a "copy" as anything tangible from which the author's work can be replicated. 17 U.S.C. sec. 102(a).
57. *Final Report of the National Commission on New Technological Uses of Copyrighted Works*, 27-31, Library of Congress, Washington, D.C., 1979.
58. *Ibid.*, at 12; subsequently enacted 17 U.S.C. sec. 101, 117, as amended P.L. 96-517, sec. 10, 94 Stat. 3028.
59. Computer Software Copyright Act of 1980 ; Act of December 12, 1980; L. No. 96-517, sec. 10; 94 Stat. 3015, 3028; 17 U.S.C. sec. 101, 117.
60. Office of the Register of Copyrights, Announcement SML-47 (May 1964); Copyright Office Circular 31D (January 1965).
61. CONTU Final Report, *op. cit.*, *supra* note 57, at 85.
62. "Computer programs are the ordered set of instructions which can operate a computer. . . . Source code can be written in languages which are English-like, such as BASIC or FORTRAN. . . . Source code instructions are either directly used by a computer or are first translated into the computer's machine language as 'object' code. Object code is usually printed as ones and zeros, but can also be printed as octal numbers (0-7) or hexadecimal numbers (0-15), with A-F representing decimal (10-15). Object code can be directly translated into 'assembly' language, in which machine instructions are represented by mnemonics. . . . Object code, the direct symbolic representation of the machine language, is intelligible to trained engineers" (e.g., like the piano player that was only readable by experts). D. M. Davidson, "Protecting Computer Software: A Comprehensive Analysis," *Jurimetrics Journal 23*:339, 341 (Summer 1983).
63. Apple Computer, Inc. v. Franklin Computer Corp., 545 F. Supp. 812 714 F. 2d 1240 (3d Cir. 1983), *cert. den.*, 104 Sup. Ct. 690 (1984).
64. *See generally* the excellent article by Duncan Davidson, *op. cit.*, *supra* note 31, which discusses the various methods of protecting software and the concerns of lawyers about the viability of each.
65. Dow Jones News Service, Doc. no. 120118-0360, January 7, 1984.
66. Dow Jones News Service, Doc. no. 120706-0544, July 6, 1984.
67. Dow Jones News Service, Doc. no. 110512-1159, May 12, 1983.
68. 17 U.S.C. sec. 109(a).
69. Dow Jones News Service, Doc. no. 120119-0661, January 19, 1984. Until that release *Flashdance* and *Jane Fonda's Workout* had been the top-selling videotapes, with 200,000 copies each. *See also* "Hollywood Thriving on Video-Cassette Boom," New York Times, Monday, May 7, 1984, pp. A1, C17.
70. Dow Jones News Service, Doc. no. 110512-1159, December 5, 1983.
71. Sony Corp. v. Universal City Studios, ___U.S. ___(1984), 104 Sup. Ct. 774, at 778.
72. 17 U.S.C. sec. 107.
73. Williams & Wilkins Co. v. United States, 420 U.S. 376 (1975).
74. Dow Jones News Service, Doc. no. 110512-1159, May 5, 1983.
75. Rule 10(b)(5).

76. *New York Times*, August 29, 1984, pp. A1, D4; *New York Times*, Sunday, May 27, 1984, pp. F1, F21.
77. S.E.C. v. Texas Gulf Sulphur Co., 401 F. 2d 833 (2d Cir. 1968).
78. *See* Chiarella v. United States, 455 U.S. 222 (1980), involving an employee of a financial printing house who decoded documents about mergers and acquisitions; S.E.C. v. Dirks, *cert. granted*, 459 U.S. 1014 (1982) involving a stockbroker; U.S. v. Newman, 664 F. 2d 12 (2d Cir. 1981) involving employees of Morgan Stanley who traded shares in a takeover target represented by their firm; S.E.C. v. Thayer (pending) involving friends of LTV Corp. CEO who may have benefitted from passing confidential information to his personal friends; and S.E.C. v. Brant (the civil case against Winans and his friends). For a discussion of all of the above cases, *see* L. Wayne, "Inside Trading by Outsiders," *New York Times*, May 27, 1984, pp. F-1, F-21.
79. Lewis v. Baxter, 368 F. Supp. 768 (D.C. Ala. 1973).
80. Public Affairs Press, Inc. v. Rickover, 369 U.S. 111 (1962). The case raises interesting questions about the copyrightability of the speeches, i.e., whether they were government documents that cannot be copyrighted under Title 17 U.S.C. sec. 105, whether they were already in the public domain because of their oral delivery and circulated copies, or whether they were the private utterances of a public official in a nonofficial capacity. On remand it was decided that the speeches were delivered in the admiral's "private capacity" and that the fact that they were typed, duplicated, and cleared by the Navy was irrelevant, 268 F. Supp. 444 (1967).
81. Nixon v. Sirica, 487 F. 2d 700 (D.C. App. 1973).
82. Harper & Row, Publishers, Inc. and the Reader's Digest Association, Inc., v. Nation Enterprises and the Nation Associates, Inc., 723 F. 2d 195 (1983).
83. Time, Inc. v. Bernard Geis Associates, 293 F. Supp. 130 (S.D.N.Y. 1968); International News Service v. Associated Press, 248 U.S. 215 (1918); Hoehling v. Universal City Studios, Inc., 618 F. 2d 972 (2d Cir.) *cert. den.*, 449 U.S. 841 (1980); Rosemont Enterprises, Inc. v. Random House, Inc., 366 F. 2d 303 (2d Cir. 1966) *cert. den.*, 385 U.S. 1009 (1967).
84. 723 F. 2d 195.
85. "Fifteen states have passed 'Son of Sam' laws freezing proceeds from moneymaking ventures such as book sales of those locked up for capital crimes until claims by victims of their survivors are satisfied." *Christian Science Monitor*, April 5, 1983, p. 1.
86. The Government in the Sunshine Act, P.L. 94-409, September 13, 1976, 90 Stat. 1241, Title 19 U.S.C. sec. 420, Title 5 U.S.C. sec. 551f., and the Freedom of Information Act, P.L. 89-487, July 4, 1966, 80 Stat. 250, Title 5 U.S.C. 552, as amended, P.L. 90-23 sec. 1, June 5, 1967, 81 Stat. 54, P.L. 93-502 sec. 1-3, November 21, 1974, 88 Stat. 15-61.
87. 18 U.S.C. sec. 2511 arguably might not include such transmissions.
88. Commission on New Information Technology, *New Views: Computers and New Media—Anxiety and Hopes* (1979). *See also* J. Freese, "The Vulnerability of Computerized Society," *Transnational Data Rep. 4(5)* at 21 (1981).
89. 50 U.S.C. sec. 2402 *et seq.*, as amended.
90. Defense Science Board Task Force on Export of U.S. Technology, *An Analysis of Export Control of U.S. Technology—A DOD Perspective*, Office of the Secretary of Defense, Washington, D.C., 1976.
91. Dow Jones News Service, Doc. no. 110325-0319, March 24, 1984.

92. For an excellent discussion of these transborder issues, *see Cultures in Collision: A Canadian-U.S. Conference on Communications Policy*, Praeger, 1984, esp. chaps. 3 and 6.

93. CRTC Public Announcement, *The Improvement and Development of Canadian Broadcasting and the Extension of U.S. Coverage in Canada by CATV*, Ottawa, December 3, 1969, p. 1.

94. CRTC Public Announcement, *The Integration of Cable Television in the Canadian Broadcasting System*, Ottawa, February 26, 1971. *See also* CRTC Policy Statement, *Cable Television: Canadian Broadcasting: A Single System*, Ottawa, July 16, 1971.

95. Canadian Bill C-58, An Act to Amend the Income Tax Act, September 1976.

96. Under sec. 301 of the Trade Act of 1974. The complaint was filed on August 29, 1978, and hearings were held in November 1978.

97. F. Fitzgerald, *America Revised*, Atlantic Little Brown, Boston, Mass., 1979.

98. *Transnational Data Report*, vol. vii, no. 4, p. 195, June-July 1984.

99. Privacy Act of 1974, 5 U.S.C.S. sec. 552a(g) and (1) (A); *see also* R.R. v. Department of Army, 482 F. Sup. 770 (D.C. 1980).

100. 28 U.S.C. sec. 315, (a); 47 C.F.R. sec. 73.123, 73.300, 73.598, 73.679.

101. Sec. 48a of the California Civil Code n2 provides in part: "1. In any action for damages for the publication of a libel in a newspaper, or of a slander by a radio broadcast, plaintiff shall recover no more than special damages unless a correction be demanded and be not published or broadcast, as herinafter provided. . . ." The California court hearing the Carol Burnett libel suit against the *Enquirer* cleared the way for the record $1.6-million verdict by ruling that the publication was a magazine not a newspaper.

102. Seattle Times v. Rhinehart, 82-1721, is on the Supreme Court docket to determine whether the Washington State Supreme Court was correct in upholding an injunction for defamation and invasion of privacy by the leader of a religious group who sought to suppress publication of information obtained during preparation for trial, *National Law Journal*, October 17, 1983, p. 5. Injunctions are more often sought to protect so-called merchandising rights or the right to publicity. *See, e.g.*, Haelan Laboratories, Inc. v. Topps Chewing Gum, Inc., 202 F. 2d 866 (2d Cir. 1953) *cert. den.* 346 U.S. 816. "This right of publicity would usually yield them no money unless it could be made the subject of an exclusive grant which barred any other advertiser from using their pictures."

103. Miami Herald v. Tornillo, 418 U.S. 241 (1974).

104. 47 U.S.C. sec. 315 (1976), *aff'd*, Red Lion Broadcasting Co. v. FCC, 395 U.S. 367 (1969).

105. Friends of Earth v. FCC, 449 F. 2d 1164 (D.C. Cir. 1971).

106. Columbia Broadcasting Systems, Inc. v. Democratic National Committee, 412 U.S. 94 (1973).

107. Muir v. Alabama Educational Television Commission, 688 F. 2d 1033 (5th Cir. 1982) *cert. den.*, ___U.S. ___, 75 L. ed. 2d (1984).

108. Midwest Video Corp. v. FCC, 571 F. 2d 1025 (8th Cir. 1978).

109. "Beyond the Global Village." Address on World Communications Day, United Nations, New York, May 17, 1983.

110. Which is only to say that we have sometimes been more and sometimes less successful in preserving and protecting them.

111. *Technologies of Freedom*, Belknap Press, Cambridge and London, 1983.